Dear NFT User,

Ever find yourself in an unfamiliar neighborhood, a hunger for some rare ethnic food in your stomach, a thirst for vino in your throat, needing a last-minute birthday present for a friend, and searching for your bank's nearest ATM? Well, have we got a book for you! Welcome to the 2006 edition of the Not For Tourists Guide to New York City—a small but powerful tool for your daily trek through the concrete jungle we call home. Whatever your need, we're sure you'll find this guide an essential go-to source for everything NYC-related.

Flip around the book, if you haven't already, to see hundreds of ways it could help you in your daily life as a New Yorker. We give you the info you really need, like which bus will get you downtown when you're broke and your train isn't running, or the location of the theater you're trying to find by curtain time. And then there are the essential daily needs, like the best places to eat, to imbibe, to shop, or to add to your credit card debt in countless other ways.

For those who've bought this book in the past, you should know that we've continued our drive to add great new content every year. In addition to expanding and updating the listings and editorial, we added **MoMA** to Arts & Entertainment, **Thru Streets** to Transit, and **NYU** to Parks & Places. Pages that received major overhauls include **JFK Airport**, **Rockefeller Center**, **Columbia University**, **Internet & Wi-Fi**, **Biking and Skating**, **Metro-North Railroad**, and **PATH/Light Rail**. And our favorite new addition: **bike lanes**, **suggested routes**, and **greenways** have been added to the transportation page of each map.

As always, our appreciation goes out to the many contributors listed to the left, and to the mighty NFT staff, whose energy and expertise help us produce not only this book, but guides to a growing number of cities. Be sure to visit our website at www.notfortourists.com for more information, and to tell us if we missed something.

Here's hoping you find what you need,

Krikor, Diana, Rob, and Jane

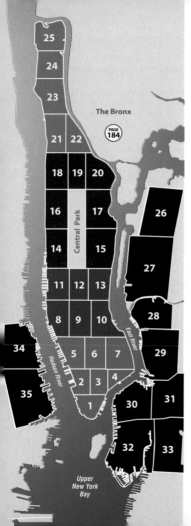

Table of Contents

Subway Map/Bus Map
foldout, last page

Map 1 • **Financial District**

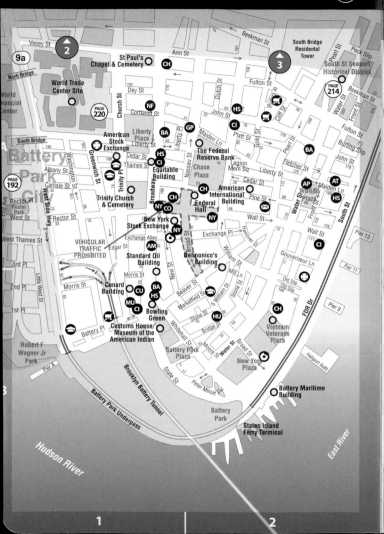

Although it's approaching four years since September 11ᵗʰ, it's hard not to feel that the financial district hasn't quite gotten back to normal—things are still a little emptier, and there are several permanent roadblocks. Look behind the skyscrapers to find such gems as Federal Hall, Trinity Church, the Cunard Building, and the Customs House.

◉ Bagels

- **Champs** · 70 Exchange Pl
- **New World Coffee** · 1 New York Plz

$ Banks

AM · **Amalgamated** · 52 Broadway
AP · **Apple** · Wall St Plz
AT · **Atlantic** · 15 Maiden Ln
BA · **Bank of America** · 150 Broadway
BA · **Bank of America (ATM)** · 175 Water St
BA · **Bank of America (ATM)** · 29 Broadway
NY · **Bank of New York** · 1 Wall St
NY · **Bank of New York** · 20 Broad St
NY · **Bank of New York** · 45 Wall St
CH · **Chase** · 1 Chase Plz
CH · **Chase** · 214 Broadway
CH · **Chase** · 55 Water St
CH · **Chase (ATM)** · 14 Wall St
CH · **Chase (ATM)** · 20 Pine St
CI · **Citibank** · 1 Broadway
CI · **Citibank** · 111 Wall St
CI · **Citibank** · 120 Broadway
CI · **Citibank (ATM)** · 100 William St
CO · **Commerce Bank** · 2 Wall St
GP · **Greenpoint Bank** · 24 Maiden Ln
HS · **HSBC** · 100 Maiden Ln
HS · **HSBC** · 110 William St
HS · **HSBC** · 120 Broadway
HS · **HSBC** · 26 Broadway
CU · **Municipal Credit Union (ATM)** · 2 Broadway
NF · **North Fork Bank** · 176 Broadway

❋ Fire Departments

- **Engine 10, Ladder 10** · 124 Liberty St
- **Engine 4, Ladder 15** · 42 South St

◯ Landmarks

- **American International Building** · 70 Pine St
- **American Stock Exchange** · 86 Trinity Pl
- **Battery Maritime Building** · 11 South St
- **Bowling Green** · Broadway & State St
- **Cunard Building** · 25 Broadway
- **Customs House/Museum of the American Indian** · 1 Bowling Green
- **Delmonico's Building** · 56 Beaver St
- **Equitable Building** · 120 Broadway
- **Federal Hall** · 26 Wall St
- **The Federal Reserve Bank** · 33 Liberty St
- **New York Stock Exchange** · 20 Broad St
- **South Street Seaport** · South St
- **St Paul's Chapel & Cemetery** · Broadway & Fulton St
- **Standard Oil Building** · 26 Broadway
- **Trinity Church & Cemetery** · Broadway & Wall St
- **Vietnam Veterans Plaza** · Coenties Slip & Water St
- **World Trade Center Site** · Church St & Vesey St

✉ Post Offices

- **Wall Street** · 73 Pine St

☎ Schools

- **High School for Economics and Finance** · 100 Trinity Pl
- **High School for Leadership & Public Service** · 90 Trinity Pl
- **John V Lindsay Wildcat Academy** · 17 Battery Pl
- **Millenium High** · 75 Broad St

⊟ Supermarkets

- **The Amish Market** · 17 Battery Pl
- **Associated** · 77 Fulton St
- **Jubilee Marketplace** · 99 John St

Map 1 · **Financial District**

With very few and notable exceptions, everything closes before 8pm. Jubilee on John Street remains the 24-hour must-go place for prepared foods and groceries, and they deliver. Zeytuna, also on John Street, is an excellent gourmet grocery/deli, open until 10pm, on weekends as well. The few bars around tend to be typical Irish places.

Coffee

- **Alfanoose** · 8 Maiden Ln
- **Andrew's Coffee Shop** · 116 John St
- **Ashby's** · 120 Broadway
- **Au Bon Pain** · 222 Broadway
- **Au Bon Pain** · 60 Broad St
- **Au Bon Pain** · 80 Pine St
- **Claudia's Coffee Shop** · 125 Broad St
- **Cosi** · 200 Vesey St
- **Cosi** · 54 Pine St
- **Cosi** · 55 Broad St
- **Dunkin' Donuts** · 139 Fulton St
- **Dunkin' Donuts** · 196 Broadway
- **Dunkin' Donuts** · 29 Broadway
- **Dunkin' Donuts** · 48 New St
- **Dunkin' Donuts** · 50 Fulton St
- **Leonidas** · 74 Trinity Pl
- **New World Coffee** · 1 New York Plz
- **Roxy Coffee Shop** · 20 John St
- **Seattle Coffee Roasters** · 110 William St
- **Starbucks** · 1 Battery Park Plz
- **Starbucks** · 100 William St
- **Starbucks** · 115 Broadway
- **Starbucks** · 165 Broadway
- **Starbucks** · 195 Broadway
- **Starbucks** · 2 Broadway
- **Starbucks** · 24 State St
- **Starbucks** · 3 New York Plz
- **Starbucks** · 45 Wall St
- **Starbucks** · 55 Broad St
- **Starbucks** · 55 Liberty St
- **Starbucks** · 80 Pine St

Copy Shops

- **Acro Photo Printing** (24 hrs) · 90 Maiden Ln
- **Administrative Resources** (7am-5:30pm) · 60 Broad, 25th Floor
- **Big Apple Copy and Printing Center** (8am-6pm) · 115 Broadway
- **Complete Mail Centers** (9am-7pm) · 28 Vesey St
- **Hard Copy Printing** (8am-6pm) · 111 John St
- **Kinko's** (7am-11pm) · 100 Wall St
- **Kinko's** (7am-11pm) · 110 William St
- **Nova Graphics** (8am-5pm) · 47 Ann St
- **Perfect Copy Center** (24hrs) · 11 Broadway
- **Sol Speedy** (8am-7pm) · 26 Broadway
- **Staples** (7am-7pm) · 200 Water St
- **The UPS Store** (8am-7:30pm) · 118A Fulton St

Farmer's Markets

- **Bowling Green Greenmarket** · Battery Park Pl & Broadway
- **Downtown PATH** · Vesey St & Church St
- **South Street Seaport** · Fulton b/w Water & Pearl Sts

Gyms

- **Crunch Fitness** · 25 Broadway
- **Curves** · 118 Water St
- **Equinox Fitness Club** · 14 Wall St
- **Heartworks Health & Fitness Center** · 180 Maiden Ln
- **John Street Fitness** · 80 John St
- **Lucille Roberts Health Club** · 143 Fulton St
- **New York Health & Racquet Club** · 39 Whitehall St
- **New York Sports Clubs** · 160 Water St
- **New York Sports Clubs** · 30 Wall St
- **Spa 88** · 88 Fulton St
- **Trinity Boxing Club** (boxing gym) · 110 Greenwich St

Hardware Stores

- **Dick's Hardware** · 205 Pearl St
- **Fulton Supply & Hardware** · 74 Fulton St
- **Whitehall Hardware** · 88 Greenwich St
- **Wolff Hardware** · 127 Fulton St

Liquor Stores

- **Famous Wines & Spirits** · 40 Exchange Pl
- **Fulton Wines & Spirits** · 110 Fulton St
- **Maiden Lane Wines & Liquors** · 6 Maiden Ln
- **New York Wine Exchange** · 9 Broadway
- **Water Street Wine & Spirit** · 79 Pine St
- **West Street Wine & Spirits** · 47 West St

Nightlife

- **John Street Bar & Grill** · 17 John St
- **Liquid Assets @ Millennium Hilton Hotel** · 55 Church St
- **Papoos** · 55 Broadway
- **Ryan Maguire's Ale House** · 28 Cliff St
- **Ryan's Sports Bar & Restaurant** · 46 Gold St
- **Ulysses** · 95 Pearl St
- **White Horse Tavern** · 25 Bridge St

Restaurants

- **The 14 Wall Street Restaurant** · 14 Wall St
- **American Café & Health Bar** · 160 Broadway
- **Battery Gardens** · Battery Park, across from 17 State St
- **Burritoville** · 36 Water St
- **Cafe Exchange** · 49 Broadway
- **Carmela's** · 30 Water St
- **Cassis on Stone** · 52 Stone St
- **Cosi Sandwich Bar** · 54 Pine St
- **Cosi Sandwich Bar** · 55 Broad St
- **Daily Soup** · 41 John St
- **Financier Patisserie** · 62 Stone St
- **Giovanni's Atrium** · 100 Washington St
- **The Grotto** · 69 New St
- **Heartland Brewery** · 93 South St
- **Lemongrass Grill** · 84 William St
- **Les Halles** · 15 John St
- **MJ Grill** · 110 John St
- **Papoos** · 55 Broadway
- **Red** · 19 Fulton St
- **Romi** · 19 Rector St
- **Rosario's** · 38 Pearl St
- **Roy's New York** · 130 Washington St
- **Sophie's** · 205 Pearl St
- **Sophie's** · 73 New St
- **St Maggie's Café** · 120 Wall St
- **Zeytuna** · 59 Maiden Ln

Shopping

- **Barclay Rex** · 75 Broad St
- **Century 21** · 22 Cortlandt St
- **Christopher Norman Chocolates** · 60 New St
- **Flowers of the World** · 80 Pine St
- **Godiva Chocolatier** · 33 Maiden Ln
- **M Slavin & Sons** · 106 South St
- **Modell's** · 200 Broadway
- **Radio Shack** · 114 Fulton St
- **Radio Shack** · 9 Broadway
- **South Street Seaport** · 19 Fulton St
- **The World of Golf** · 189 Broadway
- **Yankees Clubhouse Shop** · 8 Fulton St

Video Rental

- **Ann Street Entertainment** · 21 Ann St

Map 1 • **Financial District**

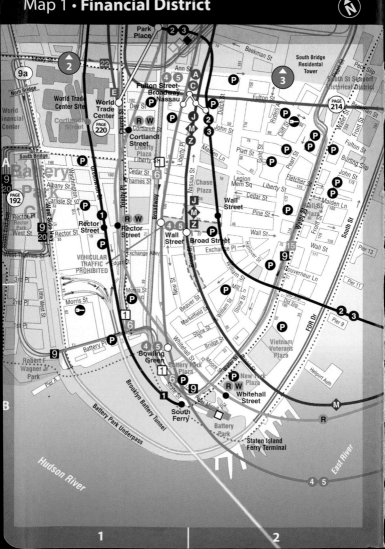

Attempting to drive---or park---during the day down here can be maddening, but you can check out the lots underneath the FDR if you really must drive. Subways are usually your best bet. The PATH Station at the WTC is now re-opened.

Subways

1	Rector St
1	South Ferry
2 3	Wall St
4 5	Bowling Green
4 5	Wall St
2 3 4 5 A C J M Z	Fulton St-Broadway-Nassau St
E	World Trade Center
J M Z	Broad St
R W	Cortlandt St
R W	Rector St
R W	Whitehall St-South Ferry

PATH

- **World Trade Center Site**

Bus Lines

1	Fifth/Madison Aves
15	First/Second Aves
20	Riverdale/246th St via Henry Hudson Pky
22	Madison/Chambers St
6	Seventh Ave/Broadway/Sixth Ave
9	Ave B/East Broadway

Bike Lanes

- • • • Recommended Route
- • • • Greenway

Car Rental

- **Enterprise** · 56 Fulton St
- **Hertz** · 20 Morris St

Parking

Map 2 · TriBeCa

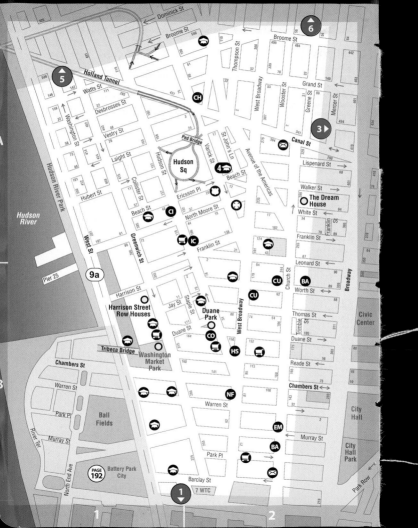

Essentials

TriBeCa's back—with a vengeance—as even more old warehouse buildings are being converted to multi-million dollar lofts that we can't afford. However, walking around and staring, and then taking a break at sublime Duane Park, keeps us happy for the moment.

$ Banks

BA · Bank of America · 100 Church St
BA · Bank of America (ATM) · 57 Worth St
CH · Chase · 423 Canal St
CI · Citibank · 127 Hudson St
CO · Commerce Bank · 25 Hudson St
EM · Emigrant · 110 Church St
HS · HSBC · 110 West Broadway
IC · Independence Community · 108 Hudson St
CU · Municipal Credit Union (ATM) · 40 Worth St
NF · North Fork Bank · 90 West Broadway
CU · Skyline Federal Credit Union · 32 Sixth Ave

Fire Departments

· **Ladder 8** · 14 N Moore St

O Landmarks

· **The Dream House** · 275 Church St
· **Duane Park** · Duane St & Hudson St
· **Harrison Street Row Houses** · Harrison St & Greenwich St
· **Washington Market Park** · Greenwich St

Police

· **1st Precinct** · 16 Ericsson Pl

Post Offices

· **Bowling Green** · 90 Church St
· **Canal Street** · 350 Canal St

Schools

· **Adelphi University** · 75 Varick St
· **The Art Institute of New York City** · 11 Beach St
· **Audrey Cohen College** · 75 Varick St
· **Borough of Manhattan Community College** · 199 Chambers St
· **College of New Rochelle DC-37 Campus** · 125 Barclay St
· **IS 289** · 201 Warren St
· **Metropolitan College of New York** · 75 Varick St
· **Montessori School** · 53 Beach St
· **New York Academy of Art** · 111 Franklin St
· **New York Law School** · 57 Worth St
· **PS 150 Tribeca Learning Center** · 334 Greenwich St
· **PS 234 Independence** · 292 Greenwich St
· **St John's University** · 101 Murray St
· **Unity High** · 121 Sixth Ave
· **Washington Market School** · 55 Hudson St

Supermarkets

· **Amish Market** · 53 Park Pl
· **Bell Bates Natural Foods** · 97 Reade St
· **Food Emporium** · 316 Greenwich St
· **Jin Market** · 111 Hudson St
· **Morgan's Market** · 13 Hudson St

Map 2 · **TriBeCa**

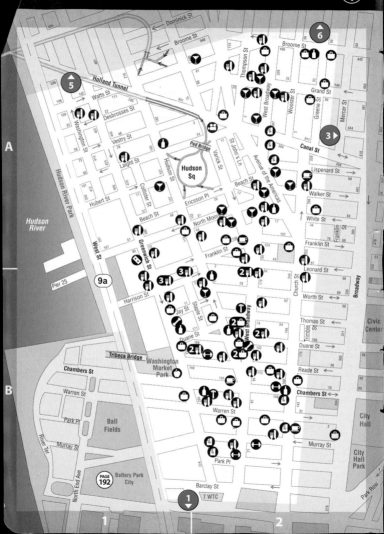

For arts, TriBeCa rocks—the film festival every year, the Knitting Factory, the MELA Foundation's "Dream House," several galleries, and experimental music at Roulette. Stalwart bars such as Puffy's and Walker's can effectively wet your whistle while you're waiting to win the lotto so you can eat at Nobu.

☕ Coffee

- **Dunkin' Donuts** · 130 Church St
- **Pecan** · 130 Franklin St
- **Starbucks** · 125 Chambers St
- **Westside Coffee Shop II** · 323 Church St

🖨 Copy Shops

- **21 Laminating & Binding Center** (9:30am-6pm) · 130 Church St
- **Bestype Imaging** (8:30am-7pm) · 285 West Broadway
- **City Copies** (8am-7pm) · 158 Church St
- **Jean Paul Duplicating Center** (8:30am-7pm) · 275 Greenwich St
- **Mail Boxes Etc** (8am-7pm) · 295 Greenwich St
- **Shield Press** (9am-6:30pm) · 9 Lispenard St
- **The UPS Store** (8:30am-7pm) · 305 West Broadway

🍎 Farmer's Markets

- **Tribeca** · Greenwich St-Chambers & Duane

🏋 Gyms

- **24/7 Fitness Club** · 107 Chambers St
- **Equinox Fitness Club** · 46 West Broadway
- **Equinox Fitness Club** · 54 Murray St
- **New York Sports Clubs** · 151 Reade St

🔧 Hardware Stores

- **Ace Hardware** · 160 West Broadway
- **Tribeca Hardware** · 154 Chambers St

🍾 Liquor Stores

- **Brite Buy Wines & Spirits** · 11 Sixth Ave
- **Chambers Street Wines** · 160 Chambers St
- **City Hall Wines & Spirits** · 108 Chambers St
- **Downtown Liquor Store** · 90 Hudson St
- **Hudson Wine & Spirits** · 165 Hudson St
- **Tribeca Wine Merchants** · 40 Hudson St
- **Tribeca Wines** · 327 Greenwich St
- **Vintage New York** · 482 Broome St

🎬 Movie Theaters

- **Tribeca Cinemas** · 54 Varick St

🌙 Nightlife

- **46 Grand** · 46 Grand St
- **Brandy Library** · 25 North Moore St
- **Bubble Lounge** · 228 West Broadway
- **Buster's Garage** · 180 West Broadway
- **Church Lounge at the Tribeca Grand Hotel** · 25 Walker St
- **Circa Tabac** · 32 Watts St
- **Lucky Strike** · 59 Grand St
- **Naked Lunch** · 17 Thompson St
- **Nancy Whisky Pub** · 1 Lispenard St
- **Puffy's Tavern** · 81 Hudson St
- **Soho Grand Hotel** · 310 West Broadway
- **Tribeca Tavern** · 247 West Broadway
- **Walker's** · 16 N Moore St

🐾 Pet Shops

- **Dudley's Paw** · 327 Greenwich St
- **Pet Bar South** · 117 West Broadway

🍴 Restaurants

- **66** · 241 Church St
- **A&M Roadhouse** · 57 Murray St
- **Azafran** · 77 Warren St
- **Bread Tribeca** · 301 Church St
- **Bubby's** · 120 Hudson St
- **Burritoville** · 144 Chambers St
- **Café Noir** · 32 Grand St
- **Capsouto Frères** · 451 Washington St
- **Chanterelle** · 2 Harrison St
- **City Hall** · 131 Duane St
- **Columbine** · 229 West Broadway
- **Danube** · 30 Hudson St
- **Della Rovere** · 250 West Broadway
- **Duane Park Café** · 157 Duane St
- **Dylan Prime** · 62 Laight St
- **Edward's** · 136 West Broadway
- **Elixir Juice Bar** · 95 West Broadway
- **Félix** · 340 West Broadway
- **Flor de Sol** · 361 Greenwich St
- **fresh** · 105 Franklin St
- **Ginger Ty** · 363 Greenwich St
- **The Harrison** · 355 Greenwich St
- **Il Giglio** · 81 Warren St
- **Ivy's Bistro** · 385 Greenwich St
- **Karahi** · 508 Broome St
- **Kitchenette** · 80 West Broadway
- **Kori** · 253 Church St
- **Landmarc** · 179 West Broadway
- **Layla** · 211 West Broadway
- **Le Zinc** · 139 Duane St
- **Lucky Strike** · 59 Grand St
- **Lupe's East LA Kitchen** · 110 Sixth Ave
- **Montrachet** · 239 West Broadway
- **Nobu** · 105 Hudson St
- **Nobu, Next Door** · 105 Hudson St
- **Odeon** · 145 West Broadway
- **Pace** · 121 Hudson St
- **Palacinka** · 28 Grand St
- **Petite Abeille** · 134 West Broadway
- **Roc** · 190 Duane St
- **Salaam Bombay** · 317 Greenwich St
- **Shore** · 41 Murray St
- **Sosa Borella** · 460 Greenwich St
- **Square Diner** · 33 Leonard St
- **Thalassa** · 179 Franklin St
- **Tribeca Grill** · 375 Greenwich St
- **Walker's** · 16 N Moore St
- **Yaffa's** · 353 Greenwich St
- **Zutto** · 77 Hudson St

🛍 Shopping

- **Assets London** · 152 Franklin St
- **Balloon Saloon** · 133 West Broadway
- **Bazzini** · 339 Greenwich St
- **Bell Bates Natural Food** · 97 Reade St
- **Boffi SoHo** · 31 1/2 Greene St
- **Canal Street Bicycles** · 417 Canal St
- **Duane Park Patisserie** · 179 Duane St
- **Gotham Bikes** · 112 West Broadway
- **Happy Baby Toys** · 51 Hudson St
- **Issey Miyake** · 119 Hudson St
- **Jack Spade** · 56 Greene St
- **Janovic Plaza** · 136 Church St
- **Kings Pharmacy** · 5 Hudson St
- **Korin Japanese Trading** · 57 Warren St
- **Let There Be Neon** · 38 White St
- **Liberty Souveniers** · 275 Greenwich St
- **Lucky Brand Dungarees** · 38 Greene St
- **MarieBelle's Fine Treats & Chocolates** · 484 Broome St
- **New York Nautical** · 158 Duane St
- **Oliver Peoples** · 366 West Broadway
- **Shoofly** · 42 Hudson St
- **Stern's Music** · 71 Warren St
- **Steven Alan** · 103 Franklin St
- **Urban Archaeology** · 143 Franklin St
- **We Are Nuts About Nuts** · 165 Church St
- **Willner Chemists** · 253 Broadway

📀 Video Rental

- **Blockbuster Video** · 368 Greenwich St

Map 2 · **TriBeCa**

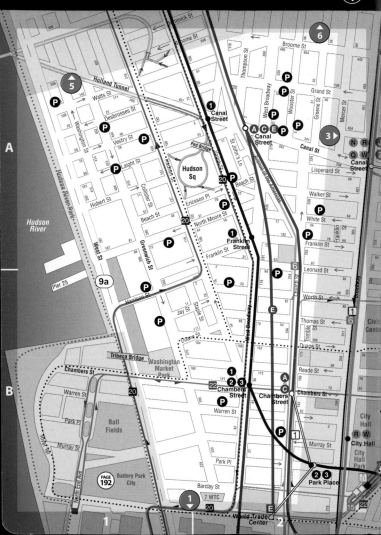

Moving around and parking in TriBeCa, especially in its northwest corner, isn't too bad, but the closer you get to City Hall and the WTC site, the more of a pain it is to find anything, especially during the week. But it's still a lot better than many other NYC neighborhoods.

Subways

2 3 .... Park Pl
1 2 3 .... Chambers St
1 .... Canal St
1 .... Franklin St
A C .... Chambers St
A C E .... Canal St
R W .... City Hall

Bus Lines

1 .... Broadway
20 .... Abingdon Sq
22 .... Seventh Ave/Sixth Ave/Broadway
6 .... Seventh Ave/Broadway/Sixth Ave
9 .... Ave B/East Broadway

Bike Lanes

• • • Recommended Route
• • • Greenway

 Parking

Map 3 · **City Hall / Chinatown**

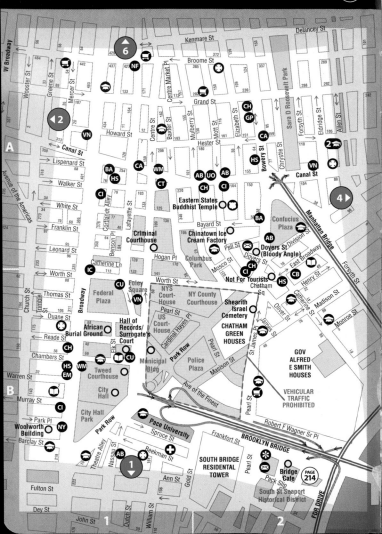

The post office on Doyers Street always has a hellish line—it's worth going somewhere else. The area's great civic architecture includes the Municipal Building, the Surrogate's Court, Foley Square, and City Hall Park. Canal Street is the major tourist area, but it's where we buy our $10 knock-offs.

$ Banks

- **AB · Abacus** · 116 Nassau St
- **AB · Abacus** · 181 Canal St
- **AB · Abacus** · 6 Bowery
- **BA · Bank of America** · 260 Canal St
- **BA · Bank of America** · 50 Bayard St
- **NY · Bank of New York** · 233 Broadway
- **CY · Cathay Bank** · 45 East Broadway
- **CH · Chase** · 180 Canal St
- **CH · Chase** · 2 Bowery
- **CH · Chase** · 231 Grand St
- **CH · Chase** · 280 Broadway
- **CT · Chinatrust Bank** · 208 Canal St
- **CA · Chinese American Bank** · 245 Canal St
- **CA · Chinese American Bank** · 77 Bowery
- **CI · Citibank** · 164 Canal St
- **CI · Citibank** · 2 Mott St
- **CI · Citibank** · 250 Broadway
- **CI · Citibank (ATM)** · 396 Broadway
- **EM · Emigrant** · 261 Broadway
- **GP · Greenpoint Bank** · 116 Bowery
- **HS · HSBC** · 254 Canal St
- **HS · HSBC** · 265 Broadway
- **HS · HSBC** · 10 East Broadway
- **HS · HSBC** · 58 Bowery
- **IC · Independence Community** · 336 Broadway
- **CU · Municipal Credit Union** · 2 Lafayette St
- **NF · North Fork Bank** · 200 Lafayette St
- **UO · United Orient Bank** · 185 Canal St
- **CU · US Courthouse Federal Credit Union** · 40 Foley Sq
- **VN · Valley National Bank** · 434 Broadway
- **VN · Valley National Bank** · 93 Canal St
- **WM · Washington Mutual** · 221 Canal St
- **WM · Washington Mutual** · 270 Broadway

❈ Community Gardens

✿ Fire Departments

- **Engine 55** · 363 Broome St
- **Engine 6** · 49 Beekman St
- **Engine 7, Ladder 1** · 100 Duane St
- **Engine 9, Ladder 6** · 75 Canal St

✚ Hospitals

- **NYU Downtown** · 170 William St

○ Landmarks

- **African Burial Ground** · Duane St & Broadway
- **Bridge Café** · 279 Water St
- **Chinatown Ice Cream Factory** · 65 Bayard St
- **City Hall** · Park Row & Broadway
- **Criminal Courthouse** · 100 Centre St
- **Doyers St (Bloody Angle)** · Doyers St
- **Eastern States Buddhist Temple** · 64 Mott St
- **Hall of Records/Surrogate's Court** · Chambers St & Park Row
- **Municipal Building** · Chambers St & Park Row
- **Not For Tourists** · 2 East Broadway
- **Shearith Israel Cemetery** · 55 St James Pl
- **Tweed Courthouse** · Chambers St & Broadway
- **Woolworth Building** · 233 Broadway

📖 Libraries

- **Chatham Square** · 33 East Broadway
- **New Amsterdam** · 9 Murray St
- **NYC Municipal Archives** · 31 Chambers St

👮 Police

- **5th Precinct** · 19 Elizabeth St

✉ Post Offices

- **Canal Street Retail** · 6 Doyers St
- **Peck Slip** · 1 Peck Slip

🎓 Schools

- **French Culinary Institute** · 462 Broadway
- **IS 131 Dr Sun Yat Sen** · 100 Hester St
- **Leadership Academy (XLDA)** · 52 Chambers St
- **M298 Pace High** · 100 Hester St
- **Murray Bergtraum High** · 411 Pearl St
- **New York Career Institute** · 15 Park Row
- **NYU School of Continuing and Professional Studies** · 14 Barclay St
- **Pace University** · 1 Pace Plz
- **PS 001 Alfred E Smith** · 8 Henry St
- **PS 124 Yung Wing** · 40 Division St
- **PS 130 DeSoto** · 143 Baxter St
- **St James** · 37 St James Pl
- **St Joseph** · 1 Monroe St
- **Transfiguration RC** · 29 Mott St

🛒 Supermarkets

- **C-Town** · 5 St James Pl
- **Dom's Fine Foods** · 202 Lafayette St
- **Gourmet Garage** · 453 Broome St
- **Italian Food Center** · 186 Grand St

19

Map 3 · **City Hall / Chinatown**

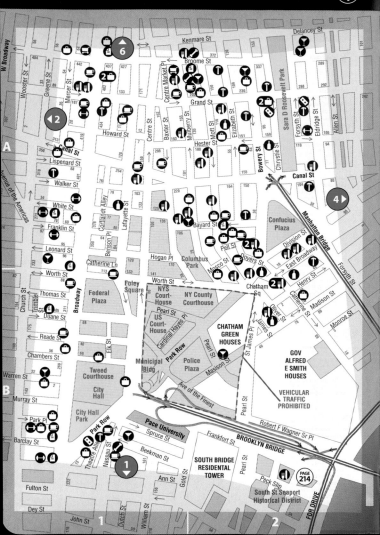

If you haven't had the crab soup dumplings at Joe's Shanghai on Pell Street, you should. For Vietnamese, Nha Trang; Thai, Pongsri Thai; Italian, Il Palazzo. If you're not in the mood for Asian or Italian cuisine, you're in the wrong area. The Bowery is still the epicenter for discount kitchen supplies and lighting fixtures.

Coffee

- **Café Palermo** · 148 Mulberry St
- **Dunkin' Donuts** · 132 Nassau St
- **Dunkin' Donuts** · 321 Broadway
- **Ferrara** · 195 Grand St
- **Green Tea Café** · 45 Mott St
- **Ho Wong Coffee House** · 146 Hester St
- **Kam Hing Coffee Shop** · 119 Baxter St
- **Maria's Bakery** · 42 Mott St
- **Mee Sum Coffee Shop** · 26 Pell St
- **Mei Lai Wah Coffee House** · 64 Bayard St
- **Nom Wah Tea Parlor** · 13 Doyers St
- **Sambuca's Café & Desserts** · 105 Mulberry St
- **Starbucks** · 111 Worth St
- **Starbucks** · 233 Broadway
- **Starbucks** · 241 Canal St
- **Starbucks** · 291 Broadway
- **Starbucks** · 38 Park Row
- **Starbucks** · 471 Broadway

Copy Shops

- **Blumberg Excelsior Copy** (8:45am-5pm) · 62 White St
- **Kinko's** (24 hrs) · 105 Duane St
- **Print Facility** (9am-6:30) · 225 Broadway
- **Soho Reprographics** (8am-7:30pm) · 381 Broome St
- **Staples** (7am-7pm) · 217 Broadway
- **Staples** (7am-8pm) · 488 Broadway
- **The UPS Store** (8:30am-7pm) · 342 Broadway
- **Visual Arts & Photo** (9:30am-8pm) · 63E Bayard St

Gyms

- **Church Street Boxing Gym** · 25 Park Pl
- **Eastern Athletic** · 80 Leonard St
- **Five Points Fitness** · 444 Broadway
- **New York Sports Clubs** · 217 Broadway
- **Peter Anthony Fitness** · 39 White St
- **Tribeca Sports Center** (boxing gym) · 381 Broadway
- **YMCA Chinatown** · 100 Hester St

Hardware Stores

- **Carl Martinez Hardware** · 88 Canal St
- **Chinatown 25 Cents Store** · 7 Elizabeth St
- **CIS Tools** · 446 Broadway
- **Design Source** · 115 Bowery
- **East Broadway Appliance Hardware** · 59 East Broadway
- **General Machinery** · 358 Broome St
- **OK Hardware** · 438 Broome St
- **T&T Hardware** · 101 Chrystie St
- **Walker Supply** · 61 Walker St
- **Weinstein & Holtzman** · 29 Park Row
- **World Construction** · 78 Forsyth St

Liquor Stores

- **Chez Choi Liquor & Wine** · 49 Chrystie St
- **Elizabeth Street Wine & Liquor** · 86 Elizabeth St
- **Royal Wine & Liquor Store** · 45 Madison St
- **Sun Wai Liquor Store** · 17 East Broadway
- **Walker Liquors** · 101 Lafayette St
- **Wine Wo Liquor Discount** · 12 Chatham Square

Nightlife

- **The Beekman** · 15 Beekman St
- **Capitale** · 130 Bowery
- **Double Happiness** · 173 Mott St
- **Happy Ending** · 302 Broome St
- **Knitting Factory** · 74 Leonard St
- **Metropolitan Improvement Company** · 3 Madison St
- **Milk & Honey** · 134 Eldridge St
- **Tribeca Blues** · 16 Warren St
- **Winnie's** · 104 Bayard St

Pet Shops

- **Aqua Star Pet Shop** · 172 Mulberry St
- **Petland Discounts** · 132 Nassau St
- **Win Tropical Aquariums** · 169 Mott St

Restaurants

- **Bridge Café** · 279 Water St
- **Canton** · 45 Division St
- **Cup & Saucer** · 89 Canal St
- **Dim Sum Go Go** · 5 East Broadway
- **Excellent Dumpling House** · 111 Lafayette St
- **Ferrara** · 195 Grand St
- **Fuleen's** · 11 Division St
- **Goody's** · 1 East Broadway
- **Il Palazzo** · 151 Mulberry St
- **Joe's Shanghai** · 9 Pell St
- **L'Ecole** · 462 Broadway
- **Lily's** · 31 Oliver St
- **Mandarin Court** · 61 Mott St
- **Mark Joseph Steakhouse** · 261 Water St
- **New York Noodle Town** · 28 Bowery
- **Nha Trang** · 87 Baxter St
- **Pho Viet Huong** · 73 Mulberry St
- **Ping's** · 22 Mott St
- **Pongsri Thai** · 106 Bayard St
- **Positano Ristorante** · 122 Mulberry St
- **Quartino** · 21 Peck Slip
- **Triple Eight Palace** · 88 East Broadway
- **Umberto's Clam House** · 178 Mulberry St
- **Wo Hop** · 17 Mott St

Shopping

- **Aji Ichiban** · 167 Hester St
- **Bangkok Center Grocery** · 104 Mosco St
- **Bloomingdale's** · 504 Broadway
- **Bowery Lighting** · 132 Bowery
- **Catherine Street Meat Market** · 21 Catherine St
- **Chinatown Ice Cream Factory** · 65 Bayard St
- **Dipalo Dairy** · 200 Grand St
- **Fountain Pen Hospital** · 10 Warren St
- **GS Food Market** · 250 Grand St
- **Hong Kong Seafood & Meat** · 75 Mulberry St
- **Industrial Plastic Supply** · 309 Canal St
- **J&R Music & Computer World** · 33 Park Row
- **Kate Spade** · 454 Broome St
- **Lung Moon Bakery** · 83 Mulberry St
- **Mitchell's Place** · 15 Park Pl
- **Modell's** · 55 Chambers St
- **New Age Designer** · 38 Mott St
- **The New York City Store** · 1 Centre St
- **Pearl Paint** · 308 Canal St
- **Pearl River Mart** · 477 Broadway
- **Radio Shack** · 280 Broadway
- **SoHo Art Materials** · 127 Grand St
- **Tan My My Market** · 253 Grand St
- **Tent & Trails** · 21 Park Pl
- **Ting's Gift Shop** · 18 Doyers St
- **Two Lines Music** · 370 Broadway
- **Vespa** · 13 Crosby St
- **Yellow Rat Bastard** · 478 Broadway

Video Rental

- **J&R Music World** · 23 Park Row
- **Laser Video Center (Chinese only)** · 97 Chrystie St
- **Terence Video** · 282 Grand St

Map 3 · City Hall / Chinatown

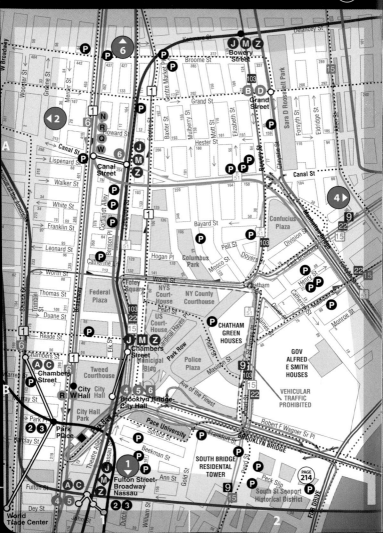

The Brooklyn Bridge is best approached from Pearl Street. Be careful about driving east on Canal Street—you have to make a right on Bowery or else you'll drive over the Manhattan Bridge. (Canal Street is one-way going west between Bowery and Chrystie.) Forget about street parking during the day.

Subways

2 3 .... Park Pl

4 5 6 J M Z .... Brooklyn Bridge-City Hall-Chambers St

B D .... Grand St

6 J M Z N Q R W .... Canal St

R W .... City Hall

J M Z .... Bowery St

A C .... Chambers St

J M Z .... Fulton St/Broadway

Bus Lines

1 .... Broadway/Centre St

103 ....Bowery/Park Row

15 .... East Broadway/Park Row

22 .... Chambers/Madison St

6 .... Church St/Broadway

9 .... Park Row

🚲 .... Lafayette/Canal Sts

Bike Lanes

- • • • Marked Bike Lane
- • • • Recommended Route
- • • • Greenway

 Parking

23

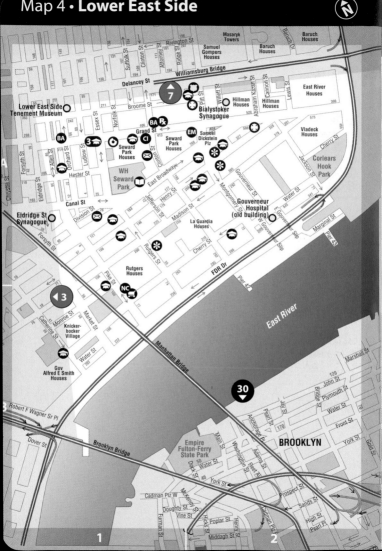

Map 4 • **Lower East Side**

The modern Lower East Side is an interesting mishmash of New York cultures, with the spillover from Chinatown abutting hipster-ville abutting bodega-ville, with the remnants of the Jewish population mixed in. Kossar's Bialys on Grand Street between Essex and Norfolk makes the best bialys ever, period. Check out Hong Kong Supermarket for Asian specialties.

24-Hour Pharmacies

· **Rite Aid** · 408 Grand St

Banks

BA · **Bank of America** · 318 Grand St
BA · **Bank of America** · 420 Grand St
CI · **Citibank** · 411 Grand St
EM · **Emigrant** · 465 Grand St
CB · **New York Community Bank** · 227 Cherry St

Bagels

· **Kossar's Bagels and Bialys** · 367 Grand St

Community Gardens

Fire Departments

· **Engine 15** · 269 Henry St
· **Ladder 18** · 25 Pitt St

Landmarks

· **Bialystoker Synagogue** · 7 Bialystoker Pl
· **Eldridge Street Synagogue** · 12 Eldridge St
· **Gouverneur Hospital** · Gouverneur Slip & Water St
· **Lower East Side Tenement Museum** · 90 Orchard St

Libraries

· **Seward Park** · 192 East Broadway

Police

· **7th Precinct** · 19 1/2 Pitt St

Post Offices

· **Knickerbocker** · 128 East Broadway
· **Pitt Station** · 185 Clinton St

Schools

· **Beth Jacob Parochial** · 142 Broome St
· **Dual Language & Asian Studies High** · 350 Grand St
· **Henry Street School for International Studies (M292)** · 220 Henry St
· **High School of History and Communication** · 350 Grand St
· **JHS 056 Corlears** · 220 Henry St
· **Mesivta Tifereth Jerusalem** · 145 East Broadway
· **New Design High** · 350 Grand St
· **PS 002 Meyer London** · 122 Henry St
· **PS 042 Benjamin Altman** · 71 Hester St
· **PS 126 Jacob Riis** · 80 Catherine St
· **PS 134 Henrietta Szold** · 293 East Broadway
· **PS 137 John L Bernstein** · 327 Cherry St
· **PS 184M Shuang Wen** · 293 East Broadway
· **Seward Park High** · 350 Grand St
· **University Neighborhood High** · 200 Monroe St

Supermarkets

· **Pathmark** · 227 Cherry St

Map 4 • Lower East Side

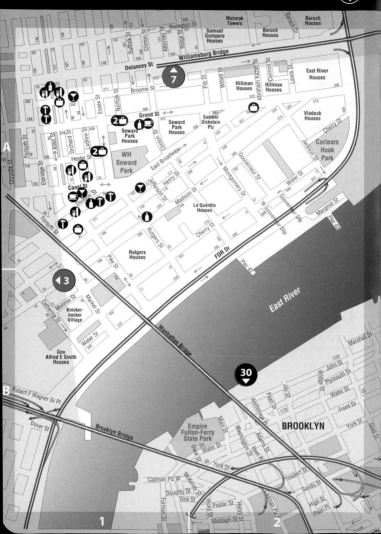

One key destination on the Lower East Side is Good World, a fabulous bar with excellent Scandinavian food. For great Jewish staples such as chocolate babka, check out Gertel's Bake Shop.

Coffee

· **Full City Coffee** · 409 Grand St
· **Happy Café** · 8 Allen St

Hardware Stores

· **International Electrical** · 77 Allen St
· **Karlee Hardware** · 98 East Broadway
· **New York Home Center** · 71 Allen St
· **Tom's Hardware** · 154 East Broadway
· **Weilgus & Sons** · 158 East Broadway

Liquor Stores

· **Madison Liquor** · 195 Madison St
· **Seward Park Liquors** · 393 Grand St
· **Wedding Banquet Liquor** · 135 Division St
· **Wing Tak Liquor** · 101 Allen St

Nightlife

· **Bar 169** · 169 East Broadway
· **Good World** · 3 Orchard St
· **Lolita** · 266 Broome St

Restaurants

· **88 Orchard** · 88 Orchard St
· **Congee Village** · 100 Allen St
· **Good World Bar & Grill** · 3 Orchard St
· **Les Enfants Terribles** · 37 Canal St
· **Pho Bang** · 3 Pike St

Shopping

· **Doughnut Plant** · 379 Grand St
· **Gertel's Bake Shop** · 53 Hester St
· **Hong Kong Supermarket** · 109 East Broadway
· **Joe's Fabric Warehouse** · 102 Orchard St
· **Kossar's Bialys** · 367 Grand St
· **Mendel Goldberg Fabrics** · 72 Hester St
· **Moishe's Kosher Bake Shop** · 504 Grand St
· **Sweet Life** · 63 Hester St

Map 4 • **Lower East Side**

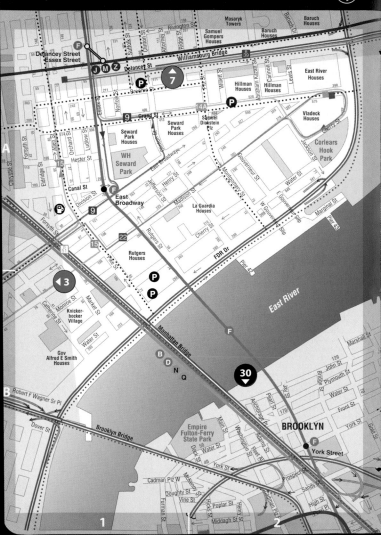

Take advantage of the reconstructed East River Esplanade off of South Street if you're biking, skating, or walking—it's got the best views of the bridges. The Williamsburg Bridge is now open for business, with a lovely new pedestrian/bike path to boot.

Subways

F	East Broadway
F	York St
F J M Z	Delancey St-Essex St

Bus Lines

14	Grand St
15	Allen St
22	Madison St
9	East Broadway/Essex St
B51	Forsyth St

Bike Lanes

- • • • Recommended Route
- • • • Greenway

Gas Stations

· **Mobil** · 2 Pike St

Parking

Map 5 • West Village

W 16th St

W 15th St

NF

8

9

HS

W 14th St

Ninth Ave

Little W 12th St

W 13th St

Greenwich Ave

W 12th St

HS

Gansevoort St

Avenue of the Americas (Sixth Ave)

Horatio St

Jane St

CH

Eighth Ave

Abingdon Sq

W 11th St

W 10th St

Washington St

W 12th St

Bethune St

Bank St

Waverly Pl

Seventh Ave S

W 9th St

W 8th St

BA

Jefferson Market Courthouse

Westbeth Building

W 11th St

Bleecker St

Stonewall

Sheridan

EM

Rx

White Horse Tavern

Perry St

Waverly Pl

W 4th St

Washington Pl

Charles Ln

Charles St

CI

CH

NF

WM

Christopher St

W 10th St

Grove St

Jones St

Cornelia St

The Cage

W 3rd St

Chumley's

Commerce St

Minetta Ln

West Side Hwy

Barrow St

Bedford St

Carmine St

Bleecker St

Hudson River Park

9a

Morton St

Downing St

6

BA

Leroy St

St Luke's

James J Walker Park

W Houston St

Hudson River

Clarkson St

HS

W Houston St

EM

King St

Varick St

MacDougal St

Sullivan St

Prince St

CH

Charlton St

Greenwich St

Washington St

Vandam St

Spring St

Spring St

Hudson St

Dominick St

Thompson St

Broome St

The Ear Inn

2

Canal St

Broome St

Watts St

Grand St

Holland Tunnel

1   2

Full of quiet, tree-lined streets, handsome houses, and tons of little shops and restaurants, the West Village is tops among many New Yorker's lists of most desirable neighborhoods. The Hudson River Greenway only adds to the sterling reputation, as the new luxury apartments on the West Side Highway demonstrate.

24-Hour Pharmacies

- **Duane Reade** · 378 Sixth Ave

Banks

BA · Bank of America · 615 Washington St
BA · Bank of America (ATM) · 390 Sixth Ave
CH · Chase · 158 W 14th St
CH · Chase · 204 W 4th St
CH · Chase · 302 W 12th St
CH · Chase · 345 Hudson St
CI · Citibank (ATM) · 75 Christopher St
EM · Emigrant · 375 Hudson St
EM · Emigrant · 395 Sixth Ave
HS · HSBC · 101 W 14th St
HS · HSBC · 207 Varick St
HS · HSBC · 80 Eighth Ave
NF · North Fork · 347 Sixth Ave
NF · North Fork Bank (ATM) · 403A W 14th St
WM · Washington Mutual · 340 Sixth Ave

Bagels

- **Bagel Buffet** · 406 Sixth Ave
- **Bagels & Much More** · 70 Greenwich Ave
- **Bagels on the Square** · 7 Carmine St
- **Bread Factory Café** · 330 Bleecker St
- **Dizzy Izzy's New York Bagels** · 185 Varick St
- **Famous Bagels Buffet** · 510 Sixth Ave
- **Hudson Bagels** · 502 Hudson St
- **Murray's Bagels** · 500 Sixth Ave
- **New World Coffee** · 488 Sixth Ave

Community Gardens

Fire Departments

- **Engine 24, Ladder 5** · 227 Sixth Ave

Hospitals

- **St Vincent's** · 153 W 11th St

Landmarks

- **The Cage (basketball court)** · 320 Sixth Ave at W 4th St
- **Chumley's** · 86 Bedford St
- **The Ear Inn** · Washington & Spring Sts
- **Jefferson Market Courthouse** · 425 Sixth Ave
- **Stonewall** · 53 Christopher St
- **Westbeth Building** · Washington St & Bethune St
- **White Horse Tavern** · 567 Hudson St

Libraries

- **Early Childhood Resource & Information Center** · 66 Leroy St
- **Hudson Park** · 66 Leroy St
- **Jefferson Market** · 425 Sixth Ave

Police

- **6th Precinct** · 233 W 10th St

Post Offices

- **Village** · 201 Varick St
- **West Village** · 527 Hudson St

Schools

- **Chelsea VHS (M615)** · 131 Sixth Ave
- **City as School** · 16 Clarkson St
- **City Country School** · 146 W 13th St
- **Elisabeth Irwin High** · 40 Charlton St
- **Empire State College - State University of New York** · 325 Hudson St
- **Greenwich House Music School** · 46 Barrow St
- **Joffrey Ballet** · 434 Sixth Ave
- **Little Red School House** · 272 Sixth Ave
- **Merce Cunningham Studio** · 55 Bethune St
- **Our Lady of Pompeii** · 240 Bleecker St
- **Pratt Institute** · 144 W 14th St
- **PS 3 The Charette** · 490 Hudson St
- **PS 41 Greenwich Village** · 116 W 11th St
- **PS 721 Manhattan Occupational Training School** · 250 W Houston St
- **St Bernard-St Francis Xavier** · 327 W 13th St
- **St Joseph's Washington Place** · 111 Washington Pl
- **St Luke's** · 487 Hudson St
- **Village Community** · 272 W 13th St
- **Village Community** · 272 W 10th St

Supermarkets

- **Associated** · 255 W 14th St
- **Balducci's** · 81 Eighth Ave
- **Citarella** · 424 Sixth Ave
- **D'Agostino** · 666 Greenwich St
- **D'Agostino** · 790 Greenwich St
- **Food Emporium** · 475 Sixth Ave
- **Gourmet Garage** · 117 Seventh Ave S
- **Gristede's** · 3 Sheridan Sq
- **Gristede's** · 585 Hudson St
- **Western Beef** · 403 W 14th St

Map 5 • **West Village**

The Corner Bistro has the best burgers in Manhattan, and the Ear Inn is one of our favorite all-time bars. We can't decide which we like most—Florent's food, vibe, or décor. The meatpacking district is now hipper-than-thou, complete with unaffordable shops, too many French restaurants, and squawking between residents and developers. Recommended.

Coffee

- **Anna Coffee Shop** · 204 W 14th St
- **Brewbar Coffee** · 13 Eighth Ave
- **Brewbar Coffee** · 327 W 11th St
- **Caffe dell'Artista** · 46 Greenwich Ave
- **Caffe Vivaldi** · 32 Jones St
- **Coffee Sweet Heart** · 69 Eighth Ave
- **Cosi** · 504 Sixth Ave
- **Doma** · 17 Perry St
- **Dunkin' Donuts** · 536 Sixth Ave
- **Dunkin' Donuts** · 75 Christopher St
- **Grey Dog's Coffee** · 33 Carmine St
- **Grounded** · 28 Jane St
- **Hudson Coffee Bar** · 350 Hudson St
- **Joe** · 141 Waverly Pl
- **Kenny's Coffee Shop** · 345 Hudson Pl
- **New World Coffee** · 488 Sixth Ave
- **Porto Rico Importing** · 201 Bleecker St
- **Sant Ambroeus** · 259 W 4th
- **Starbucks** · 150 Varick St
- **Starbucks** · 378 Sixth Ave
- **Starbucks** · 510 Sixth Ave
- **Starbucks** · 72 Grove St
- **Starbucks** · 93 Greenwich Ave
- **Sucelt Coffee Shop** · 200 W 14th St
- **Sweet Life Café** · 147 Christopher St

Copy Shops

- **Copy/Com** (9am-8pm) · 70A Greenwich Ave
- **Elite Copy Center** (9am-7pm) · 52 Carmine St
- **Mail Boxes Etc** (8:30am-7pm) · 302 W 12th St
- **Mail Boxes Etc** (8:30am-7pm) · 315 Bleecker St
- **Mail Boxes Etc** (8:30am-7pm) · 511 Sixth Ave
- **Village Copy Center** (8:30am-8pm) · 520 Hudson St

Farmer's Markets

- **Abingdon Square** · W 12th St & Hudson St

Gyms

- **Aerospace Fitness** (boxing gym) · 332 W 13th St
- **Crunch Fitness** · 152 Christopher St
- **Curves** · 345 W 14th St
- **Equinox Fitness Club** · 97 Greenwich Ave
- **Hanson Fitness** · 132 Perry St
- **New York Sports Clubs** · 125 Seventh Ave
- **Printing House Fitness & Racquet Club** · 421 Hudson St
- **YMCA McBurney** · 125 W 14th St

Hardware Stores

- **Barney's Hardware** · 467 Sixth Ave
- **Blaustein Paint & Hardware** · 304 Bleecker St
- **Colonial Hardware** · 163 Varick St
- **Garber Hardware** · 710 Greenwich St
- **Hardware Mart** · 151 W 14th St
- **Jonathan's Decorative Hardware** · 12 Perry St
- **Lock-It Hardware** · 59 Carmine St
- **The Lumber Store** · 71 Eighth Ave

Liquor Stores

- **Casa Oliveira Wines & Liquors** · 98 Seventh Ave S
- **Christopher Street Liquor Shoppe** · 45 Christopher St
- **Golden Rule Wine & Liquor** · 457 Hudson St
- **Imperial Liquors** · 579 Hudson St
- **Manley's Liquor Store** · 35 Eighth Ave
- **North Village Liquors** · 254 W 14th St
- **Pop the Cork Wine Merchant** · 168 Seventh Ave S
- **Sea Grape Wine & Spirits** · 512 Hudson St
- **Spirits of Carmine** · 52 Carmine St
- **Village Vintner** · 448 Sixth Ave
- **Village Wine & Spirits** · 486 Sixth Ave
- **Waverly Wine & Liquor** · 135 Waverly Pl

Movie Theaters

- **Film Forum** · 209 W Houston St
- **New York Public Library Jefferson Market Branch** · 425 Sixth Ave

Nightlife

- **2i's** · 248 W 14th St
- **APT** · 419 W 13th St
- **Art Bar** · 52 Eighth Ave
- **Automatic Slims** · 733 Washington St
- **Blind Tiger Ale House** · 518 Hudson St
- **Chumley's** · 86 Bedford St
- **Cielo** · 18 Little W 12th St
- **Cornelia Street Café** · 29 Cornelia St
- **Culture Club** · 179 Varick St
- **Don Hill's** · 511 Greenwich St
- **Duplex** · 61 Christopher St
- **Ear Inn** · 326 Spring St
- **Henrietta Hudson** · 438 Hudson St
- **Jazz Gallery** · 290 Hudson St
- **Lotus** · 409 W 14th St
- **The Otherroom** · 143 Perry St
- **SOB'S** · 200 Varick St
- **Trust** · 421 W 13th St
- **Village Vanguard** · 178 Seventh Ave S
- **Vol de Nuit** · 148 W 4th St
- **West** · 425 West St
- **White Horse Tavern** · 567 Hudson St

Pet Shops

- **Beasty Feast** · 630 Hudson St
- **Beasty Feast** · 680 Washington St
- **Fetch** · 43 Greenwich Ave
- **Groom-O-Rama** · 496 Sixth Ave
- **Parrots & Pups** · 45 Christopher St
- **Pet Central** · 237 Bleecker St
- **Pet Palace** · 109 W 10th St
- **Pet's Kitchen** · 116 Christopher St
- **Petland Discounts** · 389 Sixth Ave

Restaurants

- **A Salt & Battery** · 112 Greenwich Ave
- **AOC** · 314 Bleecker St
- **Aquagrill** · 210 Spring St
- **Benny's Burritos** · 113 Greenwich Ave
- **Blue Ribbon Bakery** · 33 Downing St
- **Café Asean** · 117 W 10th St
- **Caffe Torino** · 139 W 10th St
- **Chez Brigitte** · 77 Greenwich Ave

- **Chumley's** · 86 Bedford St
- **Corner Bistro** · 331 W 4th St
- **Cowgirl Hall of Fame** · 519 Hudson St
- **Day-O** · 103 Greenwich Ave
- **Dragonfly** · 47 Seventh Ave S
- **Florent** · 69 Gansevoort St
- **French Roast** · 458 Sixth Ave
- **French Roast** · 78 W 11th St
- **Gonzo Restaurant** · 140 W 13th St
- **Grey Dog's Coffee** · 33 Carmine St
- **Home** · 20 Cornelia St
- **Ivo & Lulu** · 558 Broome St
- **Jefferson** · 121 W 10th St
- **Joe's Pizza** · 233 Bleecker St
- **John's Pizzeria** · 278 Bleecker St
- **Le Gamin** · 27 Bedford St
- **Lunchbox Food Company** · 357 West St
- **Mary's Fish Camp** · 246 W 4th St
- **Mirchi** · 29 Seventh Ave S
- **Moustache** · 90 Bedford St
- **One If By Land, TIBS** · 17 Barrow St
- **Ony** · 357 Sixth Ave
- **Pastis** · 9 Ninth Ave
- **Pearl Oyster Bar** · 18 Cornelia St
- **Petite Abeille** · 466 Hudson St
- **P—** · 31 Cornelia St
- **Sapore** · 55 Greenwich Ave
- **Souen** · 210 Sixth Ave
- **Spotted Pig** · 314 W 11th St
- **Tea & Sympathy** · 108 Greenwich Ave
- **Two Boots** · 201 W 11th St
- **Yama** · 38 Carmine St

Shopping

- **Alexander McQueen** · 417 W 14th St
- **Alphabets** · 47 Greenwich Ave
- **American Apparel** · 373 6th Ave
- **Bleecker Street Records** · 239 Bleecker St
- **CO Bigelow Chemists** · 414 Sixth Ave
- **Faicco's Pork Store** · 260 Bleecker St
- **Flight 001** · 96 Greenwich Ave
- **Geppetto's Toy Box** · 10 Christopher St
- **Integral Yoga Natural Foods** · 229 W 13th St
- **Janovic Plaza** · 161 Sixth Ave
- **The Leather Man** · 111 Christopher St
- **Little Pie Company** · 407 W 14th St
- **Magnolia Bakery** · 401 Bleecker St
- **Matt Umanov Guitars** · 273 Bleecker St
- **Murray's Cheese Shop** · 254 Bleecker St
- **Mxyplyzyk** · 125 Greenwich Ave
- **Myers of Keswick** · 634 Hudson St
- **Porto Rico Importing Company** · 201 Bleecker St
- **Radio Shack** · 360 6th Ave
- **Radio Shack** · 49 Seventh Ave
- **Rebel Rebel Records** · 319 Bleecker St
- **Scott Jordan Furniture** · 137 Varick St
- **Urban Outfitters** · 374 Sixth Ave
- **Vitra** · 29 Ninth Ave

Video Rental

- **Evergreen Video** · 37 Carmine St
- **Vivid Video** · 100 Christopher St
- **World of Video** · 51 Greenwich Ave

Map 5 • West Village

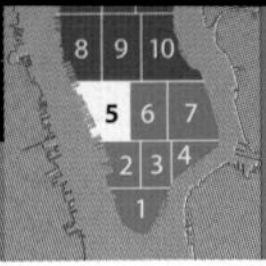

It's pretty tough to park anywhere east of Washington Street. All approaches to the Holland Tunnel suck. Thankfully, there is a great bike lane on Hudson Street, though the one on Sixth Avenue doesn't start until 9th Street. The Houston Street subway station might have the coolest mosaics of any station in Manhattan.

Subways

①②③⑤Ⓕ Ⓥ Ⓛ .... 14 St-6 Ave
① .... Christopher St-Sheridan Sq
① .... Houston St
ⒶⒸⒺⒻ Ⓥ Ⓑ Ⓓ .... W 4 St
ⒶⒸⒺⓁ .... 14 St-8 Ave
ⒸⒺ .... Spring St

Bus Lines

11	Ninth Ave/Tenth Ave
14	14th St Crosstown
20	Abingdon Sq
20	Seventh Ave/Eighth Ave/Central Park West
21	Houston St Crosstown
5	Fifth Ave/Sixth Ave/Riverside Dr
6	Seventh Ave/Sixth Ave/Broadway
8	8th St/9th St Crosstown

Bike Lanes

- • • • Marked Bike Lane
- • • • Recommended Route
- • • • Greenway

PATH

- **14 St** • 14th St & Sixth Ave
- **9th St** • 9th St & Sixth Ave
- **Christopher St** • Christopher St & Hudson St

Car Rental

- **Dollar** • 99 Charles St
- **Hertz** • 18 Morton St

Car Washes

- **Apple Management (detailer)** • 332 W 11th St
- **Lage Car Wash** • 124 Sixth Ave
- **Village Car Wash & Lube** • 160 Leroy St

Gas Stations

- **Lukoil** • 63 Eighth Ave
- **Mobil** • 140 Sixth Ave
- **Mobil** • 290 West St

Parking

Map 6 • **Washington Sq / NYU / NoHo / SoHo**

NYU may dominate here, but Washington Square Park remains a vital destination. Farther south, great shops and galleries still abound in SoHo and on Broadway, even as the chain stores move in. The whole area is an architectural "greatest hits," which is fortunate since SoHo IS becoming more like an upscale suburban mall.

24-Hour Pharmacies

- **Duane Reade** · 123 Third Ave
- **Duane Reade** · 24 E 14th St
- **Duane Reade** · 598 Broadway
- **Duane Reade** · 636 Broadway
- **Duane Reade** · 769 Broadway
- **Walgreen's** · 145 Fourth Ave

Bagels

- **Bagel Bob's** · 51 University Pl
- **The Bagel Café/Ray's Pizza** · 2 St Mark's St
- **Dizzy Izzy's New York Bagels** · 250 E 14th St
- **Giant Bagel Shop** · 120 University Pl
- **New World Coffee** · 412 West Broadway

Banks

- **AP · Apple** · 4 Irving Pl
- **AP · Apple (ATM)** · 145 Fourth Ave
- **BA · Bank of America** · 589 Broadway
- **BA · Bank of America** · 72 Second Ave
- **BA · Bank of America (ATM)** · 66 Third Ave
- **BA · Bank of America (ATM)** · 742 Broadway
- **CH · Chase** · 32 University Pl
- **CH · Chase** · 525 Broadway
- **CH · Chase** · 623 Broadway
- **CH · Chase** · 756 Broadway
- **CH · Chase** · 90 Fifth Ave
- **CI · Citibank** · 555 LaGuardia Pl
- **CO · Commerce Bank** · 666 Broadway
- **CO · Commerce Bank** · 90 Fifth Ave
- **EM · Emigrant** · 105 Second Ave
- **HS · HSBC** · 1 E 8th St
- **HS · HSBC** · 599 Broadway
- **HS · HSBC** · 769 Broadway
- **IC · Independence Community** · 43 E 8th St
- **NF · North Fork** · 594 Broadway
- **WM · Washington Mutual** · 130 Second Ave
- **WM · Washington Mutual** · 835 Broadway
- **WM · Washington Mutual** · 166 Bleecker St

Community Gardens

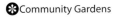

Fire Departments

- **Engine 33, Ladder 9** · 42 Great Jones St
- **Engine 5** · 340 E 14th St
- **Ladder 20** · 251 Lafayette St
- **Ladder 3** · 108 E 13th St

Hospitals

- **New York Eye & Ear Infirmary** · 310 E 14th St

Landmarks

- **The Alamo (The Cube)** · Astor Pl & Fourth Ave
- **Asch Building (Brown Building)** · 23-29 Washington St
- **Bayard-Condict Building** · 65 Bleecker St
- **CBGB & OMFUG** · 315 Bowery
- **Colonnade Row** · 428 Lafayette St
- **Con Edison Building** · 145 E 14th St
- **Cooper Union** · 30 Cooper Sq
- **Grace Church** · 802 Broadway
- **Great Jones Fire House** · Great Jones St & Bowery
- **Milano's** · 51 E Houston St
- **New York Marble Cemetery** · 41 Second Ave
- **Old Merchant's House** · 29 E 4th St
- **The Public Theater** · 425 Lafayette St
- **Salmagundi Club** · 47 Fifth Ave
- **Singer Building** · 561 Broadway
- **St Mark's-in-the-Bowery Church** · 131 E 10th St
- **The Strand Bookstore** · 828 Broadway
- **Wanamaker's** · Broadway & E 8th St
- **Washington Mews** · University Pl (entrance)
- **Washington Square Park** · Washington Sq

Libraries

- **Ottendorfer** · 135 Second Ave

Post Offices

- **Cooper** · 93 Fourth Ave
- **Patchin** · 70 W 10th St
- **Prince** · 124 Greene St

Schools

- **Alfred Adler Institute** · 594 Broadway
- **Benjamin N Cardozo School of Law** · 55 Fifth Ave
- **Cascade HS Center For Multimedia Communications (M650)** · 198 Forsyth St
- **Cooper Union** · 30 Cooper Sq
- **Eugene Lang College** · 65 W 11th St
- **Gateway** · 236 Second Ave
- **Grace Church** · 86 Fourth Ave
- **Harvey Milk** · 2 Astor Pl
- **Hebrew Union College** · 1 W 4th St
- **Institute of Audio Research** · 64 University Pl
- **La Salle Academy** · 44 E 2nd St
- **Legacy School for Integrated Studies** · 34 W 14 St
- **Legacy School for Intergrated Studies** · 33 W 13th St
- **Nativity Mission** · 204 Forsyth St
- **New School for Social Research** · 66 W 12th St
- **New York Eye and Ear Institute** · 310 E 14th St
- **New York University** · 70 Washington Sq S
- **Parson's School of Design** · 66 Fifth Ave
- **PS 751 Career Development Center** · 113 E 4th St
- **Satellite Academy High** · 198 Forsyth St
- **St Anthony** · 60 MacDougal St
- **St Patrick** · 233 Mott St
- **Third Street Music School Settlement** · 235 E 11th St
- **Tisch School of Arts - Dance** · 111 Second Ave

Supermarkets

- **Associated** · 130 Bleecker St
- **D'Agostino** · 64 University Pl
- **Dean & DeLuca** · 560 Broadway
- **Garden of Eden Gourmet** · 7 E 14th St
- **Gristede's** · 113 Fourth Ave
- **Gristede's** · 246 Mercer St
- **Gristede's** · 25 University Pl
- **Gristede's** · 333 E 14th St
- **Gristede's** · 5 W 14th St
- **Met Food** · 107 Second Ave
- **Met Food** · 251 Mulberry St
- **Whole Foods Market** · 4 Union Sq S

Map 6 • **Washington Sq / NYU / NoHo / SoHo**

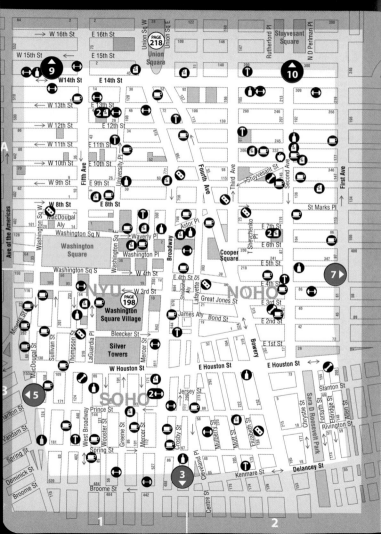

Feel like having some coffee? Welcome to the coffee shop capital of New York, at least for the non-Starbucks variety (and there's a ton of that dreaded chain as well). You can pretty much find every sundry you might need here without venturing to another neighborhood, including some great movie rental places (two Kim's, TLA and Tower).

☕ Coffee

- **Anyway Café** · 32 E 2nd St
- **Au Bon Pain** · 684 Broadway
- **Caffe Dante** · 79 MacDougal St
- **Caffe Pane e Cioccolato** · 10 Waverly Pl
- **Caffe Reggio** · 119 MacDougal St
- **Coffee Cherries** · 13 E 4th St
- **Cosi** · 841 Broadway
- **Cremcaffe** · 65 Second Ave
- **Cuppa Cuppa** · 75 E 4th St
- **Dean & DeLuca Café** · 560 Broadway
- **Dean & DeLuca Café** · 75 University Pl
- **Dunkin' Donuts** · 166 Second Ave
- **Housing Works Used Book Café** · 126 Crosby St
- **L'Angolo Café** · 108 W Houston St
- **La Lanterna di Vittorio** · 129 MacDougal St
- **Le Petite Café** · 156 Spring St
- **Mission Café** · 82 Second Ave
- **Moxa** · 552 LaGuardia Pl
- **Mudspot** · 307 E 9th St
- **Muffins & More** · 114 Fourth Ave
- **New World Coffee** · 412 West Broadway
- **Once Upon A Tart** · 135 Sullivan St
- **Oren's Daily Roast** · 31 Waverly Pl
- **Porto Rico Importing** · 107 Thompson St
- **Porto Rico Importing** · 201 Bleecker St
- **Porto Rico Importing** · 40 St Marks Pl
- **Saint Alp's Teahouse** · 170 Bleecker St
- **Simone Espresso & Wine Bar** · 134 First Ave
- **Starbucks** · 141 Second Ave
- **Starbucks** · 21 Astor Pl
- **Starbucks** · 21 E 8th St
- **Starbucks** · 51 Astor Pl
- **Starbucks** · 665 Broadway
- **Starbucks** · 72 Spring St
- **Sweet Café** · 72 Fifth Ave
- **Veniero's** · 342 E 11th St

🏢 Copy Shops

- **Advanced Copy Center** (8:30am-7pm) · 552 LaGuardia Pl
- **American Copy Center** (8am-10pm) · 201 E 10th St
- **East Side Copy Center** (8am-11pm) · 15 E 13th St
- **First Prince Center** (8:30am-7pm) · 22 Prince St
- **King Photocopy** (8am-9:30pm) · 45 E 7th St
- **Kinko's (8am-12am)** · 21 Astor Pl
- **National Reprographics** (9am-8pm) · 594 Broadway
- **New University Copy** (8am-10pm) · 11 Waverly Pl
- **New York Copy Center** (8am-9pm) · 204 E 11th St
- **New York Copy Center** (8am-9pm) · 34 E 7th St
- **Prince St Copy Center** (9am-7pm) · 159 Prince St
- **Source Unlimited Printing** (10am-5:30pm) · 331 E 9th St
- **Staples** (7am-8pm) · 5 Union Sq W
- **Staples** (7am-8pm) · 769 Broadway
- **The UPS Store** (8:30am-6:30pm) · 111 E 14th St
- **The UPS Store** (8:30am-7pm) · 7 E 8th St
- **The UPS Store** (9am-7pm) · 168 Second Ave
- **The Village Copier** (8am-12am) · 20 E 13th St
- **Unique Copy Center** (8am-11pm) · 252 Greene St

🥕 Farmer's Markets

- **St Mark's Church** · E 10th St & Second Ave

🏋 Gyms

- **24/7 Fitness Club** · 47 W 14th St
- **Crunch Fitness** · 404 Lafayette St
- **Crunch Fitness** · 54 E 13th St
- **Crunch Fitness** · 623 Broadway
- **Curves** · 580 Broadway
- **Curves** · 64 W 3rd St
- **Dolphin Fitness Clubs** · 94 E 4th St
- **Dolphin Fitness East** · 242 E 14th St
- **Hanson Fitness** · 63 Greene St
- **Hanson Fitness** · 826 Broadway
- **Lucille Roberts Health Club** · 80 Fifth Ave
- **New York Health & Racquet Club** · 24 E 13th St
- **New York Sports Clubs** · 34 W 14th St
- **New York Sports Clubs** · 503 Broadway
- **Physio Fitness** · 584 Broadway
- **Plus One Fitness Clinic** · 106 Crosby St
- **Sol Goldman YM-YWHA** · 344 E 14th St
- **Synergy Fitness Clubs** · 227 Mulberry St

🔧 Hardware Stores

- **10003 Hardware** · 90 University Pl
- **Ace Hardware** · 130 Fourth Ave
- **Allied Hardware** · 59 Second Ave
- **East Hardware** · 79 Third Ave
- **Home Locksmith** · 211 E 14th St
- **Metropolitan Lumber & Hardware** · 175 Spring St
- **Mott Hardware** · 186 Mott St
- **Shapiro Hardware** · 63 Bleecker St
- **TS Hardware** · 52 E 8th St

🍷 Liquor Stores

- **Anthony Liquors** · 52 Spring St
- **Astor Wines & Spirits** · 12 Astor Pl
- **B&S Zeeman** · 47 University Pl
- **Crossroads Wine & Liquor** · 55 W 14th St
- **Elizabeth & Vine** · 253 Elizabeth St
- **Miat Liquor Store** · 166 Second Ave
- **S&P Liquor & Wine** · 300 E 5th St
- **Soho Wine & Spirits** · 461 West Broadway
- **Spring Street Wine Shop** · 187 Spring St
- **Thompson Wine & Spirits** · 222 Thompson St
- **Warehouse Wines & Spirits** · 735 Broadway
- **Washington Square Wines** · 545 LaGuardia Pl

🐾 Pet Shops

- **Creature Features** · 21 E 3rd St
- **JBJ Discount Pet Shop** · 151 E Houston St
- **Pacific Aquarium & Plant** · 46 Delancey St
- **Whiskers** · 235 E 9th St

📼 Video Rental

- **Blockbuster Video** · 774 Broadway
- **Cinema Nolita** · 202B Elizabeth St
- **Hollywood Video** · 46 Third Ave
- **Kim's Video** · 6 St Mark's Pl
- **Kim's Video III** · 144 Bleecker St
- **TLA Video** · 52 W 8th St
- **Tower Video** · 383 Lafayette St

(39)

Map 6 • **Washington Sq / NYU / NoHo / SoHo**

There's certainly no shortage of food or drink here. SoHo has become one of the city's mainstream shopping areas, though you can still find some more interesting stuff on side streets or in the newly christened NoLita. The whole area is also a center for alternative movie theaters. The Apple Store is pretty neat.

Movie Theaters

- **Angelika Film Center** · 18 W Houston St
- **Anthology Film Archives** · 32 Second Ave
- **Cinema Classics** · 332 E 11th St
- **Cinema Village** · 22 E 12th St
- **City Cinemas: Village East Cinemas** · 189 Second Ave
- **Landmark Sunshine Cinema** · 141 E Houston St
- **Loews Cineplex Village VII** · 66 Third Ave
- **NYU Cantor Film Center** · 36 E 8th St
- **Quad Cinema** · 34 W 13th St
- **Regal Union Square Stadium 14** · 850 Broadway

Nightlife

- **13** · 35 E 13th St
- **Ace of Clubs** · 9 Great Jones St
- **B Bar** · 40 E 4th St
- **Baggot Inn** · 82 W 3rd St
- **Beauty Bar** · 231 E 14th St
- **The Bitter End** · 147 Bleecker St
- **Blue & Gold** · 74 E 7th St
- **Blue Note** · 131 W 3rd St
- **Bowery Ballroom** · 6 Delancey St
- **Bowery Poetry Club** · 308 Bowery
- **Burp Castle** · 41 E 7th St
- **CBGB and OMFUG** · 315 Bowery
- **Cedar Tavern** · 82 University Pl
- **Continental** · 25 Third Ave
- **Crash Mansion** · 199 Bowery
- **Decibel** · 240 E 9th St
- **Detour** · 349 E 13th St
- **Eight Mile Creek** · 240 Mulberry St
- **Fanelli's** · 94 Prince St
- **Fez** · 380 Lafayette St
- **The Hole** · 29 Second Ave
- **Holiday Lounge** · 75 St Mark's Pl
- **Joe's Pub** · 425 Lafayette St
- **KGB** · 85 E 4th St
- **Lion's Den** · 214 Sullivan St
- **Lit** · 93 Second Ave
- **Mannahatta** · 316 Bowery
- **Marion's Continental** · 354 Bowery
- **Mars Bar** · 25 E 1st St
- **McSorley's Old Ale House** · 15 E 7th St
- **Milady's** · 160 Prince St
- **Milano's** · 51 E Houston St
- **Nevada Smith's** · 74 Third Ave
- **Peculier Pub** · 145 Bleecker St
- **Pravda** · 281 Lafayette St
- **Red Bench** · 107 Sullivan St
- **Rififi** · 332 E 11th St
- **Sapphire Lounge** · 249 Eldridge St
- **Sin/Leopard Lounge** · 248 E 5th St
- **Sweet & Vicious** · 5 Spring St
- **Terra Blues** · 149 Bleecker St
- **Village Underground** · 130 W 3rd St
- **Webster Hall** · 125 E 11th St

Restaurants

- **A Salt & Battery** · 80 Second Ave
- **Abbondazza's** · 193 Bleecker St
- **Acme Bar & Grill** · 9 Great Jones St
- **Angelica Kitchen** · 300 E 12th St
- **Ápizz** · 217 Eldridge St
- **Around the Clock** · 8 Stuyvesant St
- **Arturo's Pizzeria** · 106 W Houston St
- **Babbo** · 110 Waverly Pl
- **Balthazar** · 80 Spring St
- **Baluchi's** · 104 Second Ave
- **Ben's Pizza** · 177 Spring St
- **Blue Hill** · 75 Washington Pl
- **Blue Ribbon** · 97 Sullivan St
- **Blue Ribbon Sushi** · 119 Sullivan St
- **Bond Street** · 6 Bond St
- **Borgo Antico** · 22 E 13th St
- **Café Colonial** · 73 E Houston St
- **Café Habana** · 17 Prince St
- **Café Spice** · 72 University Pl
- **Chez Es Saada** · 42 E 1st St
- **Cozy Soup & Burger** · 739 Broadway
- **Cuba** · 224 Thompson St
- **DeMarco's** · 146 W Houston St
- **Dojo East** · 24 St Mark's Pl
- **Dojo West** · 14 W 4th St
- **Eight Mile Creek** · 240 Mulberry St
- **Five Points** · 31 Great Jones St
- **Frank** · 88 Second Ave
- **Ghenet** · 284 Mulberry St
- **Gotham Bar & Grill** · 12 E 12th St
- **Great Jones Café** · 54 Great Jones St
- **Hampton Chutney Co** · 68 Prince St
- **Haveli** · 100 Second Ave
- **Holy Basil** · 149 Second Ave
- **Il Buco** · 47 Bond St
- **Jane** · 100 W Houston St
- **John's of 12th Street** · 302 E 12th St
- **Jules** · 65 St Mark's Pl
- **Kelley & Ping** · 127 Greene St
- **Khyber Pass** · 34 St Mark's Pl
- **L'Ulivo Focacceria** · 184 Spring St
- **La Palapa Cocina Mexicana** · 77 St Mark's Pl
- **Lupa** · 170 Thompson St
- **Mara's Homemade** · 342 E 6th St
- **Melampo Imported Foods** · 105 Sullivan St
- **Mingala Burmese** · 21 E 7th St
- **Otto** · 1 Fifth Ave
- **Paul's** · 131 Second Ave
- **Peep** · 177 Prince St
- **Penang** · 109 Spring St
- **Pravda** · 281 Lafayette St
- **Sala** · 344 Bowery
- **Sammy's Roumanian** · 157 Chrystie St
- **Snack** · 105 Thompson St
- **Soho Steak** · 90 Thompson St
- **Spice** · 60 University Pl
- **Strip House** · 13 E 12th St
- **Time Café** · 380 Lafayette St
- **Tomoe Sushi** · 172 Thompson St
- **Zo'** · 90 Prince St

Shopping

- **Academy Records & CDs** · 77 E 10th St
- **American Apparel** · 121 Spring St
- **American Apparel** · 712 Broadway
- **Apple Store SoHo** · 103 Prince St
- **Aveda Environmental Lifestyle Store** · 456 West Broadway
- **Banana Republic** · 528 Broadway
- **BCBG by Max Azria** · 120 Wooster St
- **Benetton** · 749 Broadway
- **Black Hound New York** · 170 Second Ave
- **Blades Board & Skate** · 659 Broadway
- **Burberry** · 131 Spring St
- **Canal Jean** · 718 Broadway
- **CITE Design** · 120 Wooster St
- **Coach** · 143 Prince St
- **Daily 235** · 235 Elizabeth St
- **DKNY** · 420 West Broadway
- **East Village Cheese** · 40 Third Ave
- **East Village Music Store** · 85 E 4th St
- **EMS** · 591 Broadway
- **Footlight Records** · 113 E 12th St
- **French Connection** · 700 Broadway
- **Global Table** · 107 Sullivan St
- **Guitar Center** · 25 W 14th St
- **Jam Paper & Envelope** · 135 Third Ave
- **Kar'ikter** · 19 Prince St
- **Kate's Paperie** · 561 Broadway
- **Kiehl's** · 109 Third Ave
- **Kim's Underground** · 144 Bleecker St
- **Kim's Video** · 6 St Marks Pl
- **Knit New York** · 307 E 14th St
- **Leekan Designs** · 93 Mercer St
- **Lighting by Gregory** · 158 Bowery
- **Meg** · 312 E 9th St
- **Michael Anchin Glass** · 245 Elizabeth St
- **MOMA Design Store** · 81 Spring St
- **Moss** · 146 Greene St
- **Nancy Koltes at Home** · 31 Spring St
- **National Wholesale Liquidators** · 632 Broadway
- **New York Central Art Supply** · 62 Third Ave
- **Other Music** · 15 E 4th St
- **Paul Frank Store** · 195 Mulberry St
- **Porto Rico Importing Company** · 107 Thompson St
- **Porto Rico Importing Company** · 40 St Marks Pl
- **Prada** · 575 Broadway
- **Radio Shack** · 781 Broadway
- **Ralph Lauren** · 381 West Broadway
- **Saint Mark's Comics** · 11 St Mark's Pl
- **Stereo Exchange** · 627 Broadway
- **Stuart Moore** · 128 Prince St
- **Sullivan Street Bakery** · 73 Sullivan St
- **Surprise, Surprise** · 91 Third Ave
- **Tommy Hilfiger** · 372 West Broadway
- **Tower Records** · 692 Broadway
- **Utrecht Art and Drafting Supplies** · 111 Fourth Ave
- **Veniero's** · 342 E 11th St
- **Virgin Megastore** · 52 E 14th St
- **White Trash** · 304 E 5th St

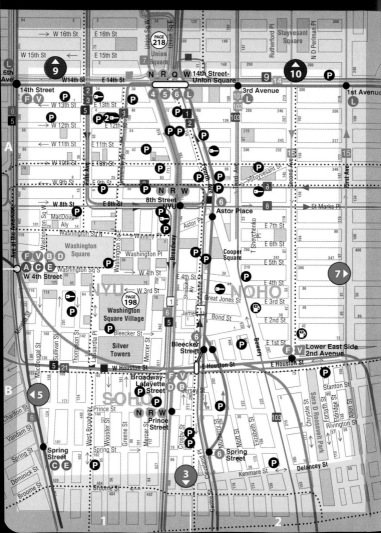

Map 6 • Washington Sq / NYU / NoHo / SoHo

Considering how exciting and vibrant this section of the city is, parking should be way worse than it is. For biking, use Lafayette Street to go north and either Fifth Avenue or Second Avenue to go south. You can only transfer to the BDFV subway from the 6 going downtown—weird.

Subways

6	Astor Pl
6	Bleecker St
6	Spring St
F V	2 Ave
B D F V	Broadway-Lafayette St
J M Z	Bowery
L	3 Ave
4 5 6 L N Q R W	14 St-Union Sq
N R W	8 St-NYU
N R W	Prince St
C E	Spring St

Bus Lines

1	Fifth/Madison Aves
101	Third Ave/Lexington Ave/Amsterdam Ave
102	Third Ave/Lexington Ave/Malcolm X Blvd
103	Third Ave/Lexington Ave
14	14th St Crosstown
15	First/Second Aves
2	Fifth/Madison Aves/Powell Blvd
21	Houston St/Avenue C
3	Fifth/Madison Aves/St Nicholas Ave
5	Fifth Ave/Sixth Ave/Riverside Dr
7	Columbus Ave/Amsterdam Ave Lenox Ave/Sixth/Seventh Aves/Broadway
8	8th/9th Sts Crosstown
9	Ave B/East Broadway

Bike Lanes

- • • • Marked Bike Lane
- • • • Recommended Route

Car Rental

- **Action Car Rental** • 741 Broadway
- **American Rent-a-Car** • 33 Great Jones St
- **Avis** • 68 E 11th St
- **Enterprise** • 221 Thompson St
- **Hertz** • 12 E 13th St
- **Liberty Car Rental** • 220 E 9th St
- **National** • 21 E 12th St

Gas Stations

- **Exxon** • 24 Second Ave
- **Gaseteria** • Houston St & Lafayette St
- **Sunoco** • Bowery & E 3rd St

Parking

Map 7 · **East Village / Lower East Side**

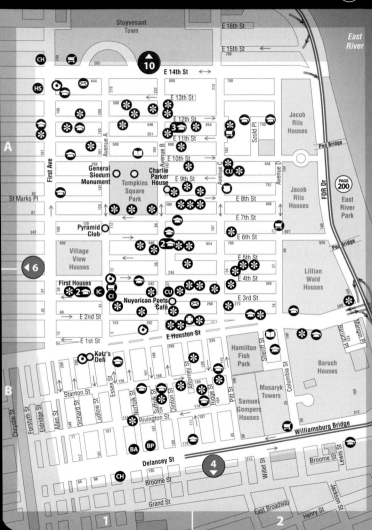

We think David's Bagels on First Avenue rocks. Tompkins Square Park is a gated community for the rich and famous ("irony," for you literalists). The farmer's market on the southwest corner of the park does remind us of crunchier days, however. Despite the many visitors, this remains one of the more "neighborhoody" neighborhoods of Manhattan.

Bagels

- **535 Self** • 203 E Houston St
- **Bagel Zone** • 50 Ave A
- **David's Bagels** • 228 First Ave
- **Houston's Bagel & Grill** • 283 E Houston St

Banks

BP • **Banco Popular** • 134 Delancey St
BA • **Bank of America** • 126 Delancey St
CH • **Chase** • 109 Delancey St
CH • **Chase** • 255 First Ave
CI • **Citibank** • 50 Ave A
HS • **HSBC** • 245 First Ave
IC • **Independence Community** • 51 Ave A
CU • **Lower East Side People's Federal Credit Union** • 134 Ave C
CU • **Lower East Side People's Federal Credit Union** • 37 Ave B

Community Gardens

Fire Departments

- **Engine 28, Ladder 11** • 222 E 2nd St

Landmarks

- **Charlie Parker House** • 151 Ave B & Tompkins Sq Pk
- **General Slocum Monument** • Tompkins Square Park
- **Katz's Deli** • 205 E Houston St
- **Nuyorican Poets Café** • 236 E 3rd St
- **Pyramid Club** • Ave A b/w 6th & 7th Sts
- **Tompkins Square Park** • Ave A & E 9th St

Libraries

- **Hamilton Fish Park** • 415 E Houston St
- **Tompkins Square** • 331 E 10th St

Police

- **9th Precinct** • 130 Ave C

Post Offices

- **Peter Stuyvesant** • 432 E 14th St
- **Tompkins Square** • 244 E 3rd St

Schools

- **Children's Workshop (M361)** • 610 E 12th St
- **CMSP- Marte Valle Secondary** • 145 Stanton St
- **Connelly Center Education/Holy Child Middle** • 220 E 4th St
- **East Side Community High** • 420 E 12th St
- **East Village Community** • 610 E 12th St
- **Immaculate Conception** • 419 E 13th St
- **JHS 025 Marta Valle** • 145 Stanton St
- **Mary Help of Christians** • 435 E 11th St
- **NEST+M** • 111 Columbia St
- **Notre Dame** • 104 St Marks Pl
- **Our Lady of Sorrows** • 219 Stanton St
- **PS 015 Roberto Clemente** • 333 E 4th St
- **PS 019 Asher Levy** • 185 First Ave
- **PS 034 F D Roosevelt** • 730 E 12th St
- **PS 061 Anna Howard Shaw** • 610 E 12th St
- **PS 063 William McKinley** • 121 E 3rd St
- **PS 064 Robert Simon** • 600 E 6th St
- **PS 097 Mangin** • 525 E Houston St
- **PS 110 F Nightingale** • 285 Delancey St
- **PS 140 Nathan Straus** • 123 Ridge St
- **PS 142 Amalia Castro** • 100 Attorney St
- **PS 188 The Island School** • 442 E Houston St
- **PS 20 Anna Silver** • 199 Essex St
- **PS 363 Neighborhood School** • 121 E 3rd St
- **PS 364 Earth School** • 601 E 6th St
- **PS 94M** • 442 E Houston St
- **St Brigid** • 185 E 7th St
- **Tompkins Square Middle Extension** • 602 E 6th St

Supermarkets

- **Associated** • 409 E 14th St
- **C-Town** • 188 Ave C
- **C-Town** • 71 Ave D
- **Key Food** • 43 Columbia St
- **Key Food** • 52 Ave A

Map 7 • **East Village / Lower East Side**

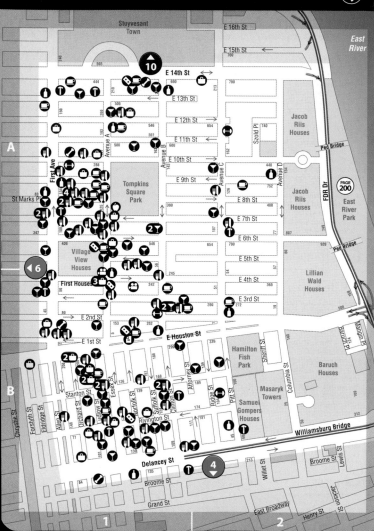

The tide of rising rents has claimed Kim's Video, sadly. Some favorite bars: 2A, 7B, Ace Bar, Bouche Bar, Bua, Mona's, Parkside, and Joe's Bar. Banjara is by far the best of the 6th Street Indians. Mama's Food Shop on 3rd Street is one of the five reasons to never leave New York City.

☕ Coffee

- **9th Street Espresso** · 700 E 9th St
- **altcoffee** · 139 Ave A
- **Café Gigi** · 417 E 9th St
- **Café Pick Me Up** · 145 Ave A
- **Ciao for Now** · 504 E 12th St
- **City Market Café** · 131 Ave A
- **Coffee Pot** · 41 Ave A
- **Dunkin' Donuts** · 140 Delancey St
- **Dunkin' Donuts** · 215 First Ave
- **Dunkin' Donuts** · 250 E Houston St
- **Dynasty Restaurant & Coffee Shop** · 600 E 14th St
- **J&J Coffee Shop** · 442 E 14th St
- **Kudo Beans** · 49 1/2 First Ave
- **Lalita Java** · 210 E 3rd St
- **Live Juice** · 85 Ave A
- **Maria's Café** · 32 Ave C
- **Pink Pony Café** · 176 Ludlow St
- **Rush Hour** · 134 Ludlow St
- **Sympathy for the Kettle** · 109 St Marks Pl

🖨 Copy Shops

- **Kinko's** (7am-11pm) · 250 E Houston St

🥕 Farmer's Markets

- **Tompkins Square Park** · E 7th St & Ave A

🏋 Gyms

- **Curves** · 114 Ridge St
- **Curves** · 182 Ave C
- **Dolphin Fitness Clubs** · 18 Ave B
- **Russian Turkish Baths** · 268 E 10th St

🔨 Hardware Stores

- **Ace Hardware** · 55 First Ave
- **Brickman and Sons** · 55 First Ave
- **CHP Hardware** · 96 Ave C
- **East Side Lumber** · 421 E 13th St
- **H&W Hardware** · 220 First Ave
- **HH Hardware** · 111 Rivington St
- **Rosa Hardware** · 85 Pitt St
- **Rothstein Hardware** · 56 Clinton St
- **Saifee Hardware** · 114 First Ave

🍾 Liquor Stores

- **6 Ave B Liquors** · 6 Ave B
- **Ave A Wine & Liquor** · 196 Ave A
- **Bee Liquors** · 225 Ave B
- **East Village Wines** · 138 First Ave
- **Gary's Liquor** · 141 Essex St
- **Jade Fountain Liquor** · 123 Delancey St
- **Loon Chun Liquor** · 47 Pitt St
- **Marty's Liquors** · 133 Ave D
- **Nizga Liquors** · 58 Ave A
- **Sale Price Liquor** · 224 Ave C
- **Wines on 1st** · 224 First Ave

🎬 Movie Theaters

- **Two Boots Pioneer Theater** · 155 E 3rd St

🍸 Nightlife

- **11th Street Bar** · 510 E 11th St
- **151** · 151 Rivington St
- **2A** · 25 Ave A
- **7B** · 108 Ave B
- **Ace Bar** · 531 E 5th St
- **Arlene Grocery** · 95 Stanton St
- **Bar 181** · 81 E 7th St
- **Barramundi** · 67 Clinton St
- **Bouche Bar** · 540 E 5th St
- **Bua** · 124 St Marks Pl
- **C-Note** · 157 Ave C
- **Cherry Tavern** · 441 E 6th St
- **DBA** · 41 First Ave
- **The Delancey** · 168 Delancey St
- **The Edge** · 95 E 3rd St
- **Guernica** · 25 Ave B
- **The Hanger** · 217 E 3rd St
- **International Bar** · 120 1/2 First Ave
- **Joe's Bar** · 520 E 6th St
- **Korova Milk Bar** · 200 Ave A
- **Lakeside Lounge** · 162 Ave B
- **Lansky Lounge** · 104 Norfolk St
- **Living Room** · 154 Ludlow St
- **Manitoba's** · 99 Ave B
- **Max Fish** · 178 Ludlow St
- **Mercury Lounge** · 217 E Houston St
- **Mona's** · 224 Ave B
- **Motor City** · 127 Ludlow St
- **Nuyorican Poet's Café** · 236 E 3rd St
- **Opaline** · 85 Ave A
- **Parkside Lounge** · 317 E Houston St
- **The Phoenix** · 447 E 13th St
- **Pianos** · 158 Ludlow St
- **The Porch** · 115 Ave C
- **Rothko** · 116 Suffolk St
- **Sidewalk** · 94 Ave A
- **Sin-é** · 150 Attorney St
- **Sophie's** · 507 E 5th St
- **Three of Cups Lounge** · 83 First Ave
- **Tonic** · 107 Norfolk St
- **WCOU Radio Bar** · 115 First Ave
- **Welcome to the Johnsons** · 123 Rivington St
- **Zum Schneider** · 107 Ave C

🐾 Pet Shops

- **Alpha Pet City** · 249 E 10th St
- **Animal Cracker** · 26 First Ave
- **Petland** · 85 Delancey St
- **Petland Discounts** · 530 E 14th St

🍴 Restaurants

- **1492 Food** · 60 Clinton St
- **71 Clinton Fresh Food** · 71 Clinton St
- **7A** · 109 Ave A
- **AKA Café** · 49 Clinton St
- **Azul Bistro** · 152 Stanton St
- **B3** · 33 Ave B
- **Banjara** · 97 First Ave
- **Benny's Burritos** · 93 Ave A
- **Bereket Turkish Kebab House** · 187 E Houston St
- **Boca Chica** · 13 First Ave
- **Café Mogador** · 101 St Mark's Pl
- **Caracas Arepa Bar** · 91 E 7th St
- **Crooked Tree Creperie** · 110 St Mark's Pl
- **The Delancey** · 168 Delancey St
- **Dish** · 165 Allen St

- **Dok Suni's** · 119 First Ave
- **El Castillo de Jaqua** · 113 Rivington St
- **Essex Restaurant** · 120 Essex St
- **Flea Market Café** · 131 Ave A
- **Flor's Kitchen** · 149 First Ave
- **Grilled Cheese NYC** · 168 Ludlow St
- **The Hat (Sombrero)** · 108 Stanton St
- **Il Bagatto** · 192 E 2nd St
- **Kate's Joint** · 58 Ave B
- **Katz's Delicatessen** · 205 E Houston St
- **Kuma Inn** · 113 Ludlow St
- **Kura Sushi** · 130 First Ave
- **La Caverna** · 122 Rivington St
- **La Focacceria** · 128 First Ave
- **Lavagna** · 545 E 5th St
- **Le Gamin** · 536 E 5th St
- **Lil' Frankie's Pizza** · 19 First Ave
- **The Lite Touch Restaurant** · 151 Ave A
- **Mama's Food Shop** · 200 E 3rd St
- **Momofuku** · 163 First Ave
- **Moustache** · 265 E 10th St
- **Odessa** · 117 Ave A
- **Old Devil Moon** · 511 E 12th St
- **Pylos** · 128 E 7th St
- **Raga** · 433 E 6th St
- **Sapporo East** · 245 E 10th St
- **Schiller's** · 131 Rivington St
- **Share** · 406 E 9th St
- **The Sunburnt Cow** · 137 Ave C
- **Takahachi** · 85 Ave A
- **Tasting Room** · 72 E 1st St
- **Teany** · 90 Rivington St
- **Two Boots** · 37 Ave A
- **Yaffa Café** · 97 St Mark's Pl
- **Zum Schneider** · 107 Ave C

🛍 Shopping

- **A Cheng** · 443 E 9th St
- **Alphabets** · 115 Ave A
- **Altman Luggage** · 135 Orchard St
- **American Apparel** · 183 E Houston St
- **Dowel Quality Products** · 91 First Ave
- **Earthmatters** · 177 Ludlow St
- **Economy Candy** · 108 Rivington St
- **Etherea** · 66 Ave A
- **Exit 9** · 64 Ave A
- **First Flight Music** · 174 First Ave
- **Gringer & Sons** · 29 First Ave
- **Lancelotti** · 66 Ave A
- **Ludlow Guitars** · 164 Ludlow St
- **Masturbakers** · 511 E 12th St
- **R&S Strauss Auto Store** · 644 E 14th St
- **Russ & Daughters** · 179 E Houston St
- **Schapiro Wine** · 126 Rivington St
- **Spectra** · 293 E 10th St
- **TG170** · 170 Ludlow St
- **Toys in Babeland** · 94 Rivington St
- **Yonah Schimmel Knishery** · 137 E Houston St

📹 Video Rental

- **Blockbuster Video** · 250 E Houston St
- **Crossbay Video** · 502 E 14th St
- **Kim's Video** · 85 Ave A
- **Two Boots** · 42 Ave A
- **The Video Store** · 128 Rivington St

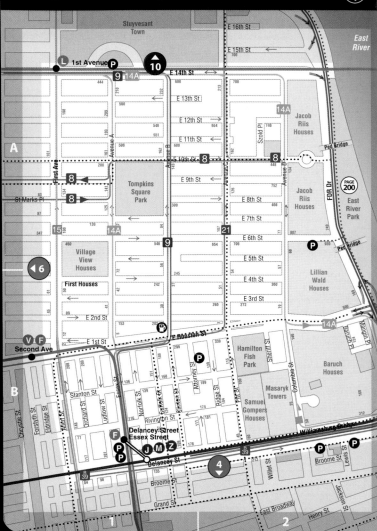

Map 7 • East Village / Lower East Side

Parking is usually pretty good except for Friday and Saturday nights when the Bridge & Tunnel crowd invades. It looks like the L train will be in and out of service through 2005 and maybe into 2006, making a trip to Williamsburg a real pain sometimes...

Subways

F **J** **M** **Z** .... Delancey St-Essex St
L .... First Ave
F **V** .... Second Ave

Bus Lines

14 .... 14th St/Ave A/Ave D
15 .... First Ave
21 .... First St/Ave C
8 .... 9th St/10th St
9 .... 14th St/Ave B
B 39 .... Delancey St

Bike Lanes

- • • • Marked Bike Lane
- • • • Recommended Route
- • • • Greenway

Gas Stations

· **Mobil** · 253 E 2nd St

Parking

Map 8 · Chelsea

The art gallery migration from SoHo is now complete---Chelsea is THE place for art. However, more services are desperately needed, especially in the Javits Center area (unless you count the services of transvestite prostitutes as "essential"). Despite controversy, it's looking increasingly like this the future home of the Jets...

24-Hour Pharmacies

- **Duane Reade** • 460 Eighth Ave

Bagels

- **Murray's Bagels** • 242 Eighth Ave
- **Unbagelievable** • 75 Ninth Ave

Banks

BA • **Bank of America (ATM)** • 312 W 34th St
CH • **Chase** • 475 W 23rd St
CH • **Chase (ATM)** • 238 Eighth Ave
CI • **Citibank** • 322 W 23rd St
CI • **Citibank (ATM)** • 111 Eighth Ave
CI • **Citibank (ATM)** • 88 Tenth Ave
WA • **Wachovia** • 66 Ninth Ave
WM • **Washington Mutual** • 111 Eighth Ave
WM • **Washington Mutual** • 601 Eighth Ave

Community Gardens

Fire Departments

- **Engine 34, Ladder 21** • 440 W 38th St

Landmarks

- **General Theological Seminary** • 175 Ninth Ave
- **High Line Elevated Railroad** • Gansevoort to 34th St, west of Tenth Ave
- **J A Farley Post Office** • 441 Eighth Ave
- **Jacob K Javits Convention Center** • 36th St & Eleventh Ave
- **Starlett-Leigh Building** • 27th St & Eleventh Ave

Police

- **Mid-Town South** • 357 W 35th St

Post Offices

- **J A Farley General** • 441 Eighth Ave
- **Port Authority** • 76 Ninth Ave

Schools

- **Bayard Rustin High School for the Humanities** • 351 W 18th St
- **Corlears** • 324 W 15th St
- **General Theological Seminary** • 175 Ninth Ave
- **Guardian Angel** • 193 Tenth Ave
- **Humanities Preparatory** • 351 W 18th St
- **The Lorge School** • 353 W 18th St
- **NYC Lab School** • 333 W 17th St
- **NYC Museum School** • 333 W 17th St
- **PS 11 William T Harris & MS 260 Clinton** • 320 W 21st St
- **PS 33 Chelsea** • 281 Ninth Ave
- **St Columba** • 331 W 25th St
- **St Michael Academy** • 425 W 33rd St
- **Technical Career Institute** • 320 W 31st St

Supermarkets

- **D'Agostino** • 257 W 17th St
- **D'Agostino** • 312 W 23rd St
- **Gristede's** • 221 Eighth Ave
- **Gristede's** • 225 Ninth Ave
- **Gristede's** • 307 W 26th St

Map 8 · Chelsea

Map 8

More and more excellent bars and restaurants are opening up, although some services are still pretty thin on Tenth and Eleventh Avenues. For food, the always amazing La Luncheonette is brilliant but pricey, and Grand Sichuan International has some interesting dishes you might not even find in Chinatown.

Coffee

- **Big Cup Tea & Coffee House** · 228 Eighth Ave
- **Dunkin' Donuts** · 215 Tenth Ave
- **Dunkin' Donuts** · 269 Eighth Ave
- **Dunkin' Donuts** · 525 Eighth Ave
- **From Earth To You Gourmet Café** · 252 Tenth Ave
- **Paradise Café & Muffins** · 139 Eighth Ave
- **Starbucks** · 124 Eighth Ave
- **Starbucks** · 177 Eighth Ave
- **Starbucks** · 255 Eighth Ave
- **Starbucks** · 352 W 30th St
- **Starbucks** · 450 W 33rd St
- **Starbucks** · 494 Eighth Ave
- **Starbucks** · 76 Ninth Ave

Copy Shops

- **Empire Graphic Service (8am-10pm)** · 347 W 36th St
- **Empire State Blue Print (8:30am-6pm)** · 555 Eighth Ave
- **Mail Boxes Etc (9am-7pm)** · 245 Eighth Ave
- **Millennium Copy (9am-5pm)** · 302 W 37th St
- **Staples (7am-8pm)** · 500 Eighth Ave

Gyms

- **Chelsea Piers Sports Center** · Chelsea Piers-Pier 60
- **New York Sports Clubs** · 128 Eighth Ave
- **New York Sports Clubs** · 270 Eighth Ave

Hardware Stores

- **Diener Park** · 194 Eighth Ave
- **Hardware Depot** · 399 Eighth Ave
- **Mercer Sq Hardware** · 286 Eighth Ave
- **MJ Hardware & Electric** · 520 Eighth Ave
- **NF Hardware** · 219 Ninth Ave
- **True Value Hardware** · 191 Ninth Ave
- **United Equipment and Supply** · 419 Ninth Ave

Liquor Stores

- **34th Street Winery** · 460 W 34th St
- **Chelsea Liquor** · 114 Ninth Ave
- **Chelsea Wine Vault** · 75 Ninth Ave
- **DeLauren Wines & Liquors** · 332 Eighth Ave
- **Kwang Koo Won** · 474 Ninth Ave
- **London Terrace Liquor** · 221 Ninth Ave
- **Philippe Wine & Liquor** · 312 W 23rd St
- **US Wine & Liquor** · 486 Ninth Ave

Movie Theaters

- **Clearview's Chelsea West** · 333 W 23rd St
- **Loews 34th Street** · 312 W 34th St

Nightlife

- **Billymark's West** · 332 Ninth Ave
- **Blarney Stone** · 340 Ninth Ave
- **Cajun** · 129 Eighth Ave
- **Chelsea Brewing Company** · Pier 59
- **Copacabana** · 560 W 34th St
- **Coral Room** · 512 W 29th St
- **Crobar** · 530 W 28th St
- **Freight** · 410 W 16th St
- **Hammerstein Ballroom** · 311 W 34th St
- **The Park** · 118 Tenth Ave
- **Red Rock West** · 457 W 17th St
- **Roxy** · 515 W 18th St
- **West Side Tavern** · 360 W 23rd St

Pet Shops

- **Barking Zoo** · 172 Ninth Ave
- **Petland Discounts** · 312 W 23rd St
- **Towne House Grooming** · 369 W 19th St

Restaurants

- **Blue Moon Mexican Café** · 150 Eighth Ave
- **Bottino** · 246 Tenth Ave
- **Bright Food Shop** · 216 Eighth Ave
- **Burritoville** · 352 W 39th St
- **Chelsea Bistro & Bar** · 358 W 23rd St
- **Cheyenne Diner** · 411 Ninth Ave
- **Cupcake Café** · 522 Ninth Ave
- **El Cid** · 322 W 15th St
- **Empire Diner** · 210 Tenth Ave
- **Frank's Restaurant** · 85 Tenth Ave
- **Grand Sichuan Int'l** · 229 Ninth Ave
- **Havana Chelsea** · 190 Eighth Ave
- **La Luncheonette** · 130 Tenth Ave
- **La Taza de Oro** · 96 Eighth Ave
- **Le Gamin** · 183 Ninth Ave
- **Manganaro Foods** · 488 Ninth Ave
- **Moonstruck Diner** · 400 W 23rd St
- **Pepe Giallo** · 253 Tenth Ave
- **The Red Cat** · 227 Tenth Ave
- **Sandwich Planet** · 534 Ninth Ave
- **Skylight Diner** · 402 W 34th St
- **Soul Fixins'** · 371 W 34th St
- **Spice** · 199 Eighth Ave
- **Tazza** · 196 Eighth Ave
- **Tick Tock Diner** · 481 Eighth Ave
- **Viceroy** · 160 Eighth Ave

Shopping

- **B&H Photo** · 420 Ninth Ave
- **Buon Italia** · 75 Ninth Ave
- **Chelsea Garden Center** · 455 W 16th St
- **Chelsea Market Baskets** · 75 Ninth Ave
- **Chelsea Wholesale Flower Market** · 75 Ninth Ave
- **Fat Witch Bakery** · 75 Ninth Ave
- **Kitchen Market** · 218 Eighth Ave
- **New Museum Store** · 556 W 22nd
- **Portico** · 75 Ninth Ave

Video Rental

- **Alan's Alley Video** · 207A Ninth Ave

Map 8 · Chelsea

N

Lincoln Tunnel
← to NJ

Hudson River Park

42 34 42

Jacob K Javits
Convention
Center
PAGE
204

11

W 40th St

W 39th St

W 38th St

W 37th St

W 36th St

16   16

W 35th St

2 P   2 P

11   11

W 34th St

A C E
34th Street
Penn Station

34

PAGE
261
Penn
Station/
MSG
PAGE
229

W 33rd St

J A Farley
Post Office

W 31st St

W 30th St

20

W 29th St

9

Hudson
River

Hudson River Park

West Side Hwy

9a

W 28th St

Chelsea Park

Penn

Station

South

Houses

W 27th St

W 26th St

Eleventh Ave

Tenth Ave

Ninth Ave

Eighth Ave

W 25th St

W 24th St

W 23rd St

C E
23rd Street

Chelsea Waterside Park

23

23

W 22nd St

W 21st St

B

W 20th St

11   11

Chelsea Piers

PAGE
222

20

W 19th St

W 18th St

W 17th St

W 16th St

Hudson River Park

14

W 15th St

W 14th St

5

A C E
14th Street

L
8th Avenue

1   2

Parking and driving in this area are quite bad during the day and quite good at night, although there just aren't many spots at all above 30th Street. Tragically, there are no subway lines west of Eighth Avenue, although they're finally studying the feasibility of running a line out to the Javits (duh!).

Subways

Ⓐ Ⓒ Ⓔ	34 St-Penn Station
Ⓐ Ⓒ Ⓔ	14th St/Eighth Ave
Ⓒ Ⓔ	23rd St

Bus Lines

10 20	Seventh Ave/Eighth Ave/Central Park W
11	Ninth Ave/Tenth Ave
14	14th St Crosstown
16	34th St Crosstown
23	23rd St Crosstown
34	34th St Crosstown

Bike Lanes

- • • • Marked Bike Lanes
- • • • Recommended Route
- • • • Greenway

Car Rental

- **U-Haul** • 562 W 23rd St

Car Washes

- **Chelsea Car Wash** • 450 W 15th St
- **Steve's Detailing & Tires** • 516 W 27th St
- **Tecknik 1 (detailer)** • 516 W 29th St

Gas Stations

- **BP** • 436 Tenth Ave
- **Exxon** • 110 Eighth Ave
- **Exxon** • 215 Tenth Ave
- **Lukoil** • 239 Tenth Ave
- **Mobil** • 309 Eleventh Ave
- **Mobil** • 70 Tenth Ave

Parking

Map 9 · **Flatiron / Lower Midtown**

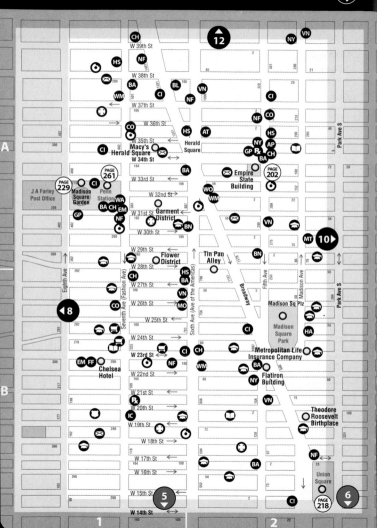

A neighborhood in flux. While the area around Madison Square Park is fairly stable, Sixth Avenue has witnessed a host of new hi-rise developments above 23rd street, mostly with luxury prices. The street hasn't quite caught up, and retains the grittiness of the Garment District.

24-Hour Pharmacies

- **Duane Reade** · 180 W 20th St
- **Duane Reade** · 358 Fifth Ave

Bagels

- **23rd St Bagel** · 170 W 23rd St
- **Bagel Maven** · 362 Seventh Ave
- **Bagels & Co** · 243 W 38th St
- **Bread Factory Café** · 470 Seventh Ave
- **Brooklyn Bagel Bakery** · 319 Fifth Ave
- **Liberty Bagel** · 876 Sixth Ave
- **Pick-a-Bagel** · 601 Sixth Ave

Banks

- **AM · Amalgamated** · 15 Union Sq W
- **AP · Apple (ATM)** · 350 Fifth Ave
- **AT · Atlantic** · 960 Sixth Ave
- **BL · Bank Leumi** · 1400 Broadway
- **BA · Bank of America** · 116 Fifth Ave
- **BA · Bank of America** · 1293 Broadway
- **BA · Bank of America** · 350 Fifth Ave
- **BA · Bank of America** · 4 Penn Plz
- **BA · Bank of America** · 515 Seventh Ave
- **BA · Bank of America** · 800 Sixth Ave
- **BA · Bank of America (ATM)** · 186 Fifth Ave
- **NY · Bank of New York** · 162 Fifth Ave
- **NY · Bank of New York** · 260 Madison Ave
- **NY · Bank of New York** · 350 Fifth Ave
- **BN · Broadway National** · 250 Fifth Ave
- **BN · Broadway National** · 855 Sixth Ave
- **CH · Chase** · 1411 Broadway
- **CH · Chase** · 2 Penn Plz
- **CH · Chase** · 305 Seventh Ave
- **CH · Chase** · 349 Fifth Ave
- **CH · Chase** · 71 W 23rd St
- **CI · Citibank** · 1107 Broadway
- **CI · Citibank** · 201 W 34th St
- **CI · Citibank** · 411 Fifth Ave
- **CI · Citibank** · 717 Sixth Ave
- **CI · Citibank (ATM)** · 1384 Broadway
- **CI · Citibank (ATM)** · 79 Fifth Ave
- **CO · Commerce Bank** · 200 W 26th St
- **CO · Commerce Bank** · 401 Fifth Ave
- **CO · Commerce Bank** · 469 Seventh Ave
- **EM · Emigrant** · 250 W 23rd St
- **EM · Emigrant** · 371 Seventh Ave
- **FF · Fourth Federal Savings** · 242 W 23rd St
- **GP · Greenpoint Bank** · 1 Penn Plz
- **GP · Greenpoint Bank** · 10 E 34th St
- **HA · Habib American Bank** · 99 Madison Ave
- **HS · HSBC** · 1350 Broadway
- **HS · HSBC** · 550 Seventh Ave
- **HS · HSBC** · 800 Sixth Ave
- **IC · Independence Community** · 169 Seventh Ave
- **MT · Manufacturers and Traders Trust** · 95 Madison Ave
- **CU · Montauk Credit Union** · 111 W 26th St
- **NF · North Fork Bank** · 1001 Sixth Ave
- **NF · North Fork Bank** · 120 W 23rd St
- **NF · North Fork Bank** · 1407 Broadway
- **NF · North Fork Bank** · 31 E 17th St
- **NF · North Fork Bank** · 370 Seventh Ave
- **NF · North Fork Bank** · 404 Fifth Ave
- **VN · Valley National Bank** · 1040 Sixth Ave
- **VN · Valley National Bank** · 145 Fifth Ave
- **VN · Valley National Bank** · 275 Madison Ave
- **VN · Valley National Bank** · 295 Fifth Ave
- **VN · Valley National Bank** · 776 Sixth Ave
- **WA · Wachovia (ATM)** · 1 Penn Plz
- **WM · Washington Mutual** · 1260 Broadway
- **WM · Washington Mutual** · 498 Seventh Ave
- **WM · Washington Mutual** · 700 Sixth Ave
- **WO · Woori America Bank** · 1250 Broadway

Fire Departments

- **Engine 1, Ladder 24** · 142 W 31st St
- **Engine 14** · 14 E 18th St
- **Engine 26** · 220 W 37th St
- **Engine 3, Ladder 12** · 146 W 19th St

Landmarks

- **Chelsea Hotel** · 23rd St b/w Seventh & Eighth Aves
- **Empire State Building** · 34th St & Fifth Ave
- **Flatiron Building** · 175 Fifth Ave
- **Flower District** · 28th St b/w Sixth & Seventh Aves
- **Garment District** · West 30s south of Herald Sq
- **Macy's Herald Square** · 151 W 34th St
- **Madison Square Garden** · 4 Penn Plz
- **Madison Square Park** · 23rd St & Broadway
- **Metropolitan Life Insurance Co** · 1 Madison Ave
- **Penn Station** · 31st St & Eighth Ave
- **Theodore Roosevelt Birthplace** · 28 E 20th St
- **Tin Pan Alley** · W 28th St b/w Sixth Ave & Broadway
- **Union Square** · 14th St-Union Sq

Libraries

- **Andrew Heiskell Library for the Blind** · 40 W 20th St
- **Muhlenberg** · 209 W 23rd St
- **Science, Industry, and Business Library** · 188 Madison Ave

Police

- **10th Precinct** · 230 W 20th St

Post Offices

- **Empire State** · 19 W 33rd St
- **Greeley Square** · 39 W 31st St
- **Midtown** · 223 W 38th St
- **Old Chelsea** · 217 W 18th St
- **Station 138 (Macy's)** · 151 W 34th St

Schools

- **American Academy of Dramatic Arts** · 120 Madison Ave
- **Apex Technical** · 635 Sixth Ave
- **Ballet Tech / NYC PS for Dance** · 890 Broadway
- **Baruch College** · 46 E 26th St
- **Community Preparatory High (M612)** · 40 E 29th St
- **Fashion Institute of Technology** · 227 W 27th St
- **High School for Fashion Industries** · 225 W 24th St
- **Institute for Culinary Education** · 50 E 23rd St
- **John A Coleman** · 590 Sixth Ave
- **Liberty High** · 250 W 18th St
- **Manhattan Village Academy** · 43 W 22nd St
- **MS 17** · 333 Seventh Ave
- **Physical City High** · 55 E 25th St
- **Satellite Academy High** · 120 W 30th St
- **Studio Semester** · 229 W 28th St
- **Touro College** · 27 W 23rd St
- **Xavier High** · 30 W 16th St

Supermarkets

- **Associated** · 244 Seventh Ave
- **Garden of Eden Gourmet** · 162 W 23rd St
- **Whole Foods Market** · 250 Seventh Ave

Map 9 • **Flatiron / Lower Midtown**

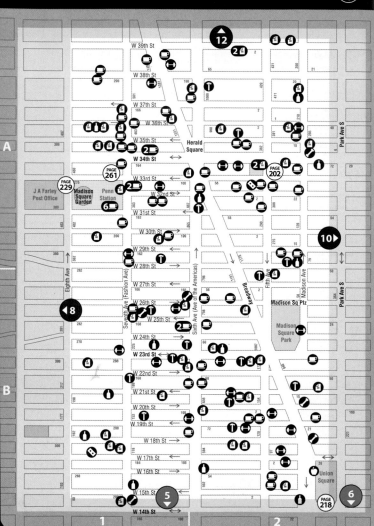

Sundries

Map 9

14 15
11 12 13
8 9 10
5 6 7

The Flatiron/Lower Midtown area contains two of New York's most famous business districts, the Garment District and the Flower District (see the "essentials" map). The big box retailers and chains have invaded Sixth Avenue (including Best Buy, Outback Steakhouse, the Olive Garden, and Home Depot. Whoopee!

☕ Coffee

- **Aleem's Coffee Shop** · 46 W 21st St
- **Andrew's Coffee Shop**
- 136 Fifth Ave · 1410 Broadway
- 246 W 38th St · 463 Seventh Ave
- **Anesis Café** · 42 W 35th St
- **Au Bon Pain** · 151 W 34th St
- **Au Bon Pain** · 350 Fifth Ave
- **Au Bon Pain** · 73 Fifth Ave
- **Café Beyond** · 620 Sixth Ave
- **Café Express** · 138 W 32nd St
- **Café Muse** · 43 W 32nd St
- **Café POM POM** · 169 W 32nd St
- **Café Space 212** · 319 Fifth Ave
- **Caffe Rafaella** · 134 Seventh Ave S
- **Coco MOKA Café (Penn Station)** · 2 Penn Plz
- **Cosi** · 498 Seventh Ave
- **Cosi** · 700 Sixth Ave
- **Dunkin' Donuts** · 1 Penn Plz
- 1286 Broadway · 150 W 30th St
- 2 Penn Plz · 24 E 23rd St
- 289 Seventh Ave · 302 Fifth Ave
- 401 Seventh Ave · 80 Madison Ave
- **Guy & Gallard** · 1001 Sixth Ave
- **Guy & Gallard** · 180 Madison Ave
- **Guy & Gallard** · 245 W 38th St
- **Guy & Gallard** · 469 Seventh Ave
- **Guy & Gallard** · 475 Park Ave S
- **Guy & Gallard IV** · 339 Seventh Ave
- **Harrie's Coffee Shop** · 1407 Broadway
- **Jamie's** · 164 Madison Ave
- **Java Shop** · 30 W 35th St
- **Kavehaz** · 37 W 26th St
- **M Café** · 901 Sixth Ave
- **Mikey's** · 44 E 32nd St
- **News Bar** · 2 W 19th St
- **Primo Cappachino** · Penn Station LIRR Concourse Level
- **Seattle Coffee Roasters** · 202 W 34th St
- **Starbucks** · 1 Penn Plz
- 1372 Broadway · 151 W 34th St
- 200 Madison Ave · 261 Fifth Ave
- 334 Fifth Ave · 370 Seventh Ave
- 41 Union Sq W · 450 Seventh Ave
- 462 Seventh Ave · 525 Sixth Ave
- 675 Sixth Ave · 684 Sixth Ave
- 750 Sixth Ave · 776 Sixth Ave
- **West Front Store** · 28 W 32nd St

🖨 Copy Shops

- **AAA Wonder Copy & Printing** (9:30am- 5:30pm) · 16 W 23rd St
- **AAA Wonder Copy & Printing** (9:30am- 5:30pm) · 174 Fifth Ave
- **Acu-Copy** (8:30am-midnight) · 26 W 39th St
- **Bernie's Copy Center / Penn Graphics** (9am–5pm) · 242 W 30th St
- **Carr & Dash** (9am-6pm) · 470 Seventh Ave
- **Century Copy Center** (8:30am-7pm) · 70 Seventh Ave
- **Chelsea Quality Copy & Printing** (9am-6pm) · 255 W 23rd St
- **Comzone** (8:30am-10pm) · 21 E 15th St
- **Copy Door Corp** (9am-7pm) · 1011 Sixth Ave
- **Copy Specialists** (8:30am-7pm) · 44 E 21st St
- **Copy Specialists** (8:30am-7pm) · 71 W 23rd St
- **Digital Data Solutions** (9am-5:30pm) · 1133 Broadway
- **Digital Output Corporation** (7:30am-10pm) · 22 W 21st St
- **Digitech Printers** (8:30am-6:30pm) · 150 W 30th St
- **Esteban** (8am-6pm) · 136 W 21st St
- **Exact** (24 hrs) · 1 W 34th St
- **Five Star** (8am-6pm) · 242 W 36th St
- **Garden Copy Center** (8:30am-7:30pm) · 234 W 35th St
- **Grant's Photo Printing** (8:30am-6:30pm) · 36 W 39th St
- **Kasray** (7am-6:30pm) · 122 W 26th St
- **Kinko's** (24 hrs) · 191 Madison Ave
- **Kinko's** (24 hrs) · 245 Seventh Ave
- **Kinko's** (24 hrs) · 500 Seventh Ave
- **Kinko's** (7am-11pm) · 650 Sixth Ave
- **Kinko's** (7am-11pm, Mon-Fri) · 350 Fifth Ave
- **Lithomatic Business Forms** (8:30am-6pm) · 233 W 18th St
- **Mail Boxes Etc** (8:30am-6:30pm) · 244 Madison Ave
- **Metropolitan Duplicating & Imaging** (24 hrs) · 216 W 18th St
- **National Reprographics** (8am-7:30pm) · 44 W 18th St
- **Oak Hill Graphics** (8:30am-5pm) · 18 E 39th St
- **Print Icon** (8am-8pm) · 7 W 18th St
- **QRC** (9am-5pm) · 256 W 36th St
- **Screen Dot Printing** (9am-6pm) · 224 W 35th St
- **Speedway Copy & Printing** (9am-5pm) · 62 W 36th St
- **Staples** (7am-8pm) · 1293 Broadway
- **Staples** (7am-8pm) · 16 E 34th St
- **Staples** (7am-8pm) · 699 Sixth Ave
- **Staples** (8:30am-8pm) · Penn Station
- **Swift Copy Printing** (9am-6pm) · 10 E 36th St
- **The UPS Store** (8:30am-7pm) · 101 W 23rd St
- **The UPS Store** (8:30am-7pm) · 130 Seventh Ave
- **The UPS Store** (8:30am-8pm) · 1357 Broadway
- **The UPS Store** (8:30am-8pm) · 243 Fifth Ave
- **Village Copier** (24 hrs) · 10 E 39th St

🛒 Farmer's Markets

- **Union Square Greenmarket** · E 17th St & Broadway

🏋 Gyms

- **19th Street Gym** · 22 W 19th St
- **Bally Sports Club** · 139 W 32nd St
- **Bally Total Fitness** · 641 Sixth Ave
- **Crunch Fitness** · 144 W 38th St
- **Curves** · 36 W 34th St
- **David Barton Gym** · 215 W 23rd St
- **Definitions** · 139 Fifth Ave
- **Empress Fitness Club** · 897 Broadway
- **Equinox Fitness Club** · 897 Broadway
- **New York Health & Racquet Club** · 60 W 23rd St
- **New York Sports Clubs** · 1372 Broadway
- **New York Sports Clubs** · 200 Madison Ave
- **New York Sports Clubs** · 50 W 34th St
- **Peak Performance Sport & Fitness Center** · 54 W 21st St
- **Steel Gym** · 146 W 23rd St
- **The Fitness Club** · 11 Madison Ave
- **Thompkins Fitness & Wellness Center** · 122 W 26th St
- **YMCA** · 333 Seventh Ave

🔧 Hardware Stores

- **727 Hardware** · 727 Sixth Ave
- **A&M 28th Street Hardware** · 31 E 28th St
- **Adco Hardware** · 23 W 35th St
- **B&N Hardware** · 12 W 19th St
- **Central Hardware & Electric** · 1055 Sixth Ave
- **Elm Electric & Hardware** · 884 Sixth Ave
- **Halmor Hardware and Supply** · 43 W 20th St
- **Harris Hardware** · 151 W 19th St
- **Home Depot** · 28 W 23rd St
- **J&M Hardware & Locksmiths** · 19 E 21st St
- **Jamali Hardware & Garden Supplies** · 149 W 28th St
- **KDM Hardware** · 147 W 26th St
- **Kove Brothers Hardware** · 189 Seventh Ave
- **Spacesaver Hardware** · 132 W 23rd St
- **Whitey's Hardware** · 244 Fifth Ave

🍷 Liquor Stores

- **A&J Kessler Liquors** · 23 E 28th St
- **Chelsea Wine Cellar** · 200 W 21st St
- **Harry's Liquors** · 270 W 36th St
- **House of Cheers** · 261 W 18th St
- **Landmark Wine & Spirit** · 167 W 23rd St
- **Lewis-Kaye Wines & Liquors** · 60 E 34th St
- **Madison Ave Liquors** · 244 Madison Ave
- **Manor House Liquor Store** · 61 W 23rd St
- **Old Chelsea Wine & Liquor Store** · 86 Seventh Ave
- **Sonest Liquors** · 878 Sixth Ave
- **Union Square Wine & Spirits** · 33 Union Sq W
- **Wine Gallery** · 576 Sixth Ave

🐾 Pet Shops

- **Doggone Purrrty** · 151 W 25th St
- **Pet Central** · 193 Madison Ave
- **Pet Central** · 776 Sixth Ave
- **Petco** · 860 Broadway
- **Spot Pets** · 78 Seventh Ave
- **Trixie & Peanut** · 23 E 20th St

📀 Video Rental

- **Koryo Video** (Korean only) · 7 W 32nd St
- **Video Blitz** · 267 W 17th St

Map 9 • **Flatiron / Lower Midtown**

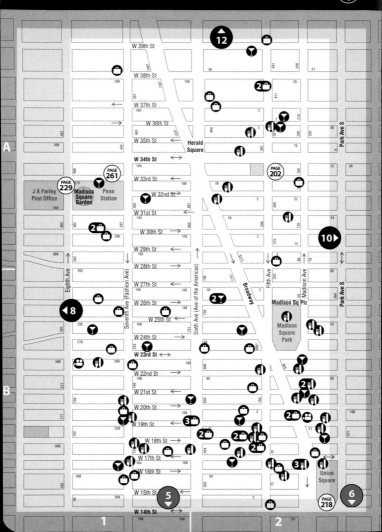

Entertainment

Map 9

14 15
11 12 13
8 9 10
5 6 7

Most of the action here is around Union Square, and if you feel like splurging on dinner, there are plenty of prime candidates here (Blue Water Grill, Craft, Gramercy Tavern, Tabla). Another option is Korean on W. 32nd Street, especially Kang Suh. The bar scene is not so great, especially north of 23rd street.

Movie Theaters

- **Clearview's Chelsea** • 260 W 23rd St
- **Loews 19th Street East** • 890 Broadway

Nightlife

- **Avalon** • 660 Sixth Ave
- **Blarney Stone** • 106 W 32nd St
- **Club Shelter** • 20 W 39th St
- **Cutting Room** • 19 W 24th St
- **Discotheque** • 17 W 19th St
- **Dusk of Miami** • 147 W 24th St
- **Ginger Man** • 11 E 36th St
- **Kavehaz** • 37 W 26th St
- **Live Bait** • 14 E 23rd St
- **Merchants** • 112 Seventh Ave
- **Old Town Bar & Restaurant** • 45 E 18th St
- **Peter McManus** • 152 Seventh Ave
- **Satalla** • 37 W 26th St
- **Splash Bar** • 50 W 17th St
- **Suede** • 161 W 23rd St
- **Tir Na Nog** • 5 Penn Plz
- **Under The Volcano** • 12 E 36th St

Restaurants

- **Basta Pasta** • 37 W 17th St
- **Blue Water Grill** • 31 Union Sq W
- **Burritoville** • 264 W 23rd St
- **Cafeteria** • 119 Seventh Ave
- **Chat 'n Chew** • 10 E 16th St
- **City Bakery** • 3 W 18th St
- **Coffee Shop** • 29 Union Sq W
- **Craft** • 43 E 19th St
- **Eisenberg's Sandwich Shop** • 174 Fifth Ave
- **Eleven Madison Park** • 11 Madison Ave
- **Elmo** • 156 Seventh Ave
- **Francisco's Centro Vasco** • 159 W 23rd St
- **Giorgio's of Gramercy** • 27 E 21st St
- **Gramercy Tavern** • 42 E 20th St
- **Hangawi** • 12 E 32nd St
- **Kang Suh** • 1250 Broadway
- **Kum Gang San** • 49 W 32nd St
- **Le Madri** • 168 W 18th St
- **Le Pain Quotidien** • 38 E 19th St
- **Le Zie 2000** • 172 Seventh Ave
- **Luna Park** • 50 E 17th St
- **Mandler's, The Original Sausage Co** • 26 E 17th St
- **Mayrose** • 920 Broadway
- **Mesa Grill** • 102 Fifth Ave
- **Periyali** • 35 W 20th St
- **Petite Abeille** • 107 W 18th St
- **Republic** • 37 Union Sq W
- **Shake Shack** • Madison Square Park
- **Silver Swan** • 41 E 20th St
- **Tabla** • 11 Madison Ave
- **Tamarind** • 41 E 22nd St
- **Toledo** • 6 E 36th St
- **Uncle Moe's** • 14 W 19th St
- **Union Square Café** • 21 E 16th St
- **Woo Chon** • 10 W 36th St

Shopping

- **17 at 17 Thrift Shop** • 17 W 17th St
- **30th Street Guitars** • 236 W 30th St
- **Al Friedman** • 44 W 18th St
- **ABC Carpet & Home** • 888 Broadway
- **Abracadabra** • 19 W 21st St
- **Academy Records & CDs** • 12 W 18th St
- **Adorama Camera** • 42 W 18th St
- **Ariston** • 69 Fifth Ave
- **Aveda Environmental Lifestyle Store** • 140 Fifth Ave
- **Bed Bath & Beyond** • 620 Sixth Ave
- **buybuyBABY** • 270 Seventh Ave
- **Capitol Fishing Tackle** • 218 W 23rd St
- **The City Quilter** • 133 W 25th St
- **CompUSA** • 420 Fifth Ave
- **The Container Store** • 629 Sixth Ave
- **Cupcake Café** • 18 W 18th St
- **DataVision** • 445 Fifth Ave
- **Fish's Eddy** • 889 Broadway
- **Housing Works Thrift Shop** • 143 W 17th St
- **Jam Paper & Envelope** • 611 Sixth Ave
- **Janovic Plaza** • 215 Seventh Ave
- **Jazz Record Center** • 236 W 26th St
- **Jensen-Lewis** • 89 Seventh Ave
- **Just Bulbs** • 5 E 16th St
- **Just Pickles** • 1 E 28th St
- **Just Pickles** • 168 Madison Ave
- **Krups Kitchen and Bath** • 11 W 18th St
- **Loehmann's** • 101 Seventh Ave
- **Lord & Taylor** • 424 Fifth Ave
- **M&J Trimmings** • 1008 Sixth Ave
- **Macy's** • 151 W 34th St
- **Manhattan Drum Shop & Music Studio** • 203 W 38th St
- **Paper Presentations** • 23 W 18th St
- **Paragon Sporting Goods** • 867 Broadway
- **Phoenix** • 64 W 37th St
- **Pleasure Chest** • 156 Seventh Ave
- **Radio Shack** • 36 E 23rd St
- **Rogue Music** • 251 W 30th St
- **Sam Flax** • 12 W 20th St
- **Sports Authority** • 636 Sixth Ave
- **Tekserve** • 119 W 23rd St

Map 9 · **Flatiron / Lower Midtown**

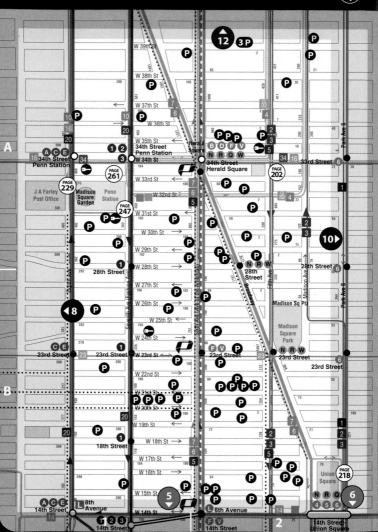

Parking during the day and on weekends is extremely difficult in this area, due to the number of business districts and commercial enterprises that are here. Driving isn't much better, since Lincoln Tunnel traffic has far-ranging repercussions. Few areas boast better subway access, however.

Subways

1 2 3	34 St-Penn Station
1	18 St
1	23 St
1	28 St
B D F V N Q R W	34 St-Herald Sq
F V	23rd St
R W	23 St
R W	28 St

Bus Lines

10 20	Seventh Ave/Eighth Ave (Central Park West)/Frederick Douglass Blvd
16	34th St Crosstown
2 3	Fifth Ave/Madison Ave
23	23rd St Crosstown
4	Fifth Ave/Madison Ave/Broadway
5	Fifth Ave/Sixth Ave/Riverdale Dr
6	Seventh Ave/Broadway/Sixth Ave
7	Columbus Ave/Amsterdam Ave/Lenox Ave/Sixth Ave/Seventh Ave/Broadway
Q 32	Penn Station/Jackson Heights, Queens

Bike Lanes

- • • • Marked Bike Lanes
- • • • Recommended Route

PATH

- **23 St** • 23rd St & Sixth Ave
- **33 St** • 33rd St & Sixth Ave

Car Rental

- **Avis** • 220 W 31st St
- **Eldan Rent-A-Car** • 350 Fifth Ave
- **Enterprise** • 106 W 24th St
- **Hertz** • 250 W 34th St

Parking

Map 10 · **Murray Hill / Gramercy**

This area is home to one of Manhattan's most pastoral and beautiful settings, Gramercy Park. It also contains two humongous and drab residential communities, Stuyvesant Town and Peter Cooper Village, plus huge Eastern Bloc-style apartment buildings like Kips Bay Towers. For juxtaposition, check out charming little Sniffen Court.

℞ 24-Hour Pharmacies

- **CVS Pharmacy** · 342 E 23rd St
- **Duane Reade** · 131 E 23rd St
- **Duane Reade** · 155 E 34th St
- **Rite Aid** · 542 Second Ave

Bagels

- **Bagel du Jour** · 478 Third Ave
- **Bagel & Schmear** · 114 E 28th St
- **Bagelry** · 429 Third Ave
- **Bagels & More** · 331 Lexington Ave
- **Daniel's Bagels** · 569 Third Ave
- **David's Bagels** · 331 First Ave
- **Ess-A-Bagel** · 359 First Ave
- **Gramercy Park Bagel** · 246 Third Ave
- **La Bagel** · 263 First Ave
- **New York Bagel** · 587 First Ave
- **NYC Bagels** · 310 E 23rd St
- **Pick-a-Bagel** · 297 Third Ave

Banks

AM · **Amalgamated** · 301 Third Ave
BP · **Banco Popular** · 441 Second Ave
BA · **Bank of America (ATM)** · 550 First Ave
BA · **Bank of America (ATM)** · 570 Second Ave
NY · **Bank of New York** · 45 Park Ave
CH · **Chase** · 225 Park Ave S
CH · **Chase** · 386 Park Ave S
CH · **Chase** · 400 E 23rd St
CH · **Chase** · 450 Third Ave
CH · **Chase (ATM)** · 390 Park Ave S
CI · **Citibank** · 1 Park Ave
CI · **Citibank** · 262 First Ave
CI · **Citibank (ATM)** · 25 Waterside Plz
CI · **Citibank (ATM)** · 481 First Ave
CO · **Commerce Bank** · 475 Park Ave S
DO · **Doral Bank** · 387 Park Ave S
FS · **Flushing Savings Bank** · 33 Irving Pl
GP · **Greenpoint Bank** · 254 E 34th St
HS · **HSBC** · 10 Union Sq E
HS · **HSBC** · 605 Third Ave
IC · **Independence Community** · 250 Lexington Ave
IB · **Interbank** · 420 Park Ave S
MT · **Manufacturers and Traders Trust** · 397 First Ave
MT · **Manufacturers and Traders Trust** · 401 E 23rd St
MT · **Manufacturers and Traders Trust (ATM)** · 385 First Ave
CU · **Municipal Credit Union (ATM)** · 462 First Ave
NF · **North Fork** · 470 Park Ave S
WM · **Washington Mutual** · 460 Park Ave S

Fire Departments

- **Engine 16, Ladder 7** · 234 E 29th St

Hospitals

- **Bellevue Hospital Center** · 462 First Ave
- **Beth Israel Medical Center** · 281 First Ave
- **Cabrini Medical Center** · 227 E 20th St
- **Hospital for Joint Diseases** · 301 E 17th St
- **NYU Medical Center: Tisch** · 560 First Ave
- **VA Hospital** · 423 E 23rd St

Landmarks

- **Gramercy Park** · Irving Pl & 20th St
- **National Arts Club** · 15 Gramercy Park S
- **Pete's Tavern** · 129 E 18th St
- **The Players** · 16 Gramercy Park S
- **Sniffen Court** · 36th St & Third Ave

Libraries

- **Epiphany** · 228 E 23rd St
- **Kips Bay** · 446 Third Ave

Police

- **13th Precinct** · 230 E 21st St

Post Offices

- **Madison Square** · 149 E 23rd St
- **Murray Hill** · 205 E 36th St
- **Murray Hill Finance** · 115 E 34th St

Schools

- **Baruch College** · 151 E 25th St
- **Baruch College High** · 17 Lexington Ave
- **The Child School** · 317 E 33rd St
- **Churchill** · 301 E 29th St
- **Epiphany Elementary** · 234 E 22nd St
- **Friends Seminary** · 222 E 16th St
- **Health Prof & Human Svcs High** · 345 E 15th St
- **HS 431 School of the Future** · 127 E 22nd St
- **Institute for Collaborative Education** · 345 E 15th St
- **JHS 104 Simon Baruch** · 330 E 21st St
- **Lee Strasberg Theater Institute** · 115 E 15th St
- **Manhattan Night Comprehensive High** · 240 Second Ave
- **MS 104 Simon Baruch** · 330 E 21st St
- **New York Film Academy** · 100 E 17th St
- **Norman Thomas High** · 111 E 33rd St
- **NYU Dental School** · First Ave & 24th St
- **NYU Medical Center** · 30th St & First Ave
- **Phillips Beth Israel School of Nursing** · 310 E 22nd St
- **PS 040 Augustus St Gaudens & MS 255 Salk** · 319 E 19th St
- **PS 116 Mary L Murray** · 210 E 33rd St
- **PS 226** · 345 E 15th St
- **PS 811 Bellevue Hospital** · 27th St & First Ave
- **PS-JHS 047 School for the Deaf** · 225 E 23rd St
- **School of Visual Arts** · 209 E 23rd St
- **Stern College for Women of Yeshiva U** · 245 Lexington Ave
- **United Nations International School** · 24 FDR Dr
- **Washington Irving High** · 40 Irving Pl

Supermarkets

- **Associated** · 278 Park Ave S
- **Associated** · 311 E 23rd St
- **D'Agostino** · 341 Third Ave
- **D'Agostino** · 528 Third Ave
- **D'Agostino** · 532 E 20th St
- **D'Agostino** · 578 Third Ave
- **Food Emporium** · 10 Union Sq E
- **Food Emporium** · 200 E 32nd St
- **Garden of Eden** · 310 Third Ave
- **Gristede's** · 25 Waterside Plz
- **Gristede's** · 355 First Ave
- **Gristede's** · 460 Third Ave
- **Gristede's** · 512 Second Ave
- **Gristede's** · 549 Third Ave
- **Met Food** · 180 Third Ave

Map 10 · **Murray Hill / Gramercy**

Sundries / Entertainment

Map 10

14 15
11 12 13
8 9 10
5 6 7

This area is a study in contrast—great ethnic Indian food on Lexington, including an NFT favorite (Pongal), but an equal number of drab eateries, especially on First Avenue. And one of the city's best bars, Pete's Tavern, balanced by ungodly "meat market" bars throughout the neighborhood. Choose wisely.

Coffee

- **71 Irving** • 71 Irving Pl
- **Aristotle Coffee Shop** • 350 Park Ave S
- **Au Bon Pain** • 600 Third Ave
- **Cosi** • 257 Park Ave S
- **Cosi** • 461 Park Ave S
- **Dunkin' Donuts** • 152 W 34th St
- **Dunkin' Donuts** • 250 Second Ave
- **Dunkin' Donuts** • 412 Third Ave
- **Dunkin' Donuts** • 476 Second Ave
- **Dunkin' Donuts** • 601 Third Ave
- **Guy & Gallard** • 120 E 34th St
- **Guy & Gallard** • 120 E 34th St
- **Oren's Daily Roast** • 434 Third Ave
- **Plaza de Café** • 51 Lexington Ave
- **Push Café** • 294 Third Ave
- **Starbucks** • 10 Union Sq E
- **Starbucks** • 145 Third Ave
- **Starbucks** • 286 First Ave
- **Starbucks** • 296 Third Ave
- **Starbucks** • 3 Park Ave
- **Starbucks** • 304 Park Ave S
- **Starbucks** • 395 Third Ave
- **Starbucks** • 424 Park Ave S
- **Starbucks** • 585 Second Ave
- **Sunburst** • 57 E 18th St
- **Trevi Coffee Shop** • 48 Union Sq E

Copy Shops

- **Alphagraphics** (8:30am-6pm) • 455 Park Ave S
- **Columbia Enterprises** (8:30am-5:30pm) • 116 E 16th St
- **Ever Ready Blue Print** (8am-5:30pm) • 200 Park Ave S
- **Graphics Service Bureau** (24 hrs) • 370 Park Ave S
- **Kinko's** (8am-11pm) • 600 Third Ave
- **Kinko's** (8am-11pm) • 257 Park Ave S
- **Mail Boxes Etc** (8:30am-7pm) • 163 Third Ave
- **Mail Boxes Etc** (8:30am-7pm) • 350 Third Ave
- **Office Depot** (7am-8pm) • 542 Second Ave
- **On-Site Sourcing** • 443 Park Ave S
- **Pro-Print** (8:30am-8pm) • 424 Park Ave S
- **Staples** (7am-7pm) • 345 Park Ave S
- **Tower Copy East** (9am-6pm) • 427 Third Ave
- **The UPS Store** (8:30am-7pm) • 527 Third Ave

Gyms

- **Club 29** • 155 E 29th St
- **Crunch Fitness** • 554 Second Ave
- **Curves** • 139 E 23rd St
- **Curves** • 150 E 39th St
- **LUYE Aquafit** • 310 E 23rd St
- **Manhattan Place Condominium Health Club** • 630 First Ave
- **New York Sports Clubs** • 10 Irving Pl
- **New York Sports Clubs** • 113 E 23rd St
- **New York Sports Clubs** • 131 E 31st St
- **New York Sports Clubs** • 3 Park Ave
- **New York Sports Clubs** • 614 Second Ave
- **Park Avenue Executive Fitness** • 90 Park Ave
- **Rivergate Fitness Center** • 401 E 34th St
- **Synergy Fitness Clubs** • 201 E 23rd St
- **Synergy Fitness Clubs** • 4 Park Ave

Hardware Stores

- **Gurell Hardware** • 132 E 28th St
- **Lumber Boys** • 698 Second Ave
- **Lumberland Hardware** • 368 Third Ave
- **Simon's Hardware & Bath** • 421 Third Ave
- **Town & Village Hardware** • 337 First Ave
- **Vercesi Hardware** • 152 E 23rd St
- **Warshaw Hardware & Electrical** • 248 Third Ave

Liquor Stores

- **Buy Rite Discount Liquors** • 398 Third Ave
- **First Avenue Wine & Spirits Supermarket** • 383 First Ave
- **Flynn Winfield Liquor** • 558 Third Ave
- **Frank's Liquor Shop** • 46 Union Sq E
- **Gramercy Park Wines & Spirits** • 104 E 23rd St
- **House of Wine & Liquor** • 250 E 34th St
- **HS Wine & Liquor** • 108 E 16th St
- **Italian Wine Merchants** • 108 E 16th St
- **New Gramercy Liquors** • 279 Third Ave
- **Quality House** • 2 Park Ave
- **Royal Wine Merchants Ltd** • 25 Waterside Plz
- **Stuyvesant Square Liquors** • 333 Second Ave
- **VINO** • 121 E 27th St
- **Windsor Wine Shop** • 474 Third Ave
- **Wine Shop** • 345 Lexington Ave
- **World Wine and Spirits** • 705 Second Ave
- **Zeichner Wine & Liquor** • 279 First Ave

Movie Theaters

- **Loews Kips Bay** • 550 Second Ave
- **Scandinavia House** • 58 Park Ave

Nightlife

- **Bar 515** • 515 Third Ave
- **Belmont Lounge** • 117 E 15th St
- **Irving Plaza** • 17 Irving Pl
- **The Jazz Standard** • 116 E 27th St
- **Joshua Tree** • 513 Third Ave
- **Mercury Bar** • 493 Third Ave
- **Molly's** • 287 Third Ave
- **Revival** • 129 E 15th St
- **Rocky Sullivan's** • 129 Lexington Ave
- **Rodeo Bar & Grill** • 375 Third Ave
- **Waterfront Ale House** • 540 Second Ave

Pet Shops

- **All Paws** • 120 E 34th St
- **Doggie-Do & Pussycats Too** • 567 Third Ave
- **Furry Paws** • 120 E 34th St
- **Furry Paws 5** • 310 E 23rd St
- **Natural Pet** • 238 Third Ave
- **New World Aquarium** • 204 E 38th St
- **Petco** • 550 Second Ave
- **Petland Discounts** • 404 Third Ave
- **Thirty-Third & Bird** • 40 E 33rd St

Restaurants

- **Angelo & Maxie's** • 233 Park Ave S
- **Artisanal** • 2 Park Ave
- **Blockheads Burritos** • 499 Third Ave
- **Coppola's** • 378 Third Ave
- **El Parador Café** • 325 E 34th St
- **Gemini Restaurant** • 641 Second Ave
- **Gramercy Restaurant** • 184 Third Ave
- **Haandi** • 113 Lexington Ave
- **I Trulli** • 122 E 27th St
- **Jackson Hole** • 521 Third Ave
- **Jaiya Thai** • 396 Third Ave
- **L'Express** • 249 Park Ave S
- **Park Avenue Country Club** • 381 Park Ave S
- **Patsy's Pizza** • 509 Third Ave
- **Pete's Tavern** • 129 E 18th St
- **Pongal** • 110 Lexington Ave
- **Pongsri Thai** • 311 Second Ave
- **Rare Bar & Grill** • 303 Lexington Ave, Shelbourne Murray Hill Hotel
- **Sarge's Deli** • 548 Third Ave
- **Shaheen's Sweets** • 130 E 29th St
- **Tatany** • 380 Third Ave
- **Totonno Pizzeria Napolitan** • 462 Second Ave
- **Turkish Kitchen** • 386 Third Ave
- **Union Pacific** • 111 E 22nd St
- **Via Emilia** • 240 Park Ave S
- **Water Club** • 500 E 30th St
- **Yama** • 122 E 17th St
- **Zen Palate** • 34 Union Sq E

Shopping

- **Alkit Pro Camera** • 222 Park Ave S
- **City Opera Thrift Shop** • 222 E 23rd St
- **Foods of India** • 121 Lexington Ave
- **Housing Works Thrift Shop** • 157 E 23rd St
- **Ligne Roset** • 250 Park Ave S
- **Nemo Tile Company** • 48 E 21st St
- **Pastrami Factory** • 333 E 23rd St
- **Pearl Paint** • 207 E 23rd St
- **Poggenpohl US** • 230 Park Ave
- **Quark Spy** • 240 E 29th St
- **Urban Angler** • 206 Fifth Ave

Video Rental

- **Blockbuster Video** • 151 Third Ave
- **Blockbuster Video** • 155 E 34th St
- **Blockbuster Video** • 312 First Ave
- **Blockbuster Video** • 344 Third Ave
- **Video Maven** • 715 Second Ave
- **Video Stop** • 367 Third Ave

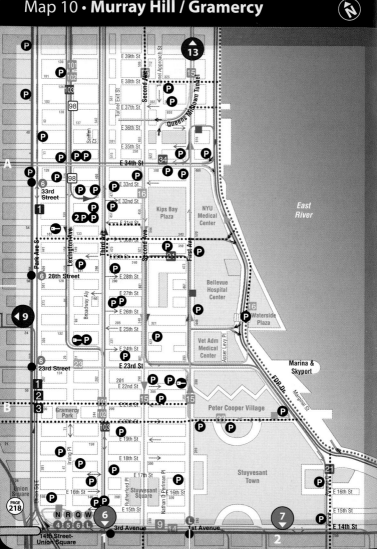

Map 10 • **Murray Hill / Gramercy**

East
River

Kips Bay
Plaza

NYU
Medical
Center

Bellevue
Hospital
Center

Vet Adm
Medical
Center

Waterside
Plaza

Marina &
Skyport

Peter Cooper Village

Stuyvesant
Town

Gramercy
Park

Union
Square

33rd
Street

28th Street

23rd Street

E 39th St
E 38th St
E 37th St
E 36th St
E 35th St
E 34th St
E 33rd St
E 32nd St
E 31st St
E 30th St
E 29th St
E 28th St
E 27th St
E 26th St
E 25th St
E 24th St
E 23rd St
E 22nd St
E 21st St
E 20th St
E 19th St
E 18th St
E 17th St
E 16th St
E 15th St
E 14th St

Park Ave S
Lexington Ave
Third Ave
Second Ave
First Ave
FDR Dr
Irving Pl
Broadway Aly
Rutherford Pl
Nathan D Perlman Pl

Queens Midtown Tunnel

3rd Avenue
1st Avenue

Overnight parking is difficult, but there are many meter spots to be had, especially on the avenues. We're very excited by the prospect of the Second Avenue subway line, even if it won't be open until after we've retired to Fort Lauderdale and monthly MetroCards cost $5000.

Subways

6	23rd St
6	28th St
6	33rd St
4 5 6 L N Q R W	14th St
L	First Ave
L	Third Ave

Bus Lines

1 2 3	Fifth Ave/Madison Ave
101	Third Ave/Lexington Ave
102	Third Ave/Lexington Ave
103	Third Ave/Lexington Ave
9	Avenue B/East Broadway
14	14th St Crosstown
34	34th St Crosstown
15	First Ave/Second Ave
16	34th St Crosstown
21	Houston St Crosstown
23	23rd St Crosstown
98	Third Ave/Lexington Ave

Bike Lanes

- • • • Marked Bike Lanes
- • • • Recommended Route
- • • • Greenway

Car Rental

- **Dollar** • 329 E 22nd St
- **Hertz** • 150 E 24th St
- **National** • 142 E 31st St

Gas Stations

- **Gulf** • E 23 St & FDR Dr

Parking

Map 11 · **Hell's Kitchen**

Essentials

14	15	
11	12	13
8	9	10
5	6	7

Map 11

A bit of a forgotten neighborhood, despite the famous name and its proximity to Times Square. Hardly any banks, bagels, or other essentials, especially west of Tenth Avenue. The area around the Port Authority Bus Terminal is still one of the most authentically seedy places in Manhattan.

Bagels
• **H&H Bagels** • 639 W 46th St

Banks
CI • **Citibank** • 401 W 42nd St
CO • **Commerce Bank** • 582 Ninth Ave
HS • **HSBC** • 330 W 42nd St

Community Gardens

Fire Departments
• **Rescue 1** • 530 W 43rd St

Hospitals
• **St Clare's** • 426 W 52nd St
• **St Luke's Roosevelt Hospital Center** •
1000 Tenth Ave

Landmarks
• **Intrepid Sea, Air & Space Museum** •
Twelfth Ave & 45th St
• **Theatre Row** • 42nd St b/w Ninth & Tenth Aves

Libraries
• **Columbus** (closed for renovation) •
742 Tenth Ave

Police
• **Mid-Town North** • 306 W 54th St

Post Offices
• **Radio City** • 322 W 52nd St
• **Times Square** • 340 W 42nd St

Schools
• **Alvin Ailey / Joan Weill Center for Dance** •
405 W 55th St
• **American Academy McAllister Institute** •
450 W 56th St
• **American Academy McAllister Institute** •
619 W 54th St
• **High School for Environmental Studies** •
444 W 56th St
• **High School of Graphic Communication Arts** •
439 W 49th St
• **Holy Cross** • 332 W 43rd St
• **Independence High (M544)** • 850 Tenth Ave
• **John Jay College** • 899 Tenth Ave
• **Park West High** • 525 W 50th St
• **Professional Performing Arts High** •
328 W 48th St
• **PS 051 Elias Howe** • 520 W 45th St
• **PS 111 Adolph S Ochs** • 440 W 53rd St
• **PS 212 Midtown West** • 328 W 48th St
• **PS 35 Manhattan** • 317 W 52nd St
• **Sacred Heart of Jesus** • 456 W 52nd St

Supermarkets
• **Amish Market** • 731 Ninth Ave
• **Associated** • 917 Ninth Ave
• **D'Agostino** • 353 W 57th St
• **D'Agostino** • 815 Tenth Ave
• **Food Emporium** • 452 W 43rd St

Map 11 • Hell's Kitchen

Sundries / Entertainment

Map 11

14	15
11	12	13
8	9	10
5	6	7

For food, try the Afghan Kebab House, Island Burgers 'N Shakes, and Hallo Berlin ("The Best Wurst" in the city), or just wander down Ninth Avenue. The Bull Moose is reliably good for a drink or two, and Rudy's is a quintessential New York bar. Only order the hot dogs when extremely drunk.

Coffee

- **The Coffee Beanery Ltd** · 601 W 54th St
- **The Coffee Pot** · 350 W 49th St
- **Dunkin' Donuts** · 580 Ninth Ave
- **Empire Coffee & Tea** · 568 Ninth Ave
- **Felix Coffee Shop** · 630 Tenth Ave
- **Flame Coffee House** · 893 Ninth Ave
- **Project Find Coffee House** · 551 Ninth Ave
- **Starbucks** · 322 W 57th St
- **Starbucks** · 325 W 49th St
- **Starbucks** · 555 W 42nd St
- **Starbucks** · 682 Ninth Ave
- **Studio Coffee Shop** · 630 Ninth Ave

Copy Shops

- **Mail Boxes Etc** (8:30am-7pm) · 331 W 57th St
- **Mail Boxes Etc** (8:30am-7pm) · 676A Ninth Ave
- **Mega Copy Center** (8am-6pm) · 738 Tenth Ave
- **Xact** (24 hrs) · 333 W 52nd St

Farmer's Markets

- **57th Street** · W 57th St & Ninth Ave

Gyms

- **Bally Sports Club** · 350 W 50th St
- **Curves** · 314 W 53rd St
- **Manhattan Plaza Health Club** · 482 W 43rd St
- **New York Underground Fitness** · 440 W 57th St
- **Strand Health Club** · 500 W 43rd St

Hardware Stores

- **Columbus Hardware** · 852 Ninth Ave
- **HT Sales** · 718 Tenth Ave
- **Lopez Sentry Hardware** · 691 Ninth Ave
- **Metropolitan Lumber & Hardware** · 617 Eleventh Ave
- **Straight Hardware & Supply** · 613 Ninth Ave

Liquor Stores

- **54 Wine & Spirits** · 408 W 55th St
- **860 Ninth Liquors** · 860 Ninth Ave
- **B&G Wine & Liquor Store** · 507 W 42nd St
- **Manhattan Plaza Winery** · 589 Ninth Ave
- **Ninth Avenue Vintner** · 669 Ninth Ave
- **Ninth Avenue Wine & Liquor** · 474 Ninth Ave
- **Ray & Frank Liquor Store** · 706 Ninth Ave
- **West 57th Street Wine & Spirit** · 340 W 57th St

Nightlife

- **Bellevue Bar** · 538 Ninth Ave
- **Birdland** · 315 W 44th St
- **Bull Moose Saloon** · 354 W 44th St
- **Don't Tell Mama** · 343 W 46th St
- **Hudson Hotel Library** · 356 W 58th St
- **Rudy's Bar & Grill** · 627 Ninth Ave
- **Siberia Bar** · 356 W 40th St
- **Xth** · 642 Tenth Ave

Pet Shops

- **Canine Castle** · 410 W 56th St
- **Metropets** · 594 Ninth Ave
- **Petland Discounts** · 734 Ninth Ave
- **Spoiled Brats** · 340 W 49th St

Restaurants

- **Afghan Kebab House** · 764 Ninth Ave
- **Ariana Afghan Kebab** · 787 Ninth Ave
- **Burritoville** · 625 Ninth Ave
- **Churruscaria Plataforma** · 316 W 49th St
- **Daisy May's BBQ USA** · 623 Eleventh Ave
- **Grand Sichuan Int'l** · 745 Ninth Ave
- **Hallo Berlin** · 402 W 51st St
- **Hallo Berlin** · 626 Tenth Ave
- **Hudson Cafeteria** · 356 W 58th St
- **Island Burgers 'N Shakes** · 766 Ninth Ave
- **Jezebel** · 630 Ninth Ave
- **Joe Allen** · 326 W 46th St
- **Les Sans Culottes** · 347 W 46th St
- **Meskerem** · 468 W 47th St
- **Munson Diner** · 600 W 48th St
- **Old San Juan** · 765 Ninth Ave
- **Orso** · 322 W 46th St
- **Ralph's** · 862 Ninth Ave
- **Tout Va Bien** · 311 W 51st St
- **Uncle Nick's** · 747 Ninth Ave
- **Zen Palate** · 663 Ninth Ave

Shopping

- **Janovic Plaza** · 771 Ninth Ave
- **Little Pie Company** · 424 W 43rd St
- **Metro Bicycles** · 360 W 47th St
- **Ninth Avenue Cheese Market** · 615 Ninth Ave
- **Ninth Avenue International** · 543 Ninth Ave
- **Pan Aqua Diving** · 460 W 43rd St
- **Poseidon Bakery** · 629 Ninth Ave
- **Radio Shack** · 333 W 57th St
- **Sea Breeze** · 541 Ninth Ave

Map 11 · **Hell's Kitchen**

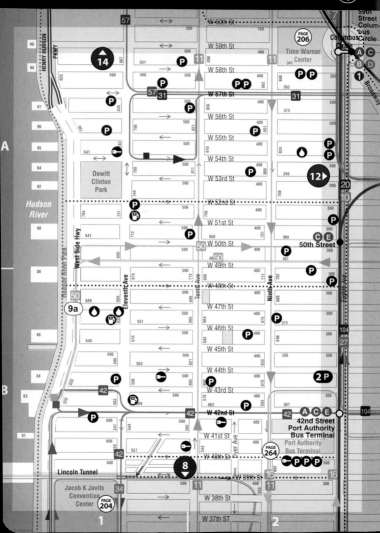

The Lincoln Tunnel jams this area up during the day. If you're coming from downtown, try taking the Tenth Avenue approach. If you're coming from uptown, you're screwed. This is also where the West Side "Highway" begins to have traffic lights and becomes a parking lot for most of the day (alternate: Eleventh Avenue). Enjoy.

Subways

C E .... 50th St
A C E .... 42nd St/Port Authority Bus Terminal
A C B D 1 .... 59th St/Columbus Cir

Bus Lines

11 .... Ninth Ave/Tenth Ave
16 .... 34th St Crosstown
27 .... 49th St/50th St Crosstown
31 .... 57th St Crosstown
42 .... 42nd St Crosstown
50 .... 49th St/50th St Crosstown
57 .... 57th St Crosstown
104 .... Broadway/42nd St

Bike Lanes

- • • • Marked Bike Lanes
- • • • Recommended Route
- • • • Greenway

Car Rental

- **All-State Auto Rental** · 540 W 44th St
- **Avis** · 460 W 42nd St
- **Courier Car Rental** · 537 Tenth Ave
- **Enterprise** · 667 Eleventh Ave
- **Hertz** · 346 W 40th St

Car Washes

- **JL Custom Car Cleaner** (detailer) · 349 W 54th St
- **New York Car Wash** · 625 Eleventh Ave
- **Westside Highway Car Wash** · 638 W 47th St

Gas Stations

- **BP** · 59th St & Eleventh Ave
- **Mobil** · 561 Eleventh Ave
- **Mobil** · 718 Eleventh Ave
- **Sunoco** · 639 Eleventh Ave

Parking

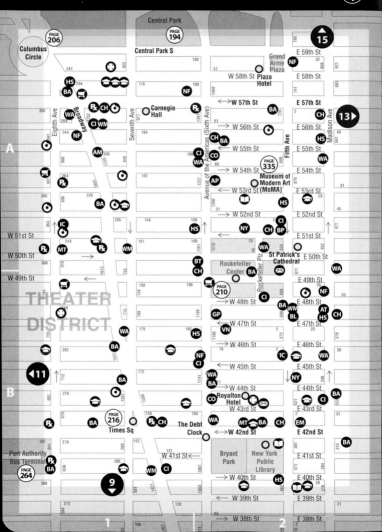

For all intents and purposes, this is the heart of New York. However, Times Square, the Theater District, and Rockefeller Center are all areas that many New Yorkers avoid. Instead, try the beautifully reconstructed Bryant Park or Phillipe Starck's utterly cool Royalton Hotel. Alas, alas for the Plaza Hotel—what an inglorious end.

24-Hour Pharmacies

- Duane Reade · 100 W 57th St
- Duane Reade · 1633 Broadway
- Duane Reade · 224 W 57th St
- Duane Reade · 4 Times Sq
- Duane Reade · 625 Eighth Ave
- Duane Reade · 661 Eighth Ave
- Duane Reade · 900 Eighth Ave
- Rite Aid · 301 W 50th St

Bagels

- Bagel Café · 850 8th Ave
- Bagel-N-Bean · 828 Seventh Ave
- Bread Factory Café · 935 Eighth Ave
- Crown Deli · 1674 Broadway
- Diamond Café · 6 E 48th St
- Pick-a-Bagel · 200 W 57th St
- Pick-a-Bagel · 891 Eighth Ave
- Times Square Bagels · 200 W 44th St
- Torino Bagel · 22 W 56th St

Banks

- AM · Amalgamated · 1745 Broadway
- AP · Apple · 1320 Sixth Ave
- AT · Atlantic · 400 Madison Ave
- BP · Banco Popular · 7 W 51st St
- BL · Bank Leumi · 579 Fifth Ave
- BA · Bank of America · 1140 Sixth Ave
- BA · Bank of America · 1515 Broadway
- BA · Bank of America · 1675 Broadway
- BA · Bank of America · 1775 Broadway
- BA · Bank of America · 335 Madison Ave
- BA · Bank of America · 4 W 57th St
- BA · Bank of America · 56 E 42nd St
- BA · Bank of America · 592 Fifth Ave
- BA · Bank of America · 625 Eighth Ave
- BA · Bank of America (ATM) · 1535 Broadway
- BA · Bank of America (ATM) · 247 W 42nd St
- BA · Bank of America (ATM) · 30 Rockefeller Plz
- BA · Bank of America (ATM) · 55 W 42nd St
- BA · Bank of America (ATM) · 77 W 55th St
- NY · Bank of New York · 51 W 51st St
- NY · Bank of New York · 530 Fifth Ave
- BT · Bank of Tokyo · 1251 Sixth Ave
- CH · Chase · 11 W 51st St
- CH · Chase · 1251 Sixth Ave
- CH · Chase · 1370 Sixth Ave
- CH · Chase · 250 W 57th St
- CH · Chase · 3 Times Sq
- CH · Chase · 401 Madison Ave
- CH · Chase · 510 Fifth Ave
- CH · Chase · 600 Madison Ave
- CI · Citibank · 1 Rockefeller Plz
- CI · Citibank · 1155 Sixth Ave
- CI · Citibank · 1345 Sixth Ave
- CI · Citibank · 1440 Broadway
- CI · Citibank · 1748 Broadway
- CI · Citibank · 330 Madison Ave
- CI · Citibank · 640 Fifth Ave
- CO · Commerce Bank · 1120 Sixth Ave
- CO · Commerce Bank · 1350 Sixth Ave
- EM · Emigrant · 5 E 42nd St
- GP · Greenpoint Bank · 1200 Sixth Ave
- HS · HSBC · 1185 Sixth Ave
- HS · HSBC · 1271 Sixth Ave
- HS · HSBC · 1790 Broadway
- HS · HSBC · 415 Madison Ave
- HS · HSBC · 452 Fifth Ave
- HS · HSBC · 555 Madison Ave
- HS · HSBC · 666 Fifth Ave
- IC · Independence Community · 550 Fifth Ave
- IC · Independence Community · 864 Eighth Ave
- MT · Manufacturers and Traders Trust · 41 W 42nd St
- MT · Manufacturers and Traders Trust · 830 Eighth Ave
- NF · North Fork · 767 Fifth Ave
- NF · North Fork Bank · 101 W 57th St
- NF · North Fork Bank · 1166 Sixth Ave
- NF · North Fork Bank · 424 Madison Ave
- VN · Valley National Bank · 62 W 47th St
- WA · Wachovia · 1156 Sixth Ave
- WA · Wachovia · 1345 Sixth Ave
- WA · Wachovia · 1755 Broadway
- WA · Wachovia · 360 Madison Ave
- WA · Wachovia · 437 Madison Ave
- WA · Wachovia · 49 Rockefeller Plz
- WA · Wachovia · 540 Madison Ave
- WA · Wachovia (ATM) · 1100 Sixth Ave
- WA · Wachovia (ATM) · 1568 Broadway
- WM · Washington Mutual · 1431 Broadway
- WM · Washington Mutual · 235 W 56th St
- WM · Washington Mutual · 589 Fifth Ave
- WM · Washington Mutual · 787 Seventh Ave

Fire Departments

- Engine 23 · 215 W 58th St
- Engine 54, Ladder 4 · 782 Eighth Ave
- Engine 65 · 33 W 43rd St

Landmarks

- Carnegie Hall · 154 W 57th St
- The Debt Clock · Sixth Ave & 42nd St
- Museum of Modern Art (MoMA) · 11 W 53rd St
- New York Public Library · Fifth Ave & 42nd St
- Plaza Hotel · 768 Fifth Ave
- Rockefeller Center · 600 Fifth Ave
- Royalton Hotel · 44th St b/w Fifth Ave & Sixth Ave
- St Patrick's Cathedral · Fifth Ave & 50th St
- Times Square · 42nd St-Times Sq

Libraries

- Donnell Library Center · 20 W 53rd St
- Humanities & Social Sciences Library · 42nd St & Fifth Ave
- Mid-Manhattan Library · 455 Fifth Ave

Post Offices

- Bryant · 23 W 43rd St
- Rockefeller Center · 610 Fifth Ave

Schools

- Berkeley College · 3 E 43rd St
- Circle in the Square Theater School · 1633 Broadway
- Coalition School for Social Change · 220 W 58th St
- Daytop Village Secondary · 54 W 40th St
- Family School W St Luke Luthrn Ch · 308 W 46th St
- Jacqueline Kennedy Onassis High · 120 W 46th St
- Katharine Gibbs · 50 W 40th St
- Laboratory Institute of Merchandising · 12 E 53rd St
- Landmark High · 220 W 58th St
- Lyceum Kennedy French School · 225 W 43rd St
- Pace University · 551 Fifth Ave
- Parsons School of Design, Midtown · 560 Seventh Ave
- Practicing Law Institute · 810 Seventh Ave
- Repertory School · 123 W 43rd St
- St Thomas Choir School · 202 W 58th St
- SUNY College of Optometry · 33 W 42nd St
- Wood Tobe-Coburn · 8 E 40th St

Supermarkets

- Associated · 225 W 57th St
- Citarella · 1250 Sixth Ave
- Food Emporium · 810 Eighth Ave
- Gristede's · 907 Eighth Ave

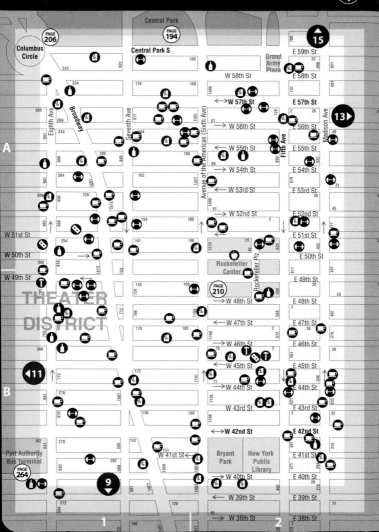

Map 12 · **Midtown**

Central Park

Columbus
Circle

Central Park S

THEATER
DISTRICT

Rockefeller
Center

Bryant
Park

New York
Public
Library

Port Authority
Bus Terminal

Grand
Army
Plaza

Eighth Ave
Broadway
Seventh Ave
Avenue of the Americas (Sixth Ave)
Fifth Ave
Madison Ave

Central Park S
W 58th St
W 57th St
W 56th St
W 55th St
W 54th St
W 53rd St
W 52nd St
W 51st St
W 50th St
W 49th St
W 48th St
W 47th St
W 46th St
W 45th St
W 44th St
W 43rd St
W 42nd St
W 41st St
W 40th St
W 39th St
W 38th St

E 59th St
E 58th St
E 57th St
E 56th St
E 55th St
E 54th St
E 53rd St
E 52nd St
E 51st St
E 50th St
E 49th St
E 48th St
E 47th St
E 46th St
E 45th St
E 44th St
E 43rd St
E 42nd St
E 41st St
E 40th St
E 39th St
E 38th St

PAGE 206
PAGE 194
PAGE 210
PAGE 264

15
13
11
9

A
B
1
2

You can find anything here, but it's probably going to be less of a pain in the butt to find it somewhere else in the city...

☕ Coffee

- **Au Bon Pain** · 1211 Sixth Ave
- **Au Bon Pain** · 125 W 55th St
- **Au Bon Pain** · 1251 Sixth Ave
- **Au Bon Pain** · 16 E 44th St
- **Café Metro** · 625 Eighth Ave
- **Cosi** · 11 W 42nd St
- **Cosi** · 1633 Broadway
- **Cosi** · 61 W 48th St
- **Cyber Café** · 250 W 49th St
- **Dean & Deluca Café** · 235 W 46th St
- **Dunkin' Donuts** · 1515 Broadway
- **Dunkin' Donuts** · 1680 Broadway
- **Dunkin' Donuts** · 761 Seventh Ave
- **Evergreen Coffee Shop Restaurant** · 145 W 47th St
- **Fluffy's Café & Bakery** · 855 Seventh Ave
- **The Greeks Coffee Shop** · 347 Madison Ave
- **La Parisienne Coffee House** · 910 Seventh Ave
- **Oren's Daily Roast** · 33 E 58th St
- **Philip's Coffee** · 155 W 56th St
- **Red Flame Coffee Shop** · 67 W 44th St
- **Starbucks** ·
  - · 1166 Sixth Ave
  - · 120 W 56th St
  - · 1320 Sixth Ave
  - · 142 W 57th St
  - · 1500 Broadway
  - · 1585 Broadway
  - · 1675 Broadway
  - · 251 W 42nd St
  - · 30 Rockefeller Plz
  - · 335 Madison Ave
  - · 400 Madison Ave
  - · 42nd St & Fifth Ave
  - · 550 Madison Ave
  - · 600 Eighth Ave
  - · 725 Fifth Ave
  - · 770 Eighth Ave
  - · Sixth Ave & 42nd St
  - · (Marriott) 1535 Broadway
  - · 1100 Sixth Ave
  - · 1185 Sixth Ave
  - · 1290 Sixth Ave
  - · 1345 Sixth Ave
  - · 1460 Broadway
  - · 156 W 52nd St
  - · 1656 Broadway
  - · 1710 Broadway
  - · 295 Madison Ave
  - · 330 Madison Ave
  - · 4 Columbus Cir
  - · 45 E 51st St
  - · 545 Fifth Ave
  - · 575 Fifth Ave
  - · 684 Sixth Ave
  - · 750 Seventh Ave
  - · 821 Eighth Ave
  - · 871 Eighth Ave
- **Teresa's Gourmet Coffee Bar** · 51 W 51st St

📋 Copy Shops

- **57th Street Copy Center** (9am-5:30pm) · 151 W 57th St
- **Accurate Copy Services** (8:30am-5pm) · 250 W 57th St
- **Atlantic Blueprint** (8:30am-5pm) · 575 Madison Ave
- **BPI** (8:30am-5pm) · 295 Madison Ave
- **The Complete Copy Center** (9am-5pm) · 1271 Sixth Ave
- **Copy Door II** (8:30am-7pm) · Sixth Ave & 40th St
- **Deanco Press** (9am-5pm) · 767 Fifth Ave
- **Discovery Copy Services** (24 hrs) · 45 W 45th St
- **Duplications Unlimited** (9am-6pm) · 149 W 55th St

- **Genie Instant Printing Center** (8am-5pm) · 37 W 43rd St
- **Kinko's** (24 hrs) · 1211 Sixth Ave
- **Kinko's** (24 hrs) · 16 E 52nd St
- **Kinko's** (24 hrs) · 233 W 54th St
- **Kinko's** (24 hrs) · 240 Central Park S
- **Kinko's** (24 hrs) · 60 W 40th St
- **Longacre Copy Center** (9am-6pm) · 235 W 56th St
- **Longacre Copy Center** (9am-6pm) · 80 W 40th St
- **Met Photo** (8am-8pm) · 1500 Broadway
- **Office Depot** (7am-9pm) · 1441 Broadway
- **Pip Printing** (9am-5pm) · 69 W 55th St
- **Pro-Print** (8am-6pm) · 18 W 45th St
- **Servco** (8:30am-8:30pm) · 1150 Sixth Ave
- **Skyline Duplication** (24 hrs) · 151 W 46th St
- **Staples** (7am-8pm) · 535 Fifth Ave
- **Staples** (7am-8pm) · 57 W 57th St
- **Staples** (7am-8pm) · 776 Eighth Ave
- **Staples** (7am-8pm) · 1065 Sixth Ave
- **The UPS Store** (10am-10pm) · 1514 Broadway
- **The UPS Store** (8am-7:30pm) · 888C Eighth Ave
- **The Village Copier** · 25 W 43rd St

🍎 Farmer's Markets

- **Rockefeller Center** · Rockefeller Plz & 50th St

💪 Gyms

- **Athletic and Swim Club at Equitable Center** · 787 Seventh Ave
- **Bally Sports Club** · 335 Madison Ave
- **Bally Total Fitness** · 45 E 55th St
- **Definitions** · 1633 Broadway
- **Drago's Gymnasium** · 50 W 57th St
- **Equinox Fitness Club** · 1633 Broadway
- **Equinox Fitness Club** · 521 Fifth Ave
- **Exude Fitness** · 16 E 52nd St
- **Fitness Center at the New York Palace** · 455 Madison Ave
- **Gold's Gym** · 250 W 54th St
- **Gravity Fitness Center** · 119 W 56th St
- **Lucille Roberts Health Club** · 300 W 40th St
- **Mid City Gym** · 244 W 49th St
- **New York Athletic Club** · 180 Central Park S
- **New York Health & Racquet Club** · 110 W 56th St
- **New York Health & Racquet Club** · 20 E 50th St
- **New York Sports Clubs** · 1221 Sixth Ave
- **New York Sports Clubs** · 1601 Broadway

- **New York Sports Clubs** · 1657 Broadway
- **New York Sports Clubs** · 19 W 44th St
- **New York Sports Clubs** · 230 W 41st St
- **New York Sports Clubs** · Rockefeller Ctr
- **The Peninsula Spa** · 700 Fifth Ave
- **Radu's Physical Culture Studio** · 24 W 57th St
- **Ritz Plaza Health Club** · 235 W 48th St
- **Sheraton New York & Manhattan Health Clubs** · 811 Seventh Ave
- **Spa & Fitness Center at the Westin** · 270 W 43rd St
- **Sports Club/LA** · 45 Rockefeller Plz
- **Ultimate Training Center** · 532 Madison Ave
- **US Athletic Training Center** · 515 Madison Ave

🔧 Hardware Stores

- **AAA Locksmiths** · 44 W 46th St
- **Garden Hardware & Supply** · 785 Eighth Ave
- **New Hippodrome Hardware** · 23 W 45th St

🍸 Liquor Stores

- **Acorn Wine & Liquor** · 268 W 46th St
- **Athens Wine & Liquor** · 302 W 40th St
- **Carnegie Spirits & Wine** · 849 Seventh Ave
- **Columbus Circle Wine & Liquor** · 1780 Broadway
- **Fifty Fifth Street Liquor Shop** · 40 W 55th St
- **Morrell & Co Wine & Spirits** · 1 Rockefeller Plz
- **O'Ryan Package Store** · 1424 Sixth Ave
- **Park Ave Liquor Shop** · 292 Madison Ave
- **Reidy Wine & Liquor** · 762 Eighth Ave
- **Shon 45 Liquors** · 840 Eighth Ave
- **Westerly Liquors** · 921 Eighth Ave

📺 Video Rental

- **Blockbuster Video** · 835 Eighth Ave
- **EC Professional Video** · 253 W 51st St
- **High Quality Video** (Japanese only) · 21 W 45th St

Map 12 • Midtown

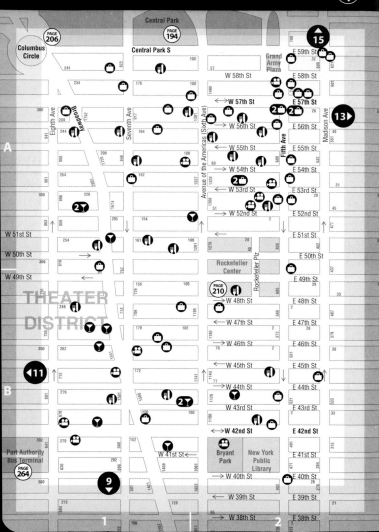

Times Square IS the center of NYC, but we try not to be caught dead in here. A few exceptions---the delicious Virgil's BBQ, the classic 21 Club, and the all-too-authentic Russian Vodka Room. Midtown has three great places to see a movie---the huge Ziegfeld, the classy Paris, and outdoors at Bryant Park.

 Movie Theaters

- **AMC Empire 25** · 234 W 42nd St
- **Bryant Park Summer Film Festival** (outdoors) · Bryant Park, b/w 40th & 42nd Sts
- **Clearview's Ziegfeld** · 141 W 54th St
- **Loews 42nd Street E Walk** · 247 W 42nd St
- **Loews Astor Plaza** · 1515 Broadway
- **Loews State** · 1540 Broadway
- **MOMA** · 11 W 53rd St
- **Museum of TV and Radio** · 25 W 52nd St
- **New York Public Library-Donnell Library Center** · 20 W 53rd St
- **Paris Theatre** · 4 W 58th St

Nightlife

- **BB King Blues Club** · 237 W 42nd St
- **China Club** · 268 W 47th St
- **Heartland Brewery** · 127 W 43rd St
- **Heartland Brewery** · 1285 Sixth Ave
- **Howard Johnson's** · 1551 Broadway
- **Iridium** · 1650 Broadway
- **Paramount Bar** · 235 W 46th St
- **Roseland** · 239 W 52nd St
- **The Royalton** · 44 W 44th St
- **Russian Vodka Room** · 265 W 52nd St
- **Show** · 135 W 41st St
- **Town Hall** · 123 W 43rd St

Restaurants

- **'21' Club** · 21 W 52nd St
- **Alain Ducasse** · 155 W 58th St
- **Aquavit** · 13 W 54th St
- **Baluchi's** · 240 W 56th St
- **Carnegie Deli** · 854 Seventh Ave
- **Cosi Sandwich Bar** · 11 W 42nd St
- **Cosi Sandwich Bar** · 1633 Broadway
- **Cosi Sandwich Bar** · 61 W 48th St
- **Haru** · 205 W 43rd St
- **Joe's Shanghai** · 24 W 56th St
- **Le Bernardin** · 155 W 51st St
- **Molyvos** · 871 Seventh Ave
- **Nation Restaurant & Bar** · 12 W 45th St
- **Norma's** · 118 W 57th St
- **Pongsri Thai** · 244 W 48th St
- **Pret a Manger** · 135 W 50th St
- **Pret a Manger** · 1350 Sixth Ave

- **The Pump Energy Food** · 40 W 55th St
- **Redeye Grill** · 890 Seventh Ave
- **Virgil's Real BBQ** · 152 W 44th St

Shopping

- **Alkit Pro Camera** · 830 Seventh Ave
- **Baccarat** · 625 Madison Ave
- **Bergdorf Goodman** · 754 Fifth Ave
- **Brooks Brothers** · 346 Madison Ave
- **Burberry** · 9 E 57th St
- **Carnegie Card & Gifts** · 56 W 57th St
- **Chanel** · 15 E 57th St
- **Colony Music** · 1619 Broadway
- **CompUSA** · 1775 Broadway
- **Crate & Barrel** · 650 Madison Ave
- **Drummer's World** · 151 W 46th St
- **Ermenegildo Zegna** · 663 Fifth Ave
- **Ermenegildo Zegna** · 743 Fifth Ave
- **ESPN Zone** · 1472 Broadway
- **FAO Schwartz** · 767 Fifth Ave
- **Felissimo** · 10 W 56th St
- **Gucci** · 685 Fifth Ave
- **Henri Bendel** · 712 Fifth Ave
- **Joseph Patelson Music House** · 160 W 56th St
- **Kate's Paperie** · 140 W 57th St
- **Klavierhaus** · 211 W 58th St
- **Manny's Music** · 156 W 48th St
- **Mets Clubhouse Shop** · 11 W 42nd St
- **Mikimoto** · 730 Fifth Ave
- **MoMA Design Store** · 44 W 53rd St
- **Museum of Arts and Design Shop** · 40 W 53rd St
- **NBA Store** · 666 Fifth Ave
- **Niketown** · 6 E 57th St
- **Orvis Company** · 522 Fifth Ave
- **Petrossian Boutique** · 911 Seventh Ave
- **Radio Shack** · 1134 Sixth Ave
- **Roberto's Woodwind Repair Shop** · 146 W 46th St
- **Saks Fifth Avenue** · 611 Fifth Ave
- **Sam Ash** · 160 W 48th St
- **Smythson of Bond Street** · 4 W 57th St
- **Steinway and Sons** · 109 W 57th St
- **Takashimaya** · 693 Fifth Ave
- **Tiffany & Co** · 727 Fifth Ave

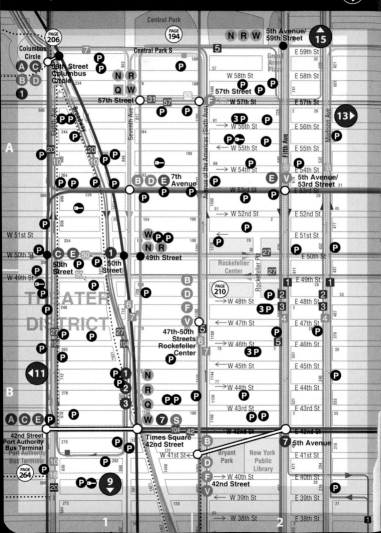

Map 12 · **Midtown**

Driving in midtown has now turned into a fate worse than post-apocalyptic with the addition of the new "through streets" and "no-turn avenues," which now means you'll have to drive fully crosstown to make a turn somewhere. We expect a boycott by the delivery folks shortly.

Subways

1	50th St
1 A C B D	59th St-Columbus Cir
A C E	42th St/Port Authority
B D E	Seventh Ave
B D F V	47th St-50th St/Rockefeller Ctr
7 B D F V	42th St/Fifth Ave
C E	50th St
E V	Fifth Ave/53rd St
F	57th St
1 2 3 7 N Q R W S	Times Sq/42th St
N R Q W	57th St
N R W	49th St
N R W	Fifth Ave/59th St

Bus Lines

1 2 3 4	Fifth Ave/Madison Ave
10 20	Seventh Ave/Eighth Ave (Central Park West)/Frederick Douglass Blvd
104	Broadway/42nd St
16	34th St Crosstown
27	49th St/50th St Crosstown
30	57th St /72nd St Crosstown
31	York Ave/57th St
42	42nd St Crosstown
5	Fifth Ave/Sixth Ave/Riverside Dr
50	49th St/50th St Crosstown
57	57th St Crosstown
6	Seventh Ave/Broadway/Sixth Ave
7	Columbus Ave/Amsterdam Ave/Lenox Ave/Sixth Ave/Seventh Ave/Broadway
Q 32	Penn Station/Jackson Heights, Queens

Bike Lanes

- • • • Marked Bike Lanes
- • • • Recommended Route

Car Rental

- **Avis** • 153 W 54th St
- **Budget** • 304 W 49th St
- **Dollar** • 263 W 52nd St
- **Hertz** • 126 W 55th St
- **National** • 252 W 40th St

Parking

Map 13 · **East Midtown**

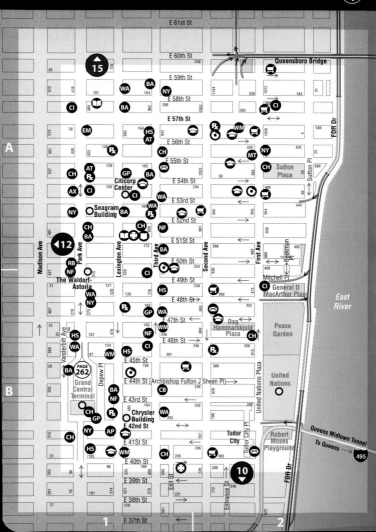

This is a busy and diverse part of town, packed with consulates, hotels, Grand Central Terminal, the United Nations, and the Queensboro Bridge. Park Avenue between 40th and 60th Streets contains some of the finest examples, if not the finest example, of every major architectural style from the past 100 years.

24-Hour Pharmacies

- **CVS Pharmacy** • 630 Lexington Ave
- **Duane Reade** • 1076 Second Ave
- **Duane Reade** • 401 Park Ave
- **Duane Reade** • 405 Lexington Ave
- **Duane Reade** • 485 Lexington Ave
- **Duane Reade** • 852 Second Ave
- **Duane Reade** • 866 Third Ave

Bagels

- **Ess-A-Bagel** • 831 Third Ave
- **Everything Bagel** • 141 E 44th St
- **Jumbo Bagels & Bialys** • 1070 Second Ave
- **Tal Bagels** • 977 First Ave

Banks

AX · AmEx Travel-Related Services • 374 Park Ave
AP · Apple • 122 E 42nd St
AT · Atlantic • 405 Park Ave
AT · Atlantic • 936 Third Ave
BA · Bank of America • 200 Park Ave
BA · Bank of America • 345 Park Ave
BA · Bank of America • 425 Lexington Ave
BA · Bank of America • 900 Third Ave
BA · Bank of America • 988 Third Ave
BA · Bank of America (ATM) • 599 Lexington Ave
BA · Bank of America (ATM) • 705 Lexington Ave
BA · Bank of America (ATM) • 825 Third Ave
NY · Bank of New York • 100 E 42nd St
NY · Bank of New York • 1006 First Ave
NY · Bank of New York • 207 E 58th St
NY · Bank of New York • 277 Park Ave
NY · Bank of New York • 360 Park Ave
CH · Chase • 410 Park Ave
CH · Chase • 60 E 42nd St
CH · Chase • 633 Third Ave
CH · Chase • 825 United Nations Plz
CH · Chase • 850 Third Ave
CH · Chase • 919 Third Ave
CH · Chase • 994 First Ave
CH · Chase (ATM) • 345 Park Ave
CH · Chase (ATM) • Grand Central lobby
CI · Citibank • 1044 First Ave
CI · Citibank • 399 Park Ave
CI · Citibank • 460 Park Ave
CI · Citibank • 734 Third Ave
CI · Citibank • 800 Third Ave
CI · Citibank • 866 United Nations Plz
CI · Citibank (ATM) • 153 E 53rd St
CO · Commerce Bank • 685 Third Ave
EM · Emigrant • 445 Park Ave
FR · First Republic Bank • 320 Park Ave
GP · Greenpoint Bank • 109 E 42nd St
GP · Greenpoint Bank • 643 Lexington Ave
GP · Greenpoint Bank • 770 Third Ave
HS · HSBC • 101 Park Ave
HS · HSBC • 250 Park Ave
HS · HSBC • 441 Lexington Ave
HS · HSBC • 777 Third Ave
HS · HSBC • 950 Third Ave
MT · Manufacturers and Traders Trust • 401 E 55th St
NF · North Fork Bank • 320 Park Ave
NF · North Fork Bank • 420 Lexington Ave
NF · North Fork Bank • 750 Third Ave
NF · North Fork Bank • 845 Third Ave
WA · Wachovia • 299 Park Ave
WA · Wachovia • 666 Third Ave
WA · Wachovia • 757 Third Ave
WA · Wachovia • 866 Third Ave
WA · Wachovia (ATM) • 230 Park Ave
WA · Wachovia (ATM) • 731 Lexington Ave
WM · Washington Mutual • 355 Lexington Ave
WM · Washington Mutual • 360 E 57th St
WM · Washington Mutual • 466 Lexington Ave
WM · Washington Mutual • 875 Third Ave

Fire Departments

- **Engine 21** • 238 E 40th St
- **Engine 8, Ladder 2** • 165 E 51st St

Landmarks

- **Chrysler Building** • 405 Lexington Ave
- **Citicorp Center** • 153 E 53rd St
- **Grand Central Terminal** • 42nd St
- **Seagram Building** • 375 Park Ave
- **United Nations** • First Ave b/w 42nd & 48th Sts
- **Waldorf-Astoria** • 301 Park Ave

Libraries

- **58th St** • 127 E 58th St
- **Terence Cardinal Cooke-Cathedral** • 560 Lexington Ave

Police

- **17th Precinct** • 167 E 51st St

Post Offices

- **Dag Hammarskjold** • 884 Second Ave
- **Franklin D Roosevelt** • 909 Third Ave
- **Tudor City** • 5 Tudor City Pl

Schools

- **The Beekman School** • 220 E 50th St
- **Cathedral High** • 350 E 56th St
- **Family School** • 323 E 47th St
- **High School of Art & Design** • 1075 Second Ave
- **Montessori School of New York** • 347 E 55th St
- **Neighborhood Playhouse** • 340 E 54th St
- **New York School of Astrology** • 370 Lexington Ave
- **NY Institute of Credit** • 380 Lexington Ave
- **PS 59 Beekman Hill** • 228 E 57th St
- **Turtle Bay Music School** • 244 E 52nd St

Supermarkets

- **Amish Market** • 240 E 45th St
- **Associated** • 908 Second Ave
- **D'Agostino** • 1031 First Ave
- **D'Agostino** • 966 First Ave
- **Food Emporium** • 405 E 59th St
- **Food Emporium** • 969 Second Ave
- **Gristede's** • 1052 First Ave
- **Gristede's** • 748 Second Ave

Map 13 · **East Midtown**

Sundries / Entertainment

14	15
11	12	13
8	9	10
5	6	7

Map 13

Some of New York's top eateries are in this map—including Vong, Smith & Wollensky, Dawat, March, and the Four Seasons. Check out the cool stores under the Queensboro Bridge—including Bridge Kitchenware and the Terence Conran Shop. The Grand Central Market houses a variety of gourmet food purveyors.

Coffee
- **Ambrosia Café** • 158 E 45th St
- **Andrew's Coffee Shop** • 138 E 43rd St
- **Au Bon Pain** • 122 E 42nd St
- **Au Bon Pain** • 600 Lexington Ave
- **Au Bon Pain** • 875 Third Ave
- **Columbus Bakery** • 957 First Ave
- **Cosi** • 320 Park Ave
- **Cosi** • 38 E 45th St
- **Cosi** • 60 E 56th St
- **Cosi** • 685 Third Ave
- **Dunkin' Donuts** • 1024 First Ave
- **Dunkin' Donuts** • 328 E 59th St
- **Dunkin' Donuts** • 47 E 42nd St
- **Dunkin' Donuts** • 800 Second Ave
- **Friars Coffee Shop** • 303 E 46th St
- **Manhattan Espresso HD** • 146 E 49th St
- **Oren's Daily Roast** • Grand Central Market
- **Palace Restaurant Coffee House** • 122 E 57th St
- **Starbucks**
  - 116 E 57th St
  - 135 E 57th St
  - 280 Park Ave
  - 400 E 54th St
  - 511 Lexington Ave
  - 560 Lexington Ave
  - 630 Lexington Ave
  - 685 Third Ave
  - 830 Third Ave
  - 125 Park Ave
  - 150 E 42nd St
  - 360 Lexington Ave
  - 450 Lexington Ave
  - 55 E 52nd St
  - 599 Lexington Ave
  - 639 Third Ave
  - 757 Third Ave
  - 943 Second Ave

Copy Shops
- **Copy Right Reprographics** (9am-6pm) • 133 E 55th St
- **Express Graphics** (8:30am-5:30pm) • 405 Lexington Ave
- **EZCopying Corp** (9am-6:30pm) • 209 E 56th St
- **Graphic Laboratory** (8:30am-11pm) • 228 E 45th St
- **Insti Copy** (8am-8pm) • 249 E 55th St
- **Kinko's** (24 hrs) • 641 Lexington Ave
- **Kinko's** (24 hrs) • 747 Third Ave
- **Kinko's** (8am-12am) • 230 Park Ave
- **Kinko's** (8am-8pm) • 153 E 53rd St
- **Kinko's** (8am-9pm) • 305 E 46th St
- **Lightning Copy Center** (8:30am-6pm) • 60 E 42nd St
- **Mail Boxes Etc** (8:30am-6pm) • 1040 First Ave
- **Mail Boxes Etc** (8:30am-7pm) • 303 Park Ave
- **Mail Boxes Etc** (8:30am-7pm) • 847 Second Ave
- **Metro Copying and Duplicating** (6:30am-2am) • 222 E 45th St
- **Pro-Print** (8:30am-6pm) • 360 Lexington Ave
- **RJP Copycenter** • 805 Third Ave
- **Staples** (7am-7pm) • 205 E 42nd St
- **Staples** (7am-7pm) • 425 Park Ave
- **Staples** (7am-7pm) • 575 Lexington Ave
- **Staples** (7am-7pm) • 730 Third Ave
- **The UPS Store** (8:30am-7pm) • 208 E 51st St
- **The UPS Store** (8:30am-8pm) • 132 E 43rd St
- **The UPS Store** (8am-8pm) • 954 Third Ave

Farmer's Markets
- **Dag Hammarskjold Plaza** • E 47th St & Second Ave

Gyms
- **Crunch Fitness** • 1109 Second Ave
- **Curves** • 240 E 56th St
- **Dolphin Fitness Clubs** • 330 E 59th St
- **Eastside Kinesthetic Center** • 133 E 55th St
- **Equinox Fitness Club** • 250 E 54th St
- **Equinox Fitness Club** • 420 Lexington Ave
- **Excelsior Athletic Club** • 301 E 57th St
- **Lift Gym** • 139 E 57th St
- **New York Health & Racquet Club** • 115 E 57th St
- **New York Health & Racquet Club** • 132 E 45th St
- **New York Sports Clubs** • 200 Park Ave
- **New York Sports Clubs** • 502 Park Ave
- **New York Sports Clubs** • 575 Lexington Ave
- **New York Sports Clubs** • 633 Third Ave
- **Upper Body** • 343 Lexington Ave
- **YMCA Vanderbilt** • 224 E 47th St
- **YWCA** • 610 Lexington Ave

Hardware Stores
- **55th Street Hardware** • 155 E 55th St
- **Home Depot** • 980 Third Ave
- **Kramer's** • 952 Second Ave
- **Midtown Hardware** • 155 E 45th St
- **Sherle Wagner International** • 60 E 57th St

Liquor Stores
- **Ambassador Wines & Spirits** • 1020 Second Ave
- **American First Liquors** • 1059 First Ave
- **Beekman Liquors** • 500 Lexington Ave
- **Diplomat Wine & Spirits** • 939 Second Ave
- **First Avenue Vintner** • 984 First Ave
- **Grand Harvest Wines** • 107 E 42nd St
- **Jeffrey Wine & Liquors** • 939 First Ave
- **Midtown Wine & Liquor Shop** • 44 E 50th St
- **Schumer's Wine & Liquors** • 59 E 54th St
- **Sussex Wine & Spirits** • 300 E 42nd St
- **Sutton Wine Shop** • 403 E 57th St
- **Turtle Bay Liquors** • 855 Second Ave
- **UN Liquor** • 885 First Ave
- **Viski Wines & Liquor** • 764 Third Ave

Movie Theaters
- **City Cinemas 1, 2, 3** • 1001 Third Ave
- **French Institute** • 55 E 59th St
- **Instituto Cervantes** • 122 E 42nd St
- **Japan Society** • 333 E 47th St
- **The ImaginAsian** • 239 E 59th St
- **YWCA** • 610 Lexington Ave

Nightlife
- **Blarney Stone** • 710 Third Ave
- **The Campbell Apartment** • Grand Central Terminal
- **Fubar** • 305 E 50th St
- **Kate Kearney's** • 251 E 50th St
- **Metro 53** • 307 E 53rd St
- **PJ Clarke's** • 915 Third Ave

Pet Shops
- **Bird Camp** (Birds) • 330 E 53rd St
- **Chic Doggie by Corey** • 400 E 54th St
- **Finishing Touches by Stephanie** • 414 E 58th St
- **Furry Paws** • 1036 First Ave
- **Furry Paws** • 1039 Second Ave
- **Petland Discounts** • 976 Second Ave

Restaurants
- **BLT Steak** • 106 E 57th St
- **Cosi Sandwich Bar** • 60 E 56th St
- **Dawat** • 210 E 58th St
- **Docks Oyster Bar** • 633 Third Ave
- **Felidia** • 243 E 58th St
- **Four Seasons** • 99 E 52nd St
- **Les Halles** • 411 Park Ave
- **March** • 405 E 58th St
- **Menchanko-tei** • 131 E 45th St
- **Oceana** • 55 E 54th St
- **Organic Harvest Café** • 235 E 53rd St
- **Oyster Bar** • Grand Central, Lower Level
- **Palm** • 837 Second Ave
- **Pershing Square** • 90 E 42nd St
- **PJ Clarke's** • 915 Third Ave
- **Rosa Mexicano** • 1063 First Ave
- **Shun Lee Palace** • 155 E 55th St
- **Smith & Wollensky** • 797 Third Ave
- **Sparks Steak House** • 210 E 46th St
- **Vong** • 200 E 54th St

Shopping
- **Adriana's Caravan** • Grand Central Station
- **Bridge Kitchenware** • 214 E 52nd St
- **Godiva Chocolatier** • 560 Lexington Ave
- **Ideal Cheese** • 942 First Ave
- **Innovative Audio** • 150 E 58th St
- **Mets Clubhouse Shop** • 143 E 54th St
- **Modell's** • 51 E 42nd St
- **New York Transit Museum** • Grand Central, Main Concourse
- **Pottery Barn** • 117 E 59th St
- **Radio Shack** • 940 Third Ave
- **Sam Flax** • 900 Third Ave
- **Sports Authority** • 845 Third Ave
- **Terence Conran Shop** • 407 E 59th St
- **The World of Golf** • 147 E 47th St
- **Yankee Clubhouse Shop** • 110 E 59th St
- **Zaro's Bread Basket** • 89 E 42nd St

Video Rental
- **American Video** • 780 Third Ave
- **Blockbuster Video** • 1023 First Ave
- **Flick's Video** • 1099 Second Ave
- **GRS Systems** • 216 E 45th St
- **International Video** • 926 Second Ave
- **New York Video** • 949 First Ave

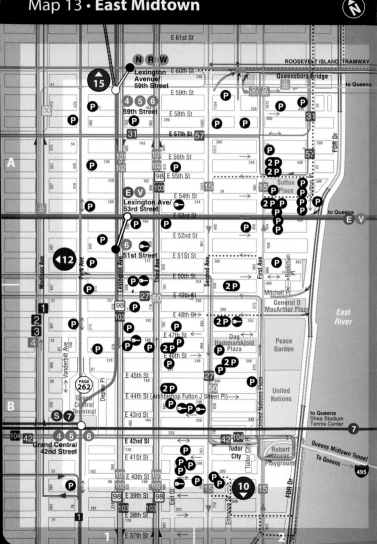

Map 13 · East Midtown

E 61st St

E 60th St

N R W
Lexington
Avenue/
59th Street

15

Roosevelt Island Tramway

Queensboro Bridge

to Queens

E 59th St

4 5 6
59th Street

E 58th St

31

E 57th St 57

E 56th St

101
102

E 55th St

98
103

E V
Lexington Ave/
53rd Street

E 54th St

15

Sutton
Place

15

E 53rd St

E 52nd St

6
51st Street

E 51st St

E V

12

E 50th St

2 P

27
50

E 49th St

98
103

E 48th St

2 P

2 P

General D
MacArthur Plaza

East
River

E 47th St

2 P

2 P

Dag
Hammarskjold
Plaza

Peace
Garden

E 46th St

27
50

E 45th St

PAGE
262

Grand
Central
Terminal

E 44th St (Archbishop Fulton J Sheen Pl)

2 P

United
Nations

to Queens
Shea Stadium
Tennis Center

7

S 7

E 43rd St

104 42

4 5 6

Grand Central
42nd Street

42 104

Tudor
City

Robert
Moses
Playground

Queens Midtown Tunnel
To Queens

495

E 42nd St

1

E 41st St

E 40th St

101
102

98 39th Street 98

103   103

10

15

FDR Dr

E 38th St

1

E 37th St

Transportation

Map 13

14	15
11	12	13
8	9	10
5	6	7

Other than the quirky ramps running around Grand Central and the snarl around the Queensboro Bridge, traffic in this area could be far worse than it is. However, it's always wise to pay attention to when the President or some other major dignitary is at the U.N., because you'll want to use mass transit that day.

Subways

4 5 6 N R W ... Lexington Ave-59th St
6 E V .... 51st St-Lexington Ave-53rd St
4 5 6 7 S .... Grand Central-42nd St

Bus Lines

104 .... Broadway
15 .... First Ave/Second Ave
27 50 .... 49th St/50th St Crosstown
30 .... 72nd St/57th St Crosstown
31 .... York Ave/57th St
42 .... 42nd St Crosstown
57 .... 57th St Crosstown
57 .... Washington Heights/Midtown Limited
98 101 102 103 .... Third Ave/Lexington Ave
Q32 .... Queens-to-Midtown

Bike Lanes

- • • • Marked Bike Lanes
- • • • Recommended Route
- • • • Greenway

Car Rental

- **Avis** · 217 E 43rd St
- **Avis** · 240 E 54th St
- **Budget** · 225 E 43rd St
- **Enterprise** · 135 E 47th St
- **Hertz** · 222 E 40th St
- **Hertz** · 310 E 48th St
- **National** · 138 E 50th St
- **Prestige Car Rental** · 151 E 51st St

P Parking

Map 14 • **Upper West Side (Lower)**

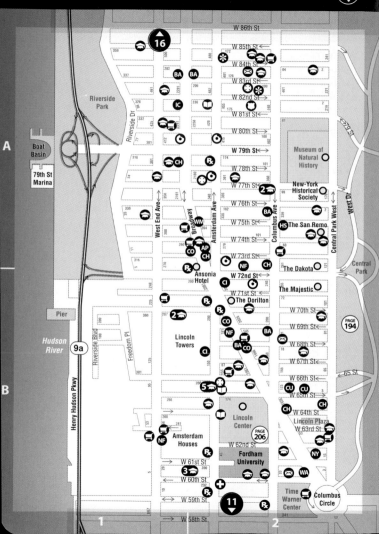

Broadway and Columbus Avenue are the main drags in this neighborhood in terms of both essentials and foot traffic, and feature the neighborhood's main anchors—Lincoln Center and the Museum of Natural History. The new Time Warner Center at Columbus Circle provides another focal point, though the shops are predictably banal.

24-Hour Pharmacies

- **CVS Pharmacy** · 400 W 59th St
- **Duane Reade** · 2025 Broadway
- **Duane Reade** · 253 W 72nd St
- **Duane Reade** · 380 Amsterdam Ave
- **Duane Reade** · 4 Amsterdam Ave
- **Duane Reade** · 4 Columbus Cir
- **Rite Aid** · 210 Amsterdam Ave

Bagels

- **72nd Street Bagel** · 130 W 72nd St
- **Bagel Talk** · 368 Amsterdam Ave
- **Bagels & Co** · 393 Amsterdam Ave
- **Bread Factory Café** · 2079 Broadway
- **H&H Bagels** · 2239 Broadway

Banks

- EF · **ABC Employees Federal** · 30 W 66th St
- EF · **ABC Employees Federal** · 77 W 66th St
- AP · **Apple** · 2100 Broadway
- BA · **Bank of America (ATM)** · 192 Columbus Ave
- BA · **Bank of America (ATM)** · 1998 Broadway
- BA · **Bank of America (ATM)** · 2301 Broadway
- BA · **Bank of America (ATM)** · 2310 Broadway
- BA · **Bank of America (ATM)** · 334 Columbus Ave
- NY · **Bank of New York** · 47 W 62nd St
- CH · **Chase** · 1 Lincoln Plz
- CH · **Chase** · 2099 Broadway
- CH · **Chase** · 2219 Broadway
- CH · **Chase** · 260 Columbus Ave
- CI · **Citibank** · 162 Amsterdam Ave
- CI · **Citibank** · 170 W 72nd St
- CO · **Commerce Bank** · 1995 Broadway
- CO · **Commerce Bank** · 2109 Broadway
- HS · **HSBC** · 301 Columbus Ave
- IC · **Independence Community** · 2275 Broadway
- NF · **North Fork Bank** · 175 W 72nd St
- NF · **North Fork Bank** · 2025 Broadway
- NF · **North Fork Bank** · 75 West End Ave
- WA · **Wachovia (ATM)** · 1841 Broadway
- WM · **Washington Mutual** · 2139 Broadway

Community Gardens

Fire Departments

- **Engine 40, Ladder 35** · 133 Amsterdam Ave
- **Engine 74** · 120 W 83rd St
- **Ladder 25** · 205 W 77th St

Landmarks

- **Ansonia Hotel** · 2109 Broadway & 73rd St
- **The Dakota** · Central Park West & 72nd St
- **The Dorilton** · Broadway & 71st St
- **Lincoln Center** · Broadway & 64th St
- **The Majestic** · 115 Central Park W
- **Museum of Natural History** · Central Park W & 79th St
- **New-York Historical Society** · 2 W 77th St
- **The San Remo** · Central Park W & 74th St

Libraries

- **New York Public Library for the Performing Arts** · 40 Lincoln Center Plz
- **Riverside** · 127 Amsterdam Ave
- **St Agnes** · 444 Amsterdam Ave

Police

- **20th Precinct** · 120 W 82nd St

Post Offices

- **Ansonia** · 178 Columbus Ave
- **Columbus Circle** · 27 W 60th St
- **Planetarium** · 127 W 83rd St

Schools

- **American Musical and Drama Academy** · 2109 Broadway
- **Art and Technology High** · 122 Amsterdam Ave
- **Beacon High** · 227 W 61st St
- **Beit Rabban Day School** · 8 W 70th St
- **Blessed Sacrement** · 147 W 70th St
- **The Calhoun** · 433 West End Ave
- **Collegiate School** · 260 W 78th St
- **Collegiate School** · 370 West End Ave
- **The Computer School (M245)** · 100 W 77th St
- **Ethical Culture-Fieldston School** · 33 Central Park W
- **Fiorello H LaGuardia High** · 100 Amsterdam Ave
- **Fordham University** · 113 W 60th St
- **IS 044 William J O'Shea** · 100 W 77th St
- **Law, Advocacy and Community Justice High** · 122 Amsterdam Ave
- **Louis D Brandeis High** · 145 W 84th St
- **Lucy Moses School For Music & Dance** · 129 W 67th St
- **Manhattan Day School** · 310 W 75th St
- **Manhattan Hunter HS of Science** · 122 Amsterdam Ave
- **Mannes College of Music** · 150 W 85th St
- **Martin Luther King High School** · 122 Amsterdam Ave
- **Metropolitan Montessori** · 325 W 85th St
- **New York Academy of Sciences** · 2 E 63rd St
- **New York Institute of Technology Metropolitan Center** · 1855 Broadway
- **Parkside** · 48 W 74th St
- **Professional Children's School** · 132 W 60th St
- **PS 009 Renaissance** · 100 W 84th St
- **PS 087 William Sherman** · 160 W 78th St
- **PS 191 Amsterdam** · 210 W 61st St
- **PS 199 Jesse Straus** · 270 W 70th St
- **PS 243 Center School** · 270 W 70th St
- **PS 244 Columbus Middle School** · 100 W 77th St
- **PS 811** · 466 West End Ave
- **PS 859 Special Music School of America** · 129 W 67th St
- **Rodeph Sholom** · 10 W 84th St
- **Stephen Gaynor School** · 22 W 74th St
- **Urban Assembly School for Media Studies** · 122 Amsterdam Ave
- **Winston Preparatory** · 4 W 76th St
- **York Prep** · 40 W 68th St

Supermarkets

- **Balducci's** · 155 W 66th St
- **Citarella** · 2135 Broadway
- **Fairway Market** · 2127 Broadway
- **Food Emporium** · 2008 Broadway
- **Gristede's** · 2109 Broadway
- **Gristede's** · 25 Central Park W
- **Gristede's** · 504 Columbus Ave
- **Gristede's** · 80 West End Ave
- **Pioneer** · 289 Columbus Ave
- **Western Beef** · 75 West End Ave
- **Whole Foods Market** · 59th St & Columbus Cir
- **Zabar's** · 249 W 80th St

Map 14 · **Upper West Side (Lower)**

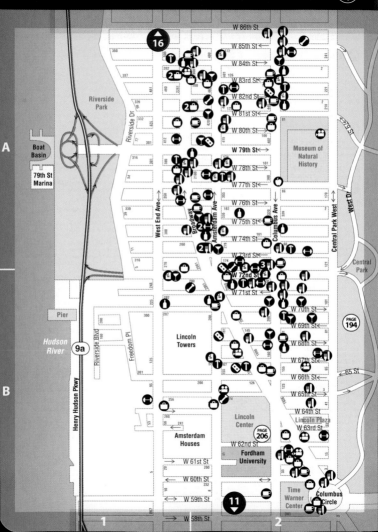

Sundries / Entertainment

The bar scene is virtually non-existent below 72nd Street and is dominated by frat bars up north (recommended haven: All-State Café). A diverse set of restaurants somewhat compensates (as does the Whole Foods at Time Warner). The new Riverside South Park on the Hudson is quite nice, though we still think Trump is, well...Trump.

Coffee

- **Columbus Bakery** • 474 Columbus Ave
- **Cosi** • 2160 Broadway
- **Dean & Deluca (Time Warner Building)** • 10 Columbus Cir
- **Edgar's Café** • 255 W 84th St
- **New World Coffee** • 416 Columbus Ave
- **Starbucks** • 152 Columbus Ave
- **1841 Broadway** • 2 Columbus Ave
- **2045 Broadway** • 2140 Broadway
- **2252 Broadway** • 267 Columbus Ave
- **338 Columbus Ave** • 444 Columbus Ave

Copy Shops

- **Gavin Printing** (9am-6pm) • 387 Amsterdam Ave
- **IBU Copy & Copy** (8am-8pm) • 517 Amsterdam Ave
- **Kinko's** (24 hrs) • 221 W 72nd St
- **Mail Boxes Etc** (8:30am-7pm) • 459 Columbus Ave
- **Mail Boxes Etc** (9:30am-7:30pm) • 163 Amsterdam Ave
- **Matrix Copy & Printing Services** (9am-4pm) • 140 W 72nd St
- **Panda Copy** (9am-8:20pm) • 2202 Broadway
- **Printing Express and Speed Copy Center** (9:30am-7pm) • 104 W 83rd St
- **Staples** (7am-9pm) • 2248 Broadway
- **Studio 305** (9am-6:45pm) • 313 Amsterdam Ave
- **Upper Westside Copy Center** (8am-10pm) • 2054 Broadway
- **The UPS Store** (8:30am-7pm) • 119 W 72nd St
- **The UPS Store** (8:30am-7pm) • 366 Amsterdam Ave

Farmer's Markets

- **77th Street** • W 77th St & Columbus Ave
- **Tucker Square** • W 66th St & Columbus Ave

Gyms

- **All Star Fitness Center** • 75 West End Ave
- **Circus Gym** • 2121 Broadway
- **Crunch Fitness** • 160 W 83rd St
- **Curves** • 76 W 85th St
- **Elysium Fitness Club** • 117 W 72nd St
- **Equinox Fitness Club** • 344 Amsterdam Ave
- **Fitness Express Manhattan** • 142 W 72nd St
- **La Palestra** • 11 W 67th St
- **New York Sports Clubs** • 2162 Broadway
- **New York Sports Clubs** • 23 W 73rd St
- **New York Sports Clubs** • 248 W 80th St
- **New York Sports Clubs** • 61 W 62nd St
- **Reebok Sports Club NY** • 160 Columbus Ave
- **Synergy Fitness Clubs** • 2130 Broadway
- **The Training Ground** • 118 W 72nd St
- **YMCA West Side** • 5 W 63rd St

Hardware Stores

- **A&I Hardware** • 207 Columbus Ave
- **AJA Decorative Hardware** • 381 Amsterdam Ave
- **Amsterdam Hardware** • 147 Amsterdam Ave
- **Beacon Paint & Wallpaper** • 371 Amsterdam Ave
- **Ben Franklin Paints** • 2193 Broadway

- **Gartner's Hardware** • 134 W 72nd St
- **Gracious Home** • 1992 Broadway
- **Klosty Hardware** • 471 Amsterdam Ave
- **Roxy Hardware and Paint** • 469 Columbus Ave
- **Supreme Hardware & Supply** • 65 W 73rd St

Liquor Stores

- **67 Wine & Spirits** • 179 Columbus Ave
- **79th Street Wine & Spirits** • 230 W 79th St
- **Acker Merrall** • 160 W 72nd St
- **Bacchus Wine Made Simple** • 2056 Broadway
- **Beacon Wines & Spirits** • 2120 Broadway
- **Candlelight Wine** • 2315 Broadway
- **Central Wine & Liquor Store** • 227 Columbus Ave
- **Ehrlich Liquor Store** • 222 Amsterdam Ave
- **Nancy's Wines** • 313 Columbus Ave
- **Rose Wine & Liquor** • 449 Columbus Ave
- **West End Wine** • 204 West End Ave
- **West Side Wine & Spirits Shop** • 481 Columbus Ave
- **Wines for Food Limited** • 161 W 75th St

Movie Theaters

- **American Museum of Natural History IMAX** • Central Park W & 79th St
- **Clearview's 62nd & Broadway** • 1871 Broadway
- **Lincoln Plaza Cinemas** • 30 Lincoln Plz
- **Loews 84th St** • 2310 Broadway
- **Loews Lincoln Square & IMAX Theatre** • 1992 Broadway
- **Makor** • 35 W 67th St
- **Walter Reade Theater** • 70 Lincoln Plz

Nightlife

- **All-State Café** • 250 W 72nd St
- **Beacon Theater** • 2124 Broadway
- **Café Des Artistes** • 1 W 67th St
- **Dead Poet** • 450 Amsterdam Ave
- **Dublin House** • 225 W 79th St
- **Emerald Inn** • 205 Columbus Ave
- **Jake's Dilemma** • 430 Amsterdam Ave
- **Makor** • 35 W 67th St
- **P&G** • 279 Amsterdam Ave
- **Prohibition** • 503 Columbus Ave
- **Raccoon Lodge** • 480 Amsterdam Ave
- **Shalel Lounge** • 65 W 70th St

Pet Shops

- **Furry Paws 4** • 141 Amsterdam Ave
- **Pet Health Store** • 440 Amsterdam Ave
- **Pet Market** • 210 W 72nd St
- **Petland Discounts** • 137 W 72nd St
- **Red Rover International** • 77 W 85th St

Restaurants

- **All-State Café** • 250 W 72nd St
- **Asiate** • 80 Columbus Cir, 35th fl
- **Baluchi's** • 283 Columbus Ave
- **Big Nick's** • 2175 Broadway
- **Café Des Artistes** • 1 W 67th St
- **Café Lalo** • 201 W 83rd St
- **Café Luxembourg** • 200 W 70th St
- **Caprice** • 199 Columbus Ave

- **China Fun** • 246 Columbus Ave
- **Edgar's Café** • 255 W 84th St
- **EJ's Luncheonette** • 447 Amsterdam Ave
- **Fairway Café** • 2127 Broadway
- **The Firehouse** • 522 Columbus Ave
- **French Roast** • 2340 Broadway
- **Gabriel's** • 11 W 60th St
- **Gray's Papaya** • 2090 Broadway
- **Harry's Burrito Junction** • 241 Columbus Ave
- **Hunan Park** • 235 Columbus Ave
- **Jackson Hole** • 517 Columbus Ave
- **Jean Georges** • 1 Central Park W
- **Jean-Luc** • 507 Columbus Ave
- **Josie's** • 300 Amsterdam Ave
- **Krispy Kreme** • 141 W 72nd St
- **La Caridad 78** • 2197 Broadway
- **La Fenice** • 2014 Broadway
- **Land Thai Kitchen** • 450 Amsterdam Ave
- **Le Pain Quotidien** • 50 W 72nd St
- **Lenge** • 200 Columbus Ave
- **Manhattan Diner** • 2180 Broadway
- **Penang** • 240 Columbus Ave
- **Picholine** • 35 W 64th St
- **Planet Sushi** • 380 Amsterdam Ave
- **Rain West** • 100 W 82nd St
- **Rosa Mexicano** • 61 Columbus Ave
- **Ruby Foo's Dim Sum & Sushi Palace** • 2182 Broadway
- **Santa Fe** • 73 W 71st St
- **Sarabeth's** • 423 Amsterdam Ave
- **Taco Grill** • 146 W 72nd St
- **Vince and Eddie's** • 70 W 68th St
- **Vinnie's Pizza** • 285 Amsterdam Ave
- **Whole Foods Café** • 10 Columbus Cir, downstairs

Shopping

- **Alphabets** • 2284 Broadway
- **Assets London** • 464 Columbus Ave
- **Balducci's** • 155 W 66th St
- **Bed Bath & Beyond** • 1932 Broadway
- **Bonne Nuit** • 30 Lincoln Plz
- **Bruce Frank** • 215 W 83rd St
- **Bruno the King of Ravioli** • 2204 Broadway
- **Claire's Accessories** • 2267 Broadway
- **Eastern Mountain Sports** • 20 W 61st St
- **EMS** • 20 W 61st St
- **Ethan Allen** • 103 West End Ave
- **Fish's Eddy** • 2176 Broadway
- **Godiva Chocolatier** • 245 Columbus Ave
- **Gracious Home** • 1992 Broadway
- **Harry's Shoes** • 2299 Broadway
- **Housing Works Thrift Shop** • 306 Columbus Ave
- **Janovic Plaza** • 159 W 72nd St
- **Lincoln Stationers** • 1889 Broadway
- **NYCD** • 173 W 81st St
- **Patagonia** • 426 Columbus Ave
- **Tower Records/Video** • 1961 Broadway
- **Tumi** • 10 Columbus Cir
- **West Side Records** • 233 W 72nd St
- **Whole Foods Market** • 10 Columbus Cir
- **Yarn Co** • 2274 Broadway
- **Zabar's** • 2245 Broadway

Video Rental

- **Blockbuster Video** • 197 Amsterdam Ave
- **Champagne Video** • 213 W 79th St
- **Channel Video** • 472 Columbus Ave
- **Flick's Video** • 175 W 72nd St
- **Tower Records-Video-Books** • 1961 Broadway

(93)

Map 14 • **Upper West Side (Lower)**

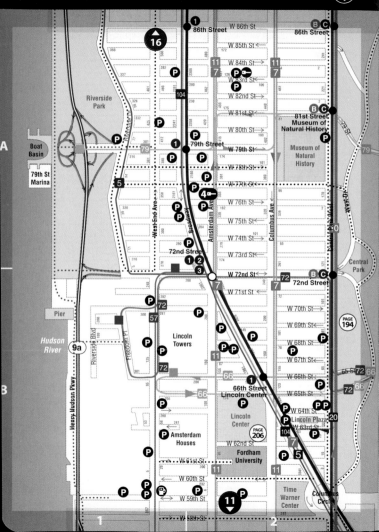

Parking and driving are both actually doable in this area, with most of the available spots on or near Riverside Drive. We recommend the 79th Street Transverse for crossing Central Park to the east side. The Lincoln Center area is by far the messiest traffic problem here— you can avoid it by taking West End Avenue.

Subways

① ② ③ .... 72 St
① .... 66 St-Lincoln Center
① .... 79 St
Ⓑ Ⓒ .... 72 St
Ⓑ Ⓒ .... 81 St-Museum of Natural History

Bus Lines

10 20 ... Seventh Ave/Eighth Ave/Douglass Blvd
104 .... Broadway/42nd St
11 .... Ninth Ave/Tenth Ave
5 ....Fifth Ave/Sixth Ave/Riverside Dr
57 .... 57th St Crosstown
66 .... 66th St/67th St Crosstown
7 ....Columbus Ave/Amsterdam Ave/
Lenox Ave/Sixth Ave/Broadway
72 ....72nd St Crosstown
79 .... 79th St Crosstown

Bike Lanes

- • • • Marked Bike Lanes
- • • • Recommended Route
- • • • Greenway

Car Rental

- **Avis** • 216 W 76th St
- **Dollar** • 207 W 76th St
- **Enterprise** • 147 W 83rd St
- **Hertz** • 210 W 77th St
- **National** • 219 W 77th St

Ⓟ Parking

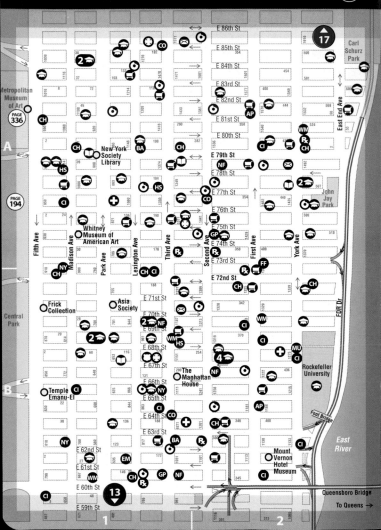

Map 15 • **Upper East Side (Lower)**

The southern half of the Upper East Side is a hotbed of culture, research, and education, containing one of the world's top museums (the Metropolitan Museum of Art); several top schools, including Cornell University Medical Center and Rockefeller University; and perhaps the foremost cancer hospital in the world, Memorial Sloan-Kettering Cancer Center.

24-Hour Pharmacies

- **CVS Pharmacy** • 1396 Second Ave
- **Duane Reade** • 1191 Second Ave
- **Duane Reade** • 1279 Third Ave
- **Duane Reade** • 1345 First Ave
- **Duane Reade** • 1498 York Ave
- **Duane Reade** • 773 Lexington Ave

Bagels

- **Bagel Mill Café** • 1461 Third Ave
- **Bagel Shoppe** • 1421 Second Ave
- **Bagels & Co** • 500 E 76th St
- **Bagelworks** • 1229 First Ave
- **Bread Factory Café** • 785 Lexington Ave
- **Eastside Bagel** • 1496 First Ave
- **Elaine's Bagel** • 941 Park Ave
- **H&H Midtown Bagel East** • 1551 Second Ave
- **Healthy Bagel & Things** • 1355 Second Ave
- **Hot & Tasty Bagels** • 1323 Second Ave
- **Monsieur Bagel** • 874 Lexington Ave
- **New World Coffee** • 1046 Third Ave
- **New World Coffee** • 1246 Lexington Ave
- **NYC Bagels** • 1228 Second Ave
- **Pick A Bagel** • 1101 Lexington Ave
- **Pick A Bagel** • 1475 Second Ave
- **Tal Bagel** • 1228 Lexington Ave

Banks

- **AP • Apple** • 1168 First Ave
- **AP • Apple** • 1555 First Ave
- **BA • Bank of America** • 1143 Lexington Ave
- **BA • Bank of America (ATM)** • 1065 Third Ave
- **NY • Bank of New York** • 1100 Third Ave
- **NY • Bank of New York** • 706 Madison Ave
- **NY • Bank of New York** • 909 Madison Ave
- **CH • Chase** • 1003 Lexington Ave
- **CH • Chase** • 1025 Madison Ave
- **CH • Chase** • 201 E 79th St
- **CH • Chase** • 300 E 64th St
- **CH • Chase** • 35 E 72nd St
- **CH • Chase** • 360 E 72nd St
- **CH • Chase** • 501 E 79th St
- **CH • Chase** • 770 Lexington Ave
- **CH • Chase (ATM)** • 1000 Fifth Ave
- **CI • Citibank** • 1078 Third Ave
- **CI • Citibank** • 1285 First Ave
- **CI • Citibank** • 1512 First Ave
- **CI • Citibank** • 171 E 72nd St
- **CI • Citibank** • 757 Madison Ave
- **CI • Citibank** • 785 Fifth Ave
- **CI • Citibank** • 976 Madison Ave
- **CI • Citibank (ATM)** • 1266 First Ave
- **CI • Citibank (ATM)** • 1275 York Ave
- **CI • Citibank (ATM)** • 501 E 62nd St
- **CO • Commerce Bank** • 1091 Third Ave
- **CO • Commerce Bank** • 1470 Second Ave
- **CO • Commerce Bank** • 1504 Third Ave
- **EM • Emigrant** • 812 Lexington Ave
- **FF • Fourth Federal Savings** • 1355 First Ave
- **GP • Greenpoint Bank** • 1010 Third Ave
- **GP • Greenpoint Bank** • 1432 Second Ave
- **HS • HSBC** • 1002 Madison Ave
- **HS • HSBC** • 1165 Third Ave
- **HS • HSBC** • 1340 Third Ave
- **CU • Municipal Credit Union (ATM)** • 525 E 68th St
- **NF • North Fork Bank** • 1011 Third Ave
- **NF • North Fork Bank** • 1180 Third Ave
- **NF • North Fork Bank** • 1258 Second Ave
- **NF • North Fork Bank** • 300 E 79th St
- **WM • Washington Mutual** • 1191 Third Ave
- **WM • Washington Mutual** • 1308 First Ave
- **WM • Washington Mutual** • 1520 York Ave
- **WM • Washington Mutual** • 510 Park Ave

Fire Departments

- **Engine 22, Ladder 13** • 159 E 85th St
- **Engine 39, Ladder 16** • 157 E 67th St
- **Engine 44** • 221 E 75th St

Hospitals

- **Lenox Hill** • 120 E 77th St
- **Manhattan Eye, Ear & Throat** • 210 E 64th St
- **New York Presbyterian–Weill Cornell Medical Center** • 525 E 68th St

Landmarks

- **Asia Society** • 725 Park Ave
- **Frick Collection** • 1 E 70th St
- **The Manhattan House** • 200 E 66th St
- **Metropolitan Museum of Art** • 1000 Fifth Ave
- **Mount Vernon Hotel Museum** • 421 E 61st St
- **New York Society Library** • 53 E 79th St
- **Temple Emanu-El** • 1 E 65th St
- **Whitney Museum of American Art** • 945 Madison Ave

Libraries

- **67th St (closed for renovation)** • 328 E 67th St
- **New York Society Library** • 53 E 79th St
- **Webster** • 1465 York Ave
- **Yorkville** • 222 E 79th St

Police

- **19th Precinct** • 153 E 67th St

Post Offices

- **Cherokee** • 1483 York Ave
- **Gracie** • 229 E 85th St
- **Lenox Hill** • 217 E 70th St

Schools

- **Abraham Lincoln** • 12 E 79th St
- **All Souls** • 1157 Lexington Ave
- **Allen-Stevenson School** • 132 E 78th St
- **Birch Wathen Lenox School** • 210 E 77th St
- **Brearly** • 610 E 83rd St
- **Browning School** • 52 E 62nd St
- **Buckley School** • 113 E 73rd St
- **Caedmon School** • 416 E 80th St
- **Cathedral School** • 319 E 74th St
- **Chapin School** • 100 East End Ave
- **Cornell University Medical College** • 1300 York Ave
- **Dominican Academy** • 44 E 68th St
- **East Side Middle** • 1458 York Ave
- **Eleanor Roosevelt High** • 411 E 76th St
- **Ella Baker** • 317 E 67th St
- **Episcopal School** • 35 E 69th St
- **Geneva School of Manhattan** • 583 Park Ave
- **Hewitt School** • 45 E 75th St
- **Hunter College** • 695 Park Ave
- **JHS 167 Robert F Wagner** • 220 E 76th St
- **Loyola School** • 980 Park Ave
- **Lycée Français de New York** • 505 E 75th St
- **Manhattan High School for Girls** • 154 E 70th St
- **Manhattan International High** • 317 E 67th St
- **Martha Graham** • 316 E 63rd St
- **Marymount Manhattan College** • 221 E 71st St
- **Marymount School** • 1026 Fifth Ave
- **New York School of Interior Design** • 170 E 70th St
- **PS 006 Lillie D Blake** • 45 E 81st St
- **PS 158 Bayard Taylor** • 1458 York Ave
- **PS 183 R L Stevenson** • 419 E 66th St
- **PS 290 Manhattan New School** • 311 E 82nd St
- **Rabbi Arthur Schneier Park East Day** • 164 E 68th St
- **Ramaz Lower** • 125 E 85th St
- **Ramaz Middle** • 114 E 85th St
- **Ramaz Upper** • 60 E 78th St
- **Regis High** • 55 E 84th St
- **Rockefeller University** • 1230 York Ave
- **Rudolf Steiner Lower** • 15 E 79th St
- **Rudolf Steiner Upper** • 15 E 78th St
- **The Smith School** • 1393 York Ave
- **Sotheby's Educational Studies** • 1334 York Ave
- **Spanish Institute** • 684 Park Ave
- **St Ignatius Loyola School** • 50 E 84th St
- **St Jean Baptiste High** • 173 E 75th St
- **St Stephan of Hungary School** • 408 E 82nd St
- **St Vincent Ferrer High** • 151 E 65th St
- **Talent Unlimited High** • 300 E 68th St
- **Town School** • 540 E 76th St
- **Ukrainian Institute of America** • 2 E 79th St
- **Urban Academy Lab High** • 317 E 67th St
- **Vanguard High** • 317 E 67th St

Supermarkets

- **Agata & Valentina** • 1505 First Ave
- **Associated** • 1565 First Ave
- **Citarella** • 1313 Third Ave
- **D'Agostino** • 1410 Lexington Ave
- **D'Agostino** • 1233 Lexington Ave
- **D'Agostino** • 1507 York Ave
- **Eli's Manhattan** • 1411 Third Ave
- **Food Emporium** • 1066 Third Ave
- **Food Emporium** • 1175 Third Ave
- **Food Emporium** • 1331 First Ave
- **Food Emporium** • 1450 Third Ave
- **Gourmet Garage East** • 301 E 64th St
- **Grace's Marketplace** • 1237 Third Ave
- **Gristede's** • 1180 Second Ave
- **Gristede's** • 1208 First Ave
- **Gristede's** • 1350 First Ave
- **Gristede's** • 1365 Third Ave
- **Gristede's** • 1446 Second Ave
- **Gristede's** • 40 East End Ave

97

Map 15 · **Upper East Side (Lower)**

With plenty of services spread throughout this neighborhood (aside from the area around Fifth Avenue, but they can afford to have everything delivered!), along with decent housing and Central Park close by, this part of the Upper East Side is quite desirable.

Coffee

- Café Bacio • 1316 First Ave
- Café Bacio • 1223 Third Ave
- DT * UT • 1626 Second Ave
- Dunkin' Donuts • 1225 First Ave
- Dunkin' Donuts • 1433 Second Ave
- Dunkin' Donuts • 1593 First Ave
- First Avenue Coffee Shop • 1433 First Ave
- Genes Coffee Shop • 26 E 60th St
- Gotham Coffee House • 1298 Second Ave
- Java Girl • 348 E 66th St
- Nectar Coffee Shop • 1022 Madison Ave
- Nectar Coffee Shop • 1090 Madison Ave
- Neil's Coffee Shop • 961 Lexington Ave
- New World Coffee • 1046 Third Ave
- New World Coffee • 1246 Lexington Ave
- Oren's Daily Roast • 1144 Lexington Ave
- Oren's Daily Roast • 1574 First Ave
- Oren's Daily Roast • 985 Lexington Ave
- Rohrs M • 303 E 85th St
- Starbucks
  - 1102 First Ave
  - 1128 Third Ave
  - 1445 First Ave
  - 1488 Third Ave
  - 1631 First Ave
  - 1117 Lexington Ave
  - 1290 Third Ave
  - 1449 Second Ave
  - 1559 Second Ave
  - 444 E 80th St
- Tramway Coffee Shop • 1143 Second Ave
- Viand Coffee Shop • 1011 Madison Ave

Copy Shops

- Complete Copy Center (9am-7pm) • 349 E 82nd St
- Copycats (8:30am-9pm) • 1646 Second Ave
- Copycats (8am-9pm) • 968 Lexington Ave
- Copyland Center (8am-10pm) • 1579 Second Ave
- Copyland Center (8am-10pm) • 335 E 65th St
- Kinko's (24 hrs) • 1122 Lexington Ave
- Mail Boxes Etc (8:30am-7pm) • 1461 First Ave
- Mail Boxes Etc (9am-7pm) • 1202 Lexington Ave
- Mail Boxes Etc (9am-7pm) • 954 Lexington Ave
- Universal Copy (8am-9pm) • 1343 Second Ave
- The UPS Store (8:30am-7:30pm) • 1173 Second Ave
- The UPS Store (8:30am-7:30pm) • 1275 First Ave
- The UPS Store (9am-7pm) • 1562 First Ave
- Yorkville Copy Service (8:30am-5:45pm) • 133 E 84th St

Gyms

- Casa at the Regency • 540 Park Ave
- Curves • 1460 Second Ave
- David Barton Gyms • 30 E 85th St
- Definitions • 39 E 78th St
- Elissa's Personal Best Gym • 334 E 79th St
- Equinox Fitness Club • 140 E 63rd St
- Equinox Fitness Club • 205 E 85th St
- Hampton House Health Club • 404 E 79th St
- Lenox Hill Neighborhood House • 331 E 70th St
- Liberty Fitness Center • 244 E 84th St
- New York Health & Racquet Club • 1433 York Ave
- New York Sports Clubs • 349 E 76th St
- Promenade Health Club • 530 E 76th St
- Sports Club/LA • 330 E 61st St
- Strathmore Swim & Health Club • 400 E 84th St
- Synergy Fitness Clubs • 1438 Third Ave

Hardware Stores

- 72nd Street Hardware • 1400 Second Ave
- ATB Locksmith & Hardware • 1603 York Ave
- Gracious Home • 1220 Third Ave
- Kraft Hardware • 315 E 62nd St
- Lexington Hardware & Electric • 797 Lexington Ave
- New York Paint & Hardware • 1593 Second Ave
- Queensboro Hardware • 1157 Second Ave
- Rainbow Ace Hardware • 1449 First Ave
- S&V General Supply • 1450 First Ave
- Sutton Hardware & Home Center • 1153 First Ave
- Thalco Maintenance Supply • 1462 Second Ave
- Third Ave Supply • 1301 Third Ave

Liquor Stores

- 1375 First Liquors • 1375 First Ave
- 76 Liquors • 1473 First Ave
- Aulden Cellars • 1334 York Ave
- Big Apple Wine & Spirits • 1408 Second Ave
- City Liquor • 1145 Second Ave
- Cork and Bottle Liquor Store • 1158 First Ave
- Crown Wine & Liquor • 1587 Second Ave
- East River Liquors • 1364 York Ave
- Embassy Liquors • 796 Lexington Ave
- Garnet Wines & Liquors • 929 Lexington Ave
- Headington Wines & Liquors • 1135 Lexington Ave
- Lumers Fine Wines & Spirits • 1479 Third Ave
- McCabe's Wines & Spirits • 1347 Third Ave
- Milli Liquors • 1496 Second Ave
- Monro Wines & Liquors • 68 East End Ave
- Morrell Wine Exchange • 1035 Third Ave
- Sherry-Lehman • 679 Madison Ave
- Windsor Wine Shop • 1103 First Ave
- The Wine Cart • 235 E 69th St
- The Wine Shop • 1585 First Ave
- Woody Liquor & Wine • 1450 Second Ave
- York Wines & Spirits • 1291 First Ave

Pet Shops

- American Kennels • 798 Lexington Ave
- Animal Attractions • 343 E 66th St
- Bark Place • 415 E 72nd St
- Calling All Pets • 1590 York Ave
- Calling All Pets • 301 E 76th St
- Canine Styles • 830 Lexington Ave
- Dogs Cats & Co • 208 E 82nd St
- Just Cats • 244 E 60th St
- Karen's for People Plus Pets • 1195 Lexington Ave
- Le Chien Pet Salon • 1044 Third Ave
- Pet Market • 1570 First Ave
- Pet Market • 1400 Second Ave
- Pet Necessities • 236 E 75th St
- Pets on Lex • 1275 Lexington Ave
- Sutton Dog Parlour Kennel & Daycare Center • 311 E 60th St

Video Rental

- Blockbuster Video • 1251 Lexington Ave
- Blockbuster Video • 1270 First Ave
- Champagne Video • 1194 First Ave
- Champagne Video • 1416 Third Ave
- Champagne Video • 1577 First Ave
- Fifth Dimension Video • 1427 York Ave
- Filmfest Video • 1594 York Ave
- Video Room • 976 Lexington Ave
- Videoroom • 1487 Third Ave
- York Video • 1472 York Ave
- Zitomer Department Store & Electronics • 969 Madison Ave

Map 15 · **Upper East Side (Lower)**

Maya may well serve the best Mexican food in the city. If you want to go slumming, the Subway Inn is the place. The bar scene is centered in the east 70s and 80s, where the post-college crowd resides, resulting in plenty of standard "Irish" bars.

Movie Theaters

- **Asia Society** • 725 Park Ave
- **Cineplex Odeon: Beekman Theater** • 1254 Second Ave
- **Clearview's First & 62nd Street** • 400 E 62nd St
- **Czech Center** • 1109 Madison Ave
- **Loews 72nd Street East** • 1230 Third Ave
- **Metropolitan Museum of Art** • 1000 Fifth Ave
- **New York Twin** • 1271 Second Ave
- **New York Youth Theater** • 593 Park Ave
- **UA 64th & Second** • 1210 Second Ave
- **UA East 85th Street** • 1629 First Ave
- **Whitney Museum** • 945 Madison Ave

Nightlife

- **Banshee Pub** • 1373 First Ave
- **Brandy's Piano Bar** • 235 E 84th St
- **Brother Jimmy's** • 1485 Second Ave
- **Café Carlyle and Bemelmans Bar** • 35 E 76th St
- **David Copperfield's** • 1394 York Ave
- **Feinstein's at the Regency** • 540 Park Ave
- **Finnegan's Wake** • 1361 First Ave
- **Hi-Life** • 1340 First Ave
- **Session 73** • 1359 First Ave
- **Ship of Fools** • 1590 Second Ave
- **Subway Inn** • 143 E 60th St
- **Vudu** • 1487 First Ave

Restaurants

- **Afghan Kebab House** • 1345 Second Ave
- **Atlantic Grill** • 1341 Third Ave
- **Aureole** • 34 E 61st St
- **Baluchi's** • 1149 First Ave
- **Baluchi's** • 1565 Second Ave
- **Barking Dog Luncheonette** • 1453 York Ave
- **Brunelli** • 1409 York Ave
- **Canyon Road** • 1470 First Ave
- **Daniel** • 60 E 65th St
- **EJ's Luncheonette** • 1271 Third Ave
- **Ethiopian Restaurant** • 1582 York Ave
- **Haru** • 1329 Third Ave
- **Heidelberg** • 1648 Second Ave
- **Jackson Hole** • 1611 Second Ave
- **Jackson Hole** • 232 E 64th St
- **JG Melon** • 1291 Third Ave
- **John's Pizzeria** • 408 E 64th St
- **JoJo** • 160 E 64th St
- **Le Pain Quotidien** • 1131 Madison Ave
- **Le Pain Quotidien** • 1336 First Ave
- **Le Pain Quotidien** • 833 Lexington Ave
- **Mary Ann's** • 1503 Second Ave
- **Maya** • 1191 First Ave
- **Our Place** • 1444 Third Ave
- **Park Avenue Café** • 100 E 63rd St
- **Pearson's Texas Barbecue** • 170 E 81st St
- **Penang** • 1596 Second Ave
- **Pintaile's Pizza** • 1237 Second Ave
- **Pintaile's Pizza** • 1443 York Ave
- **Pintaile's Pizza** • 1577 York Ave
- **Post House** • 28 E 63rd St
- **Rain East** • 1059 Third Ave
- **rm** • 33 E 60th St
- **Serafina Fabulous Grill** • 29 E 61st St
- **Totonno Pizzeria Napolitano** • 1544 Second Ave
- **Viand** • 1011 Madison Ave
- **Viand** • 673 Madison Ave

Shopping

- **A Bear's Place** • 789 Lexington Ave
- **American Apparel** • 1090 3rd Ave
- **Aveda Environmental Lifestyle Store** • 1122 Third Ave
- **Bang & Olufsen** • 952 Madison Ave
- **Barneys New York** • 660 Madison Ave
- **Bed Bath & Beyond** • 410 E 61st St
- **Bloomingdale's** • 1000 Third Ave
- **Bra Smyth** • 905 Madison Ave
- **Diesel** • 770 Lexington Ave
- **DKNY** • 655 Madison Ave
- **Dolce & Gabbana** • 825 Madison Ave
- **Donna Karan** • 819 Madison Ave
- **Dylan's Candy Bar** • 1011 Third Ave
- **Elk Candy** • 1628 Second Ave
- **Garnet Wines & Liquors** • 929 Lexington Ave
- **Giorgio Armani** • 760 Madison Ave
- **Gracious Home** • 1217 Third Ave
- **Hermes** • 691 Madison Ave
- **Housing Works Thrift Shop** • 202 E 77th St
- **Janovic Plaza** • 1150 Third Ave
- **Kate's Paperie** • 1282 Third Ave
- **Lyric Hi-Fi** • 1221 Lexington Ave
- **Morgane Le Fay** • 746 Madison Ave
- **Neuhaus Chocolate Boutique** • 922 Madison Ave
- **Ottomanelli Brothers** • 1549 York Ave
- **Radio Shack** • 1267 Lexington Ave
- **Radio Shack** • 1477 Third Ave
- **Radio Shack** • 782 Lexington Ave
- **Radio Shack** • 925 Lexington Ave
- **Steuben** • 667 Madison Ave
- **Venture Stationers** • 1156 Madison Ave
- **Yorkville Meat Emporium** • 1560 Second Ave

Map 15 · **Upper East Side (Lower)**

Parking is extremely difficult during the day due to the number of schools in this area. It gets a bit better (but not much) at night, especially in the upper 70s and lower 80s near the FDR. (You'll never find legal street parking near Bloomingdale's, however.) Park Avenue is the best street to travel downtown during rush hour.

Subways

6	.68 St-Hunter College
6	77 St
4 5 6	86 St
F	Lexington Ave/63 St
N R W	5 Ave/59 St
4 5 6 N R W	Lexington Ave/59 St

Bus Lines

1 2 3	Fifth Ave/Madison Ave
101 102 103 32	Third Ave/Lexington Ave
15	First Ave/Second Ave
30	72nd St/57th St Crosstown
31	York Ave/57th St Crosstown
4	Fifth Ave/Madison Ave/Broadway
66	67th St/68th St Crosstown
72	72nd St Crosstown
79	79th St Crosstown
98	Washington Heights/Midtown
101	Astoria
60	Jamaica

Bike Lanes

- • • Marked Bike Lanes
- • • Recommended Route
- • • Greenway

Car Rental

- **Avis** • 310 E 64th St
- **Dollar** • 157 E 84th St
- **Enterprise** • 425 E 61st St
- **Hertz** • 327 E 64th St
- **Hertz** • 355 E 76th St
- **National** • 305 E 80th St

Gas Stations

- **Mobil** • 1132 York Ave

Parking

Map 16 · **Upper West Side (Upper)**

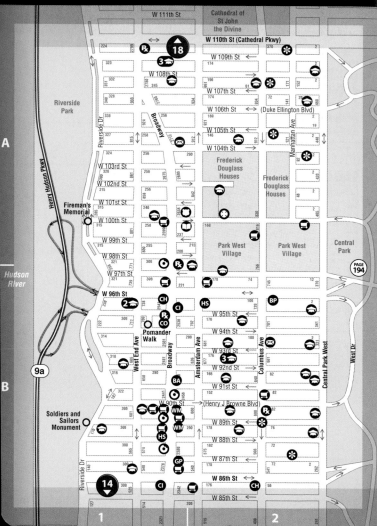

This part of the Upper West Side is extremely residential. Riverside Drive, West End Avenue, and Central Park West are all highly desirable addresses—if you can afford them. Gentrification continues to creep up past 96th Street towards Columbia, especially towards the west. Check out Riverside Park for all sorts of amusements.

24-Hour Pharmacies

- **Duane Reade** · 2522 Broadway
- **Duane Reade** · 2589 Broadway
- **Duane Reade** · 609 Columbus Ave
- **Rite Aid** · 2833 Broadway

Bagels

- **Bagel Basket** · 2415 Broadway
- **Hot & Crusty Bagel Café** · 2387 Broadway
- **Lenny's Bagels** · 2601 Broadway
- **Tal Bagels** · 2446 Broadway

Banks

- BP · **Banco Popular** · 90 W 96th St
- BA · **Bank of America (ATM)** · 2461 Broadway
- CH · **Chase** · 2551 Broadway
- CH · **Chase** · 59 W 86th St
- CI · **Citibank** · 2350 Broadway
- CI · **Citibank** · 2560 Broadway
- CO · **Commerce Bank** · 2521 Broadway
- GP · **Greenpoint Bank** · 2379 Broadway
- HS · **HSBC** · 2401 Broadway
- HS · **HSBC** · 739 Amsterdam Ave
- NF · **North Fork Bank** · 2460 Broadway
- WM · **Washington Mutual** · 2438 Broadway
- WM · **Washington Mutual** · 2554 Broadway

Community Gardens

Fire Departments

- **Engine 76, Ladder 22** · 145 W 100th St

Landmarks

- **Fireman's Memorial** · W 100th St & Riverside Dr
- **Pomander Walk** · 261 W 94th St
- **Soldiers and Sailors Monument** · Riverside Dr & 89th St

Libraries

- **Bloomingdale** · 150 W 100th St

Police

- **24th Precinct** · 151 W 100th St

Post Offices

- **Cathedral** · 215 W 104th St
- **Park West** · 693 Columbus Ave

Schools

- **Abraham Joshua Heschel** · 270 W 89th St
- **Aichhorn** · 23 W 106 St
- **Alexander Robertson** · 3 W 95th St
- **Ascension** · 224 W 108th St
- **Columbia Grammar and Prepatory** · 5 W 93rd St
- **Dwight** · 291 Central Park W
- **Edward A Reynolds West Side HS (M505)** · 140 W 102nd St
- **Holy Name School & De La Salle Academy** · 202 W 97th St
- **JHS 054 B Washington** · 103 W 107th St
- **Morningside Montessori** · 251 W 100th St
- **Mott Hall II** · 234 W 109th St
- **MS 246 Crossroads** · 234 W 109th St
- **MS 250 Collaborative** · 735 West End Ave
- **MS 256 Academic and Athletic Excellence** · 154 W 93rd St
- **MS 258 Community Action School** · 154 W 93rd St
- **PS 075 Emily Dickinson** · 735 West End Ave
- **PS 084 Lillian Weber School/MS 247 Dual Language** · 32 W 92nd St
- **PS 145 Bloomingdale** · 150 W 105th St
- **PS 163 Alfred E Smith** · 163 W 97th St
- **PS 165 Robert E Simon** · 234 W 109th St
- **PS 166 Arts & Sciences** · 132 W 89th St
- **PS 333 Manhattan School for Children** · 154 W 93rd St
- **PS 38 Roberto Clemente** · 232 E 103rd St
- **Solomon Schechter High** · 1 W 91st St
- **St Agnes Boys School** · 555 West End Ave
- **St Gregory the Great** · 138 W 90th St
- **Studio Elementary** · 124 W 95th St
- **Trinity School** · 139 W 91st St
- **Upper Trevor Day School** · 1 W 88th St
- **West Side Montessori** · 309 W 92nd St
- **Yeshiva Ketana of Manhattan** · 346 W 89th St

Supermarkets

- **Associated** · 13 W 100th St
- **Associated** · 755 Amsterdam Ave
- **C-Town** · 818 Columbus Ave
- **D'Agostino** · 633 Columbus Ave
- **Food Emporium** · 2415 Broadway
- **Gourmet Garage West** · 2567 Broadway
- **Gristede's** · 251 W 86th St
- **Gristede's** · 2633 Broadway
- **Gristede's Mega Store** · 262 W 96th St
- **Kosher Marketplace** · 2442 Broadway
- **Met Food** · 530 Amsterdam Ave
- **Whole Foods Market** · 2421 Broadway

Map 16 • **Upper West Side (Upper)**

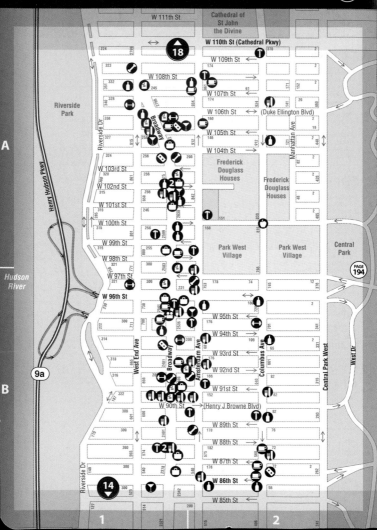

This area is saved from being totally bland by the proliferation of excellent and cheap Latin American cuisine, as well as by the Broadway Dive. For something more upscale, hit Docks Oyster Bar on Broadway.

Coffee

- **108 Mini Café** · 196 W 108th St
- **964 Jumbo Pizza Coffee Shop** · 964 Amsterdam Ave
- **Columbus Café** · 556 Columbus Ave
- **Dunkin' Donuts** · 2547 Broadway
- **Dunkin' Donuts** · 929 Amsterdam Ave
- **Silver Moon Bakery** · 2740 Broadway
- **Starbucks** · 2498 Broadway
- **Starbucks** · 2521 Broadway
- **Starbucks** · 2600 Broadway
- **Starbucks** · 2681 Broadway
- **Starbucks** · 540 Columbus Ave
- **Three Star Coffee Shop** · 541 Columbus Ave

Copy Shops

- **Columbia Copy Center** (8am-11pm) · 2790 Broadway
- **Copy Concept** (8am-9pm) · 216 W 103rd st
- **Copy Experts & Computer Center** (8am-11pm) · 2440 Broadway
- **Foxy Copy** (7:30am-8pm) · 211 W 92nd St
- **Global Copy** (8am-9pm) · 2578 Broadway
- **Mail Boxes Etc** (8:30am-7pm) · 2444 Broadway
- **Mail Boxes Etc** (8:30am-7pm) · 2565 Broadway
- **Riverside Resumes** (9am-8pm) · 248 W 106th St
- **The UPS Store** (8am-7pm) · 2753 Broadway

Farmer's Markets

- **97th Street** · W 97th St & Columbus Ave

Gyms

- **Body Strength Fitness** · 250 W 106th St
- **Equinox Fitness Club** · 2465 Broadway
- **New York Sports Clubs** · 2527 Broadway
- **Paris Health Club** · 752 West End Ave
- **Synergy Fitness Clubs** · 700 Columbus Ave

Hardware Stores

- **Ace Hardware** · 610 Columbus Ave
- **Ace Hardware** · 817 Amsterdam Ave
- **Altman Hardware** · 641 Amsterdam Ave
- **Aquarius Hardware & Houseware** · 601 Columbus Ave
- **B Cohen & Son** · 969 Amsterdam Ave
- **C&S Hardware** · 788 Amsterdam Ave
- **Garcia Hardware Store** · 995 Columbus Ave
- **Grand Metro Home Centers** · 2554 Broadway
- **Leo Hardware** · 716 Amsterdam Ave
- **Mike's Lumber Store** · 254 W 88th St
- **World Houseware** · 2617 Broadway

Liquor Stores

- **86th Corner Wine & Liquor** · 536 Columbus Ave
- **Adel Wine & Liquor** · 925 Columbus Ave
- **Best Liquor & Wine** · 2648 Broadway
- **Columbus Ave Wine & Spirits** · 730 Columbus Ave
- **Gotham Wines And Liquors** · 2517 Broadway
- **H&H Broadway Wine Center** · 2669 Broadway
- **Hong Liquor Store** · 2616 Broadway
- **Martin Brothers Liquor Store** · 2781 Broadway
- **Mitchell's Wine & Liquor Store** · 200 W 86th St
- **Polanco Liquor Store** · 948 Amsterdam Ave
- **Riverside Liquor** · 2746 Broadway
- **Roma Discount Wine & Liquor** · 737 Amsterdam Ave
- **Turin Wines & Liquors** · 609 Columbus Ave
- **Vintage New York** · 2492 Broadway
- **Westlane Wines & Liquor** · 689 Columbus Ave
- **Wine Place** · 2406 Broadway

Movie Theaters

- **Leonard Nimoy Thalia** · 2537 Broadway

Nightlife

- **Abbey Pub** · 237 W 105th St
- **Broadway Dive** · 2662 Broadway
- **Dive Bar** · 732 Amsterdam Ave
- **The Parlour** · 250 W 86th St
- **Smoke** · 2751 Broadway

Pet Shops

- **Amsterdog Groomers** · 586 Amsterdam Ave
- **Little Creatures** · 770 Amsterdam Ave
- **Pet Market** · 2821 Broadway
- **Pet Stop** · 564 Columbus Ave
- **Petco** · 2475 Broadway
- **Petland Discounts** · 2708 Broadway

Restaurants

- **A** · 947 Columbus Ave
- **Afghan Kebob House** · 2680 Broadway
- **AIX** · 2398 Broadway
- **Barney Greengrass** · 541 Amsterdam Ave
- **Bella Luna** · 584 Columbus Ave
- **Café Con Leche** · 726 Amsterdam Ave
- **Carmine's** · 2450 Broadway
- **City Diner** · 2441 Broadway
- **Docks Oyster Bar** · 2427 Broadway
- **Flor de Mayo** · 2651 Broadway
- **Gabriela's** · 685 Amsterdam Ave
- **Gennaro** · 665 Amsterdam Ave
- **Henry's** · 2745 Broadway
- **Lemongrass Grill** · 2534 Broadway
- **Mary Ann's** · 2452 Broadway
- **Pampa** · 768 Amsterdam Ave
- **Popover Café** · 551 Amsterdam Ave
- **Saigon Grill** · 620 Amsterdam Ave
- **Talia's Steakhouse** · 668 Amsterdam Ave
- **Trattoria Pesce Pasta** · 625 Columbus Ave

Shopping

- **Ann Taylor** · 2380 Broadway
- **Banana Republic** · 2360 Broadway
- **Ben & Jerry's** · 2722 Broadway
- **Gothic Cabinet Craft** · 2652 Broadway
- **Gourmet Garage** · 2567 Broadway
- **Health Nuts** · 2611 Broadway
- **Janovic Plaza** · 2680 Broadway
- **Metro Bicycles** · 231 W 96th St
- **Mommy Chic** · 2449 Broadway
- **Planet Kids** · 2688 Broadway

Video Rental

- **Blockbuster Video** · 2510 Broadway
- **Blockbuster Video** · 2689 Broadway
- **Hollywood Video** · 535 Columbus Ave
- **Movie Place** · 237 W 105th St

Map 16 • **Upper West Side (Upper)**

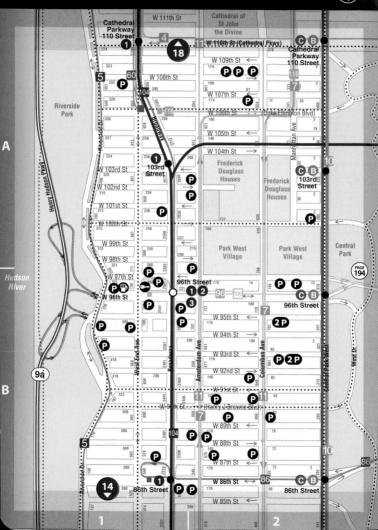

The 96th Street Transverse is by far the best way to cross Central Park. And isn't it nice that the Upper West Side has two separate subway lines?

Subways

1 2 3	96 St
1	103 St
1	86 St
B C	103 St
B C	86 St
B C	96 St

Bus Lines

10	Seventh Ave/Central Park W
104	Broadway
106	106th St Crosstown
11	Columbus Ave/Amsterdam Ave
116	116th St Crosstown
5	Fifth Ave/Sixth Ave/Riverside Dr
60	LaGuardia Airport
7	Columbus Ave/Amsterdam Ave
86	86th St Crosstown
96	96th St Crosstown

Bike Lanes

- • • • Marked Bike Lanes
- • • • Recommended Route
- • • • Greenway

Car Rental

· **AAMCAR** · 303 W 96th St

Gas Stations

· **Exxon** · 303 W 96th St

Parking

Map 17 · **Upper East Side / East Harlem**

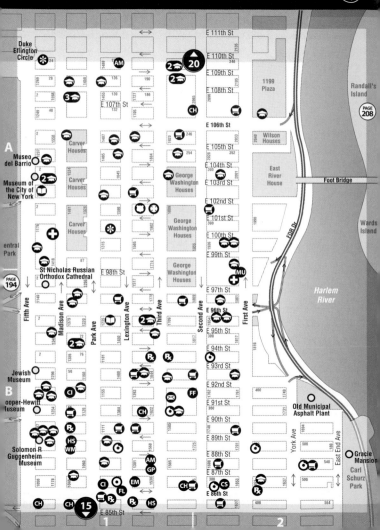

If you were unsure as to whether or not New York had enough cultural institutions, Museum Mile should convince you. The Guggenheim is one of the greatest architectural tours de force in Manhattan, notwithstanding its rapaciously high admission fees. Great bank and supermarket coverage---below 96th Street anyway.

24-Hour Pharmacies

- **CVS Pharmacy** · 1622 Third Ave
- **Duane Reade** · 1231 Madison Ave
- **Duane Reade** · 125 E 86th St
- **Duane Reade** · 1675 Third Ave
- **Duane Reade** · 401 E 86th St
- **Rite Aid** · 146 E 86th St

Bagels

- **Bagel Bob's** · 1638 York Ave
- **Bagel Express** · 1804 Second Ave
- **Bagel Mill** · 1700 Third Ave
- **Corner Bagel Market** · 1324 Lexington Ave
- **New York Hot Bagel** · 1585 Third Ave
- **Tal Bagels** · 333 E 86th St

Banks

- **BA · Bank of America (ATM)** · 1276 Lexington Ave
- **BA · Bank of America (ATM)** · 1538 Third Ave
- **CH · Chase** · 12 E 86th St
- **CH · Chase** · 126 E 86th St
- **CH · Chase** · 181 E 90th St
- **CH · Chase** · 2065 Second Ave
- **CH · Chase** · 255 E 86th St
- **CH · Chase** · 453 E 86th St
- **CI · Citibank** · 123 E 86th St
- **CI · Citibank** · 1275 Madison Ave
- **CS · City and Suburban FSB** · 345 E 86th St
- **EM · Emigrant** · 1270 Lexington Ave
- **FF · Fourth Federal Savings** · 1751 Second Ave
- **GP · Greenpoint Bank** · 1536 Third Ave
- **HS · HSBC** · 186 E 86th St
- **HS · HSBC** · 45 E 89th St
- **CU · Municipal Credit Union (ATM)** · 1901 First Ave
- **WM · Washington Mutual** · 1221 Madison Ave

Community Gardens

Fire Departments

- **Engine 53, Ladder 43** · 1836 Third Ave

Hospitals

- **Metropolitan** · 1901 First Ave
- **Mt Sinai Medical Center** · 1468 Madison Ave

Landmarks

- **Cooper-Hewitt Museum** · 2 E 91st St
- **Gracie Mansion** · Carl Schulz Park & 88th St
- **Jewish Museum** · 1109 Fifth Ave
- **Museo del Barrio** · Fifth Ave & 104th St
- **Museum of the City of New York** · Fifth Ave & 103rd St
- **Old Municipal Asphalt Plant (Asphalt Green)** · 90th St & FDR Dr
- **Solomon R Guggenheim Museum** · 1071 Fifth Ave
- **St Nicholas Russian Orthodox Cathedral** · 15 E 97th St

Libraries

- **96th Street** · 112 E 96th St
- **New York Academy of Medicine Library** · 1216 Fifth Ave

Police

- **23rd Precinct** · 162 E 102nd St

Post Offices

- **Yorkville** · 1617 Third Ave

Schools

- **Amber Charter** · 220 E 106th St
- **Ballet Academy East** · 1651 Third Ave
- **The Bilingual Bicultural School (M182)** · 219 E 109th St
- **Brick Church School** · 62 E 92nd St
- **Central Park East I Elementary** · 1573 Madison Ave
- **Central Park East II (M964)** · 19 E 103rd St
- **Central Park East Secondary** · 1573 Madison Ave
- **Convent of the Sacred Heart** · 1 E 91st St
- **Coop Tech** · 320 E 96th St
- **Dalton** · 108 E 89th St
- **East Harlem Block** · 1615 Madison Ave
- **East Harlem School at Exodus House** · 309 E 103rd St
- **Harbor Science & Arts Charter** · 1 E 104th St
- **Heritage** · 1680 Lexington Ave
- **HS 580 Richard Green High School of Teaching** · 421 E 88th St
- **Hunter College Elementary** · 71 E 94th St
- **Hunter College High** · 71 E 94th St
- **JHS 013 Jackie Robinson** · 1573 Madison Ave
- **JHS 099 Julio De Burgos School & Environmental Science** · 410 E 100th St
- **Life Sciences Secondary** · 320 E 96th St
- **Lower Trevor Day School** · 11 E 89th St
- **Lycée Français de New York** · 3 E 95th St
- **Manhattan Country School** · 7 E 96th St
- **Manhattan West Art Institute (M277)** · 19 E 103rd St
- **Mount Sinai School of Medicine** · 1 Gustave Levy Pl
- **MS 224 Manhattan East Center for Arts & Academics** · 410 E 100th St
- **National Academy School of Fine Arts** · 5 E 89th St
- **Nightingale-Bamford** · 20 E 92nd St
- **Our Lady of Good Counsel** · 323 E 91st St
- **Park East High** · 234 E 105th St
- **PS 072** · 131 E 104th St
- **PS 083 Luis Munoz Rivera** · 219 E 109th St
- **PS 108 Angelo Del Toro** · 1615 Madison Ave
- **PS 146 Anna M Short** · 421 E 106th St
- **PS 169 Robert F Kennedy** · 110 E 88th St
- **PS 171 Patrick Henry** · 19 E 103rd St
- **PS 198 Isador and Ida Straus** · 1700 Third Ave
- **PS 77 Lower Lab School** · 1700 Third Ave
- **Reece** · 180 E 93rd St
- **School of Cooperative Technical Education** · 321 E 96th St
- **Solomon Schechter** · 50 E 87th St
- **Spence** · 22 E 91st St
- **St Bernard's** · 4 E 98th St
- **St David's** · 12 E 89th St
- **St Francis de Sales** · 116 E 97th St
- **St Joseph Yorkville** · 420 E 87th St
- **St Lucy's Academy** · 340 E 104th St
- **Tag Young Scholars JHS (M012)** · 240 E 109th St
- **Tito Puente Educational Complex (M117)** · 240 E 109th St
- **Young Women's Leadership High** · 105 E 106th St

Supermarkets

- **Associated** · 1486 Lexington Ave
- **Associated** · 1635 Lexington Ave
- **Associated** · 1968 Second Ave
- **C-Town** · 1721 First Ave
- **Food Emporium** · 1211 Madison Ave
- **Food Emporium** · 1660 Second Ave
- **Gristede's** · 120 E 86th St
- **Gristede's** · 1343 Lexington Ave
- **Gristede's** · 1356 Lexington Ave
- **Gristede's** · 1644 York Ave
- **Gristede's** · 202 E 95th St
- **Gristede's Mega Store** · 350 E 86th St
- **Key Food** · 1769 Second Ave
- **Met Food** · 235 E 106th St
- **Pioneer** · 1407 Lexington Ave
- **Pioneer** · 2076 First Ave

Map 17 · **Upper East Side / East Harlem**

A popular landing spot for kids right out of school, the bar scene is heavily college-influenced. There's a dramatic change in the number of services north of 96th Street, much of which is due to several large housing projects. However, a few new building projects on 97th and 98th Streets illustrate the creep of gentrification north of 96th Street.

Coffee

- **Dunkin' Donuts** · 1276 Lexington Ave
- **Dunkin' Donuts** · 1391 Madison Ave
- **Dunkin' Donuts** · 1630 Madison Ave
- **Dunkin' Donuts** · 1760 Second Ave
- **Dunkin' Donuts** · 1880 Third Ave
- **Juliano Gourmet Coffee** · 1378 Lexington Ave
- **London Coffee Company** · 1817 Second Ave
- **Starbucks** · 120 E 87th St
- **Starbucks** · 1378 Madison Ave
- **Starbucks** · 1642 Third Ave
- **Starbucks** · 400 E 90th St
- **Viand Coffee Shop** · 300 E 86th St

Copy Shops

- **Copy Quest** (8am-6pm) · 159 E 92nd St
- **Desktop USA** · 1476 Lexington Ave
- **Mail Boxes Etc** (8am-6:30pm) · 1369 Madison Ave
- **Mail Boxes Etc** (8am-7pm) · 1710 First Ave
- **SDS Duplicating Service** (9am-7pm) · 2069 Second Ave
- **Staples** (7am-9pm) · 1280 Lexington Ave
- **The UPS Store** (8:30am-7pm) · 1636 Third Ave
- **The UPS Store** (8:30am-7pm) · 217 E 86th St

Gyms

- **92nd St Y–May Center** · 1395 Lexington Ave
- **Asphalt Green** · 555 E 90th St
- **Bally Total Fitness** · 144 E 86th St
- **Bally Total Fitness** · 1915 Third Ave
- **Carnegie Park Swim & Health Club** · 200 E 94th St
- **Curves** · 1711 First Ave
- **Monterey Sports Club** · 175 E 96th St
- **New York Sports Clubs** · 151 E 86th St
- **New York Sports Clubs** · 1637 Third Ave
- **Pumping Iron Gym** · 403 E 91st St
- **Synergy Fitness Clubs** · 1781 Second Ave
- **Trainer's Place** · 210 E 86th St

Hardware Stores

- **El Barrio Hardware** · 1876 Third Ave
- **Feldmans IV** · 1190 Madison Ave
- **Johnny's Hardware** · 1708 Lexington Ave
- **K&G Hardware & Supply** · 401 E 90th St
- **M&E Madison Hardware** · 1396 Madison Ave
- **Morales Brothers Hardware** · 1959 Third Ave
- **Service Hardware** · 1338 Lexington Ave
- **Wankel's Hardware & Paint** · 1573 Third Ave

Liquor Stores

- **86th Street Wine & Liquor** · 306 E 86th St
- **Best Cellars** · 1291 Lexington Ave
- **East 87th Street Wine Traders** · 1693 Second Ave
- **Edwin's Wines & Liquors** · 176 E 103rd St
- **House of J&H** · 2073 Second Ave
- **K&D Wines & Spirits** · 1366 Madison Ave
- **Mercedes Liquor Store** · 102 E 103rd St
- **Mister Wright** · 1593 Third Ave
- **Normandie Wines** · 1834 Second Ave
- **Park East Liquors** · 1657 York Ave
- **Pet Wines & Spirits** · 415 E 91st St
- **Rivera Liquor Store** · 2025 First Ave
- **Uptown Wine Shop** · 1361 Lexington Ave
- **West Coast Wine & Liquor** · 1440 Lexington Ave
- **Yorkshire Wines & Spirits** · 1646 First Ave

Movie Theaters

- **92nd Street Y** · Lexington Ave & 92nd St
- **City Cinemas: East 86th Street** · 210 E 86th St
- **Goethe Institute** · 1014 Fifth Ave
- **Loews Cineplex Orpheum** · 1538 Third Ave
- **Solomon R Guggenheim Museum** · 1071 Fifth Ave

Nightlife

- **Auction House** · 300 E 89th St
- **Big Easy** · 1768 Second Ave
- **Kinsale Tavern** · 1672 Third Ave
- **Rathbones Pub** · 1702 Second Ave
- **Ruby's Tap House** · 1754 Second Ave

Pet Shops

- **Furry Paws** · 1705 Third Ave
- **Petco** · 147 E 86th St
- **Petland Discounts** · 1954 Third Ave
- **Petland Discounts** · 304 E 86th St
- **Shaggy Dog** · 400 E 88th St
- **World Wide Kennel** · 1661 First Ave

Restaurants

- **Barking Dog Luncheonette** · 1678 Third Ave
- **El Paso Taqueria** · 1642 Lexington Ave
- **Elaine's** · 1703 Second Ave
- **Jackson Hole** · 1270 Madison Ave
- **La Fonda Boricua** · 169 E 106th St
- **Pintaile's Pizza** · 26 E 91st St
- **Saigon Grill** · 1700 Second Ave
- **Sarabeth's** · 1295 Madison Ave
- **Viand** · 300 E 86th St

Shopping

- **Best Buy** · 1280 Lexington Ave
- **Blacker & Kooby** · 1204 Madison Ave
- **Blades Board & Skate** · 120 W 72nd St
- **Capezio** · 1651 Third Ave
- **Cooper-Hewitt National Design Museum Shop** · 2 E 91st St
- **Eli's Vinegar Factory** · 431 E 91st St
- **FACE Stockholm** · 1263 Madison Ave
- **La Tropezienne** · 2131 First Ave
- **Martha Frances Mississippi Cheesecake** · 1707 Second Ave
- **New York Replacement Parts Corp** · 1456 Lexington Ave
- **Piece of Cake Bakery** · 1370 Lexington Ave
- **Schatzie's Prime Meats** · 1200 Madison Ave
- **Soccer Sport Supply** · 1745 First Ave
- **Steve Madden** · 150 E 86th St
- **Super Runners Shop** · 1337 Lexington Ave
- **Williams-Sonoma** · 1175 Madison Ave

Video Rental

- **Blockbuster Video** · 1646 First Ave
- **Blockbuster Video** · 1707 Third Ave
- **Blockbuster Video** · 1924 Third Ave
- **We Deliver Videos** · 1716 First Ave
- **York Video** · 1428 Lexington Ave

Map 17 · **Upper East Side / East Harlem**

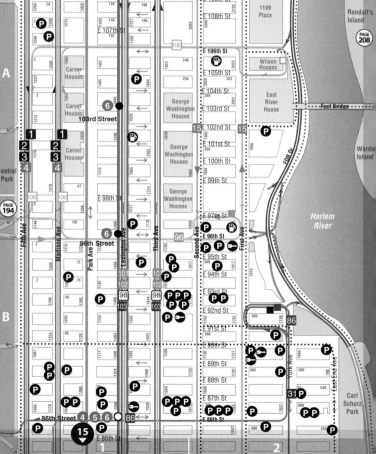

How anyone ever thought that one subway was enough for the Upper East Side is beyond us. It isn't. However, parking is about the best here that it's going to ever get in Manhattan. The 96th Street entrance to the FDR is jammed most of the day, usually with really, really bad drivers. A popular portal for the bridge and tunnel crowd?

Subways

4 5 6	86 St
6	96 St
6	103 St

Bus Lines

1 2 3	Fifth Ave/Madison Ave
101	Third Ave/Lexington Ave
102	Third Ave/Lexington Ave
103	Third Ave/Lexington Ave
106	96th St/106th St Crosstown
15	First Ave/Second Ave
31	York Ave/57th St
4	Fifth Ave/Madison Ave/Broadway
86	86th St Crosstown
96	96th St Crosstown
98	Washington Heights/Midtown

Bike Lanes

- • • • Marked Bike Lanes
- • • • Recommended Route
- • • • Greenway

Car Rental

- **Avis** · 420 E 90th St
- **Budget** · 152 E 87th St
- **Enterprise** · 1833 First Ave
- **Hertz** · 412 E 90th St

Gas Stations

- **Amoco** · 1599 Lexington Ave
- **BP** · 1855 First Ave
- **Getty** · 348 E 106th St

Parking

Map 18 · Columbia / Morningside Heights

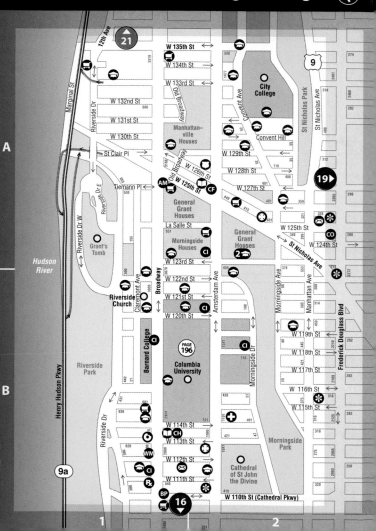

This is perhaps one of the most truly economically diverse parts of the city, with tons of Columbia students mixing with high-, middle-, and low-income professionals and families. Change could be on its way, however, if the university's expansion plans go through. The Cathedral of St. John the Divine is the most eclectic and astounding building in Manhattan.

℞ 24-Hour Pharmacies

- **Duane Reade** · 2864 Broadway

Bagels

- **Nussbaum & Wu** · 2897 Broadway

$ Banks

AM · Amalgamated · 564 W 125th St
BP · Banco Popular · 2852 Broadway
CF · Carver Federal Savings (ATM) · 503 W 125th St
CH · Chase · 2824 Broadway
CI · Citibank · 1310 Amsterdam Ave
CI · Citibank · 2861 Broadway
CI · Citibank (ATM) · 3009 Broadway
CI · Citibank (ATM) · 420 W 118th St
CI · Citibank (ATM) · 525 W 120th St
CO · Commerce Bank · 300 W 125th St
WM · Washington Mutual · 2875 Broadway

Community Gardens

Fire Departments

- **Engine 37, Ladder 40** · 415 W 125th St
- **Engine 47** · 502 W 113th St

Hospitals

- **St Luke's** · 1111 Amsterdam Ave

Landmarks

- **Cathedral of St John the Divine** · 112th St & Amsterdam Ave
- **City College** · 138th St & Convent Ave
- **Columbia University** · 116th St & Broadway
- **Grant's Tomb** · 122nd St & Riverside Dr
- **Riverside Church** · 490 Riverside Dr

Libraries

- **George Bruce** · 518 W 125th St
- **Morningside Heights Library** · 2900 Broadway

Police

- **26th Precinct** · 520 W 126th St

Post Offices

- **Columbia University** · 534 W 112th St
- **Manhattanville** · 365 W 125th St

Schools

- **A Philip Randolph Campus High** · 443 W 135th St
- **Annunciation School** · 461 W 131st St
- **Bank Street College of Education** · 610 W 112th St
- **Barnard College** · 3009 Broadway
- **Cathedral School** · 1047 Amsterdam Ave
- **City College** · 138th St & Convent Ave
- **Columbia University** · 2960 Broadway
- **The Cooke Center For Learning** · 475 Riverside Dr
- **Corpus Christi** · 535 W 121st St
- **IS 172 Adam C Powell** · 509 W 129th St
- **IS 195 Roberto Clemente** · 625 W 133rd St
- **IS 223 Mott Hall** · 71 Convent Ave
- **IS 286 Renaissance Military** · 509 W 129th St
- **Jewish Theological Seminary of America** · 3080 Broadway
- **Kipp Starr College Preparatory (M726)** · 433 W 123rd St
- **Manhattan School of Music** · 120 Claremont Ave
- **PS 036 Margaret Douglas** · 123 Morningside Dr
- **PS 125 Ralph Bunche** · 425 W 123rd St
- **PS 129 John H Finley** · 425 W 130th St
- **PS 161 Pedro A Campos** · 499 W 133rd St
- **PS 180 Hugo Newman** · 370 W 120th St
- **St Hilda and Hugh School** · 619 W 114th St
- **St Joseph's School of the Holy Family** · 168 Morningside Ave
- **Teachers College, Columbia University** · 525 W 120th St

Supermarkets

- **Associated** · 2943 Broadway
- **C-Town** · 3320 Broadway
- **C-Town** · 560 W 125th St
- **Citarella** · 461 W 125th St
- **D'Ag Fresh Market** · 2828 Broadway
- **Fairway Market** · 2328 Twelfth Ave
- **Met Food** · 1316 Amsterdam Ave

Map 18 · **Columbia / Morningside Heights**

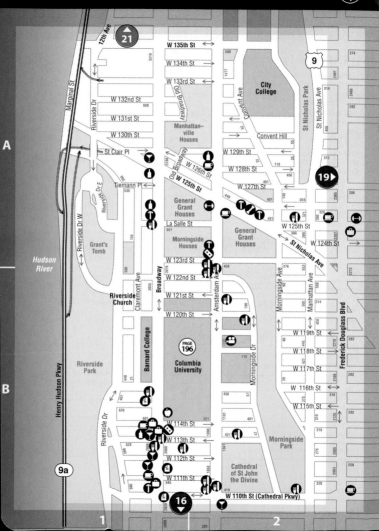

Many services can be found near Columbia University on Broadway. Labyrinth Books is a great place to blow some money. Columbia's plans to expand its campus north and westward towards the river will no doubt spur development of services. And community meetings. For some decent grub, check out Toast on Broadway.

Coffee

- **Dunkin' Donuts** • 1342 Amsterdam Ave
- **Dunkin' Donuts** • 321 W 125th St
- **Jimbo's Coffee Shop** • 1345 Amsterdam Ave
- **Oren's Daily Roast** • 2882 Broadway
- **Saurin Parke Café** • 301 W 110th St
- **Starbucks** • 2853 Broadway
- **Starbucks** • 2929 Broadway

Copy Shops

- **Broadway Copy Center** (9am-6pm) • 3062 Broadway
- **The UPS Store** (8am-7pm) • 603 W 115th St
- **The Village Copier** • 2872 Broadway

Farmer's Markets

- **Columbia** • Broadway b/w 114 & 115th Sts

Gyms

- **Dream Shape Xpress** • 251 W 125th St
- **Lucille Roberts Health Club** • 505 W 125th St

Hardware Stores

- **Academy Hardware & Supply** • 2869 Broadway
- **Clinton Supply** • 1256 Amsterdam Ave
- **Columbia Hardware** • 2905 Broadway
- **Philip Glick Supply** • 421 W 125th St
- **TriBoro Hardware** • 433 W 125th St

Liquor Stores

- **Amsterdam Liquor Mart** • 1356 Amsterdam Ave
- **Caro Wines & Liquor** • 3139 Broadway
- **International Wines and Spirits** • 2903 Broadway
- **Wine & Liquors Authority** • 574 W 125th St

Movie Theaters

- **Italian Academy** • 1161 Amsterdam Ave

Nightlife

- **1020 Bar** • 1020 Amsterdam Ave
- **Cotton Club** • 666 W 125th St
- **Heights Bar & Grill** • 2867 Broadway
- **Nacho Mama's Kitchen Bar** • 2893 Broadway
- **West End** • 2911 Broadway

Pet Shops

- **NYC Pet Place** • 431 W 125th St

Restaurants

- **Bistro Ten 18** • 1018 Amsterdam Ave
- **Hungarian Pastry Shop** • 1030 Amsterdam Ave
- **Kitchenette Uptown** • 1272 Amsterdam Ave
- **Le Monde** • 2885 Broadway
- **M&G Soul Food Diner** • 383 W 125th St
- **Massawa** • 1239 Amsterdam Ave
- **Max SoHa** • 1274 Amsterdam Ave
- **The Mill Korean Restaurant** • 2895 Broadway
- **Ollie's** • 2957 Broadway
- **Pisticci** • 125 La Salle St
- **Sezz Medi** • 1260 Amsterdam Ave
- **Symposium** • 544 W 113th St
- **Terrace in the Sky** • 400 W 119th St
- **Toast** • 3157 Broadway
- **V&T Pizzeria** • 1024 Amsterdam Ave

Shopping

- **JAS Mart** • 2847 Broadway
- **Kim's Mediapolis** • 2906 Broadway
- **Labyrinth Books** • 536 W 112th St
- **Mondel Chocolates** • 2913 Broadway

Video Rental

- **Blockbuster Video** • 1280 Amsterdam Ave
- **Kim's Mediapolis** • 2906 Broadway

Map 18 · **Columbia / Morningside Heights**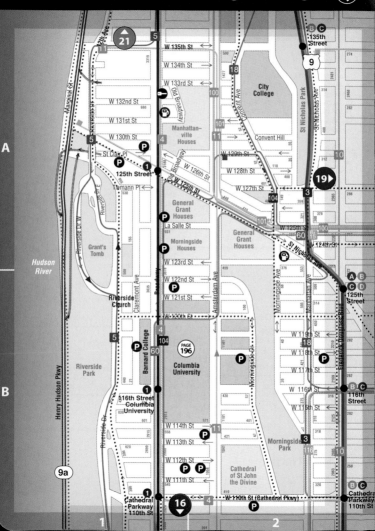

Driving and parking are both pretty decent around here, and the area is also served well by subway. We wish we could say that about the rest of the city. Riverside Drive is always a good alternative to the West Side Highway if the latter is jammed up.

Subways

1 .... 116th St Columbia University
1 .... 125th St
1 .... Cathedral Pkwy (110th St)
B C .... 135th St
A C B D .... 125th St

Bus Lines

100 .... 86th St Crosstown
101 .... 96th St Crosstown
104 .... 106th St Crosstown
11 .... Columbus Ave/Amsterdam Ave
18 .... Convent Ave
3 .... Fifth Ave/Madison Ave
4 .... Fifth Ave/Sixth Ave/Riverside Dr
5 .... Columbus Ave/Amsterdam Ave
15 .... 116th St Crosstown

Bike Lanes

- • • • Marked Bike Lanes
- • • • Recommended Route
- • • • Greenway

Car Rental

· **U-Haul** · 3270 Broadway

Gas Stations

· **Mobil** · 3260 Broadway
· **Sunoco** · 619 W 125th St

Parking

Map 19 · **Harlem (Lower)**

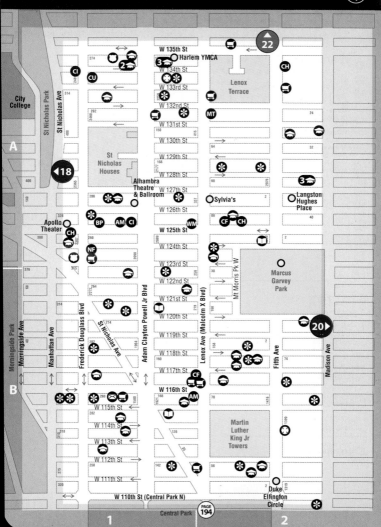

This neighborhood revolves around all the shops and services on 125th Street, which continues to attract big box retailers, banks, and other signs of mass consumer culture. This is also the location of the famous Apollo Theater. And don't forget to stop by and say hello to Mr. Clinton.

💲 Banks

BP · Banco Popular · 231 W 125th St
BA · Bank of America · 215 W 125th St
BA · Bank of America (ATM) · 102 W 116th St
CF · Carver Federal Savings · 142 Malcolm X Blvd
CF · Carver Federal Savings · 75 W 125th St
CH · Chase · 2218 Fifth Ave
CH · Chase · 322 W 125th St
CH · Chase · 55 W 125th St
CI · Citibank · 201 W 125th St
CI · Citibank · 2518 Frederick Douglass Blvd
MT · Manufacturers and Traders Trust · 420 Lenox Ave
CU · Municipal Credit Union (ATM) ·
  2518 Frederick Douglass Blvd
NF · North Fork · 2310 Frederick Douglass Blvd
WM · Washington Mutual · 105 W 125th St

❇️ Community Gardens

🔥 Fire Departments

· **Engine 58, Ladder 26** · 1367 Fifth Ave
· **Engine 59, Ladder 30** · 111 W 133rd St

🅾 Landmarks

· **Alhambra Theatre and Ballroom** ·
  2116 Adam Clayton Powell Jr Blvd
· **Apollo Theater** · 253 W 125th St
· **Duke Ellington Circle** · 110th St & Fifth Ave
· **Harlem YMCA** · 180 W 135th St
· **Langston Hughes Place** · 20 E 127th St
· **Marcus Garvey Park** · E 120-124th Sts & Madison Ave
· **Sylvia's** · 328 Lenox Ave

📖 Libraries

· **115th St (closed for renovation)** · 203 W 115th St
· **Harlem** · 115th St (temporary location)
· **Harlem** · 9 W 124th St

🚓 Police

· **28th Precinct** · 2271 Eighth Ave
· **32nd Precinct** · 250 W 135th St

✉️ Post Offices

· **Morningside** · 232 W 116th St

🎓 Schools

· **Center for Continuing Education** · 22 E 128th St
· **Christ Crusader Academy** · 302 W 124th St
· **College of New Rochelle Rosa Parks Campus** ·
  144 W 125th St
· **Eight Plus Academy** · 212 W 120th St
· **Fellowship Of Learning** · 70 W 126th St
· **Frederick Douglass Academy II** · 215 W 114th St
· **Harlem Children's Zone/Promise Academy Charter
  School M284** · 175 W 134th St
· **Harlem Renaissance High** · 22 E 128th St
· **Helene Fuld School of Nursing North** · 26 E 120th St
· **Henry Highland Garnet** · 175 W 134th St
· **IS 275** · 175 W 134th St
· **JA Reisenbach Charter (M701)** · 257 W 117th St
· **JHS 088 Wadleigh** · 215 W 114th St
· **Opportunity Charter** · 222 W 134th St
· **Pregnant and Parenting Students School** ·
  22 E 128th St
· **PS 076 A Philip Randolph** · 220 W 121st St
· **PS 092 Mary M Bethune Academy** · 222 W 134th St
· **PS 133 Fred R Moore** · 2121 Fifth Ave
· **PS 144 Hans C Anderson** · 134 W 122nd St
· **PS 149 Sojourner Truth** · 41 W 117th St
· **PS 154 Harriet Tubman** · 250 W 127th St
· **PS 162** · 34 W 118th St
· **PS 185 John M Langston** · 20 W 112th St
· **PS 208 Alain L Locke** · 21 W 111th St
· **PS 41 Family Academy** · 240 W 113th St
· **Rice High** · 74 W 124th St
· **Sister Clara Mohammed** · 102 W 116th St
· **Sisulu Children's Charter** · 125 W 115th St
· **St Aloysius** · 223 W 132nd St
· **Thurgood Marshall Academy** · 200 W 135th St
· **Wadleigh Arts High** · 215 W 114th St

🛒 Supermarkets

· **Associated** · 2170 Fifth Ave
· **Associated** · 2296 Eighth Ave
· **Associated** · 448 Lenox Ave
· **C-Town** · 2217 Adam Clayton Powell Jr Blvd
· **C-Town** · 24 W 135th St
· **Met Food** · 101 W 116th St
· **Met Food** · 238 W 116th St
· **Met Food** · 37 Lenox Ave
· **Pioneer** · 134 Lenox Ave

Map 19 • **Harlem (Lower)**

Sundries / Entertainment

The Magic Johnson Multiplex on 124th Street is a great thing for the neighborhood. Sylvia's really is as good as everyone says it is, but it's definitely not the only great place for food anymore. Look for the beginnings of revitalization/gentrification (depending on your politics) on Lenox Avenue near Marcus Garvey Park.

Coffee
- **Dunkin' Donuts** • 105 W 125th St
- **Dunkin' Donuts** • 53 W 116th St
- **Farafena Coffee Shop** • 219 W 116th St
- **Starbucks** • 77 W 125th St

Copy Shops
- **Harvest Information & Tech Center** (8:30am-5pm) • 2261 Adam Clayton Powell Jr Blvd
- **Staples** (7am-8pm) • 105 W 125th St
- **The UPS Store** (8:30am-7:30pm) • 55 W 116th St
- **The UPS Store** (8am-7:30pm) • 2216 Frederick Douglas Blvd

Gyms
- **Curves** • 2103 Frederick Douglass Blvd
- **Curves** • 6 E 126th St
- **Harlem World Sports Club** • 1400 Fifth Ave
- **New York Sports Clubs** • 2311 Frederick Douglass Blvd
- **YMCA Harlem** • 180 W 135th St

Hardware Stores
- **Citi General Hardware** • 100 St Nicholas Ave
- **Concordia Electrical & Plumbing** • 2297 Adam Clayton Powell Jr Blvd
- **Harlem Locksmith** • 106 Malcolm X Blvd
- **Manhattan Paint Fair** • 17 W 125th St

Liquor Stores
- **115th Street Liquor Store** • 5 E 115th St
- **312 Lenox Liquor Outlet** • 312 Malcolm X Blvd
- **458 Lenox Liquors** • 458 Lenox Ave
- **A&D Liquor** • 23 Lenox Ave
- **D&L Liquor** • 2178 Fifth Ave
- **Fred's Wine & Liquors** • 77 Lenox Ave
- **Grand Liquors** • 2049 Frederick Douglass Blvd
- **Harlem Retail Wine & Liquor** • 1902 Adam Clayton Powell Jr Blvd
- **Olympic Wine and Liquor** • 2391 Eighth Ave
- **Palace Liquors** • 2215 Adam Clayton Powell Jr Blvd

Movie Theaters
- **Magic Johnson Harlem USA** • 124th St & Frederick Douglass Blvd

Nightlife
- **Apollo Theatre** • 253 W 125th St
- **Lenox Lounge** • 288 Lenox Ave

Pet Shops
- **Petland Discounts** • 56 W 117th St

Restaurants
- **Amy Ruth's** • 113 W 116th St
- **Bayou** • 308 Lenox Ave
- **Home Sweet Harlem Café** • 270 W 135th St
- **Keur Sokhna** • 225 W 116th St
- **Manna's Too** • 486 Lenox Ave
- **Native** • 161 Lenox Ave
- **Papaya King** • 121 W 125th St
- **Slice of Harlem** • 308 Lenox Ave
- **Sylvia's** • 328 Lenox Ave
- **Yvonne Yvonne** • 301 W 135th St

Shopping
- **The Body Shop** • 1 E 125th St
- **Champs** • 208 W 125th St
- **Dr Jays Harlem NYC** • 256 125th St
- **H&M** • 125 W 125th St
- **Harlem Underground Clothing Co** • 2027 Fifth Ave
- **Harlemade** • 174 Lenox Ave
- **Jimmy Jazz** • 132 W 125th St
- **MAC Cosmetics** • 202 W 125th St
- **Malcolm Shabazz Harlem Market** • 58 W 116th St
- **Settepani** • 196 Lenox Ave
- **Studio Museum of Harlem Gift Shop** • 144 W 125th St
- **Wimp's Southern Style Bakery** • 29 W 125th St
- **Xukuma** • 183 Lenox Ave

Video Rental
- **Big Apple Video** • 1330 Fifth Ave
- **Blockbuster Video** • 121 W 125th St
- **Bus Stop Video** • 9 W 110th St

(125)

Map 19 • **Harlem (Lower)**

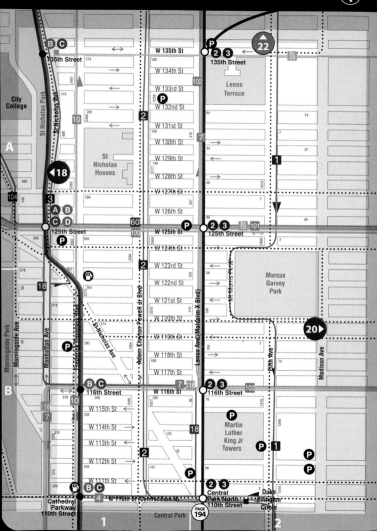

Driving across 110th Street should be good, but it's usually a pain. 116th Street is much better. Parking is pretty good, even on the major avenues. There's a bike lane on St. Nicholas Avenue.

Subways

②③ .... 116 St
②③ .... 125 St
②③ .... 135 St
②③ .... Central Park N (110 St)
ⒷⒸ .... 116 St
ⒷⒸ .... Cathedral Pkwy (110 St)

Bus Lines

1 .... Fifth Ave/Madison Ave
10 .... Seventh Ave/Eighth Ave/
                         Frederick Douglass Blvd
100 .... Amsterdam Ave/Broadway/125th St
101 .... Third Ave/Lexington Ave/Amsterdam Ave
102 .... Third Ave/Lexington Ave/Malcolm X Blvd
116 .... 116th St Crosstown
2 .... Fifth Ave/Madison Ave/Powell Blvd
4 .... Fifth Ave/Madison Ave/Broadway
60 .... LaGuardia Airport via 125th St
7 .... Columbus Ave/Amsterdam Ave/
            Lenox Ave/Sixth Ave/Seventh Ave/Broadway
Bx15 .... 125th St Crosstown
Bx33 .... 135th St Crosstown

Bike Lanes

- • • • Marked Bike Lanes
- • • • Recommended Route

🅿 Gas Stations

- **Exxon** • 2040 Frederick Douglass Blvd
- **Shell** • 235 St Nicholas Ave

Parking

Map 20 · El Barrio

Rich and vibrant in history and culture, exploring El Barrio is highly recommended. Both Marcus Garvey and Jefferson Parks are excellent places to take a break, too.

Banks

AP · Apple · 124 E 125th St
BP · Banco Popular · 164 E 116th St
BA · Bank of America · 157 E 125th St
BA · Bank of America (ATM) · 2250 Third Ave
CH · Chase · 160 E 125th St
CI · Citibank · 2261 First Ave

Community Gardens

Fire Departments

· **Engine 35, Ladder 14 ·** 2282 Third Ave
· **Engine 36 ·** 120 E 125th St
· **Engine 91 ·** 242 E 111th St

Hospitals

· **North General ·** 1879 Madison Ave

Landmarks

· **Church of Our Lady of Mt Carmel ·** 448 E 115th St
· **Harlem Courthouse ·** 170 E 121st St
· **Harlem Fire Watchtower ·** Marcus Garvey Park
· **Keith Haring "Crack is Wack" Mural ·** Second Ave & 127th St

Libraries

· **125th St ·** 224 E 125th St
· **Aguilar ·** 174 E 110th St

Police

· **25th Precinct ·** 120 E 119th St

Post Offices

· **Oscar Garcia Rivera ·** 153 E 110th St
· **Triborough ·** 167 E 124th St

Schools

· **Academy for Health/Sciences(M03T) ·** 2351 First Ave
· **All Saints ·** 52 E 130th St
· **Bilingual 45 RCBS (M055) ·** 2351 First Ave
· **Children's Storefront School ·** 70 E 129th St
· **The Choir Academy of Harlem ·** 2005 Madison Ave
· **East Harlem Tech (M02P) ·** 2351 First Ave
· **East Harlem Village Academy Charter (M709) ·** 413 E 120th St
· **Harlem Day Charter ·** 240 E 123rd St, 4th Fl
· **Highway Christian Academy ·** 132 E 111th St
· **Issac Newton JHS for Science & Math (M825) ·** 260 Pleasant Ave
· **JHS 045 J C Roberts ·** 2351 First Ave
· **Kappa II (M317) ·** 144 E 128th St
· **King's Academy ·** 2341 Third Ave
· **Manhattan Center for Science & Math ·** 260 Pleasant Ave
· **Mount Carmel-Holy Rosary ·** 371 Pleasant Ave
· **NY College of Podiatric Medicine ·** 1800 Park Ave
· **Our Lady Queen of Angels ·** 232 E 113th St
· **PS 007 Samuel Stern ·** 160 E 120th St
· **PS 057 James W Johnson ·** 176 E 115th St
· **PS 079 Horan ·** 55 E 120th St
· **PS 096 Joseph Lanzetta ·** 216 E 120th St
· **PS 101 Draper ·** 141 E 111th St
· **PS 102 Cartier ·** 315 E 113th St
· **PS 112 Jose Celso Barbasa ·** 535 E 119th St
· **PS 138 ·** 144 E 128th St
· **PS 155 William Paca ·** 319 E 117th St
· **PS 206 Jose Celso Babosa ·** 508 E 120th St
· **PS 30 Hernandez-Hughes Learning Academy ·** 144 E 128th St
· **River East (M037) ·** 260 Pleasant Ave
· **St Ann ·** 314 E 110th St
· **St Paul ·** 114 E 118th St
· **Urban Peace Academy (M695) ·** 2351 First Ave

Supermarkets

· **Associated ·** 125 E 116th St
· **Associated ·** 160 E 110th St
· **Associated ·** 2212 Third Ave
· **C-Town ·** 309 E 115th St
· **Pathmark ·** 160 E 125th St
· **Pioneer ·** 1666 Madison Ave

Map 20 · El Barrio

Patsy's Pizza really is the "original" New York thin-crust pizza, and Rao's is another New York landmark restaurant. El Barrio is also the unofficial "bakery" capital of New York.

Coffee

- **Dunkin' Donuts** · 1773 Lexington Ave
- **Dunkin' Donuts** · 255 E 125th St
- **The Harlem Tea Room** · 1793 Madison Ave
- **Juana's Luncheonette** · 242 E 116th St
- **Kahlua's Café** · 2117 Third Ave
- **Treichville** · 343 E 118 St

Farmer's Markets

- **La Marqueta** · E 115th St & Park Ave

Gyms

- **Curves** · 2246 First Ave

Hardware Stores

- **B&B Supply & Hardware** · 2338 Second Ave
- **N&J Locksmith & Hardware** · 1637 Park Ave
- **Novelle** · 218 E 125th St
- **SM Hardware** · 2139 Third Ave
- **Third Ave Home Center** · 2196 Third Ave

Liquor Stores

- **249 E 115th Liquor** · 249 E 115th St
- **Harlem Liquor World** · 63 E 125th St
- **IC Liquors** · 2255 First Ave
- **JM Liquor** · 1861 Lexington Ave
- **Lexington Wine and Liquor** · 2010 Lexington Ave
- **RA Landrau Liquors & Wines** · 2334 Second Ave
- **Ramos Liquor Store** · 1814 Madison Ave
- **Third Ave Liquors** · 2030 Third Ave

Pet Shops

- **Ideal Pet Warehouse** · 356 E 116th St
- **Petland Discounts** · 167 E 125th St

Restaurants

- **Camaradas** · 2241 First Ave
- **Creole Restaurant** · 2167 Third Ave
- **La Hacienda** · 219 E 116th St
- **Orbit East Harlem** · 2257 First Ave
- **Patsy's Pizza** · 2287 First Ave
- **Rao's** · 455 E 114th St
- **Sandy's Restaurant** · 2261 Second Ave

Shopping

- **Capri Bakery** · 186 E 116th St
- **Casa Latina** · 151 E 116th St
- **The Children's Place** · 163 E 125th St
- **Don Paco Lopez Panaderia** · 2129 Third Ave
- **Gothic Cabinet Craft** · 2268 Third Ave
- **La Marqueta** · Park Ave & 114th St
- **Mexico Lindo Bakery** · 2267 Second Ave
- **Morrone Bakery** · 324 E 116th St
- **Motherhood Maternity** · 163 E 125th St
- **Payless Shoe Source** · 2143 Third Ave
- **R&S Strauss Auto** · 2005 Third Ave
- **VIM** · 2239 Third Ave

Video Rental

- **First Run Video** · 1147 1/2 Second Ave

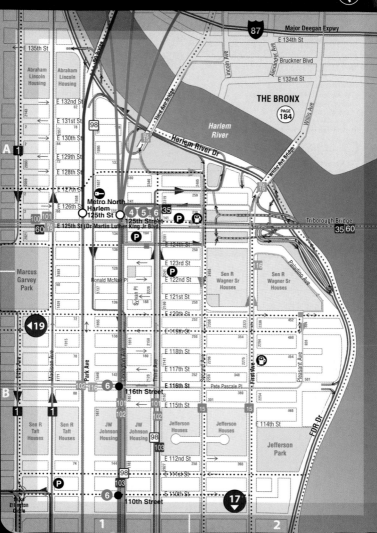

Map 20 · **El Barrio**

The best route to the Triborough is to go up Third Avenue and make a right on 124th Street, especially when the FDR is jammed. We feel for the folks who live over on Pleasant Avenue and have to hike five miles to the nearest subway (or worse yet, wait for the bus).

Subways

6 .... 110 St
6 .... 116 St
4 5 6 .... 125 St

Bus Lines

1 .... Fifth/Madison Aves
101 ..... Third Ave/Lexington Ave/Amsterdam Ave
102 ..... Third Ave/Lexington Ave/Malcolm X Blvd
103 .... Third/Lexington Aves
116 .... 116th St Crosstown
15 .... First Ave/Second Ave
35 .... Randall's Island/Ward Island
60 .... LaGuardia Airport
98 .... Washington Heights/Midtown
Bx 15 .... 125th St Crosstown

Bike Lanes

- • • Marked Bike Lanes
- • • Recommended Route
- • • Greenway

Car Rental

• **A-Value Rent-A-Car** • 1851 Park Ave

Gas Stations

• **Amoco** • 125th St & Second Ave
• **Amoco** • 2276 First Ave

Parking

Map 21 • **Manhattanville / Hamilton Heights**

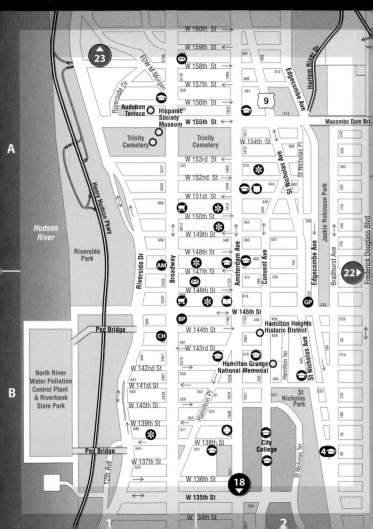

This neighborhood is quite varied, both in its extremely hilly topography and in the side-by-side existence of run-down areas with overlooked Manhattan landmarks such as Trinity Cemetery, Audubon Terrace, and Sugar Hill. Convent Avenue and Hamilton Terrace are two of the prettiest streets in Manhattan.

$ Banks

BP · Banco Popular · 3540 Broadway
BA · Bank of America (ATM) · 3579B Broadway
CH · Chase · 3515 Broadway
GP · Greenpoint Bank · 700 St Nicholas Ave

Community Gardens

Fire Departments

· **Engine 80, Ladder 23** · 503 W 139th St

Landmarks

· **Audubon Terrace** · Broadway & W 155th St
· **Hamilton Grange National Memorial** · 287 Convent Ave
· **Hamilton Heights Historic District** · W 141st-W 145th Sts & Convent Ave
· **Hispanic Society Museum** · 613 W 155th St & Broadway
· **Trinity Church Cemetery's Graveyard of Heroes** · 3699 Broadway

Libraries

· **Hamilton Grange** · 503 W 145th St

Police

· **30th Precinct** · 451 W 151st St

Post Offices

· **Fort Washington** · 556 W 158th St
· **Hamilton Grange** · 521 W 146th St

Schools

· **Boricua College** · 3755 Broadway
· **Childs' Memorial Christian Academy** · 1763 Amsterdam Ave
· **Dance Theatre of Harlem** · 466 W 152nd St
· **Harlem School of the Arts** · 645 St Nicholas Ave
· **HS 685 Bread & Roses Integrated Arts High** · 6 Edgecombe Ave
· **HS for Math, Science & Engineering @ CCNY (M692)** · 138th St & Convent Ave
· **Kappa IV (M302)** · 6 Edgecombe Ave
· **Manhattan Theatre Lab (M283)** · 6 Edgecombe Ave
· **The Moore Learning Center** · 614 W 157 St
· **Mott Hall High (M304)** · 6 Edgecombe Ave
· **Our Lady of Lourdes** · 468 W 143rd St
· **PS 028 Wright Brothers** · 475 W 155th St
· **PS 153 Adam C Powell** · 1750 Amsterdam Ave
· **PS 192 Jacob H Schiff** · 500 W 138th St
· **Thurgood Marshall Academy** · 6 Edgecombe Ave

Supermarkets

· **C-Town** · 3550 Broadway
· **C-Town** · 3632 Broadway

Map 21 · **Manhattanville / Hamilton Heights**

New construction along 145th Street is certainly sending the message that this neighborhood is on the cusp of big changes. Expect the retail along 145th to turn over accordingly. For live music and drinks, it's St. Nick's Pub or bust.

Coffee

- **Astron Coffee Shop** · 3795 Broadway
- **Coffee Shop** · 398 W 145th St
- **Dunkin' Donuts** · 3455 Broadway

Gyms

- **NYC Fitness** · 3552 Broadway

Hardware Stores

- **Cohen & Cohen** · 1982 Amsterdam Ave
- **Felix Supply** · 3650 Broadway
- **O&J Hardware** · 3405 Broadway
- **Westside Home Center** · 3447 Broadway

Liquor Stores

- **2001 Liquor** · 3671 Broadway
- **Brand's Liquor** · 550 W 145th St
- **JOCL Liquor Store** · 561 W 147th St
- **Jumasol Liquors** · 1963 Amsterdam Ave
- **La Alta Gracia Liquor Store** · 3435 Broadway
- **Reliable Wine & Liquor Shop** · 3375 Broadway
- **Unity Liquors** · 708 St Nicholas Ave

Nightlife

- **St Nick's Pub** · 773 St Nicholas Ave

Restaurants

- **Copeland's** · 547 W 145th St
- **Devin's Fish and Chips** · 747 St Nicholas Ave

Shopping

- **Foot Locker** · 3549 Broadway
- **VIM** · 508 W 145th St

Video Rental

- **Santos Variety** · 3766 Broadway

Map 21 • **Manhattanville / Hamilton Heights**

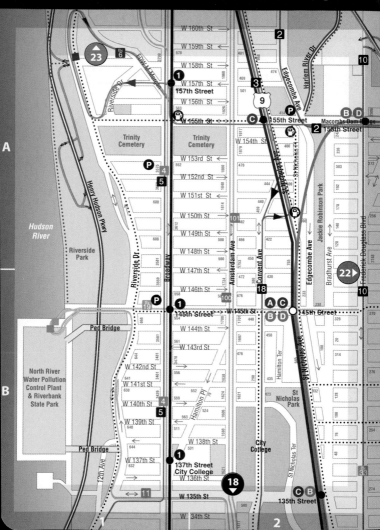

Despite the fact that the signs outside the 135th and 155th Street stations list the A and C trains, the A train stops at them only during late nights, when it runs local. Riverside Drive can be an intriguing alternative to traffic during rush hour as one moves closer to the George Washington Bridge.

Subways

1	....	137 St-City College
1	....	145 St
1	....	157 St
A **C** **B** **D**	....	145 St
C	....	155 St

Bus Lines

100	....	Amsterdam Ave/Broadway/125th St
101	..	Third Ave/Lexington Ave/Broadway/125th St
11	....	Ninth (Columbus)/Tenth (Amsterdam Ave)/Convent Ave
18	....	Convent Ave
2	....	Fifth Ave/Madison Ave/Powell Blvd
3	......	Fifth Ave/Madison Ave/St Nicholas Blvd
4	....	Fifth Ave/Madison Ave/Broadway
5	....	Fifth Ave/Sixth Ave/Riverside Dr
Bx 19	....	145th St Crosstown
Bx 6	....	E 161st St/E 163rd St

Bike Lanes

- • • • Marked Bike Lanes
- • • • Recommended Route
- • • • Greenway

Gas Stations

- **Getty** • 155 St Nicholas Pl
- **Mobil** • 3740 Broadway
- **Mobil** • 800 St Nicholas Ave

Parking

Map 22 · **Harlem (Upper)**

This part of New York remains troubled, but it does boast a number of historic buildings such as the Dunbar Houses, Striver's Row, and many other notable Harlem Renaissance locales. As much as people who live in the Polo Grounds Houses need housing, we really wish the Polo Grounds itself was still there.

$ Banks

CI · **Citibank** · 2481 Adam Clayton Powell Jr Blvd
CU · **Municipal Credit Union (ATM)** ·
  506 Lenox Ave

✳ Community Gardens

✪ Fire Departments

· **Engine 69, Ladder 28** · 248 W 143rd St

➕ Hospitals

· **Harlem Hospital Center** · 506 Lenox Ave

O Landmarks

· **The 369th Regiment Armory** · 2366 Fifth Ave
· **Abyssinian Baptist Church** · 132 Odell Clark Pl
· **The Dunbar Houses** · Frederick Douglass Blvd &
  W 149th St
· **St Nicholas Historic District** · 202 W 138th St

📖 Libraries

· **Countee Cullen** · 104 W 136th St
· **Macomb's Bridge** ·
  2650 Adam Clayton Powell Jr Blvd
· **Schomburg Center for Research in Black Culture** ·
  515 Malcolm X Blvd

✉ Post Offices

· **College Station** · 217 W 140th St
· **Colonial Park** · 99 Macombs Pl
· **Lincolnton** · 2266 Fifth Ave

🏫 Schools

· **Frederick Douglass Secondary School** ·
  2581 Seventh Ave
· **PS 046 Tappan** · 2987 Frederick Douglass Blvd
· **PS 123 Mahalia Jackson** · 301 W 140th St
· **PS 194 Countee Cullen** · 244 W 144th St
· **PS 197 John Russwurm** · 2230 Fifth Ave
· **PS 200 James Smith** · 2589 Seventh Ave
· **Resurrection School** · 282 W 151st St
· **St Charles Borromeo** · 214 W 142nd St
· **St Mark the Evangelist** · 55 W 138th St

🛒 Supermarkets

· **Associated** · 2927 Eighth Ave
· **Met Food** · 2541 Adam Clayton Powell Jr Blvd
· **Met Food** · 592 Lenox Ave
· **Pathmark** · 300 W 145th St
· **Pioneer** · 2497 Adam Clayton Powell Jr Blvd

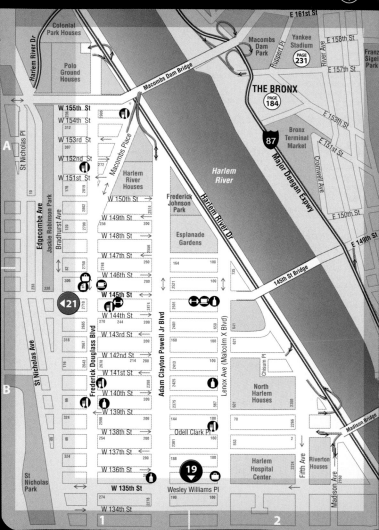

Map 22 · **Harlem (Upper)**

Charles' Southern-Style Chicken doesn't look very impressive, but the fried chicken is better, and way cheaper, than any 10 downtown faux-southern hipster restaurants. For a classic Italian throwback, hit the oddly-named Flash Inn, which sounds more like a strip club in LA. (It was named after a race horse back in the '30s.)

Coffee

- **Dunkin' Donuts** · 110 W 145th St
- **Dunkin' Donuts** · 2730 Frederick Douglass Blvd

Copy Shops

- **Kev's Copy Center** (8:30am-8pm) ·
  2730 Eighth Ave

Gyms

- **Curves** · 274 W 145th St
- **Serge Gym** · 104 W 145th St

Liquor Stores

- **All-Rite Liquors** · 2651 Frederick Douglass Blvd
- **Friedland Wine & Liquor Store** · 605 Lenox Ave
- **Harlem Discount Liquors** ·
  2302 Adam Clayton Powell Jr Blvd
- **Luis Liquor** · 108 W 145th St

Restaurants

- **Charles' Southern-Style Chicken** ·
  2841 Eighth Ave
- **Flash Inn** · 107 Macombs Pl
- **Londel's Supper Club** ·
  2620 Frederick Douglass Blvd
- **Margie's Red Rose** · 267 W 144th St
- **Miss Maude's** · 547 Lenox Ave
- **Sugar Shack** · 2611 Frederick Douglass Blvd

Shopping

- **Baskin-Robbins** · 2730 Frederick Douglass Blvd
- **New York Public Library Shop** ·
  515 Malcolm X Blvd, Schomburg Ctr

Map 22 • **Harlem (Upper)**

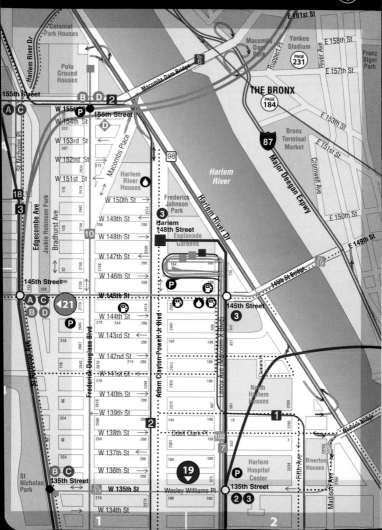

If the FDR Drive is jammed, feel free to drive up Frederick Douglass Boulevard, grab some fried chicken, and jump back on the FDR at 155th Street before heading out to the shopping paradise that is New Jersey.

Subways

3 .... 145 St
3 .... Harlem-148 St
B D .... 155 St

Bus Lines

1 .... Fifth Ave/Madison Ave
10 .... Seventh Ave/Eighth Ave
(Central Park West)/Frederick Douglass Blvd
102 ..... Third Ave/Lexington Ave/Malcolm X Blvd
2 .... Fifth Ave/Madison Ave/Powell Blvd
7 .... Columbus Ave/Amsterdam Ave/
Sixth Ave/Seventh Ave/Broadway
98 .... Washington Heights/Midtown
Bx 19 .... 145th St Crosstown
Bx 33 .... 135th St Crosstown
Bx 6 .... E 161st St/E 163rd St

Bike Lanes

- • • • Marked Bike Lanes
- • • • Recommended Route
- • • • Greenway

Car Washes

- **Harlem Hand Car Wash** • 2600 Adam Clayton
  Powell Jr Blvd
- **Los Amigos** • 119 W 145th St

Gas Stations

- **Amoco** • 232 W 145th St
- **Getty** • 119 W 145th St
- **Hess** • 128 W 145th St
- **Mobil** • 150 W 145th St

Parking

Map 23 • **Washington Heights**

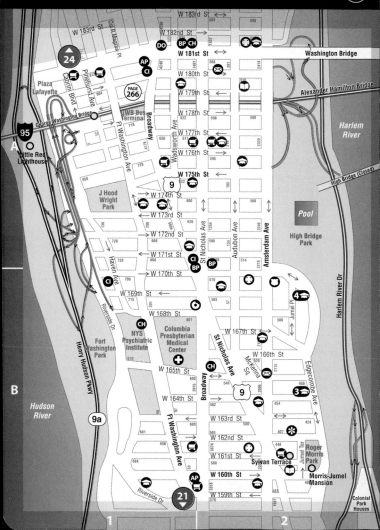

One of New York's more notorious neighborhoods of the last 20 years, Washington Heights has improved quite a bit since its days as the one-stop drug shop for Jersey, though it still has some problems. Sylvan Terrace is the most un-Manhattan-looking place in Manhattan—it's way cool.

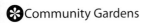 Bagels

• **Mike's Bagels** • 4005 Broadway

Banks

AP • Apple • 3815 Broadway
AP • Apple • 706 W 181st St
BP • Banco Popular • 1200 St Nicholas Ave
BP • Banco Popular • 4043 Broadway
BP • Banco Popular • 615 W 181st St
CH • Chase • 1421 St Nicholas Ave
CH • Chase • 180 Ft Washington Ave
CH • Chase • 3940 Broadway
CI • Citibank • 4249 Broadway
CI • Citibank (ATM) • 4058 Broadway
CI • Citibank (ATM) • 60 Haven Ave
DO • Doral Bank • 4246 Broadway

Community Gardens

Fire Departments

• **Engine 67** • 518 W 170th St
• **Engine 84, Ladder 34** • 515 W 161st St
• **Engine 93, Ladder 45** • 515 W 181st St

Hospitals

• **Columbia-Presbyterian Medical Center** •
622 W 168th St

Landmarks

• **George Washington Bridge** • W 178th St
• **Little Red Lighthouse** •
under the George Washington Bridge
• **Morris-Jumel Mansion** • Edgecombe Ave &
161st St
• **Sylvan Terrace** • b/w Jumel Ter & St Nicholas Ave

Libraries

• **Fort Washington** • 535 W 179th St
• **Washington Heights** • 1000 St Nicholas Ave

Police

• **33rd Precinct** • 2207 Amsterdam Ave

Post Offices

• **Audubon** • 511 W 165th St
• **Washington Bridge** • 555 W 180th St

Schools

• **HS 552 Gregorio Luperon** • 516 W 181st St
• **Incarnation Elementary** • 570 W 175th St
• **Interboro** • 206 Audubon Ave
• **IS 164 Edward W Stitt** • 401 W 164th St
• **Mirabel Sisters IS 90** • 21 Jumel Pl
• **The Modern School** • 870 Riverside Dr
• **MS 319 Minerva** • 21 Jumel Pl
• **MS 321 Maria Teresa** • 21 Jumel Pl
• **Patria (MS 324)** • 21 Jumel Pl
• **PS 004 Duke Ellington** • 500 W 160th St
• **PS 008 Luis Belliard** • 465 W 167th St
• **PS 115 Humboldt** • 586 W 177th St
• **PS 128 Audubon** • 560 W 169th St
• **PS 173** • 306 Ft Washington Ave
• **PS 210 21st Century Academy** • 4111 Broadway
• **St Rose of Lima** • 517 W 164th St
• **St Spyridon Parochial School** •
120 Wadsworth Ave

Supermarkets

• **Associated** • 3871 Broadway
• **Bravo Supermarket** • 1331 St Nicholas Ave
• **C-Town** • 1016 St Nicholas Ave
• **C-Town** • 1314 St Nicholas Ave
• **Gristede's** • 4037 Broadway
• **Jins Superette** • 804 W 181st St
• **Karrot Cabrini** • 854 W 181st St
• **Super Extra** • 3835 Broadway

Map 23 • **Washington Heights**

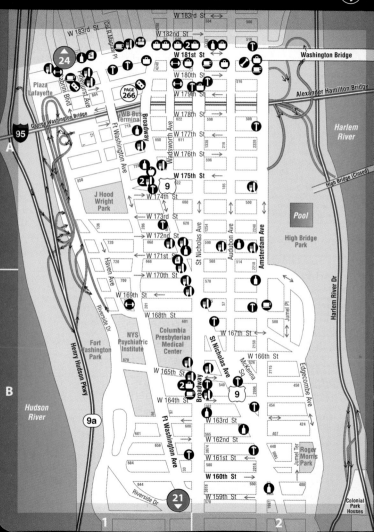

Check out Hispaniola for excellent food and bridge views, but you'll have to move slightly further uptown or slightly further downtown for much else in the way of excellence. Most of the entertainment here comes from watching the always-percolating street life.

Coffee

- **Chris Coffee Shop** · 500 W 168th St
- **Dunkin' Donuts** · 1416 St Nicholas Ave
- **Dunkin' Donuts** · 2420 Amsterdam Ave
- **Dunkin' Donuts** · 728 W 181st St
- **Hathie's Coffee Shop** · 3915 Broadway
- **Starbucks** · 803 W 181st St
- **X Caffe** · 3952 Broadway

Copy Shops

- **The UPS Store** (8:30-7) · 809 W 181st St
- **The UPS Store** (8:30am-7pm) · 4049 Broadway

Farmer's Markets

- **175th Street** · W 175th St & Broadway

Gyms

- **Big Gym** · 625 W 181st St
- **Curves** · 216 Ft Washington Ave
- **Curves** · 854 W 181st St
- **Lucille Roberts Health Club** · 1387 St Nicholas Ave

Hardware Stores

- **3841 Hardware** · 3841 Broadway
- **756 Hardware** · 756 W 181st St
- **AT Mini Hardware** · 1388 St Nicholas Ave
- **AHS Hardware** · 2416 Amsterdam Ave
- **Blue Bell Lumber** · 2360 Amsterdam Ave
- **Chavin Hardware** · 1348 St Nicholas Ave
- **Cibao Hardware** · 1045 St Nicholas Ave
- **E&T Hardware** · 4087 Broadway
- **Ernesto's Hardware Store** · 2180 Amsterdam Ave
- **EZ Open Hardware** · 2304 Amsterdam Ave
- **Ferreteria Hardware** · 1087 St Nicholas Ave
- **Fort Washington Hardware** · 3918 Broadway
- **Nunez Hardware** · 4147 Broadway
- **Taveras Hardware** · 2029 Amsterdam Ave
- **Washington Heights Hardware** · 736 W 181st St

Liquor Stores

- **All-Star Spirits** · 4189 Broadway
- **Cabrina Wines & Liquors** · 831 W 181st St
- **Galicia Liquors** · 3906 Broadway
- **Guadalupe Barbara** · 4084 Broadway
- **Heights Liquor Supermarket** · 547 W 181st St
- **In Good Spirits** · 3819 Broadway
- **McLiquor Store** · 2208 Amsterdam Ave
- **Mora Liquor** · 2001 Amsterdam Ave
- **O&J Liquors** · 1045 St Nicholas Ave
- **Vargas Liquor Store** · 114 Audubon Ave

Movie Theaters

- **New Coliseum Theatre** · 703 W 181st St

Pet Shops

- **Pet Place** · 518 W 181st St

Restaurants

- **Aqua Marina** · 4060 Broadway
- **Bohio** · 4055 Broadway
- **Carrot Top Pastries** · 3931 Broadway
- **Coogan's** · 4015 Broadway
- **Dallas BBQ** · 3956 Broadway
- **El Conde Steak House** · 4139 Broadway
- **El Malecon** · 4141 Broadway
- **El Ranchito** · 4129 Broadway
- **Empire Szechuan** · 4041 Broadway
- **Hispaniola** · 839 W 181st St
- **International Food House** · 4073 Broadway
- **Jessie's Place** · 812 W 181st St
- **Jimmy Oro Restaurant** · 711 W 181st St
- **Malibu Restaurant** · 1091 St Nicholas Ave
- **Parrilla** · 3920 Broadway
- **Reme Restaurant** · 4021 Broadway
- **Restaurant Tenares** · 2306 Amsterdam Ave
- **Taino Restaurant** · 2228 Amsterdam Ave
- **Tipico Dominicano** · 4172 Broadway
- **Tu Sonrisa** · 132 Audubon Ave

Shopping

- **Baskin-Robbins** · 728 W 181st St
- **Carrot Top Pastries** · 3931 Broadway
- **The Children's Place** · 600 W 181st St
- **Fever** · 1387 St Nicholas Ave
- **FootCo** · 599 W 181st St
- **Footlocker** · 621 W 181st St
- **Goodwill Industries** · 512 W 181st St
- **Modell's** · 606 W 181st St
- **Payless Shoe Source** · 617 W 181st St
- **Planet Girls** · 3923 Broadway
- **Range** · 659 W 181st St
- **Santana Banana** · 661 W 181st St
- **Tribeca** · 655 W 181st St
- **VIM** · 561 W 181st St

Video Rental

- **Blockbuster Video** · 4211 Broadway
- **Kappy's Record & Video World** · 91 Pinehurst Ave

Map 23 • **Washington Heights**

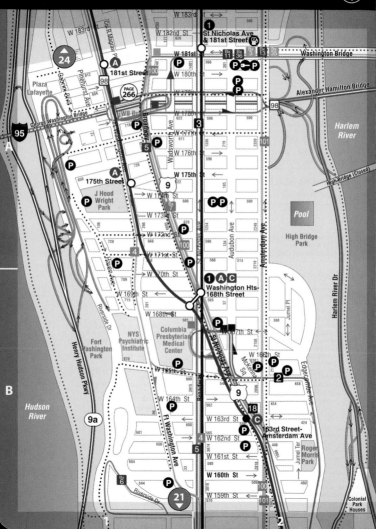

Pay close attention when you cross over into Manhattan from New Jersey on the George Washington Bridge, because if you miss the "Harlem River Drive–Last Exit in Manhattan" exit, you'll be crossing over into the Bronx and sitting in traffic on what is categorically the most miserable highway in all the world, the Cross Bronx Expressway.

Subways

1	.... 181 St
A	.... 175 St
A	.... 181 St
1 **A** **C**	.... 168 St-Washington Hts
C	.... 163 St-Amsterdam Ave

Bus Lines

100	.... Amsterdam Ave/Broadway/125th St
101	.... Third and Lexington Aves/Malcolm X Blvd
18	.... Convent Ave
2	.... Fifth and Madison Aves/ Adam Clayton Powell Jr Blvd
3	...... Fifth and Madison Aves/St Nicholas Ave
4	.... Fifth and Madison Aves/Broadway
5	.... Fifth Ave/Sixth Ave/Riverside Dr
98	.... Washington Heights/Midtown
Bx 11	.... to Southern Blvd via 170th St
Bx 13	.... to Yankee Stadium via Ogden Ave
Bx 3	.... to Riverdale, 238th St-Broadway
Bx 35	.... to West Farms Rd via 167th St
Bx 36	..... to Olmstead Ave/Randall Ave via 180th St
Bx 7	.... Riverdale Ave/Broadway

Bike Lanes

- • • • Marked Bike Lanes
- • • • Recommended Route
- • • • Greenway

Car Rental

- **Uptown Car Rental** • 506 W 181st St

Gas Stations

- **Shell** • 2420 Amsterdam Ave

Parking

Map 24 · **Fort George / Fort Tryon**

You'll get a workout walking up and down all the hills and stairs in this neighborhood. Fort Tryon Park, including the Cloisters Museum, is a treasure that allows visitors to gaze over the Hudson and go for a hike right in the city. ATM coverage is pretty much confined to bodegas.

$ Banks

CH · Chase · 596 Ft Washington Ave

✳ Community Gardens

O Landmarks

· **Fort Tryon Park** · Ft Washington Ave
· **Yeshiva University Main Building (Zysman Hall)** ·
  Amsterdam Ave & W 187th St

🚔 Police

· **34th Precinct** · 4295 Broadway

✉ Post Offices

· **Fort George** · 4558 Broadway

🎓 Schools

· **Academic Universe** · 93 Nagle Ave
· **Business & Finance High** · 549 Audubon Ave
· **Health Careers & Sciences High** ·
  549 Audubon Ave
· **IS 143 Eleanor Roosevelt** · 511 W 182nd St
· **IS 218 Salome Ukena** · 4600 Broadway
· **Law & Public Service High** · 549 Audubon Ave
· **Media & Communications High** ·
  549 Audubon Ave
· **Mesivta Rabbi Samson Raphael** · 8593 Bennet Ave
· **Mother Cabrini High** · 701 Ft Washington Ave
· **Our Lady Queen of Martyrs** · 71 Arden St
· **Prof Juan Boch Public School** · 12 Ellwood St
· **PS 005 Ellen Lurie** · 3703 Tenth Ave
· **PS 048 Officer Buczek** · 4360 Broadway
· **PS 132 Juan Pablo Duarte** · 185 Wadsworth Ave
· **PS 152 Dyckman Valley** · 93 Nagle Ave
· **PS 187/IS 287 Hudson Cliffs** · 349 Cabrini Blvd
· **PS 189** · 2580 Amsterdam Ave
· **PS 528 Bea Fuller Rodgers** · 180 Wadsworth Ave
· **Shabak Christian** · 362 Audubon Ave
· **St Elizabeth School** · 612 W 187th St
· **Yeshiva University** · 500 W 185th St
· **Yeshiva University High** · 2540 Amsterdam Ave

🛒 Supermarkets

· **Associated** · 592 Ft Washington Ave
· **Frank's Meat Market** · 707 W 187th St
· **Key Food** · 4365 Broadway
· **Pioneer** · 72 Nagle Ave

Map 24 • **Fort George / Fort Tryon**

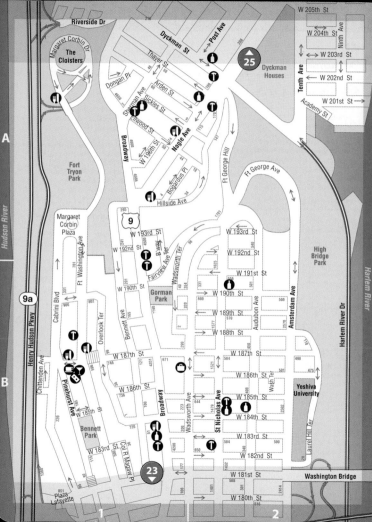

Anyone who says northern Manhattan has nothing cool to do hasn't been here. Lots of small independent restaurants combine downtown ambience with small-town feel and uptown prices—check out Bleu Evolution and the rest of W 187th Street near Ft Washington.

Coffee

- **Angela's Coffee Shop** · 805 W 187th St

Hardware Stores

- **Apex Supply** · 4580 Broadway
- **Castillo Hardware** · 1449 St Nicholas Ave
- **Century Hardware** · 4309 Broadway
- **Geomart Hardware** · 607 Ft Washington Ave
- **Nagle Hardware Store** · 145 Nagle Ave
- **St Nicholas Hardware** · 1488 St Nicholas Ave
- **Supreme Hardware** · 106 Dyckman St
- **Victor Hardware Store** · 25 Sherman Ave
- **VNJ Hardware** · 4476 Broadway

Liquor Stores

- **185 Street Liquor Store** · 4329 Broadway
- **Alex's Liquor Store** · 1598 St Nicholas Ave
- **Dyckman Liquors** · 121 Dyckman St
- **J&P Discount Liquors** · 377 Audubon Ave
- **Las Vegas Wine & Liquor** · 154 Nagle Ave
- **Sherman Liquor** · 25 Sherman Ave
- **Yuan & Yuan Wine & Liquors** ·
  1492 St Nicholas Ave

Nightlife

- **The Monkey Room** · 589 Ft Washington Ave

Restaurants

- **107 West** · 811 W 187th St
- **Bleu Evolution** · 808 W 187th St
- **Caridad Restaurant** · 4311 Broadway
- **Frank's Pizzeria** · 94 Nagle Ave
- **New Leaf Café** · 1 Margaret Corbin Dr
- **Rancho Jubilee** · 1 Nagle Ave

Video Rental

- **Ft Washington Video** · 805 W 187th St

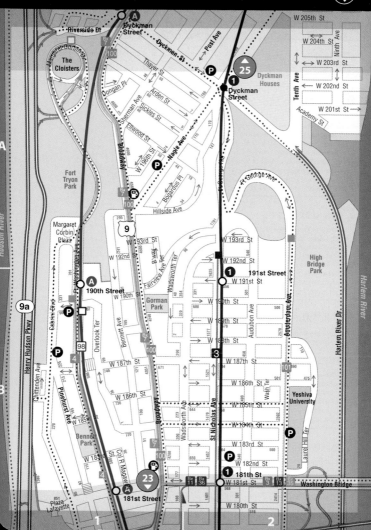

Map 24 • Fort George / Fort Tryon

Living on the A line is a blessing before 11 pm, when it runs express, but beware at night when you'll have to sit through every stop between 59th and 125th and beyond. Tight streets, double parking, and bad drivers always makes driving in this area "interesting".

Subways

1	.... Dyckman St
1	.... 191 St
A	.... 190 St

Bus Lines

100	.... Broadway
100	.... Amsterdam Ave
3	.... St Nicholas Ave
4	.... Ft Washington Ave
98	.... Ft Washington Ave
Bx 7	.... Broadway

Bike Lanes

- • • • Marked Bike Lanes
- • • • Recommended Route
- • • • Greenway

Gas Stations

· **Rammco Service Station** · 4275 Broadway

Parking

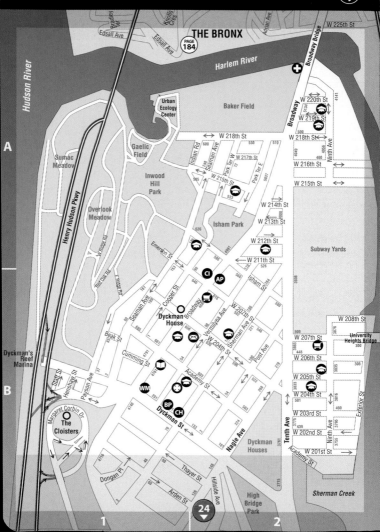

Map 25 • Inwood

Inwood is definitely Manhattan's best-kept housing secret—the houses along Payson Avenue and Seaman Avenue are very nice. Inwood Hill Park is a shady, overgrown, semi-wild park with a killer view of the Cloisters and Fort Tryon Park. Inwood also contains one of Manhattan's oldest buildings, the Dyckman House (it looks it!).

$ Banks

AP · Apple · 4950 Broadway
BP · Banco Popular · 175 Dyckman St
CH · Chase · 161 Dyckman St
CI · Citibank · 4949 Broadway
WM · Washington Mutual ·
    211 Dyckman St

Fire Departments

· **Engine 95, Ladder 36 ·** 29 Vermilyea Ave

+ Hospitals

· **Columbia-Presbyterian Allen Pavilion ·**
    5141 Broadway

O Landmarks

· **The Cloisters ·** Ft Tryon Park
· **Dyckman House ·** 4881 Broadway

Libraries

· **Inwood ·** 4790 Broadway

Post Offices

· **Inwood Post Office ·** 90 Vermilyea Ave

Schools

· **Good Shepherd ·** 620 Isham St
· **IS 052 Inwood ·** 650 Academy St
· **Manhattan Christian Academy ·** 401 W 205th St
· **Northeastern Academy ·** 532 W 215th St
· **PS 018 ·** 4124 Ninth Ave
· **PS 098 Shorac Kappock ·** 512 W 212nd St
· **PS 176 ·** 4862 Broadway
· **PS/IS 278 (M278) ·** 407 W 219th St
· **St Jude ·** 433 W 204th St
· **St Matthew Lutheran ·** 200 Sherman Ave

Supermarkets

· **C-Town ·** 4918 Broadway
· **Pathmark ·** 410 W 207th St

Map 25 • Inwood

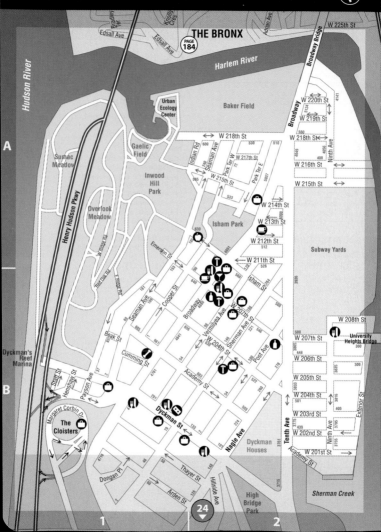

Sundries / Entertainment

Even though more people are moving to Inwood, it's still only about 3.3 on our Gentrification Scale. Check out Bobby's for fresh seafood.

Coffee

- **Dunkin' Donuts** · 4932 Broadway
- **JCT Coffee Shop** · 5009 Broadway

Farmer's Markets

- **Inwood** · Isham St b/w Seaman Ave & Cooper St

Hardware Stores

- **Dick's Hardware** · 4947 Broadway
- **Inwood Paint & Hardware** · 165 Sherman Ave
- **J&A Hardware** · 132 Vermilyea Ave

Liquor Stores

- **PJ Liquor Warehouse** · 4898 Broadway
- **Q Royal** · 529 W 207th St

Nightlife

- **Piper's Kilt** · 4944 Broadway

Pet Shops

- **Pic-A-Pet** · 4791 Broadway

Restaurants

- **Bobby's Fish and Seafood Market and Restaurant** · 3842 Ninth Ave
- **Capitol Restaurant** · 4933 Broadway
- **Cloisters Restaurant Pizza** · 4754 Broadway
- **DR-K** · 114 Dyckman St
- **Hoppin' Jalapenos Bar & Grill** · 597 W 207th St
- **Mirage Restaurant** · 185 Dyckman St

Shopping

- **Carrot Top Pastries** · 5025 Broadway
- **The Cloisters** · Ft Tryon Park
- **Foot Locker** · 146 Dyckman St
- **K&R Florist** · 4955 Broadway
- **Payless Shoe Source** · 560 W 207th St
- **Radio Shack** · 180 Dyckman St
- **Radio Shack** · 576 W 207th St
- **Tread Bicycles** · 225 Dyckman St
- **VIM** · 565 W 207th St

Video Rental

- **Blockbuster Video** · 165 Dyckman St

Map 25 • **Inwood**

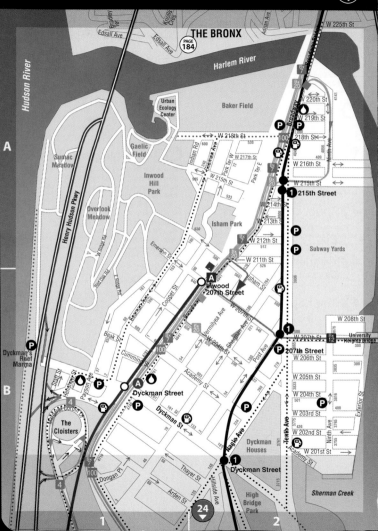

The stupid toll plaza at the tip of the Henry Hudson is only one of many reasons why driving in New York is nothing short of a nightmare. You might as well be getting your car washed at one of Inwood's many fine establishments. Parking is usually not too much of a problem, even close to Inwood Hill Park.

Subways

1 .... 215 St
1 .... 207 St
A .... Dyckman St
A .... Inwood-207 St

Bus Lines

100 .... Amsterdam Ave/Broadway/125th St
4 .... Fifth/Madison Aves/Broadway
Bx 12 .... Riverdale/263rd St via Riverdale Ave
Bx 20 ..... Riverdale/246th St via Henry Hudson Pky
Bx 7 .... Riverdale Ave/Broadway

Bike Lanes

- • • • Marked Bike Lanes
- • • • Recommended Route
- • • • Greenway

Car Washes

- **Broadway Bridge Car Wash** • 5134 Broadway
- **Broadway Hand Car Wash** • 4778 Broadway
- **Dyckman Car Wash** • 284 Dyckman St

Gas Stations

- **BP** • 204th St & Tenth Ave
- **BP** • 3936 Tenth Ave
- **Getty** • 242 Dyckman St
- **Getty** • 4880 Broadway
- **Shell** • 3761 Tenth Ave
- **Sunoco** • 5080 Broadway

Parking

Map 26 • **Astoria**

Centuries after Peter Minuet claimed it as a part of his famous $24 purchase of the island we know and love, Astoria is still considered a "mini-Manhattan" and a haven for city-dwellers in search of lower rents. On a half-hour stroll through Astoria, one can discover hundreds of ethnic shops, dozens of magnificent sculptures, and a fabulous view of Manhattan across the East River. Anything and everything can be found on Astoria's Steinway Street. You'll find a fabulous beer garden at Bohemian Hall, a Greek cafe on nearly every block, a handful of Irish pubs, an Egyptian coffee shop or two, and a few spots that are just plain trendy. Great restaurants are plentiful, also—check out Christos and Stamatis for Greek, and Ubol's Kitchen for Thai. The brand-new all-weather track and miles of trails at Astoria Park are suitable for burning the calories gained from such fine dining.

💲 Banks

AT · **Astoria Federal** · 3716 30th Ave
AT · **Atlantic** · 28-07 Steinway St
AT · **Atlantic** · 29-10 Ditmars Blvd
AT · **Atlantic** · 33-12 30th Ave
AT · **Atlantic** · 36-10 Broadway
CH · **Chase** · 22-45 31st St
CH · **Chase** · 31-05 30th Ave
CH · **Chase** · 38-18 Broadway
CI · **Citibank** · 22-16 31st St
CI · **Citibank** · 25-91 Steinway St
CO · **Commerce** · 3104 Ditmars Blvd
FC · **First Central Savings** · 35-01 30th Ave
IC · **Independence Community** · 22-59 31st St
IC · **Independence Community** · 24-28 34th St
IC · **Independence Community** · 37-10 Broadway
IN · **Interbank of NY** · 31-01 Broadway
QC · **Queens County Savings** · 31-09 Ditmars Blvd
RS · **Roslyn Savings** · 30-75 Steinway St

🍴 Restaurants

· **31 Pasta Pizza & Panni** · 2248 31st St
· **Amici Amore I** · 29-35 Newtown Ave
· **Christos Hasapo-Taverna** · 41-08 23rd Ave
· **Eastern Nights** · 25-35 Steinway St
· **Elias Corner** · 24-02 31st St
· **Esperides** · 37-01 30th Ave
· **Fatty's Cafe** · 2501 Ditmars Blvd
· **Kabab Café** · 25-12 Steinway St
· **Lorusso Foods** · 18-01 26th Rd
· **Rizzo's Pizza** · 30-13 Steinway St
· **Stamatis** · 29-12 23rd Ave
· **Taverna Kyclades** · 33-07 Ditmars Blvd
· **Tierras Colombianas** · 33-01 Broadway
· **Tierras Colombianas** · 82-18 Roosevelt Ave
· **Trattoria L'Incontro** · 21-76 31st St
· **Ubol's Kitchen** · 24-42 Steinway St
· **Uncle George's** · 33-19 Broadway

⭕ Landmarks

· **Socrates Sculpture Park** · Broadway &
  Vernon Blvd
· **Bohemian Hall** · 29-19 24th Ave

🛍 Shopping

· **Bagel House** · 3811 Ditmars Blvd
· **Book Value** · 3318 Broadway
· **Top Tomato** · 33-15 Ditmars Blvd
· **Mediterranean Foods** · 23-18 31st St

🍸 Nightlife

· **Bohemian Hall** · 29-19 24th Ave
· **Brick Café** · 30-95 33rd St
· **Byzantio** · 28-31 31st St
· **Café Athens** · 32-07 30th St
· **Crescent Lounge** · 32-05 Crescent St
· **Gibney's** · 32-01 Broadway
· **McCann's Pub & Grill** · 3615 Ditmars Blvd
· **McLoughlin's Bar** · 31-06 Broadway

Map 27 · **Long Island City**

Unfortunately, the island of Manhattan cannot grow in tandem with its population. Akin to that in Brooklyn, a yuppie invasion of Long Island City has made it acceptable, even trendy, for Manhattanites to set foot into their neighbor to the east. Gentrification of this former industrial town has led to small battles between the natives and those who began the renaissance. In the case of P.S.1's solid concrete wall, good fences do not make good neighbors. Long Island City is the place to be if you want to check out great modern art. P.S.1 thankfully kept its reasonable entrance price tag even when MoMA temporarily moved in next door. Near Queens Plaza, The Space provides decorative public art that makes a statement, sometimes political, often puzzling. Although not as romantic as the Brooklyn Bridge or the Staten Island Ferry, a walk over the Pulaski Bridge provides a great view of midtown Manhattan's skyline. In contrast to the rest of the borough, public transportation serves people in this area of Queens well. A special treat is a newly implemented Hunters Point Ferry that travels to E 34th Street or Pier 11 near Wall Street.

$ Banks

NY · Bank of NY · 29-37 41st Ave
CH · Chase · 10-51 Jackson Ave
CI · Citibank · One Court Sq
QC · Queens County Savings · 4202 Northern Blvd

O Landmarks

· **American Museum of the Moving Image** ·
  35th Ave & 36th St
· **Center for the Holographic Arts** · 45-10 Court Sq
· **Citicorp Building** · 1 Court Sq
· **Isamu Noguchi Museum** · 32-37 Vernon Blvd
· **Long Island City Courthouse** ·
  25-10 Court Square
· **Kaufman-Astoria Studios** · 34-12 36th St
· **NY Center for Media Arts** · 45-12 Davis St
· **PS 1** · 22-25 Jackson Ave
· **Silvercup Studios** · 42-22 22nd St
· **The Space** · 42-16 West St

Movie Theaters

· **Regal/UA** · 35-30 38th St

Y Nightlife

· **Café Bar** · 32-90 36th St

Restaurants

· **Brooks 1890 Restaurant** · 24-28 Jackson Ave
· **Court Square Diner** · 45-30 23rd St
· **Jackson Ave Steakhouse** · 12-23 Jackson Ave
· **La Vuelta** · 10-43 44th Dr
· **Manducatis** · 13-27 Jackson Ave
· **Manetta's** · 10-76 Jackson Ave
· **S'Agapo** · 34-21 34th St
· **Sage American Kitchen** · 26-21 Jackson Ave
· **Tournesol** · 50-12 Vernon Blvd
· **Water's Edge** · 44th Dr & East River

Map 28 · **Greenpoint**

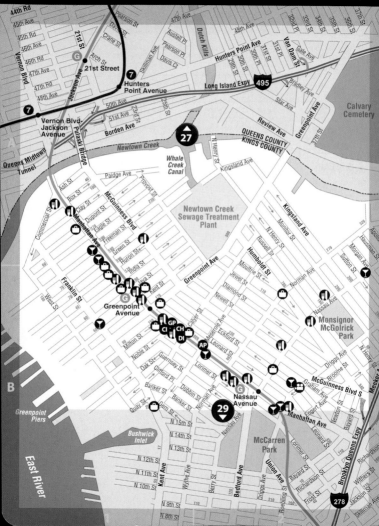

Whole lotta Polish, but not for much longer. In search of lower rents in a close proximity to their mecca, Williamsburg, the hipsters are making it less possible for Greenpoint to keep its "Little Warsaw" distinction. Great second-hand clothing, especially jeans, can be found at Pop's. The Warsaw on Driggs has great live music and here's a tip for wine drinkers—Z&J Liquor gives a 20% discount when you buy three bottles at a time.

💲 Banks

AP · Apple Bank · 776 Manhattan Ave
CH · Chase · 798 Manhattan Ave
CI · Citibank · 836 Manhattan Ave
DI · Dime · 814 Manhattan Ave
GP · Greenpoint · 807 Manhattan Ave

🎬 Movie Theaters

· **Cinema Warsaw** · 261 Driggs Ave

🍸 Nightlife

· **Enid's** · 560 Manhattan Ave
· **Europa** · 765 Manhattan Ave
· **Lyric Lounge** · 278 Nassau Ave
· **Matchless** · 557 Manhattan Ave
· **The Mark Bar** · 1025 Manhattan Ave
· **Pencil Factory** · 142 Franklin St
· **Tommy's Tavern** · 1041 Manhattan Ave
· **Warsaw** · 261 Driggs Ave

🍴 Restaurants

· **Acapulco Deli & Restaurant** ·
  1116 Manhattan Ave
· **Amarin Café** · 617 Manhattan Ave
· **Bleu Drawes Cafe** · 97 Commericial St
· **Casanova** · 338 McGuinness Blvd
· **Christina's** · 853 Manhattan Ave
· **Divine Follie Café** · 929 Manhattan Ave
· **Enid's** · 560 Manhattan Ave
· **God Bless Deli** · 818 Manhattan Ave
· **Kam Loon** · 975 Manhattan Ave
· **Manhattan 3 Decker Restaurant** ·
  695 Manhattan Ave
· **Old Poland Restaurant** · 181 Nassau Ave
· **OTT** · 970 Manhattan Ave
· **Relax** · 68 Newell St
· **SunView Luncheonette** · 221 Nassau Ave
· **Thai Café** · 925 Manhattan Ave
· **Valdiano** · 659 Manhattan Ave
· **Wasabi** · 638 Manhattan Ave

🛍️ Shopping

· **The City Mouse** · 1015 Manhattan Ave
· **Dee & Dee** · 777 Manhattan Ave
· **Mini Me** · 123 Nassau Ave
· **Polam** · 952 Manhattan Ave
· **Pop's Popular Clothing** · 7 Franklin St
· **Syrena Bakery** · 207 Norman Ave
· **The Thing** · 1001 Manhattan Ave
· **Uncle Louie G's** · 172 Greenpoint Ave
· **The Vortex** · 1084 Manhattan Ave
· **Wizard Electrolad** · 863 Manhattan Ave
· **Z&J Liquor** · 761 Manhattan Ave

Map 29 · **Williamsburg**

As far as food and fun go, you don't have to leave Williamsburg to find tasty eats, cheap beer, and a night on the town. A self-contained little community one stop from Manhattan, this 'hood continues to lure Manhattanites in search of trends. Check out great stores such as Spoonbill & Sugartown (books), Earwax Records (music), and Beacon's Closet (resale items).

Banks

AP · Apple Bank · 44 Lee Avenue
CH · Chase · 225 Havemeyer St
CC · Cross County Federal · 175 Bedford Ave
CC · Cross County Federal · 731 Metropolitan Ave
DI · Dime · 209 Havemeyer St
HS · HSBC · 175 Broadway

Landmarks

· **Brooklyn Brewery ·** 79 N 11th St

Nightlife

· **The Abbey ·** 536 Driggs Ave
· **Black Betty ·** 366 Metropolitan Ave
· **Boogaloo ·** 168 Marcy Ave
· **BQE ·** 300 N 6th St
· **Brooklyn Ale House ·** 103 Berry St
· **Brooklyn Brewery ·** 79 N 11th St
· **Charleston ·** 174 Bedford Ave
· **Galapagos ·** 70 N 6th St
· **Greenpoint Tavern ·** 188 Bedford Ave
· **Iona ·** 180 Grand St
· **Laila Lounge ·** 113 N 7th St
· **Northsix ·** 66 N 6th St
· **Pete's Candy Store ·** 709 Lorimer St
· **Stinger Club ·** 241 Grand St
· **Sweetwater Tavern ·** 105 N 6th St
· **Trash ·** 256 Grand St
· **Turkey's Nest ·** 94 Bedford Ave
· **Union Pool ·** 484 Union Ave

Restaurants

· **Acqua Santa ·** 556 Driggs Ave
· **Allioli ·** 291 Grand St
· **Anna Maria Pizza ·** 179 Bedford Ave
· **Anytime ·** 93 N 6th St
· **Bliss ·** 191 Bedford Ave
· **Bonita ·** 338 Bedford Ave
· **Buffalo Cantina ·** 149 Havemeyer St
· **Diner ·** 85 Broadway
· **Du Mont ·** 432 Union Ave
· **Foodswings ·** 295 Grand St
· **Kellogg's Diner ·** 518 Metropolitan Ave
· **M Shanghai Bistro & Den ·** 129 Havemeyer St
· **Miss Williamsburg Diner ·** 206 Kent Ave
· **Oznot's Dish ·** 79 Berry St
· **Peter Luger Steak House ·** 178 Broadway
· **Planet Thailand ·** 133 N 7th St
· **Relish ·** 225 Wythe St
· **Teddy's Bar and Grill ·** 96 Berry St
· **Vera Cruz ·** 195 Bedford Ave

Shopping

· **American Apparel ·** 104 N 6th St
· **Artist & Craftsman ·** 221 N 8th St
· **Beacon's Closet ·** 88 N 11th St
· **Bedford Cheese Shop ·** 218 Bedford Ave
· **Brooklyn Industries ·** 154 Bedford Ave
· **Domsey's Warehouse ·** 431 Broadway
· **Earwax Records ·** 218 Bedford Ave
· **Isa ·** 88 N 6th St
· **The Mini-Market ·** 218 Bedford Ave
· **MTC Drum Shop ·** 536 Metropolitan Ave
· **Spacial Etc ·** 199 Bedford Ave
· **Spoonbill & Sugartown ·** 218 Bedford Ave
· **Yarn Tree ·** 347 Bedford Ave

Map 30 · **Brooklyn Heights / DUMBO / Downtown**

A rather dizzying mix of fast food, hipster joints, and neighborhood stalwarts show the difference in these neighborhoods. Some institutions, however, include Junior's, Grimaldi's, and Henry's End. A new Barnes & Noble and googol-plex has changed the tenor of Court Street north of Atlantic, though not enough—it's still somewhat seedy. For more indie viewing fare, try the Heights Cinema.

💲 Banks

- **AT · Atlantic** · Gristedes, 101 Clark St
- **AL · Atlantic Liberty** · 186 Montague St
- **BP · Banco Popular** · 166 Livingston St
- **BF · Brooklyn Federal** · 81 Court St
- **CH · Chase** · 1 MetroTech Ctr
- **CH · Chase** · 16 Court St
- **CH · Chase** · 177 Montague St
- **CH · Chase** · 4 MetroTech Ctr
- **CI · Citibank** · 1 University Plz
- **CI · Citibank** · 181 Montague St
- **CC · Community Capital** · 111 Livingston St
- **FL · Fleet** · 205 Montague St
- **GP · Greenpoint** · 356 Fulton St
- **HS · HSBC** · 200 Montague St
- **HS · HSBC** · 342 Fulton St
- **IC · Independence Community** · 195 Montague St
- **IC · Independence Community** · 40 Washington St
- **NF · North Fork** · 50 Court St
- **WM · Washington Mutual** · 9 Dekalb Ave

⭕ Landmarks

- **Brooklyn Borough Hall** · 209 Joralemon St
- **Brooklyn Bridge** · Adams St & East River
- **Brooklyn Heights Promenade** ·
- **Brooklyn Historical Society** · 128 Pierrepont St
- **Brooklyn Ice Cream Factory** · Fulton Ferry Pier
- **Brooklyn Navy Yard** · Waterfront
- **Fulton Street Mall** · Fulton St b/w Flatbush Ave & Boerum Hall
- **Junior's Cheesecakes** · 386 Flatbush Ave
- **New York Transit Museum** · Boerum Place & Schermerhorn St

🎥 Movie Theaters

- **Pavilion Brooklyn Heights** · 70 Henry St
- **Regal/UA Court Street** · 108 Court St

🍸 Nightlife

- **Eamonn Doran** · 174 Montague St
- **Henry St Ale House** · 62 Henry St
- **Lunatarium** · 10 Jay St
- **St Ann's Warehouse** · 38 Water St
- **Water Street Bar** · 66 Water St

🍴 Restaurants

- **Bubby's** · 1 Main St
- **Fascati Pizzeria** · 80 Henry St
- **Five Front** · 5 Front St
- **Grimaldi's** · 19 Old Fulton St
- **Henry's End** · 44 Henry St
- **Noodle Pudding** · 38 Henry St
- **River Café** · 1 Water St
- **Superfine** · 126 Front St
- **Sushi California** · 71 Clark St

🛍️ Shopping

- **ABC Carpet & Home** · 20 Jay St
- **Heights Prime Meats** · 59 Clark St
- **Lassen & Hennigs** · 114 Montague St
- **Soho Art Materials** · 111 Front St
- **Tapestry the Salon** · 107 Montague St
- **West Elm** · 75 Front St

Map 31 · **Fort Greene / Clinton Hill**

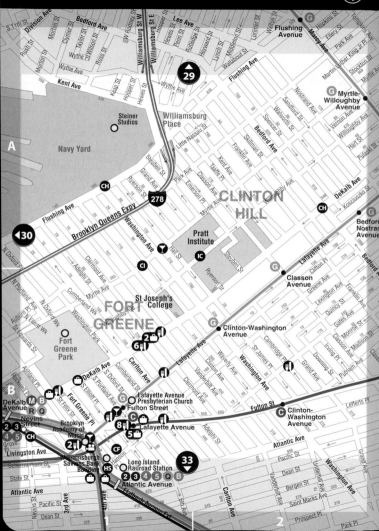

Today, this up-and-coming neighborhood is one of Brooklyn's finest, being not only close to Manhattan (just two subway stops away), but home to the Brooklyn Academy of Music (BAM), Madiba and Cambodian Cuisine (the only South African and Cambodian restaurants in the city, respectively), and Frank's Lounge. A good green grocer is sorely need, however.

💲 Banks

CF · Carver Federal · Hanson Pl & Fort Greene
CH · Chase · 20 Flatbush Ave
CH · Chase · 210 Flushing Ave
CH · Chase · 975 Bedford Ave
CI · Citibank · 430 Myrtle Ave
HS · HSBC · 1 Hanson Pl
IC · Independence Community · 200 Willoughby Ave

⊙ Landmarks

· **Brooklyn Academy of Music** · 30 Lafayette Ave
· **Fort Greene Park** · DeKalb Ave & Washington Park
· **Lafayette Ave Presbyterian Church** · 82 S Oxford St
· **Long Island Railroad Station** · Hanson Pl & Flatbush Ave
· **Steiner Studios** · 15 Washington Ave
· **Williamsburg Savings Bank Building** · 15 Washington Ave

😀 Movie Theaters

· **BAM Rose Cinemas** · 30 Lafayette Ave

🍸 Nightlife

· **BAM Café** · 30 Lafayette Ave
· **Five Spot** · 459 Myrtle Ave
· **Frank's Lounge** · 660 Fulton St
· **Moe's** · 80 Lafayette Ave

🍴 Restaurants

· **1 Greene Sushi and Sashimi** · 1 Greene Ave
· **Ë Table** · 171 Lafayette Ave
· **Academy Restaurant** · 69 Lafayette Ave
· **BAM Café** · 30 Lafayette Ave
· **Black Iris** · 228 DeKalb Ave
· **Brooklyn Moon Cafe** · 747 Fulton St
· **Café Lafayette** · 99 S Portland Ave
· **Cambodian Cuisine** · 87 S Elliot Pl
· **Chez Oskar** · 211 DeKalb Ave
· **Good Joy Chinese Takeout** · 216 DeKalb Ave
· **Ici** · 246 DeKalb Ave
· **Liquors** · 219 DeKalb Ave
· **Locanda Vini & Olii** · 129 Gates Ave
· **Madiba** · 195 DeKalb Ave
· **Mario's Pizzeria** · 224 DeKalb Ave
· **Mo-Bay** · 112 DeKalb Ave
· **Pequena** · 86 S Portland Ave
· **Scopello** · 63 Lafayette Ave
· **Thomas Beisl** · 25 Lafayette Ave
· **Veliis** · 773 Fulton St

🛍 Shopping

· **Cake Man Raven Confectionary** · 708 Fulton St
· **Carol's Daughter** · 1 S Elliot Pl
· **The Greene Grape** · 756 Fulton St
· **Indigo Café and Books** · 672 Fulton St
· **Jacob Eyes** · 114 Dekalb Ave
· **L'Epicerie** · 270 Vanderbilt Ave
· **Malchijah Hats** · 225 DeKalb Ave
· **The Midtown Greenhouse Garden Center** · 115 Flatbush Ave
· **My Little India** · 96 S Elliot Pl
· **Target** · 139 Flatbush Ave
· **Yu Interiors** · 15 Greene Ave

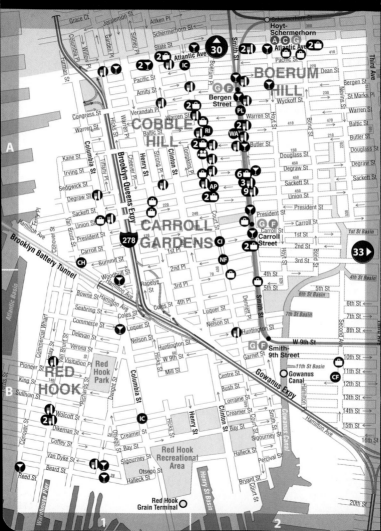

Map 32 • BoCoCa / Red Hook

Map 32

Five years ago, Smith Street was bodegas, dollar stores and junk shoes. Today, over 20 furniture/design/clothing/hipster shops line it from First Place up to Pacific Street, as well as over a dozen restaurants and several bars. Most of it's quite good and there's tons more to explore on Court Street if you get bored. For peace and quiet, stroll Hentry and Clinton Streets and the surrounding blocks.

$ Banks

- **AP · Apple Bank ·** 326 Court St
- **CF · Carver Federal ·** 1-37 12th St
- **CH · Chase ·** 79 Hamilton Ave
- **CI · Citibank ·** 375 Court St
- **IC · Independence Community ·** 130 Court St
- **IC · Independence Community ·** 498 Columbia St
- **NF · North Fork ·** 420 Court St
- **PL · Ponce De Leon ·** 169 Smith St
- **RW · Ridgewood ·** 244 Court St
- **WM · Washington Mutual ·** 192 Smith St

Landmarks

- **Gowanus Canal**
- **Red Hook Grain Terminal**

Movie Theaters

- **Cobble Hill Cinema ·** 265 Court St

Nightlife

- **The Boat ·** 175 Smith St
- **Brazen Head ·** 228 Atlantic Ave
- **Brooklyn Inn ·** 148 Hoyt St
- **Brooklyn Social Club ·** 335 Smith St
- **Gowanus Yacht Club ·** 323 Smith St
- **The Hook ·** 18 Commerce St
- **Kili ·** 81 Hoyt St
- **Last Exit ·** 136 Atlantic Ave
- **Liberty Heights Tap Room ·** 34 Van Dyke St
- **Lillie's ·** 46 Beard St
- **Magnetic Field ·** 97 Atlantic Ave
- **Moonshine ·** 317 Columbia St
- **Quench ·** 282 Smith St
- **Sunny's ·** 253 Conover St
- **Waterfront Ale House ·** 155 Atlantic Ave
- **Zombie Hut ·** 263 Smith St

Restaurants

- **360 ·** 360 Van Brunt St
- **Alma ·** 187 Columbia St
- **Bar Tabac ·** 128 Smith St
- **Buddy's Burrito & Taco Bar ·** 260 Court St
- **Cafe Luluc ·** 214 Smith St
- **Chance ·** 223 Smith St
- **Cobble Hill Grill ·** 212 DeGraw St
- **Delicatessen ·** 264 Clinton St
- **Donut House ·** 314 Court St
- **El Chulo ·** 272 Smith St
- **El Portal ·** 217 Smith St
- **Faan ·** 209 Smith St
- **Fatoosh ·** 330 Hicks St
- **Ferdinando's ·** 151 Union St
- **The Grocery ·** 288 Smith St
- **Hill Diner ·** 231 Court St
- **Hope & Anchor ·** 347 Van Brunt St
- **Joya ·** 215 Court St
- **Le Petite Cafe ·** 502 Court St
- **Leonardo's Brick Oven Pizza ·** 383 Court St
- **Liberty Heights Tap Room ·** 34 Van Dyke St
- **Margaret Palca Bakes ·** 191 Columbia St
- **Osaka ·** 272 Court St
- **Panino'teca ·** 275 Smith St
- **Patois ·** 255 Smith St
- **Sal's Pizzeria ·** 305 Court St
- **Savoia ·** 277 Smith St
- **Schnack ·** 122 Union St
- **Sherwood Café/Robin des Bois ·** 195 Smith St
- **Siam Garden ·** 172 Court St
- **Sonny's Bar & Grill ·** 305 Smith St
- **Tuk Tuk ·** 204 Smith St
- **Zaytoons ·** 283 Smith St

Shopping

- **American Beer Distributors ·** 256 Court St
- **Astro Turf ·** 290 Smith St
- **Bopkat ·** 113 Union St
- **Breukelen ·** 369 Atlantic Ave
- **Caputo's Fine Foods ·** 460 Court St
- **D'Amico Foods ·** 309 Court St
- **Frida's Closet ·** 296 Smith St
- **Granny's Attic ·** 305 Smith St
- **The Green Onion ·** 274 Smith St
- **Kimera ·** 366 Atlantic Ave
- **Knitting Hands ·** 398 Atlantic Ave
- **Lowes ·** 118 Second Ave
- **Marquet ·** 221 Court St
- **Mazzola Bakery ·** 192 Union St
- **Monte Leone's Pasticceria ·** 355 Court St
- **Refinery ·** 254 Smith St
- **Sahadi Importing Company ·** 187 Atlantic Ave
- **Stacia ·** 267 Smith St
- **Staubitz Meat Market ·** 222 Court St
- **Swallow ·** 361 Smith St
- **Sweet Melissa ·** 276 Court St
- **Tuller ·** 199 Court St
- **Uncle Louie G's ·** 517 Henry St
- **Urban Monster ·** 396 Atlantic Ave
- **Zipper ·** 333 Smith St

Blue Ribbon's arrival was a big deal for the neighborhood, which has seen an influx of incredible restaurants in the past few years. The Food Coop on Union Street is the largest member- owned and operated co-op in the nation. Prospect Heights has much to call its own and, for a great (but pricey) night out, check out the cats at Up Over Jazz Café

$ Banks

AS · **Astoria Federal** · 110 Seventh Ave
AS · **Astoria Federal** · 459 Fifth Ave
CH · **Chase** · 127 Seventh Ave
CH · **Chase** · 401 Flatbush Ave
CH · **Chase** · 444 Fifth Ave
CI · **Citibank** · 114 Seventh Ave
CF · **CSF** · Pathmark, 625 Atlantic Ave
GP · **Greenpoint** · 516 Fifth Ave
GP · **Greenpoint** · 856 Washington Ave
HS · **HSBC** · 325 9th St
IC · **Independence Community** · 234 Prospect Park W
MT · **M&T Bank** · 354 Flatbush Ave
WM · **Washington Mutual** · 533 Fifth Ave

O Landmarks

· **Brooklyn Botanic Garden** · 900 Washington Ave
· **Brooklyn Conservatory of Music** · 58 7th Ave
· **Brooklyn Museum** · 200 Eastern Pkwy
· **Brooklyn Public Library (Central Branch)** · Grand Army Plaza
· **Brooklyn Tabernacle** · 290 Flatbush Ave
· **Grand Army Plaza** · Flatbush Ave & Plaza St
· **Park Slope Food Coop** · 782 Union St

Movie Theaters

· **Pavilion Flatbush** · 314 Flatbush Ave
· **Pavilion Movie Theatres** · 188 Prospect Park W

Nightlife

· **Babinga** · 78 St Marks Ave
· **Bar 4** · 444 Seventh Ave
· **Bar Reis** · 375 Fifth Ave
· **Bar Toto** · 411 11th St
· **Barbes** · 376 9th St
· **Blu Lounge** · 197 Eighth St
· **Excelsior** · 390 Fifth Ave
· **Freddy's** · 485 Dean St
· **The Gate** · 321 Fifth Ave
· **Ginger's** · 363 Fifth Ave
· **Great Lakes** · 284 Fifth Ave
· **Loki Lounge** · 304 Fifth Ave
· **Mooney's Pub** · 353 Flatbush Ave
· **O'Connor's** · 39 Fifth Ave
· **Park Slope Ale House** · 356 Sixth Ave
· **Patio Lounge** · 179 Fifth Ave
· **Southpaw** · 125 Fifth Ave
· **Up Over Jazz Café** · 351 Flatbush Ave

Restaurants

· **12th Street Bar and Grill** · 1123 Eighth Ave
· **2nd Street Café** · 189 Seventh Ave
· **360 Restaurant** · 360 Van Brunt St
· **Al Di La Trattoria** · 248 Fifth Ave
· **Beso** · 210 Fifth Ave
· **Bistro St Mark's** · 76 St Mark's Ave
· **Blue Ribbon Brooklyn** · 280 Fifth Ave
· **Café Steinhof** · 422 Seventh Ave
· **ChipShop** · 383 Fifth Ave
· **Christie's Jamaican Patties** · 334 Flatbush Ave
· **Convivium Osteria** · 68 Fifth Ave
· **Cousin John's Café and Bakery** · 70 Seventh Ave
· **Dizzy's** · 511 Ninth Ave
· **Franny's** · 295 Flatbush Ave
· **Garden Café** · 620 Vanderbilt Ave
· **Junior's** · 386 Flatbush Ave
· **La Taqueria** · 72 Seventh Ave
· **Long Tan** · 196 Fifth Ave
· **Los Pollitos II** · 148 Fifth Ave
· **Mamma Duke** · 243 Flatbush Ave
· **Maria's Mexican Bistro** · 669 Union St
· **The Minnow** · 442 9th St
· **Mitchell's Soul Food** · 617 Vanderbilt Ave
· **Nana** · 155 Fifth Ave
· **New Prospect Café** · 393 Flatbush Ave
· **Olive Vine Café** · 441 Seventh Ave
· **Olive Vine Pizza** · 81 Seventh Ave
· **Parkside Restaurant** · 355 Flatbush Ave
· **Rose Water** · 787 Union St
· **Santa Fe Grill** · 62 Seventh Ave
· **Tom's** · 782 Washington Ave
· **Tutta Pasta** · 160 Seventh Ave
· **Two Boots** · 514 2nd St

Shopping

· **Barnes & Noble** · 267 Seventh Ave
· **Beacon's Closet** · 220 Fifth Ave
· **The Bicycle Station** · 560 Vanderbilt Ave
· **Bird** · 430 Seventh Ave
· **Bob and Judi's Collectibles** · 217 Fifth Ave
· **Boing Boing** · 204 Sixth Ave
· **Brooklyn Industries** · 152 Fifth Ave
· **Brooklyn Superhero Supply** · 372 Fifth Ave
· **Castor & Pollux** · 76 Sixth Ave
· **Clay Pot** · 162 Seventh Ave
· **Community Book Store** · 143 Seventh Ave
· **Eidolon** · 233 Fifth Ave
· **Heidi Story** · 453 Seventh Ave
· **Hibiscus** · 564A Vanderbilt Ave
· **Hooti Couture** · 321 Flatbush Ave
· **JackRabbit Sports** · 151 Seventh Ave
· **Kimera** · 274 Fifth Ave
· **Leaf and Bean** · 83 Seventh Ave
· **Nancy Nancy** · 244 Fifth Ave
· **Nkiru International Bookstore** · 732 Washington Ave
· **Pieces** · 671 Vanderbilt Ave
· **RedLipstick** · 64 Sixth Ave
· **Sound Track** · 119 Seventh Ave
· **Uncle Louie G's** · 741 Union St
· **Uprising Bread Bakery** · 138 Seventh Ave
· **Uprising Bread Bakery** · 328 Seventh Ave

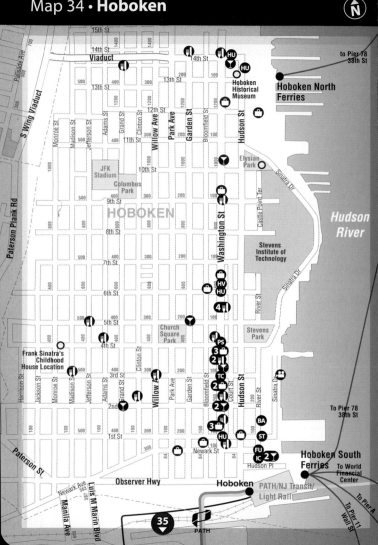

Map 34 · Hoboken

Just 9 minutes away from Manhattan by PATH train or 10 minutes by ferry, Hoboken is almost another borough of New York City. Wall Street types have driven the dizzying gentrification of this once gritty longshoreman town. Sinatra denied his Hoboken heritage because of the seedy reputation, but this "city on the waterfront" seems to be morphing before our eyes into one of the most desirable locales in the area; it has the new condos, high rises, day spas, trendy boutiques, and sushi restaurants to prove it. Every weekend, recent grads pour in from all over NJ for pub-crawls and good-time college partying, but the old-time Italian roots still show in the brick-oven bread, fresh mozzarella, Feast of St. Ann street festival, and house-dressed ladies sitting on front porches.

 Banks

- **BA · Bank of America** · 1 Firehouse Plz
- **FU · First Union National** · 95 River St
- **HS · Haven Savings** · 621 Washington St
- **HU · Hudson United** · 101 Washington St
- **HU · Hudson United** · 60 14th St
- **HU · Hudson United** · 1325 Hudson St
- **HU · Hudson United** · 609 Washington St
- **IC · Independence Community** · 86 River St
- **PS · Pamrapo Savings** · 401 Washington St
- **ST · Sumitomo Trust** · 111 River St
- **TC · Trust Co** · 301 Washington St

Landmarks

- **First recorded baseball game** · Elysian Fields
- **Frank Sinatra's Childhood Home Location** · 415 Monroe St
- **Hoboken Historical Museum** · 1301 Hudson St

Movie Theaters

- **Hudson Street Cinemas** · 5 Marineview Plz

Nightlife

- **Black Bear** · 205 Washington St
- **City Bistro** · 56 14th St
- **Leo's Grandezvous** · 200 Grand St
- **Louise & Jerry's** · 329 Washington St
- **Maxwell's** · 1039 Washington St
- **Mile Square** · 221 Washington St
- **Moran's** · 501 Garden St
- **Oddfellows** · 80 River St
- **Texas Arizona** · 76 River St

Restaurants

- **Amanda's** · 908 Washington St
- **Arthur's Tavern** · 237 Washington St
- **Baja** · 104 14th St (b/w Bloomfield & Washington)
- **Bangkok City** · 335 Washington St
- **Biggies Clam Bar** · 318 Madison St
- **Brass Rail** · 135 Washington St
- **Cucharamama** · 233 Clinton St
- **Delfino's** · 500 Jefferson St
- **East LA** · 508 Washington St
- **Far Side Bar & Grill** · 531 Washington St
- **Frankie & Johnnie's** · 14th St & Garden St
- **Gas Light** · 400 Adams St
- **Hoboken Gourmet Company** · 423 Washington St
- **Karma Kafe** · 505 Washington St
- **La Isla** · 104 Washington St
- **La Tartuferia** · 1405 Grand St
- **Robongi** · 520 Washington St
- **Trattoria Saporito** · 328 Washington St
- **Zafra** · 301 Willow Ave

Shopping

- **Air Studio** · 55 First St
- **Arts on Sixth** · 155 Sixth St
- **Basic Foods** · 204 Washington St
- **Battaglia's** · 319 Washington St
- **Big Fun Toys** · 602 Washington St
- **City Paint & Hardware** · 130 Washington St
- **Gallatea** · 1224 Washington St
- **Hand Mad** · 116 Washington St
- **Heidi Story** · 453 Seventh Ave
- **Hoboken Farmboy** · 127 Washington St
- **JackRabbit Sports** · 151 Seventh Ave
- **Makeovers** · 302 Washington St
- **Peper** · 1030 Washington St
- **Sobsey's Produce** · 92 Bloomfield St
- **Sparrow Wine and Liquor** · 1224 Washington St
- **Sparrow Wine and Liquor** · 126 Washington St
- **Tunes New & Used CDs** · 225 Washington St
- **Yes I Do** · 312 Washington St

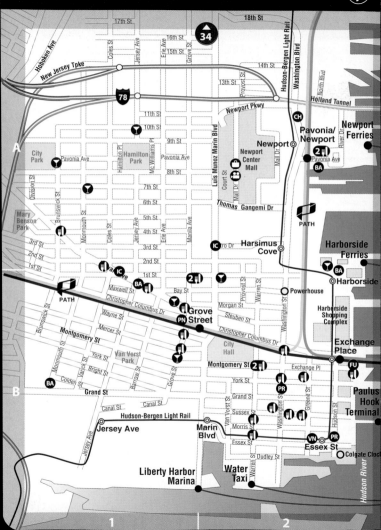

Map 35 · **Jersey City**

If you are taking the ferry from Manhattan, you will quickly notice that the entire waterfront of Jersey City is under construction. (You'll see at least ten new buildings going up.) Is Jersey City the "Sixth Borough" of New York? Not yet, but when all of the building is complete, it will be interesting to see what has evolved. With many fine restaurants and an increasing number of after-work hangouts popping up, Jersey City is growing as a neighborhood that is well worth checking out.

$ Banks

BA · **Bank of America** · 123 Harborside Financial Ctr
BA · **Bank of America** · 125 Pavonia Ave
BA · **Bank of America** · 186 Newark Ave
BA · **Bank of America** · 235 Monmouth St
CH · **Chase** · 575 Washington Blvd
FU · **First Union National** · 10 Exchange Pl
IC · **Independence Community** · 224 Newark Ave
IC · **Independence Community** · 400 Marin Blvd
PN · **PNC** · 95 Christopher Columbus Dr
PR · **Provident Savings** · 239 Washington St
PR · **Provident Savings** · 30 Hudson St (Goldman Sachs Tower)
VN · **Valley National** · 46 Essex St

O Landmarks

· **Colgate Clock** · 105 Hudson St
· **Powerhouse** · 344 Washington St

Movie Theaters

· **Loews Cineplex Newport Center 11** · 30 Mall Dr W

Nightlife

· **Dennis and Maria's Bar** · 322 1/2 7th St
· **Hamilton Park Ale House** · 708 Jersey Ave
· **LITM** · 140 Newark Ave
· **Lamp Post Bar and Grille** · 382 2nd St
· **Markers** · Harborside Financial Ctr, Plz II
· **The Merchant** · 279 Grove St
· **PJ Ryan's** · 172 First St
· **White Star** · 230 Brunswick St

Restaurants

· **Amelia's Bistro** · 187 Warren St
· **Casablanca Grill** · 354 Grove St
· **Ibby's Falafel** · 303 Grove St
· **Iron Monkey** · 97 Greene St
· **Kitchen Café** · 60 Sussex St
· **Komegashi** · 103 Montgomery St
· **Komegashi Too** · 99 Pavonia Ave
· **Light Horse Tavern** · 199 Washington St
· **Madame Claude Café** · 364 4th St
· **Marco and Pepe** · 289 Grove St
· **Miss Saigon** · 249 Newark Ave
· **Nicco's Restaurant** · 247 Washington St
· **Oddfellows Restaurant** · 111 Montgomery St
· **Presto's Restaurant** · 199 Warren St
· **Pronto Cena Ristorante** · 87 Sussex St
· **Rosie Radigans** · 10 Exchange Pl (Lobby)
· **Saigon Café** · 188 Newark Ave
· **Tania's** · 348 Grove St
· **Unlimited Pizza Café & Diner** · 116 Newark Ave
· **Uno Chicago Bar & Grill** · 286 Washington St
· **ZZ's Brick Oven Pizza** · 118 Pavonia Ave

Shopping

· **Harborside Shopping Complex** ·
· **Newport Center Mall** · 30 Mall Dr W

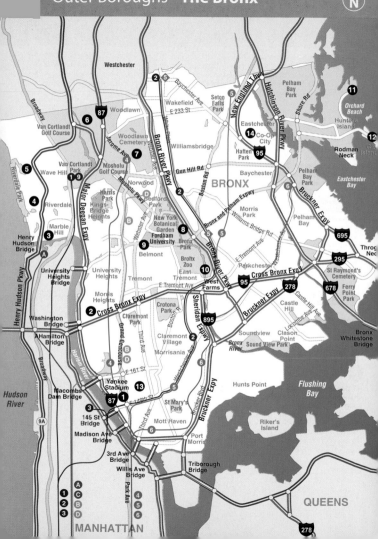

The Bronx probably gets the worst rap of any of the five boroughs, but it's really not deserved. And since part of the Bronx's problems were caused by Robert Moses, you really can't blame it. But blame or no blame, it still feels like a nice neighborhood in the Bronx remains the exception and not the rule.

Communities

The Bronx has one of the largest dichotomies between communities—the private, wooded mansions of Riverdale **4** greatly contrast with the problematic South Bronx **13**, around Yankee Stadium **1**. To add to the mix, the Bronx also contains a huge co-op complex (named "Co-Op City") **14**, quiet streets around Pelham Parkway, several waterfront communities including City Island **12** (one of those rare, interesting places that feels totally un-New York), and one of New York's major universities, Fordham **9**. (And in case you were wondering, the community of Marble Hill **3**, physically located in the Bronx, is technically part of New York County.)

Culture

Some of the Bronx's most interesting cultural spots are actually vestiges of long-gone institutions (or people). For instance, beautiful Woodlawn Cemetery **7** holds the remains of Mayor Fiorello LaGuardia, Duke Ellington, and Herman Melville. The bizarre and interesting "Hall of Fame" at Bronx Community College **2** is actually leftover from New York University's dismantled University Heights campus. And Wave Hill, a wonderful park and occasional concert venue, **5** was formerly a private estate.

Sports

Yankee Stadium **1**, perhaps the Bronx's best-known landmark, has been a fixture on the Harlem River for over seventy years. Since opening, it's hosted over 20 Yankee World Series championships. Another major Bronx sports institution is one of America's oldest golf courses, Van Cortlandt Golf Course **6**, or "Vanny" to regulars. You'll see a beautiful lily pond with ducks before dealing with dry, brown fairways, and garbage-strewn roughs. Ah, New York.

Nature

Besides an excellent and underrated system of parks—including Pelham Bay Park, Soundview Park, Van Cortlandt Park, and Ferry Point Park—the Bronx is also home to the notable New York Botanical Garden **8** and the Bronx Zoo **10**. Orchard Beach **11** is another of the borough's popular outdoor destinations.

Food

Belmont:
- Dominick's, 2335 Arthur Ave, 718-733-2807—Quintessential Italian eatery.

City Island:
- The Lobster Box, 34 City Island Ave, 718-885-1952—When in Rome, eat seafood.

Riverdale:
- Café Blue, 3509 Johnson Ave, 718-884-2020—Italian-American
- Josephina Restaurant, 3522 Johnson Ave, 718-796-7997—Italian neighborhood fave, with reasonably priced, delicious food.
- Kappock Café, 17 Knolls Cres, 718-601-5500—New American and Italian in a homey setting.
- Nonno Tony's, 554 W 235th St (& Johnson Ave), 718-884-5700—Replaced the old Bellavista Café.
- Riverdale Garden, 4574 Manhattan College Pkwy, 718-884-5232—Upscale New American cooked in wood-fired oven, friendly staff, lovely garden.
- Siam Square Thai Restaurant, 564 Kappock St, 718-432-8200—Order anything that comes served in a pineapple.

Belmont:
- Ann & Tony's, 2407 Arthur Ave, 718-933-1469—Slightly off the beaten track, this place does mouth-watering calamari.
- Giovanni, 2343 Arthur Ave, 718-933-4141—Excellent pizza, good pasta, and the chicken's not bad either.
- Mario's Restaurant, 2342 Arthur Ave, 718-584-1188—Traditional Italian served by traditional wait staff.
- Pasquale Rigoletto Restaurant 2311 Arthur Ave, 718-365-6644—Authentic Italian with friendly staff.

University Heights:
- Webster Café, 2873 Webster Ave, 718-733-9634—24-hour gem that serves regular diner food, as well as some Mexican delights.
- University Pizza & Restaurant, 574 E Fordham Rd, 718-220-1959—Cheap, delicious pizza.

Castle Hill:
- Sabrosura, 1200 Castle Hill Ave, 718-597-1344—Latin-Chinese fusion.

Morris Park:
- Patricia's, 1080 Morris Park Ave, 718-409-9069—Famous brick-oven pizza.

Wakefield:
- Vernon's New Jerk House, 987 East 233rd St, 718-655-8348—Tasty, spicy Jamaican.

Landmarks

1 Yankee Stadium
2 Hall of Fame at Bronx Community College
3 Marble Hill
4 Riverdale
5 Wave Hill
6 Van Cortlandt Golf Course
7 Woodlawn Cemetery
8 New York Botanical Garden
9 Fordham University
10 Bronx Zoo
11 Orchard Beach
12 City Island/South Bronx/Co-op City

Until 1898, Brooklyn was its own autonomous city. Today, it could still make a damn fine city all on its own, but with glittering Manhattan just across the water, Brooklyn gets second billing when it's not ignored altogether. This, of course, makes Brooklynites seethe with justifiable anger, for they believe that their borough is just as beautiful and interesting as Manhattan. But since Manhattan rents are skyrocketing, hipsters, yuppies, and just plain folks are moving to Brooklyn in hordes—which might make long-time residents start wishing they hadn't been bragging so much for the last 100 years. C'est la vie.

Communities

With 2.5 million residents, Brooklyn is one of the largest cities in the US. Here you can find pretty much every type of community you could wish for and, of course, some you really wouldn't wish for. Many Brooklyn neighborhoods are in transition, including—but not limited to—Park Slope, Boerum Hill, Carroll Gardens, Bushwick, Red Hook, Williamsburg, Greenpoint, and Fort Greene (the communities closest to Manhattan).

If you've never explored further out into Brooklyn than the obligatory trip to Coney Island, you're missing some interesting, and very different, neighborhoods. For instance, Bay Ridge **4** has beautiful single-family homes along its western edge, a killer view of the Verrazano Bridge, and a host of excellent shops and restaurants. Dyker Heights **6** is composed of almost all single-family homes, many of which go all-out with Christmas light displays during the holiday season. Brighton Beach **8** continues to be a haven to many Russian expatriates. The quiet, tree-lined streets of both Ocean Parkway **10** and Midwood **11** can make one forget all about the hustle and bustle of downtown Brooklyn, or downtown anywhere else for that matter. Finally, while Bedford-Stuyvesant **12** does have its problems, it also has a host of cool public buildings, fun eateries, and beautiful brownstones.

Sports

Brooklynites can't wait for the San Andreas Fault Line to give its final heave and toss all of California into the Pacific Ocean. Why? Because deep down, they know that it's the only way the Dodgers will ever come back to Brooklyn. Until then, check out the Brooklyn Cyclones, the Mets' Class A affiliate, at 1904 Surf Avenue in Coney Island.

Attractions

There are plenty of reasons to dislike Coney Island **7**, but they're simply not good enough when you stack them up against the Cyclone, the ferris wheel, Nathan's, Totonno's, the beach, the freaks, and *The Warriors*. Close by is the Aquarium **13**. Nature trails, parked blimps, views of the water, and scenic marinas all make historical Floyd Bennett Field **9** a worthwhile trip. For more beautiful views, you can check out Owl's Point Park **3** in Bay Ridge, or the parking lot underneath the Verrazano-Narrows Bridge **5** (located right off the Shore Parkway). The Verrazano might not be New York's most beautiful bridge, but it's hands-down the most awe-inspiring. Both Greenwood Cemetery **2** and Prospect Park **1** provide enough greenery to keep you happy until you get to Yosemite. Finally, Brooklyn Heights **14** is the most beautiful residential neighborhood in all of New York. Don't believe us? Go stand on the corner of Willow & Orange Streets.

Food

Here are some restaurants in some of the outlying areas of Brooklyn: See pages 168 to 179 for other Brooklyn eateries.
Bay Ridge: Tuscany Grill, 8620 Third Ave, 718-921-5633—The gorgonzola steak is a must.
Coney Island: Totonno Pizzeria Napolitano,1524 Neptune Ave, 718-372-8606—Paper-thin pizza. Bizarre hours.
Midwood: DiFara's Pizzeria, E 15th St & Ave J, 718-258-1367—Dirty, cheap, disgusting…awesome!
Sunset Park: Nyonya, 5223 Eighth Ave, 718-633-0808—Good quality Malaysian.

Landmarks

1 Prospect Park	6 Dyker Heights	11 Midwood
2 Green-Wood Cemetery	7 Coney Island	12 Bedford-Stuyvesant
3 Owl's Point Park	8 Brighton Beach	13 New York Aquarium
4 Bay Ridge	9 Floyd Bennett Field	14 Brooklyn Heights
5 Verrazano-Narrows Bridge	10 Ocean Parkway	

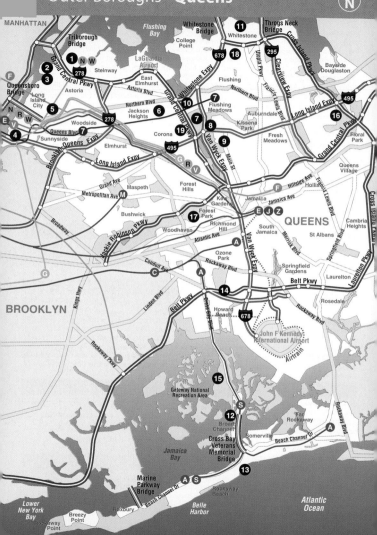

Queens has everything you'd expect from a big city—great art, great food, ethnic diversity, beautiful parks, sporting events, etc. However, since Queens is New York's largest borough, this is all spread out over 100 square miles. And as Mets fans discovered long ago, it's more than a hop, skip, and a jump to Flushing—and then there's another 5 miles of Queens east of Flushing that's not even serviced by subway. But if you've got wheels or large, unfinished Thomas Pynchon novels for the train ride, exploring Queens can be a blast.

Communities

Queens has almost 2 million people, and they are far from homogenized. Astoria **1** has the largest concentration of Greek people outside of Greece, Jackson Heights **6** has a vibrant Indian and Pakistani community, and that's just for starters. Mix in the relatively upscale communities of Whitestone **11** and Forest Hills, working-class Howard Beach, industrial Maspeth, sprawling Jamaica, and sleepy Broad Channel **12**, and you've got endless diversity.

Culture

We can't say enough about how cool Socrates Sculpture Park **2** is. Located on the waterfront (next to founder Mark Di Suvero's sculpture studio) at the end of Broadway (take the Ⓝ train to the Broadway stop and walk west), this park has had some of New York's best outdoor sculpture for the last ten years. Right down the street is the excellent Noguchi Museum **3** featuring a comprehensive collection of the sculptor's work. Astoria is also home to the American Museum of the Moving Image **5**, located in the Kaufman-Astoria Studios district. In Hunter's Point, the expanded and brilliant P.S. 1 Art Museum **4** is a must-see. In Flushing Meadows-Corona Park, check out the gigantic Hall of Science **8**. Finally, if you've never seen the scale model of New York City at the Queens Museum **9** in Corona Park, you should.

Sports

Home to the lovable New York Mets, Shea Stadium **10** is right off the ❼ train and the Port Washington branch of the LIRR. Aqueduct Racetrack **14** has its own Ⓐ train stop (open 11 am-7 pm on racing days). Rockaway Beach **13** is great for swimming (especially mid-week!), and, if there doesn't happen to be anything you want to do at 3 am in Manhattan, drive out to Whitestone Lanes **18**, off the Linden Place exit of the Whitestone Expressway, for 24-hour bowling pleasure. Every Labor Day, the popular U.S. Open is held at the National Tennis Center **7**.

Nature

Queens is home to the vast Gateway National Recreation Area, which has some excellent trails at its Jamaica Bay Wildlife Refuge **15** facility. Alley Pond Park **16** also has several sections of interest, including the quiet "Upper Alley" area. The Queens Zoo **19** in Flushing Meadows features only American animals and is definitely worth a look-see. Finally, the 165 wooded acres of Forest Park **17** provide excellent walks, ponds, and stands of trees.

Food

Below is an insanely short list of Queens eateries, but at least we can say that what's listed is great:
Astoria: Stamatis, 29-12 23rd Ave, 718-932-8596—Really great, unpretentious Greek food.
Corona: Park Side, 107-01 Corona Ave, 718-271-9274—Great neighborhood Italian.
Forest Hills: Nick's Pizza, 108-26 Ascan Ave, 718-263-1126—Queens' best pizza.
Jackson Heights: Jackson Diner, 37-47 74th St, 718-672-1232—Excellent, cheap Indian in a busy neighborhood.
Sunnyside: Hemsin, 39-17 Queens Blvd, 718-937-1715—Turkish. Recommended.

Landmarks

1 Astoria
2 Socrates Sculpture Park
3 Noguchi Museum
4 P.S. 1 Art Museum
5 American Museum of the Moving Image
6 Jackson Heights
7 U.S. Open/National Tennis Center
8 Hall of Science
9 Queens Museum
10 Shea Stadium

11 Whitestone
12 Broad Channel
13 Rockaway Beach
14 Aqueduct Racetrack
15 Jamaica Bay Wildlife Refuge
16 Alley Pond Park
17 Forest Park
18 Whitestone Lanes
19 Queens Zoo

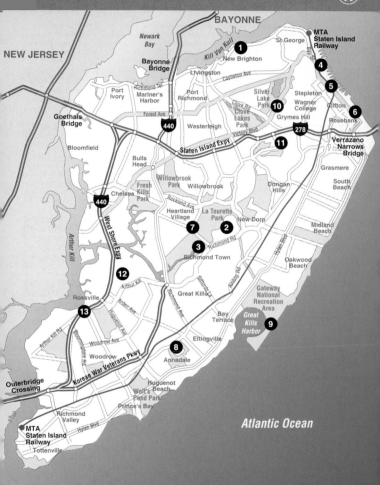

Every borough has an identity—Manhattan is the center of the universe, Brooklyn is the new capital of hip, the Bronx is the old capital of notoriety, and Queens is, well, Queens. But Staten Island? When most people think of Staten Island, the first thing that comes to mind is the Fresh Kills landfill. Thankfully Staten Island has a lot more to offer, if you have the time and the inclination to travel there and back. By the time you take the ferry from Battery Park or drive across the Verrazano, you'll be ready to turn around and head back. If you do have the fortitude to make the journey, you'll be rewarded with ample Staten Island highlights. The following activities are all highly recommended.

Culture

1 **Snug Harbor Cultural Center**, 1000 Richmond Ter, 718-448-2500. Staten Island's premiere cultural hotspot. This interesting complex of buildings was once a maritime hospital and home for retired sailors. Now it hosts excellent art exhibits and concerts in its 83-acre garden setting filled with walking paths, a children's museum, and Greek Revival architecture.

2 **Jacques Marchais Museum of Tibetan Art**, 338 Lighthouse Ave, 718-987-3500. An impressive collection of Staten Island art, courtesy of former New York art collector Edna Coblentz, a.k.a Jacques Marchais.

3 **Historic Richmondtown**, 441 Clark Ave, 718-351-1611. A 30-acre complex of historic buildings on the site of an early Dutch settlement—the oldest building dates back to 1695.

4 **Civic Center**, 10 Richmond Ter, 718-816-2000. After Staten Island became part of New York City in 1898, plans to build a civic center in St. George were devised. The full plan was never entirely realized, but the resulting Borough Hall, Supreme Courthouse (formerly the County Courthouse), and Family Courthouse are an impressive collection of buildings nonetheless.

5 **Staten Island Village Hall**, 111 Canal St. Last remaining village hall building in Staten Island, a reminder of the borough's rural past.

6 **Alice Austen House**, 2 Hylan Blvd, 718-816-4506. Alice Austen was an early twentieth-century amateur photographer and a contemporary of Jacob Riis. Some of her 8,000 images are always on view at her house, which also provides a great view of lower New York Harbor.

Nature

7 **The Staten Island Greenbelt**, 200 Nevada Ave, 718-667-2165. Although this 2,500-acre swath of land (comprising several different parks) in the center of the island houses a golf course, a hospital, a scout camp, and several graveyards, plenty of woodsy areas remain relatively undeveloped and can be accessed only by walking trails. A good starting point is High Rock Park, accessible from Nevada Avenue. Great views abound.

8 **Blue Heron Nature Center**, 222 Poillon Ave, 718-967-3542. Accessible from Poillon Avenue in southwestern Staten Island, this quiet 147-acre park has a unique serenity to it. Good ponds, bird-watching, wetlands, streams, etc.

9 **Great Kills Park**, 718-987-6790. Part of the Gateway National Recreation Area, Great Kills Park is home to some excellent beaches, a marina, and a nature preserve. It's right off Hylan Boulevard.

10 **Wagner College**, 1 Campus Rd, 718-390-3100. Wagner's tranquil hilltop location rewards visitors with beautiful views of the serene surroundings. Worth the winding drive up the hill. Accessible from Howard Avenue.

Other

11 **110/120 Longfellow Road.** The estate owned by the Corleone family in *The Godfather*. You might have to wait a while for Johnny Fontaine to show up and sing, though.

12 **Fresh Kills Landfill**, off Route 440. Excellent hiking, backcountry camping, and scavenging. Bring the whole family.

13 **Ship Graveyard**, at Arthur Kill Rd and Rossville Ave. Excellent views of rotting ships and other industrial wonders. Recommended.

Food

Snug Harbor:
RH Tugs, 1115 Richmond Ter, 718-447-6369.
Overlooks Kill Van Kull so there's a lot of tug and tanker action.

Rosebank:
Aesop's Tables, 1233 Bay St & Maryland Ave, 718-720-2005.
Seasonal dishes and a lush outdoor garden for the warmer months. Open for dinner, Tues-Sat.
Marina Café, 154 Mansion Ave, 718-967-3077.
Pricey seafood joint where the best feature is the view!

Richmondtown:
Parsonage, 74 Arthur Kill Rd & Clarke Ave, 718-351-7879.
Charming atmosphere offering reasonable food at reasonable prices.

Driving In/ Through Staten Island

At certain times, the drive from Brooklyn to New Jersey via Staten Island is a quick trip. Take the Verrazano to the Staten Island Expressway (Route 278) to Route 440 to the Outerbridge Crossing, and you're almost halfway to Princeton or the Jersey shore. However...the Staten Island Expressway often gets jammed. Two scenic, though not really quicker, alternatives: one, take Hylan Boulevard all the way south to almost the southwest tip of Staten Island, and then cut up to the Outerbridge Crossing; two, take Richmond Terrace around the north shore and cross to New Jersey at the Goethals Bridge. Remember, neither is really faster, but at least you'll be moving.

General Information

Battery Park Parks Conservancy:
212-267-9700

Websites: www.batteryparkcity.org
www.lowermanhattan.info
www.batteryparkcityonline.com
www.bpcparks.org
www.bpcdogs.org

Overview

Battery Park City is a 92-acre planned community on Manhattan's southwest tip. Built on landfill from the construction of the World Trade Center, it ranked among the hardest hit neighborhoods by the September 11th attacks, but is now well on the path to recovery. Its ability to carry on comes as little surprise, since the neighborhood possesses intrinsic worth—views of the harbor, green space galore, and overall good community planning (sparing it from the shortcomings of Roosevelt Island). The Battery Park City Authority keeps track of changes to the area on its interesting and informative website, www.batteryparkcity.org.

BPC has gone through many stages of urban planning, but the latest plan—42% residential, 30% open space, 19% streets, and 9% commercial—seems to include something for everyone. 14,000 new living units are in the works, with a potential occupancy of 25,000 residents. There are big plans for "green" apartment buildings—each equipped

with energy-saving features. The first of these buildings, the Solaire, opened its doors in July 2003 to rave reviews. BPC's network of parks—Robert F. Wagner, Jr., South Cove, Rector, North Cove, the Esplanade, and Governor Nelson A. Rockefeller—is swiftly gaining a reputation for beautiful views, excellent outdoor sculptures (by Louise Bourgeois, Tom Otterness, Martin Puryear, Jim Dine, and Brian Tolle), and great places to just chill out. The looming presences of Stuyvesant High School, Siah Armajani's the Tribeca Bridge, Kevin Roche's Museum of Jewish Heritage, Caesar Pelli's Winter Garden, and the World Financial Center make the architecture of Battery Park City something to look at. Despite all this, BPC is still a bit un-NY—too planned and too boring (there's no nightlife). A nice place to visit but, unless you have a family, not a great place to live.

🥯 Bagels

· **Pick A Bagel** · 102 North End Ave (Embassy Suites)

💲 Banks

CH · **Chase** · 331 South End Ave
BA · **Bank of America** · 4 World Financial Ctr

🌙 Nightlife

· **Rise Bar @ the Ritz** · 2 West St

🏫 Schools

· **PS 89** · 201 Warren St
· **Stuyvesant High School** · 345 Chambers St

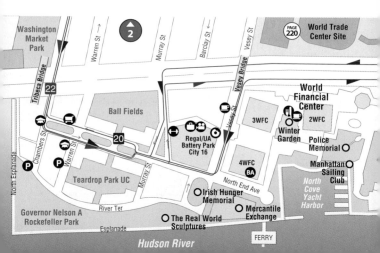

○ Landmarks

- **The Irish Hunger Memorial** · Vesey St & North End Ave
- **Manhattan Sailing Club** · North Cove (Liberty St & North End Ave)
- **Mercantile Exchange** · 1 North End Ave
- **Police Memorial** · Liberty St & South End Ave
- **The Real World Sculptures**
- **Skyscraper Museum** · 39 Battery Pl
- **Winter Garden** · 37 Vesey St

☕ Coffee

- **Financier Patisserie** · 225 Liberty St (Winter Garden, courtyard)
- **Starbucks** · 3 World Financial Ctr

🏋 Gyms

- **Battery Park Swim & Fitness Center** · 375 South End Ave (Gateway Plz)
- **Liberty Club MCB** · 200 Rector Pl
- **New York Sports Club** · 102 North End Ave (Embassy Suites)

🍸 Liquor Stores

- **Bulls & Bears Winery** · 309 South End Ave

🎬 Movie Theaters

- **Regal Battery Park City 16** · 102 North End Ave (Embassy Suites)

🍴 Restaurants

- **Cove Restaurant** · 2 South End Ave
- **Foxhounds** · 320 South End Ave
- **Gigino at Wagner Park** · 20 Battery Pl
- **Grill Room** · Winter Garden, World Financial Ctr
- **Picasso Pizza** · 303 South End Ave
- **Samantha's Fine Foods** · 235 South End Ave
- **Steamer's Landing** · 375 South End Ave
- **Wave Japanese Restaurant** · 21 South End Ave
- **Zen** · 311 South End Ave

◈ Video Rental

- **Video Room** · 300 Rector Pl

🛍 Shopping

- **DSW Shoe Warehouse** · 102 North End Ave (Embassy Suites)

🛒 Supermarkets

- **Gourmet Heaven** · 450 North End Ave
- **Gristede's** · 315 South End Ave
- **Gristede's** · 71 South End Ave

🔑 Car Rental

Avis · 345 South End Ave

🅿 Parking

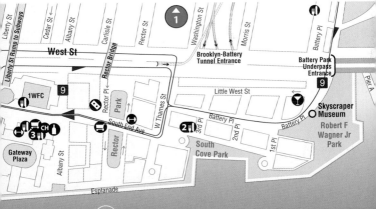

General Information

Website: www.centralpark.org
Central Park Conservancy: 212-310-6600
Shakespeare in the Park: 212-539-8750

Overview

Central Park, designed by Frederick Law Olmsted (with help from Calvert Vaux) in the 1850s, is an 843-acre haven for many New Yorkers. On any given summer Saturday, the park is full of jugglers, magicians, disco roller-skater-bladers, Hungarian folk dancing, skateboarders, joggers, operas, rock concerts, ball players, *Troilus and Cressida*, boaters, art, turtles, frogs, birds, and...oh, yes, billions of people. But the park is so big that there are more than enough quiet spots where you can still feel alone, including official "quiet zones" such as the Shakespeare Gardens **17** for reading, picnicking, and napping.

Central Park, like the city itself, is made up of a diverse mix of attractions. Just when you think that Central Park is nothing more than an overcrowded noisy place crawling with sweaty rollerbladers, you'll stumble upon a quiet glade that houses a small sculpture and a few solitary people reading books.

Practicalities

Central Park is easily accessible by subway, since the Ⓐ Ⓒ Ⓑ Ⓓ Ⓝ Ⓡ Ⓦ ❶ ❷ ❸ trains all circle the park. (Oddly enough, there are no stations within the park.) Parking along Central Park West is usually not difficult. Unless you're heading to the park for a big concert, a softball game, or for Shakespeare in the Park, walking or hanging out (especially alone!) in the park at night is not recommended.

Nature

There are an amazing number of both plant and animal species that inhabit the park (and we're not just talking about the creatures housed in its two zoos **4** & **8**). A good source of information on all of the park's flora and fauna is schoolteacher Leslie Day's web site, www.nysite.com/nature/index.htm.

Architecture & Sculpture

The Bethesda Fountain and Terrace **11,** designed by Emma Stebbins, has become the park's main attraction for many people. The view of Turtle Pond from Belvedere Castle **16** (home of the Central Park Learning Center) is also not to be missed. The Arsenal **5** is a wonderful ivy-clad building that houses several Parks Department offices. The park is teeming with sculptures and two of the most notable are Alice in Wonderland **15** and the Obelisk **19**. Oh and one other tiny point of interest...the Metropolitan Museum of Art **24** also happens to be in the park.

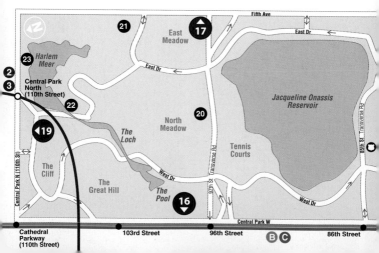

Open Spaces

The word "space" is not often used to describe the average New Yorker's apartment (unless you're talking about the lack thereof), so it comes as little surprise that large areas such as Strawberry Fields 10, the Great Lawn 26, the Ramble 27, and Sheep's Meadow 28 are taken advantage of by New Yorkers.

Performance

Central Park is a microcosm of the great cultural attractions New York has to offer. The Delacorte Theater 18 is the home of Shakespeare in the Park, a New York tradition begun by famous director Joseph Papp. SummerStage 9 is now an extremely popular summer concert venue for all types of music, including the occasional killer rock concert. Opera companies and classical philharmonics also show up in the park frequently, as does the odd mega-star (Garth Brooks, Diana Ross, etc.).

Sports

Rollerblading and roller skating are very popular (not just at the Roller Skating Rink 7—see www.centralparkskate.com, www.cpdsa.org, www.skatecity.com), as is jogging, especially around the reservoir (1.57 mi). The Great Lawn 26 boasts beautiful softball fields. Central Park has 30 tennis courts (and a long waiting list to use them), fishing at Harlem Meer, gondola rides and boat rentals at the Loeb Boathouse 13, model boat rentals at the Conservatory Water, chess and checkers at the Chess & Checkers House 25, and rock-climbing lessons at the North Meadow Rec Center 20. There are also volleyball, basketball, skateboarding, bicycling, and many pick-up soccer, frisbee, football, and kill-the-carrier games to join. If horseback riding is more your speed, you can rent a steed from Claremont Riding Academy (212-724-5100) on W 89th Street at Amsterdam Avenue and ride into the park. Finally, Central Park is where the NYC Marathon ends each year.

Landmarks

1 Wollman Rink
2 Carousel
3 The Dairy
4 Central Park Zoo
5 The Arsenal
6 Tavern on the Green
7 Roller Skating Rink
8 Children's Zoo
9 SummerStage

10 Strawberry Fields
11 Bethesda Fountain
12 Bow Bridge
13 Loeb Boathouse
14 Model Boat Racing
15 Alice in Wonderland
16 Belvedere Castle
17 Shakespeare Gardens
18 Delacorte Theater

19 The Obelisk
20 North Meadow Recreation Center
21 Conservatory Garden
22 Lasker Rink
23 Dana Discovery Center
24 Metropolitan Museum of Art

25 Chess & Checkers House
26 The Great Lawn
27 The Ramble
28 Sheep's Meadow

Police Precinct
86th St & Transverse Rd

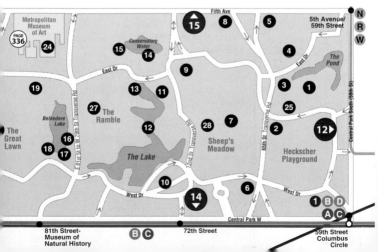

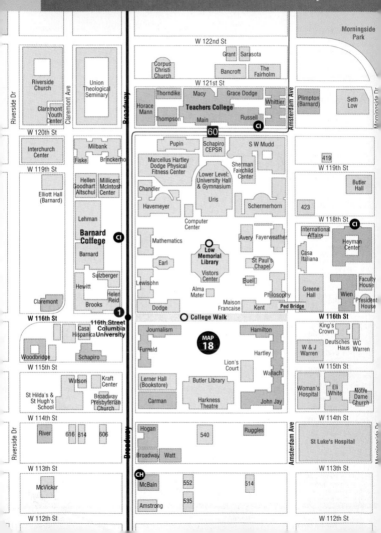

General Information

NFT Map: 18
Morningside Heights: 2960 Broadway & 116th St
Medical Center: 601 W 168th St
Phone: 212-854-1754
Website: www.columbia.edu
Students Enrolled: 23,650
Endowment: Market value as of June 30, 2003
$4.343 billion

Overview

Founded in 1754 and originally known as King's College, Columbia University is one of the country's most prestigious universities.

After residing in two different downtown locations, Columbia moved to its present campus (designed by McKim, Mead, and White) in 1897. At the time, the surrounding area was sparsely populated, but during the more than one hundred years since, the neighborhood of Morningside Heights has expanded considerably. Today, the town/gown relations in Morningside Heights are complicated. On the one hand, Columbia is a focal point for the neighborhood, providing local businesses with students ready to part with their cash. On the other hand, community members often oppose the school's policies, and there's resentment for what some perceive as heavy-handedness on Columbia's part. The most famous of these struggles came in response to Columbia's plans to build a gymnasium in Morningside Park. Thankfully, the park was saved, so that today people can continue to avoid walking through it.

Undeterred by previous setbacks (or perhaps having learned how to get around them), Columbia's most recent plan is to expand its campus into Manhattanville, north of 125th Street between Broadway and Twelfth Avenue. The Manhattanville campus will be conveniently located between the Morningside Campus and the Columbia University Medical Center. The plans have sparked opposition from the neighborhood, but Columbia is trying a more collaborative approach than it has in the past.

Columbia's medical school was the first in the nation. The school is affiliated with the Columbia-Presbyterian Medical Center in Washington Heights and encompasses the graduate schools of medicine, dentistry, nursing, and public health. Columbia is the only Ivy League university with a journalism school. The school is also affiliated with Barnard College, Jewish Theological Seminary, Teachers College, and Union Theological Seminary.

Numerous movies have been filmed on or around the campus including *Ghostbusters*, *Hannah and Her Sisters*, and *Spiderman I* and *II*.

Notable alums and faculty include artists James Cagney, Art Garfunkel, Georgia O'Keeffe, Rodgers and Hammerstein, Paul Robeson, and Twyla Tharp; critic Lionel Trilling; baseball player Lou Gehrig; and writers Isaac Asimov, Joseph Heller, Zora Neale Hurston, and Herman Wouk. Business alumni include Warren Buffet, Alfred Knopf, Joseph Pulitzer, and Milton Friedman, while politicians Madeline Albright, Dwight Eisenhower, Alexander Hamilton, Robert Moses, Franklin Delano Roosevelt, and Teddy Roosevelt all graced the university's classrooms. In the field of law, Benjamin Cardozo, Ruth Bader Ginsburg, Charles Evans Hughes, and John Jay called Columbia home, and Stephen Jay Gould, Margaret Mead, and Benjamin Spock make the list of notable science alumni.

Tuition

Columbia undergraduate tuition and fees for the 2004-05 academic year were $30,260 plus $9,096 for room and board. Graduate school fees vary by college.

Sports

Columbia's football team, the Lions, was really, really bad back in the '80s. In fact, they almost set the record for straight losses by a major college football team when they dropped 44 consecutive games between 1983 and 1988. Not much has changed—their 1-9 record in 2004 was par for the course. The Lions play their mostly Ivy league opponents at Lawrence A. Wein Stadium (Baker Field), located way up at the top of Manhattan.

Columbia excels in other sports including crew, fencing, golf, tennis, and sailing. The university is represented by 29 men's and women's teams in the NCAA Division I. It also has the oldest wrestling team in the country.

Culture on Campus

Columbia features dance, film, music, theater, readings, and talks. Venues include: the Macy Gallery at the Teacher's College, which exhibits works by a variety of artists, including faculty and children's artwork; the Miller Theatre at 2960 Broadway, which primarily features musical performances; the student-run Postcrypt Art Gallery in the basement of St. Paul's Chapel; the Theatre of the Riverside Church for theatrical performances; and the Wallach Art Gallery on the 8th floor of Schermerhorn Hall, featuring art and architecture exhibits. Check the website for a calendar of events.

Phone Numbers

Morningside Campus 212-854-1754
Health Services Campus 212-305-2500
Visitors Center 212-854-4900
Public Affairs 212-854-5573
University Development and Alumni Relations 212-870-3100
Library Information 212-854-2271
School of Architecture 212-854-3510
School of the Arts 212-854-2875
Graduate School of the Arts 212-854-4737
School of Dental and Oral Surgery 212-305-6726
School of Engineering 212-854-2522
Graduate School of Engineering 212-854-2931
School of General Studies 212-854-2772
School of International Affairs 212-854-6216
Graduate School of Journalism 212-854-8608
School of Law 212-854-2670
School of Nursing 212-305-5756
School of Public Health 212-305-3927
School of Social Work 212-854-2856

Parks & Places · **New York University**

General Information

NFT Map: 6
Phone: 212-998-INFO
Website: www.nyu.edu
Enrollment: 51,901

Overview

New York University is such a presence in the Village these days that people forget (or don't even know) that the school used to have its main campus in the Bronx and was on the brink of bankruptcy in the mid-'70s. The financial strain required the school to abandon its University Heights campus, as well as drop its engineering school and other programs. Of course, now that NYU is on its feet again, it's considering re-acquiring an engineering school by subsuming Polytechnic University.

The expansion of NYU during recent years has not been seen by local residents as a positive development. Some Village folks blame NYU's sprawl for higher rents and diminished quirkiness. On the other hand, the students are a financial boon for businesses in the area, and many historical buildings (such as the row houses on Washington Square) are owned and kept in good condition by the university.

NYU comprises fifteen colleges, schools, and faculties, including the well-regarded Stern School of Business, the School of Law, and the Tisch School of Arts. It also has a school of Continuing and Professional Studies. Almost 34,000 people applied to NYU for undergraduate school last year; 12,008 were accepted. About 35% of the freshman class was from the NYC metro area.

It's also worth noting that the school holds a precious culinary pearl: the only Chick-fil-A location for miles (the next closest is in Paramus, NJ). Located within the Weinstein Hall dining facility (5-11 University Pl) members of the general public are welcome to indulge in their delicious crispy chicken sandwiches complete with sweet, buttered buns and two tangy pickles. Perfection.

Tuition

Tuition costs roughly $16,000 per semester for undergrads (closer to $18,000 for Tisch), while graduate schools generally charge by points taken (except for Stern, which costs nearly $20,000 per semester). Check the NYU website for specific tuition information.

Sports

NYU isn't big on athletics. They don't have a football team. (Where would they play anyway?) It does have a number of other sports teams, though. The school competes in Division III and its mascot is the Bobcat.

Culture on Campus

The Grey Art Gallery usually has something cool (www.nyu.edu/greyart), and the new Skirball Center for the Performing Arts hosts live performances (www.skirballcenter.nyu.edu). But NYU doesn't host nearly as many events as decent liberal arts schools in the middle of nowhere. Why should it? It's in Greenwich Village, surrounded by some of the world's best rock and jazz clubs, and on the same island as 700+ art galleries, thousands of restaurants, tons of revival and new cinema, etc...so why bother? This is both the blessing and the curse of NYU—no true "campus," but situated in the middle of the greatest cultural square mileage in the world.

Transportation

NYU runs its own campus transportation service for students, faculty, staff, and alumnus with school ID cards. They run 7 am to 2 am weekdays and 10 am to 2 am weekends.

Route A: 200 Water St (South Street Seaport) to 715 Broadway (near 4th St), stopping at the Lafayette and Broome Street dorms on the way.
Route B: Woolworth Building to 715 Broadway, passing through the same areas as Route A.
Route C: Sixth Ave to Spring St and 14th Street to First Ave, passing through SoHo, NoHo, and the East Village.
Route D: 715 Broadway loop through the West Village via the Greenwich Street dorm.
Route E: Midtown Center (SCPS near 42nd St and Fifth Ave) to 715 Broadway, stopping at the NYU Medical Center on the east side and passing through the Gramercy Park area.

General Phone Numbers

NYU Information Center: 212-998-INFO (4636)
NYU Protection Services: 212-998-2222
Undergraduate Admissions: 212-998-4500
Financial Aid: 212-998-4444
University Registrar: 212-998-4800
University Employment Office: 212-998-1250
Student Health Services: 212-443-1000
Kimmel Center for University Life: 212-998-4900
Bobst Library: 212-998-2505
Coles Sports Center: 212-998-2020
NYU Card: 212-443-CARD (2273)

Academic Phone Numbers

All undergraduate programs: 212-998-4500
Summer Session: 212-998-2292
Dental School: 212-998-9818
School of Education: 212-998-5030
Ehrenkranz School of Social Work: 212-998-5910
Gallatin School of Individualized Study: 212-998-7370
Graduate School of Arts & Science 212-998-8050
Graduate Computer Science 212-998-3063
Law School 212-998-6060
School of Medicine 212-263-5290
School of Continuing and Professional 212-998-7100
 Studies Degree Program
School of Continuing and Professional 212-790-1335
 Studies Real Estate Institute
School of Continuing and Professional 212-998-7080
 Studies Non-Credit Program
Stern School of Business 212-998-0600
Tisch School of the Arts 212-998-1918
Wagner School of Public 212-998-7414
 Administration

Overview

Popular among residents of the East Village and the Lower East Side, East River Park is a long, thin slice of land, sandwiched between FDR Drive and the East River, that runs from Jackson Street up to 14th Street. East River Park was built in the early '40s as part of FDR Drive (another Robert Moses project). The Park's recent refurbishments have made its sporting facilities some of the best Manhattan has to offer. The East River Esplanade, a walkway encircling many parts of the East Side, is a constant work-in-progress. The city's plan is to some day create one continuous green stretch from Battery Park to 125th street. This plan is part of a larger, ambitious East Coast Greenway initiative (www.greenway.org), which could eventually connect the esplanade with a continuous greenway stretching from Boston to Washington DC.

Attractions

The usually quiet park comes alive in the summer and on weekends. Hundreds of families barbeque in the areas between the athletic fields, blaring music and eating to their hearts' content. Others take leisurely strolls or jogs along the East River Esplanade, which offers some of the most dramatic views of the East River and Brooklyn. Many have turned the park's unused areas into unofficial dog runs, places for pick-up games of ultimate frisbee or soccer, and sunbathing areas. It's common to see fishermen along the water trying to catch fish—believe it or not, people actually catch bluefish and striped bass. Not that we have to tell you, but nothing caught in the East River should be eaten—while the water quality has improved dramatically, it's still full of pollutants.

Sports

The sports facilities at East River Park have undergone heavy reconstruction. The park now includes facilities for football, softball, basketball, cricket, soccer, and tennis. Call 212-387-7678 for information on reserving a field or court. Thankfully, many of the fields have been re-surfaced with a resilient synthetic turf—a smart move, given the amount of use the park gets by all the different sports leagues.

Facilities

There are three bathroom facilities located in the park—one at the tennis courts, one at the soccer/

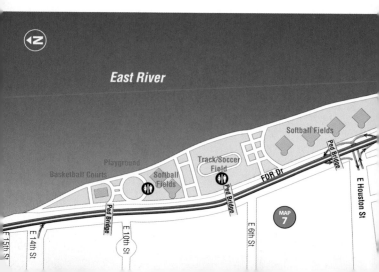

track field, and one up in the northern part of the park by a children's playground. The reconstruction has provided the park with new benches, game tables, a harbor seals spray sprinkler with animal art, and new drinking fountains. Aside from the occasional guy with a grocery cart full of cold drinks or a pushcart with flavored ice, there aren't any food or drink facilities close by. Your best bet is to arrive at the park with any supplies you might need—if that's too difficult, try a bodega on Avenue D.

Safety

The park is relatively safe, especially during the daytime, but we would not recommend hanging out there—or in any other city park, for that matter—after dark, even if you're just passing through.

Esoterica

Plans for the fancy $3.5 million amphitheater/restaurant that was to replace the sad-looking, abandoned, graffiti-covered Corlears Hook Pavilion band shell have been canned. Built in 1941, and closed since 1971, the Corlears Hook Pavilion was the original home of Joseph Papp's Shakespeare in the Park. A less ambitious reconstruction took place

in 2001, and with new seating, a renovated band shell, and a good scrubbing, the facility is currently open for use.

How to Get There

Two FDR Drive exits will get you very close to East River Park—the Houston Street exit and the Grand Street exit. Technically, cars are not allowed in the park. There is some parking available at the extreme south end of the park by Jackson Street off the access road, but it's hard to get to and poorly marked. Plan to find street parking just west of the FDR and cross over on a footbridge.

If you are taking the subway, you'd better have your hiking boots on—the fact that the closest subway (the **F** train at Delancey/Essex Street) is so far away (at least four avenue blocks) is one of the reasons East River Park has stayed mainly a neighborhood park. Fortunately, if you're into buses, the **14** and the **8** get you pretty close. Regardless of the bus or subway lines, you will have to cross one of the five pedestrian bridges that traverse the FDR Drive, unless you approach via the East River Esplanade.

General Information

NFT Map:	9
Address:	350 Fifth Ave (& 34th St)
Phone:	212-736-3100
Website:	www.esbnyc.com
Observatory Hours:	9:30 am to midnight, last admission 11:15 pm.

Observatory Admission: $13 for adults, $12 for children aged 12-17, seniors, military with ID, and $8 children aged 6-11. Toddlers (under 5) and military personnel in uniform get in free.

Overview

The 1,454-foot Empire State Building was built during the depths of the depression in around fourteen months—an average rate of four-and-a-half stories per week. After constructing the building in record time, all subsequent projects in New York have achieved the opposite.

There are two observation areas—the open terrace on the 86th floor is open to the general public, the glass-enclosed 102nd floor has been closed for some time. The ESB does not accommodate private events, but the chapel on the 80th floor hosts a giant group wedding on Valentine's Day—sign up by November 30th. Also of note is the NYC Roadrunners Club's annual Run-Up, where runners try to bound up all 1,860 steps in under eleven minutes.

The Empire State Building is more than an attraction. Its antenna is used by more than twenty radio and TV stations to broadcast to the metro area. The building also contains over 2.1 million square feet of office space. The ESB website has information on leasing, as well as building history, trivia, and a complete schedule of events.

The Lights

The top 30 floors of the ESB have automated color fluorescent lighting, which is lit for holidays and other days of recognition, celebration, and memoriam. Between holidays and events, white lighting is used. The following semi-official lighting schedule lists colors from bottom to top as they appear from the street. Since there are additions to the schedule every year, some color patterns you see may not be listed.

Lighting Schedule (for updates/changes, check www.esbnyc.com)

- January · Martin Luther King, Jr Day
- January · March of Dimes
- January/Febuary · Lunar New Year
- February 14 · Valentine's Day
- February · President's Day
- February · Westminster Kennel Club
- February · Swisspeaks Festival for Switzerland
- February · World Cup Archery Championship
- March 17 · St Patrick's Day
- March · Greek Independence Day
- March · Equal Parents Day/ Childrens' Rights
- March · Wales/St David's Day
- March · Oscar Week in NYC
- March · Colon Cancer Awareness
- March · Red Cross Month
- March–April · Spring/Easter Week
- April · Earth Day
- April · Child Abuse Prevention
- April · National Osteoporosis Society
- April · Rain Forest Day
- April · Israel Independence Day
- April · Dutch Queen's Day
- April · Tartan Day
- May · Muscular Dystrophy
- May · Armed Forces Day
- May · Memorial Day
- May · Police Memorial Day
- May · Fire Department Memorial Day
- May · Haitian Culture Awareness
- June 14 · Flag Day
- June · Portugal Day
- June · NYC Triathlon
- June · Stonewall Anniversary/Gay Pride
- July 4 · Independence Day
- July · Bahamas Independence Day
- July · Bastille Day
- July · Peru Independence

- July · Columbia Heritage & Independence
- August · US Open
- August · Jamaica Independence Day
- August · India Independence Day
- August · Pakistan Independence Day
- September · Mexico Independence Day
- September · Labor Day
- September · Brazil Independence Day
- September · Pulaski Day
- September · Race for the Cure
- September · Switzerland admitted to the UN
- September · Qatar Independence
- September · Fleet Week/Support our Servicemen and Servicewomen/ Memorial for 9/11
- September · Feast of San Gennaro
- October · Breast Cancer Awareness
- October · German Reunification Day
- October · Columbus Day
- October 24 · United Nations Day
- October · Big Apple Circus
- October · Pennant/World Series win for the Yankees
- October · Pennant/World Series win for the Mets [Ha!]
- October · NY Knicks Opening Day
- October–November · Autumn
- October · Walk to End Domestic Violence
- November · NYC Marathon
- November · Veterans' Day
- November · Alzheimer's Awareness
- December · First night of Hannukah
- December · "Day Without Art/Night Without Lights"/AIDS Awareness
- December-January 7 (with interruptions) · Holiday Season

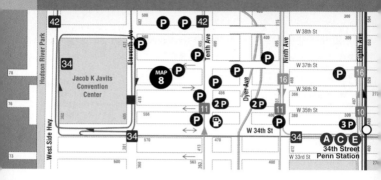

LEVEL ONE

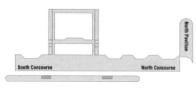

1E | 1D | 1C | 1B | 1A

LEVEL THREE

3E | 3D | 3B | 3A

LEVEL TWO

North Pavilion

South Concourse | North Concourse

LEVEL FOUR

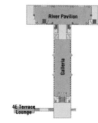

River Pavilion

Galleria

4E Terrace Lounge

General Information

NFT Map: 8
Address: 655 W 34th St
Website: www.javitscenter.com
Phone Number: 212-216-2000
Fax Number: 212-216-2588

Overview

The Jacob K. Javits Center, designed by the firm I.M. Pei & Partners and completed in 1986, is a massive glass-and-steel behemoth of a convention hall next to the Hudson River between 34th and 40th Streets. It was built with the purpose of providing a place for big trade shows, conventions, and expositions, but its true purpose is clearly to annoy anyone who has to go there, since it's in the middle of nowhere with no subway link. If you do get there, you might find that the glass walls and ceiling are impressive, as is the center's capacity and flexibility, but as far as convention centers go, it's definitely not up to the standards of other big cities (it now ranks about 14th in terms of its size). Still, it replaced the Coliseum, which somehow managed to be worse than the Javits.

There's been talk of expanding the center, along with building an on-site hotel and a stadium for the Jets nearby, but, as of now, there is no groundbreaking ceremony in sight.

Usually a massive build-up of expensive buildings in a small-scale neighborhood is a bad idea, but in this case it might be an okay compromise, since the surrounding area is currently quite bleak and sketchy. Exactly why nice restaurants and hotels didn't spring up around the city's biggest meeting place for business travelers is a mystery, but as it is, Eleventh Avenue and the surrounding streets offer little in the way of eating options and accommodations.

ATMs

CH · Chase · Level One
CH · Chase · Level Three

Services

Coat Check   Lost and Found
Concierge Services   Mailboxes Etc
First Aid   My New York Office
Hudson News   Shoeshine
Information

Food

The food at the Javits Center is, of course, rapaciously expensive, and, if you're exhibiting, usually sold out by 2:30 in the afternoon. Our suggestion is to look for people handing out Chinese food menus and have them deliver to your booth. (And yes, they take credit cards. And yes, it's bad Chinese food.)

Asian Star   Gourmet Coffee Bar
The Bakery   The Grille
Boar's Head Deli   Korean Market
Caliente Cab Company   Kosher Food and Sushi
Carvel Ice Cream Bakery   Nathan's
Cocktail Lounge   Panini
Dai Kichi Sushi   Villa Cucina Italiana
The Dining Car   Villa Pizza
Feast of the Dragon

How to Get There—Mass Transit

Until they extend that **7** train, there's no direct subway access to the center. The closest subway stop is at 34th Street/Penn Station **A C E 1 2 3** but even that's a good 4- to 5-block hike away. You can also take the buses from the 42nd Street **42** and 34th Street **34** subway stops, which will both drop you off right outside the center.

There are also numerous shuttle buses that run to various participating hotels and other locales free of charge for convention goers. Schedules and routes vary for each convention, so ask at the information desk on the first floor.

From New Jersey, the NY Waterway operates a ferry from Weehawken, NJ that ships you across the Hudson River to 39th Street and Twelfth Avenue in 4 minutes, dropping you just one block from the Javits Center. The ferry leaves every 10-15 minutes during peak hours. Call 1-800-53-FERRY for a schedule and more information

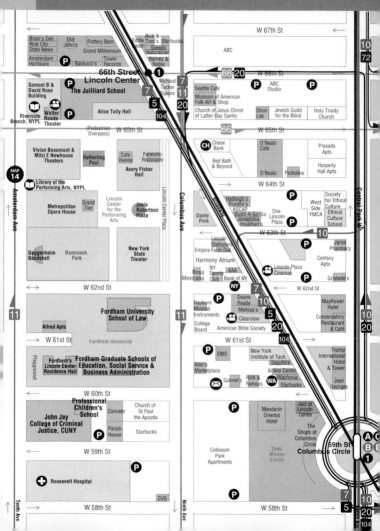

Lincoln Center / Columbus Circle

Lincoln Center / Columbus Circle

General Information

Website: . . . . www.lincolncenter.org
General Information: 212-546-2656 (212-LINCOLN)
Customer Service: 212-875-5456
Alice Tully Hall: 212-875-5050
Avery Fisher Hall: 212-875-5030
The Chamber Music Society: 212-875-5775
Film Society of Lincoln Center: 212-875-5600
Guided Tours: 212-875-5350
Jazz at Lincoln Center: 212-258-9800
The Juilliard School: 212-799-5000
Lincoln Center Theater: 212-362-7600

The Metropolitan Opera House: 212-362-6000
New York City Ballet and Opera: 212-870-5500
New York Philharmonic: 212-875-5700
New York State Theater: 212-870-5570
Parking Garage: 212-874-9021
Walter Reade Theater: 212-875-5601
Ticket Purchase Phone Numbers
Alice Tully and Avery Fisher Halls: 212-721-6500
Film Society of Lincoln Center: 212-496-3809
MovieFone, Walter Reade Theater: 212-777-FILM
TeleCharge, Lincoln Center Theater: 212-239-6200
Ticketmaster, New York State Theater: 212-307-4100
Ticketmaster, Met & Ballet: 212-307-4100

Overview

Lincoln Center is one of Manhattan's most vibrant and romantic spots. It's almost obscene how much culture is packed into this four-square-block area—not bad for what was once a terrible, poverty-ridden section of New York. Even Robert Moses got some things right.

In addition to its performance spaces, Lincoln Center also boasts some of the city's signature art and architectural gems. Henry Moore's "Reclining Figure" is the centerpiece of the reflecting pool and Mark Chagall's murals grace the foyer of the Metropolitan Opera House. Philip Johnson's Plaza Fountain anchors the entire center, creating an intimate space where New Yorkers can go to forget about their appallingly high rents and pretend they're in the scene from *Moonstruck* where Cher and Nicholas Cage meet to see *La Boheme*.

Who Lives Where

Lincoln Center is home to so many different companies, groups, and troupes that we figured we'd provide a list of who is where. Perhaps the most confusing thing about Lincoln Center is that the "Lincoln Center Theater" is actually two theaters—the Vivian Beaumont and the Mitzi E. Newhouse Theaters. Jazz at Lincoln Center moved into the Frederick P. Rose Hall in new AOL/Time Warner Center; it's the first space in the world designed specifically for jazz education, performance, and broadcast.

American Ballet Theater — Metropolitan Opera House
Chamber Music Society — Samuel B. and David Rose Building
Film Society of Lincoln Center — Samuel B. and David Rose Building
Jazz at Lincoln Center — Frederick P. Rose Hall
Julliard Orchestra & Symphony — Alice Tully Hall
Metropolitan Opera Company — Metropolitan Opera House
Mitzi E. Newhouse Theater — Lincoln Center Theater Building

Mostly Mozart Festival — Avery Fisher Hall
New York City Ballet — New York State Theater
New York City Opera — New York State Theater
New York Philharmonic — Avery Fisher Hall
School of American Ballet — Samuel B. and David Rose Building
Stanley Kaplan Penthouse Performance Space — Samuel B. and David Rose Building
Vivian Beaumont Theater — Lincoln Center Theater
Walter Reade Theater — Samuel B. and David Rose

Columbus Circle

Columbus Circle has seen a major overhaul in the past several years, including the addition of an always understated Trump International Hotel and Tower, the destruction of the New York Coliseum, and completion of the new AOL/Time Warner Center and Mandarin Oriental Hotel. With a mammoth Whole Foods, offices, movies, and new condominiums, Columbus Circle is proving to be a virtual epicenter (or maybe just a glorified shopping mall) in the city that's already considered "The Center of the Universe."

How to Get There

Lincoln Center is right off Broadway and only a few blocks north of Columbus Circle, which makes getting there easy. The closest subway is the 66th Street 1, 9, which has an exit right on the edge of the center. Lincoln Center is also an easy walk from the trains that roll into Columbus Circle Ⓐ Ⓒ Ⓑ Ⓓ ❶. If you prefer above-ground transportation, the ⑤ ⑦ ⑩ ⑪ ⑯ ⑩④ bus lines all stop within one block of Lincoln Center. There is also a parking lot underneath Lincoln Center for those bent on driving.

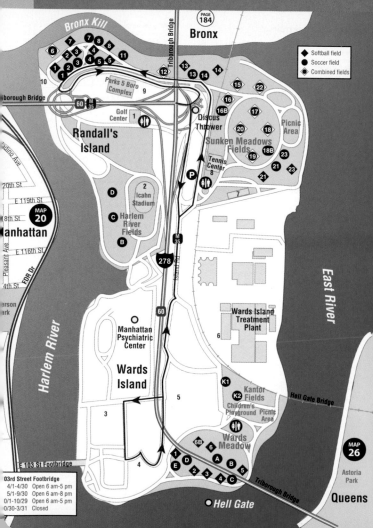

Bronx Kill

PAGE
184

Bronx

◆ Softball field
● Soccer field
◉ Combined fields

Triborough Bridge

10

Parks 5 Boro
Complex

9

Triborough Bridge

60

M
35

Golf
Center 1

Discus
Thrower

Randall's
Island

15 22

16

16B

17

20 18

Picnic
Area

Sunken Meadows
Fields

18B

19 23

21 23

21

Tennis
Center 8

P

7

M
35

278

2

Icahn
Stadium

D

C Harlem
River
Fields

B

20th St

E 119th St

8th St

Manhattan

E 116th St

MAP
20

Pleasant Ave

4th St

Pelham Ave

FDR Dr

erson
Park

60

Harlem River

Manhattan
Psychiatric
Center

Wards
Island

East River

Wards Island
Treatment
Plant

6

Hell Gate Bridge

K1

K2 Kantor
Fields

Children's
Playground Picnic
Area

3

5

Wards
Meadow

6B 6

A

1 D

B

E

D

A B

2 3 4 C 5

4

E 103 ST Footbridge

Triborough Bridge

MAP
26

Astoria
Park

Hell Gate

Queens

03rd Street Footbridge
4/1-4/30   Open 6 am-5 pm
5/1-9/30   Open 6 am-8 pm
0/1-10/29   Open 6 am-5 pm
0/30-3/31   Closed

General Information

Randall's Island Sports Foundation: 212-830-7722; www.risf.org

Overview

Most New Yorkers associate Randall's Island solely with the Triborough Bridge, not realizing the island has 440 acres of parkland for public use. In fact, Randall's and Wards Islands, connected by landfill, contain some of Manhattan's best athletic fields and parks. Originally conceived of and built by the infamous Robert Moses, Randall's and Wards Island Park is now administered by the Randall's Island Sports Foundation. Their mission is to continue to improve and upgrade the park for the residents of New York City.

Phase I of their very big plan included replacing Downing Stadium with the recently completed, state-of-the-art Icahn Track & Field Stadium and the adjacent amphitheater for concerts. The Foundation is also improving all bike and pedestrian trails and renovating the soccer and softball fields. Future phases include adding a cricket field and ferry service, and there's even talk of a water park opening in 2006. Hopefully part of their plan will include some food facilities. As it is, the only food available is the snack bar in the golf center, and the lunch trucks scattered around Icahn Stadium and the Fire Training Center.

Just south of Wards Island lies Hell Gate, a treacherous body of water where the Harlem and East Rivers meet. Many commercial and private vessals have come to grief in this stretch of water.

How to Get There

By Car: Take the Triborough Bridge, exit left to Randall's Island. There's a $3.50 toll to get on the island with your car. It's free to leave!

By Subway/Bus: From Manhattan: take the **4** **5** **6** train to 125th Street, then transfer on the corner of 125th Street and Lexington Avenue for the **35** bus to Randall's Island. There's a bus about every 40 minutes during the day. From Queens: take the **51** from 61st Street-Woodside.

By Foot: A pedestrian footbridge at 103rd Street was built by Robert Moses in the '50s to provide Harlem residents access to the recreational facilities of the parks after then-City Council President Newbold Morris criticized the lack of facilities in Harlem. Today, the bridge's hours are seasonal and limited. See timetable on map.

1 **Randall's Island Golf Center** · 212-427-5689 · The golf center on Randall's Island has a driving range open year-round with 80 heated stalls, along with two 18-hole mini-golf courses, nine batting cages, and a snack bar. A weekend shuttle service is available every hour on the hour, 10 am-5 pm from Manhattan (86th Street and Third Avenue) and costs $10 round-trip. Summer hours are 6 am-11 pm Tuesday-Sunday and 11 am-11 pm on Mondays, with off-season hours from 8 am-8 pm Tuesday-Sunday and 1 am-8 pm on Mondays.

2 **Icahn Track & Field Stadium** · Named for financier Carl Icahn, the 10,000-seat stadium is the only state-of-the-art outdoor track and field venue in New York City with a 400-meter running track and a regulation-size soccer field.

3 **Supportive Employment Center** · 212-534-3866

4 **Charles H. Gay Shelter Care Center for Men** —Volunteers of America - Greater New York · 212-369-8900 · www.voa-gny.org

5 **Odyssey House Drug Rehab Center**—Mabon Building · 212-426-6677

6 **DEP Water Pollution Control Plant** · 718-595-6600 · www.ci.nyc.ny.us/html/dep/html/drainage.html

7 **Fire Department Training Center** · The NYC Fire Academy is located on 27 acres of landfill on the east side of Randall's Island. In an effort to keep the city's "bravest" in shape, the academy utilizes the easily accessible 68 acres of parkland for physical fitness programs. The ultra-cool training facility includes 11 Universal Studios-like buildings for simulations training, a 200,000 gallon water supply tank, gasoline and diesel fuel pumps, and a 300-car parking lot. In addition, the New York Transit Authority installed tracks and subway cars for learning and developing techniques to battle subway fires and other emergencies. It's really too bad they don't sell tickets and offer tours!

8 **Tennis Center** · 212-860-2863 · 11 outdoor courts. Indoor courts heated for winter use.

9 **Robert Moses Building** · We're sure many an urban planning student has made a pilgrimage here.

10 **NYPD** · They launch cool-looking police boats from here.

(209)

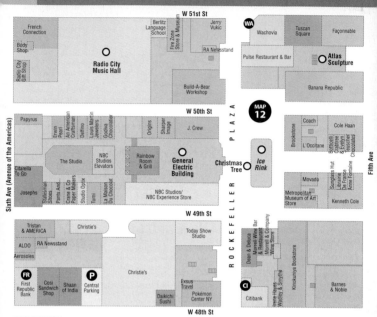

W 51st St

French Connection

Body Shop

Radio City Gift Shop

Radio City Music Hall

Berlitz Language School

Fire Zone Store & Museum

Jerry Vukic

RA Newsstand

Build-A-Bear Workshop

WA Wachovia

Tuscan Square

Façonnable

Pulse Restaurant & Bar

Atlas Sculpture

Banana Republic

W 50th St

Sixth Ave (Avenue of the Americas)

Papyrus

Erwin Pearl

An American Craftsman

Delfino

Louis Martin Jewelers

Godiva Chocolatier

The Studio

NBC Studios Elevators

Rainbow Room & Grill

Citarella To Go

Crane & Co Paper Makers

Josephs

Statesman Shoes

Parts And...

Studio Optix

La Maison Du Chocolat

Tumi

NBC Studios/ NBC Experience Store

Origins

Sharper Image

J. Crew

MAP 12

PLAZA

Christmas Tree

Ice Rink

General Electric Building

Coach

Cole Haan

Brookstone

L'Occitane

Botticelli, Crabtree & Evelyn, De France, Teuscher Chocolates

Movado

Metropolitan Museum of Art Store

Sunglass Hut, Librairie, Anne Fontaine

Kenneth Cole

Fifth Ave

W 49th St

Tristan & AMERICA

Christie's

Today Show Studio

ALDO

RA Newsstand

Aerosoles

FR First Republic Bank

Cosi Sandwich Shop

Shaan of India

P Central Parking

Christie's

Daikichi Sushi

Exsus Travel

Pokémon Center NY

Dean & Deluca

Morrell Wine Bar & Restaurant

Morrell & Company Wine Store

ROCKEFELLER

Irene Hayes Wadley & Smythe

Kinokuniya Bookstore

CI Citibank

Barnes & Noble

W 48th St

STREET LEVEL

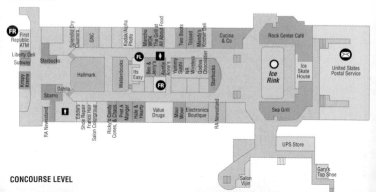

FR First Republic ATM

Liberty Deli Subway

Krispy Kreme

Starbucks

Dahlia

Sbarro

RA Newsstand

Splenda Dry Cleaners

GNC

Hallmark

Edstie's Shoe Repair Franco Hair Salon Colorgroup

Ricky's Candy Cones, & Chocs

Koda/Alpha Photo

Waldenbooks

Its Easy

FL

Ben & Jerry's

Pret A Manger

Hale & Hearty

Mancha Wok

Aunte's

Yummy Sushi

Value Drugs

FR

Maui Wowi

The Grillat All About Food

Anne's

NR Wireless

Electronics Boutique

Two Boots

Tossed

Mendy's Kosher Deli

Godiva Chocolatier

Starbucks

Cucina & Co

Rock Center Café

Ice Rink

Ice Skate House

Sea Grill

United States Postal Service

UPS Store

Gary's Top Shoe

Salon Vijin

CONCOURSE LEVEL

General Information

NFT Map:	12
Phone:	212-632-3975
Website:	www.rockefellercenter.com
Rink Phone:	212-332-7654
Rink Website:	www.therinkatrockcenter.com
NBC Tour Phone:	212-664-3700

Overview

Rockefeller Center is a three-square-block complex of retail, entertainment, dining, and office facilities. Architect Hugh Hardy put it best when he said that the center "invented Midtown," and it remains one of the focal points of the area to this day. Like the Empire State Building, Rockefeller Center was built in the midst of the Great Depression. Its exterior and interior possess the flourishes and flamboyant characteristics of Art Deco architecture.

Among the prominent businesses that operate out of "Rock Center" are the Associated Press, General Electric, and NBC (the *Today Show* studio overlooks the main plaza of the center). Quite a few television shows tape at "30 Rock," including *Saturday Night Live* and *Late Night with Conan O'Brien*.

Rockefeller Center is perhaps most associated with Christmas, thanks to its gargantuan tree and the ice-skating rink, St. Patrick's holiday services, and the Rockettes at Radio City Music Hall. With all of the stores in the center and on Fifth Avenue, Rock Center is also a major holiday shopping haunt.

Where to Eat

Rock Center isn't a prime dining destination, but you won't starve if you find yourself in the area. For cheaper fare, try places down in the Concourse such as **Cosi**, **Pret A Manger**, or **Two Boots**. Don't forget about **Ben & Jerry's** and **Krispy Kreme** for dessert, as well as the magnificently named **Ricky's Candy, Cones, and Chaos**. For fancier food, try the **Sea Grill** (overlooking the skating rink), or the **Rainbow Room** on the center's 65th floor. The food may not be the best New York has to offer—you're essentially paying for the view. **Tuscan Square**, 16 W 51st St, offers pretty decent Italian, though prices are a bit inflated here as well. Many restaurants in Rockefeller Center are open on Saturdays but, aside from the "nice" restaurants, only a few open their doors on Sundays.

Where to Shop

Some have called Rockefeller Center the "first mall," which is ironic, since New Yorkers have such an aversion to them. But the concourse level is undeniably mall-like—heck, there's a S**harper Image** *and* a **Brookstone**. There are, however, a few interesting stores in Rockefeller Center and the surrounding area:

FireZone Store and Museum • 34 W 51st St • Official seller of FDNY merchandise.
Kinokuniya Bookstore • 10 W 49th St • Japanese language and Asian-themed English language books.
La Maison Du Chocolat • 30 Rockefeller Center • French chocolates.
Librairie De France • 610 Fifth Ave • Foreign bookseller, including French language texts, children's books, travel guides, and maps.
Teuscher Chocolates • 620 Fifth Ave • German chocolates.

There are also some useful services on the Concourse, including **Dahlia** (flowers), **Eddie's Shoe Repair**, **Kodak/Alpha Photo**, and **Splendid Cleaners**. They are all conveniently located near the entrance to the Sixth Avenue subway (Ⓑ Ⓓ Ⓕ Ⓥ). There's a **UPS** office in the area perpendicular to the **Sea Grill**. But they, like many of the stores in the Concourse, are closed on weekends. Unless you work in Rockefeller Center, it's not likely that you'll need to use them anyway.

The Rink

The skating rink opens during Columbus Day weekend and closes in early April to make way for the Rink Bar. Each skating day is divided into hour and a half-long skating sessions, with a half-hour break for the Zamboni to clear the ice. The rink opens at 8:30 am and each new session starts at two-hour intervals after that (10:30, 12:30, etc) until midnight. Skating prices range between $9 and $17 for adults, depending on the day you visit. (Weekends and holidays are the most expensive times to skate.) The skating rate for children ranges from $7 to $12 per session. Skate rental costs an additional $8 for all skaters. Lessons are available for $30 during the week and $32 during the weekend—call 212-332-7655 for more information. In spite of the hefty skating rates, the rink gets crowded, so plan your skating for the morning or early afternoon of a weekday, or very early on the weekend.

Overview

Once upon a time, Roosevelt Island was populated by criminals, the sick, and the mentally ill, but that's all changed (no shortage in Manhattan, however). This slender tract of land between Manhattan and Queens has become prime real estate for families, UN officials, and "Grandpa" Al Lewis from *The Munsters*.

The 147-acre island, formerly known as "Welfare Island" because of its population of outcasts, was re-named after Franklin D. Roosevelt in 1973, when the island began changing its image. The first residential housing complex opened in 1975. Visitors can check out some of the island's monuments, including the Smallpox Hospital, the Blackwell House (fourth oldest house in the city), and the dreaded Octagon (site of a 19th-century mental hospital). The lighthouse that stands on the island's northern tip was designed by James Renwick, Jr., of St. Patrick's Cathedral fame. The island's northern tip is also a popular destination for fishermen with iron gullets. If you experience a major medical emergency on Roosevelt Island, you're in luck—the tiny island is home to two hospitals. The island's main drag, Main Street (where did they come up with the name?), resembles a cement-block college campus built around 1968.

Residents of Roosevelt Island take pride in their 30-year-old community, describing it as a place where people greet each other in the street and kids of all stripes play together. The housing situation on the island is becoming increasingly complicated, with many landlords looking to switch from rent-controlled status to market rates. Merchants have experienced problems too—lack of foot traffic, high rent, and high utility bills have forced many businesses to close. On a more positive note, Roosevelt Island offers dramatic views of midtown Manhattan. Unless you live there, the superb view is really the only reason to stay after dark; Roosevelt Island's only bar closed in early 2005 due to lack of patronage and noise complaints.

How to Get There

Roosevelt Island can be reached via the 🄵 subway line, but its much more fun to take the tram. You can board it at 60th Street and Second Avenue in Manhattan—look for the big hulking mass drifting through the sky. To get there by car, take the Queensboro Bridge and follow signs for the 21st Street-North exit. Go north on 21st Street and make a left on 36th Avenue. Go west on 36th Avenue and cross over the red Roosevelt Island Bridge. The only legal parking is at Motorgate Plaza at the end of the bridge at Main Street.

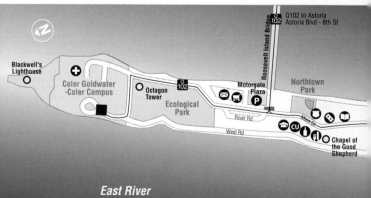

Parks & Places · **Roosevelt Island**

$ Banks

CU · **Montauk Credit Union** · 559 Main St

✚ Hospitals

· **Coler Goldwater-Coler Campus (no ER)** · 900 Main St
· **Coler Goldwater-Goldwater Campus (no ER)** ·
  1 Main St

O Landmarks

· **Blackwell House** · 591 Main St
· **Blackwell's Lighthouse**
· **Chapel of the Good Shepherd**
· **Octagon Tower**
· **Smallpox Hospital**
· **Tramway** · Tramway Plz

📖 Libraries

· **Roosevelt Island** · 524 Main St

🍾 Liquor Stores

· **Grog Shop** · 605 Main St

✉ Post Offices

· **Roosevelt Island** · 694 Main St

🎓 Schools

· **IS 217 Roosevelt Island** · 645 Main St
· **Lillies Internation Christian** · 504 Main St

🛒 Supermarkets

· **Gristede's** · 686 Main St

📹 Video Rentals

· **KIO Enterprise** · 544 Main St

Subways

🄕 ....Roosevelt Island

Bus Lines

🚍102 ....Main St / East and West Rds

P Parking

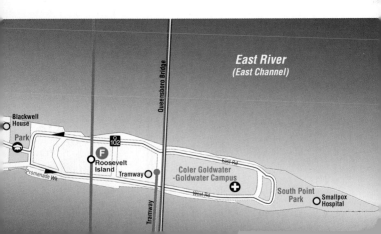

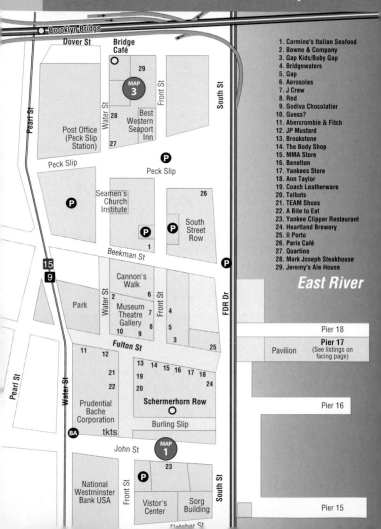

Brooklyn Bridge

Dover St

Bridge Café

29

MAP 3

Best Western Seaport Inn

28

27

Post Office (Peck Slip Station)

Water St

Front St

South St

Pearl St

Peck Slip

Peck Slip

Seamen's Church Institute

26

South Street Row

1

Beekman St

15
9

Cannon's Walk

Park

Water St

Museum Theatre Gallery

2

6

7

8

Front St

4

5

3

25

10

9

Fulton St

Pearl St

11

12

13 14 15 16 17 18

21

19

22

20

24

Water St

Prudential Bache Corporation

Schermerhorn Row

Burling Slip

BA

tkts

John St

MAP 1

National Westminster Bank USA

Front St

23

Visitor's Center

Sorg Building

South St

Fletcher St

FDR Dr

East River

Pier 18

Pier 17
(See listings on facing page)

Pavilion

Pier 16

Pier 15

1. Carmine's Italian Seafood
2. Bowne & Company
3. Gap Kids/Baby Gap
4. Bridgewaters
5. Gap
6. Aerosoles
7. J Crew
8. Red
9. Godiva Chocolatier
10. Guess?
11. Abercrombie & Fitch
12. JP Mustard
13. Brookstone
14. The Body Shop
15. MMA Store
16. Benetton
17. Yankees Store
18. Ann Taylor
19. Coach Leatherware
20. Talbots
21. TEAM Shoes
22. A Bite to Eat
23. Yankee Clipper Restaurant
24. Heartland Brewery
25. Il Porto
26. Paris Café
27. Quartino
28. Mark Joseph Steakhouse
29. Jeremy's Ale House

In some ways, South Street Seaport is the most unabashed tourist destination in New York, with its museums and malls—certainly the stores in the Pier 17 pavilion are not at all "New York." But the Seaport has its own interesting history if you bother looking for it. Take, for instance, the large ships docked in the harbor, including the *Peking*, *Wavertree*, and *Ambrose*. There are some finely preserved and renovated 19th-century buildings in the area as well, not just on Fulton Street, but also on Beekman, Peck Slip, and Dover Street. The Seaport itself houses about 25 restaurants, but we recommend the Bridge Café, Mark Joseph Steakhouse, or Quartino, all of which are located north of the Seaport and just south of the Brooklyn Bridge.

The Bridge looms over the whole area—the back decks of the Pier 17 Pavilion have a great view, as does the East Side Promenade, which passes underneath it. Sadly, the most authentic part of the neighborhood, the Fulton Fish Market, has moved to the Bronx, leaving only the sweet stench of seafood from two centuries past lingering in the air. We suggest going down to South Street and having a drink at the bar in the Paris Café one night at 2 am to mourn its passing…

If you're downtown and looking for discounted theater tickets, the tkts booth that was formerly located in the World Trade Center is now at the corner of Front and John Streets. Check the electronic board for show times and discounts, then go inside and book. For matinee shows, you need to book the day before from this downtown location.

General Information

NFT Map: 1
Phone: 212-SEA-PORT
Phone (museum): 212-748-8600
Museum:
www.southstseaport.org
Retail:
www.southstreetseaport.com

Landmarks

Schermerhorn Row
Bridge Café
Brooklyn Bridge

Banks

BA · Bank of America ·
175 Water St

Subways

②③④⑤Ⓙ🅼Ⓩ
Fulton Street
ⒶⒸ........Broadway-Nassau

Bus Lines

15........First and Second Aves
9........Ave B/East Broadway

Pier 17 Pavilion

9000 Perfumery Inc
A.B.C.D.E.
Alamo Flags
American Eagle Outfitters
Art A La Carte
Bath & Body Works
Beyond The Wall
Broadway Beat
Christmas Dove
City Streets
Claire's Accessories
EB Games
Filmline Gallery
Footlocker
Jewelry Mine
Lids
Mariposa The Butterfly Gallery
Neighborhoodies
New York: A View of the World
The New York Shell Shop
The NY Yankees Club Shop
Nutcracker Sweets
Purple-icious
Sam Goody
Seaport News
Seaport Watch Co
The Sharper Image
Sunglass Hut & Watch Station
Teazeria
Victoria's Secret
Waxology

Food

Athenian Express
Bergin's Wine & Beer Garden
Cabana
Cajun Café
China Max Asian Cuisine
Cyber Cigar and Coffee Bar
Daikichi Sushi
Haagen Dazs
Harbour Lights
Heavenly Soup & Smoothie
Little Tokyo
MacMenamin's Irish Pub
Murph's
Nathan's Famous
Pizza on the Pier
Pizzeria Uno
Salad Mania
Seaport Café
Sedutto Ice Cream
Sequoia
Simply Seafood
Subway
Taqueria Mexicali
Yorkville Burgers

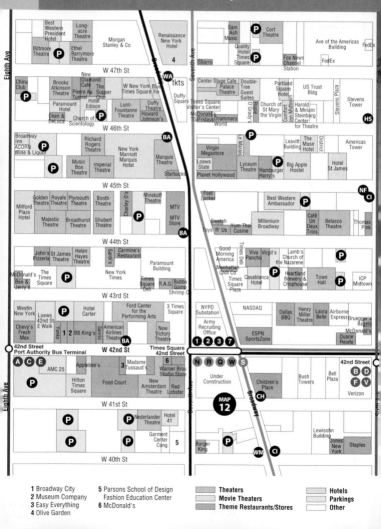

1 Broadway City
2 Museum Company
3 Easy Everything
4 Olive Garden
5 Parsons School of Design
  Fashion Education Center
6 McDonald's

Theaters
Movie Theaters
Theme Restaurants/Stores

Hotels
Parkings
Other

For an area named after a high-brow newspaper, Times Square has seen mostly middle- and low-brow entertainment over the last hundred years, from Vaudeville to the golden age of Broadway to the "golden age" of porn and finally to the current "Disney-fication." Of all the neighborhoods in New York for a New Yorker to avoid, this has to be at the top, but inevitably your cousin from out of town is going to want to see it, so…

Helpful Websites

www.timessquare.com
www.timessquarenyc.org

Transit

Take the ❶ ❷ ❸ ❼ ❾ Ⓝ Ⓡ Ⓠ Ⓦ and Ⓢ trains to get to the center of everything at the 42nd Street/Times Square stop.

ATMs

BA · Bank of America · 1515 Broadway
BA · Bank of America · 1523 Broadway
BA · Bank of America · 247 W 42nd St
CH · Chase · 3 Times Sq
CI · Citibank · 1155 Sixth Ave
CI · Citibank · 1440 Broadway
HS · HSBC · 1185 Sixth Ave
NF · North Fork · 1166 Sixth Ave
WM · Washington Mutual · 1431 Broadway
WA · Wachovia · 1568 Broadway

Hotels

Best Western President Hotel · 234 W 48th St
Best Western Ambassador · 132 W 45th St
Big Apple Hostel · 119 W 45th St
Broadway Inn · 264 W 46th St
Casablanca Hotel · 147 W 43rd St
Comfort Inn Midtown · 129 W 46th St
Doubletree Guest Suites · 1568 Broadway
Hilton Times Square · 234 W 42nd St
Hotel 41 · 206 W 41st St
Hotel Carter · 250 W 43rd St
Hotel St James · 109 W 45th St
Milford Plaza Hotel · 270 W 45th St
Millennium Hotel Broadway · 145 W 44th St
The Muse Hotel · 130 W 46th St
New York Marriott Marquis Hotel · 1535 Broadway
Paramount Hotel · 235 W 46th St
Portland Square Hotel · 132 W 47th St
Hotel Edison · 228 W 47th St
Quality Hotel Times Square · 157 W 47th St
Renaissance New York Hotel · 714 Seventh Ave
W New York Times Square · 1567 Broadway
Westin New York · 270 W 43rd St

Movie Theaters

AMC Empire 25 · 234 W 42nd St
Loews State · 1540 Broadway
Loews 42nd St E-Walk · 247 W 42nd St

Theaters

American Airlines Theater · 227 W 42nd St
Belasco Theatre · 111 W 44th St
Biltmore Theatre · 261 W 47th St
Booth Theatre · 222 W 45th St
Broadhurst Theatre · 235 W 44th St
Brooks Atkinson Theatre · 256 W 47th St
Cort Theatre · 138 W 48th St
Duffy Theatre · 1553 Broadway
Ethel Barrymore Theatre · 243 W 47th St
Ford Center for the Performing Arts · 213 W 42nd St
John Golden Theatre · 252 W 45th St
Harold & Miriam Steinberg Center for Theatre/ Laura Pels Theatre · 111 W 46th St
Helen Hayes Theatre · 240 W 44th St
Henry Miller Theatre · 124 W 43rd St
Imperial Theatre · 249 W 45th St
Longacre Theatre · 220 W 48th St
Lunt-Fontanne Theatre · 205 W 46th St
Lyceum Theatre · 149 W 45th St
Majestic Theatre · 274 W 44th St
Marquis Theatre · 1535 Broadway
Minskoff Theatre · 200 W 45th St
Music Box Theatre · 239 W 45th St
Nederlander Theatre · 208 W 41st St
New Amsterdam Theatre · 214 W 42nd St
New Victory Theatre · 209 W 42nd St
Palace Theatre · 1564 Broadway
Plymouth Theatre · 236 W 45th St
Richard Rogers Theatre · 226 W 46th St
Royale Theatre · 242 W 45th St
Shubert Theatre · 225 W 44th St
St James Theatre · 246 W 44th St
Town Hall · 123 W 43rd St

* Here's a tip: You can win $20 Rent tickets in the random drawing if you line up at the Nederlander by 6:30 pm, just in case that cousin wants to see "a show."

Theme Restaurants/ Stores

Applebee's · 234 W 42nd St
Pierre Au Tunnel · 250 W 47th St
BB King's Blues Club · 237 W 42nd St
Ben & Jerry's · 680 Eighth Ave
Blue Fin · 1567 Broadway
Broadway City · 241 W 42nd St
Bruegger's Bagels Bakery · 1115 Sixth Ave
Bubba Gump Shrimp Co · 1501 Broadway
Burger King · 561 Seventh Ave
Café Un Deux Trois · 123 W 44th St
Carmine's Restaurant · 200 W 44thSt
Center Stage Cafe · 1568 Broadway
Charley O's · 218 W 45th St
Chevy's Fresh Mex · 243 W 42nd St

The Children's Place · 1460 Broadway
China Club 268 W 47th St
Dallas BBQ · 132 W 43rd St
Dean & DeLuca · 235 W 46th St
District · 130 W 46th St
Drummers World · 151 W 46th St
Duane Reade Pharmacy · 115 W 42nd St
Easy Everything · 234 W 42nd St
ESPN Sportszone · 4 Times Sq
Food Court · 234 W 42nd St
Foot Locker · 1530 Broadway
Hamburger Harry's · 145 W 45th St
Heartland Brewery · 127 W 43rd St
Howard Johnson's · 1551 Broadway
John's Brick Oven Pizzeria · 260 W 44th St
Jones New York · 1190 W 40th St
Laura Belle · 120 W 43rd St
Le Marais · 150 W 46th St
Manhattan Chili Co · 1500 Broadway
McDonald's · 220 W 42nd St
McDonald's · 688 8th Ave
McDonald's · 1109 Sixth Ave
McDonald's · 1560 Broadway, 220 W 42nd St
MTV · 1515 Broadway
MTV Store · 1515 Broadway
Museum Company · 239 W 42nd St
New Diamond Café · 224 W 47th St
Olive Garden · 2 Times Square
Planet Hollywood · 1540 Broadway
RAG · 1501 Broadway
Red Lobster · 5 Times Square
Rosie O'Grady's · 149 W 46th St
Sam Ash Music · 160 W 48th St
Sanrio · 233 W 42nd St
Sardi's · 234 W 44th St
Sbarro · 701 Seventh Ave
Staples · 1065 Sixth Ave
Swatch · 1528 Broadway
TGI Friday's · 1552 Broadway
The Supper Club · 240 W 47th St
Thomas Pink · 1155 Sixth Ave
Times Deli · 158 W 44th St
Times Square Deli · 211 W 43rd St
Toys 'R' Us · 1514-1530 Broadway
Virgil's Real Barbecue · 152 W 44th St
Virgin Megastore · 1540 Broadway
Viva Pancho · 156 W 44th St
Warner Bros Studio Store · 1 Times Square Plz
Yankee Clubhouse Shop · 245 W 42nd St
Yum Thai Cuisine · 129 W 44th St

Other

Army Recruiting Office · Want to join the Army? Opened in 1946, this Army Recruiting Office has turned more civilians into soldiers than any other recruiting station (43rd St & Broadway),
Fox News Channel Studios · 133 W 47th St
tkts · Discount theater tickets (47th & Broadway).

217

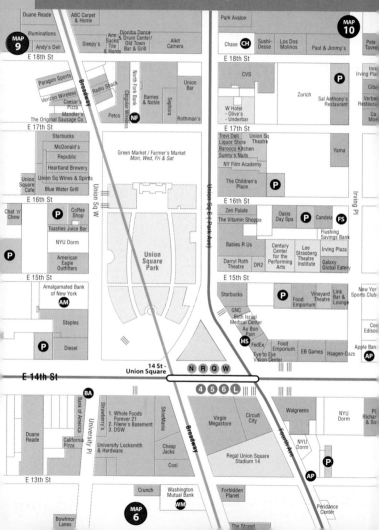

The large square at the union of Broadway and Fourth Avenue (originally Bloomingdale and Bowery, New York's most important streets) has been many things to many New Yorkers over the years—posh residential neighborhood, center of retail, center of Vaudeville, center of depravity, center of chain stores. But throughout it all, the square has retained a vitality not found in other open spaces around New York; it's the place where downtown's grunginess meets midtown sophistication. The large crowds of people gathered there on any particularly sunny afternoon could just as likely be protesters, hipsters, office workers eating lunch outside, or NYU students.

The domain of the rich in the early 19th-century, the square gradually became a commercial area, with theaters moving in once retail moved farther uptown. In the early 20th-century, the square became a major focal point for labor activity and leftist political rallies, which led, in turn, to the art scene in

the '50s and '60s centered around Andy Warhol's Factory. In 1983, after the area had been declining for years, a Business Improvement District was created to bring the area back from the brink of total deprivation. Today, the square has become quite safe and mainstream (to its detriment, some would say). One thing that remains, though, is its role as a locus for political rallies, protests, and other events of social significance. In the past few years, Union Square has been the center of September 11th remembrances and protests against the war in Iraq and the 2004 Republican National Convention.

Quite a few of New York's best restaurants are near Union Square, including Gotham Bar & Grill, Gramercy Tavern, Blue Water Grill, Mesa Grill, and the Union Square Café. For less extravagant food, the Farmer's Market on the northwest side of the park sells fresh fruit, home baked cakes, and the most delicious hard sourdough pretzels you'll ever taste!

ATMs

AM · Amalgamated Bank of NY · 15 Union Sq
AM · Amalgamated Bank of NY · 31 E 17th St
AP · Apple · 4 Irving Pl
AP · Apple · 145 Fourth Ave
BA · Bank of America · 36 E 14th St
CH · Chase · 225 Park Ave S
FS · Flushing Savings · 33 Irving Pl
HS · HSBC · 10 Union Sq E
WM · Washington Mutual · 835 Broadway

Hotels

Inn at Irving Place · 56 Irving Pl
W Hotel · 201 Park Avenue S

Stores/Restaurants

13 · 35 E 13th St
ABC Carpet & Home · 888 Broadway
Alkit Camera · 222 Park Ave S
American Eagle Outfitters· 19 Union Sq W
Andy's Deli · 873 Broadway
Angelo & Maxie's Steakhouse · 233 Park Ave S
Ann Sacks Tile & Stone · 37 E 18th St
Au Bon Pain · 6 Union Sq E
Babies R Us · 24 Union Sq E
Barnes & Noble · 33 E 17th St
Blue Water Grill · 31 Union Sq W
Caesar's Pizza · 861 Broadway
California Pizza · 122 University Pl
Candela · 116 E 16th St
Casa Mono · 52 Irving Pl
Chat 'n' Chew · 10 E 16th St
Cheap Jack's · 841 Broadway
The Children's Place · 36 Union Sq E
Cibar · 56 Irving Pl
Cingular Wireless · 31 E 17th St
Circuit City · 52-64 E 14th St
City Bakery · 3 W 18th St
City Crab & Seafood Co · 235 Park Ave S
Coffee Shop · 29 Union Sq W
Cosi · 841 Broadway
CVS · 215 Park Ave S (not 24 hours)

Diesel · 1 Union Sq W
Duane Reade · 873 Broadway
DSW · 40 E14th St, 3rd fl
EB Games · 107 E 14th St
Fed Ex · 4 Union Sq E
Filene's Basement · 4 Union Sq S
Food Emporium · 10 Union Sq E
Forbidden Planet · 840 Broadway
Forever 21 · 4 Union Sq S
Galaxy Global Eatery · 15 Irving Pl
Garden of Eden · 7 E 14th Street
GNC · 10 Union Sq E
Gotham Bar & Grill · 12 E 12th St
Gramercy Tavern · 42 E 20th St
Haagen-Dazs · 117 E 14th St
Heartland Brewery · 35 Union Sq W
Illuminations · 873 Broadway
Link Bar & Lounge · 120 E 15th St
Los Dos Molinos · 119 E 18th St
Luna Park · 29 Union Sq W
Mandler's The Original Sausage Co · 26 E 17th St
McDonald's · 39 Union Sq W
Mesa Grill · 102 Fifth Ave
Oasis Day Spa · 108 E 16th St
Old Town Bar & Grill · 45 E 18th St
Paragon Sports · 867 Broadway
Park Avalon · 225 Park Ave S
Paul & Jimmy's · 123 E 18th St
PC Richard & Son · 120 E 14th St
Petco · 860 Broadway
Pete's Tavern · 129 E 18th St
Radio Shack · 866 Broadway
Republic · 37 Union Sq W
Rothman's · 200 Park Ave S
Sal Anthony's Restaurant · 55 Irving Pl
ShoeMania · 853 Broadway
Shija Day Spa · 37 Union Sq W
Sephora · 200 Park Ave S
Sleepy's · 874 Broadway
Staples · 5-9 Union Sq W
Starbucks · 10 Union Sq E
Starbucks · 41 Union Sq W
The Strand · 828 Broadway
Strawberry's · 38 E 14th St
Sushi-Desse · 113 E 18th St
Toasties Juice Bar · 25 Union Sq W
Union Bar · 204 Park Ave S
Union Square Café · 21 E 16th St
Union Square Wines & Spirits · 33 Union Sq W

University Locksmith & Hardware · 121 University Pl
Verbena Restaurant · 54 Irving Pl
Verizon Wireless · 859 Broadway
Virgin Megastore · 52 E 14th St
The Vitamin Shoppe · 25-30 Union Sq E
Whole Foods · 4 Union Sq S
Wiz · 17 Union Sq W
Yama · 122 E 17th St
Zen Palate · 34 Union Sq E

Entertainment

Century Center for the Performing Arts · 111 E 15th St
Classic Stage Company · 136 East 13th St
Darryl Roth Theatre/DR2 · 20 Union Sq E
Djoniba Dance and Drum Centre · 37 E 18th St
Irving Plaza · 17 Irving Pl
Lee Strasberg Theatre Institute · 115 E 15th St
Union Square Theatre · 100 E 17th St
Regal Union Square Stadium14 · 850 Broadway
Vineyard Theatre · 108 E 15th St

24 Hour Services

Duane Reade · 24 E 14th Street
Walgreens · 145 Fourth Ave

Other

Amalgamated Bank of New York · 11 Union Sq W
Beth Israel Phillips Ambulatory Center · 10 Union Sq E
Bowlmor Lanes · 110 University Pl
Carlyle Court · 25 Union Sq W
Con Edison · 4 Irving Pl
Crunch · 54 E 13th St
New York Sports Clubs · 10 Irving Pl
NY Film Academy · 100 E 17th St
The Palladium · 140 E 14th St
Peridance Center · 132 Fourth Ave
Zurich · 105 E 17th St

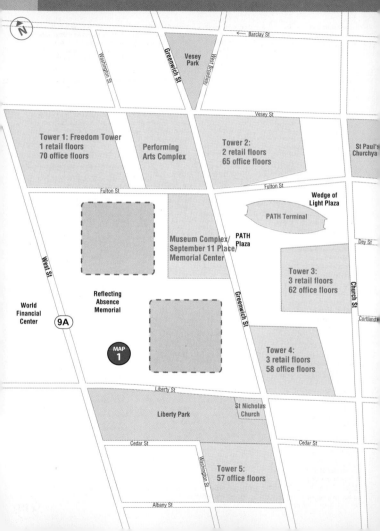

N

Barclay St →

Washington St

Greenwich St

Vesey Park

West Broadway

Vesey St

Tower 1: Freedom Tower
1 retail floors
70 office floors

Performing Arts Complex

Tower 2:
2 retail floors
65 office floors

St Paul's Churchya

Fulton St

Fulton St

Wedge of Light Plaza

PATH Terminal

Dey St

Museum Complex/ September 11 Place/ Memorial Center

PATH Plaza

Tower 3:
3 retail floors
62 office floors

Church St

West St

Reflecting Absence Memorial

World Financial Center

9A

MAP 1

Greenwich St

Cortland

Tower 4:
3 retail floors
58 office floors

Liberty St

Liberty Park

St Nicholas Church

Cedar St

Cedar St

Washington St

Tower 5:
57 office floors

Albany St

The rebuilding of the World Trade Center site has proven extremely complicated because of the numerous groups competing to see that their vision for the project is fulfilled. The Port Authority originally built the buildings and, just before September 11th, they were leased to Larry Silverstein. As leaseholder, he had the right to collect insurance and redevelop the site. Created by Governor Pataki, the Lower Manhattan Development Corporation was assigned the task of overseeing the development of the site. The families of victims and the rest of the public have been vocal in expressing their desires for the rebuilding project.

In the fall of 2002, a single design was selected from over 400 submissions to the LMDC. Studio Daniel Libeskind's proposal, "Memory Foundations," achieved the nearly impossible task of getting the approval of the LMDC, Port Authority, city, and state of New York. The plans included a 4.5-acre memorial garden, an Interpretive Museum, and a striking 1,776-foot-tall spire-like building (expected to be the tallest building in the world). Despite the Libeskind design being accepted as the official master plan, the architects have since stepped in; Silverstein hired architect Larry Childs because of his extensive experience in designing office buildings. Under pressure from the LMDC, Childs collaborated with Libeskind on creating designs based on the master plan. Throughout late 2003, local papers suggested that the two were feuding over designs. However, late in the year, Libeskind and Childs emerged with an amicable compromise, changing the arrangement of the buildings and parks on the ground and altering the look of the Freedom Tower. The current plan for the tower includes a clear-top section with energy-generating wind turbines and a large broadcast antenna. In early 2004, revised plans were released for a memorial at the site called "Reflecting Absence." The memorial was designed by architect Michael Arad and incorporates waterfalls flowing into sunken "footprints" of the twin towers, cascading onto the names etched in stone of those who died there. The plans also include a performing arts and museum space designed by Norwegian firm Snøhetta.

Debate still rages regarding many aspects of the project, from the height and look of the other towers (Silverman hired three other architects to design the remaining buildings in Libeskind's plan) to the design of a memorial space, to how many streets will be allowed to run through the site (many were demapped when the WTC was originally built).

Larry Silverstein's court cases involving insurance payments ended in 2004 with one jury deciding the attacks were a single incident, and the other deeming it two, resulting in Silverstein receiving about $4.6 billion of the $6.8 billion he was hoping for. Silverstein received more bad news when his company and the four construction companies responsible for the post-attack cleanup became the target of a class action lawsuit alleging that there had been inadequate protection for workers against the dangerous toxins that emerged during the effort. And while Silverstein has managed to get enough money in the form of Liberty Bonds to rebuild 7 World Trade Center, there are still no tenants signed for the building, which is set to open in 2006.

Transit has been restored to pre-September 11th order, with all subway lines resuming service to the area, along with PATH service to the newly constructed PATH station. By 2009, a large station designed by Spanish architect Santiago Calatrav, connecting the subway, PATH, and trains to JFK airport, will be completed on the site.

Useful Websites

- The World Trade Center Health Registry will track the health survey of thousands of people directly exposed to the events of 9/11: www.nyc.gov/html/doh/html/wtc/index.html

- The findings of the National Commission on Terrorist Attacks Upon the United States (the 9/11 Commission): www.9-11commission.gov

- Website of the largest Sept. 11 advocacy group, representing the WTC memorial position of over 4,000 Sept. 11 family members, survivors, rescue workers, and others: www.coalitionof911families.org

- "New York New Visions," is a coalition of several groups looking at different options for rebuilding the area: http://nynv.aiga.org

- The New York Skyscraper Museum continues to add information about the WTC and downtown NYC in general; they also contributed to the historical panels placed on the viewing wall around the site: www.skyscraper.org

- *New York Newsday's* compendium of articles and plans about the WTC site: www.nynewsday.com/news/local/manhattan/wtc

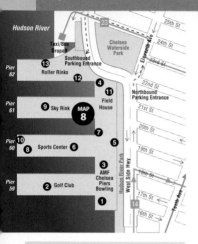

Overview

Website: www.chelseapiers.com

Opened in 1910 as a popular port for trans-Atlantic ships, Chelsea Piers found itself neglected and deteriorating by the 1960s. In 1992, Roland W. Betts began the plan to renovate and refurbish the piers as a gargantuan 30-acre sports and entertainment center. In 1995, Chelsea Piers re-opened its doors to the public at a final cost of $120 million—all private money. The only help from the state was a very generous 49-year lease. By 1998, Chelsea Piers was the third-most popular attraction in New York City.

How to Get There

Unless you live in Chelsea, it's a real pain to get to the Piers. The closest subway is the **C E** to 23rd Street and Eighth Avenue, and then it's still a three-avenue block hike there. If you're lucky, you can hop a **23** bus on 23rd Street and expedite the last leg of your journey. **L** train commuters should get off at the Eighth Avenue stop and take the **14** bus across to the West Side Highway where you'll be dropped off at 18th Street.

If you drive, entering from the south can be a little tricky. It's pretty well signed, so keep your eyes peeled. Basically you exit right at Eleventh Avenue and 22nd Street, turn left onto 24th Street and then make a left onto the West Side Highway. Enter Chelsea Piers the same way you would if you were approaching from the north. Parking costs $9 for the first hour, $12 for two, $16 for three. Street parking in the west 20s is an excellent alternative in the evenings after 6 pm.

Facilities

Chelsea Piers is amazing. There are swimming pools, ice skating rinks, a bowling alley, spa, restaurants, shops, batting cages—you name it. So, what's the catch? Well, it's gonna cost ya. Like Manhattan rents, only investment bankers can afford this place.

1 **Chelsea Brewing Company** · 212-336-6440. Micro-brewery and restaurant. Try the amber ale, wings, nachos, spinach dip, and cheesy fries—all excellent.

2 **Golf Club** · 212-336-6400. Aside from potentially long wait times, the 200-yard driving range with 52 heated stalls and automated ball-feed (no buckets or bending over!) is pretty awesome. $25 buys you 100 balls (peak) or 148 balls (off-peak). If you don't bring your own, club hire is $4/one club, $5/two, $6/three, or $12/ten. Before 5 pm on weekdays, you can whack all the balls you want for an hour for $20 plus free club rental.

3 **AMF Chelsea Piers** · 212-835-BOWL. A very schmancy 40-lane bowling alley equipped with video games and bar. $7.50/game plus $4.50 shoe rental.

4 **Ruthy's Bakery & Café** · 212-336-6333. Pastries and sandwiches.

5 **New York Presbyterian Sports Medicine Center** · 212-366-5100.

6 **The Spa at Chelsea Piers** · 212-336-6780. It's not Canyon Ranch. A basic 50-minute massage is $100, a basic 50-minute facial is $80. They also have a range of scrubs, wraps, polishes, manicures, pedicures, and waxes.

7 **College Sports Television** · Street-level broadcast center accessible to the public with interactive events and activities for college sports fans.

8 **The Sports Center** · 212-336-6000. A very expensive, monster health club with a 10,000-square-foot climbing wall, a quarter-mile track, swimming pool, and enough fitness equipment for a small army in training. If you have to ask how much the membership is, you can't afford it.

9 **Sky Rink** · 212-336-6100. Two 24/7 ice rinks mainly used for classes, training, and bar mitzvahs.

10 **The Lighthouse** · 212-336-6144. 10,000-square-foot event space for private gatherings catered by Abigail Kirsch.

11 **The Field House** · 212-336-6500. The Field House is an 80,000-square-foot building with a 30-foot climbing wall, a gymnastics training center, four batting cages, two basketball courts, and two indoor soccer fields. A season (ten games plus playoffs) of league soccer costs $220/person, league basketball costs $150/person, rock-climbing costs $15/class, and gymnastics costs $25/class.

12 **Spirit Cruise** · 212-727-7735; www.spiritofnewyork.com. Ships run out of Chelsea Piers and Weehawken, NJ. Dinner cruises are approximately $67/person, and if you're having a big function, you can rent the entire boat!

13 **Roller Rinks** · 212-336-6200. Two regulation-size outdoor skating rinks and an "extreme" skate park. The Skate Park costs $10/day for members, otherwise each session costs $14 (on weekends, sessions are only three hours long). Closed from October 31 until spring.

Unfortunately, but not surprisingly, there are no golf courses on the island of Manhattan. Thankfully, there are two driving ranges where you can at least smack the ball around until you can get to a real course, as well as a golf simulator at Chelsea Piers that lets you play a full round "at" various popular courses (Pebble Beach, St. Andrews, etc.). NYC has a number of private and public courses throughout the outer boroughs and Westchester; however, they don't even come close to satisfying the area's huge demand for courses.

Golf Courses

	Borough	Address	Par	Phone
Mosholu Golf Course (9-hole)	Bronx	3700 Jerome & Bainbridge Aves	35	718-655-9164
Pelham/Split Rock Golf Course	Bronx	870 Shore Rd (in Pelham Bay Park)	71	718-885-1258
Van Cortlandt Golf Course	Bronx	Van Cortlandt Pk S & Bailey Ave	70	718-543-4595
Dyker Beach Golf Course	Brooklyn	86th St & Seventh Ave	71	718-836-9722
Marine Park Golf Club	Brooklyn	2880 Flatbush Ave	72	718-338-7149
Clearview Golf Course	Queens	202-12 Willets Point Blvd	70	718-229-2570
Douglaston Golf Course	Queens	6320 Marathon Pkwy	67	718-428-1617
Flushing Meadows Pitch & Putt	Queens	Flushing Meadows–Corona Park	54	718-271-8182
Forest Park Golf Course	Queens	101 Forest Park Dr	70	718-296-0999
Kissena Park Golf Course	Queens	164-15 Booth Memorial Ave	64	718-939-4594
LaTourette Golf Course	Staten Island	1001 Richmond Hill Rd	72	718-351-1889
Silver Lake Golf Course	Staten Island	915 Victory Blvd	69	718-447-5686
South Shore Golf Course	Staten Island	200 Huguenot Ave	72	718-984-0101

Fees are generally as follows (reservations are a must, and usually cost an extra $2):

Weekdays before 1 pm—$22   Weekends before 1 pm—$25
Weekdays after 1 pm—$19   Weekends after 1 pm—$21
Carts $13.75 per person

Golf Simulator – Chelsea Piers Golf Club (see previous Chelsea Piers page): $40 for one hour, $340 for a 10-hour package

Driving Ranges in Manhattan

		Fees	Phone
Chelsea Piers: Pier 59	59, Chelsea Piers (at 23rd St)	$25/100 balls (peak), $25/148 balls (off-peak) Clubs: 1 for $4, 2 for $5, 3 for $6, 10 for $12 Till 5 pm: $20 an hour, all you can hit, one club rental included.	212-336-6400
Randall's Island Golf Center	1 Randalls Rd	$6/small bucket, $10/large bucket	212-427-5689

Bowling Alleys

	Address	Phone	Fees
Bowlmor Lanes	110 University Pl b/w 12th & 13th Sts	212-255-8188	$6.45-$8.95 per person per game $5 for shoes
AMF Chelsea Piers Bowl	Pier 60	212-835-2695	$7.50-$8.25 per person per game $4.50 for shoes
Leisure Time	625 Eighth Ave, 2nd Fl, Port Authority	212-268-6909	$8 per person per game $5 for shoes

For swimming pools in Manhattan, you pretty much have two options: Pay exorbitant gym fees or health club fees in order to use the private swimming facilities, or wait until the summer to share the city's free outdoor pools with freely-urinating summer camp attendees. OK, so it's not that bad! Some YMCAs and YWCAs have nice indoor pools and their fees are reasonable. And several of the same New York public recreation centers that have outdoor pools (and some that do not) have indoor pools for year-round swimming. Though plenty of kids use the pools, there are dedicated adult swim hours in the mornings, at lunch time, and in the evenings (pee-free if you get there early).

And then there's the Hudson. Yes, we're serious. There are about eight races in the Hudson each year and the water quality is tested before each race. New York City also has some great beaches for swimming including Coney Island, Manhattan Beach, and the Rockaways. If you prefer your swimming area enclosed, check out the pool options in Manhattan:

Pools

	Address	Phone	Type — Fees	Map
14th Street Y	344 E 14th St	212-780-0800	Indoor — $15 per day	13
All Star Fitness Club	75 West End Ave	212-265-8200	Indoor — call for membership fees	14
Asphalt Green	1750 91st St	212-369-8890	Indoor — $25 per day	17
Asser Levy	E 23rd St & Asser Levy Pl	212-447-2020	Indoor — $75 per year (not open during summer) / Outdoor — Free*	10
Athletic and Swim Club at the Equitable Center	787 Seventh Ave	212-265-3490	Indoor — call for membership fees	12
Bally's Sports Club	335 Madison Ave	212-983-5320	Indoor — $25 per day	12
Bally's Sports Club	139 W 32nd St	212-465-1750	Indoor — $25 per day	9
Bally's Sports Club	350 W 50th St	212-265-9400	Indoor — $25 per day	12
Battery Park Swim & Fitness Center	375 South End Ave	212-321-1117	Indoor — call for membership fees	BPC
Carmine Recreation Center	1 Clarkson St	212-242-5228	Indoor — $725 per year Outdoor — Free*	5
Chelsea Piers Sports Center	Pier 60	212-336-6000	Indoor — $50 per day	8
Coles Sports and Recreation Center	181 Mercer St	212-998-2020	Indoor — call for membership fees	6
Crowne Plaza	1601 Broadway	212-977-4000	Indoor — $25 per day	12
Excelsior Athletic Club	301 E 57th St	212-688-5280	Indoor — call for membership fees	7
New York Sports Club	1637 Third Ave	212-987-7200	Indoor — $25 per day	19
Gravity Fitness and Spa	119 W 56th St	212-708-7340	Indoor — $50 per day	12
Hamilton Fish Recreation Center	128 Pitt St	212-387-7687	Outdoor — Free*	23
Hansborough Recreation Center	35 W 134th St	212-234-9603	Indoor — $75 per year	11
Highbridge	173rd St & Amsterdam	212-927-2400	Outdoor — Free	21
Holiday Inn	440 W 57th St	212-581-8100	Outdoor — call for rate information	11
Jackie Robinson Pool	89 Bradhurst Ave	212-234-9607	Outdoor — Free*	21
John Jay	E 77th St & Cherokee Pl	212-794-6566	Outdoor — Free*	15
Lasker Pool	110th St & Lenox Ave	212-534-7639	Outdoor — Free*	19
Lenox Hill Neighborhood House	331 E 70th St	212-744-5022	Indoor — $10 per day	15
Manhattan Plaza Health Club	482 W 43rd St, 2nd Fl	212-563-7001	Indoor — $25.03 per day (no day pass during summer)	11
Marcus Garvey Swimming Pool	13 E 124th St	212-410-2818	Outdoor — Free*	20
Monterey Sports Club	175 E 96th St	212-996-8200	Indoor — call for membership fees	17
New York Health & Racquet Club	132 E 45th St	212-986-3100	Indoor – $50 per day	13
New York Health & Racquet Club	110 W 56th St	212 541-7200	Indoor – $50 per day	12
New York Sports Club	1637 3rd Ave	212-987-7200	Indoor – $15 per day	17
New York Sports Club	1614 Second Ave	212-213-5999	Indoor – $25 per day	15
Paris Health Club	752 West End Ave	212-749-3500	Indoor — call for membership fees	16
Recreation Center 54	348 E 54th St	212-754-5411	Indoor-- $75 per year	13
Recreation Center 59	533 W 59th St	212-397-3159	Indoor — $75 per year	11
Reebok Sports Club	160 Columbus Ave	212-362-6800	Indoor — $35 with a member, or call for membership fees	14
Riverbank State Park	679 Riverside Dr	212-694-3600	Indoor — $2 per day	21
Sheltering Arms	W 129th St & Amsterdam Ave	212-662-6191	Outdoor — Free*	18
Sheraton New York Health Club	811 Seventh Ave	212-621-8591	Indoor — $40 per day, free for hotel guests	12
Dry Dock Swimming Pool	408 E 10th St	212-677-4481	Outdoor — Free*	7
Thomas Jefferson Swimming Pool	2180 First Ave	212-860-1372	Outdoor — Free*	20
Tompkins Square Mini Pool	500 E 9th St	212-387-7685	Outdoor — Free*	7
UN Plaza Health Club	1 UN Plz 41st Floor	212-702-5016	Indoor — $35 per day	13
YMCA	180 W 135th St	212-281-4100	Indoor — $10 per day	19
YMCA	1395 Lexington Ave	212-415-5700	Indoor — $30 per day	17
YMCA	224 E 47th St	212-756-9600	Indoor — $25 per day	13
YWCA	610 Lexington Ave	212-755-4500	Indoor — $20 per day	13

* summer only (Fourth of July–Labor Day)

General Information

Manhattan Parks Dept: 212-360-8131 • website: www.nycgovparks.org
Permit Locations: The Arsenal, 830 5th Ave @ 64th St; Paragon Sporting Goods Store, 867 Broadway & 18th St

Overview

There are more tennis courts on the island of Manhattan than you might think, although getting to them may be a bit more than you bargain for. Most of the public courts in Manhattan are either smack in the middle of Central Park or are on the edges of the city—East River Park, for instance, and Riverside Park. These courts in particular can make for some pretty windy playing conditions.

Public Courts—Outdoor	Address	# of Cts.	Type	Phone
Central Park Tennis Center	96th St & Central Park W	30	Clay/Hard	212-280-0205
East River Park Tennis Courts	FDR Dr & Broome St	12	Hard	212-529-7185
Fort Washington Park	Hudson River & 170th St	10	Hard	212-304-2322
F Johnson Playground	151st St, east of Seventh Ave	8	Hard	212-234-9609
Inwood Park	207th St & Seaman Ave	9	Hard	212-304-2381
Randall's Island	East and Harlem Rivers	11	Hard	212-860-1827
Riverbank State Park	W 145th St & Riverside Dr	4	Hard	212-694-3600
Riverside Park	Riverside Dr & W 96th St	10	Clay	212-469-2006
Riverside Park	Riverside Dr & W 119th St	10	Hard	212-496-2006

Public Courts—Indoor	Address	# of Cts.	Type	Phone
Randall's Island Indoor Tennis*	Randall's Island Park	4	Hard	212-427-6150
Sutton East Tennis Club*	York Ave and 60th St	8	Clay	212-751-3452

*Courts are only available October through April. Please call for more information.

Private Clubs	Address	# of Cts.	Type	Phone
Columbia Tennis Center	575 W 218th St	6	Hard	212-942-7100
Manhattan Plz Racquet Club	450 W 43rd St	5	Hard	212-594-0554
Midtown Tennis Club	341 Eighth Ave	8	Har-Tru	212-989-8572
River Club	447 E 52nd St	2	Clay	212-751-0100
Roosevelt Island Racquet Club	281 Main St	11	Clay	212-935-0250
The Tennis Club	15 Vanderbilt Ave, 3rd Floor	2	Hard	212-687-3841
Tower Tennis Courts	1725 York Ave	2	Hard	212-860-2464
Town Tennis Club	430 E 56th St	3	Hard/Clay	212-752-4059
Millennium UN Plaza Hotel Gym	44th & First Ave	1	Supreme	212-702-5016

Schools	Address	# of Cts.	Type	Phone
Coles Center, NYU	181 Mercer St	9	Rubber	212-998-2020
PS 125	425 W 123rd St	3	Hard	N/A
PS 137	327 Cherry St	5	Hard	N/A
PS 144	134 W 122nd St	4	Hard	N/A
PS 146	421 E 106th St	3	Hard	N/A
PS 187	349 Cabrini Blvd	4	Hard	N/A
Rockefeller University	1230 York Ave	1	Hard	212-327-8000

Getting a Permit

The tennis season, according to the NYC Parks Department, lasts from April 3 to November 23. Permits are good for use until the end of the season at all public courts in all boroughs, and are good for one hour of singles or two hours of doubles play. Fees are:

Juniors (17 yrs and under) $10		Adults (18-61 yrs) $100	
Senior Citizen (62 yrs and over) $20		Single-play tickets $7	

Yoga

Finding a Class

Looking for a studio where you can perfect your down-ward-facing dog can seem overwhelming in NYC—almost as daunting as picking a restaurant or a bar for the evening. Whether you're seeking stress relief or looking to improve your physical and spiritual well-being, you're bound to find something in the city that appeals to your inner pretzel. Once you've familiarized yourself with the different branches of yoga, you're going to want to find a studio that best suits your needs. Contact studios in advance for information about their different approaches to classes, what branches of yoga they teach, class sizes, appropriate attire, cost, and schedules.

Word to the wise: you may want to begin with an introductory class wherever you land. Even seasoned yogis will want to familiarize themselves with the methods of each studio before jumping in head-stand first.

Recommended Studios In Manhattan…

Jivamukti Yoga Center • 404 Lafayette St • 212-353-0214 • www.jivamuktiyoga.com
BeYoga • 37 W 65th St, 4th Fl, 160 E 56th St, 1319 Third Ave, 138 Fifth Ave • 212-769-9642 • www.karmayogany.com
OM Yoga Center • 826 Broadway, 6th Fl • 212-254-YOGA • www.omyoga.com
exhale • 980 Madison Ave, 150 Central Park S • 212-561-6400 • www.exhalespa.com

Sonic Yoga • 54th St & Ninth Ave • 212-397-6344 • www.sonicyoga.com
Bikram Yoga NYC • 797 Eighth Ave • 212-245-2525 • www.bikramyoganyc.com
Laughing Lotus • 59 W 19th St, 3rd Fl • 212-414-2903 • www.laughinglotus.com
Virayoga • 580 Broadway, Ste 1109 • 212-334-9960 • www.virayoga.com
Himalayan Institute - Yoga Science • 78 Fifth Ave • 212-243-5995 • www.hinyc.org
Integral Yoga Institute • 227 W 13th St • 212-929-0586 • www.integralyogany.org
Ashtanga Yoga Shala • 295 E 8th St • 718-614-9537 • www.ashtangayogashala.net
Kula Yoga Project • 28 Warren St, 4th Fl • 212-945-4460 • www.kulayoga.com

And Some in Brooklyn…

Yoga People • 157 Remsen St, Brooklyn Heights • 718-522-9642 • www.yoga-people.com
Hot Yoga People • (offers Hot and Vinyasa style classes) 659 Fulton St, Fort Greene • 718-237-2300 • www.yoga-people.com
Park Slope Yoga Center • 792 Union St, 2nd Fl (above Dixon's Bike Shop) • 718- 789-2288 • www.parkslopeyoga.com
Bikram Yoga Brooklyn Heights • 106 Montague St, 2nd Floor, Brooklyn Heights • 718-797-2100 • www.bikramyogabrooklyn.com
Go Yoga • 218 Bedford Ave, Williamsburg • 718-486-5602 • www.goyoga.ws

Billiards

	Address	Phone	Fee	Hours
128 Billiards	128 Elizabeth St	212-925-8219	$6 per hour	Until 3 am
Amsterdam Billiards & Bar	344 Amsterdam Ave	212-496-8180	$5-7.50 per hour	12 pm-3 am weekdays, 11 am-3 am weekends
Broadway Billiard Café	10 E 21st St	212-388-1582	$4 per person/hour	Open 24 hours
Corner Billiards	110 E 11th St	212-995-1314	$7-9 per person/hour	12 pm-2 am, 12 pm- 3 am, weekends
East Side Billiard Club	163 86th St	212-831-7665	$5- $6.50per person/hour	11 am-3 am
Fat Cat Billiards	75 Christopher St	212-675-6056	$4.50 per person/per hour	2 pm-2 am
Guys & Gals Billiard Parlor	500 W 207th St	212-567-9279	$5 per hour	1 pm-dawn
Mammoth Billiards	558 Eighth Ave	212-535-0331	$3-$4 per person/hour	24 hours
Post Billiards Café	154 Post Ave	212-569-1840	$8-$10 per person/hour	12 pm-dawn
Pressure	110 University Pl	212-352-1161	$26 per table/hour	Fri-Sat 9 pm-4 am
Q Lounge	220 W 19th St	212-206-7665	$15-18 per person/hour	3 pm-2 am weekdays, 3 pm-4 am weekends
Slate Restaurant Bar Billiards	54 W 21st St	212-989-0096	$7-9 per person/hour	11 am-4 am
Soho Billiard Sport Center	Mott & Houston	212-925-3753	$7-12 per person/hour	11 am-5 am

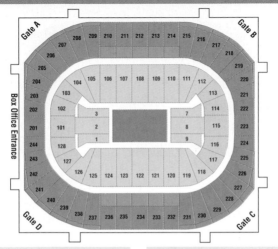

General Information

Address:	East Rutherford, NJ 07073
Website:	www.meadowlands.com/coarenafaq.asp
Devils:	www.newjerseydevils.com
Nets:	www.nba.com/nets
Ticketmaster:	212-307-7171, www.ticketmaster.com

Overview

Once upon a time, this place was called Brendan Byrne Arena and was the home of two very bad pro teams: the New Jersey Nets and the New Jersey Devils. Today, it's called the Continental Airlines Arena and is the home of two suddenly very good teams. Though things seem to be going well game-wise for the Nets, they've been engulfed in financial troubles for quite sometime. NJ Nets management is currently in talks to sell and move the team to Brooklyn. Developer Bruce Ratner hopes to move the team to a proposed $435 million arena as a part of a residential, shopping, and office complex development to be built in the Prospect Heights area within the next five years. Residents who don't want their brownstone neighborhoods infringed upon by this mammoth complex are protesting the plan. The NJ Storm lacrosse team up and relocated to Anaheim, CA as well. And then there were two.

How to Get There—Driving

Continental Airlines Arena is only five miles from the Lincoln Tunnel. Luckily, since the fan base for the teams that play hails primarily from New Jersey, you won't have to deal with the same New York City and Long Island traffic that plagues Giants Stadium games. Additionally, attendance rates are much smaller than for football, even on the rare occasions when the Nets or Devils sell out. You can take the Lincoln Tunnel to Route 3 W to Route 120 N, or you can try either the Holland Tunnel to the New Jersey Turnpike (North) to Exit 16W, or the George Washington Bridge to the New Jersey Turnpike (South) to Exit 16W. Accessing the stadium from Exit 16W feeds you directly into the parking areas.

How to Get There–Mass Transit

The direct bus from the Port Authority Bus Terminal to the arena costs $7 round trip for advance-purchase tickets, and $4 each way on the bus, which accepts exact change only. Buses usually start running two hours before game time.

How to Get Tickets

The box office is open Monday–Saturday from 11 am to 6 pm and is closed Sunday, unless there is an event. For ticket information, call 201-935-3900. To purchase tickets without going to the box office, call Ticketmaster at 212-307-7171, or visit their website.

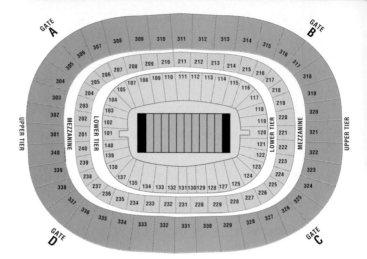

General Information

Address:	East Rutherford, NJ 07073
Phone:	201-935-3900
Website:	www.giantsstadium.com
Giants:	www.giants.com
Jets:	www.newyorkjets.com
Metrostars:	www.metrostars.com
Ticketmaster:	212-307-7171, www.ticketmaster.com

Overview

Giants Stadium, located in New Jersey's scenic and smelly Meadowlands Sports Complex, is the home of both the New York Giants and New York Jets football teams. It's the only stadium in the country that hosts two professional football teams, but that may all change if Bloomberg's plan for a west side stadium eventually happens. For now, the two NFL teams play on alternating Sundays throughout the fall, and the only way to get regular-priced tickets is to inherit them, since both teams are sold out through the next ice age. Giants Stadium also houses Major League Soccer's Metrostars (for which many, many tickets are available) and is the site of several concerts and other sporting and religious events throughout the year. The stadium's field is made of synthetic FieldTurf.

How to Get There—Driving

Giants Stadium is only five miles from the Lincoln Tunnel (closer to Midtown than Shea Stadium, even), but leave early if you want to get to the game on time—remember that the Giants and the Jets are a) sold out for every game and b) have tons of fans from both Long Island and the five boroughs. You can take the Lincoln Tunnel to Route 3 W to Route 120 N, or you can try either the Holland Tunnel to the New Jersey Turnpike N to Exit 16W, or the George Washington Bridge to the New Jersey Turnpike S to Exit 16W. Accessing the stadium from Exit 16W allows direct access to parking areas.

How to Get There–Mass Transit

Less stressful than driving to Giants Stadium is taking a bus from the Port Authority Bus Terminal directly to the stadium. Pre-paid bus trips cost $7 round trip (and $4 each way when purchased on the bus), and buses usually start running two hours before kickoff.

How to Get Tickets

For the Jets and the Giants, scalpers and friends are the only options. For the MetroStars and for concerts, you can call Ticketmaster or visit the website.

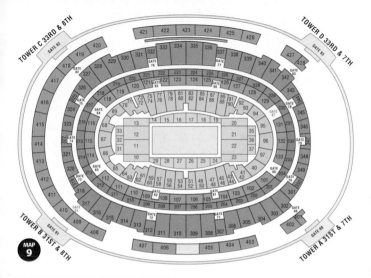

General Information

NFT Map: 9
Address: 4 Pennsylvania Plz
                New York, NY 10001
Phone: 212-465-6741
Website: www.thegarden.com
Knicks: www.nyknicks.com
Liberty: www.nyliberty.com
Rangers: www.newyorkrangers.com
Ticketmaster: 212-307-7171, www.ticketmaster.com

Overview

Madison Square Garden is home to the Knicks, the Rangers, and the Liberty. If you don't know which sports these teams play, then we can't help you. With the Knicks performing poorly in recent years, tickets that were formerly hard to acquire are suddenly easy to come by. When the NHL season is not cancelled due to salary disputes, Rangers tickets are a little harder to find. Liberty games are the most fun, especially when they take on west coast teams such as Los Angeles, Seattle, and Houston. Liberty tickets are reasonably priced and readily available. The bad boys of St John's also call the Garden home.

MSG hosts a ton of other events throughout the year, including rock concerts, tennis tournaments, political conventions, and, for those of you with 2+ years of graduate school, monster truck rallies and "professional" wrestling. Check out MSG's website for a full calendar of events.

How to Get There–Mass Transit

MSG is right above Penn Station, which makes getting there very easy. You can take the Ⓐ Ⓒ Ⓔ and ① ② ③ lines to 34th Street and Penn Station, or the Ⓝ Ⓡ Ⓠ Ⓦ, Ⓑ Ⓓ Ⓕ Ⓥ, and PATH lines to 34th Street and 6th Avenue. The Long Island Rail Road also runs right into Penn Station.

How to Get Tickets

For single seats for the Knicks and the Rangers, you can try Ticketmaster, but a better bet would be to try the "standby" line (show up a half-hour before game time and wait). The ubiquitous ticket scalpers surrounding the Garden are a good last resort for when your rich out-of-town friends breeze in to see a game. Liberty tickets (and tickets for other events) are usually available through Ticketmaster.

Sports • Shea Stadium

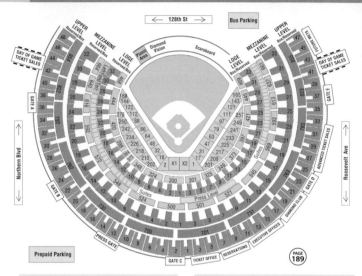

PAGE 189

General Information

Mets Clubhouse Shops: 143 E 54th St & 11 W 42nd St
Shea Stadium Box Office: 718-507-TIXX
Website: www.mets.com
Address: 126th St & Roosevelt Ave,
Flushing, Queens
Ferry: 800-53-FERRY

Overview

Shea Stadium is the home of the New York Mets. It's painted in those lovely garish colors of Dodger Blue and Giant Orange (homage to the two baseball teams that deserted New York City for the west coast) and is located in Flushing Meadows in Queens. Although the Mets had one of the most abysmal starts in baseball history in 1962 (going 40-120), since that time, they've won two World Series (in 1969 and 1986), appeared in two others, and have been competitive in at least some portion of every decade. As always, hope springs eternal among Mets fans, whose team looks great on paper with the acquisition of Pedro Martinez, Carlos Beltran, and manager Willie Randolph. This being the Mets, the smart money is on another disappointing season.

How To Get Tickets

You can order Mets tickets by phone through the Mets' box office, on the internet through the Mets' website, or at the Mets Clubhouse Shops.

How To Get There—Driving

Driving to Shea Stadium is easy, although commuter traffic during the week can cause tie-ups. You can take the Triborough Bridge to the Grand Central Parkway; the Mid-Town Tunnel to the Long Island Expressway to the Grand Central; or the Brooklyn-Queens Expressway to the LIE to the Grand Central. If you want to try and avoid the highways, get yourself over to Astoria Boulevard in Queens, make a right on 108th Street, then a left onto Roosevelt Avenue.

How To Get There–Mass Transit

The good news is that the ⑦ train runs straight to Shea Stadium. The bad news is: 1) it's the ⑦ train, usually rated the worst among all train lines; and 2) it's the only train that goes there. However, it will get you there and back (eventually), and the ⑦ is accessible from almost all the other train lines in Manhattan. Alternately, you can take the ⑤ to Roosevelt Avenue and pick up the ⑦ there, saving about 30 minutes. Also, New York Waterway runs a ferry service (the "Mets Express") to Shea from the South Street Seaport, E 34th Street, and E 94th Street. The other option is the Port Washington LIRR from Penn Station, which stops at Shea on game days.

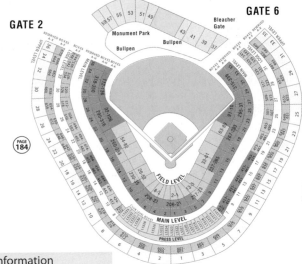

GATE 2

GATE 6

Bleacher Gate

Monument Park

Bullpen

Bullpen

GATE 4

General Information

Address: 161st St & River Ave, Bronx
Box Office: 718-293-6000
Website: www.yankees.com
Yankees Store: 393 5th Ave
Ferry: 800-53-FERRY
Ticketmaster: 212-307-7171; www.ticketmaster.com

Overview

Hellish ticket prices and extremely mediocre food won't stop us from going to Yankee Stadium, the Bronx's most famous landmark since the 1920's. Since moving in, the Yankees have won almost a quarter of the World Series that have been played, making them one of the most successful sports franchises in history. Last fall's historic Game Seven loss to the Red Sox has been pushed out of our minds for now. We expect the Yanks back in the playoffs next fall, just like everyone else does…

How to Get There—Driving

Driving to Yankee Stadium from Manhattan isn't as bad as you might think. Your best bet is to take the Willis Avenue Bridge from either First Avenue or FDR Drive and get on the Major Deegan for about one mile until you spot the stadium exit. From the Upper West Side, follow Broadway

up to 155th Street and use the Macombs Dam Bridge to cross over the river to the stadium (thus avoiding crosstown traffic). Parking (in contrast to ticket prices) is cheap, especially at lots a few blocks away from the stadium.

How to Get There–Mass Transit

Getting to the stadium by subway is easy. The **4**, **D**, and the **B** (on weekdays) all run express to the stadium, and you can easily hook up with those lines at several junctions in Manhattan. It should take no more than 45 minutes to get to the stadium from any point in Manhattan—even less from Midtown. New York Waterway also runs a wonderful ferry (the "Yankee Clipper") from South Street Seaport, E 34th Street, and E 94th Street.

How to Get Tickets

You can purchase tickets by phone through Ticketmaster, at the box office or the Yankee store, or online through either Ticketmaster or the Yankees web site.

Airline	Phone	JFK	EWR	LGA
Aer Lingus	888-474-7424	■		
Aeroflot	800-340-6400	■		
Aerolineas Argentinas	800-333-0276	■		
Aeromar	877-237-6627	■		
Aeromexico	800-237-6639	■		
Aerosvit Ukranian	212-661-1620	■		
Air Canada	888-247-2262	■	■	■
Air France	800-237-2747	■	■	
Air India	212-751-6200	■	■	
Air Jamaica	800-523-5585	■	■	
Air Malta	800-756-2582	■		
Air Plus Comet	877-999-7587	■		
Air Tran	800-247-8726	■	■	
Air Ukraine	212-230-1001	■		
Alaska Airlines	800-426-0333	■		
Alitalia	800-223-5730	■	■	
All Nippon	800-235-9262	■		
America West (domestic)	800-235-9292	■	■	
America West (international)	800-363-2597	■		
American (domestic)	800-433-7300	■	■	■
American (international)	800-433-7300	■	■	
American Eagle	800-433-7300	■		
Asiana	800-227-4262	■		
ATA	800-435-9282		■	
Austrian Airlines	800-843-0002	■		
Avianca	800-284-2622	■		
Biman Bangladesh	212-808-4477	■		
British Airways	800-247-9297	■		
BWIA	800-538-2942	■		
Casino Express	775-738-6040			■
Cathay Pacific	800-233-2742	■		
China Airlines	800-227-5118	■		
Colgan	800-428-4322			■
Comair	800-354-9822	■		
Continental (domestic)	800-525-0280	■	■	■
Continental (international)	800-231-0856		■	
Corsair (seasonal)	800-677-0720	■		
Czech Airlines	212-765-6545	■		
Delta (domestic)	800-221-1212	■	■	■
Delta (international)	800-241-4141	■	■	
Delta Express	800-235-9359	■	■	■
Egyptair	212-315-0900	■		
El Al	800-223-6700	■	■	
Ethiopian Airlines	212-867-0095	■		
Eva Airways	800-695-1188	■		
Finnair	800-950-5000	■		
Frontier Airlines	800-432-1359			■
Guyana Airways	718-523-2300	■		
Hooters Air	888-359-4668		■	
Iberia	800-772-4642	■		
Icelandair	800-223-5500		■	

Airline	Phone	JFK	EWR	LGA
Japan Airlines	800-525-3663	■		
Jet Blue	800-538-2583	■		
KLM	800-374-7747	■		
Korean Air	800-438-5000	■		
Kuwait Airways	800-458-9248	■		
Lacsa	800-225-2272	■		
Lan Chile	800-735-5526	■		
Lan Peru	800-735-5590	■		
LOT Polish	800-223-0593	■	■	
Lufthansa	800-645-3880	■	■	
Malaysia	800-582-9264		■	
Malev Hungarian	800-223-6884	■		
Mexicana	800-531-7921	■		
Miami Air (charter)	305-871-3300	■	■	
Midwest Express	800-452-2022	■	■	■
National Airlines	888-757-5387	■		
Nigeria Airlines	212-972-4565	■		
North American	718-656-2650	■	■	
Northwest (domestic)	800-225-2525	■	■	■
Northwest (international)	800-447-4747	■		
Olympic	800-223-1226	■		
Pakistan Int'l Airlines	212-370-9157	■		
Pan American Airways	800-FLY-PANAM		■	
Qantas	800-227-4500	■	■	
Royal Air Maroc	800-344-6726	■		
Royal Jordanian	212-949-0050	■		
SAS	800-221-2350		■	
Saudi Arabian Airlines	800-472-8342	■		
Singapore Airlines	800-742-3333	■	■	
Song	800-359-7664	■		
South African Airways	800-722-9675	■		
Southeast	800-359-7325			■
Spirit	800-772-7117			■
Swiss Airlines	800-221-4750	■	■	
TACA	800-535-8780	■		
TACV Cabo Verde	617-472-2431	■		
Tap Air Portugal	800-221-7370		■	
Tarom Romanian	212-560-0840	■		
Thai Airways	800-560-0840	■		
Turkish	800-874-8875	■		
United Airlines (domestic)	800-241-6522	■	■	■
United Airlines (international)	800-241-6522	■	■	
Universal	718-441-4900	■		
US Airways	800-428-4322	■	■	
USA3000	800-577-3000	■		
Uzbekistan	212-245-1005	■		
Varig	800-468-2744	■		
Virgin Atlantic	800-862-8621	■	■	
World Airways	770-632-8000	■		

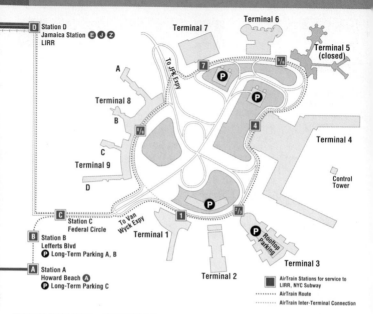

Station D
Jamaica Station **E J Z**
LIRR

Terminal 7

Terminal 6

Terminal 5
(closed)

To JFK Expy

A

Terminal 8

B

C

Terminal 9

D

Terminal 4

Control
Tower

Station C
Federal Circle

To Van
Wyck Expy

Terminal 1

Station B
Lefferts Blvd
P Long-Term Parking A, B

Station A
Howard Beach **A**
P Long-Term Parking C

Terminal 2

Rooftop
Parking

Terminal 3

■ AirTrain Stations for service to
LIRR, NYC Subway
···· AirTrain Route
···· AirTrain Inter-Terminal Connection

Airline	Terminal	Airline	Terminal	Airline	Terminal	Airline	Terminal
Aer Lingus	4	American (intl/Carib)	8	JetBlue Airways	6	Royal Air Maroc	1
Aero Mexico	3	Asiana	4	KLM	4	Royal Jordanian	3
Aeroflot	3	Austrian Airlines	1	Korean	4	Saudi Arabian	
Aerolineas Argentinas	4	Avianca	3	Kuwait	4	Airlines	
Aeromar	1	Biman Bangladesh	4	Lacsa	4	Singapore	1
Aerosvit Ukrainian	4	British Airways	7	Lan Chile	4	Song	2
Air Canada	7	BWIA	4	Lan Peru	4	South African	3
Air China	1	Cathay Pacific	7	LOT Polish	8	Swiss International	4
Air France	1	China Airlines	3	Lufthansa	1	TACA International	4
Air India	4	Continental Airlines	4	Malev	4	TACV Cabo Verde	4
Air Jamaica	2	Czech Airlines	3	Miami Air	4	TAP Air Portugal	4
Air Malta	4	Delta	3	National	4	Tarom Romanian	4
Air Plus Comet	4	Egypt Air	4	Nigeria Airways	4	Turkish	1
Air Ukraine	4	El Al	4	North American	4	United	7
Alitalia	1	Finnair	8	Northwest	4	Universal	4
All Nippon Airways	3	Ghana Airways	4	Olympic	1	Uzbekistan Airlines	4
America West	7	Iberia	8	PACE Airlines	4	Varig	4
American (dom/		Icelandair	7	Pakistan	4	Virgin Atlantic	4
San Juan)	9	Japan	1	Qantas	7	World Airways	4

General Information

Address:	JFK Expy
	Jamaica, NY 11430
Phone:	718-244-4444
Lost & Found:	718-244-4225
Website:	www.kennedyairport.com
AirTrain:	www.airtrainjfk.com
AirTrain Phone:	718-570-1048
Long Island Rail Road:	www.mta.info/lirr

Overview

Ah, JFK. It's long been a nemesis to Manhattanites due to the fact that it's the furthest of the three airports from the city. Nonetheless, more than 32 million people use JFK every year. A $9.5 billion expansion and modernization program is well underway, including the recently completed AirTrain (a direct rail link to the Jamaica LIRR Station), as well as the addition of some chi-chi retail options (Hermes, Bulgari, H. Stern, Cartier). But our best advice remains the same: if you live in Manhattan, try Newark instead.

However, if you're already at JFK, have some time to kill, and want to give the AirTrain a whirl, all terminal-to-terminal connections are free. Terminals 1 and 4 have far-and-away the best shops and food, and architecture buffs can catch a glimpse of Eero Saarinen's masterful Terminal 5 (temporarily unoccupied).

Rental Cars (On-Airport)

The rental car offices are all located along the Van Wyck Expressway near the entrance to the airport. Just follow the signs.

1 · **Avis** · 718-244-5406 or 800-230-4898
2 · **Budget** · 718-656-6010 or 800-527-0700
3 · **Dollar** · 718-656-2400 or 800-800-4000
4 · **Hertz** · 718-656-7600 or 800-654-3131
5 · **Enterprise** · 718-659-1200 or 800-RENT-A-CAR
6 · **National** · 718-632-8300 or 800-CAR-RENT

Hotels

Crown Plaza JFK · 151-20 Baisley Blvd · 718-489-1000
Comfort Inn JFK · 144-36 153rd Ln · 718-977-0001
Holiday Inn JFK Airport · 144-02 135th Ave · 718-659-0200
Radisson Hotel at JFK · 135-40 140th St · 718-322-2300
Ramada Plaza Hotel · Van Wyck Expy · 718-995-9000

Car Services & Taxis

All County Express · 914-381-4223 or 800-914-4223
Classic Limousine · 631-567-5100 or 800-666-4949
Dial 7 Car & Limo Service · 212-777-7777 or 800-222-9888
Super Saver by Carmel · 800-924-9954 or 212-666-6666
Tel Aviv Limo Service · 800-222-9888 or 212-777-7777

Taxis from the airport to Manhattan cost a flat $45 + tolls, while fares to the airport are metered + tolls. The SuperShuttle (800-258-3826) will drop you anywhere between Battery Park and 227th, including all hotels, for $17-$19 but it could end up taking a while, depending on where your fellow passengers are going—nevertheless, a good option if you want door-to-door service, have a lot of time to kill, but not a lot of cash.

235

How to Get There–Driving

You can take the lovely and scenic Belt Parkway straight to JFK, as long as it's not rush hour. The Belt Parkway route is about 30 miles long, even though JFK is only 15 or so miles from Manhattan. You can access the Belt by taking the Brooklyn-Battery Tunnel to the Gowanus (the best route) or by taking the Brooklyn, Manhattan, or Williamsburg Bridges to the Brooklyn-Queens Expressway to the Gowanus. If you're sick of stop-and-go highway traffic, and you prefer an alternate route using local roads, take Atlantic Avenue in Brooklyn and drive east until you hit Conduit Avenue. Follow this straight to JFK—it's direct and fairly simple. You can get to Atlantic Avenue from any of the three downtown bridges (look at one of our maps first!). From Midtown, you can take the Queens Midtown Tunnel to the Long Island Expressway to the Van Wyck Expressway S (there's never much traffic on the LIE, of course…). From uptown, you can take the Triboro Bridge to the Grand Central Parkway to the Van Wyck Expressway S. JFK also has two new AM frequencies solely devoted to keeping you abreast of all of the airport's endeavors that may affect traffic. Tune into 1630AM for general airport information and 1700AM for construction updates en route to your next flight. It might save you a sizeable headache.

How to Get There—Mass Transit

This is your chance to finish *War and Peace*. The new AirTrain will make your journey marginally smoother, but it will also make your wallet a little lighter. Where there was once a free shuttle bus service from the Howard Beach/JFK Airport stop on the Ⓐ subway line, the AirTrain will now whisk you across for a mere five bucks extra. Depending on where you're traveling from in Manhattan, Queens or Brooklyn, the Ⓔ, Ⓙ, and Ⓜ subway lines to Sutphin Blvd/Archer Ave also connect with the AirTrain.

All subway-AirTrain combos will set you back a total of $7. If you're anywhere near Penn Station and your time is valuable, the LIRR to Jamaica will cost you $5 off-peak, $7 during peak times, and the journey takes roughly 20 minutes. The AirTrain portion of the trip will still cost you an additional $5 and round out your travel time to more than an hour.

If you want to give your MetroCard a workout, you can take the Ⓔ or the Ⓕ to the Turnpike/Kew Gardens stop, and transfer to the Ⓑ. Another possibility is the Ⓑ to New Lots Avenue, where you transfer to the Ⓜ to JFK. The easiest and most direct option is to take a New York Airport Service Express bus (718-875-8200) from either Grand Central Station, Penn Station, or the Port Authority for $15 or you can hop on the Trans-Bridge Bus Line (800-962-9135) at Port Authority for $12. Since the buses travel on service roads, Friday afternoon is not an advisable time to try them out.

Parking

Rates for the Central Terminal Area lots cost $3 for the first half-hour, $6 for up to one hour, $3 for every hour after that, and $24 per day. Long-term parking costs $10 per day, for a maximum of 30 days. Be warned, though—many of the ongoing construction projects at JFK affect both their short-term and long-term lots, so be sure to allow extra time for any unpleasant surprises.

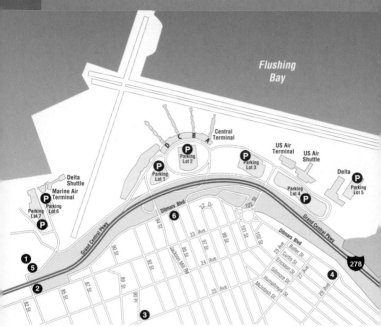

Airline	Terminal
Air Canada	A
Air Tran	B
American	D
American Eagle	C
ATA	B
Colgan	US Airways
Comair	Delta
Continental	A
Continental Express	A
Delta	Delta
Delta Shuttle	Marine
Frontier Airlines	B
Midwest Express	B
Northwest	Delta
Spirit	B
United	B
United (to DCA & BOS)	US Air Shuttle
United Express	C
US Airways	US Airways
US Airways Express	US Airways
US Airways Shuttle	US Air Shuttle

General Information

Address:	LaGuardia Airport
	Flushing, NY 11371
Recorded Information:	718-533-3400
Lost & Found:	718-533-3988
Police:	718-533-3900
Website:	www.laguardiaairport.com

Overview

The best thing we can say about LaGuardia Airport is that it's named for a most excellent former New York City mayor, Fiorello LaGuardia. Although LaGuardia has improved in recent years, it still has away to go before it can hold its own against the nation's other airports. However, a number of new food stands and retail establishments have opened up in the Central Terminal and US Airways Terminal, including places like Brooks Brothers, National Geographic, and the Metropolitan Museum of Art store.

Although LaGuardia remains inconvenient to public transportation, with the nearest subway station miles and miles away, it's still closer to the city than either Kennedy or Newark (especially from the Upper West or Upper East Sides).

How to Get There—Driving

LaGuardia is mere inches away from Grand Central Parkway, which can be reached from both the Brooklyn-Queens Expressway (BQE) or from the Triboro Bridge. From Lower Manhattan, take the Brooklyn, Manhattan, or Williamsburg Bridges to the BQE to Grand Central Parkway E. From Midtown Manhattan, take FDR Drive to the Triboro to Grand Central. A potential alternate route (and money-saver) would be to take the 59th Street Bridge to 21st Street in Queens. Once you're heading north on 21st Street, you can make a right on Astoria Boulevard and follow it all the way to 94th Street, where you can make a left and drive straight into LaGuardia. This alternate route is good if the FDR and/or the BQE is jammed, although that probably means that the 59th Street Bridge won't be much better.

How to Get There—Mass Transit

Alas, no subway line goes to LaGuardia (although there SHOULD be one running across 96th Street in Manhattan, through Astoria, and ending at LaGuardia—but that's another story). The closest the subway comes is the **7** **E** **F** **G** **R** Jackson Heights/Roosevelt Avenue/74th Street stop in Queens, where you can transfer to the 🚌 or 🚌 bus to LaGuardia. Sound exciting? Well, it's not. A better bus to take is the M60, which runs across 125th Street to the airport. An even better bet would be to pay the extra few bucks and take the New York Airport Service Express Bus ($12 one-way, 718-875-8200) from Grand Central Station. It departs every 20-30 minutes and takes approximately 45 minutes; also catch it on Park Avenue between 41st and 42nd Streets, Penn Station, and the Port Authority Bus Terminal. The improbably named SuperShuttle Manhattan, is a shared mini-bus that picks you up anywhere within the city limits ($13-$22 one-way, 212-258-3826). Or you could just pay a cab driver with your firstborn.

How to Get There—Really

Two words: car service. Call them, they'll pick you up at your door and drop you at the terminal. Simple. Allstate Car and Limousine: 212-333-3333 ($30 in the am & $38 in the pm + tolls from Union Square); Tri-State: 212-777-7171 ($30 + tolls from Union Square; best to call in the morning); Tel Aviv: 212-777-7777 ($30 in the am & $40 in the pm + tolls from Union Square).

Parking

Parking rates at LaGuardia cost $3 for the first half-hour, $6 for up to one hour, $3 for every hour thereafter, and $24 per day. Long-term parking is $24 maximum for the first day and then $10 per day thereafter (though only in Lot 3). Another option is independent parking lots, such as Clarion Airport Parking (Ditmars Blvd & 94th St, 718-335-6713) and AviStar (23rd Ave & 90th St, 718-507-8162). They run their own shuttle buses from their lots, and they usually charge $14-$17 per day. If all the parking garages onsite are full, follow the "P" signs to the airport exit and park in one of the off-airport locations.

Rental Cars

1 Avis · LGA		800-230-4898
2 Budget · 83-34 23rd Ave		800-527-0700
3 Dollar · 90-05 25th Ave		800-800-4000
4 Enterprise · 104-04 Ditmars Blvd		718-457-2900
5 Hertz · LGA		800-654-3131
6 National · Ditmars Blvd & 95th St		800-227-7368

Hotels

Clarion · 94-00 Ditmars Blvd · 718-335-1200
Courtyard · 90-10 Grand Central Pkwy · 718-446-4800
Crowne Plaza · 104-04 Ditmars Blvd · 718-457-6300
Best Western · 113-10 Corona Ave · 718-699-4500
LaGuardia Marriott · 102-05 Ditmars Blvd · 718-565-8900
Paris Suites · 109-17 Horace Harding Expy · 718-760-2820
Sheraton · 135-20 39th Ave · 718-460-6666
Wyndham Garden · 100-15 Ditmars Blvd · 718-426-1500

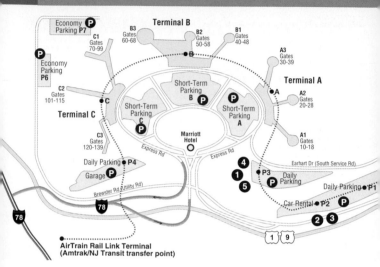

Airline	Terminal
Air Canada	A
Air France	B
Air India	B
Air Jamaica	B
Air Tran	A
Alaska Airlines	A
Alitalia	B
America West	A
American (domestic)	A
American (international)	A/B*
ATA (domestic)	A
ATA (international)	A/B*
British Airways	B
Casino Express	A
Continental	C
Continental (Chicago/Atlanta/Dallas)	A
Czech Airlines	B
Delta	B
El Al	B
Ethiopian Airlines	B
Eva Airways	B

Airline	Terminal
Hooters Air	B
LOT Polish	B
Lufthansa	B
Malaysia	B
Mexicana	B
Miami Air	B
Midwest Express	B
Northwest	B
Pan American Airways	A
Qantas	A
SAS	B
Singapore Airlines	B
Swiss International Air Lines	B
TAP Air Portugal	B
United (domestic)	A
United (international)	A/B*
United Express	A
USA3000	B
US Airways	A
US Airways Express	A
Virgin Atlantic	B

* Departs Terminal A, arrives Terminal B.

General Information

Address:	10 Toler Pl, Newark, NJ 07114
Phone:	888-EWR-INFO
Police/Lost & Found:	973-961-6230
Airport Information:	973-961-6000
Transportation Info:	800-AIR-RIDE (247-7533)
Radio Station:	530 AM
Website:	www.newarkairport.com

Overview

Newark Airport is easily the nicest of the three major metropolitan airports. The monorail and the AirTrain link from Penn Station, as well as a diverse food court, make it the city's preferred point of departure and arrival. Newark's burgeoning international connections are increasing its popularity, which means you might be languishing in Holland Tunnel traffic long after your plane has left the ground.

If your flight gets delayed or you find yourself with time on your hands, check out the new d-parture spa in Terminal C, Gate 92 (with another new location at Gate 48 in Terminal B). They offer everything from massage and facials to haircuts and make-up, and their friendly staff watches the clock so you don't have to. www.departurespa.com, 973-242-3444.

How to Get There—Driving

The route to Newark Airport is easy—just take the Holland Tunnel or the Lincoln Tunnel to the New Jersey Turnpike South. You can use either Exit 14 or Exit 13A. If you want a cheaper and slightly more scenic (from an industrial standpoint) ride, follow signs for the Pulaski Skyway once you exit the Holland Tunnel. It's free, it's one of the coolest bridges in America, and it leads you to the airport just fine. If possible, check a traffic report before leaving Manhattan—sometimes there are viciously long tie-ups, especially at the Holland Tunnel. It's always worth it to see which outbound tunnel has the shortest wait.

How to Get There—Mass Transit

If you're allergic to traffic, try taking the AirTrain service from Penn Station. It's run by Amtrak ($27-$35 one-way) and NJ Transit ($11.55 one-way). If you use NJ Transit, choose a train that runs on the Northeast Corridor or North Jersey Coast Line with a scheduled stop for Newark Airport. If you use Amtrak, choose a train that runs on the Northeast Corridor Line with a scheduled stop for Newark Airport. You can also catch direct buses departing from Port Authority Bus Terminal (with the advantage of a bus-only lane running right out of the station and into the Lincoln Tunnel), Grand Central Terminal, and Penn Station (the New York version) on Olympia for $12. The SuperShuttle will set you back $19 and a taxi from Manhattan will cost you around $50.

How to Get There–Car Services

Car services are always the simplest option, although they're a bit more expensive for Newark Airport than they are for LaGuardia. Allstate Car and Limousine: 212-333-3333 ($44 in the am & $52 in the pm + tolls from Union Square); Tri-State: 212-777-7171 ($43 + tolls from Union Square; best to call in the morning); Tel Aviv: 212-777-7777 ($44 in the am & $54 in the pm + tolls from Union Square).

Parking

Regular parking rates are $3 for the first half-hour, $6 for up to one hour, $3 for every hour after that, and now an excessive $20 per day for the P1, P3, and P4 monorail-serviced lots. The P6 parking lot is much farther away, only serviced by a shuttle bus, and costs $10 per day. Valet parking costs $36 per day.

Rental Cars

1 · **Avis**	800-230-4898
2 · **Budget**	800-527-0700
3 · **Dollar**	973-824-2002
4 · **Hertz**	800-654-3131
5 · **National**	800-227-7368
6 · **Alamo** (Off-Airport)	800-327-9633
7 · **Enterprise** (Off-Airport)	800-325-8007

Hotels

Marriott(On-Airport) · 973-623-0006
Courtyard Marriott · 600 Rte 1 9 · 973-643-8500
Hilton · 1170 Spring St · 908-351-3900
Howard Johnson · 50 Port St · 201-344-1500
Sheraton · 128 Frontage Rd · 973-690-5500
Hampton Inn · 1128-38 Spring St · 908-355-0500
Best Western · 101 International Wy · 973-621-6200
Holiday Inn North · 160 Frontage Rd · 973-589-1000
Days Inn · 450 Rte 1 South · 973-242-0900
Ramada Inn · US Hwy 1/9 & Haynes Ave · 973-824-4000
Four Points Sheraton · 901 Spring St · 908-527-1600

Transit · **Bridges & Tunnels**

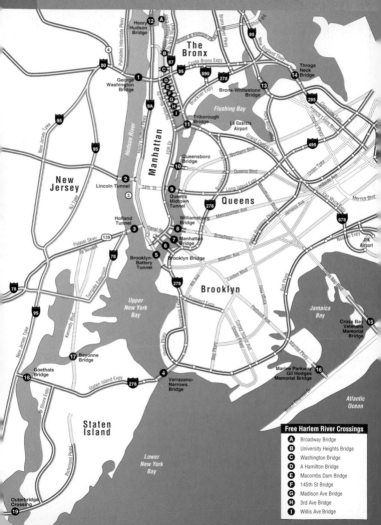

Free Harlem River Crossings

Ⓐ	Broadway Bridge
Ⓑ	University Heights Bridge
Ⓒ	Washington Bridge
Ⓓ	A Hamilton Bridge
Ⓔ	Macombs Dam Bridge
Ⓕ	145th St Bridge
Ⓖ	Madison Ave Bridge
Ⓗ	3rd Ave Bridge
Ⓘ	Willis Ave Bridge

Henry Hudson Bridge

The Bronx

George Washington Bridge

Throgs Neck Bridge

Bronx-Whitestone Bridge

Flushing Bay

Triborough Bridge

La Guardia Airport

New Jersey

Hudson River

Manhattan

Lincoln Tunnel

Queensboro Bridge

Queens

Holland Tunnel

Queens Midtown Tunnel

Williamsburg Bridge

Manhattan Bridge

Brooklyn-Battery Tunnel

Brooklyn Bridge

Brooklyn

JFK Airport

Jamaica Bay

Upper New York Bay

Cross Bay Veterans Memorial Bridge

Bayonne Bridge

Goethals Bridge

Marine Parkway Gil Hodges Memorial Bridge

Verrazano-Narrows Bridge

Staten Island

Atlantic Ocean

Lower New York Bay

Outerbridge Crossing

General Information

Port Authority of NY and NJ:	www.panynj.gov
DOT:	www.ci.nyc.ny.us/html/dot/home.html • 212 or 718-CALLDOT
MTA:	www.mta.info
EZPass:	www.e-zpassny.com • 1-800-333-TOLL
Transportation Alternatives:	www.transalt.org
Best overall site:	www.nycroads.com

Overview

Since NYC is an archipelago, it's no wonder there are so many bridges and four major tunnels. Most of the bridges listed in the chart below are considered landmarks, either for their sheer beauty or because they were the first of their kind at one time. The traffic-jammed Holland Tunnel, finished in 1927, was the first vehicular tunnel connecting New Jersey and New York. King's Bridge, built between Manhattan and the Bronx in 1693, was sadly demolished in 1917. Highbridge, the oldest existing bridge in NYC, (built in 1843) is no longer open to vehicles or pedestrians. Brooklyn Bridge, built in 1883, is the city's oldest functioning bridge, still open to vehicles and pedestrians alike, and is considered one of the most beautiful bridges ever built.

The '70s was a decade of neglect for city bridges. Inspections in the '80s and maintenance and refurbishment plans in the '90s/'00s have made the bridges stronger and safer than ever before. On certain holidays when the weather permits, the world's largest free-flying American flag flies from the upper arch of the New Jersey tower on the George Washington Bridge.

		Toll/EZPass peak/EZPass off-peak	# of lanes	Pedestrians/bicyclists?	# of vehicles/day (in thousands)	Original cost (in millions)	Engineer	Main span	Operated by	Opened to traffic
1	Geo. Washington Bridge	6.00/5.00/4.00 (inbound only)	14	yes	300	59	Othmar H. Ammann	4,760'	PANYNJ	10/25/31
2	Lincoln Tunnel	6.00/5.00/4.00 (inbound only)	6	no	120	75	Othmar H. Ammann / Ole Singstad	8,216'	PANYNJ	12/22/37
3	Holland Tunnel	6.00/5.00/4.00 (inbound only)	4	no	100	54	Clifford Holland / Ole Singstad	8,558'	PANYNJ	11/13/27
4	Verrazano-Narrows Bridge	*	12	no	190	320	Othmar H. Ammann	4,260'	MTA	11/21/64
5	Brooklyn-Battery Tunnel	4.50/4.00	4	no	60	90	Ole Singstad	9,117'	MTA	5/25/50
6	Brooklyn Bridge	free	6	yes	140	15	John Roebling / Washington Roebling	1,595.5'	DOT	5/24/1883
7	Manhattan Bridge	free	7	yes	150	31	Leon Moisseiff	1,470'	DOT	12/31/09
8	Williamsburg Bridge	free	8	yes	140	24.2	Leffert L. Buck	1,600'	DOT	12/19/03
9	Queens-Midtown Tunnel	4.50/4.00	4	no	80	52	Ole Singstad	6,414'	DOT	11/15/40
10	Queensboro Bridge	free	10	yes	200	20	Gustav Lindenthal	1,182'	DOT	3/30/70
11	Triborough Bridge	4.50/4.00	8/6/8	yes	200	60.3	Othmar H. Ammann	1,380'/	MTA	7/11/36
12	Henry Hudson Bridge	2.25/1.75	7	yes	75	5	David Steinman	840'	MTA	12/12/36
13	Whitestone Bridge	4.50/4.00	6	no	110	20	Othmar H. Ammann	2300'	MTA	4/29/39
14	Throgs Neck Bridge	4.50/4.00	6	no	100	92	Othmar H. Ammann	1800'	MTA	1/11/61
15	Cross Bay Veterans Memorial Bridge	2.25/1.50	6	yes	20	29	N/A	3000'	MTA	5/28/70
16	Marine Parkway Gil Hodges Memorial Bridge	2.25/1.50	4	no	25	12	Madigan and Hyland	540'	MTA	7/3/37
17	Bayonne Bridge	6.00/5.00/4.00	4	yes	20	13	Othmar H. Ammann	5,780'	PANY/NJ	11/13/31
18	Goethals Bridge	6.00/5.00/4.00	4	no	75	7.2	Othmar H. Ammann	8,600'	PANY/NJ	6/29/28
19	Outerbridge Crossing	6.00/5.00/4.00	4	no	80	9.6	Othmar H. Ammann	750'	PANY/NJ	6/29/28

* $9.00/$8.00 with EZPass to Staten Island ($6.40/4.80 for registered Staten Island residents with EZPass),
$2.25 with three or more occupants—cash only). Free to Brooklyn.

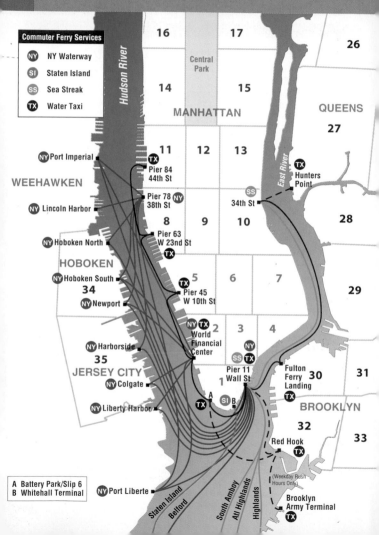

Commuter Ferry Services

- NY NY Waterway
- SI Staten Island
- SS Sea Streak
- TX Water Taxi

16   17   26

Central Park

14   15

MANHATTAN   QUEENS

27

Hudson River

WEEHAWKEN

NY Port Imperial

NY Lincoln Harbor

11   12   13

TX Pier 84 44th St

Pier 78 NY 38th St

SS 34th St

28

East River

TX Hunters Point

8   9   10

NY Hoboken North

HOBOKEN

NY Hoboken South

34

NY Newport

TX Pier 63 W 23nd St

5   6   7

TX Pier 45 W 10th St

29

NY Harborside

JERSEY CITY

NY Colgate

35

NY Liberty Harbor

NY TX 2   3   4
World Financial Center

SS TX

1 Pier 11 Wall St

NY

Fulton Ferry Landing 30   31

TX

BROOKLYN

A
TX SI B

32   33

Red Hook

TX

(Weekday Rush Hours Only)

A Battery Park/Slip 6
B Whitehall Terminal

NY Port Liberte

Staten Island
Belford

South Amboy
Atl Highlands
Highlands

Brooklyn Army Terminal

TX

Ferries/Boat Tours, Rentals, & Charters

Name	Contact Info
Staten Island Ferry	311 • www.nyc.gov/html/dot/html/masstran/ferries/statfery.html
	This free ferry travels between Battery Park and Staten Island. On weekdays it leaves every 15-20 minutes from 6:30 am-9 am and 4 pm-8 pm. On weekends, it leaves every hour between 12:30 am-7:30 am, and every half hour at all other times.
NY Waterway	800-53-FERRY • www.nywaterway.com
	The largest ferry service in NY, NYWaterway offers many commuter routes (mostly from New Jersey), sightseeing tours, and shuttles to Yankees and Mets games. However, recent financial troubles have them closing many commuter lines.
NY Water Taxi	1-212-742-1969 • www.nywatertaxi.com
	Available for commuting, sightseeing, and charter. Commuter tickets range between $4 and $6 and tours cost $20 to $35. For chartered trips or tours, call for a quote.
Sea Streak	1-800-BOAT-RIDE • www.seastreakusa.com
	Catamarans that go pretty fast from the Highlands in NJ to Wall Street, E 34th Street, and the Brooklyn Army Terminal.
Circle Line	212-269-5755 • www.circleline.com
	Circle Line offers many sightseeing tours, including a visit to Ellis Island (departs from Pier 16 at South Street Seaport - $10 for adults, $4 for kids)
Spirit of New York	212-727-7735 • www.spiritcruises.com
	Offers lunch and dinner cruises. Prices start at $43. Leaves from Pier 61 at Chelsea Piers. Make a reservation at least one week in advance, but the earlier the better.
Loeb Boathouse	212-517-2233 • www.centralpark.org/virtualpark/thegreatlawn/loebboathouse/
	You can rent rowboats from April through October at the Lake in Central Park, open seven days a week, weather permitting, during the spring and summer seasons. Boat rentals cost $10 for the first hour and $2.50 for every additional 15 minutes (rentals also require a $30 cash deposit). The boathouse is open 10 am-5 pm, but the last boat goes out at 4:30 pm. Up to five people per boat. No reservations needed.
World Yacht Cruises	212-630-8100 or 800-498-4271 • www.worldyacht.com
	These fancy, three-hour dinner cruises start at $69.95 per person. The cruises depart from Pier 81 (41st Street) and require reservations. The cruise boards at 6 pm, sails at 7 pm, and returns at 10 pm. There's also a Sunday brunch cruise April–December that costs $41.90 per person.

Marinas/Passenger Ship Terminal

Name	Contact Info	Map
Surfside III	212-336-7873 • www.surfside3.com	8
	Dockage at Chelsea Piers. They offer daily, weekly, and seasonal per foot rates (there's always a waiting list).	
NY Skyports Inc	212-686-4547	10
	Located on the East River at E 23rd Street. Transient dockage costs $3 per foot.	
79th St Marina	212-496-2105	14
	This city-operated dock is filled with long-term houseboat residents. It's located at W 79th Street and the Hudson River. Open from May to October.	
Dyckman Marina	212-567-5120	25
	Transient dockage on the Hudson River at 348 Dyckman Street	
Passenger Ship Terminal	212-246-5450 • www.nypst.com	11
	If Love Boat re-runs aren't enough and you decide to go on a cruise yourself, you'll leave from the Passenger Ship Terminal. W 55th Street at 12th Avenue. Take the West Side Highway to Piers 88-92.	
North Cove Yacht Harbor	212-786-1200 • www.thenorthcove.com	BPC
	A very, very fancy place to park your yacht in Battery Park City.	

Helicopter Services

Name	Contact Info	Map
Helicopter Flight Services	212-355-0801 • www.heliny.com	3, 8
	For a minimum of $109, you can hop on a helicopter at the Downtown Manhattan Heliport at Pier 6 on the East River on weekdays, or at the W 30th Street Heliport on weekends and spend 15 minutes gazing down on Manhattan. Reservations are recommended, and there's a minimum of two passengers per flight.	
Liberty Helicopter Tours	212-967-6464 • www.libertyhelicopters.com	3, 8
	Leaves from the heliport at W 30th Street and 12th Avenue (9 am-9 pm) or the Downtown Manhattan Heliport at Pier 6 on the East River (9 am-6 pm). Prices start at $56, and reservations are needed only when boarding at the Seaport. Flights depart every 5-10 minutes. Minimum of four passengers per flight.	
Wall Street Helicopter	212-943-5959 • www.wallstreetheli.qpg.com	3
	Leaves from any heliport in Manhattan. Executive/corporate helicopter and twin engine aircraft charters. No sightseeing.	

General Information

E-ZPass Information: 800-333-TOLL
Radio Station Traffic Updates: 1010 WINS on the 1s for a 5 Boroughs focus and 880 on the 8s for a suburbs focus
DOT Website: www.ci.nyc.ny.us/html/dot/html/motorist/motorist.html
Real-Time Web Traffic Info: www.metrocommute.com

Driving in Manhattan

Hardware requirements: Small, durable car with big, wide tires. New York plates. Plenty of dents and scratches. Loud, obnoxious horn. Stick shift. Semi-automatic tripod-mounted tommy gun.

Software requirements: Copy of NFT. Hagstrom 5-Borough Atlas. E-ZPass. Sweet'N Low. Fix-A-Flat can.

Basic rules: Never look in your rear-view mirror.

    Always assume that the cab that looks like it's about to cut you off, will.

    Always assume that the bus that looks like it's about to cut you off, will.

    Never, ever pull into an intersection unless you're SURE you can make it all the way through before the light turns red.

    The rule of the jungle applies; bigger and meaner have the right of way.

    The pecking order starts at fire engines, ambulances, cops, and most dangerous of all, sanitation trucks. The hyena level consists of buses, delivery trucks, and particularly crazy cabbies. The amoeba level encompasses everyone else, but even they will devour those with out-of-state plates.

    Never let them see the whites of your eyes.

But seriously, driving in Manhattan is not for the timid, clueless, or otherwise emotionally fragile.

The following are some tips that we've encountered over the years:

Hudson River Crossings

The George Washington Bridge is by far the best Hudson River crossing. It's got more lanes and better access than the two crappy tunnels. If you're going anywhere in the country that's north of central New Jersey, take it. The Lincoln Tunnel is pretty good inbound, but check 1010 AM (WINS) if you have the chance—even though they can be horribly inaccurate and frustrating. If you have to take the Holland Tunnel outbound, try the Broome Street approach, but don't even bother between 5 and 7-pm on weekdays.

East River Crossings

Brooklyn

Pearl Street to the Brooklyn Bridge is the least-known approach. Only the Williamsburg Bridge has direct access (i.e. no traffic lights) to the northbound BQE in Brooklyn, and only the Brooklyn Bridge has direct access to the FDR Drive in Manhattan. Again, listen to the radio if you can, but all three bridges can suck hard simultaneously, especially since they are all perpetually being worked on. Now that construction on the Williamsburg is complete, it is by far the best free route into Brooklyn, but make sure to take the outer roadway to keep your options open in case the BQE is jammed. Your best option to go anywhere in Brooklyn is usually the Brooklyn-Battery Tunnel, which can be reached from the FDR as well as the West Side Highway. It's not free ($4.50), but you've got E-ZPass anyway ($4) (if you're not a schmuck).

Queens

There are three options for crossing into Queens by car. The Queens Midtown Tunnel is usually miserable, since it feeds directly onto the always-busy Long Island Expressway. The 59th Street Bridge is the only free crossing to Queens. The best approach to it is First Avenue to 57th Street. If you're in Queens and want to go downtown in Manhattan, you can take the lower level of the 59th Street Bridge since it will feed directly onto Second Avenue, which of course goes downtown. The Triborough Bridge is usually the best option (especially if you're going to LaGuardia, Shea, or Astoria for Greek food). The FDR to the Triborough is good except for rush hour—then try Third Avenue to 124th Street.

Harlem River Crossings

The Triborough ($4.50) will get you to the Bronx in pretty good shape, especially if you are heading east on the Bruckner towards 95 or the Hutchinson (which will take you to eastern Westchester and Connecticut). To get to Yankee Stadium, take the Willis or the Macomb's Dam (which are both free). The Henry Hudson Bridge will take you up to western Westchester along the Hudson, and, except for the antiquated and completely unnecessary toll plaza, is pretty good. (The booth attendants there win the "most disarmingly nice in NY" award.) Always attempt to avoid the Cross-Bronx Expressway.

Manhattan's "Highways"

There are two so-called highways in Manhattan—the Harlem River Drive/FDR Drive (which prohibits commercial vehicles) and the Henry Hudson Parkway/West Side Highway. The main advantage of the FDR is that it has no traffic lights, while the West Side Highway has lights from Battery Park up through 57th Street. If there's been a lot of rain, both highways will flood, so you're out of luck. We also think that FDR Drive drivers are one percent better than West Side Highway drivers.

Driving Uptown

The 96th Street transverse across Central Park is usually the best one, although if there's been a lot of rain, it will flood too. If you're driving on the west side, Riverside Drive is the best route, followed next by West End Avenue. People drive like morons on Broadway, and Columbus jams up in the mid 60s before Lincoln Center. Amsterdam is a good uptown route if you can get to it. For the east side, you can take Fifth Avenue downtown to about 65th Street, whereupon you should bail out and cut over to Park Avenue for the rest of the trip. NEVER try driving on Fifth Avenue below 65th Street within a month of Christmas. The 96th Street entrance to the FDR screws up First and Third Avenues going north and the 59th Street Bridge screws up Lexington and Second Avenues going downtown. Getting stuck in 59th Street Bridge traffic is one of the most frustrating things in the universe because there is absolutely no way out of it.

Driving in Midtown

Good luck! Sometimes Broadway is best because everyone's trying to get out of Manhattan, jamming up the west side (via the Lincoln Tunnel) and the east side (via the 59th Street Bridge and the Queens Midtown Tunnel). The "interior" city is the last place to get jammed up—it's surprisingly quiet at 8 am. At 10 am, however, it's a parking lot.

The city's latest "innovation" in Midtown is the demarcation of several "THRU Streets" running east-west. See the next page for more information.

Driving in the Village

If you're coming into the Village from the northwest, 14th Street is the safest crosstown route heading east. However, going west, take 13th Street. Houston Street is usually okay in both directions and has the great benefit of direct access to FDR Drive, both getting onto it and coming off of it. If you want to get to Houston Street from the Holland Tunnel, take Hudson Street to King Street to the Avenue of the Americas to Houston Street (this is the **only** efficient way to get to the Village from the Holland Tunnel). First Avenue is good going north and Fifth Avenue is good going south. Washington Street is the only way to make any headway in the West Village.

Driving Downtown

Don't do it unless you have to. Western TriBeCa is okay and so is the Lower East Side—try not to "turn in" to SoHo, Chinatown, or City Center. Canal Street is a complete mess during the day (avoid it at all costs), since on its western end everyone is trying to get to the Holland Tunnel, and on its eastern end everyone is mistakenly driving over the Manhattan Bridge (your only other option when heading east on Canal is to turn **right** onto Bowery!).

DMV Locations in Manhattan

If you're going to the DMV to get your first NY license (including drivers with other states' licenses), you'll need extensive documentation of your identity. The offices have a long list of accepted documents, but your best bet is a US Passport and a Social Security card. If you don't have these things, birth certificates from the US, foreign passports, and various INS documents will be ok under certain conditions.

Greenwich Street Office
11 Greenwich St
New York, NY 10004
(Cross Streets Battery Park Pl & Morris St)
M-F 8:30 am-4 pm
212-645-5550 or 718-966-6155

Harlem Office
159 E 125th St, 3rd Fl
New York, NY 10035
(Lexington and Third)
M, T, W & F 8:30 am-4 pm, Thursday 8:30 am-6 pm
212-645-5550 or 718-966-6155

Herald Square Office
1293-1311 Broadway, 8th Fl
New York, NY 10001
(Between W 33 & W 34 Sts)
M-F 8:30 am-4 pm
212-645-5550 or 718-966-6155

Manhattan
License X-Press Office*
300 W 34th St
New York, NY 10001
(Between Eighth & Ninth Ave)
*Service Limited: Only NY State renewals. You also can't renew your boat or snowmobile license here, only stuff for cars and trucks.
M, T, W & F 8:30-5:30 pm, Thursday 8 am-7 pm,
Closed Fridays; 212-645-5550 or 718-966-6155

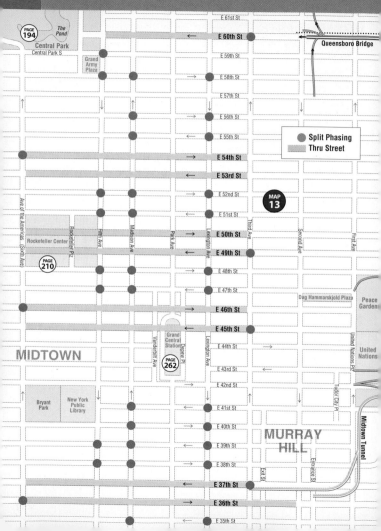

The Pond

PAGE 194

Central Park

Central Park S

Grand Army Plaza

E 61st St

E 60th St

Queensboro Bridge

E 59th St

E 58th St

E 57th St

E 56th St

E 55th St

E 54th St

E 53rd St

E 52nd St

E 51st St

MAP 13

● Split Phasing

▨ Thru Street

Ave of the Americas (Sixth Ave)

Rockefeller Center

Rockefeller Plz

Fifth Ave

Madison Ave

Park Ave

Lexington Ave

Third Ave

Second Ave

First Ave

PAGE 210

E 50th St

E 49th St

E 48th St

E 47th St

Dag Hammarskjold Plaza

Peace Gardens

E 46th St

E 45th St

Grand Central Station

Vanderbilt Ave

Depew Pl

PAGE 262

E 44th St

E 43rd St

Lexington Ave

United Nations Pl

United Nations

MIDTOWN

E 42nd St

Bryant Park

New York Public Library

E 41st St

E 40th St

E 39th St

MURRAY HILL

Tudor City Pl

Midtown Tunnel

E 38th St

E 37th St

Exit St

Entrance St

E 36th St

E 35th St

General Information

DOT Website: www.nyc.gov/html/dot/html/motorist/streetprog.html
DOT Phone: 311

Overview

In the tradition of "don't block the box" and other traffic solutions (such as randomly arresting political protesters), the city introduced "THRU Streets" in 2002. The plan was implemented on some crosstown streets in Midtown in order to reduce travel times, relieve congestion, and provide a safer environment for pedestrians and cyclists. After an initial testing period (where all driver feedback was probably completely ignored), the THRU Streets were made permanent in 2004.

On certain streets, cars are not allowed to make turns between Sixth and Third Avenues (with the exception of Park Avenue). The regulations are in effect between 10 am and 6 pm on weekdays. The affected streets are:

> 36th & 37th Streets
> 45th & 46th Streets
> 49th & 50th Streets
> 53rd & 54th Streets
> 60th Street (between Third and Fifth Avenues)

The above streets are easily identifiable by big, purple "THRU Streets" signs. With everything that's going on in midtown Manhattan though, you'd be forgiven for missing a sign (by us, not by the NYPD). If you happen to unwittingly find yourself on a THRU Street, you're going to have to suck it up until you get to Sixth Avenue or Third Avenue, depending on the direction you're heading. If you attempt to turn before the designated avenue, you'll find yourself with an insanely expensive ticket. Of course, if you're trying to drive crosstown, it's in your best interests to take one of these streets.

According to the DOT, THRU Streets are working—since the program began, travel times have fallen by 25 % (as people have decided to emigrate to New Zealand) and vehicle speeds have increased by an average of 33 % (from 4 mph to 5.3 mph). The THRU Streets combined now carry 4,854 vehicles per hour (up from 4,187), which means that each of the THRU Streets accommodates an average of 74 additional vehicles per hour.

Split Signal Phasing

Another traffic innovation in Midtown is "split signal phasing", which allows pedestrians to cross the street without having to worry about vehicles turning in their path. Of course, this system relies on New Yorkers acknowledging pedestrian crossing signals—a dubious assumption. In spite of the disregard that most New Yorkers display for crossing signals, the number of pedestrian accidents in the eight-month trial period (compared to the 8 months prior to implementation) fell from 81 to 74. The number of cycling accidents fell from 30 to 17. Accidents not related to pedestrians or bikes fell from 168 to 102. We have to admit that something must be working—though there would be no accidents if no one ever left their house...

Now if the DOT and NYPD could get traffic to flow smoothly onto bridges and into tunnels, they might actually be onto something. They can save you 1.5 minutes getting crosstown, just don't try leaving the city. Ever.

Information

Department of Transportation (DOT):
212-225-5368 (24 hours)
TTY Hearing-Impaired: 212-442-9488
Website: www.ci.nyc.ny.us/html/dot/
Parking Violations Help Line: 718-422-7800
TTY Automated Information
  for the Hearing Impaired: 718-802-3555
Website:
www.ci.nyc.ny.us/finance (parking ticket info)

Parking Meter Zones

All "No Parking" signs in meter zones are suspended on ASP (alternate side parking) and MLH (major legal holidays); however, coins must be deposited during posted hours.

Meters

At a broken meter, parking is allowed **only** up to one hour. Where a meter is missing, parking is still allowed for the maximum time on the posted sign (an hour for a one-hour meter, two hours for a two-hour meter, etc.).

Signs

New York City Traffic Rules state that one parking sign per block is sufficient notification. Check the entire block and read all signs carefully before you park. Then read them again.

If there is more than one sign posted for the same area, the more restrictive sign takes effect (of course). If a sign is missing on a block, the remaining posted regulations are the ones in effect.

The Blue Zone

The Blue Zone is a "No Parking" (Mon–Fri 7 am–7 pm) area in Lower Manhattan. Its perimeter has been designated with blue paint; however, there are no individual "Blue Zone" signs posted. Any other signs posted in that area supersede Blue Zone regulations. Confused yet?

General

- All of NYC was designated a Tow Away Zone under the State's Vehicle & Traffic Law and the NYC Traffic Rules. This means that any vehicle parked or operated illegally, or with missing or expired registration or inspection stickers, may, and probably will, be towed.

- On major legal holidays, stopping, standing, and parking are permitted except in areas where stopping, standing, and parking rules are in effect seven days a week (for example, "No Standing Anytime").

- Double-parking of passenger vehicles is illegal at all times, including street-cleaning days, regardless of location, purpose, or duration. Everyone, of course, does this anyway.

- It is illegal to park within 15 feet of either side of a fire hydrant. The painted curbs at hydrant locations do not indicate where you can park. Isn't New York great?

- If you think you're parked legally in Manhattan, you're probably not, so go and read the signs again.

- There is now clearly an all-out effort to harass everyone who is insane enough to drive and/or park during the day in downtown Manhattan. Beware.

Alternate Side Parking Suspension Calendar 2006 (estimated*)

Holiday	Date	Day	Rules
New Year's Day	Jan 1	Sun	MHL
Martin Luther King Jr's Birthday	Jan 16	Mon	ASP
Idul Adha	Jan 10-12	Fri-Sun	ASP
Asian Lunar New York	Jan 29	Sun	ASP
Ash Wednesday	Mar 1	Wed	ASP
Lincoln's Birthday	Feb 12	Sun	ASP
President's Day	Feb 20	Mon	ASP
Holy Thursday	Apr 13	Thurs	ASP
Good Friday	Apr 14	Fri	ASP
Purim	Mar 25	Fri	ASP
Passover, 1st/2nd Day	April 13-14	Sun-Mon	ASP
Passover, 7th/8th Day	April 19-20	Sat-Sun	ASP
Memorial Day	May 29	Mon	MHL
Solemnity of Ascension	May 25	Thurs	ASP
Shavout, 1st/2nd Day	June 2-3	Mon-Tues	ASP
Independence Day	July 4	Tues	MHL
Assumption of the Blessed Virgin	Aug 15	Tues	ASP
Labor Day	Sept 4	Mon	MHL
Rosh Hashanah, 1st/2nd Day	Sept 23-24	Tues-Wed	ASP
Columbus Day	Oct 9	Mon	ASP
Yom Kippur	Oct 2	Sun	ASP
Succoth, 1st/2nd Day	Oct 7-8	Tues-Wed	ASP
Shemini Atzereth	Oct 14	Sat	ASP
Simchat Torah	Oct 15	Sun	ASP
All Saints Day	Nov 1	Wed	ASP
Idul-Fitr, 1st/2nd/3rd Day	Oct 24-26	Tues-Thurs	ASP
Veterans Day	Nov 11	Sat	ASP
Thanksgiving Day	Nov 23	Thurs	MHL
Immaculate Conception	Dec 8	Fri	ASP
Christmas Eve	Dec 24	Sun	MHL
Christmas Day	Dec 25	Mon	MHL
New Year's Eve	Dec 31	Sun	MHL

* Note: We go to press before the DOT issues its official calendar. However, using various techniques, among them a Ouija Board, a chainsaw, and repeated phone calls to said DOT, we think it's pretty accurate. Nonetheless, caveat parkor.

- **Street Cleaning Rules** (SCR)
  Most SCR signs are clearly marked by the "P" symbol with the broom through it. Some SCR signs are the traditional 3-hour ones ("8 am-11 am" etc.) but many others vary considerably. Check the times before you park. Then check them again.
- **Alternate Side Parking Suspended** (ASP)
  "No Parking" signs in effect once a day a week or on alternate days are suspended on days designated ASP; however, all "No Stopping" and "No Standing" signs remain in effect.
- **Major Legal Holiday Rules in Effect** (MLH)
  "No Parking" and "No Standing" signs than are in effect fewer than seven days a week are suspended on days designated MLH in the above calendar.
- If the city finds that a neighborhood keeps its streets clean enough, it may lessen the number of street cleaning days, or even eliminate them all together. So listen to your mother and don't litter.

Tow Pounds

Manhattan
Pier 76 at W 38th St & Twelfth Ave
Monday: 7 am-11 pm, Tuesday-Saturday: 7 am, open 24 hours through Sunday: 6 am
212-971-0771 or 212-971-0772

Bronx
745 E 141st St b/w Bruckner Expy & East River
Monday-Friday: 8 am-9 pm, Saturday: 8 am-3 pm, Sunday: Closed
718-585-1385 or 718-585-1391

Brooklyn
Brooklyn Navy Yard; corner of Sands St & Navy St
Monday-Friday: 8 am-9 pm, Saturday: 8 am-4 pm, Sunday: 12 pm-8 pm; 718-694-0696

Queens
Under the Kosciusko Bridge at 56th Rd & Laurel Hill Blvd
Monday-Friday: 8 am-6 pm, Saturday: 7 am-3 pm, Sunday: 12 pm-8 pm; 718-786-7122, 718-786-7123, or 718-786-7136

Find out if your car was towed (and not stolen or disintegrated): 718-422-7800 or 718-802-3555
www.nyc.gov/html/dof/html/nycserv_epayment.html

Once you've discovered that your car has indeed been towed, your next challenge is to find out which borough it's been towed to. This depends on who exactly towed your car—the DOT, the Marshal, etc. Don't assume that since your car was parked in Manhattan that they will tow it to Manhattan—always call first.

So you've located your car, now come the particulars: If you own said towed car, you're required to present your license, registration, insurance, and payment of your fine before you can collect the impounded vehicle. If you are not the owner of the car, you can usually get it back with all of the above, if your last name matches the registration (i.e. the car belongs to a relative or spouse); otherwise, you'll need a notarized letter with the owner's signature authorizing you to take the car. The tow fee is $185, plus $20 for each day it's in the pound. If they've put a boot on it instead, it's still $185. You can pay with cash or debit card; if you own the car, you can also pay by credit card or certified check.

(251)

Transit · LIRR

General Information

New York City: 718-217-LIRR
Nassau County: 516-822-LIRR
Suffolk County: 631-231-LIRR
TTY Information (Hearing Impaired):   718-558-3022
Group Travel and Tours: 718-558-7498
                                                  (M-F 8 pm-4 pm)
Mail & Ride: 800-649-NYNY
MTA Police Eastern Region: 718-558-3300
                                              or 516-733-3900
Lost & Found (M-F 7:20 am-7:20 pm):   212-643-5228
Ticket Refunds (M-F 8 am-4 pm):   718-558-3488
Ticket Machine Assistance: 877-LIRR-TSM
Hamptons Reserve Service: 718-558-8070
Website: www.mta.info/lirr

Overview

The Long Island Railroad is the busiest railroad in North America. It has eleven lines with 124 stations stretching from Penn Station in midtown Manhattan, to the eastern tip of Long Island, Montauk Point. An estimated 81 million people ride the LIRR every year. If you enjoy traveling on overcrowded, smelly trains with intermittent air-conditioning, then the LIRR is for you.

If you're not a regular LIRR user, you might find yourself taking the train to Shea Stadium for a Mets game (Port Washington Branch), Long Beach for some summer surfing (Long Beach Branch), or to Jamaica to transfer to the AirTrain to JFK.

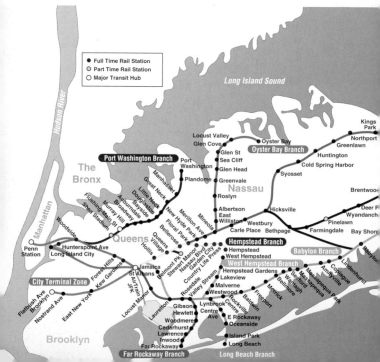

Fares and Schedules

Fares and schedules can be obtained by calling one of the general information lines, depending on your area. They can also be found on the LIRR website. Make sure to buy your ticket before you get on the train at a ticket window or at one of the ticket vending machines in the station. Otherwise it'll cost you an extra $2.75 to $3.50 depending on your destination. As it is a commuter railroad, the LIRR offers weekly and monthly passes, as well as ten-trip packages for on- or off-peak hours.

Pets on the LIRR

Trained service animals accompanying passengers with disabilities are permitted on LIRR trains. Other small pets are allowed on trains, but they must be confined to closed, ventilated containers.

Bikes on the LIRR

You need a permit ($5) to take your bicycle onto the Long Island Railroad. Pick one up at a ticket window, or online at the LIRR website.

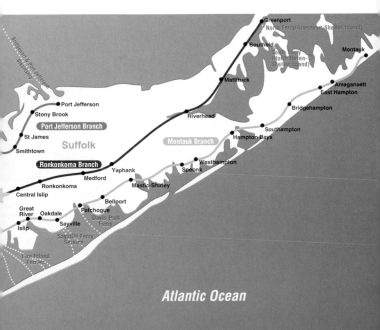

Transit · **Metro-North Railroad**

Key

- Rail Station
- Wheelchair or ADA Accessible station
- Major transit hub
- Connecting rail service

© 2004 Metropolitan Transportation Authority
Design: Michael Hertz Associates, NYC

Amtrak to Albany

Poughkeepsie &

HUDSON LINE

DUTCHESS

New Hamburg

Beacon &

Breakneck Ridge
Cold Spring &

Garrison &

PUTNAM

Manitou

Peekskill &

Cortlandt

WESTCHESTER

Croton–Harmons &

Ossining &

Scarborough

Philipse Manor

Tarrytown &

Irvington

Ardsley-on-Hudson

Dobbs Ferry &

Hastings-on-Hudson

Greystone

Glenwood

Yonkers &

Ludlow

Riverdale &

Spuyten Duyvil

Marble Hill &

University Hts &

Morris Hts &

NEW YORK

Penn Station & PATH

Grand Central Terminal &

BROOKLYN

QUEENS

NASSAU

Wassaic &
Tenmile River &
Dover Plains &

Harlem Valley–Wingdale &

Appalachian Trail &

Pawling &

HARLEM LINE

Patterson &

NEW YORK CONNECTICUT

Southeast &
Brewster &

Croton Falls &

Purdy's &

Golden's Bridge &

Katonah &

Bedford Hills &

Mount Kisco &

Chappaqua &

Pleasantville &

Hawthorne &
Mt Pleasant

Walhalla &

North White Plains &

White Plains &

Hartsdale

Scarsdale

Crestwood
Tuckahoe &
Bronxville &

Fleetwood

Mt Vernon West

Woodlawn
Wakefield

Williams Bridge
Botanical Garden &
Fordham &
Tremont
Melrose

THE BRONX

Harlem–125 St &

Danbury Branch

Danbury &

Bethel &

Redding &

Branchville &

Cannondale &
Wilton &

New Canaan Branch

New Canaan &

Talmadge Hill &

Springdale &
Glenbrook &

Stamford, CT
Old Greenwich &
Riverside &
Cos Cob &
Greenwich &
Port Chester, NY
Rye &
Harrison &
Mamaroneck &
Larchmont &
New Rochelle &
Pelham
Mt Vernon East

Merritt 7 &

NEW YORK CONNECTICUT

LITCHFIELD

Housatonic River

NEW HAVEN

FAIRFIELD

NEW HAVEN LINE

Fairfield &
Southport
Green's Farms
Westport &
East Norwalk
South Norwalk &
Rowayton
Darien &
Noroton Heights

Long Island Sound

Waterbury Branch

Waterbury &

Naugatuck

Beacon Falls

Seymour

Ansonia

Derby–Shelton

New Haven–Union Station &

New Haven State St &

Milford &

Stratford &
Bridgeport &

Bridgeport Port Jefferson Steamboat Co.

Amtrak to Hartford & Springfield

Shore Line East
New London
Amtrak to Boston

General Information

NYC Phone:	212-532-4900
All other areas:	800-METRO-INFO
Website:	www.mta.info/mnr
Lost and Found (Grand Central):	212-712-4500
MTA Inspector General:	800-MTA-IG4U

Overview

Metro-North is an extremely accessible and efficient railroad with three of its main lines (Hudson, Harlem, and New Haven) originating in Grand Central Station in Manhattan (42nd St & Park Ave). Those three lines east of the Hudson River, along with two lines west of the Hudson River that operate out of Hoboken, NJ (not shown on map), form the second-largest commuter railroad system in the US. Approximately 250,000 commuters use the tri-state Metro-North service each day for travel between New Jersey, New York, and Connecticut. Metro-North rail lines cover roughly 2,700 square miles of territory.

Fares and Schedules

Fare information is available on Metro-North's extraordinarily detailed website (along with in-depth information on each station, full timetables, and excellent maps) or at Grand Central Station. The cost of a ticket to ride varies depending on your destination so you should probably check the website before setting out. If you wait until you're on the train to pay, it'll cost you an extra $2.75-$3.50. Monthly and weekly rail passes are also available for commuters. Daily commuters save 50% on fares when they purchase a monthly travel pass.

Hours

Train frequency depends on your destination and the time of day that you're traveling. On weekdays, peak-period trains run every 20-30 minutes; off-peak trains run every 30-60 minutes; and weekend trains run hourly. Hours of operation are approximately 5 am to 3 am.

Bikes on Board

If you're planning on taking your two-wheeler onboard, you'll need to apply for a bicycle permit first. An application form can be found on the Metro-North website at http://mta.info/mnr/html/mnrbikepermit.htm. The $5 permit fee and application can either be mailed into the MTA, or processed right away at window 27 at Grand Central Terminal.

Common sense rules for taking bikes on board include: no bikes on escalators, no riding on the platform, and board the train after other passengers have boarded. Unfortunately there are restrictions on bicycles during peak travel times. Bicycles are not allowed on trains departing from Grand Central Terminal 7 am-9 am and 3:01 pm-8:15 pm. Bikes are not permitted on trains arriving at Grand Central 5 am-10 am and 4 pm-8 pm. Don't even think about taking your bike with you on New Year's Eve, New Year's Day, St. Patrick's Day, Mother's Day, eve of Rosh Hashanah, eve of Yom Kippur, eve of Thanksgiving, Thanksgiving Day, Christmas Eve, or Christmas Day—they're not allowed. The Friday before any long weekend is also a no-no. There's a limit of two bikes per carriage, and four bikes per train at all times. What happens if there are five riders waiting on the platform? Rock, paper, scissors?

Riders of folding bikes do not require a permit and do not have to comply with the above rules, provided that the bike is folded at all times at stations and on trains.

Pets

Only seeing-eye dogs and small pets, if restrained or confined, are allowed aboard the trains.

One-Day Getaways

Metro-North offers "One-Day Getaway" packages on its website. Packages include reduced rail fare and discounted entry to destinations along MNR lines including Dia:Beacon ($27), Foxwoods Casino ($41.25), Hudson River Museum/Andrus Planetarium ($14.50), Maritime Aquarium at Norwalk ($27.75), Mohegan Sun Casino ($38.25), New York Botanical Garden ($18.25), and Nyack ($14.50). The website also suggests one-day hiking and biking excursions.

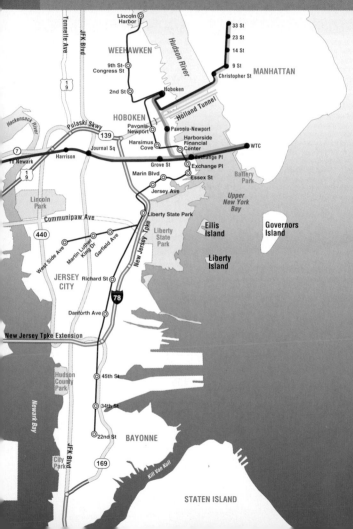

PATH Train

General Information
Website: www.panynj.gov/path
Phone: 800-234-7284
Police/Lost & Found: 201-216-6078

Overview

The PATH (Port Authority Trans-Hudson Corp.) is an excellent small rail system that services Newark, Jersey City, Hoboken, and Manhattan. There are a few basic lines that run between 33rd Street and the WTC site (now the busiest PATH station in the system) in Manhattan and Hoboken and Newark in New Jersey. Transfers between the lines are available at most stations. Two uses for the PATH other than basic commuting: you can take it to Newark's train station and then catch a relatively cheap cab to Newark Airport; and you can take it back to the Village late at night when you've finished seeing a show at Maxwell's in Hoboken.

Check the front or the sides of incoming trains to determine their destination. Don't be fooled by the TV screens installed at stations—they're merely for advertising, not for announcing which train is next scheduled to arrive. Also, don't assume that if a Journal Square train just passed through, the next train is going to Hoboken. Often there will be two Journal Square trains in a row, followed by two Hoboken trains.

The Port Authority is in the process of installing seven new escalators at the Journal Square Station. Each one will take approximately 6 months to install, so expect some disruption over the next few years.

Fares

The PATH costs a buck fifty one-way. Regular riders can purchase 11-trip, 20-trip, and 40-trip QuickCards, which reduce the fare per journey to $1.20-$1.36. The fare for seniors (65+) is $1 per ride. New turnstiles are being installed that will allow the use of pay-per-ride MTA MetroCards for easy transition between the PATH and subway.

Hours

The PATH runs 24/7 (although a modified service operates between 12 am and 5 am). The night schedule for the PATH is a bit confusing, so make sure to look at the map while you're waiting (you'll have plenty of time). Trains run half an hour apart so that they can run on the same track through the tunnel, allowing for maintenance to be completed on the unused track.

Hudson-Bergen Light Rail

General Information
Website: www.njtransit.com
Phone: 800-772-2222

Overview

The Hudson-Bergen Light Rail system (operated by NJ Transit) is the newest rail line in the New York area, and has brought about some exciting changes (a.k.a. "gentrification") in Jersey City and Bayonne, NJ. Currently there are 20 stops in the system, including service to Jersey City, Hoboken, and Weehawken. Transfer at the Hoboken stop for the PATH into Manhattan. Expansion plans include: a Port Imperial station in Weehawken, a Bergenline Avenue stop in Union City, and a Tonnelle Avenue station in North Bergen. We're psyched.

Fares

The Light Rail is $1.50 per trip; reduced fare is 75 cents. Ten-trip tickets are $13, monthly passes cost $53, and monthly passes with parking are $93. Unless you have a monthly pass, you need to validate your ticket before boarding at a Ticket Validating Machine (TVM).

Hours

Light rail service operates between 4 am and 2 am. Check the website for exact schedules on each line.

Bikes on Board

Bikes are allowed (no permit or fee required) on board during off-peak times—weekdays from 9:30 am to 4 pm and 7 pm to 6 am, and all day Saturday, Sunday, and NJ state holidays. Bicycles have to be accompanied on the low-floor vestibule section of each rail car.

Pets

Small pets are allowed, as long as they're confined to a carry container. Service animals are permitted at all times.

Transit · **NJ Transit**

Port Jervis Line

Otisville
Middletown
Campbell Hall
Salisbury Mills - Cornwall

PENNSYLVANIA
NEW YORK

Port Jervis

Harriman

Orange

Tuxedo

Rockland

Sloatsburg

Suffern
Spring Valley
Nanuet

Pascack Valley Line

Mahwah
Pearl River
Ramsey
Montvale
Allendale
Park Ridge
Waldwick
Woodcliff Lake
Ho-Ho-Kus
Hillsdale
Ridgewood
Westwood
Glen Rock-Main Line
Glen Rock-Boro Hall
Emerson
Hawthorne
Oradell
River Edge
Paterson
North Hackensack
Anderson St
Essex St
HACKENSACK

● Station
◉ Under Contruction Station

Sussex

Main Line & Bergen County Line

Passaic

Lincoln Park

Montclair-Boonton Line
MidTOWN DIRECT Service to
New York from Montclair Heights
Note: no weekend service

Mt Olive
Lake Hopatcong
Netcong
Dover
Denville
Towaco
Mtn View-Wayne
Boonton
Little Falls
Great Notch
Mountain Lakes
Mountain Ave
Montclair Heights
Upper Montclair
Watchung Ave
Walnut St
Bay St
Glen Ridge
Bloomfield
Watsessing

Clifton
Passaic
Delawanna
Lyndhurst
Kingsland

Radburn-Fair Lawn
Broadway-Fair Lawn
Plauderville
Garfield

Teterboro-Williams L
Woon-Ridge
Rutherford

NEW YORK CITY

Warren

Hackettstown

Mt Tabor

Morris Plains

Morristown

Convent

Madison

Morris

Morris and Essex Lines
MidTOWN DIRECT Service to New York
from Dover and Gladstone

Highland Ave
Mountain Station
South Orange

Secaucus
Junction

New York
Penn Static

Hoboken

Basking Ridge
New Providence
Chatham

Brick Church
Orange
East Orange

Newark
Penn Station

Gladstone
Bernardsville
Lyons
Murray Hill
Berkeley Heights
Summit
Short Hills
Millburn
Maplewood
Roseland Park

Newark Broad St
Newark Liberty
International Airport

Peapack
Far Hills
Millington
Stirling
Gillette

Essex

North Elizabeth

Elizabeth

Staten
Island

High Bridge
Annandale
Lebanon
White House

Union
Roselle
Cranford
Garwood
Westfield
Fanwood
Netherwood
Plainfield
Dunellen

Linden

Rahway

Avenel
Woodbridge

Raritan Valley Line

North Branch

Bound Brook
Bridgewater
Somerville
Raritan
Manville

Metuchen

Metropark

Perth Amboy

Atlantic Ocean

Hunterdon

Somerset

Edison

South Amboy

New Brunswick
Jersey Ave.

Middlesex

Aberdeen-Matawan
Hazlet

Middletown

Northeast Corridor Line

Princeton

Princeton Junction

Red Bank
Little Silver

Mercer

Monmouth Park
(seasonal service)

Long Bra

Hamilton

Monmouth

Elberon
Allenhurst
Asbury Park
Bradley Beac

NEW JERSEY
PENNSYLVANIA

Trenton

North Jersey Coast Line

Belmar
Spring Lake
Manasquan
Point Pleasant Be
Bay Head

Bucks

Burlington

Ocean

General Information

Address:	1 Penn Plz E
	Newark, NJ 07105
Phone:	973-762-5100 or
	800-772-3606
Website:	www.njtransit.com
Mail Tik (monthly passes):	973-491-8491
Emergency Hotline:	973-491-7400
Newark Lost and Found:	973-491-8792
Hoboken Lost and Found:	201-714-2739
New York Lost and Found:	212-630-7389
AirTrain:	973-961-6230
Atlantic City Terminal:	609-343-7174

Overview

NJ Transit carries hundreds of thousands of New Jersey commuters to New York every morning—well, almost. The trains are usually clean (and immune to the weirdness that plagues the LIRR), but some lines (like the Pascack Valley Line) seem to just creep along, and many lines involve transfers before reaching the Big Apple. But with many new stations, including the renovated transfer station at Secaucus, and an expanded Light Rail system (see PATH page), NJ Transit is staying competitive with all other modes of transportation into and out of the city. NJ Transit also runs an AirTrain to Newark Airport. While NJ Transit won't be competing with Japanese rail systems any time soon, riding their rails still beats waiting in traffic at the three main Hudson River automobile crossings. NJ Transit also offers bus lines to Hoboken and Newark for areas not served by train lines.

Secaucus Transfer Station

The new, three-level train hub at Secaucus cost around $450 million and took 14 years to complete. The new building is dedicated to Democratic New Jersey senator, Frank R. Lautenberg, who was responsible for securing the federal funds necessary for construction. The former Secaucus Transfer Station

is now officially known as the Frank R. Lautenberg Station at Secaucus Junction. We're certain that most commuters will adopt this new name whenever referring to the station.

For riders, the biggest advantage of the new station is that they no longer have to travel out to Hoboken to get to Penn Station (Secaucus is just an 8-minute ride from Penn Station). The Secaucus hub connects ten of NJ Transit's 11 rail lines, and also offers service to Newark Airport, downtown Newark, Trenton, and the Jersey Shore.

Fares and Schedules

Fares and schedules can be obtained at Hoboken, Newark, Penn Station, on NJ Transit's website, or by calling NJ Transit. If you wait to pay until you're on the train, you'll pay extra for the privilege. NJ Transit also offers discounted monthly, weekly, weekend, and ten-trip tickets for regular commuters.

Pets

Only seeing-eye dogs and small pets in carry-on containers are allowed aboard the trains and buses.

Bikes

You can take your bicycle onboard a NJ Transit train only during off-peak hours (weekdays from 9:30 am to 4 pm, and from 7 pm to 5 am) and during all hours on the weekends. Bikes are not allowed on board on most holidays; however a folding frame bicycle can be taken onboard at any time. Most NJ Transit buses participate in the "Rack 'n Roll" program, which allows you to load your bike right on to the front of the bus.

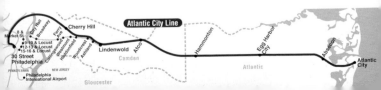

Overview

Phone: 800-USA-RAIL
Website: www.amtrak.com

General Information

Amtrak is our national train system, and while it's not particularly punctual or affordable, it *will* take you to many major northeastern cities in half a day or less. Cheap airlines like Southwest and JetBlue have made flying to many cities faster and cheaper than Amtrak. But if you plan a trip at the last minute and miss the requisite advance on buying airline tickets, you might want to at least shop Amtrak's fares.

Amtrak was created by the federal government in 1971. Today, Amtrak services 500+ stations in 46 states (Alaska, Hawaii, South Dakota, and Wyoming sadly do not have the pleasure of being serviced by Amtrak). Amtrak serves over 24 million passengers a year, employs 22,000 people, and provides "contract-commuter services" for several state and regional rail lines.

Amtrak in New York

In New York City, Amtrak runs out of Pennsylvania Station, which is currently located in a rat's maze underneath Madison Square Garden at Seventh Avenue and 33rd Street. But don't despair—chances are, the city you'll wind up in will have a very nice station, and, if all goes well, so will we, once the front half of the Farley Post Office is converted to a "new" Penn Station.

Popular Destinations

Many New Yorkers use Amtrak to get to Boston, Philadelphia, or Washington, DC. Amtrak also runs a line up to Montreal and through western New York state (making stops in Buffalo, Rochester, Albany, etc.) Check Amtrak's website for a complete listing of all Amtrak stations.

Going to Boston

Amtrak usually runs 18 trains daily to Boston, MA. One-way fares cost $66 and the trip, which ends at South Station in downtown Boston, takes about four-and-a-half hours door-to-door. For $99 one-way, you can ride the high speed Acela ("acceleration" and "ex-cellence" combined into one word, though perhaps "expensive" would have been more appropriate) and complete the journey in three to three-and-a-half hours.

Going to Philadelphia

About 40 Amtrak trains pass through Philadelphia every day. One-way tickets cost about $52 on a regular Amtrak train; if you're really in a hurry, you can take the special "Metroliner" service for $87, which will get you there in an hour and fifteen minutes, or the Acela for $95, which takes about one hour from station to station. The cheapest rail option to Philly is actually to take NJ Transit to Trenton and then hook up with Eastern Pennsylvania's excellent SEPTA service—this will take longer, but will cost you under $25.

Going to Washington, DC

(Subtitle: *How Much is Your Time Worth?*)
Amtrak runs over 40 trains daily to DC and the prices vary dramatically. The cheapest trains cost $76 one-way and take just under four hours. The Acela service costs almost double at $147 one-way, and delivers you to our nation's capital in less than three hours. Worth it? Only you can say.

A Note About Fares

While the prices quoted above for Boston, Philly, and DC destinations tend to remain fairly consistent, fare rates to other destinations, such as Cleveland, Chicago, etc., can vary depending on how far in advance you book your seat. For "rail sales" and other discounts, check www.amtrak.com.

Baggage Check (Amtrak Passengers)

A maximum of three items may be checked up to thirty minutes before departure. Up to three additional bags may be checked for a fee of $10 (two carry-on items allowed). No electronic equipment, plastic bags, or paper bags may be checked. See the "Amtrak Policies" section of their website for details.

General Information

NFT Map:	9
Address:	7th Ave & 33rd St
General Information (Amtrak):	800-872-7245
MTA Subway Stops:	❶❷❸ⒶⒸⒺ
MTA Bus Lines:	4 10 16 34
Train Lines:	LIRR, Amtrak, NJ Transit
Newark Airport Bus Service:	Olympia, 212-964-6233, $12
LaGuardia Airport Bus Service:	NY Airport Service, 718-706-9658, $10
JFK Airport Bus Service:	NY Airport Service, 718-706-9658, $13
Passengers per day:	600,000

Overview

Penn Station, designed by McKim, Mead & White (New York's greatest architects), is a Beaux Arts treasure, filled with light and…oh wait, that's the one that was torn down. Penn Station today is essentially a basement, minus the bowling trophies and the Johnny Walker Black.

BUT…good news seems to be coming around the corner, in the form of a plan to convert the eastern half of the Farley Post Office (also designed by McKim, Mead, & White) to a new, above-ground (a novel concept), light-filled station. We can't wait. Until then, Penn Station will go on being the country's busiest railway station, servicing 600,000 people per day in the crappy terminal under Madison Square Garden.

Penn Station services Amtrak, the LIRR, and NJ Transit trains. Amtrak, which is surely the worst national train system of any first-world country, administers the station. While we're hoping the new station proposal will come through, affording ridiculously high Amtrak fares to DC, Philly, and Boston is another issue altogether.

Terminal Shops

On the LIRR Level
Food & Drink
Blimpie
Caruso's Pizza
Central Market
Carvel
Cinnabon
Colombo Frozen Yogurt
Dunkin' Donuts
Haagen Dazs
Hot & Crusty
Island Dine
KFC
Knot Just Pretzels
Le Bon Café
McDonald's
Nedick's
Pizza Hut
Primo! Cappuccino
Rose Pizza and Pasta
Salad Chef
Seattle Coffee Roasters

Soup Man/Smoothie
  King (2)
Starbucks
TGI Friday's
Tracks Raw Bar & Grill

Other
Carlton Cards
Dreyfus Financial Center
GNC
Hudson News (3)
K-Mart
Penn Books
Perfumania
Soleman—Shoe repair,
  locksmith
Verizon Wireless

On the Amtrak Level
Food & Drink
Auntie Anne's Soft
  Pretzels (2)

Baskin Robbins
Dunkin' Donuts
Don Pepi Pizza
Don Pepi's Delicatessen
Houlihan's Restaurant
  & Bar
Nathan's
Kabooz's Bar and Grille
Krispy Kreme Doughnuts
Pizza Hut
Primo! Cappuccino (2)
Roy Rogers
Soup Man/Smoothie King
The Grove
Zaro's Bread Basket

Other
Book Corner
Duane Reade
Elegance
Gifts & Electronics
GNC

Hudson News (3)
Joseph Lawrence
  Jewelers
New York New York
Shoetrician—Shoe repair
  and shine
Tiecoon
The Petal Pusher
Staples
Tourist Information
  Center
Verizon Wireless

There is a Wachovia 24-hour ATM and a PNC Bank ATM located on the Amtrak level. There is a Fleet 24-hour ATM located on the LIRR level, in addition to the generic (money-thieving) ATMs located in several stores throughout the station.

Temporary Parcel/Baggage Check

The only facility for storing parcels and baggage in Penn Station is at the Baggage Check on the Amtrak level (to the left of the ticket counter). There are no locker facilities at Penn Station. The Baggage Check is open from 5 am until midnight and costs $4.50 per item for each 24-hour period.

261

Main Concourse

Tracks 42 — 35

Tracks 34 — 11

Biltmore Room

58
57
2
1
4

Station Master's Office

6

13

Graybar Passage

14 15 16 17 18 19

21 22 23 24 25

Grand Central Market

26a 26b 27 28 29 30 31 32 33

34 35 36 37 38 39 40 41

Lexington Passage

Exit to MetLife Building

Information

7

CH

Ticketing/ Train Board

Ticketing/ Train Board

20

9
8
10

Ramp Down

11

12

56

Banana Republic

54

Ramp Down

50

53

55

Vanderbilt Hall

Kenneth Cole

42 59 43 44b 44a 45 46 47 48 49

4 5 6 7 S

51

52

4
5
4 5 6
7 S 6

Vanderbilt Ave

Lexington Ave

7 S
4 5 6

EXIT

EXIT

EXIT

42nd St

Balcony

Michael Jordan's The Steakhouse NYC

Metrazur

EXIT

Cipriani Dolce

EXIT

The Campbell Apartment

MAP **13**

Vanderbilt Ave

Dining Concourse

Tracks 117

101

West Dining

Information

East Dining

Ramp from Main Concourse Level

Oyster Bar & Restaurant

Stores

1. Eddie's Shoe Repair
2. Eastern News
3. Dahlia
4. Junior's
5. Starbucks
6. New York Transit Museum
7. Zaro's Bread Basket
8. Discovery Channel Store
9. Posman Books
10. Rite Aid
11. Central Market
12. Hot & Crusty
13. Zaro's Bread Basket
14. Olivers & Co
15. Grande Harvest Wines
16. Cobbler & Shine
17. Stop'N Go Wireless
18. O' Henry's Film Works
19. GNC
20. Hudson News

21. Greenwich Produce
22. Koglin German Hams
23. Murray's Cheese
24. Ceriello Fine Foods
25. Greenwich Produce
26a. Pescatore Seafood Company
26b. Dishes at Home
27. Li-Lac Chocolates
28. Oren's Daily Roast
29. Adriana's Caravan
30. Zaro's Bread Basket
31. Wild Edibles
32. Corrado Bread & Pastry
33. Forever Silver
34. Grand Central Optical
35. Tumi
36. L'Occitane
37. Bose
38. Our Name is Mud

40. Watch Station
41. Starbucks
42. Matt Hunter & Co
43. Origins
44a. Children's General Store
44b. Leeper Kids
45. Altitunes
46. Pink Slip
47. TOTO
48. LaCrasia Gloves & Creative Accessories
49. Godiva Chocolatier
50. Super Runners Shop
51. Papyrus
52. Oren's Daily Roast
53. Douglas Cosmetics
54. Joon Stationary
55. Super Runners Shop
56. Neuhaus Boutique
57. Grand Central Raquet
58. Central Watch Band Stand
59. Flowers on Lexington

General Information

NFT Map:	13
Address:	42nd St & Park Ave
General Information:	212-340-2210
Lost and Found:	212-712-4500
Website:	www.grandcentralterminal.com
MTA Subway Stops:	④ ⑤ ⑥ ⑦ Ⓢ
MTA Bus Lines:	① ② ③ ④ 42 98 101 102 104 ⑤
Other Rail Lines:	Metro North
Newark Airport Bus Service:	Olympia, 212-964-6233, $12
LaGuardia Airport Bus Service:	NY Airport Express, 718-875-8200, $10
JFK Airport Bus Service:	NY Airport Express, 718-875-8200, $13

Overview

Grand Central Terminal, designed in the Beaux Arts style by Warren & Wetmore, is by far the most beautiful of Manhattan's major terminals, and is considered one of the most stunning terminals in the world. It's convenient location (right in the heart of Midtown), and its refurbishments only add to its intrinsic appeal. The only downside is that the station only services Metro North—you'll have to venture over to ugly Penn Station for LIRR and NJ Transit trains.

If you ever find yourself underestimating the importance of the Grand Central renovations, just take a peek at the ceiling towards the Vanderbilt Avenue side—the small patch of black shows how dirty the ceiling was previously. And it was really dirty…

If you've got time for a drink, check out the exceptionally cool and snotty (no sneakers!) bar, The Campbell Apartment, near the Vanderbilt Avenue entrance. You can also snag some seafood at the Oyster Bar & Restaurant, then go right outside its entrance to hear a strange audio anomaly: if you and a friend stand in opposite corners and whisper, you'll be able to hear each other clearly.

Grand Central Station offers three tours: the hour-long LaSalle Tour (212-340-2347), the Municipal Arts Society Tour (212-935-3960), and the Grand Central Partnership Tour (212-697-1245). The last two tours are free.

ATMs

Chase
Numerous generic (money-thieving) ATMs at stores throughout the station.

East Dining

Brother Jimmy's BBQ
Café Spice
Central Market Grill
Golden Krust Patties
Jaques-Imo's to Geaux
Little Pie Company
Pepe Rosso
Two Boots
Zaro's Bread Basket
Zócalo Bar and Restaurant

West Dining

Dishes
Ciao Bella Gelateria
Chirping Chicken
Eata Pita
Feng Shui
Hale and Hearty Soups
Junior's
Masa Sushi
Mendy's Kosher Dairy
Mendy's Kosher Delicatessen
New York Pretzel
Paninoteca Italiana

Transit • **Port Authority Bus Terminal**

General Information

NFT Map:	11
Address:	41st St & 8th Ave
General Information:	212-564-8484
Kinney Garage:	212-502-2341
Website:	www.panynj.gov/tbt/pabframe.HTM
Subway:	**A C E** Port Authority
	1 2 3 7 N R Q W S Times Square
MTA Bus Lines:	10 11 16 20 27 42 104
Newark Airport Bus Service:	Olympia, 212-964-6233, $10
LaGuardia Airport Bus Service:	NY Airport Express, 718-875-8200, $10
JFK Airport Bus Service:	NY Airport Express, 718-875-8200, $13

Overview

In 1939, eight separate bus terminals scattered throughout the city were increasing traffic congestion. While one larger central terminal seemed like the obvious solution, many of the smaller terminals refused to give up their autonomy and merge. Mayor Fiorello LaGuardia finally put his foot down and asked the Port Authority of New York and New Jersey to take over the project and develop one central terminal. Construction began on January 27, 1949 at the site bordered by Eighth Avenue, 40th Street, Ninth Avenue, and 41st Street. After a $24 million investment, Port Authority Bus Terminal opened in 1950.

That original investment has now grown to $443 million, and while the terminal is located in perhaps Manhattan's last genuinely shady neighborhood, the dozens of terminal shops and amenities (including a post office, bank, refurbished bathrooms, a blood bank, subway access, and even a bowling alley) make Port Authority a convenient point of departure and arrival. The grungiest area of the terminal is the lower bus level, which is a dirty, exhaust-filled space, best visited just a few minutes before you need to board your bus. The chart on the right shows which bus companies run out of the Port Authority and provides a basic description of their destinations.

On Easter Sunday, Christmas Eve, or Thanksgiving, one can see all the angst-ridden sons and daughters of suburban New Jersey parents joyfully waiting in cramped, disgusting corridors for that nauseating bus ride back to Leonia or Morristown or Plainfield or wherever. A fascinating sight.

Terminal Shops

South Wing—Lower Bus Level
Green Trees
Hudson News

South Wing—Subway Mezzanine
Au Bon Pain
Hudson News
Music Explosion

South Wing—Main Concourse
Au Bon Pain
California Burrito
Casa Java
Deli Plus
Duane Reade
First Stop-Last Stop Cafe
GNC
Hudson News

Hudson News
Book Corner
Marrella Men's Hair Stylist
NY Blood Center
Radio Shack
Ruthie's Hallmark
Stop 'n Go Wireless
Villa Pizza
World's Fare Restaurant Bar
Zaro's Bakery

South Wing—Second Floor
Café Metro
Drago Shoe Repair
Fleet Bank
Hudson News Book Corner
Kelly Film Express
Leisure Time Bowling Center

McAnn's Pub
Mrs Fields Bakery Café
Munchy's Gourmet
Sak's Florist
Sweet Factory

South Wing—Fourth Floor
First Stop-Last Stop Café
Hudson News

North Wing-Lower Bus Level
Snacks-N-Wheels
North Wing—Subway Mezzanine
Fleet Bank (ATM)
Green Trees
Hudson News

North Wing—Main Concourse

Continental Airlines
Hudson News
Mrs Fields Cookies

North Wing—on 42nd Street
Big Apple Café

North Wing—Second Floor
Fleet Bank (ATM)
Hudson News
Jay's Hallmark Bookstore
Tropica Juice Bar
USO
US Postal Service

North Wing—Third Floor
Hudson News
Tropica Juice Bar

Bus Company	Phone	Area Served
Academy Bus Transportation	800-242-1339	Serves New York City, including Staten Island, Wall Street and Port Authority, and New Jersey, including Hoboken.
Adirondack Trailways	800-858-8555	Serves all of New York State with coach connections throughout the U.S.
Bonanza Bus	800-556-3815	Serves many points between New York and New England, including Cape Cod and the Berkshires.
Capitol Trailways	800-333-8444	Service between Pennsylvania, Virginia, New York State, and New York City.
Carl Bieber Bus	800-243-2374	Service to and from Port Authority and Wall Street in New York and Reading, Kutztown, Wescosville, Hellertown, and Easton, Pennsylvania.
Coach USA	800-522-4514	Service between New York City and W Orange, Livingston, Morristown, E Hanover, Whippany, and Floram Park, New Jersey.
DeCamp Bus	800-631-1281	Service between New York City and New Jersey, including the Meadowlands.
Greyhound Bus	800-229-9424	Serves most of the US and Canada.
Gray Line Bus	212-397-2620	Service offered throughout the US and Canada.
Hudson Bus	201-653-2222	Serves 48 states.
Lakeland Bus	973-366-0600	Service between New York and New Jersey.
Martz Group	800-233-8604	Service between New York and Pennsylvania.
New Jersey Transit	800-772-2222 (NJ) 973-762-5100 (all other)	Serves New York, New Jersey, and Philadelphia.
NY Airport Service	212-875-8200	Service between Port Authority and Kennedy and LaGuardia Airports.
Olympia Trails	212-964-6233	Provides express bus service between Manhattan and Newark Airport. Makes stops all over New York City, including Penn Station, Grand Central, and many connections with hotel shuttles.
Peter Pan Lines	800-343-9999	Serves the East, including New Hampshire, Maine, Philly, DC. Also goes to Canada.
Rockland Coaches/ Red and Tan Services	201-384-2400	Services New York's Port Authority, GW bridge, 44th Street, and 8th Street to and from most of Bergen County and upstate New York.
ShortLine Bus	800-631-8405	Serves the New York City airports, Atlantic City, and the Hudson Valley.
Suburban	732-249-1100	Offers commuter service from Central New Jersey to and from Port Authority and Wall Street. Also services between the Route 9 Corridor and New York City.
Susquehanna Trailways	800-692-6314	Service to and from New York City and Newark (Greyhound Terminal) and Summerville, New Jersey and many stops in Central Pennsylvania, ending in Williamsport and Lock Haven.
Trailways	800-858-8555	Services New York state area.
Trans-Bridge Lines	610-868-6001 800-962-9135	Offers service between New York, Pennsylvania, and New Jersey, including Newark and Kennedy airports.
Trans-Hudson Express	201-876-9000	Serves New York City and Hudson County, New Jersey.

General Information

NFT Map:	23
Address:	4211 Broadway & 178th St
Phone:	800-221-9903
Website:	www.panynj.gov/tbt/gwbframe.htm
Subway:	Ⓐ (175th St), Ⓐ ❶ (181st St)
Buses:	10X 98 5 4 3 7

Overview

Completed in 1963, the George Washington Bridge Bus Terminal, located between 178th and 179th Streets on Fort Washington Avenue, is a bit like the bastard sibling of the 42nd Street terminal. It's fairly reminiscent of its downtown brother, but for the wrong reasons: the omnipresent smell of gasoline, assorted strange people hanging around, and a slightly seedy aura. To be fair, it's been getting better over the last few years thanks to some timely renovations, but any place where one of the centerpiece establishments is OTB has a long way to go.

Stores

Concourse:
ATM
Bridge Opticians—Edward Friedman, OD
Bridge Stop Newsstand
Dentists—Howard Bloom, DDS; Steve Kaufman DDS
E-Z Visions Travel
Food Plus Café
GW Books and Electronics
Joseph's Leather Designs
Neighborhood Trust Federal Credit Union
New York National Bank
Off Track Betting
Pizza Palace
Terminal Barber Shop

Street Level:
Blockbuster Video
Rite-Aid Pharmacy
Urban Pathways—Homeless Outreach Office
Port Authority Business Outreach Center (179th St underpass)

Bus Companies

Astro-Eastern Bus Company · 201-865-2230 ·
www.easternbuses.com
Trips to Florida (purchase tickets on the upper level).

Express Bus Service · 973-881-9122 ·
www.spanishtransportation.com
To Clifton, Passaic, Paterson, and Willowbrook Mall.

New Jersey Transit · 800-772-3606 ·
www.njtransit.com/sf_bus.shtm
Services to Bergenfield, Bogota, Cliffside Park, Edgewater (including Edgewater Commons Mall), Englewood, Fair Lawn (including the Radburn section), Fort Lee, Glen Rock, Guttenberg, Hackensack (including NJ Bus Transfer), Hoboken, North Hackensack (Riverside Square), Leonia, Maywood, North Bergen, Paramus (including the Bergen Mall and Garden State Plaza), Paterson (including Broadway Terminal), Ridgewood, Rochelle Park, Teaneck (including Glenpointe and Holy Name Hospital), Union City, Weehawken, and West New York.

Red & Tan Lines/Coach USA · 845-356-0877 ·
www.redandtanlines.com
Trips to Alpine, Bergenfield, Blauvelt, Bradlees Shopping Center, Closter, Congers, Creskill, Demarest, Dumont, Emerson, Englewood, Englewood Cliffs, Grandview, Harrington Park, Haverstraw, Haworth, Hillsdale, Linwood Park, Montvale, Nanuet, (including Nanuet Shopping Mall), Nauraushaun, New City, New Milford, Northvale (including Northvale Industrial Park), Norwood, Nyack, Oradell, Orangeburg, Palisades, Park Ridge, Pearl River, Piermont, Rivervale, Rockland Lake, Rockland Psych Center, Rockleigh (including Rockleigh Industrial Park), South Nyack, Sparkill, Spring Valley, Stony Point, Tappan, Tenafly, Upper Nyack, Valley Cottage, West Haverstraw, Westwood, and Woodcliff Lake.

Shortline/Coach USA · 800-631-8405 ·
www.shortlinebus.com
To Atlantic City, Harriman, Paramus, Park Ridge, and Ridgewood.

Vanessa Express · 201-583-0999.
To Cliffside Park, Jersey City, North Bergen, Union City, and West New York.

General Information

NFT Map:	3
Websites:	www.ivymedia.com
	www.chinatown-bus.com

Overview

There are several inexpensive bus lines running from Chinatown in New York City to the respective Chinatowns in Boston, Philadelphia, Washington DC, and even Atlanta. If you're lucky, you'll even catch an in-bus kung-fu movie on the way. Tickets usually cost $15-20 each way, and can be purchased online or in person at pick-up locations.

The buses are certainly cheaper than trains and other bus services, but are they worth it? There's a good chance that you'll experience at least one problem at some point during your trip including, but not limited to, poor customer service, unmarked bus stops, late departures, less than ideal bus conditions, and hucking and spitting from other passengers. More pertinent problems include cancelled or delayed trips without warning, luggage being stolen from underneath buses, and drop-offs on the side of the road by the highway because bus companies don't have permission to deliver passengers to central transportation hubs. On the other hand, many people have enjoyed dirt-cheap, hassle-free experiences on the Chinatown buses. If you're game and you need to save some cash, give it a try.

Passengers should arrive at least 30 minutes prior to take-off and, as always, schedules and prices are subject to change, so call or consult the company's website before planning your trip. If you walk down East Broadway under the Manhattan Bridge, chances are you'll be solicited by people on the street without even having to ask. Buy your "chickets" before boarding the bus. Buses vary in quality from company to company and even from day to day. Fung Wah has been around the longest and is generally considered the best line. To read user reviews, visit www.chinatown-bus.com.

Bus Companies

Fung Wah Bus Transportation • 212-925-8889 • www.fungwahbus.com
• To Boston every hour on the hour between 7 am-10 pm. From **139 Canal Street** to South Station: one-way $15, round trip $30.

Lucky Star Bus Transportation • 617-426-8801 • www.luckystarbus.com.
• To Boston every hour 7 am-10 pm. From **Chrystie & Hester Sts** to South Station: one-way $15, round trip $30.

Boston Deluxe • 617-354-2101 • www.ivymedia.com/bostondeluxe
• To Boston at 9 am, 12:30 pm, and 6 pm. From **Broadway & 32nd St** or **E 86th St & 2nd Ave** to 175 Huntington Ave: one-way $15, round trip $30.
• To Hartford at 8:30 am and 5:30 pm. From the same pick-up points to 365 Capital Ave: one-way $15, round trip $30.

Washington Deluxe • 866-BUS-NY-DC • www.washny.com
• To Washington several times a day; From **34th St & 8th Ave**. Additional departures from **Delancey & Allen Sts**, and several locations in **Williamsburg** to various locations in DC. Schedule varies by day of the week, so it's recommended that you check the website for info. One-way $20, round-trip $35.

Dragon Coach • 617-354-2101 • www.ivymedia.com/dragoncoach
• To Washington DC eight times a day between 8 am and 11:30 pm. From **2 Mott St** or **Broadway & 8th Ave** to 14th & L Sts: one-way $20, round trip $35.
• To Baltimore eight times a day between 8 am and 11:30 pm. From the same pick-up points to 5600 Odonnell St: one-way $20, round trip $35.
• To Albany at 9 am, 1:15 pm, and 5:30 pm. From the same pick-up points to Collins Circle at SUNY and 420 Broadway: one-way $20, round trip $35
• To Woodbury Commons at 9 am and 1:15 pm. From the same pick-ups points to Woodbury Commons: one-way $10, round trip $20.

Eastern Travel • 617-354-2101 • www.ivymedia.com/eastern
• To Washington DC 12 times a day between 7:30 am and 7 pm; From **88 E Broadway, 42nd St & 7th Ave,** or **Penn Station** to 715 H Street NW in Washington DC and 430 Hungerford Dr in Rockville, MD: one-way $20, round trip $35.
• To Baltimore 12 times a day between 7:30 am and 7 pm. From same pickup-point to 5625 Odonnell St: one-way $20, round trip $35.

New Century Travel • 215-627-2666 • www.2000coach.com
• To Philadelphia every hour between 7 am and 11 pm. From **88 E Broadway** or **5994 8th Ave, Williamsburg** (7 am only) to 55 N 11th St: one-way $12, round trip $20.
• To DC eight times between 7 am and 11 pm; From **88 E Broadway** to 513 H St NW: one-way $20, round trip $35.
• To Richmond at 5 pm and 1 am. From **88 E Broadway** to 121 W Broad St: one-way $40, round-trip $60.

Today's Bus • 617-354-2101 • www.ivymedia.com/todaysbus
• To Philadelphia 14 times a day between 7:15 am and 11 pm. From **88 E Broadway** to 121 N 11th St: one-way $12, round trip $20.
• To DC 11 times a day between 7:15 am and 11 pm. From **88 E Broadway** to 610 I St NW: one-way $20, round trip $36.
• To Atlantic City at 10 am, 1 pm, and 11 pm. From **37 Division St** to Resorts Casino: round trip $20 (but they give you $25 cash back and $20 in chips if you're over 21).
• To Norfolk, VA at 6 pm. From **88 E Broadway** to 649 Newton Rd: one-way $35, round trip $66.
• To Richmond, VA at 5 pm. From **88 E Broadway** to 106 W Broad St: one-way $40, round trip $64.
• To Atlanta, GA at 10 pm. From **109 E Broadway** to 5150 Buford Hwy NE: one-way $90, round trip $176.

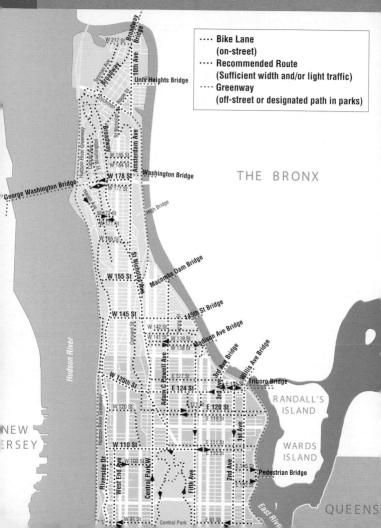

Bike Lane
(on-street)

Recommended Route
(Sufficient width and/or light traffic)

Greenway
(off-street or designated path in parks)

THE BRONX

George Washington Bridge

W 217 St
Broadway Bridge
10th Ave
Broadway
Seaman Ave
Broadway
Univ Heights Bridge
Dyckman Avenue
St Nicholas Ave
Broadway
Ft Washington
Hudson River Greenway
Amsterdam Ave
10th Ave
Cabrini
W 185 St
W 184 St
Washington Bridge
W 178 St
W 177 St
High Bridge
W 172 St
W 171 St
W 165 St
St Nicholas Ave
W 155 St
Macombs Dam Bridge
W 145 St
145th St Bridge
W 142 St
W 141 St
W 139 St
W 138 St
Madison Ave Bridge
3rd Ave Bridge
Willis Ave Bridge
Convent Ave
Adam C Powell Ave
W 125th St
E 127 St
E 124 St
E 125 St
Triboro Bridge
3rd Ave
E 123 St
W 120 St
E 120 St
E 119 St
RANDALL'S ISLAND
WARDS ISLAND
W 110 St
E 111 St
E 110 St
1st Ave
Hudson River Greenway
Riverside Dr
West End Ave
Central Park W
W 100 St
Central Park
Fifth Ave
E 105 St
2nd Ave
Pedestrian Bridge
E 102 St
W 91 St
E 91 St
Central Park

Hudson River

NEW JERSEY

East River

QUEENS

General Information

Bike New York, Five Borough Bike Tour: www.bikenewyork.org
Century Road Club Association (CRCA): www.crca.net
Department of City Planning: www.ci.nyc.ny.us/html/dcp/html/bike
Fast & Fabulous Lesbian & Gay Bike Club: www.fastnfab.org
Five Boro Bicycle Club: www.5bbc.org
League of American Bicyclists: www.bikeleague.org
New York Bicycle Coalition: www.nybc.net
New York Cycle Club: www.nycc.org
Empire Skate Club: www.empireskate.org
Time's Up! Bicycle Advocacy Group: www.times-up.org
Transportation Alternatives: www.transalt.org; 212-629-8080

Overview

While not for the faint of heart, biking and skating around Manhattan can be one of the most efficient and exhilarating forms of transportation (insight into the abundance of bike messengers careening around town). Manhattan is relatively flat, and the fitness and environmental advantages of using people power are incontrovertible. However, there are also some downsides, including, but not limited to: psychotic cab drivers, buses, traffic, pedestrians, pavement with potholes, glass, and debris, and poor air quality. In 1994, the Bicycle Network Development Program was created to increase bicycle usage in the NYC area. Since then, many bike lanes have been created on streets and in parks (see map on previous page). These tend to be the safest places to ride, though they sometimes get blocked by parked or standing cars. Central Park is a great place to ride, as are the newly developed paths from Battery Park that run along the Hudson River. East River Park is another nice destination for recreational riding and skating—just not after dark! In addition to bicycle rentals, Pedal Pusher Bike Shop (1306 Second Ave, 212-288-5592) offers recorded tours of Central Park, so you can learn about the park and exercise at the same time.

Recreational skating venues in Manhattan include Wollman and Lasker Rinks in Central Park, Chelsea Piers, The Roxy (515 W 18th St), Riverbank State Park (Riverside Drive at 145th St), and Rivergate Ice Rink (401 E 34th St). If you're looking for a place to get your skates sharpened to your own personal specifications before hitting the ice, contact Westside Skate & Stick (115 W 23rd St, 212-228-8400), a custom pro shop for hockey & figure skaters that's by appointment only. For more information on skating venues throughout the boroughs, check out www.skatecity.com. For organized events, visit the Empire Skate Club at www.empireskate.org.

Bikes are sometimes less convenient than skates. Where skates can be tucked in a bag and carried onto subways, indoors, or on buses, bikes have to be locked up on the street and are always at risk of being stolen (always lock them to immovable objects with the best lock you can afford). On the upside, bikes provide a much faster, less demanding form of transportation around the city.

Crossing the Bridges by Bike

Crossing the Brooklyn, Manhattan, or Williamsburg Bridges by bike is a great way for Brooklynites to commute to work (unless, of course, it's really windy and cold out). All bridges afford great views of the Manhattan and Brooklyn skylines and waterfronts. In the fall of 2003, the DOT estimated that nearly 4,000 cyclists crossed the East River bridges each day. It just isn't healthy to stay underground so much, so gear up and give it a go.

Brooklyn Bridge

Separate bicycle and pedestrian lanes run down the center of the bridge, with the bicycle lane on the north side and the pedestrian lane on the south. Cyclists should beware of wayfaring tourists taking photographs. We do not recommend rollerblading across the bridge—the wooden planks make for quite a bumpy ride. The bridge is quite level and, aside from the tourists and planks, fairly easy to traverse.

Brooklyn Access: Ramp at Adams St & Tillary St or stairs at
Cadman Plz E & Prospect St in DUMBO
Manhattan Access: Chambers St & Centre St

Manhattan Bridge

The last of the Brooklyn crossings to be outfitted with decent pedestrian and bike paths, the Manhattan Bridge bike and pedestrian paths are on separate sides of the bridge. The walking path is on the south side, and the bike path is on the north side of the bridge. The major drawback to walking across the Manhattan Bridge is that you have to climb a steep set of stairs on the Brooklyn side (not the best conditions for lugging around a stroller or suitcase). Fortunately, the bike path on the north side of the bridge is ramped on both approaches.

Brooklyn Access: Jay St & Sands St
Manhattan Access: Bike Lane–Canal St & Forsyth St
Pedestrian Lane–Bowery, just south of Canal St

Williamsburg Bridge

The 'Billyburg bridge has the widest pedestrian/bike path of the three bridges to Brooklyn. The path on the north side, shared by cyclists and pedestrians, is 12 feet wide. The southern path, at 8 feet wide, is also shared by bikers and walkers while construction continues. Usually only one of the paths is open at any give time. The steep gradient on both the Manhattan and Brooklyn sides of the Williamsburg Bridge gives bikers and pedestrians a good workout. Bikers beware: the steel bumps on the Manhattan side of the bridge create quite a jerky (and potentially dangerous) ride—definitely no fun for roller blades, bikes, or wheelchairs. Transportation Alternatives continues to push the city to replace the protruding bridge joiners with something more rider-friendly; we can't wait!

Brooklyn Access: North Entrance–Driggs Ave, right by the Washington Plz
South Entrance–Bedford Ave b/w S 5th & S 6th Sts
Manhattan Access: Delancey St & Clinton St/Suffolk St

George Washington Bridge
Bikers get marginalized by the pedestrians on this crossway to New Jersey. The north side is for pedestrians only, and the south side is shared by pedestrians and bikers. Cyclists had to fight to keep their right to even bike on this one walkway, as city officials wanted to institute a "walk your bike across" rule to avoid bicycle/pedestrian accidents during construction. The bikers won the battle but are warned to "exercise extra caution" when passing pedestrians.

Manhattan Access: W 178th St & Fort Washington Ave
New Jersey Access: Hudson Terrace in Fort Lee

Triboro Bridge
Biking is officially prohibited on this two-mile span that connects the Bronx, Queens, and Manhattan. Unofficially, people ride between the boroughs and over to Wards Island all the time. The bike path is quite narrow, compared to the paths on other bridges, and the lighting at night is mediocre at best. The tight path sees less pedestrian/cycling traffic than other bridges, which, paired with the insufficient lighting, gives the span a rather ominous feeling after dark. If you're worried about safety, or keen on obeying the laws, the 103rd Street footbridge provides an alternative way to reach Wards Island sans car. This pedestrian pass is open only during the warmer months, and then only during daylight hours. See page [208] for more information about the footbridge schedule.

Bronx Access: 134th St & Cypress Ave
Manhattan Access: 124/126th Sts & First Ave
Queens Access: 26th St & Hoyt Ave (beware of extremely steep stairs).

Queensboro Bridge
The north outer roadway of the Queensboro Bridge is open exclusively to bikers, 24 hours a day, seven days a week, except for the day of the New York Marathon. More than 2,500 cyclists and pedestrians per day traverse the bridge. Bikers complain about safety issues on the Manhattan side of the bridge: with no direct connection from Manhattan onto the bridge's West Side, bikers are forced into an awkward five block detour to get to Second Avenue, where they can finally access the bridge.

Manhattan Entrance: 60th St, b/w First Ave & Second Ave
Queens Entrance: Queens Plz & Crescent St

Bike Rentals (and Sales)

Metro Bicycle Stores:
• 88th St & Lexington Ave • 212-427-4450 • Map 17
• 360 W 47th St & Ninth Ave • 212-581-4500 • Map 11
• 213 W 96th St & Broadway • 212-663-7531 • Map 16
• 14th St, b/w First & Second Aves • 228-4344 • Map 9
• Sixth Ave & W 15th St • 255-5100 • Map 9
• Sixth Ave b/w Canal & Grand • 212-334-8000 • Map 2
Anewgen Bicycles • 832 Ninth Ave • 757-2418 • Map 11
Toga Bike Shop • 110 West End Ave & 64th St• 212-799-9625 • Map 14
Gotham Bikes • 112 W Broadway • 212-732-2453 • Map 2
Bicycle Habitat • 244 Lafayette St b/w Spring & Prince Sts • 212-431-3315 • Map 6
Bicycle Heaven • 348 E 62 St b/w First & Second Aves • 212-230-1919 • Map 15
Bike Works • 106 Ridge St b/w Stanton & Rivington Sts • 212-388-1077 • Map 7
City Bicycles • 315 W 38th St b/w Eighth & Ninth Aves• 212-563-3373 • Map 11
Eddie's Bicycles Shop • 490 Amsterdam Ave b/w 83rd & 84th Sts • 212-580-2011 • Map 14
Larry and Jeff's Bicycles Plus • 1690 Second Ave b/w 87th & 88th Sts • 212-722-2201 • Map 17
Pedal Pusher Bike Shop • 1306 Second Ave b/w 68th & 69th Sts • 212-288-5592 • Map 15
Manhattan Bicycles • 791 Ninth Ave b/w 52nd & 53rd Sts• 212-262-0111 • Map 11
New York Cyclist • 301 Cathedral Pkwy • 212-864-4449 • Map 16

Bikes and Mass Transit

Surprisingly, you can take your bike on trains and some buses—just make sure it's not during rush hour and you are courteous to other passengers. The subway requires you to carry your bike down staircases, use the service gate instead of the turnstile, and board at the very front or back end of the train. To ride the commuter railroads with your bike, you'll need to purchase a bike permit. For appropriate contact information, see transportation pages.

Amtrak: Train with baggage car required.
LIRR: $5 permit required.
Metro-North: $5 permit required.
New Jersey Transit: Free permit required.
PATH: No permit required.
NY Waterway: $1 fee.
Staten Island Ferry: Enter at lower level.
Bus companies: Call individual companies.

January

- Winter Antiques Show — Park Ave at 67th St — Selections from all over the country.
- Three Kings Day Parade — El Museo del Barrio — Features a cast of hundreds from all over the city dressed as kings or animals–camels, sheep, and donkeys (early Jan).
- Outsider Art Fair — Corner of Lafayette & Houston — Art in many forms of media from an international set. $15 admits one for one day.
- National Boat Show — Jacob Javits Convention Center — Don't go expecting a test drive (early Jan).
- Chinese New Year — Chinatown — Features dragons, performers, and parades.

February

- Empire State Building Run-Up — Empire State Building — Run until the 86th floor (0.2 miles) or heart seizure.
- The Art Show — Park Ave at 67th St — A very large art fair.
- Westminster Dog Show — Madison Square Garden — Fancy canines.
- Seventh on Sixth Fall Fashion Show — Bryant Park — Weeklong celeb-studded event.

March

- International Cat Show — Madison Square Garden — Fine felines.
- St Patrick's Day Parade — Fifth Avenue — Irish pride (March 17).
- Orchid Show — Bronx River Parkway — Brought to you by the New York Botanical Garden
- Ringley Brothers Circus — Madison Square Garden — Greatest Show on Earth (March–April).
- Whitney Biennial — Whitney Museum — Whitney's most important American art, every other year (March–June).
- Greek Independence Day Parade — Fifth Avenue — Floats and bands representing area Greek Orthodox churches and Greek federations and organizations. (Late March)
- Small Press Book Fair — Small Press Center — Sometimes-interesting fair of small publishers and self-published authors.
- Macy's Flower Show — Broadway and 34th St — Flowers.
- New Directors/New Films — MoMA — Film festival featuring new films by emerging directors.

April

- Easter Parade — Fifth Avenue — Starts at 11 am, get there early (Easter Sunday).
- New York Antiquarian Book Fair — Park Ave at 67th St — 170 international booksellers exhibition.
- New York International Auto Show — Jacob Javits Convention Center — Traffic jam.
- Spring Spectacular — Radio City Music Hall — The Rockettes in bunny costumes? (Easter week)
- New York City Ballet Spring Season — Lincoln Center — Features new and classical ballet. (April–June)

May

- Tribeca Film Festival — Various locations including Regal 16 at BPC, BMCC Chambers St, Battery Park — Festival includes film screenings, panels, lectures, discussion groups, and concerts (Early May).
- The Great Five Boro Bike Tour — Battery Park to Staten Island — Tour de NYC (first Sunday in May).
- Ninth Avenue International Food Festival — Ninth Avenue from 37th to 57th Sts — A truly fabulous experience!
- Fleet Week — USS Intrepid — Boats and sailors from many navies (last week in May).
- New York AIDS Walk — Central Park — 10K walk whose proceeds go toward finding a cure.
- Lower East Side Festival of the Arts — Theater for the New City, 155 First Ave — Celebrating Beatniks and Pop Art (last weekend in May).
- Spring Flower Exhibition — NY Botanical Garden, Bronx — More flowers.
- Cherry Blossom Festival — Brooklyn Botanic Garden — Flowering trees.
- Martin Luther King, Jr Parade — Fifth Avenue — Celebration of equal rights (third Sunday in May).
- Thursday Night Concert Series — South Street Seaport — Free varied concerts (May–September).

June

• Toyota Comedy Festival	Various locations	Japan's dullest cars, America's funniest comics.
• Puerto Rican Day Parade	Fifth Avenue	Puerto Rican pride (First Sunday in June).
• Metropolitan Opera Parks Concerts	Various locations	Free performances through June and July.
• Museum Mile Festival	Fifth Avenue	Museum open-house (second Sunday in June).
• Gay and Lesbian Pride Parade	Columbus Circle, Fifth Ave & Christopher St	Commemorates the 1969 Stonewall riots (last Sunday in June).
• New York Jazz Festival	Various locations	All kinds of jazz.
• JVC Jazz Festival	Various locations	Descends from the Newport Jazz Festival.
• Mermaid Parade	Coney Island	Showcase of sea-creatures and freaks.
• Feast of St Anthony of Padua	Little Italy	Patron saint of expectant mothers, mail, Portugal, seekers of lost articles, shipwrecks, Tigua Indians, and travel hostesses, among other things. (Saturday before summer solstice)
• Central Park SummerStage	Central Park	Free concerts (June–August).
• Bryant Park Free Summer Season	Sixth Ave at 42nd St	Free music, dance, and film (June–August).
• Midsummer Night Swing	Lincoln Center	Performances with free dance lessons (June–July).

July

• Macy's Fireworks Display	East River	Independence Day's literal highlight (July 4).
• American Crafts Festival	Lincoln Center	Celebrating quilts and such (first two weekends in July).
• Washington Square Music Festival	W 4th St at LaGuardia Pl	Open-air concert (July–August).
• New York Philharmonic Concerts	Various locations	Varied programs (July–August).
• Summergarden	MoMA	Free classical concerts (July–August).
• Celebrate Brooklyn! Performing Arts Festival	Prospect Park Bandshell	9 weeks of free outdoor events (July–August).
• Mostly Mozart	Lincoln Center	The name says it all (July–August).
• New York Shakespeare Festival	Delacorte Theater in Central Park	Two free plays every summer (July–August).
• Music on the Boardwalk	Coney Island	"Under the Boardwalk" not on the set list, presumably... (July–August).

August

• Harlem Week	Harlem	Black and Latino culture. The celebration lasts all month.
• Hong Kong Dragon Boat Festival	Flushing-Meadows Park Lake, Queens	39-foot boats race.
• Greenwich Village Jazz Festival	Greenwich Village	10-day festival ending with a free concert in Washington Square Park.
• The Fringe Festival	Various locations, Lower East Side	Avant-garde theater.
• US Open Tennis Championships	USTA National Tennis Center, Flushing	Final Grand Slam event of the year (August–September).
• Howl Festival	Tompkins Square Park	Jazz, East Village merchants, art, etc. Recommended.

September

• West Indian Day Carnival	Eastern Parkway from Utica—Grand Army Plaza, Brooklyn	Children's parade on Saturday, adult's parade on Labor Day (Labor Day Weekend).
• Richmond County Fair	441 Clarke Ave, Staten Island	Best agricultural competitions (Labor Day).
• Wigstock	Pier 54 b/w 12th–13th Sts, west side	Celebration of drag, glamour, and artificial hair (Labor Day Weekend).
• Feast of San Gennaro	Little Italy	Plenty of greasy street food (third week in September).
• Downtown Arts Festival	Various locations, SoHo	Mammoth art exhibitions.
• Broadway on Broadway	Times Square	Sneak peak at old and new plays.

September—*continued*

Event	Location	Description
Brooklyn BeerFest	N 11th St between B erry and Wythe, Brooklyn	Taste test of over 100 beers.
Atlantic Antic	Brooklyn Heights	Multicultural street fair (last Sunday in September).
New York Is Book Country	Fifth Avenue	Publishers and bookstores from around NYC (third Sunday in September).
Race for the Mayor's Cup	NY Harbor	And the winner gets to find out what he's been drinking! (September–November)
New York City Opera Season	Lincoln Center	Popular and classical operas.

October

Event	Location	Description
New York Film Festival	Lincoln Center	Features film premieres (early October).
Fall Crafts Park Avenue	Seventh Regiment Armory on Park Avenue, b/w 66th and 67th Sts	Display and sale of contemporary American crafts by 175 of the nation's finest craft artists.
Columbus Day Parade	Fifth Avenue	Celebrating the second person to discover America (Columbus Day).
Halloween Parade	West Village	Brings a new meaning to costumed event (October 31).
Fall Antique Show	Pier 92	Look at old things you can't afford.
Chrysanthemum and Bonsai Festival	NY Botanical Garden, Bronx	Even more flowers.
Blessing of the Animals	St John the Divine, Morningside Heights	Where to take your gecko.
Big Apple Circus	Lincoln Center	Step right up! (October–January)
Hispanic Day Parade	Fifth Ave b/w 44th and 86th Sts	A celebration of Latin America's rich heritage (mid-October).

November

Event	Location	Description
New York City Marathon	Verrazano to Central Park	26 miles of NYC air (first Sunday of November).
Veteran's Day Parade	Fifth Ave from 42nd St to 79th St	Service at Eternal Light Memorial in Madison Square Park following the parade.
Macy's Thanksgiving Day Parade	Central Park West at 79th St to Macy's	Santa starts the holiday season.
Chase Championships, Corel WTA Tour	Madison Square Garden	Women's tennis.
The Nutcracker Suite	Lincoln Center	Christmas tradition (November–December).
Singing Christmas Tree	South Street Seaport	Warning: might scare small children, family pets, and stoners (November–December).
Christmas Spectacular	Radio City Music Hall	Rockettes star (November–January).
A Christmas Carol	Madison Square Garden	Dickens a la New York City (Nov–Jan).
Origami Christmas Tree	Museum of Natural History	Hopefully not decorated with candles (Nov–Jan).

December

Event	Location	Description
Christmas Tree Lighting Ceremony	Rockefeller Center	Most enchanting spot in the city during the holidays.
Messiah Sing-In	Call 212-333-5333	Handel would be proud.
New Year's Eve Fireworks	Central Park	Hot cider and food available (December 31).
New Year's Eve Ball Drop	Times Square	Welcome the new year with a freezing mob (Dec 31).
Blessing of the Animals	Central Presbyterian Church	Where to take your other gecko (December 24).
Menorah Lighting	Fifth Avenue	Yarmulke required.
Kwanzaa Holiday Expo	Jacob Javits Convention Center	Black pride retail.
New Year's Eve Midnight Run	Central Park	5k for the brave.

"New York is the concentrate of art and commerce and sport and religion and entertainment and finance, bringing to a single compact arena the gladiator, the evangelist, the promoter, the actor, the trader and the merchant." —E.B. White

Useful Phone Numbers

Emergencies:	911
General City Information:	311
City Board of Elections:	212-VOTE-NYC
Con Edison:	800-752-6633
Time Warner Cable:	212-358-0900
Verizon:	212-890-1550
Police Headquarters:	646-610-5905
Public Advocate:	212-669-7200

Bathrooms

When nature calls, New York can make your life excruciatingly difficult. The city-sponsored public bathroom offerings, including dodgy subway restrooms and the sporadic experimentation with self-cleaning super porta-potties, leave a lot to be desired. Your best bet, especially in an emergency, remains bathrooms in stores and other buildings that are open to the public.

The three most popular bathroom choices for needy New Yorkers (and visitors) are Barnes & Noble, Starbucks, and any kind of fast food chain. Barnes & Noble bathrooms are essentially open to everyone (as long as you're willing to walk past countless shelves of books during your navigation to the restrooms). They're usually clean enough, but sometimes you'll find yourself waiting in line during the evening and weekends. Although Starbucks bathrooms are more prevalent, they tend to be more closely guarded (in most places you have to ask for a key) and not as clean as you'd like. Fast food restrooms are similarly unhygienic but easy to use inconspicuously without needing to purchase anything.

For a comprehensive listing of bathrooms in NYC (including hours and even ratings), try www.allny.com (look under "NYC Bathroom Guide") and the Bathroom Diaries at www.thebathroomdiaries.com/usa/new+york.

If you're busting to go and there's no Barnes & Noble, Starbucks, or fast food joint in sight, consider the following options:

- **Public buildings**—including train stations (Grand Central, Penn Station), and malls (South Street Seaport, World Financial Center, Manhattan Mall, The Shops at Columbus Circle).
- **Government buildings**—government offices, courthouses, police stations.
- **Department stores**—Macy's, Bloomingdale's, Saks, Kmart, etc.
- **Other stores**—Old Navy, Bed Bath & Beyond, FAO Schwartz, NBA store, The Strand, etc.
- **Restaurants**—McDonald's, Burger King, Starbucks, etc.
- **Supermarkets**—Pathmark, Food Emporium, D'Agostino, Gristedes, Key Food, etc. You'll probably have to ask, because the restrooms in supermarkets are usually way in the back amongst the employee lockers.
- **Bars**—a good choice at night when most other places are closed. Try to choose a busy one so as not to arouse suspicion. Most bars have those intimidating signs warning you that the restrooms are for customers only!
- **Museums**—most are closed at night and most require an entry fee during the day. How desperate are you?
- **Colleges**—better if you're young enough to look like a student.
- **Parks**—great during the day, closed at night.
- **Hotels**—you might have to sneak past the desk though.
- **Times Square visitors centers**—1560 Broadway and 810 Seventh Avenue.
- **Places of worship**—unpredictable hours and not all have public restrooms.
- **Subways**—how bad do you have to go? Your best bets are express stops on the IND lines, for example, 34th Street and 6th Avenue. Some stations have locked bathrooms, with keys available at the booths.
- **Gyms**—i.e. places where you have a membership.
- **Outdoor public bathrooms**—try these once in a while (if you can find one)—apparently the city signed on for 20 of them in 2004.

Websites

www.allny.com · The most detailed and varied site about anything you can imagine that relates to NY.
www.downtowninfocenter.org · Current listing of Downtown events.
www.downtowny.com/gettingaround/?sid=19 · Information and map of the FREE Downtown Connection bus service that shuttle passengers between Battery Park City and the South Street Seaport with many stops in between.
www.fieldtrip.com/ny/index_ny.htm · Hundreds of suggestions for places to visit in the city.
www.forgotten-ny.com · Fascinating look at the relics of New York's past.
www.gothamist.com · Blog detailing various daily news and goings-on in the city.
www.lowermanhattan.info · An excellent resource for information about what's happening in Lower Manhattan.
www.lowermanhattanmap.com · Maps with icons of all the neighborhoods in Lower Manhattan.
www.menupages.com · Menus for almost every restaurant in Manhattan below 96th Street.
www.newyork.citysearch.com · Still a good overview of businesses, landmarks, and attractions in the city, though somewhat less useful in recent years because of too many paid listings, pop-up ads, and the like.
www.newyork.craigslist.org · Classifieds in almost every area, including personals, apartments for rent, musicians, and more.
www.notfortourists.com/ny-home.aspx · The ultimate NYC website.
www.ny1.com · Local news about the city; weather.
www.nyc.gov · New York City government resources.
www.nycsubway.com · Complete history and overview of the subways.
www.nycvisit.com · The official NYC tourism site.

New York Timeline — a timeline of significant events in New York history (by no means complete)

1524: Giovanni de Verrazano enters the New York harbor.
1609: Henry Hudson explores what is now called the Hudson River.
1625: The Dutch purchase Manhattan and New Amsterdam is founded.
1647: Peter Stuyvesant becomes Director General of New Amsterdam.
1664: The British capture the colony and rename it New York.
1754: King's College/Columbia founded.
1776: British drive colonial army from New York and hold it for the duration of the war.
1776: Fire destroys a third of the city.
1788: Washington takes the Oath of Office as the first President of the United States.
1811: The Commissioners Plan dictates a grid plan for the streets of New York.
1812: City Hall completed.
1835: Great Fire destroys 300 buildings and kills 30 New Yorkers.
1859: Central Park opens.
1863: The Draft Riots terrorize New York for three days.
1868: Prospect Park opens.
1880: The population of Manhattan reaches over 1 million.
1883: Brooklyn Bridge opens.
1886: The Statue of Liberty is dedicated, inspires first ticker tape parade.
1888: The Blizzard of '88 incapacitates the city for two weeks.
1892: Ellis Island opens; 16 million immigrants will pass through in the next 32 years.
1897: Steeplechase Park opens, first large amusement park in Coney Island.
1898: The City of Greater New York is founded when the five boroughs are merged.
1904: The subway opens.
1906: First New Year's celebration in Times Square.
1911: Triangle Shirtwaist Fire kills 146, impels work safety movement.
1920: A TNT-packed horse cart explodes on Wall Street, killing 30; the crime goes unsolved.
1923: The Yankees win their first World Championship.
1929: Stock market crashes, signaling the beginning of the Great Depression.
1929: The Chrysler Building is completed.
1930: The Empire State Building is built, then tallest in the world.
1927: The Holland Tunnel opens, making it the world's longest underwater tunnel.
1931: The George Washington Bridge is completed.
1933: Fiorello LaGuardia elected mayor.
1934: Robert Moses becomes Parks Commissioner.
1939: The city's first airport, LaGuardia, opens.
1950: United Nations opens.
1955: Dodgers win the World Series; they move to LA two years later.
1964: The Verrazano-Narrows Bridge is built, at the time the world's longest suspension bridge.
1965: Malcolm X assassinated in the Audubon Ballroom.
1965: Pennsylvania Station is demolished to the dismay of many; preservation efforts gain steam.
1965: Blackout strands hundreds of thousands during rush hour.
1969: The Stonewall Rebellion marks beginning of the gay rights movement.
1969: The Miracle Mets win the World Series.
1970: Knicks win their first championship.
1970: First New York City Marathon takes place.
1971: World Trade Center opens.
1975: Ford to City: Drop Dead.
1977: Thousands arrested for various mischief during a city-wide blackout.
1977: Ed Koch elected mayor to the first of three terms.
1987: Black Monday—stock market plunges.
1993: Giuliani elected mayor.
1993: A bomb explodes in the parking garage of the World Trade Center, killing 5.
1994: Rangers win the Stanley Cup after a 40-year drought.
1999: NFT publishes its first edition.
2000: Yankees win their 26th World Championship.
2001: The World Trade Center is destroyed in a terrorist attack; New Yorkers vow to rebuild.
2003: Tokens are no longer accepted in subway turnstiles.
2004: Yankees lose the World Series to the Boston Red Sox. We don't want to talk about it.

Essential New York Songs

"Sidewalks of New York" — Various, written by James Blake and Charles Lawlor, 1894

"Give My Regards to Broadway" — Various, written by George Cohan, 1904

"I'll Take Manhattan" — Various, written by Rodgers and Hart, 1925

"Puttin' on the Ritz" — Various, written by Irving Berlin, 1929

"42nd Street" — Various, written by Al Dubin and Harry Warren, 1929

"Take the A Train" — Duke Ellington, 1940

"Autumn in New York" — Frank Sinatra, 1947

"Spanish Harlem" — Ben E. King, 1961

"Car 54 Where Are You?" — Nat Hiken and John Strauss, 1961

"On Broadway" — Various, written by Weil/Mann/Leiber/Stoller, 1962

"Talkin' New York" — Bob Dylan, 1962

"Up on the Roof" — The Drifters, 1963

"59th Street Bridge Song" — Simon and Garfunkel, 1966

"I'm Waiting for My Man" — Velvet Underground, 1967

"Crosstown Traffic" — Jimi Hendrix, 1969

"Personality Crisis" — The New York Dolls, 1973

"New York State of Mind" — Billy Joel, 1976

"53rd and 3rd" — The Ramones, 1977

"Shattered" — Rolling Stones, 1978

"New York, New York" — Frank Sinatra, 1979

"Life During Wartime" — Talking Heads, 1979

"New York New York" — Grandmaster Flash and the Furious 5, 1984

"No Sleep Til Brooklyn" — Beastie Boys, 1987

"Christmas in Hollis" — Run-D.M.C., 1987

"New York" — U2, 2000

"I've Got New York" — The 6th's, 2000

"New York, New York" — Ryan Adams, 2001

"New York" — Ja Rule f. Fat Joe, Jadakiss, 2004

Essential New York Movies

The Crowd (1928)
42nd Street (1933)
King Kong (1933)
On the Town (1949)
The Blackboard Jungle (1955)
An Affair to Remember (1957)
The Apartment (1960)
Breakfast at Tiffany's (1961)
West Side Story (1961)
Barefoot in the Park (1967)
Midnight Cowboy (1969)
French Connection (1970)

Shaft (1971)
Mean Streets (1973)
Godfather II (1974)
The Taking of Pelham One Two Three (1974)
Taxi Driver (1976)
Saturday Night Fever (1977)
Superman (1978)
Manhattan (1979)
The Warriors (1979)
Escape From New York (1981)
Nighthawks (1981)

Ghostbusters (1984)
The Muppets Take Manhattan (1984)
Wall Street (1987)
Moonstruck (1987)
Working Girl (1988)
Do the Right Thing (1989)
When Harry Met Sally (1989)
A Bronx Tale (1993)
Men in Black (1997)
Chelsea Walls (2001)
Gangs of New York (2002)
Spider-Man (2002)

Essential New York Books

A Tree Grows in Brooklyn, by Betty Smith	Coming of age story set in the slums of Brooklyn.
The Bonfire of the Vanities, by Tom Wolfe	The story of a Wall Street tycoon, set in New York in the 1980's.
Bright Lights, Big City, by Jay McInerney	1980's yuppie and the temptations of the city.
Catcher in the Rye, by J.D. Salinger	Classic portrayal of teenage angst.
The Cricket in Times Square, by George Selden	Classic children's book.
The Death and Life of Great American Cities, by Jane Jacobs	Influential exposition on what matters in making cities work.
The Encyclopedia of New York City, . by Kenneth T. Jackson, ed	Huge and definitive reference work.
Gotham: A history of New York City to 1898, by Edwin G. Burrows and Mike Wallace	Authorative history of New York.
Here is New York, by E.B. White	Reflections on the city.
House of Mirth, by Edith Wharton	Climbing the social ladder in upper crust, late 19th-century NY.
Knickerbocker's History of New York, by Washington Irving	Very early (1809) whimsical "history" of NY.
The Power Broker, by Robert Caro	Biography of Robert Moses, you'll never look at the city the same way after reading it.
Washington Square, by Henry James	Love and marriage in upper-middle-class 1880's NY.

General Information • Media

Television

2	WCBS (CBS)	www.cbsnewyork.com
4	WNBC (NBC)	www.wnbc.com
5	WNYW (FOX)	www.fox5ny.com
7	WABC (ABC)	abclocal.go.com/wabc
9	WWOR (UPN)	www.upn9.com
11	WPIX (WB)	www.wb11.com
13	WNET (PBS)	www.thirteen.org
21	WLIW (Long Island Public)	www.wliw.org
25	WNY (Public)	www.wnye.nycenet.edu
31	PXN (Pax)	www.pax.tv
41	WXTV (Univision)	www.univision.com
47	WNJU (Telemundo)	www.telemundo.com
50	CPTV (Conn. Public)	www.cptv.org
50	WNJN (NJ Public)	www.njn.net
55	WLNY (Public)	www.wlnytv.com
63	WMBC (Religious)	www.wmbctv.com

AM Stations

570	WFME	Religious
620	WSNR	Sports
660	WFAN	Sports
710	WOR	Talk
770	WABC	Talk
820	WNYC	Talk
880	WCBS	Talk
930	WPAT	Talk
1010	WINS	News
1050	WEVD	Sports
1130	WBBR	Talk
1190	WLIB	Talk
1280	WADO	Sports
1600	WWRL	Talk
1660	WWRU	Talk

FM Stations

88.3	WBGO	Jazz
88.9	WSIA	College
89.1	WFDU	College
89.1	WNYU	College
89.5	WSOU	Alternative/Hard Rock
89.9	WKCR	Jazz
90.3	WHCR	College
90.3	WHPC	College
90.7	WFUV	Adult Alternative
90.9	WKPB	College
91.1	WFMU	College
91.5	WNYE	Talk
92.3	WXRK	Alternative/Hard Rock
92.7	WLIR	Latin
93.1	WPAT	Latin
93.9	WNYC	Talk
94.7	WFME	Religious
95.5	WPLJ	Top 40
96.3	WQXR	Classical
97.1	WQHT	Hip-Hop/R&B
97.9	WSKQ	Latin
98.7	WRKS	Hip-Hop/R&B
99.5	WBAI	Talk
100.3	WHTZ	Top 40
101.1	WCBS	Oldies
101.9	WQCD	Jazz
102.3	WBAB	Classic Rock
102.7	WNEW	Top 40
103.5	WKTU	Top 40/Dance
104.3	WAXQ	Classic Rock
105.1	WWPR	Hip-Hop/R&B
105.9	WWPR	Latin
106.7	WLTW	Adult Comtemporary
107.1	WCAA	Latin
107.5	WBLS	R&B

Print Media

amNY	145 W 30th St, 9th Fl	212-239-5398	Free daily, general news.
Daily News	450 W 33rd St	212-210-2100	Daily tabloid, rival of the Post.
El Diario	345 Hudson St	212-807-4600	Daily, America's oldest Spanish language newspaper.
Metro NYC	44 Wall St	212-952-1500	Free daily, pick it up at the subway.
New York Observer	54 E 64th St	212-755-2400	Weekly.
New York Post	1211 Avenue of the Americas	212-997-9272	Daily tabloid, known for its sensationalist headlines.
New York Sun	105 Chambers St	212-406-2000	Daily, only a couple of years old.
New York Times	229 W 43rd St	212-556-1234	Daily, one of the world's best known papers.
Newsday	235 Pinelawn Rd,	516-843-2700	Daily, based in Long Island. Melville, NYC
NY Press	333 Seventh Ave	212-244-2282	Free, mostly opinion/editorial.
The Onion	515 W 20th St	212-627-1972	Weekly, news satire.
The Village Voice	36 Cooper Sq	212-475-3300	Free, alternative weekly.
Wall Street Journal	200 Liberty St	212-416-2500	Daily, famous financial paper.
New York Magazine	444 Madison Ave	212-508-0700	Weekly, geared towards well-to-do, various topics.
New York Review of Books	1755 Broadway	212-757-8070	Bi-weekly, intellectual lit review.
The New Yorker	4 Times Square	212-286-5400	Weekly, intellectual news, lit and arts.
Time Out New York	627 Broadway, 7th Fl	212-539-4444	Weekly, guide to goings on in the city.

The Best of the Best

With all the culture the city has to offer, finding activities to amuse children is easy enough. From fencing classes to the funnest parks, our guide will provide you with great ideas for entertaining your little ones.

★ **Neatest Time-Honored Tradition:** The Central Park Carousel (830 Fifth Ave, 212-879-0244) features the largest hand-carved figures ever constructed and has been in residence in the park since 1950. $1 will buy you a memory to last forever. Open 10 am to 6 pm on weekdays and 10 am to 7 pm weekends, weather permitting.

★ **Coolest Rainy Day Activity:** Our Name is Mud (59 Greenwich Ave, 212-647-7899) is a paint-your-own pottery studio, with four locations throughout the city. Pick out what you want to paint and the studio will provide paint, stencils, and all the other equipment to produce a masterpiece. A great activity for creative kids and a fantastic destination for birthday parties.

★ **Sweetest Place to Get a Cavity:** Dylan's Candy Bar (1011 Third Ave, 646-735-0078) is a two-story candy land, chock full of every confectionary delight you can think of, plus a tasty ice cream bar. A great place for birthday parties, they'll provide enough candy-related activities to keep

kids on a permanent sugar high. Watch out, Willy Wonka. Open Sun-Thurs: 10 am–9 pm, Fri-Sat: 10 am–10 pm.

★ **Best Spots for Sledding:** Central Park's Pilgrim Hill and Cedar Hill. Kids pray for a snow day for the chance to try out these slick slopes. BYO sled or toboggan.

★ **Funnest Park:** Hudson River Park Playground (Pier 51, Gansevoort St) With a beautiful view of the Hudson River, the park features several sprinklers, a winding "canal" and a boat-themed area complete with prow, mast, and captain's wheel.

★ **No Tears Hair Cuts:** Whipper Snippers (106 Reade St, 212-227-2600) is a children's salon that calms the most fearful of scissor-phobes. An on-site toy store helps to distract timid tots and promises a prize for the well-behaved. The salon also provides birthday parties.

★ **Best Halloween Costume Shopping:** Halloween Adventure (104 Fourth Ave, 212-673-4546) is the city's costume emporium that has every disguise you can possibly imagine, along with wigs, make-up supplies, and magic tricks to complete any child's dress-up fantasy. Open year-round.

Rainy Day Activities

When splashing in puddles has lost its novelty and ruined far too many of their designer duds:

• **American Museum of Natural History** (Central Park West and 79th St, 212- 769-5100) Fantastic for kids of all ages, with something to suit every child's interest. From the larger-than-life dinosaur fossils and the realistic animal dioramas to the out-of-this-world Hayden Planetarium, all attention will be rapt. The hands-on exhibits of the Discovery Room and the IMAX theater are also worth a visit. Open 10 am–5:45 pm daily.

• **Bowlmor Lanes** (110 University Pl, 212-255-8188) Great bowling alley with a retro décor that kids will love. Bumpers are available to cut down on those pesky gutter balls. Children are welcome every day before 5 pm and all day Sunday—a popular birthday spot.

• **Brooklyn Children's Museum** (145 Brooklyn Ave, 718-735-4400) The world's first museum for children (opened in 1899) engages the kids in educational hands-on activities and exhibits. Kids can learn about life in New York in the "Together in the City" exhibit and find out why snakes are so slimy in the "Animal Outpost."

• **Children's Museum of the Arts** (182 Lafayette St, 212-941-9198) Through special exhibitions, workshops, and activities, as well as after school art classes in music, ceramics, painting, and mixed media, the museum provides a creative outlet for children, aged 1-12. The museum is open Wed-Sun, 12 pm-5 pm.

• **Children's Museum of Manhattan** (212 W 83rd St, 212-721-1234) As soon as you arrive at the museum, sign up for some of the day's activities. While you're waiting, check out the other exhibits in the museum. There's the Word Play area designed for the younger children in your group and the

Time/Warner Media Center for the older set, where kids can produce their own television shows. The museum is open Wed-Sun, 10 pm–5 pm.

• **Intrepid Sea Air Space Museum** (Pier 86, 46th St and 12th Ave, 212-245-0072) Tour The Growler, a real submarine that was once a top-secret missile command center, or take a virtual trip on one of the simulator rides. After you've taken a look at the authentic aircrafts on deck, visit the museum of The Intrepid to see an extensive model airplane collection and a Cockpit Challenge flight video game for those aspiring pilots. The museum is open Mon-Fri, 10 am–5pm, and Sat-Sun, 10 am–6 pm.

• **Lower East Side Tenement Museum** (90 Orchard St, 212-431-0233) The museum offers insight into immigrant life in the late 19th and early 20th centuries by taking groups on tours of historic tenements throughout the Lower East Side. One tour called "Visit the Confino Family" is led by "Victoria Confino," a young girl dressed in authentic costume who teaches children about the lives of immigrants in the early 1900's. A great way to take your kids, if they haven't already been there on a school field trip.

• **The Metropolitan Museum of Art** (1000 Fifth Ave, 212-535-7710) A great museum to explore with audio guides designed specifically for children. From the armor exhibits to the Egyptian Wing, the museum offers art exhibits from all historical periods.

• **Sydney's Playground** (66 White St, 212-431-9125) A 6,000-square-foot indoor playground featuring a giant sandbox, climbing play town, and a book nook. There's also a Womb Room, a quiet, dimly lit space with a view of the play area for moms who need to quiet baby while big brother plays.

Shopping Essentials

Kid's designer couture sounds like a recipe for disaster, with threats of grass stains, paint stains, and dirt lurking around every corner. But it exists and thrives in New York City, nonetheless (e.g. Julian & Sara). buybuyBABY has nursing rooms which are very helpful. Here's a list of shops for the best party clothes and party gifts and everything in between:

- **American Girl Place** · 609 Fifth Ave · 877-AGPLACE· dolls
- **Bambini** · 1088 Madison Ave · 212-717-6742 · European clothing
- **A Bear's Place** · 789 Lexington Ave · 212-826-6465 · furniture & toys
- **Bellini** · 1305 Second Ave · 212-517-9233 · furniture
- **Betwixt** · 245 W 10th St · 212-243-8590 · pre-teen clothing
- **Big Fun** · 636 Hudson St · 212-414-4138 · toys & trinkets
- **Bombalulus** · 101 W 10th St · 212-463-0897 · unique clothing & toys
- **Bonpoint** · pricey clothing
  - 1269 Madison Ave · 212-722-7720
  - 811 68th St · 212-879-0900
- **Books of Wonder** · 18 W 18th St · 212- 989-3270 · books
- **Boomerang Toys** · 173 West Broadway · 212-226-7650 · infant toys
- **Bu and the Duck** · 106 Franklin St · 212-431-9226 · vintage-inspired clothing/toys
- **buybuyBABY** · 270 Seventh Ave · 917-344-1555 · furniture/clothing/toys
- **Calypso Enfant & Bebe** · 426 Broome St · 212-966-3234 · hand-made clothing
- **Catimini** · 1284 Madison Ave · 212-987-0688 · French clothing
- **The Children's General Store** · Central Passage Grand Central Terminal · 212-682-0004 · toys
- **The Children's Place** · chain clothing store
  - 1460 Broadway · 212-398-4416
  - 901 Sixth Ave · 212-268-7696
  - 173 E 86th St · 212-831-5100
  - 22 W 34th St · 212-904-1190
  - 2187 Broadway · 917-441-9807
  - 36 Union Sq E · 212-529-2201
  - 600 W 181 St · 212-923-7244
  - 1164 Third Ave · 212-717-7187
  - 248 W 125th St · 212-866-9616
  - 650 Sixth Ave · 917-305-1348
  - 153 E 125th St · 212-348-3607
  - 142 Delancey St · 212-979-5071
- **Classic Toys** · 218 Sullivan St · 212-674-4434 · toys
- **Dinosaur Hill** · 306 E 9th St · 212-473-5850 · toys & clothes
- **Disney Store** · 711 Fifth Ave · 212-702-0702 · Disney merchandise
- **Discovery Channel Store** · Grand Central Station · 212-808-9144 · educational toys
- **East Side Kids** · 1298 Madison Ave · 212-360-5000 · shoes
- **EAT Gifts** · 1062 Madison Ave · 212-861-2544 · toys & trinkets
- **Estella** · 493 Sixth Ave · 212-255-3553 · boutique clothing
- **FAO Schwarz** · 767 Fifth Ave · 212-644-9400 · toy land

- **Funky Fresh Children's Boutique** · 9 Clinton St · 212-254-5584 · unique clothing
- **GapKids/baby Gap** · chain clothing store
  - 1 Astor Pl · 212-253-0145
  - 11 Fulton St · 212-374-1051
  - 1535 Third Ave · 212-423-0033
  - 750 Broadway · 212-674-1877
  - 2300 Broadway · 212-873-2044
  - 335 Columbus Ave · 212-875-9196
  - 734 Lexington Ave · 212-327-2614
  - 225 Liberty St · 212-945-4090
  - 1988 Broadway · 212-721-5304
  - 122 Fifth Ave · 917-408-5580
  - 250 W 57th St · 212-315-2250
  - 545 Madison Ave · 212-980-2570
  - 657 Third Ave · 212-697-3590
  - 680 Fifth Ave · 212-977-7023
  - 60 W 34th St · 212-760-1268
  - 1212 Sixth Ave · 212-730-1087
  - 1466 Broadway · 212-382-4500
- **Geppetto's Toy Box** · 10 Christopher St · 212 620-7511 · toys
- **Granny-Made** · 381 Amsterdam Ave · 212-496-1222 · hand-made sweaters
- **Greenstone's** · hats & clothing
  - 442 Columbus Ave · 212-580-4322
  - 1184 Madison Ave · 212-427-1665
- **Gymboree** · chain clothing store
  - 1049 Third Ave · 212- 688-4044
  - 2015 Broadway · 212- 595-7662
  - 1332 Third Ave · 212-517-5548
  - 2271 Broadway · 212- 595-9071
  - 1120 Madison Ave · 212-717-6702
- **Halloween Adventure** · 104 Fourth Ave · 212-673-4546 · costumes & magic tricks
- **Jacadi** · expensive French clothing
  - 1296 Madison Ave · 212-369-1616
  - 787 Madison Ave · 212-535-3200
  - 1260 Third Ave · 212-717-9292
- **Jane's Exchange** · 207 Avenue A · 212-674-6268 · consignment clothing
- **Jay Kos** · boys' clothing
  - 986 Lexington Ave · 212-327-2382
  - 475 Park Ave · 212-319-2770
- **Julian & Sara** · 103 Mercer St · 212-226-1989 · European clothing
- **Just for Tykes** · 83 Mercer St · 212-274-9121 · clothing & furniture
- **KB Toys** · chain toy store
  - 901 Sixth Ave · 212-629-5386
  - 2411 Broadway · 212-595-4389
- **Karin Alexis** · 490 Amsterdam Ave · 212-769-9550 · clothing & toys
- **Kendall's Closet** · 162 W 84th St · 212-501-8911 · clothing
- **Kidding Around** · 60 W 15th St · 212-645-6337 · toy store
- **Kidrobot** · 126 Prince St · 212-966-6688 · toy store
- **Leeper Kids** · Grand Central Station, Lexington Terminal · 212-499-9111 · pricey clothing & toys
- **Lester's** · 1522 Second Ave · 212-734-9292 · clothing

- **Lilliput** · pricey clothing
  - 240 Lafayette St · 212-965-9201
  - 265 Lafayette St · 212-965-9567
- **Little Eric** · 1118 Madison Ave · 212-717-1513 · shoes
- **Magic Windows** · 1186 Madison Ave · 212-289-0181 · clothing
- **Manhattan Dollhouse Shop** · 428 Second Ave · 212-725-4520 · dolls
- **Mary Arnold Toys** · 1010 Lexington Ave · 212-744-8510 · toys
- **Oilily** · 212-772-8686 · unique clothing
- **Oshkosh B'Gosh** · 586 Fifth Ave · 212-827-0098 · play clothes
- **Peanut Butter and Jane** · 617 Hudson St · 212-620-7952 · clothing & toys
- **Penny Whistle Toys** · toys & trinkets
  - 448 Columbus Ave · 212-873-9090
  - 1283 Madison Ave · 212-369-3868
- **Pipsqueak** · 248 Mott St · 212-226-8824 · clothing
- **Planet Kids** · infant gear
  - 247 E 86th St · 212-426-2040
  - 2688 Broadway · 212-864-8705
- **Pokemon Center** · 10 Rockefeller Plz · 212-307-0900 · Pokemon
- **Promises Fulfilled** · 1592 Second Ave · 212-472-1600 · toys & trinkets
- **The Scholastic Store** · 557 Broadway · 212-343-6166 · books & toys
- **ShooFly** · 42 Hudson St · 212-406-3270 · shoes & accessories
- **Space Kiddets** · 46 E 21st St · 212-420-9878 · girls' clothing
- **Spring Flowers** · shoes & clothes
  - 538 Madison Ave · 212-207-4606
  - 905 Madison Ave · 212-717-8182
  - 1050 Third Ave · 212-758-2669
- **Stinky & Minky** · 171 Sullivan St · 212-253-2530 · vintage clothing
- **Talbot's Kids and Babies** · clothing
  - 527 Madison Ave · 212-758-4152
  - 1523 Second Ave · 212-570-1630
- **Tannen's Magical Development Co** · 45 W 34st,Ste 608 · 212-929-4500 · magic shop
- **Tigers, Tutu's and Toes** · fun clothing & shoes
  - 128 Second Ave · 212-228-7990
  - 56 University Pl · 212-375-9985
- **Tiny Doll House** · 1179 Lexington Ave · 212-744-3719 · dolls
- **Toys R Us** · toy superstore
  - 1514 Broadway · 800-869-7787
- **West Side Kids** · 498 Amsterdam Ave · 212-496-7282 · toys
- **Yoya** · 636 Hudson St · 646-336-6844 · clothing
- **Z'baby** · clothing
  - 100 W 72nd St · 212-579-BABY
  - 996 Lexington Ave · 212-472-BABY
- **Zitamor** · 969 Madison Ave, 3rd Fl · 212-737-2040 · toys & books

Outdoor *and* Educational

They can't learn *everything* from the Discovery Channel.

- **Central Park Zoo** · 830 Fifth Ave, 212-439-6500 · Houses more than 1,400 animals, including some endangered species. Take a walk through the arctic habitat of the polar bears and penguins in the steamy tropical Rain Forest Pavilion. The Tisch Children's Zoo nearby is more suited for the younger crowd with its smaller, cuddlier animals.

- **Fort Washington Park** · W 155 St to Dyckman, at the Hudson River · 301-763-4600. Call the Urban Park Rangers to arrange a tour of the little red lighthouse located at the base of the George Washington Bridge. The lighthouse affords some spectacular views—better than anything they'd see from atop dad's shoulders. The park offers a "Junior Ranger Program" for kids, as well as a playground in Picnic Area "B".

- **Historic Richmond Town** · 441 Clarke Ave, Staten Island, 718-351-1611 · A 100-acre complex with over 40 points of interest and a museum that covers over three centuries of the history of Staten Island. People dressed in authentic period garb lead demonstrations and tours.

Classes

With all of their after-school classes and camps, the children of New York City are some of the most well-rounded in the country. Help them beef up their college applications with some fancy extracurriculars. It's never too early…

- **92nd Street Y After-School Programs** · 1395 Lexington Ave, 212-415-5500 · The center provides children of all ages with tons of activities, ranging from music lessons and chess to flamenco and yoga. 92nd St is known as "the Y to beat all Y's."

- **Abrons Arts Center/Henry Street Settlement** · 466 Grand St, 212-598-0400 · The Arts Center offers classes and workshops for children of all ages in music, dance, theater, and visual arts.

- **Archikids** · 44 E 32 St, 718-768-6123 · After-school classes and summer camp for children ages 5 and up that teach kids about architecture through hands-on building projects.

- **The Art Farm** · 419 E 91st St, 631-537-1634 · "Mommy & Me" art and music classes, baking courses, and small animal care for the very young.

- **Asphalt Green** · 1750 York Ave, 212-369-8890 · Swimming and diving lessons, gymnastics, teams sports, and art classes. They've got it all for kids one and up.

- **Baby Moves** · 139 Perry St, 212-255-1685 · A developmental play space that offers classes for infants to 6 year-olds in movement, music, and play.

- **Children and Art** · 747 Amsterdam Ave, 917-841-9651 · After-school art lessons for children ages 5 and up that focus on art history and developing the skills to create masterpieces.

- **The Children's Studio** · 307 E 84th St, 212-737-3344 · The Studio offers hands-on courses in art, science, and yoga, with an emphasis on process and discovery.

- **Church Street School for Music and Art** · 74 Warren St, 212-571-7290 · This community arts center offers a variety of classes in music and art involving several different media, along with private lessons and courses for parents and children.

- **Claremont Riding Academy** · 175 W 89th St, 212-724-5100 · Horseback riding lessons offered by the oldest continuously operating stable in the United States.

- **Dieu Donné Papermill** · 433 Broome St, 212-226-0573 · Workshops in hand papermaking offered for children ages 7 and up.

- **free2be** · 24 Fifth Ave, 212-598-9760 · A holistic enrichment program that combines yoga, art, drama, storytelling, music, and poetry in classes where children are encouraged to be unabashedly creative and free with their self-expression.

- **Greenwich House Music School** · 27 Barrow St, 212-242-4140 · Group classes and private lessons in music and ballet for children of all ages.

- **Greenwich Village Center** · 219 Sullivan St, 212-254-3074 · Run by the Children's Aid Society, the center provides arts and after-school classes ranging from gymnastics to origami, as well as an early childhood program and nursery school.

- **Hamilton Fish Recreation Center** · 128 Pitt St, 212-387-7687 The center offers free swimming lessons in two outdoor pools along with free after-school programs with classes like astronomy and photography.

- **Hi Art!** · 601 W 26th St, Studio 1425I, 212-362-8190 · For children ages 2-12, the classes focus on the exploration of art in museums and galleries in the city and giving kids the freedom to develop what they've seen into new concepts in a spacious studio setting.

- **Institute of Culinary Education** · 50 W 23rd St, 212-847-0700 · Hands-on cooking classes.

- **Irish Arts Center** · 553 W 51st St, 212-757-3318 · Introductory Irish step dancing classes for children five and up.

- **Jewish Community Center** · 334 Amsterdam Ave, 646-505-4444 · The center offers swimming lessons, team sports, and courses in arts and cooking. There's even a rooftop playground.

- **Kids at Art** · 1349 Lexington Ave, 212-410-9780 · Art program that focuses on the basics in a non-competitive environment for kids ages 2-11.

- **Marshall Chess Club** · 23 W 10th St, 212-477-3716 · Membership to the club offers access to weekend chess classes, summer camp, and tournaments for children ages five and up.

- **Metropolis Fencing** · 45 W 19st St, 212-463-8044 · Fencing classes offered for children ages 7 and up.

- **Tannen's Magical Development Co** · 24 W 25th St, 2nd Fl, 212-929-4500 · Private magic lessons for children 8 and up on weekday evenings, or group lessons of 3-4 teens on Monday nights. Their week-long summer sleep-away camp is also very popular.

- **The Mixing Bowl** · 243 E 82nd St, 212-585-2433 · Cooking classes for the aspiring young chef, ages 2 and up.

- **The Techno Team** · 160 Columbus Ave, 212-501-1425 · Computer technology classes for children ages 3-12.

- **Trapeze School** · West St, south of Canal, 917-797-1872 · Kids ages one and up can learn how to fly through the air with the greatest of ease.

Babysitting/Nanny Services

Baby Sitter's Guild · 60 E 42nd St, 212-682-0227
Barnard College of Babysitting Services · 11 Milbank Hall, 212-854-7678
My Child's Best Friend · 239 E 73rd St, 212-396-4090
New York City Explorers · 212-591-2619
The NYC Babysitters Club · 212-396-4090

Where to go for more info

www.gocitykids.com

General Information · **Places of Worship**

Whether you never miss a Friday/Saturday/Sunday worship, or see religion as an archaic bastion of hypocrisy, there may be a time when you need to find a place of worship in the city. Maybe because it's Easter and it'd make your mom feel better if you went, or your nephew is getting bar mitzvahed, or because they'll probably let you use the bathroom…

The faiths practiced in New York are as diverse as the people who live here, ranging from Catholic and Protestant churches to Buddhist temples to quasi-religious fringe freak faiths. In other words, for people on a spiritual quest, there are plenty of options. If none of the below places attract you in a religious way, many are worth visiting for their significant historical, cultural, or architectural appeal. Some notable places of worship:

Abyssinian Baptist Church—famous politically active Harlem church. Previous pastors include Adam Clayton Powell Sr. and Jr. [Map 22]

African Methodist Episcopal—first African American church in the city, played a crucial role in the Underground Railroad. [Map 21]

Brooklyn Tabernacle—home of the famous Brooklyn Tabernacle Choir. [Map 30]

Cathedral of St. John the Divine—largest Gothic cathedral in the world. [Map 18]

Mosque no. 7/Masjid Malcolm Shabazz—Malcolm X served as imam here from 1954-1965. [Map 19]

Riverside Church—boasts the world's largest carillon bell tower. [Map 18]

St. Patrick's Cathedral—largest Roman Catholic cathedral in the US. [Map 12]

St. Paul's Chapel—NY's only church built before the Revolution; relief center during 9/11 aftermath. [Map 1]

Temple Emanu-El—largest Jewish house of worship in the world. [Map 15]

Trinity Church—downtown landmark since 1698; current building dates to1846. [Map 1]

The Watchtower—international headquarters of the Jehovah's Witness. [Map 30]

Denomination Key:

B=Baptist	Mo=Morman
Bu=Buddhist	Mu=Muslim
C=Catholic	ND=Non-denominational
E=Episcopal	O=Orthodox
J=Jewish	OP=Other Protestant
L=Lutheran	P=Presbyterian
M=Methodist	Pe=Pentacostal

Map 1 · Financial District

Bu	True Buddha Diamond Temple	105 Washington St
C	Our Lady of Victory Church	60 William St
C	St Elizabeth Ann Seton Shrine	7 State St
C	St Joseph's Chapel	385 South End Ave
E	St Paul's Chapel	209 Broadway
E	Trinity Church	Broadway & Wall St
M	St John's United Methodist Church	44 John St

Map 3 · City Hall / Chinatown

B	Chinese Conservative Baptist	103 Madison St
B	Mariners' Temple Buddhist Church	3 Henry St
Bu	Eastern States Buddhist Temple	64 Mott St
Bu	Faith Vow Ded Buddhist Association	130 Lafayette St # 2
Bu	Mahayana Temple Buddhist Association	133 Canal St
Bu	Society of Buddhist Studies	214 Centre St
Bu	Transworld Buddhist Association	7 East Broadway
C	Most Precious Blood Church	113 Baxter St
C	St Andrew's Roman Catholic Church	20 Cardinal Hayes Pl
C	St Joseph's Church	5 Monroe St
C	Transfiguration Catholic Church	29 Mott St
C	Church Our Saviour	48 Henry St
E	Seamen's Church	241 Water St
J	Civic Center Synagogue (Orthodox)	49 White St
L	True Light Lutheran Church	195 Worth St
M	Chinese United Methodist Church	69 Madison St
Mo	Church of Jesus Christ of Latter Day Saints	401 Broadway
Or	St Barbara Greek Orthodox Church	27 Forsyth St
P	First Chinese Presbyterian Church	61 Henry St

Map 4 · Lower East Side

C	St Mary's Church	440 Grand St
C	St Teresa's Church	141 Henry St
E	St Augustine's Episcopal Church	333 Madison St
J	Mesivtha Tifereth Jerusalem (Orthodox)	145 East Broadway
J	Young Israel Synagogue	225 East Broadway
Pe	Primitive Christian Church	207 East Broadway

Map 5 · West Village

B	Legree Baptist Church	362 W 125th St
C	Our Lady of Guadalupe C Church	328 W 14th St
C	Our Lady of Pompeii Church	25 Carmine St
E	St John's in the Village	224 Waverly St
E	St Luke in the Fields Church	487 Hudson St
J	A Greenwich Village Synagogue	53 Charles St
L	St John's Lutheran Church	81 Christopher St
M	Metropolitan-Duane United Church	201 W 13th St
ND	Village Church	232 W 11th St
ND	Abounding Grace	9 E 7th St
OP	Manhattan Seventh Day Adventist Church	232 W 11th St

Map 6 · Washington Sq/NY/NoHo/SoHo

	Baha'i Faith (Islamic)	53 E 11th St
	Dianetics Temple Hubbard (Scientology)	4 W 43th St
B	Judson Memorial Church	55 Washington Sq
C	Nativity Church	44 Second Ave
C	Old St Patrick's Cathedral	263 Mulberry St
C	Our Lady of Loreto	18 Bleecker St
C	St Cyril's Church	62 St Mark's Pl
C	St George's Ukrainian C	30 E 7th St
E	Church of the Ascension	Fifth Ave & 10th St
E	First Presbyterian Church	12 W 12th St
E	Grace Church	802 Broadway
J	Conservative Synagogue-5th Ave	11 E 11th St
M	Church of All Nations	48 St Mark's Pl
M	Washington Square United M	135 W 4th St

General Information · **Places of Worship**

Map 6 · *continued*

O Russian Orthodox Cathedral of the Holy Virgin Protection	59 E 2nd St
OP Christian Science Church 10th	171 MacDougal St
OP Middle Church (Dutch Reformed)	50 E 7th St
OP NY Chinese Alliance Church	162 Eldridge St

Map 7 · East Village / Lower East Side

- Islamic Council of America (Islamic)	401 E 11th St
B Greater New Hope Missionary Baptist Church of Christ	507 E 11th St
C Church of Mary Help-Christians	440 E 12th St
C Immaculate Conception Church	414 E 14th St
C Most Holy Redeemer Church	173 E 3rd St
C St Emeric's Church	740 E 13th St
C St Stanislaus B&M Church	101 E 7th St
J Congregation Meseritz Synagogue (Orthodox)	451 E 6th St
L Trinity Lower East Side Lutheran	602 E 9th St
ND East Side Tabernacle	6163 Rivington St
ND Father's Heart Church	545 E 11th St
OP Church of Christ	257 E 10th St
OP DeWitt Reformed Church	280 Rivington St
Pe Citylight Church	121 E 7th St

Map 8 · Chelsea

C St Columba Church	343 W 25th St
C St Michael's C Church	424 W 34th St
E Holy Apostles Episcopal Church	296 Ninth Ave
E St Peter's E Church	346 W 20th St
J Congregation Beth Israel (Modern Orthodox)	347 W 34th St
ND Chelsea Community Church	346 W 20th St
ND Metropolitan Community Church	446 W 36th St

Map 9 · Flatiron / Lower Midtown

B Madison Ave Baptist Church	129 Madison Ave
Bu Shambhala Meditation Center of NY (Tibetan)	118 W 22nd St #6
C Church of Holy Innocents	128 W 37th St
C Church of Holy Innocents	128 W 37th St
C Church of St Francis	135 W 31st St
C St Francis Church	135 W 31st St
C St Francis Xavier Church	30 W 16th St
C St Vincent de Paul Church	116 W 24th St
E Church of the Incarnation	209 Madison Ave
J Congregation Emunath Israel (Orthodox)	236 W 23rd St
J Metropolitan Synagogue of NY (Reformed)	40 E 35th St
J United Synagogue of America (Conservative)	155 Fifth Ave
J Young Israel of 5th Ave (Orthodox)	3 W 16th St
M Japanese American United Church	255 Seventh Ave
ND Aquarian Foundation	139 W 35th St
OP Community Church of New York (Unitarian)	40 E 35th St
OP French Evangelical Church	126 W 16th St
OP Unity Church of New York	230 W 29th St

Map 10 · Murray Hill / Gramercy

C Church of Our Saviour	59 Park Ave
C Our Lady of the Scapular & St Stephen's Church	149 E 29th St
C Sacred Hearts Church	307 E 33rd St
E St Ann's Church for the Deaf	209 E 16th St
J East End Temple (Reformed)	245 E 17th St
J Society of Jewish Science	109 E 39th St
L Christ Lutheran Church (Evangelical)	355 E 19th St
L Lutheran Church of Gustavus	155 E 22nd St
O Diocese of the Armenian Church	630 Second Ave
O Greek Orthodox Church of St John the B	143 E 17th St
O St Illuminators Cathedral (Armenian)	221 E 27th St
OP Armenian Evangelical Church	152 E 34th St
OP First Moravian Church	154 Lexington Ave
OP Manhattan Mennonite Fellowship	15th St & Second Ave
P Remnant Presbyterian Church	206 E 29th St

Map 11 · Hell's Kitchen

B Metro Baptist Church	410 W 40th St
C Church of the Sacred Heart of Jesus	457 W 51st St
C St Paul the Apostle Church	415 W 59th St
E St Clement's Episcopal Church	423 W 46th St
J Congregation Ezrath Israel (Conservative)	339 W 47th St
ND Rauschenbusch Memorial United Church in Christ	422 W 57th St
OP Crossroads Seventh Day Church	410 W 45th St
P First Presbyterian Church	424 W 51st St
P Trinity Presbyterian Church	422 W 57th St

Map 12 · Midtown

B First Corinthian Baptist Church	1912 Seventh Ave
B Shiloh Baptist Church	2226 Seventh Ave
C St Patrick's Cathedral	460 Fifth Ave
E St Mary the Virgin Church	145 W 46th St
E St Thomas Church Fifth Ave	1 W 53rd St
J Chabad Lubavitch of Midtown (Orthodox)	509 Fifth Ave
J Garment Center Congregation (Modern Orthodox)	205 W 40th St
L St Luke's Lutheran Church	308 W 46th St
L Swedish Seamen's Church	5 E 48th St
M Salem United M Church	2190 Seventh Ave
ND Harvest Christian Fellowship	130 W 56th St
O St George Greek Orthodox Church	307 W 54th St
OP Christian Science Church	9 E 43rd St
OP Fifth Church of Christ Scientist	9 E 43rd St
OP First Church of Religious Science (Metaphysical)	14 E 48th St
OP Lamb's Church of the Nazarene	130 W 44th St
P Fifth Ave Presbyterian Church	7 W 55th St

Map 13 · East Midtown

C Church of St Agnes	143 E 43rd St
C Holy Family Church	315 E 47th St
C St John Evangelist Church	348 E 55th St
J Central Synagogue	123 E 55th St
J Conservative Synagogue (Conservative)	308 E 55th St
L St Peter's Lutheran Church	619 Lexington Ave
OP Sacred Center for Spiritual Living (New Thought Church)	111 E 59th St

Map 14 · Upper West Side (Lower)

B First Baptist Church	265 W 79th St
Bu Karma Thegwum Choling	412 West End Ave
C Blessed Sacrament Church	152 W 71st St
C Holy Trinity Roman Catholic	213 W 82nd St
E All Angels Church	251 W 80th St
E Church-St Matthew & St Timothy	26 W 84th St
E St Matthew & St Timothy Church	26 W 84th St
J Congregation Habonim (Conservative)	44 W 66th St
J Congregation Rodeph Sholom (Reformed)	7 W 83rd St
J Congregation Shearith Israel (Sephardic Orthodox)	8 W 70th St
J Lincoln Square Synagogue (Modern Orthodox)	200 Amsterdam Ave
J West End Synagogue (Reconstructionist)	190 Amsterdam Ave
J West Side Synagogue (Modern Orthodox)	120 W 76th St
L Holy Trinity Lutheran Church	3 W 65th St
L Lutheran Church of the Holy Trinity	65 Central Park W
ND Church of Humanism & Humanist	250 W 85th St
ND Vision Church	2 W 64th St
OP Christian Science Church	10 W 68th St
OP Collegiate Reformed Church	368 West End Ave
OP West End Collegiate Church (Dutch Reform)	368 West End Ave
OP World Wide Church of God (Evangelical)	2 W 64th St
P Good Shepherd-Faith Church	152 W 66th St
P Rutgers Church	236 W 73rd St

General Information · **Places of Worship**

Map 15 · Upper East Side (Lower)

-	Dianetics Foundation Hubbard (Scientology)	65 E 82nd St
B	Trinity Baptist Church	250 E 61st St
Bu	Zen Studies Society	223 E 67th St
C	Our Lady of Peace	237 E 62nd St
C	St Catherine of Siena Church	411 E 68th St
C	St Ignatius Church (Jesuit)	53 E 83rd St
C	St Jean Be Church	184 E 76th St
C	St John Nepomucene Church	411 E 66th St
C	St Monica's Church	413 E 79th St
C	St Stephens of Hungary Church	414 E 82nd St
E	Church of the Epiphany	1393 York Ave
E	Church of the Resurrection	115 E 74th St
E	St James' Episcopal Church	865 Madison Ave
J	Congregation of Zarua (Conservative Traditional)	127 E 82nd St
J	Congregation Zichron Ephraim (Orthodox)	164 E 68th St
J	Fifth Avenue Synagogue (Modern Orthodox)	5 E 62nd St
J	Lisker Congregation	163 E 69th St
J	Manhattan Sephardic Congregation (Orthodox)	325 E 75th St
J	Temple Emanu-El (Reformed)	1 E 65th St
J	Temple Israel-City-NY (Reformed)	112 E 75th St
J	Temple Shaaray Tefila (Reformed)	250 E 79th St
J	Temple-Universal Judaism (Reformed)	1010 Park Ave
L	Zion St Mark's Church	424 E 84th St
M	Christ Church United Methodist	520 Park Ave
M	Koryo United Methodist Church	150 E 62nd St
M	Lexington United Methodist Church	150 E 62nd St
O	Greek Orthodox Cathedral	319 E 74th St
O	Hellenic Eastern Orthodox Church (Greek)	319 E 74th St
O	Holy Trinity Cathedral (Greek)	319 E 74th St
OP	Christian Science Church	103 E 77th St
OP	Christian Science Church	583 Park Ave
OP	Unitarian Church of All Souls	1157 Lexington Ave
P	Madison Ave Presbyterian Church	921 Madison Ave

Map 16 · Upper West Side (Upper)

B	Central Baptist Church of NY	166 W 92nd St
B	Southern Baptist Church	12 W 108th St
Bu	New York Buddhist Church	332 Riverside Dr
C	Ascension Catholic Church	221 W 107th St
C	Church of St Gregory	144 W 90th St
E	St Ignatius Episcopal Church	552 West End Ave
J	Ansche Chesed Temple (Conservative)	251 W 100th St
J	Congregation Ohab Zedek (Orthodox)	118 W 95th St
J	Congregation Shaare Zedek (Conservative)	212 W 93rd St
L	Advent Lutheran Church	2504 Broadway
L	Trinity Lutheran Church	168 W 100th St
M	St Paul & St Andrew Methodist	West End Ave & W 86th St
O	Evangelismos Greek Orthodox	302 W 91st St
O	Greek Orthodox Community	149 W 105th St
P	Second P Church	6 W 96th St
P	West End Presbyterian Church	165 W 105th St
P	West Park Presbyterian Church	165 W 86th St

Map 17 · Upper East Side / East Harlem

-	Ramakrishna-Vivekananda Center (Hindu)	17 E 94th St
B	East Ward Missionary Baptist	2011 First Ave
C	Church of the Holy Agony	1834 Third Ave
C	Church of St Thomas More	65 E 89th St
C	Our Lady of Good Counsel Church	230 E 90th St
C	St Cecilia's Parish Service	125 E 105th St
C	St Francis De Sales Church	135 E 96th St
C	St Joseph's Church	404 W 87th St
C	St Lucy Catholic Church	344 E 104th St
E	Church of the Heavenly Rest	2 E 90th St
E	Church of the Holy Trinity	316 E 88th St
E	Church of the Holy Trinity	316 E 88th St
E	St Edward the Martyr	14 E 109th St
J	Park Avenue Synagogue (Conservative)	50 E 87th St
L	Immanuel Lutheran Church	122 E 88th St
M	Park Avenue Church	106 E 86th St
ND	Church of the Resurrection	325 E 101st St
ND	City Church New York	111 E 87th St
O	Synod of Bishops Russian Church	75 E 93rd St
OP	Bethany Christian Church (Spanish-speaking Assembly of God)	131 E 103rd St
OP	Church of Advent Hope (Seventh Day Adventist)	111 E 87th St
OP	Church of the Living Hope (United Church of Christ)	161 E 104th St
P	Brick Presbyterian Church	62 E 92nd St
Pe	Healing Stream Deliverance Church	121 E 106th St

Map 18 · Columbia / Morningside Hts

B	Antioch Buddhist Church	515 W 125th St
B	St Luke Baptist Church	103 Morningside Ave
C	Annunciation Rectory	88 Convent Ave
C	Church of Notre Dame	405 W 114th St
C	Corpus Christi Catholic Church	529 W 121st St
C	Timplo Biblico Church	503 W 126th St
E	Cathedral of St John the Divine	1047 Amsterdam Ave
E	St Mary's Episcopal Church	521 W 126th St
J	Congregation Ramath Orah (Orthodox)	550 W 110th St
M	Emanuel African Methodist Episcopal Church	3741 W 119th St
M	Korean Methodist Church	633 W 115th St
ND	Manhattan Grace Tabernacle	2929 Broadway
ND	Riverside Church	91 Claremont Ave
P	Broadway Presbyterian Church	601 W 114th St
Pe	Gethsemane Revival Holiness	463 W 125th St
Pe	Manhattan Pentecostal Church	541 W 125th St

Map 19 • Harlem (Lower)

B	Beulah Baptist Church	125 W 130th St
B	Canaan Baptist Church	132 W 116th St
B	Christ Temple Baptist Church	161 W 131st St
B	Friendship Baptist Church	144 W 131st St
B	Greater Central Baptist Church	2152 Fifth Ave
B	Greater Metropolitan Baptist Church	147 W 123rd St
B	Memorial Baptist Church	141 W 115th St
B	Metropolitan Baptist Church	151 W 128th St
B	Mt Nebo Baptist Church	1883 Seventh Ave
B	Mt Pisgah Baptist Church	30 W 126th St
B	Second Canaan Baptist Church	10 Lenox Ave
B	Second Providence Baptist Church	11 W 116th St
B	St Thomas the Apostle	262 W 118th St
E	All Souls Church	88 St Nicholas Ave
E	St Ambrose Episcopal Church (Episcopal/British)	9 W 130th St
E	St Andrew's Episcopal Church	2067 Fifth Ave
E	St Martin's E Church	230 Lenox Ave
E	St Philips Church	204 W 134th St
L	Church of Transfiguration	74 W 126th St
M	Bethel African Methodist Episcopal Church	60 W 132nd St
M	St James African M E Church	2010 Fifth Ave
Mu	Masjid Malcolm Shabazz Mosque	102 W 116th St
ND	Bethelite Community Church	38 W 123rd St
ND	Faith Mission Christian Church	160 W 129th St
ND	Harlem Grace Tabernacle	180 W 135th St
ND	New Covenent Life Christian	2433 Eighth Ave
ND	Salvation & Deliverance Church	37 W 116th St
OP	Ephesus 7th Day Adventist Church of Harlem	101 W 123rd St
OP	Lively Stone Church Apostolic	161 W 122nd St
OP	NY United Sabbath Day Church (Seventh Day Adventist)	145 W 110th St
OP	Shiloh Church of Christ	5 W 128th St #7
OP	Tabernacle of Prayer	139 W 126th St
Pe	Kelly Temple Church of God in Christ	8 E 130th St
Pe	Pilgrim Cathedral of Harlem	15 W 126th St
Pe	Refuge Temple	2081 Seventh Ave
Pe	United House of Prayer For All	2320 Eighth Ave

Map 20 • El Barrio

-	Church of Scientology (Scientology)	2250 Third Ave
B	Church of the Crucified Christ	350 E 120th St
C	All Saints Church	47 E 129th St
C	Church of Our Lady of Mt Carmel	448 E 116th St
C	St Ann's Roman Catholic Church	312 E 110th St
M	Madison Ave United Methodist Church	1723 Madison Ave
M	Metropolitan Community Church	1975 Madison Ave
ND	Holy Tabernacle Church	407 E 114th St
ND	Hosanna City Church	240 E 123rd St
ND	United Moravian Church	200 E 127th St
OP	Elmendorf Reformed Church	171 E 121st St
OP	Kingdom Hall of Jehovah's Witness	1763 Madison Ave
Pe	Christ Apostolic Church	160 E 112th St
Pe	Community Pentecostal Church	214 E 111th St
Pe	Greater Highway Church of Christ	132 E 111th St

Map 21 • Manhattanville / Hamilton Hts

C	Church of Our Lady of Esperanza (Spanish speaking)	624 W 156th St
C	Our Lady of Lourdes Church	463 W 142nd St
C	Convent Avenue Baptist Church	420 W 145th St
B	Jehovah-Jireh Baptist Church	536 W 148th St
B	Macedonia Baptist Church	452 W 147th St
B	St John Baptist Church	448 W 152nd St
E	African Methodist Episcopal	140 W 137th St
E	Church of the Intercession	550 W 155th St
E	St Luke's Episcopal Church	435 W 141st St
M	Mt Calvary Methodist Church	116 Edgecombe Ave
M	United Methodist Church	53 Edgecombe Ave
O	Russian Holy Fathers Church	524 W 153rd St
OP	Christian Science Church	555 W 141st St
P	North Presbyterian Church	525 W 155th St
P	St James Presbyterian Church	409 W 141st St
Pe	Bethel Holy Church of Mt Sinai	922 St Nicholas Ave

Map 22 • Harlem (Upper)

B	Abyssinian Baptist Church	132 W 138th St
B	Bethany Baptist Church	303 W 153rd St
B	Mt Calvary Baptist Church	231 W 142nd St
C	Church of St Mark	65 W 138th St
C	Resurrection Roman Catholic Church	276 W 151st St
C	St Charles Church	211 W 141st St
C	St Mark Evangelist Catholic	65 W 138th St
C	St Thomas Liberal Catholic Church	147 W 144th St
ND	Calvery Christian Fellowship	2350 Fifth Ave
ND	Harlem Tabernacle	2350 Fifth Ave
Pe	First Emmanuel Church of Jesus	270 W 153rd St
P	Rendall Memorial Presbyterian	59 W 137th St

Map 23 • Washington Heights

B	Primera Iglesia Ba	96 Wadsworth Ave
C	Christ United Church & the United Palace	4140 Broadway
C	Church of the Incarnation	1290 St Nicholas Ave
C	St Rose of Lima Church	510 W 165th St
J	Congregation Shaare (Orthodox)	711 W 179th St
M	Christ United Church	4140 Broadway
O	St Spyridon Church (Greek)	124 Wadsworth Ave
O	Washington Heights Hellenic Orthodox (Greek)	124 Wadsworth Ave
OP	Collegiate Reformed Church	729 W 181st St
OP	Correa Miguel (Evangelical)	507 W 159th St

Map 24 • Fort George / Fort Tryon

B	Wadsworth Ave B Church	210 Wadsworth Ave
C	Our Lady Queen of Martyrs	71 Arden St
C	St Elizabeth's Church	268 Wadsworth Ave
L	Our Saviors Atonement	178 Bennett Ave
J	Congregation K'Hal Adath Jeshurun (Orthodox)	85 Bennett Ave
J	Fort Tryon J Center (Reformed)	524 Ft Washington Ave

Map 25 • Inwood

C	Church of the Good Shepherd	4967 Broadway
C	St Jude's Roman C Church	431 W 204th St
E	Holy Trinity E Church	20 Cumming St
Mo	The Church of Jesus Christ of Latter Day Saints (Inwood 1st Ward) (Mormon meeting house)	1815 Riverside Dr
ND	Manhattan Bible Church	3816 Ninth Ave
Pe	Narrow Door Church	161 Sherman Ave

Roosevelt Island

C	Sacred Heart of Jesus Church	206 Main St
C	St Mary's Roman C Church	201 Main St

285

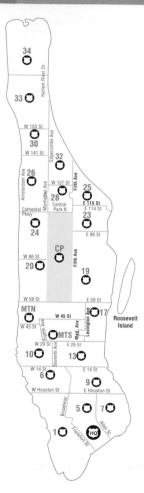

Important Phone Numbers

All Emergencies:	911
Non-Emergencies:	311
Terrorism Hot Line:	888-NYC-SAFE
Crime Stoppers:	800-577-TIPS
Crime Stoppers (Spanish):	888-57-PISTA
Sex Crimes Report Line:	212-267-RAPE
Crime Victims Hotline:	212-577-7777
Cop Shot:	800-COP-SHOT
Missing Persons Case Status:	646-610-6914
Missing Persons Squad:	212-473-2042
Operation Gun Stop:	866-GUNSTOP
Organized Crime Control	
Bureau Drug Line:	888-374-DRUG
Complaints (Internal Affairs):	212-741-8401
Website:	www.ci.nyc.ny.us/html/nypd/home.html

Statistics

	2003	2002	2001	2000
Uniformed Personnel	37,200			39,778
Murders	596	584	643	671
Rapes	1,877	2,013	1,917	2,067
Robberies	25,890	27,124	27,863	32,231
Felony Assaults	18,717	20,700	22,994	25,854
Burglaries	29,120	31,250	32,663	38,241
Grand Larcenies	46,518	45,461	46,115	49,381
Grand Larcenies (cars)	23,144	26,339	29,619	35,602

Precinct	Address	Phone	Map
1	16 Ericsson Pl	212-334-0611	2
5	19 Elizabeth St	212-334-0711	3
6	233 W 10th St	212-741-4811	5
7	19 1/2 Pitt St	212-477-7311	4
9	130 Ave C	212-477-7811	7
10	230 W 20th St	212-741-8211	9
13	230 E 21st St	212-477-7411	10
Mid-Town South	357 W 35th St	212-239-9811	8
17	167 E 51st St	212-826-3211	13
Mid-Town North	306 W 54th St	212-760-8300	11
19	153 E 67th St	212-452-0600	15
20	120 W 82nd St	212-580-6411	14
Central Park	86th St & Transverse Road	212-570-4820	
23	162 E 102nd St	212-860-6411	17
24	151 W 100th St	212-678-1811	16
25	120 E 119th St	212-860-6511	20
26	520 W 126th St	212-678-1311	18
28	2271 Eighth Ave	212-678-1611	19
30	451 W 151st St	212-690-8811	21
32	250 W 135th St	212-690-6311	19
33	2207 Amsterdam Ave	212-927-3200	23
34	4295 Broadway	212-927-9711	24

General Information • **Fire Departments**

Since its inception in 1648 (when "prowlers" walked the streets with buckets, hooks, and ladders, looking for fires), the FDNY has grown to include more than 11,400 Fire Officers and fire-fighters, 2,800 Emergency Medical Technicians, Paramedics and Supervisors, and 1,200 civilian employees.

In 2004, the FDNY responded to 27,718 structural fires, 22,437 non-structural fires, and 189,162 medical emergencies, as well as 37,332 malicious false alarms. The Fire Department is currently overseen by Fire Commissioner Nicholas Scoppetta, appointed by Mayor Bloomberg. The Fire Officers and fire-fighters are under the command of the Chief of Department. You can read about the history of each engine and ladder company on the FDNY website at http://nyc.gov/html/fdny. Also check out the history of New York's fire service at http://nyc.gov/html/fdny/html/history/index.shtml.

For those of you who are wondering, an "engine" company runs the smaller trucks with the hoses, while a "ladder" company manages the larger trucks with the large (you guessed it) ladders on the back. An engine and a ladder company may be located together or separately, but usually arrive together when fighting fires.

Map 1 • Financial District	
Engine 10, Ladder 10	124 Liberty St
Engine 4, Ladder 15	42 South St

Map 2 • TriBeCa	
Ladder 8	14 N Moore St

Map 3 • City Hall / Chinatown	
Engine 55	363 Broome St
Engine 6	49 Beekman St
Engine 7, Ladder 1	100 Duane St
Engine 9, Ladder 6	75 Canal St

Map 4 • Lower East Side	
Engine 15	269 Henry St
Ladder 18	25 Pitt St

Map 5 • West Village	
Engine 24, Ladder 5	227 Sixth Ave

Map 6 • Washington Sq/NYU/NoHo/SoHo	
Engine 33, Ladder 9	42 Great Jones St
Engine 5	340 E 14th St
Ladder 20	251 Lafayette St
Ladder 3	108 E 13th St

Map 7 • East Village / Lower East Side	
Engine 28, Ladder 11	222 E 2nd St

Map 8 • Chelsea	
Engine 34, Ladder 21	440 W 38th St

Map 9 • Flatiron / Lower Midtown	
Engine 1, Ladder 24	142 W 31st St
Engine 14	14 E 18th St
Engine 26	220 W 37th St
Engine 3, Ladder 12	146 W 19th St

Map 10 • Murray Hill / Gramercy	
Engine 16, Ladder 7	234 E 29th St

Map 11 • Hell's Kitchen	
Rescue 1	530 W 43rd St

Map 12 • Midtown	
Engine 23	215 W 58th St
Engine 54, Ladder 4	782 Eighth Ave
Engine 65	33 W 43rd St

Map 13 • East Midtown	
Engine 21	238 E 40th St
Engine 8, Ladder 2	165 E 51st St

Map 14 • Upper West Side (Lower)	
Engine 40, Ladder 35	133 Amsterdam Ave
Engine 74	120 W 83rd St
Ladder 25	205 W 77th St

Map 15 • Upper East Side (Lower)	
Engine 22, Ladder 13	159 E 85th St
Engine 39, Ladder 16	157 E 67th St
Engine 44	221 E 75th St

Map 16 • Upper West Side (Upper)	
Engine 76, Ladder 22	145 W 100th St

Map 17 • Upper East Side / East Harlem	
Engine 53, Ladder 43	1836 Third Ave

Map 18 • Columbia/Morningside Heights	
Engine 37, Ladder 40	415 W 125th St
Engine 47	502 W 113th St

Map 19 • Harlem (Lower)	
Engine 58, Ladder 26	1367 Fifth Ave
Engine 59, Ladder 30	111 W 133rd St

Map 20 • El Barrio	
Engine 35, Ladder 14	2282 Third Ave
Engine 36	120 E 125th St
Engine 91	242 E 111th St

Map 21 • Manhattanville/Hamilton Heights	
Engine 80, Ladder 23	503 W 139th St

Map 22 • Harlem (Upper)	
Engine 69, Ladder 28	248 W 143rd St

Map 23 • Washington Heights	
Engine 67	518 W 170th St
Engine 84, Ladder 34	515 W 161st St
Engine 93, Ladder 45	515 W 181st St

Map 25 • Inwood	
Engine 95, Ladder 36	29 Vermilyea Ave

General Information • **Hospitals**

Generally, if you have to get to a hospital, it's best to go to the closest one. As a quick reference, this is a list of largest hospitals by neighborhood. Obviously, we recommend going to the map page for your neighborhood to see the location of these and all hospitals in your area:

Lower Manhattan: NYU Downtown Hospital • William & Beekman Sts, just south of the Brooklyn Bridge • [Map 3]

West Village/Chelsea: St Vincent's • Seventh Ave & 12th St [Map 5]

East Village: Beth Israel Medical Center • 14th St & Broadway/Union Square • [Map 10]

Murray Hill: Bellevue Hospital Center • First Ave & 27th St [Map 10]

Hell's Kitchen/Upper West Side: St Luke's Roosevelt Hospital • 10th Ave & 58th St [Map 10]

East Side: New York Presbyterian • York Ave & 68th St [Map 15]; Lenox Hill Hospital • Lexington Ave & 77th St [Map 15]; Mt Sinai Medical Center • Madison Ave & 101st St [Map 17]

Columbia/Morningside Heights: St Luke's Hospital Center • Amsterdam Ave & 114th St [Map 18]

El Barrio: North General Hospital • Madison Ave & 125th St [Map 20]

Farther Uptown: Columbia Presbyterian Medical Center • 168th St & Broadway [Map 23]

If you have a condition that isn't immediately threatening, certain hospitals in New York specialize and excel in specific areas of medicine:

Cancer: Memorial Sloan-Kettering

Birthing Center/Labor & Delivery: St Luke's Roosevelt

Digestive Disorders: Mt Sinai

Ear, Nose and Throat: Mt Sinai

Eyes: New York Eye and Ear Infirmary

Geriatrics: Mt Sinai, New York Presbyterian

Heart: New York Presbyterian

Hormonal Disorders: New York Presbyterian

Kidney Disease: New York Presbyterian

Mental Health: Bellevue

Neurology: New York Presbyterian, NYU Medical Center

Orthopedics: Hospital for Special Surgery, New York Presbyterian

Pediatrics: Children's Hospital of New York Presbyterian

Psychiatry: New York Presbyterian, NYU Medical Center

Rheumatology: Hospital for Special Surgery, Hospital for Joint Diseases Orthopedic Institute, NYU Medical Center

Hospital	Address	Phone	Map
Bellevue Hospital Center	462 First Ave	212-562-4141	10
Beth Israel Medical Center	281 First Ave	212-420-2000	10
Brooklyn Hospital Center	121 DeKalb Ave	718-250-8000	31
Cabrini Medical Center	227 E 20th St	212-995-6000	10
Coler Goldwater-Coler Campus(No ER)	900 Main St	212-848-6000	p212
Coler Goldwater-Goldwater Campus	1 Main St	212-848-6000	p212
Columbia-Presbyterian Allen Pavilion	5141 Broadway	212-932-4000	25
Columbia-Presbyterian Medical Center	622 W 168th St	212-305-2500	23
Harlem Hospital Center	506 Lenox Ave	212-939-1000	22
Hospital for Joint Diseases	301 E 17th St	212-598-6000	10
Lenox Hill	120 E 77th St	212-434-2000	15
Long Island College	339 Hicks St	718-780-1000	32
Manhattan Eye, Ear & Throat	210 E 64th St	212-838-9200	15
Metropolitan	1901 First Ave	212-423-6262	17
Mt Sinai Medical Center	1468 Madison Ave	212-241-6500	17
New York Eye & Ear Infirmary	310 E 14th St	212-979-4000	6
New York Presbyterian–Weill Cornell Medical Center	525 E 68th St	212-746-5454	15
North General	1879 Madison Ave	212-423-4000	20
New York Methodist	506 6th St	718-780-3000	33
NYU Downtown	170 William St	212-312-5000	3
NYU Medical Center: Tisch	560 First Ave	212-263-7300	10
St Clare's	426 W 52nd St	212-586-1500	11
St Luke's Hospital Center	1111 Amsterdam Ave	212-523-4000	18
St Luke's Roosevelt Hospital Center	1000 Tenth Ave	212-523-4000	11
St Vincent's Hospital & Medical Center	153 W 11th St	212-604-7000	5
VA Hospital	423 E 23rd St	212-686-7500	10

In addition to the regular branch system of the New York Public Library, there are several specialized "research" libraries in Manhattan. The **Schomburg Center for Research in Black Culture** contains a wealth of material on the history of African-Americans. The **Science, Industry, and Business Library** is perhaps the newest and swankiest of all of Manhattan's libraries. **The Library for the Performing Arts** contains a wonderful archive of New York City theater on film and tape. **The Early Childhood Resource and Information Center** runs workshops for parenting and reading programs for children. And, of course, the main branch of the **New York Public Library** (one of Manhattan's architectural treasures, designed by Carrere and Hastings in 1897) has several special collections and services, such as the Humanities and Social Sciences Library, the Map Division, Exhibition galleries, and divisions dedicated to various ethnic groups. The main branch contains 88 miles of shelves and has over 10,000 current periodicals from almost 150 countries. There is also the **Andrew Heiskell Library for the Blind and Physically Handicapped,** designed to be barrier-free. The library contains large collections of special format materials and audio equipment for listening to recorded books and magazines. You can check out the full system online at www.nypl.org.

Library	Address	Phone	Map
115th St (closed for renovation)	203 W 115th St	212-666-9393	19
125th St	224 E 125th St	212-534-5050	20
58th St	127 E 58th St	212-759-7358	13
67th St (closed for renovation)	328 E 67th St	212-734-1717	15
96th Street	112 E 96th St	212-289-0908	17
Aguilar	174 E 110th St	212-534-2930	20
Andrew Heiskell Library for the Blind	40 W 20th St	212-206-5400	9
Bloomingdale	150 W 100th St	212-222-8030	16
Chatham Square	33 East Broadway	212-964-6598	3
Columbus (closed for renovation)	742 Tenth Ave	212-586-5098	11
Countee Cullen	104 W 136th St	212-491-2070	22
Donnell Library Center	20 W 53rd St	212-621-0618	12
Early Childhood Resource & Information Center	66 Leroy St	212-929-0815	5
Epiphany	228 E 23rd St	212-679-2645	10
Fort Washington	535 W 179th St	212-927-3533	23
George Bruce	518 W 125th St	212-662-9727	18
Hamilton Fish Park	415 E Houston St	212-673-2290	7
Hamilton Grange	503 W 145th St	212-926-2147	21
Harlem	115th St (temporary location)	212-666-9393	19
Harlem	9 W 124th St	212-348-5620	19
Hudson Park	66 Leroy St	212-243-6876	5
Humanities & Social Sciences Library	42nd St & Fifth Ave	212-930-0830	12
Inwood	4790 Broadway	212-942-2445	25
Jefferson Market	425 Sixth Ave	212-243-4334	5
Kips Bay	446 Third Ave	212-683-2520	10
Macomb's Bridge	2650 Adam Clayton Powell Jr Blvd	212-281-4900	22
Mid-Manhattan Library	455 Fifth Ave	212-340-0833	12
Morningside Heights Library	2900 Broadway	212-864-2530	18
Muhlenberg	209 W 23rd St	212-924-1585	9
New Amsterdam	9 Murray St	212-732-8186	3
New York Academy of Medicine Library	1216 Fifth Ave	212-822-7200	17
New York Public Library for the Performing Arts	40 Lincoln Center Plz	212-870-1630	14
New York Society Library	53 E 79th St	212-288-6900	15
NYC Municipal Archives	31 Chambers St	212-788-8580	3
Ottendorfer	135 Second Ave	212-674-0947	6
Riverside	127 Amsterdam Ave	212-870-1810	14
Roosevelt Island	524 Main St	212-308-6243	p212
Schomburg Center for Research in Black Culture	515 Malcolm X Blvd	212-491-2200	22
Science, Industry, and Business Library	188 Madison Ave	212-592-7000	9
Seward Park	192 East Broadway	212-477-6770	4
St Agnes	444 Amsterdam Ave	212-877-4380	14
Terence Cardinal Cooke-Cathedral	560 Lexington Ave	212-752-3824	13
Tompkins Square	331 E 10th St	212-228-4747	7
Washington Heights	1000 St Nicholas Ave	212-923-6054	23
Webster	1465 York Ave	212-288-5049	15
Yorkville	222 E 79th St	212-744-5824	15

From the "Muscle Marys" of Chelsea to the grungy rock-and-roll homos of the East Village, New York offers a diverse range of men and the places they play. Strangely, the gay scene in NYC is barely visible in daylight, as most clubs don't get busy before midnight. To see the boys during the day, check out the **Big Cup** coffee shop on Eighth Avenue and 22nd Street. Otherwise, enjoy the museums and shopping before taking your disco-nap to explore the city that never sleeps—perhaps as a result of all the "Tina" in this town.

If you're a lesbian venturing into New York City with high hopes of finding a hot soccer mom, turn around, girlfriend, because they live on the other side of the tunnel. And even if you think you might find her sipping on a Miller Light at old **Henrietta Hudson**, stay away, because the bar is notorious for its intolerable bathroom line. There are few venues in Manhattan that cater to the lesbian crowd full-time—instead you'll need to hit the weeknight girl parties dotted around the island. Check out **Starlight** on Sunday nights for the hotties. For an up-to-the-minute list, visit www.gonycmagazine.com. In Brooklyn, check out the patio at **Ginger's** (363 Fifth Ave).

Websites

The Lesbian, Gay, Bisexual & Transgender Community Center: www.gaycenter.org — Information about center programs, meetings, publications, and events.

Out & About: www.outandabout.com — Travel website for gays and lesbians including destination information, a gay travel calendar, health information, and listings of gay tour operators.

Gayellow Pages: www.gayellowpages.com — Yellow pages of gay/lesbian-owned and gay/lesbian-friendly businesses in the US and Canada.

Dyke TV: www.dyketv.org — Whether you're interested in viewing or contributing, this website has all the info you'll need.

Edwina: www.edwina.com — A NY online meeting place for gays and lesbians looking for love, lust, or just friendship.

Publications

Free at gay and lesbian venues and shops, and some street corners.

HX — Weekly magazine featuring information about bars, clubs, restaurants, events, meetings, and loads of personals. www.hx.com

Gay City News (formerly LGNY) — Newspaper for lesbian and gay New Yorkers including current local and national news items. www.gaycitynews.com

The New York Blade — NYC's only gay-owned and operated weekly newspaper featuring local and national news coverage, as well as guides to theater, nightlife, food, and local arts and entertainment. www.nyblade.com

GO NYC — Monthly magazine for the urban lesbian on the go with free arts and entertainment listings, weekly event picks, plus information on community organizations and LGBT-owned and LGBT friendly-businesses. www.gonycmagazine.com

Bookshops

Creative Visions, 548 Hudson St (212-645-7573) — Gay and lesbian magazines and videos. http://www.creativevisionsbooks.com

Bluestockings, 172 Allen St (212-777-6028) — Lesbian/radical bookstore and activist center with regular readings and a fair-trade café. www.bluestockings.com

Health Centers and Support Organizations

Callen-Lorde Community Health Center, 356 W 18th St (212-271-7200) — Primary Care Center for GLBT New Yorkers. www.callen-lorde.org

Gay Men's Health Crisis, 119 W 24th St (212-367-1000; Hotline: 212-807-6655) — Non-profit organization dedicated to AIDS awareness and support for those with the disease. www.gmhc.org

The Lesbian, Gay, Bisexual & Transgender Community Center, 208 W 13th (212-620-7310) — The largest LGBT multi-service organization on the East Coast. www.gaycenter.org

Gay and Lesbian National Hotline, (212-989-0999) — Switchboard for referrals, advice, and counseling. www.glnh.org

PFLAG, 109 E 50th St (212-463-0629) — Parents, Families, and Friends of Lesbians and Gays meet on the second Sunday of every month 3 pm-5 pm for mutual support. www.pflagnyc.org

Lesbian and Gay Immigration Rights Task Force (LGIRTF), 350 W 31st St, Ste 505 (212-714-2904) — Advocates for changing US policy on immigration of permanent partners. www.lgirtf.org

GLAAD (Gay and Lesbian Alliance Against Defamation), 248 W 35th St, 8th fl (212-629-3322) — These are the folks who go to bat for you in the media. www.glaad.org

OUTdancing @ Stepping Out Studios, 37 W 26th St (646-742-9400) — The first GLBT partner dance program in the US. www.steppingoutstudios.com

Annual Events

Pride Week — Usually the last full week in June; www.hopinc.org (212-807-7433)

New York Gay and Lesbian Film Festival — Showcase of international gay and lesbian films, May/June; www.newfestival.org (212-571-2170)

AIDS Action Ride — Replacing the old NYC to Boston AIDS ride, this version is a three-day, 225-mile ride across Massachusetts. The ride begins in Pittsfeld and finishes in Salem, mid-August; www.aidsactionride.org (617-450-1100 or 888-MASSRIDE)

Venues — Lesbian

- **Bar d'O** (Mon) · 29 Bedford St · 212-627-1580
- **Club Fahrenheit** (second, fourth Fri) · 95 Leonard St · 917-299-1975
- **Cubbyhole** · 281 W 12th St · 212-243-9041
- **Escuelita** (Fri) · 301 W 39th St · 212-631-1093
- **Girlsroom** · 210 Rivington St · 212-677-6149 · girlsroomnyc.com
- **Halo** (first Mon) · 49 Grove St · 212-243-8885
- **Heaven** (Wed, Fri, Sat) · 579 Sixth Ave · 212-243-6100
- **Henrietta Hudson** · 438 Hudson St · 212-924-3347 · www.henriettahudsons.com
- **Nowhere** (Mon) · 322 E 14th St · 212-477-4744
- **Opaline** (Fri) · 85 Avenue A · 212-995-8684
- **Rubyfruit** · 531 Hudson St · 212-929-3343
- **Slipper Room** (Tues) · 167 Orchard St · 212-253-7246
- **Starlight** (Sun) · 167 Avenue A · 212-475-2172
- **Wonderbar** · 167 Avenue A · 212-475-2172 · www.wonderbarnyc.com

Venues — Gay

- **219 Flamingo** · 219 Second Ave · 212-533-2860
- **Avalon** · 47 W 20th St · 212-807-7780 · www.jblair.com
- **Babalu** · 327 W 44th St · 212-262-1111
- **Barracuda** · 275 W 22nd St · 212-645-8613
- **Barrage** · 401 W 47th St · 212-586-9390
- **Boots & Saddle** · 76 Christopher St · 212-929-9684
- **Boysroom** · 9 Avenue A · 212-995-8684
- **Candle Bar** · 309 Amsterdam Ave · 212-874-9155
- **Chi Chiz** · 135 Christopher St · 212-462-0027
- **Cleo's Ninth Avenue Salon** · 656 Ninth Ave · 212-307-1503

- **The Cock** · 188 Avenue A · 212-777-6254
- **Crobar** · 530 W 28th St · 212-629-9000 · www.crobar.com
- **Dick Bar** · 192 Second Ave · 212-475-2071
- **The Dugout** · 185 Christopher St · 212-242-9113
- **The Duplex** · 61 Christopher St · 212-255-5438 · www.theduplex.com
- **Eagle** · 554 W 28th St · 646-473-1866 · www.eaglenyc.com
- **Escuelita** · 301 W 39th St · 212-631-0588
- **G Lounge** · 225 W 19th St · 212-929-1085 · www.glounge.com
- **Hangar Bar** · 115 Christopher St · 212-627-2044
- **Heaven** · 579 Sixth Ave · 212-243-6100
- **The Hole** · 29 Second Ave · 212-473-9406
- **Marie's Crisis** · 59 Grove St · 212-243-9323
- **The Monster** · 80 Grove St · 212-924-3558 · www.manhattan-monster.com
- **Nowhere** · 322 E 14th St · 212-477-4744
- **OW Bar** · 221 E 58th St · 212-355-3395 · www.owbar.com
- **Pegasus** · 119 E 60th St · 212-888-4702
- **The Phoenix** · 447 E 13th St · 212-477-9979
- **Pieces Bar** · 8 Christopher St · 212-929-9291 · www.piecesbar.com
- **Posh** · 405 W 51st St · 212-957-2222
- **Pyramid Club** · 101 Avenue A · 212-473-7184
- **Rawhide** · 212 Eighth Ave · 212-242-9332
- **Regents** · 317 E 53rd St · 212-593-3001
- **Roxy** · 515 W 18th St · 212-645-5156
- **The Slide** · 356 Bowery · 212-420-8885
- **Splash (SBNY)** · 50 W 17th St · 212-691-0073 · www.splashbar.com
- **Starlight** · 167 Avenue A · 212-475-2172 · www.starlightbarlounge.com
- **Stonewall** · 53 Christopher St · 212-463-0950 · www.stonewall-place.com
- **Tenth Avenue Lounge** · 642 Tenth Ave · 212-245-9088
- **Therapy** · 348 W 52nd St · 212-397-1700 · www.therapy-nyc.com
- **Tool Box** · 1742 Second Ave · 212-348-1288
- **Townhouse** · 236 E 58th St · 212-754-4649 · www.townhouseny.com
- **Ty's** · 114 Christopher St · 212-741-9641
- **Urge** · 33 Second Ave · 212-533-5757
- **View Bar** · 232 Eighth Ave · 212-929-2243
- **The Web** · 40 E 58th St · 212-308-1546
- **XL** · 357 W 16th St · 646-336-5574 · www.XLnewyork.com

New York has more landmarks than you can shake a foam Statue of Liberty crown at, which is good because it means that New Yorkers can enjoy some of them without tackling a crowd of out-of-towners. The landmarks discussed are really idiosyncratic choices, and this list is by no means complete or even logical, but we've included an array of places, from world famous to little known, all worth visiting.

Coolest Skyscrapers

Most visitors to New York go to the top of the **Empire State Building**, but it's far more familiar to New Yorkers from afar—as a directional guide, a tip-off to current holidays, and something you hope your apartment has a view of. If it's class you're looking for, the **Chrysler Building** has it in spades. Unfortunately, this means that only the "classiest" are admitted to the top floors. Other midtown highlights include the **Citicorp Center**, a building that breaks out of the boxy tower form, and the **RCA Building**, one of the steepest looking skyscrapers in the city. More neck-craning excitement can be found in the financial district, including the **Woolworth Building**, the **City Services Building** at 70 Pine Street (with private spire rooms accessible only to the connected), **40 Wall Street**, the **Bankers Trust Company Building**, and **20 Exchange Place**.

Best Bridges

The **Brooklyn Bridge** is undoubtedly the best bridge in New York—aesthetically, historically, and practically (as the constant flow of walkers and bikers proves). It's also worth walking across the **George Washington Bridge**, though it takes more time than you'd expect (trust us). The **Henry Hudson Bridge** expresses the tranquility of that part of the island—view it from Inwood Hill Park to see its graceful span over to Spuyten Duyvil. The **Verrazano-Narrows Bridge** between Brooklyn and Staten Island is the most awe-inspiring in the city.

Great Architecture

Grand Central Terminal stands as New York's great transit hub, and is notable as being more famous for its interior than its exterior. If you're looking for cast-iron buildings, head to SoHo to see the **Singer Building**. The **Flatiron**, once among the tallest buildings in the city, remains one of the most distinctive. The **Lever House**, the **Seagram's Building**, and the **Marine Midland Bank Building** are great examples of Modernism. The **Guggenheim** is one of New York's most unique and distinctive buildings (apparently there's some art inside too). The **Cathedral of St. John the Divine** is the world's largest and coolest unfinished cathedral—a much better destination that competing with the hordes clamoring to get into **St. Patrick's Cathedral**.

Great Public Buildings

If you're looking to boost your civic pride, there are quite a few old city buildings to admire (once upon a time, the city felt that public architecture should aspire to great architecture). Head downtown to view **City Hall** (1812), **Tweed Courthouse** (1880), **Jefferson Market Courthouse** (1877 - now a library), the **Municipal Building** (1914), and a host of other courthouses built in the early 20th century. The **Old Police Headquarters** would be a more celebrated building if it wasn't located in a forgotten corner of Little Italy/Chinatown. And what are the chances a firehouse built today would have the same charm as the **Great Jones Firehouse**?

Outdoor Spaces

Central Park, obviously. **Madison Square Park** is not as well known as many other central city parks, but it succeeds in being a peaceful respite from the city, which is more than you can say for Tompkins or Washington Square. For better or worse, **Washington Square** is a landmark (the arch is nice to look at), although there's a ton of other parks we'd rather spend time in. In addition to **Union Square** housing a bunch of great statues (Gandhi, Washington, Lincoln), it also hosts an amazing Farmer's Market (Mon, Wed, Fri, and Sat) and is close to great shopping. Tiny **Duane Park** is a perfect place to read a book on a nice day. The same goes for **Bryant Park**, and they've got movies in the summer, too. Next door, the **New York Public Library** steps are a classic NY set piece. **Rockefeller Center** tends to get overrun by tourists, but it's still a neat place to visit, especially to view the Art Deco styling. **Trinity Church** is nice building and the view of it from Wall Street is pretty cool; the graveyard next door has some famous names and is worth a stroll too. The **Cloisters** and **Inwood Hill Park** are great uptown escapes. Thanks to Stuyvesant Street's diagonal path, **St. Marks-in-the-Bowery** gives a nice little corner of land in front for a park, which gives a hint of its rural past. **Yankee Stadium**—less for the architecture and more for the gargoyles within.

Lowbrow Landmarks

The **Chinatown Ice Cream Factory** is worth a slog through Chinatown crowds on a hot day. Just around the corner is **Doyers Street**, which retains the slight air of danger from its gang war past. Among other positive attributes, **CBGB's** is dingy, dark, and loud.

Some classic and historic New York bars, known mainly for their famous patrons of drinks past, include: **Pete's Tavern**, the **White Horse Tavern**, **Chumleys**, and the **Ear Inn**.

Lame, Bad & Overrated Landmarks

Even the most cynical New Yorker would have to admit that **Times Square** is a unique place, but the truth is that it sucks to go there. **South Street Seaport** is essentially a lame mall with some old ships parked nearby. **Madison Square Garden** is often given vaunted status as a great sports arena, but the accolades aren't really deserved. Aside from a few shining moments, the teams there usually stink, and the architecture is mostly banal. The worst part is that the gorgeous old Penn Station was torn down to make room for it. You can see pictures of the old station when you walk through

the new **Penn Station**, which is famous not for its totally drab and depressing environs, but because of the sheer volume of traffic it handles. The **Cross Bronx Expressway** gets a mention as the worst highway ever.

Underrated Landmarks

Many of these get overlooked because they are uptown. **Grant's Tomb** was once one of New York's most famous attractions, but these days it's mostly a destination for history buffs. The **City College** campus is quite beautiful, even though a few newer buildings muck things up. Further north, **Sylvan Terrace** and the **Morris Jumel Mansion**, a unique block of small row houses and a revolutionary war era house, offer a truer glimpse of old New York than the Seaport or Frances Tavern.

Map 1 · Financial District

American International Building	70 Pine St	Great Art Deco skyscraper.
American Stock Exchange	86 Trinity Pl · 212-306-1000	New York's other stock exchange.
Battery Maritime Building	11 South St	Ready-to-be-converted riverfront building.
Bowling Green	Broadway & State St	Watch the tourists take pics of the bull. New York's first park.
Cunard Building	25 Broadway · 212-363-9490	Great mosaics on the ceiling.
Customs House/Museum of the American Indian	1 Bowling Green · 212-514-3700	Stately Cass Gilbert building; check out the oval staircases.
Delmonico's Building	56 Beaver St · 212-509-3130	Once the site of THE restaurant in New York.
Equitable Building	120 Broadway · 212-490-0666	It's massiveness gave momentum to zoning laws for skyscrapers.
Federal Hall	26 Wall St · 212-825-6888	Where George the First was inaugurated.
The Federal Reserve Bank	33 Liberty St · 212-720-6130	Where *Die Hard* took place.
New York Stock Exchange	20 Broad St · 212-656-5168	Where Wall Street took place.
South Street Seaport	South St · 212-732-7678	Mall with historic ships as backdrop.
St Paul's Chapel & Cemetery	Broadway & Fulton St · 212-602-0874	Old-time NYC church and cemetery.
Standard Oil Building	26 Broadway	Sweeping wall of a building overlooking Bowling Green.
Trinity Church & Cemetery	Broadway & Wall St	Formerly the tallest building in New York.
Vietnam Veterans Plaza	Coenties Slip & Water St	A nice quiet spot to contemplate our faded dreams of empire.
World Trade Center Site	Church St & Vesey St	We still can't believe what happened.

Map 2 · TriBeCa

The Dream House	275 Church St · 212-925-8270	Cool sound + light installation by LaMonte Young. Closed during summer.
Duane Park	Duane St & Hudson St	One of the nicest spots in all of New York.
Harrison Street Row Houses	Harrison St & Greenwich St	Some old houses.
Washington Market Park	Greenwich St · 212-274-8447	One of the city's oldest marketplaces.

Map 3 · City Hall / Chinatown

African Burial Ground	Duane St & Broadway	Colonial burial ground for 20,000+ African American slaves.
Bridge Café	279 Water St · 212-227-3344	The oldest bar in NYC. Great vibe, good food too.
Chinatown Ice Cream Factory	65 Bayard St · 212-608-4170	The best mango ice cream, ever.
City Hall	Park Row & Broadway · 212-788-6879	Beautiful and now heavily barricaded.
Criminal Courthouse	100 Centre St · 212-374-4423	Imposing.
Doyers St (Bloody Angle)	Doyers St	One of the few angled streets in New York. Has a decidedly otherworldly feel.
Eastern States Buddhist Temple	64 Mott St · 212-966-6229	The oldest Chinese Buddhist temple on the east coast.

General Information • Landmarks

Map 3 • City Hall / Chinatown—continued

Hall of Records/Surrogate's Court	Chambers St & Park Row	Great lobby and zodiac-themed mosaics.
Municipal Building	Chambers St & Park Row	Wonderful McKim, Mead & White masterpiece.
Not For Tourists	2 East Broadway • 212-365-8650	Where the sh** goes down!
Shearith Israel Cemetery	55 St James Pl	Oldest Jewish cemetary in New York.
Tweed Courthouse	Chambers St & Broadway	Great interior dome, but will we ever see it?
Woolworth Building	233 Broadway	A Cass Gilbert classic. Now partly condominium.

Map 4 • Lower East Side

Bialystoker Synagogue	7 Bialystoker Pl • 212-475-0165	The oldest building in NY to currently house a synagogue. Once a stop on the Underground Railroad.
Eldridge Street Synagogue	12 Eldridge St	The first large-scale building constructed by Eastern European immigrants in NY.
Gouverneur Hospital	Gouverneur Slip & Water St	One of the oldest hospital buildings in the world.
Lower East Side Tenement Museum	90 Orchard St • 212-431-0233	Great illustration of turn-of-the-century (20th, that is) life.

Map 5 • West Village

The Cage (basketball court)	320 Sixth Ave at W 4th St	Where everybody's got game…
Chumley's	86 Bedford St • 212-675-4449	Former speakeasy; still one of the coolest bars around.
The Ear Inn	Washington & Spring Sts • 212-226-9060	Second-oldest bar in New York; great space.
Jefferson Market Courthouse	425 Sixth Ave • 212-243-4334	Now a library.
Stonewall	53 Christopher St • 212-463-0950	Site of a very important uprising in the late '60s.
Westbeth Building	Washington St & Bethune St • 212-989-4650	Cool multifunctional arts center.
White Horse Tavern	567 Hudson • 212-243-9260	Another old, cool bar. Dylan Thomas drank here (too much).

Map 6 • Washington Square / NYU / NoHo / SoHo

The Alamo (The Cube)	Astor Pl & Fourth Ave	Give it a spin sometime…
Asch Building (Brown Building)	23-29 Washington Pl	Site of the Triangle Shirtwaist Fire.
Bayard-Condict Building	65 Bleecker St	Louis Sullivan's only New York building.
CBGB & OMFUG	315 Bowery • 212-982-4052	Stands for: Country, BlueGrass, Blues, and Other Music For Uplifting Gourmandizers.
Colonnade Row	428 Lafayette St	Remains of a very different era.
Con Edison Building	145 E 14th St	Cool top.
Cooper Union	30 Cooper Sq • 212-353-4195	Great brownstone-covered building.
Grace Church	802 Broadway • 212-254-2000	Another old, small, comfortable church.
Great Jones Fire House	Great Jones St & Bowery	The coolest firehouse in NYC.
Milano's	51 E Houston St • 212-226-8844	One of our favorite bars. An utter dump.
New York Marble Cemetery	41 Second Ave	Oldest public non-sectarian cemetery in New York City.
Old Merchant's House	29 E 4th St	The merchant is now dead.
The Public Theater	425 Lafayette St • 212-260-2400	Great building, great shows.
Salmagundi Club	47 Fifth Ave • 212-255-7740	Cool building.
Singer Building	561 Broadway	Now houses Kate's Paperie; a fine building by Ernest Flagg.
St Mark's-in-the-Bowery Church	131 E 10th St • 212-674-6377	Old church with lots of community ties.
The Strand Bookstore	828 Broadway • 212-473-1452	One of a kind. All others are imitations.
Wanamaker's	Broadway & 8th St	Once the classiest department store in the city, now houses a Kmart.
Washington Mews	University Pl (entrance)	Where horses and servants used to live. Now coveted NYU space.
Washington Square Park	Washington Sq	Dime bag, anyone?

Map 7 • East Village / Lower East Side

Charlie Parker House	151 Ave B & Tompkins Sq Pk	Bird lived here. Great festival every summer in Tompkins Square.
General Slocum Monument	Tompkins Square Park	Memorial to one of the worst disasters in NYC history.
Katz's Deli	205 E Houston St • 212-254-2246	Classic NY deli, interior hasn't changed in decades.
Nuyorican Poets Café	236 E 3rd St • 212-505-8183	Home of the poetry slam, among other things.
Pyramid Club	Ave A b/w 6th & 7th Sts • 212-473-7184	Classic '80s and '90s club.
Tompkins Square Park	Ave A & E 9th St • 212-387-7685	Home to many.

General Information · **Landmarks**

Map 8 · Chelsea

General Theological Seminary	175 Ninth Ave · 212-243-5150	Oldest seminary of the Episcopal Church; nice campus.
High Line Elevated Railroad	Gansevoort to 34th St, west of Tenth Ave	Elevated railroad trestle, soon to be a park. Maybe.
J A Farley Post Office	441 Eighth Ave · 212-967-2781	Another McKim, Mead & White masterpiece.
Jacob K Javits Convention Center	36th St & Eleventh Ave · 212-216-2000	I M Pei's attempt to make sense out of New York. Love the location.
Starlett-Leigh Building	27th St & Eleventh Ave	One of the coolest factories ever built.

Map 9 · Flatiron / Lower Midtown

Chelsea Hotel	23rd St b/w Seventh & Eighth Aves · 212-243-3700	The scene of many, many crimes.
Empire State Building	34th St & Fifth Ave · 212-736-3100	The roof deck at night is unmatched by any other view of New York.
Flatiron Building	175 Fifth Ave · 212-633-0200	A lesson for all architects: design for the actual space.
Flower District	28th St b/w Sixth & Seventh Aves	Lots of flowers by day, lots of nothing by night.
Garment District	West 30s south of Herald Sq	Clothing racks by day, nothing by night. Gritty, grimy.
Macy's Herald Square	151 W 34th St · 212-494-4662	13 floors of wall-to-wall tourists! Sound like fun?
Madison Square Garden	4 Penn Plz · 212-465-6000	Crappy, uninspired venue for Knicks, Rangers, Liberty, and over-the-hill rock bands.
Madison Square Park	23rd St & Broadway · 212-360-8111	One of the most underrated parks in the city. Lots of great weird sculpture.
Metropolitan Life Insurance Co	1 Madison Ave · 212-578-3700	Cool top, recently refurbished.
Penn Station	31st St & Eighth Ave	Well, the old one was a landmark, anyway…
Theodore Roosevelt Birthplace	28 E 20th St · 212-645-1242	Teddy was born here, apparently.
Tin Pan Alley	W 28th St b/w Sixth Ave & Broadway	Where all that old-timey music came from.
Union Square	14th St-Union Sq	Famous spot for protests and rallys. Now bordered on all sides by chain stores.

Map 10 · Murray Hill / Gramercy

Gramercy Park	Irving Pl & 20th St	New York's only keyed park. This is where the revolution will doubtlessly start.
National Arts Club	15 Gramercy Park S · 212-477-2389	One of two beautiful buildings on Gramercy Park South.
Pete's Tavern	129 E 18th St · 212-473-7676	Where O Henry hung out. And so should you, at least once.
Pete's Tavern	66 Irving Pl · 212-473-7676	Classic NY literary pub.
The Players	16 Gramercy Park S	The other cool building on Gramercy Park South.
Sniffen Court	36th St & Third Ave	Great little space.

Map 11 · Hell's Kitchen

Intrepid Sea, Air & Space Museum	Twelfth Ave & 45th St · 212-957-3700	Lots of tourists.
Theatre Row	42nd St b/w Ninth & Tenth Aves	This is that "Broadway" place that everyone keeps talking about, isn't it?

Map 12 · Midtown

Carnegie Hall	154 W 57th St · 212-247-7800	Great classic performance space. The Velvet Underground's first gig was here.
The Debt Clock	Sixth Ave & 42nd St	How much we all owe.
Museum of Modern Art (MoMA)	11 W 53rd St · 212-708-9400	Moved to Queens for three years in a vain attempt to get some street cred.
New York Public Library	Fifth Ave & 42nd St · 212-930-0787	A wonderful Beaux Arts building. Great park behind it. The map room rules.
Plaza Hotel	768 Fifth Ave · 212-759-3000	The best lobby and bars of any hotel in New York. Might soon be closing its doors.
Rockefeller Center	600 Fifth Ave · 212-632-3975	Sculpture, ice skating, and a mall!
Royalton Hotel	44th St b/w Fifth Ave & Sixth Ave · 212-869-4400	Starck + Schrager = cool.
St Patrick's Cathedral	Fifth Ave & 50th St · 212-753-2261	NYC's classic cathedral. Always empty.
Times Square	42nd St-Times Sq	It looks even cooler than it does on TV!

Map 13 · East Midtown

Chrysler Building	405 Lexington Ave · 212-682-3070	The stuff of Art Deco dreams. Wish the Cloud Club were public.
Citicorp Center	153 E 53rd St	How does it stand up?

General Information · **Landmarks**

Map 13 · East Midtown—*continued*

Grand Central Terminal	42nd St · 212-340-2583	Another Beaux Arts masterpiece by Warren & Wetmore. Ceiling, staircases, tiles, clock, Oyster Bar, all great.
Seagram Building	375 Park Ave	Or, "how to be a modernist in 3 easy steps!"
United Nations	First Ave b/w 42nd & 48th Sts · 212-963-8687	The diplomatic version of the World Cup.
Waldorf-Astoria	301 Park Ave · 212-355-3000	Great hotel, although the public spaces aren't up to the Plaza's.

Map 14 · Upper West Side (Lower)

Ansonia Hotel	2109 Broadway & 73rd St · 212-724-2600	Truly unique residence on Broadway.
The Dakota	Central Park West & 72nd St	Classic Central Park West apartment building, designed by Henry J Hardenbergh.
The Dorilton	Broadway & 71st St	Cool, weird arch. Flashy facade.
Lincoln Center	Broadway & 64th St · 212-875-5000	A rich and wonderful complex. Highly recommended—movies, theater, music, opera.
The Majestic	115 Central Park W	Great brick by Chanin.
Museum of Natural History	Central Park W & 79th St · 212-769-5100	Includes the new planetarium and lots and lots of stuffed animals.
New-York Historical Society	2 W 77th St · 212-873-3400	Oldest museum in New York City.
The San Remo	Central Park W & 74th St · 212-877-0300	Emery Roth's contribution to the Upper West Side skyline.

Map 15 · Upper East Side (Lower)

Asia Society	725 Park Ave · 212-288-6400	Small-scale modernism.
Frick Collection	1 E 70th St · 212-288-0700	Lots of furniture.
The Manhattan House	200 E 66th St	Seminal UES "white-brick" building.
Metropolitan Museum of Art	1000 Fifth Ave · 212-879-5500	The mother of all art musuems. Check out: temple, roof garden, Clyfford Still room, baseball cards.
Mount Vernon Hotel Museum	421 E 61st St · 212-838-6878	Nice old building.
New York Society Library	53 E 79th St · 212-288-6900	A 250-year-old library. Wow!
Temple Emanu-El	1 E 65th St · 212-744-1400	Way cool building.
Whitney Museum of American Art	945 Madison Ave · 212-570-3676	It almost always has something to talk about—not the least of which is their typically controversial Biennial.

Map 16 · Upper West Side (Upper)

Fireman's Memorial	W 100th St & Riverside Dr	Memorial to fallen fire fighters.
Pomander Walk	261 W 94th St	Great little hideaway.
Soldiers and Sailors Monument	Riverside Dr & 89th St	It's been seen in *Law & Order*, along with everything else in New York.

Map 17 · Upper East Side / East Harlem

Cooper-Hewitt Museum	2 E 91st St · 212-860-8400	Great design shows; run by the Smithsonian.
Gracie Mansion	Carl Schulz Park & 88th St · 212-570-4751	Our own Buckingham Palace, and right above the FDR Drive.
Jewish Museum	1109 Fifth Ave · 212-423-3200	Over 28,000 artifacts of Jewish culture and history.
Museo del Barrio	Fifth Ave & 104th St · 212-831-7272	NYC's only Latino museum.
Museum of the City of New York	Fifth Ave & 103rd St · 212-534-1672	Nice space, but we were excited when they were going to move to the Tweed Courthouse.
Old Municipal Asphalt Plant (Asphalt Green)	90th St & FDR Dr · 212-369-8890	Industrial architecture turned sports facility.
Solomon R Guggenheim Museum	1071 Fifth Ave · 212-423-3500	Wright's only building in NYC, but it's one of the best.
St Nicholas Russian Orthodox Cathedral	15 E 97th St	This UES cathedral, built in 1902, remains the center of Russian Orthodoxy in the US.

Map 18 · Columbia / Morningside Heights

Cathedral of St John the Divine	112th St & Amsterdam Ave · 212-316-7540	Our favorite cathedral. Completely unfinished and usually in disarray—just the way we like it.
City College	138th St & Convent Ave · 212-650-7000	Once known for academic excellence and free tuition, now has open admissions and hefty fees.
Columbia University	116th St & Broadway · 212-854-1754	Peaceful campus. A nice little sanctuary amid the roiling masses.

Grant's Tomb	122nd St & Riverside Dr · 212-666-1640	A totally underrated experience—interesting, great grounds.
Riverside Church	490 Riverside Dr	Gothic, great views from 392-foot tower.

Map 19 · Harlem (Lower)

Alhambra Theatre and Ballroom	2116 Adam Clayton Powell Jr Blvd · 212-222-6940	Last Harlem dance hall.
Apollo Theater	253 W 125th St · 212-531-5300	Live, the Hardest Working Man in Show Business, Mr. James Brown!
Duke Ellington Circle	110th St & Fifth Ave	Nice monument to a jazz great.
Harlem YMCA	180 W 135th St · 212-281-4100	Sidney Poitier, James Earl Jones, and Eartha Kitt have performed at this Y's "Little Theatre."
Langston Hughes Place	20 E 127th St · 212-534-5992	Where the prolific poet lived and worked from 1947-1967.
Marcus Garvey Park	E 120-124th Sts & Madison Ave · 212-201-PARK	Appealingly mountainous park.
Sylvia's	328 Lenox Ave · 212-996-0660	This restaurant is worth the trip.

Map 20 · El Barrio

Church of Our Lady of Mt Carmel	448 E 115th St 8 212-534-0681	The first Italian parish in NYC.
Harlem Courthouse	170 E 121st St	Cool.
Harlem Fire Watchtower	Marcus Garvey Park	It's tall.
Keith Haring "Crack is Wack" Mural	Second Ave & 127th St	Keith was right.

Map 21 · Manhattanville / Hamilton Heights

Audubon Terrace	Broadway & W 155th St	American Academy and Institute of Arts and Letters, American Numismatic Museum, Hispanic Society of America. Pleasant, if lonely, Beaux Arts complex. What's it doing here?
Hamilton Grange National Memorial	287 Convent Ave · 212-368-9133	Elegant buildings on a serene street.
Hamilton Heights Historic District	W 141st- W 145th Sts & Convent Ave	Hamilton's old dig moved here from its original location and now facing the wrong way. Damn those Jeffersonians.
Hispanic Society Museum	613 W 155th St & Broadway · 212-690-0743	Free museum (Tues-Sat) with Spanish masterpieces.
Trinity Church Cemetery's Graveyard of Heroes	3699 Broadway	Hilly, almost countryish cemetery.

Map 22 · Harlem (Upper)

The 369th Regiment Armory	2366 Fifth Ave	Home of the Harlem Hellfighters.
Abyssinian Baptist Church	132 Odell Clark Pl · 212-862-7474	NY's oldest black congregation.
The Dunbar Houses	Frederick Douglass Blvd & W 149th St	Historic multi-family houses.
St Nicholas Historic District	202 W 138th St	Beautiful neo-Georgian townhouses.

Map 23 · Washington Heights

George Washington Bridge	W 178th St	Try to see it when it's lit up. Drive down from Riverdale on the Henry Hudson at night and you'll understand.
Little Red Lighthouse	under the George Washington Bridge · 212-304-2365	It's there, really!
Morris-Jumel Mansion	Edgecombe Ave & 161st St · 212-923-8008	The oldest building in New York, at least until someone changes it again.
Sylvan Terrace	b/w Jumel Ter & St Nicholas Ave	The most un-Manhattanlike place in all the world.

Map 24 · Fort George / Fort Tryon

Fort Tryon Park	Ft Washington Ave	A totally beautiful and scenic park on New York's north edge.
Yeshiva University Main Building (Zysman Hall)	Amsterdam Ave & W 187th St · 212-960-5224	Interesting Byzantine-style building.

Map 25 · Inwood

The Cloisters	Ft Tryon Park · 212-923-3700	The Met's storehouse of medieval art. Great herb garden, nice views.
Dyckman House	4881 Broadway · 212-643-1527	Needs some work.

Map 26 · Astoria

Bohemian Hall	29-19 24th Ave · 718-274-4925	Last remaining beer garden in NYC.
Socrates Sculpture Park	Broadway & Vernon Blvd	Constantly revolving sculpture collection resides on this former illegal dump. Great view of the Manhattan skyline from the river.

Map 27 · Long Island City

American Museum of the Moving Image	35th Ave & 36th St · 718-784-4520	Educates about the art, history, technique, and technology of film, television, and digital media.
Center for the Holographic Arts	45-10 Court Sq · 718-784-5065	Promotes the art of holography.
Citicorp Building	1 Court Sq	This 48-story structure in blue glass is the tallest New York building outside of Manhattan.
The Isamu Noguchi Museum	32-37 Vernon Blvd · 718-204-7088	Showcases the work of Isamu Noguchi.
Kaufman-Astoria Studios	34-12 36th St · 718-706-5300	The US's largest studio outside of Los Angeles sits on a 13-acre plot with 8 sound stages. Films made here include *Scent of a Woman* and *The Secret of My Success*. Television's *The Cosby Show* and *Sesame Street* were also taped here.
Long Island City Courthouse	25-10 Court Sq · 718-298-1000	Grand building in the middle of less-than-grand LIC.
NY Center for Media Arts	45-12 Davis St · 718-472-9414	Educates on traditional and modern artistic methods.
PS1	22-25 Jackson Ave · 718-784-2084	A contemporary art center partly owned by MoMA.
Silvercup Studios	42-22 22nd St · 718-906-2000	Former bakery that now produces hundreds of commercials, films, television shows, and music videos.
The Space	42-16 West St · 718-706-6697	Organization to encourage public arts in Long Island City.

Map 29 · Williamsburg

Brooklyn Brewery	79 N 11th St · 718-486-7422	Brooklyn's only commerial brewery—check out the free tours on Saturdays. You get free samples!

Map 30 · Brooklyn Heights / DUMBO / Downtown

Brooklyn Borough Hall	209 Joralemon St · 718-802-3700	Built in the 1940's, this Greek Revival landmark was employed as the official City Hall when Brooklyn was an independent city.
Brooklyn Bridge	Adams St & East River	Opened in 1883, the Brooklyn Bridge is the oldest NYC bridge open to vehicles and pedestrians and is still considered one of the most beautiful bridges ever built.
Brooklyn Conservatory of Music	58 7th Ave · 718-622-3957	This five-story Victorian Gothic brownstone in Park Slope is home to the conservatory of music, which hosts regular performances by its students and guest artists.
Brooklyn Heights Promenade		Killer views of lower Manhattan.
Brooklyn Historical Society	128 Pierrepoint St · 718-222-4111	This newly renovated historical landmark building houses a new exhibition, Brooklyn Works: 300 Years of Making a Living in Brooklyn.
Brooklyn Ice Cream Factory	Fulton Ferry Pier · 718-246-3963	Expensive, old fashioned ice cream beneath the bridge.
Brooklyn Navy Yard	Waterfront	Nation's first navy yard—employed 70,000 people during WWII. Today, it houses a diverse range of businesses.
Fulton Street Mall	Fulton St b/w Flatbush Ave & Boerum Hall	NYC's first pedestrian mall with hundreds of retail outlets.
Junior's Cheesecakes	386 Flatbush Ave · 800-458-6467	World-famous cheesecakes, serving 4,000 Brooklyn patrons daily.
New York Transit Museum	Boerum Place & Schermerhorn St · 718-243-8601	Housed appropriately in an old subway station, the museum exhibits old subway cars, photographs, and maps from bygone eras.

Map 31 · Fort Greene / Clinton Hill

Brooklyn Academy of Music	30 Lafayette Ave · 718-636-4100	America's oldest continuously operating performing arts center.
Fort Greene Park	DeKalb Ave & Washington Park	It just has a great feel!
Lafayette Avenue Presbyterian Church	85 S Oxford St · 718-625-7515 (b/w Lafayette & Green Aves)	Nationall known church with performance arts; former Underground Railroad stop.

| Long Island Railroad Station | Hanson Pl & Flatbush Ave
• 718-217-5477 | A low red brick building which is used by more than 20 million passengers annually. A total craphole. |
| Steiner Studios | 15 Washington Ave | Spanking new film studios in the Brooklyn Navy Yard. |

Map 32 · BoCoCa / Red Hook

Gowanus Canal		Brooklyn's answer to the Seine.
Red Hook Grain Terminal		Abandoned grain terminal that looks really cool.
Williamsburgh Savings Bank Building	1 Hanson Pl	Known as "willie," it is the tallest structure in Brooklyn.

Map 33 · Park Slope / Prospect Heights / Windsor Ter

Brooklyn Botanic Garden	900 Washington Ave • 718-623-7200	More than 12 individual gardens and 12,000 species of plants inhabit this peaceful public garden.
Brooklyn Museum	200 Eastern Pkwy • 718-638-5000	Excellent permanent collection including a highly regarded collection of American paintings.
Brooklyn Public Library (Central Branch)	Grand Army Plz • 718-230-2100	The building looks like a book!
Brooklyn Tabernacle	290 Flatbush • 718-783-0942	Home of the Grammy Award-winning Brooklyn Tabernacle Choir.
Grand Army Plaza	Flatbush Ave & Plaza St	Site of John H. Duncan's Soldiers' and Sailors' Memorial Arch.
Park Slope Food Co-op	782 Union St • 718-622-0560	One of the largest food coops in the country. Best place to buy groceries in all of New York!
Prospect Park Wildlife Center	450 Flatbush Ave • 718-399-7339	Home to approximately 400 animals.

Map 34 · Hoboken

| First recorded baseball game | Elysian Fields | On 19 June 1846, the first officially recorded, organized baseball match was played on Hoboken's Elysian Fields. |

Map 35 · Jersey City

| Colgate Clock | 105 Hudson St | The world's largest clock's dial is 50 feet in diameter and has a minute hand weighing 2,200 pounds. |
| Powerhouse | 344 Washington St | This coal-powered railway powerhouse connected New York to New Jersey by train via Hudson River tunnels. Today the Powerhouse is being considered for residential development. |

Battery Park City

The Irish Hunger Memorial	corner of Vesey St & North End Ave	A memorial to the "The Great Irish Famine & Migration" to the US in the mid-1800's.
Manhattan Sailing Club	North Cove (Liberty St & North End Ave) • 212-786-3323	Membership required.
Mercantile Exchange	1 North End Ave	A great, big financial building in Battery Park.
Police Memorial	Liberty St & South End Ave	A fountain commemorating the career of a policeman and those killed in the line of duty.
Skyscraper Museum	39 Battery Pl • 212-968-1961	The place to go to learn what's up in New York.
The Real World		Tom Otterness sculptures of a tiny, whimsical society. Cooler than Smurfs.
Winter Garden	37 Vesey St	A cavernous marble and glass atrium.

Roosevelt Island

Blackwell House	591 Main St	Fifth-oldest wooden house in New York City.
Blackwell's Lighthouse		Built by institutionalized 19th-century convicts.
Chapel of the Good Shepherd		1888 Chapel given as a gift to island inmates and patients.
Smallpox Hospital		New York City's only landmarked ruin.
Tramway	Tramway Plz	Short but great thrill ride; see *Nighthawks* for more thrills.
Octagon Tower		Former lunatic asylum; now another cool ruin.

299

General Information · **Dog Runs**

Useful websites: www.doglaw.com, www.nycparks.org, www.allny.com/pets, www.nyc.dogslife.com, www.nycpetinfoline.com/home_page

NYC is full of dog runs—both formal and informal—scattered throughout the city's parks and neighborhood community spaces. While the city takes no active role in the management of the dog runs, it provides space to the community groups who do. These community groups are always eager for help—volunteer time or financial contributions) and many post volunteer information on park bulletin boards. Formal runs are probably the safest bet for pets, as most are enclosed and maintained. Dog owners are advised to remove from their pets any choke or pronged collars, to prevent them from getting tangled with other dogs or fences (both of which can result in serious injury). The dog's flat collar and identification tag should remain on. Most runs prohibit dogs in heat, aggressive dogs, and dogs without inoculations. Many runs do not allow toys, balls, or frisbees.

Map · Name · Address · Comments

2   **P.S. 234** · 300 Greenwich St at Chambers St · Private run. $50/year membership.
3   **Fish Bridge Park** · Pearl and Dover Sts · Concrete-surfaced run. Features water hose, wading pool, and lock box with newspapers.
5   **West Village D.O.G. Run** · Little W 12th St · Features benches, water hose, and drink bowl. Membership costs $40 annually, but there's a waiting list.
6   **Washington Square Park** · MacDougal St at W 4th St · Located in the southwest corner of the park, this is a large, gravel-surfaced run with many spectators. This popular run gets very crowded, but is well-maintained nonetheless.
6   **LaGuardia Place** · Mercer St at Houston St · This is a private run with a membership (and a waiting list). The benefits to this run include running water and a plastic wading pool for your dog to splash in.
6   **Union Square** · Broadway at 16th St · Crushed stone surface.
7   **Tompkins Square Park** · Avenue B at 10th St · New York City's first dog run is quite large and has a wood chip surface. Toys, balls, frisbees, and dogs in heat are all prohibited. This community-centered run offers lots of shade, benches, and running water.
8   **Thomas Smith Triangle** · Eleventh Ave at 23rd St · Concrete-surfaced run.
8   **Chelsea** · 18th St at the West Side Hwy
10 **Madison Square Park** · Madison Ave at 25th St · Medium-sized run with gravel surface and plenty of trees.
11 **DeWitt Clinton Park** · Eleventh Ave at 52nd & 54th Sts · Two small concrete-surfaced runs.
11 **Hell's Kitchen/Clinton Dog Run** · W 39th St at Tenth Ave · A private dog run (membership costs $15 a year) featuring chairs, umbrellas, fenced garden, and woodchip surface.
13 **E 60th Street Pavilion** · 60th St at the East River · Concrete-surfaced run.
13 **Peter Detmold Park** · Beekman Pl at 51st St · Large well-maintained run with cement and dirt surfaces and many trees.
13 **Robert Moses Park** · First Ave and 42nd St · Concrete surface.
14 **Theodore Roosevelt Park** · Central Park W at W 81st St · Gravel surface.
14 **Riverside Park** · Riverside Dr at 72nd St
14 **Margaret Mead Park** · Columbus Ave at 81st St
15 **Balto Monument** · Fifth Ave at E 67th St (Central Park)
15,17 **Carl Shurz Park** · East End Ave at 85/86th Sts · Medium-sized enclosed run with pebbled surface and separate space for small dogs. This run has benches and shady trees, and running water is available in the bathrooms.
15 **Riverside Park** · Riverside Dr at 77/78th Sts
16 **Riverside Park** · Riverside Dr at 87th St · Medium-sized run with gravel surface.
16 **Riverside Park** · Riverside Dr at 105/106th Sts · Medium-sized run with gravel surface.
18 **Morningside Park** · Morningside Ave b/w 114th & 119th Sts
20 **Thomas Jefferson Park** · E 112nd St at First Ave · Woodchips surface.
21 **Harlem** · Riverside Dr at 140th St
23 **J. Hood Wright Park** · Haven Ave at W 173rd St · An enclosed dirt-surfaced run.
24 **Fort Tryon Park** · Margaret Corbin Dr, Washington Heights
25 **Inwood Hill Dog Run** · W 207th St · Gravel surface.
BPC **Battery Park City (south end)** · Third Pl at Battery Pl · This long, narrow, concrete-surfaced enclosed run is located along the West Side Highway and offers a pleasant view of the river and some shade.
BPC **Battery Park City** · Along River Ter between Park Pl W and Murray St · Concrete-surfaced run with a view of the river.

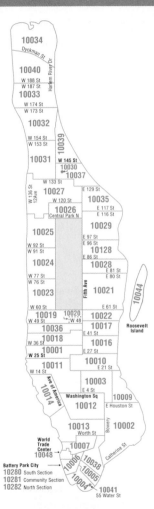

The phone number for all branches is now one central number: 800-275-8777.

Branch	Address	Zip	Map
Ansonia	178 Columbus Ave	10023	14
Audubon	511 W 165th St	10032	23
Bowling Green	90 Church St	10004	2
Bryant	23 W 43rd St	10036	12
Canal Street	350 Canal St	10013	2
Canal Street Retail	6 Doyers St	10013	3
Cathedral	215 W 104th St	10025	16
Cherokee	1483 York Ave	10021	15
College Station	217 W 140th St	10030	22
Colonial Park	99 Macombs Pl	10039	22
Columbia University	534 W 112th St	10025	18
Columbus Circle	27 W 60th St	10023	14
Cooper	93 Fourth Ave	10003	6
Dag Hammarskjold	884 Second Ave	10017	13
Empire State	19 W 33rd St	10118	9
Fort George	4558 Broadway	10040	24
Fort Washington	556 W 158th St	10032	21
Franklin D Roosevelt	909 Third Ave	10022	13
Gracie	229 E 85th St	10028	15
Greeley Square	39 W 31st St	10001	9
Hamilton Grange	521 W 146th St	10031	21
Inwood Post Office	90 Vermilyea Ave	10034	25
J A Farley General	441 Eighth Ave	10001	8
Knickerbocker	128 East Broadway	10002	4
Lenox Hill	217 E 70th St	10021	15
Lincolnton	2266 Fifth Ave	10037	22
Madison Square	149 E 23rd St	10010	10
Manhattanville	365 W 125th St	10027	18
Midtown	223 W 38th St	10018	9
Morningside	232 W 116th St	10026	19
Murray Hill	205 E 36th St	10016	10
Murray Hill Finance	115 E 34th St	10016	10
Old Chelsea	217 W 18th St	10011	9
Oscar Garcia Rivera	153 E 110th St	10029	20
Park West	693 Columbus Ave	10025	16
Patchin	70 W 10th St	10011	6
Peck Slip	1 Peck Slip	10038	3
Peter Stuyvesant	432 E 14th St	10009	7
Pitt Station	185 Clinton St	10002	4
Planetarium	127 W 83rd St	10024	14
Port Authority	76 Ninth Ave	10011	8
Prince	124 Greene St	10012	6
Radio City	322 W 52nd St	10019	11
Rockefeller Center	610 Fifth Ave	10020	12
Roosevelt Island	694 Main St	10044	p212
Station 138 (Macy's)	151 W 34th St	10001	9
Times Square	340 W 42nd St	10036	11
Tompkins Square	244 E 3rd St	10009	7
Triborough	167 E 124th St	10035	20
Tudor City	5 Tudor City Pl	10017	13
Village	201 Varick St	10014	5
Wall Street	73 Pine St	10005	1
Washington Bridge	555 W 180th St	10033	23
West Village	527 Hudson St	10014	5
Yorkville	1617 Third Ave	10128	17

(301)

General Information · **FedEx**

The latest FedEx dropoffs are at 9:30 pm Monday-Friday at 880 Third Ave (Map 13), 606 W 49th St and 621 W 48th St (Map 11), 130 Leroy (Map 5) and 537 W 33rd St (Map 8). However, many Manhattan FedEx delivery trucks have a drop-off slot on the side of the truck itself, in case you're on your way to a service center at 9:15 pm and see one. Please note that locations, hours of operation, and pickup times may change. If in doubt, call 1-800-Go-FedEx or visit www.fedex.com.

* Last pick-up

Map 1 · Financial District

FedEx Kinko's	110 William St	9:00
FedEx Service	100 William St	9:00
FedEx Service	110 Wall St	9:00
FedEx Service	55 Broadway	9:00
Drop Box	1 New York Plz	8:30
Drop Box	32 Old Slip	8:30
Drop Box	85 Broad St	8:30
Drop Box	88 Pine St	8:30
Drop Box	1 Battery Park Plz	8:00
Drop Box	1 Chase Manhattan Plz	8:00
Drop Box	1 State St Plz	8:00
Drop Box	11 Broadway	8:00
Drop Box	125 Maiden Ln	8:00
Drop Box	14 Wall St	8:00
Drop Box	150 Broadway	8:00
Drop Box	17 Battery Pl	8:00
Drop Box	180 Maiden Ln	8:00
Drop Box	2 Chase Manhattan Plz	8:00
Drop Box	26 Broadway	8:00
Drop Box	4 New York Plz	8:00
Drop Box	40 Exchange Pl	8:00
Drop Box	44 Wall St	8:00
Drop Box	60 Wall St	8:00
Drop Box	7 Hanover Sq	8:00
Drop Box	90 Broad St	8:00
Drop Box	95 Wall St	8:00
FedEx Kinko's	100 Wall St	8:00
Drop Box	33 Liberty St	7:30
Drop Box	40 Rector St	7:30
Postnet	29 John St	7:00
Complete Mail Centers	28 Vesey St	6:30
Post Office	73 Pine St	5:00

Map 2 · TriBeCa

Drop Box	100 Sixth Ave	8:00
Drop Box	32 Sixth Ave	8:00
Drop Box	145 Hudson St	7:30
Bestype Imaging	285 West Broadway	6:00
Mail Boxes Etc	295 Greenwich St	5:30
Postnet	130 Church St	5:30

Map 3 · City Hall / Chinatown

FedEx Kinko's	105 Duane St	9:00
FedEx Service	4 Barclay St	9:00
Drop Box	11 Park Pl	8:30
Drop Box	401 Broadway	8:30
Howard Shipping and Trading	33 Howard St	8:30
Drop Box	109 Lafayette St	8:00
Drop Box	434 Broadway	8:00
Drop Box	361 Broadway	7:00
FedEx Service Center	383 Broadway	7:00
Far East Shipping	28 Bowery	6:30
Quick Global Shipping	25 Howard St	6:00
Staples	488 Broadway	6:00
Wird Inc	125 Canal St	6:00
Post Office	1 Peck Slip	4:30
Post Office	6 Doyers St	4:30

Map 4 · Lower East Side

Drop Box	357 Grand St	8:00

Map 5 · West Village

FedEx Service	130 Leroy St	9:30
FedEx Service	229 W 4th St	9:00
Drop Box	180 Varick St	8:30
Drop Box	350 Hudson St	8:30
Drop Box	375 Hudson St	8:30
Drop Box	201 Varick St	8:00
Drop Box	80 Eighth Ave	8:00
Drop Box	95 Morton St	8:00
Drop Box	139 Charles St	7:30
Drop Box	315 Hudson St	7:30
Village Copy & Computer	520 Hudson St	7:00
Your Neighborhood Office	332 Bleecker St	7:00
Mail Boxes Etc	511 Sixth Ave	6:00
Mail Boxes Etc	302 W 12th St	5:30
Mail Boxes Etc	315 Bleecker St	5:15

Map 6 · Washington Sq / NYU / NoHo / SoHo

FedEx Service	70 Spring St	9:00
Drop Box	375 Lafayette St	8:30
Drop Box	799 Broadway	8:30
Drop Box	270 Lafayette St	8:00
Drop Box	580 Broadway	8:00
FedEx Kinko's	21 Astor Pl	8:00
Staples	5-9 Union Sq W	7:00
United Shipping	200 E 10th St	6:30
First Prince Copy Center	22 Prince St	6:00
Village Postal	532 LaGuardia Pl	5:00
Mail Call	341 Lafayette St	4:30
Post Office	124 Greene St	4:30

Map 7 · East Village / Lower East Side

FedEx Kinko's	250 E Houston St	9:00
Keepers Packaging	444 E 10th St	8:00
Little Village Postal	151 First Ave	5:00
Drop Box	84 Clinton St	4:00

Map 8 · Chelsea

FedEx Service	537 W 33rd St	9:30
FedEx Service	450 W 15th St	8:30
Drop Box	111 Eighth Ave	8:00
Drop Box	322 Eighth Ave	8:00
Drop Box	505 Eighth Ave	8:00
Drop Box	508 W 26th St	8:00
Drop Box	519 Eighth Ave	8:00
Drop Box	520 Eighth Ave	8:00
Drop Box	538 W 34th St	8:00
Drop Box	545 Eighth Ave	8:00
Drop Box	75 Ninth Ave	8:00
Drop Box	547 W 27th St	7:30
Direct Rush	356 W 37th St	8:00
Drop Box	450 W 33rd St	8:00
Mail Boxes Etc	245 Eighth Ave	6:00
Post Office	234 Tenth Ave	4:30

Map 9 · Flatiron

FedEx Service	1 Penn Plz	9:00
FedEx Service	112 W 39th St	9:00
FedEx Service	125 Fifth Ave	9:00
FedEx Service	125 W 33rd St	9:00
FedEx Service	1350 Broadway	9:00
FedEx Service	149 Madison Ave	9:00
FedEx Service	157 W 35th St	9:00
FedEx Service	20 E 20th St	9:00
FedEx Service	261 Madison Ave	9:00
FedEx Service	326 Seventh Ave	9:00
FedEx Service	525 Seventh Ave	9:00
FedEx Service	8 E 23rd St	9:00
Drop Box	1133 Broadway	9:00
Drop Box	121 W 27th St	8:00

Drop Box	207 W 25th St	8:00
Drop Box	21 Penn Plz	8:00
Drop Box	220 Fifth Ave	8:00
Drop Box	225 W 34th St	8:00
Drop Box	230 Fifth Ave	8:00
Drop Box	390 Fifth Ave	8:00
Drop Box	41 Madison Ave	8:00
Drop Box	45 W 18th St	8:00
Drop Box	450 Seventh Ave	8:00
Drop Box	463 Seventh Ave	8:00
Drop Box	469 Seventh Ave	8:00
Drop Box	485 Seventh Ave	8:00
Drop Box	5 Penn Plz	8:00
Drop Box	875 Sixth Ave	8:00
FedEx Kinko's	191 Madison Ave	8:00
FedEx Kinko's	245 Seventh Ave	8:00
FedEx Kinko's	500 Seventh Ave	8:00
FedEx Kinko's	650 Sixth Ave	8:00
Drop Box	132 W 31st St	7:30
Drop Box	1370 Broadway	7:30
Drop Box	1385 Broadway	7:30
Drop Box	5 W 37th St	7:30
Drop Box	100 W 33rd St	7:00
Drop Box	1250 Broadway	7:00
Drop Box	1407 Broadway	7:00
Drop Box	28 E 28th St	7:00
Drop Box	37 E 28th St	7:00
Drop Box	50 W 34th St	7:00
Drop Box	699 Sixth Ave	7:00
Drop Box	330 Fifth Ave	6:00
Drop Box	366 Fifth Ave	6:00
Staples	16 E 34th St	6:00
Drop Box	220 W 19th St	5:00
Drop Box	233 W 18th St	5:00
Post Office	217 W 18th St	5:00
Post Office	223-241 W 38th St	5:00
Drop Box	39 W 31st St	4:30

Map 10 · Murray Hill

FedEx Service	108 E 28th St	9:00
FedEx Service	2 Park Ave	9:00
FedEx Service	4 Union Sq E	9:00
FedEx Service	90 Park Ave	9:00
Drop Box	200 Park Ave S	8:15
Drop Box	200 Lexington Ave	8:00
Drop Box	220 E 23rd St	8:00
Drop Box	3 Park Ave	8:00
Drop Box	30 Waterside Plz	8:00
Drop Box	345 Park Ave S	8:00
Drop Box	475 Park Ave S	8:00
Drop Box	545 First Ave	8:00
Drop Box	550 First Ave	8:00
FedEx Kinko's	257 Park Ave S	8:00
FedEx Kinko's	600 Third Ave	8:00
Sx/Moonlite Courier	125 E 23rd St	8:00
Drop Box	240 E 38th St	7:30
Drop Box	425 E 25th St	7:30
Back Office NYC	345 E 18th St	7:00
Drop Box	192 Lexington Ave	7:00
The Villager	338 First Ave	7:00
Mail Boxes Etc	303 Park Ave S	6:30
Drop Box	660 First Ave	6:00
Mail Boxes Etc	163 Third Ave	6:00
Mail Boxes Etc	350 Third Ave	6:00
Staples	345 Park Ave S	6:00

Map 11 · Hell's Kitchen

FedEx Service	560 W 42nd St	9:30
FedEx Service	606 W 49th St	9:30
FedEx Service	621 W 48th St	9:30
Drop Box	405 W 55th St	8:00

Drop Box	429 W 53rd St	8:00
Drop Box	630 Ninth Ave	8:00
Drop Box	690 Ninth Ave	8:00
Post Office	322 W 52nd St	7:00
Drop Box	432 W 58th St	6:00
Mail Boxes Etc	331 W 57th St	6:00
Mail Boxes Etc	676 A Ninth Ave	5:00
Post Office	340 W 42nd St	4:30

Map 12 • Midtown *

Drop Box	51 E 44th St	9:00
FedEx Kinko's	1211 Sixth Ave	9:00
FedEx Service	10 E 53rd St	9:00
FedEx Service	1120 Sixth Ave	9:00
FedEx Service	1290 Sixth Ave	9:00
FedEx Service	135 W 50th St	9:00
FedEx Service	200 W 57th St	9:00
FedEx Service	43 W 42nd St	9:00
FedEx Service	437 Madison Ave	9:00
FedEx Service	6 W 48th St	9:00
Drop Box	1230 Sixth Ave	8:30
Drop Box	1325 Sixth Ave	8:30
Drop Box	1515 Broadway	8:30
Drop Box	1700 Broadway	8:30
Drop Box	444 Madison Ave	8:30
Drop Box	51 W 52nd St	8:30
Drop Box	10 E 40th St	8:00
Drop Box	1185 Sixth Ave	8:00
Drop Box	120 W 45th St	8:00
Drop Box	1285 Sixth Ave	8:00
Drop Box	1350 Sixth Ave	8:00
Drop Box	1466 Broadway	8:00
Drop Box	1500 Broadway	8:00
Drop Box	1501 Broadway	8:00
Drop Box	152 W 57th St	8:00
Drop Box	1775 Broadway	8:00
Drop Box	3 E 54th St	8:00
Drop Box	41 W 48th St	8:00
Drop Box	477 Madison Ave	8:00
Drop Box	488 Madison Ave	8:00
Drop Box	555 Madison Ave	8:00
Drop Box	575 Madison Ave	8:00
Drop Box	590 Madison Ave	8:00
Drop Box	600 Madison Ave	8:00
Drop Box	712 Fifth Ave	8:00
Drop Box	787 Seventh Ave	8:00
Drop Box	825 Eighth Ave	8:00
FedEx Kinko's	16 E 52nd St	8:00
FedEx Kinko's	240 Central Park S	8:00
FedEx Service	233 W 54th St	8:00
FedEx Service	60 W 40th St	8:00
La Boutique	2 E 55th St	8:00
Drop Box	1095 Sixth Ave	7:30
Drop Box	1370 Sixth Ave	7:30
Drop Box	156 W 56th St	7:30
Drop Box	335 Madison Ave	7:30
Staples	1065 Sixth Ave	7:00
Staples	57 W 57th St	7:00
Post Office	224 W 57th St	6:00
Post Office	23 W 43rd St	4:30
Post Office	610 Fifth Ave	4:30

Map 13 • East Midtown *

FedEx Service	880 Third Ave	9:30
Drop Box	270 Park Ave	9:15:00
FedEx Kinko's	305 E 46th St	9:00
FedEx Service	405 Park Ave	9:00
FedEx Service	750 Third Ave	9:00
Drop Box	280 Park Ave	8:45
Drop Box	150 E 58th St	8:30
Drop Box	299 Park Ave	8:30
Drop Box	60 E 42nd St	8:15
Drop Box	100 Park Ave	8:00
Drop Box	110 E 59th St	8:00
Drop Box	220 E 42nd St	8:00
Drop Box	355 Lexington Ave	8:00
Drop Box	420 Lexington Ave	8:00
Drop Box	55 E 59th St	8:00
Drop Box	630 Third Ave	8:00
Drop Box	633 Third Ave	8:00
Drop Box	866 United Nations Plz	8:00
Drop Box	885 Third Ave	8:00
FedEx Kinko's	641 Lexington Ave	8:00
FedEx Kinko's	747 Third Ave	8:00
Post Office	450 Lexington Av	8:00
Drop Box	353 Lexington Ave	7:30
Drop Box	135 E 57th St	7:00
Drop Box	150 E 42nd St	7:00
Drop Box	211 E 43rd St	7:00
Drop Box	350 Park Ave	7:00
Drop Box	500 Park Ave	7:00
Drop Box	575 Lexington Ave	7:00
Drop Box	805 Third Ave	7:00
Drop Box	979 Third Ave	7:00
FedEx Kinko's	153 E 53rd St	7:00
Post Office	909 Third Ave	6:30
Staples	205 E 42nd St	6:00
Staples	425 Park Ave	6:00
Mail Boxes Etc	1040 First Ave	5:00
Mail Boxes Etc	847A Second Ave	5:00
Drop Box	45 E 45th St	4:45

Map 14 • Upper West Side (Lower) *

FedEx	2211 Broadway	9:00
FedEx Service Center	156 W 72 St	9:00
Drop Box	2112 Broadway	8:00
Drop Box	517 Amsterdam Ave	7:00
FedEx Kinko's	221 W 72nd St	7:00
Post Office	168 Columbus Ave	6:30
Drop Box	101 West End Ave	6:00
Drop Box	211 W 61st St	6:00
Mail Boxes Etc	163 Amsterdam Ave	6:00
Mail Boxes Etc	459 Columbus Ave	6:00
Post Office	127 W 83rd St	6:00
Staples	2248 Broadway	5:00
The Padded Wagon	215 W 85th St	5:00
Post Office	27 W 60th St	3:30

Map 15 • Upper East Side (Lower) *

Drop Box	1300 York Ave	8:30
Drop Box	1343 Second Ave	8:30
Drop Box	667 Madison Ave	8:30
FedEx Kinko's	1122 Lexington Ave	8:30
Drop Box	525 E 68th St	8:00
Drop Box	650 Madison Ave	7:30
Drop Box	695 Park Ave	7:30
Big Apple	1456 Second Ave	6:00
Drop Box	428 E 72nd St	6:00
Drop Box	968 Lexington Ave	6:00
Mail Boxes Etc	1461 First Ave	6:00
Post Office	217 E 70th St	6:00
Postal Express	1382 Third Ave	6:00
The Padded Wagon	1431 York Ave	6:00
The Padded Wagon	1569 Second Ave	6:00
Mail Boxes Etc	954 Lexington Ave	5:45
Drop Box	425 E 61st St	5:30
Drop Box	645 E 69th St	5:30
Senderos Ltd	1471 Third Ave	5:00

Map 16 • Upper West Side (Upper) *

Columbia Copy Center	2790 Broadway	8:00
Drop Box	70 W 86th St	8:00
Copy Experts	2440 Broadway	7:30
Foxy Graphic Services	211 W 92nd St	6:30
Mail Boxes Etc	2444 Broadway	6:00
Mail Boxes Etc	2565 Broadway	6:00

Map 17 • Upper E Side/E Harlem *

Drop Box	225 E 95th St	8:30
Staples	1280 Lexington Ave	8:00
Drop Box	1 E 104th St	6:30
Mail Boxes Etc	1369 Madison Ave	6:00
Mail Boxes Etc	1710 First Ave	6:00
Compu Sign Plus	1598 Third Ave	5:30
Post Office	1619 Third Ave	5:00

Map 18 • Morningside Heights *

FedEx Service	600 W 116th St	9:00
Drop Box	3022 Broadway	8:00
Drop Box	435 W 116th St	8:00
Drop Box	525 W 120th St	8:00
Drop Box	475 Riverside Dr	7:00

Map 19 • Harlem (Lower) *

Drop Box	163 W 125th St	7:00
Drop Box	2261 Adam C Powell Jr Blvd	7:00
Drop Box	55 W 125th St	7:00

Map 20 • El Barrio *

Drop Box	1879 Madison Ave	6:45

Map 21 • Manhattanville / Hamilton Heights *

La Nacional	3351 Broadway	6:00
La Nacional	3480 Broadway	6:00
La Nacional	3609 Broadway	6:00

Map 23 • Washington Heights *

Drop Box	1051 Riverside Dr	7:30
Doc Q Pack	2201 Amsterdam Ave	7:00
Drop Box	100 Haven Ave	7:00
Drop Box	161 Ft Washington Ave	7:00
Drop Box	177 Ft Washington Ave	7:00
Drop Box	3960 Broadway	7:00
Drop Box	60 Haven Ave	7:00
Drop Box	622 W 168th St	7:00
Drop Box	630 W 168th St	7:00
Drop Box	1150 St Nicholas Ave	6:30
La Nacional	113 Audubon Ave	6:00
La Nacional	1342 St Nicholas Ave	6:00
La Nacional	2174 Amsterdam Ave	6:00
La Nacional	3914 Broadway	6:00
Rel Express	2140 Amsterdam Ave	6:00

Map 24 • Ft George / Ft Tryon *

Drop Box	701 W 168th St	7:00
Drop Box	710 W 168th St	7:00
Quisqueyana Express	4468 Broadway	7:00
La Nacional	1443 St Nicholas Ave	6:00
La Nacional	151 Nagle Ave	6:00
La Nacional	1533 St Nicholas Ave	6:00
Drop Box	722 W 168th St	5:00
Mibandera Cargo Express	570 W 189th St	5:00

Map 25 • Inwood *

Atlas Travel Group	4742 Broadway	5:00
Adam Enterprises	165 Sherman Ave	4:30
La Nacional	566 W 207th St	3:00

Pharmacies

	Address	Phone	Map
Rite Aid	408 Grand St	212-529-7115	4
Duane Reade	378 Sixth Ave	212-674-5357	5
Duane Reade	123 Third Ave	212-529-7140	6
Duane Reade	24 E 14th St	212-989-3632	6
Duane Reade	598 Broadway	212-343-2567	6
Duane Reade	636 Broadway	212-979-2142	6
Duane Reade	769 Broadway	646-602-8274	6
Walgreen's	145 Fourth Ave	212-677-0054	6
Duane Reade	460 Eighth Ave	212-244-4026	8
Duane Reade	180 W 20th St	212-243-0129	9
Duane Reade	358 Fifth Ave	212-279-0208	9
CVS Pharmacy	342 E 23rd St	212-473-5750	10
Duane Reade	131 E 23rd St	212-674-7704	10
Duane Reade	155 E 34th St	212-683-3042	10
Rite Aid	542 Second Ave	212-213-9887	10
Duane Reade	100 W 57th St	212-956-0464	12
Duane Reade	1633 Broadway	212-586-0374	12
Duane Reade	224 W 57th St	212-541-9708	12
Duane Reade	4 Times Sq	646-366-8047	12
Duane Reade	625 Eighth Ave	212-273-0889	12
Duane Reade	661 Eighth Ave	212-977-1562	12
Duane Reade	900 Eighth Ave	212-582-3463	12
Rite Aid	301 W 50th St	212-247-8384	12
CVS Pharmacy	630 Lexington Ave	917-369-8688	13
Duane Reade	1076 Second Ave	212-223-1130	13
Duane Reade	401 Park Ave	212-213-9730	13
Duane Reade	405 Lexington Ave	212-808-4743	13
Duane Reade	485 Lexington Ave	212-682-5338	13
Duane Reade	852 Second Ave	212-983-1810	13
Duane Reade	866 Third Ave	212-759-9412	13
CVS Pharmacy	400 W 59th St	212-245-0617	14
Duane Reade	2025 Broadway	212-579-9955	14
Duane Reade	253 W 72nd St	212-580-0497	14
Duane Reade	380 Amsterdam Ave	212-579-7246	14
Duane Reade	4 Amsterdam Ave	212-581-5527	14
Duane Reade	4 Columbus Cir	212-265-2302	14
Rite Aid	210 Amsterdam Ave	212-787-2903	14
CVS Pharmacy	1396 Second Ave	212-249-5699	15
Duane Reade	1191 Second Ave	212-355-5944	15
Duane Reade	1279 Third Ave	212-744-2668	15
Duane Reade	1345 First Ave	212-535-9816	15
Duane Reade	1498 York Ave	212-879-8990	15
Duane Reade	773 Lexington Ave	212-829-0651	15
Duane Reade	2522 Broadway	212-663-1580	16
Duane Reade	2589 Broadway	212-864-5246	16
Duane Reade	609 Columbus Ave	212-724-4270	16
Rite Aid	2833 Broadway	212-663-3135	16
CVS Pharmacy	1622 Third Ave	212-876-7212	17
Duane Reade	1231 Madison Ave	212-360-6586	17
Duane Reade	125 E 86th St	212-996-5261	17
Duane Reade	1675 Third Ave	212-348-7400	17
Duane Reade	401 E 86th St	917-492-8801	17
Rite Aid	146 E 86th St	212-876-0600	17
Duane Reade	2864 Broadway	212-316-5113	18

* These stores are open 24 hours, but the pharmacy in the store closes at this time.

Hardware Store

	Address	Phone	Map
HomeFront	202 E 29th St	212-545-1447	10

Copying

	Address	Phone	Map
Acro Photo Printing	90 Maiden Ln	212-809-8999	1
Perfect Copy Center	11 Broadway	212-425-4818	1
Kinko's	105 Duane St	212-406-1220	3
Exact	1 W 34th St	212-643-6699	9
Kinko's	191 Madison Ave	212-685-3449	9
Kinko's	245 Seventh Ave	212-929-0623	9
Kinko's	500 Seventh Ave	646-366-9166	9
Metropolitan Duplicating & Imaging	216 W 18th St	212-620-0087	9
Village Copier	10 E 39th St	212-599-3344	9
Graphics Service Bureau	370 Park Ave S	212-684-3600	10
Xact	333 W 52nd St	212-581-9595	11
Discovery Copy Services	45 W 45th St	212-827-0039	12
Kinko's	1211 Sixth Ave	212-391-2679	12
Kinko's	16 E 52nd St	212-308-2679	12
Kinko's	233 W 54th St	212-977-2679	12
Kinko's	240 Central Park S	212-258-3750	12
Kinko's	60 W 40th St	212-921-1060	12
Skyline Duplication	151 W 46th St	212-302-5153	12
Kinko's	641 Lexington Ave	212-572-9995	13
Kinko's	747 Third Ave	212-753-7778	13
Kinko's	221 W 72nd St	212-362-5288	14
Kinko's	1122 Lexington Ave	212-628-5500	15

Post Office

	Address	Phone	Map
J A Farley GPO	421 Eighth Ave	212-330-5557	8

Delivery and Messengers

	Phone
Moonlite Courier	212-473-2246
Alliance Courier & Freight	212-302-3422
Same Day Express	800-982-5910
Need It Now	212-989-1919
Urban Express	212-855-5555
Parkes Messenger Service	212-997-9023

Private Investigators

	Phone
Sherlock Investigations	212-579-4302
	888-354-2174
Matthew T Cloth, PI	718-449-4100
North American Investigations	800-724-8080

Laundromats

	Address	Phone	Map
69 Avenue C Laundromat	69 Ave C	212-388-9933	7
Clean Rite Center	262 W 145th St	917-507-4865	22
106 Audubon Avenue Laundromat	106 Audubon Ave	212-795-8717	23
D&D Laundromat	568 W 184th St	212-923-3409	24

Plumbers

	Address	Phone	Map
New York Plumbing & Heating Service	Multiple Locations	212-496-9191	N/A
Effective Plumbing	Multiple Locations	212-545-0100	N/A
Roto-Rooter Plumbing	Multiple Locations	212-687-1661	N/A
Sanitary Plumbing and Heating	211 E 117th St	212-734-5000	20

Gyms

	Address	Phone	Map
Crunch (Mon-Fri only)	Lafayette St & 4th St	212-614-0120	6
Synergy Fitness Clubs	2130 Broadway	212-501-9069	14

Car Rental

	Address	Phone	Map
Avis	217 E 43rd St	212-593-8378	13

Car Washes

	Address	Phone	Map
Cars A-Poppin Carwash	124 Sixth Ave	212-925-3911	5
Broadway Car Wash	614 Broadway (Houston St)	212-673-5115	6
Westside Highway Car Wash	638 W 47th St	212-757-1141	11
Eastside Car Wash	1770 First Ave (92nd St)	212-722-2222	17

Gas Stations

		Map			Map
Mobil	Allen St & Division St	4	Mobil	Eleventh Ave & W 57th St	11
Getty	Eight Ave & W 13th St	5	Amoco	Eighth Ave & 110th St	19
Mobil	Sixth Ave & Spring St	5	Exxon	110th St & Central Park W	19
Amoco	Broadway & Houston St	6	Merit	Seventh Ave & W 145th St	22
Citgo	Bowery & 3rd St	6	Mobil	Seventh Ave & W 145th St	22
Gaseteria	Houston & Lafayette Sts	6	Amoco	Amsterdam Ave & 165th St	23
Mobil	Houston St & Ave C	7	Shell	Amsterdam Ave & W 167th St	23
Getty	Tenth Ave & W 20th St	8	Shell	Amsterdam Ave & W 181st St	23
Gulf	Tenth Ave & 23rd St	8	Gaseteria	Broadway & 193rd St	24
Gaseteria	West End Ave & W 59th St	11	Amoco	Tenth Ave & 207th St	25
Mobil	Eleventh Ave & W 51st St	11	Jerusalem	Tenth Ave & 201st St	25

Newsstands

	Map		Map
Sixth Ave (South of 8th St)	5	First Ave & 57th St	13
Sixth Ave & 3rd St	5	59th St & Third Ave	13
St Marks Pl (8th St)/Bowery (Third Ave)	6	72nd St & Broadway	14
Second Ave & St Marks Pl	6	76th St & Broadway	14
Delancey & Essex Sts	7	Columbus Ave & 81st St	14
23rd St & Third Ave	10	Second Ave (60th/61st Sts)	15
Third Ave (34th/35th Sts)	10	79th St & York (First Ave)	15
49th St & Eighth Ave	12	First Ave & 63rd St	15
42nd St & Seventh Ave	12	86th St & Lexington Ave	17
Broadway & 50th St	12	Broadway & 116th St	18

Locksmiths

	Phone		Phone
A&V Locksmith	212-226-0011	Emergency Locksmith	212-231-7627
Aaron-Hotz Locksmith	212-243-7166	KC Manhattan Locksmith	212-398-5500
Abbey Locksmiths	212-535-2289	LockDoctors	212-935-6600
Always Ready Locksmiths	888-490-4900	Lockmasters Locksmith	212-690-4018
American Locksmiths	212-888-8888	Night and Day Locksmith	212-722-1017
CBS Locksmith	212-410-0090	Paragon Security & Locksmith	212-620-9000
Champion Locksmiths	212-362-7000	Speedway Locksmith	877-917-6500
East Manhattan Locksmiths	212-369-9063		

Veterinary

	Address	Phone	Map
St Marks Veterinary Hospital	348 E 9th St	212-477-2688	6
Animal Emergency Clinic	1 W 15th St	212-924-3311	9
Animal Medical Center	510 E 62nd St	212-838-8100	15
Park East Animal Hospital	52 E 64th St	212-832-8417	15
Center for Veterinary Care	236 E 75th St	212-734-7480	15

These listings will be of limited use to New Yorkers, unless cousin Becky's coming to town and you don't have room in your studio apartment, or you really, really can't make it home after a long night. Hotels are a good option if you want to make a romantic (or slightly less than romantic) getaway without leaving the city. Prices are generally highest during the holiday season and the summer, and lowest during the in-between times. Not all hotels have a star rating, and those that do are sometimes inaccurate. The quoted rates will give you a pretty good idea of the quality of each hotel. Rates are ballpark and subject to change—go to one of the many travel websites (Hotels.com, Priceline, Hotwire, Travelocity, Expedia, etc.) or individual company websites (hilton.com, spg.com, holiday-inn.com) to get the best rates. Or call the hotel and ask if they have any specials.

Map 1 · Financial District

	Address	Phone	Rate $	Rating
Hilton Millennium Hotel	55 Church St	212-693-2001	159-299	★★★★
Holiday Inn Wall Street	15 Gold St	212-232-7700	249	★★★1/2*
Manhattan Seaport Suites	129 Front St	212-742-0003	179-229	
New York Marriott Financial Center	85 West St	212-385-4900	165-265	★★★★
Wall Street Inn	9 S William St	212-747-1500	169-249	★★★★

Map 2 · TriBeCa

Cosmopolitan Hotel	95 West Broadway	212-566-1900	119-149	★★★
Soho Grand Hotel	310 West Broadway	212-965-3000	239-259	
Tribeca Grand Hotel	2 Sixth Ave	212-519-6600	269-319	★★★★

Map 3 · City Hall / Chinatown

Best Western Seaport Inn	33 Peck Slip	212-766-6600	159	★★★
Hampton Inn Seaport	320 Pearl St	212-571-4400	195	
Holiday Inn Downtown	138 Lafayette St	212-966-8898	189-199	★★★
Pioneer of Soho Hotel	341 Broome St	212-226-1482	80-91 (69*)	
Windsor Hotel	108 Forsyth St	212-226-3009	155	

Map 5 · West Village

Abingdon Guest House	13 Eighth Ave	212-243-5384	149-229	
Chelsea Pines Inn	317 W 14th St	212-929-1023	79-119	
Hotel Gansevoort	18 Ninth Ave	212-206-6700	325-395	
Hotel Riverview	113 Jane St	212-929-0060	40	
Incentra Village House	32 Eighth Ave	212-206-0007	119	
Liberty Inn	51 Tenth Ave	212-741-2333	150, 55-65*	
Mini Suites of Minetta	9 Minetta St	212-475-6952	110	★★
Rooms to Let	83 Horatio St	212-675-5481	110	
West Eleventh	278 W 11th St	212-675-7897	190	

Map 6 · Washington Square / NYU / NoHo / SoHo

60 Thompson	60 Thompson St	877-431-0400	370	★★★★
Howard Johnson Express Inn	135 E Houston St	212-358-8844	129-149	
Larchmont Hotel	27 W 11th St	212-989-9333	70-80	
Off Soho Suites Hotel	11 Rivington St	212-353-0860	149 (89*)	
Second Home on Second Avenue	221 Second Ave	212-677-3161	$105	
St Marks Hotel	2 St Mark's Pl	212-674-2192	110 (90*)	
Union Square Inn	209 E 14th St	212-614-0500	140	
Village House	45 W 9th St	212-473-5500	120-140	
Washington Square Hotel	103 Waverly Pl	212-777-9515	161	★★★
White House Hotel	340 Bowery	212-477-5623	32	

Map 7 · East Village / Lower East Side

East Village Bed & Coffee	110 Ave C	212-533-4175	60-90	
Hotel on Rivington	107 Rivington St	212-475-2600		

Map 8 · Chelsea

Allerton Hotel	302 W 22nd St	212-243-6017	68	
Best Western Convention Center Hotel	522 W 38th St	212-405-1700	165	★★
Chelsea Inn	184 Eleventh Ave	212-929-4096	45	
Chelsea International Hostel	251 W 20th St	212-647-0010	65	
Chelsea Lodge Suites	318 W 20th St	212-243-4499	90	
Chelsea Star Hotel	300 W 30th St	212-244-7827	69-99	
Colonial House Inn	318 W 22nd St	212-243-9669	125 -140, (80-99*)	
Manhattan Inn	303 W 30th St	212-629-4064	32 dorm, 95 private	
New Yorker Ramada Hotel	481 Eighth Ave	212-971-0101	130	★★★

General Information · **Hotels**

Map 9 · Flatiron / Lower Midtown

	Address	Phone	Rate $	Rating
Americana Inn	69 W 38th St	212-840-2019	65	★
Arlington Hotel	18 W 25th St	212-645-3990	85-100	★★
The Avalon	16 E 32nd St	212-299-7000	199	★★★★
Broadway Plaza Hotel	1155 Broadway	877-50-HOTEL	99-169	★★1/2*
Carlton Hotel	22 E 29th St	212-532-4100	129-159	★★★
Chelsea Grand Hotel	160 W 25th St	212-627-1888	139	★★★
Chelsea Hotel	222 W 23rd St	212-243-3700	150-165	
Chelsea Inn	46 E 17th St	212-645-8989	139, 99*	
Chelsea Savoy Hotel	204 W 23rd St	212-929-9353	99-125	
Churchill Residence Suites	50 W 34th St	877-424-7848	170-250	★★★
Comfort Inn Manhattan	42 W 35th St	212-947-0200	129	★★★
Comfort Inn New York	442 W 36th St	212-714-6699	99-159	★★★
Gershwin Hotel	7 E 27th St	212-545-8000	99-119	
Hampton Inn Manhattan/Chelsea	108 W 24th St	212-414-1000	159	
Herald Square Hotel	19 W 31st St	212-279-4017	85-99 (65*)	
Holiday Inn Martinique on Broadway	49 W 32nd St	212-736-3800	129-189	★★★1/2*
Hotel Chandler	12 E 31st St	212-889-6363	245	★★★★
Hotel Grand Union	34 E 32nd St	212-683-5890	120	★★1/2*
Hotel Metro	45 W 35th St	212-947-2500	170	★★★
Hotel Stanford	43 W 32nd St	212-563-1500	120	
Hotel Thirty Thirty	30 E 30th St	212-689-1900	119	★★★
Howard Johnson Penn Station	215 W 34th St	212-947-5050	125	★1/2*
Inn on 23rd	131 W 23rd St	212-463-0330	189	
Jolly Hotel Madison Towers	22 E 38th St	212-802-0600	169-199	★★★
La Quinta Inn - Manhattan	17 W 32nd St	212-790-2710	89-119	★★★
La Samanna	25 W 24th St	212-255-5944	139, 169	
LaQuinta Inn	17 W 32nd St	212-736-1600	139	★★★
Madison Hotel on the Park	21 E 27th St	212-532-7373	64	
Manhattan Broadway Hotel	273 W 38th St	212-921-9791	89	
Morgan's Hotel	237 Madison Ave	212-686-0300	210-290	★★★★
New York Hotel Pennsylvania	401 Seventh Ave	212-736-5000	119, 200	★★★★
Red Roof Inn	6 W 32nd St	212-643-7100	99 -119	★★
Roger Williams Hotel	131 Madison Ave	212-448-7000	260	★★★
Senton Hotel	39 W 27th St	212-684-5800	78	
Southgate Tower Hotel	371 Seventh Ave	212-563-1800	189-209	★★★
Wolcott Hotel	4 W 31st St	212-268-2900	180	★★★

Map 10 · Murray Hill / Gramercy

	Address	Phone	Rate $	Rating
70 Park Ave Hotel	70 Park Ave	212-687-7050	325	★★★
Carlton Arms Hotel	160 E 25th St	212-679-0680	70-85	
Clarion Park Avenue	429 Park Ave S	212-532-4860	139	★★
Deauville Hotel	103 E 29th St	212-683-0990	99	★★
Dumont Plaza	150 E 34th St	212-481-7600	199-229	★★★1/2*
Eastgate Tower Suite Hotel	222 E 39th St	212-687-8000	179-199	★★★
Envoy Club	377 E 33rd St	212-481-4600	209	
Hotel 17	225 E 17th St	212-475-2845	65	★★★
Hotel 31	120 E 31st St	212-685-3060	100 (70*)	
Hotel Giraffe	365 Park Ave S	212-685-7700	265-325	★★★★
Inn at Irving Place	56 Irving Pl	212-533-4600	325	★★★★
Kitano Hotel New York	66 Park Ave	212-885-7000	210-230	★★★★
Marcel Hotel	201 E 24th St	888-664-6835	180-200	★★★
Maritime Hotel	363 16th St	212-242-4300	155-245	
Murray Hill East Suites	149 E 39th St	212-661-2100	199	★★★
Murray Hill Inn	143 E 30th St	212-545-0879	79-119	
Park South Hotel	122 E 28th St	212-448-0888	189-229	★★★1/2*
Ramada Inn Eastside	161 Lexington Ave	212-545-1800	99-109	★★★
Shelburne	303 Lexington Ave	212-689-5200	150-219	★★★
Sheraton Russell Hotel	45 Park Ave	212-685-7676	199-239	★★★
W New York - The Court	130 E 39th St	212-685-1100	209-229	★★★
W New York - The Tuscany	120 E 39th St	212-686-1600	389	★★★★★
W Union Square	201 Park Ave S	212-253-9119	379	★★★★★

Map 11 · Hell's Kitchen	Address	Phone	Rate $	Rating
414 Inn New York	414 W 46th St	212-399-0006	120-140	★★★
Belvedere Hotel	319 W 48th St	212-245-7000	160-170	★★★
Elk Hotel	360 W 42nd St	212-563-2864	40*	
Holiday Inn Midtown	440 W 57th St	212-581-8100	159-214	★★★
Hudson Hotel	356 W 58th St	212-554-6000	165-210	★★★
Skyline Hotel	725 Tenth Ave	212-586-3400	119-159	★★★
Travel Inn	515 W 42nd St	212-695-7171	125	★★★
Washington Jefferson Hotel	318 W 51st St	212-246-7550	139	★★★
Westpark Hotel	308 W 58th St	866-937-8727	119-149	★★1/2*

Map 12 · Midtown	Address	Phone	Rate $	Rating
Algonquin Hotel	59 W 44th St	212-840-6800	269	★★★1/2
Ameritania Hotel	230 W 54th St	212-247-5000	257	★★★
Amsterdam Court Hotel	226 W 50th St	212-459-1000	125-185	★★★
Best Western Ambassador	132 W 45th St	212-921-7600	129	★★1/2
Best Western President Hotel	234 W 48th St	212-246-8800	129	★★★
Big Apple Hostel	119 W 45th St	212-302-2603	90	
Blakely Hotel	136 W 55th St	212-245-1800	255	★★★
Broadway Bed & Breakfast Inn	264 W 46th St	212-997-9200	129	★★★
Bryant Park Hotel	40 W 40th St	212-869-0100	295-595	★★★★
Buckingham Hotel	101 W 57th St	212-246-1500	199-269	★★★1/2
Carter Hotel	250 W 43rd St	212-944-6000	90	
Casablanca Hotel	147 W 43rd St	212-869-1212		
Chambers Hotel	15 W 56th St	212-974-5656	235-275	★★★★
City Club Hotel	55 W 44th St	212-921-5500	295	★★★★
Clarion Hotel	3 E 40th St	212-447-1500	160-180	★★★
Comfort Inn (Remington) Midtown	129 W 46th St	212-221-2600	120-140	★★★
Courtyard by Marriott Times Square South	114 W 40th St	212-391-0088	150-220	★★★
Crowne Plaza Times Square	1605 Broadway	212-977-4000	210, 170	★★★★
Da Vinci Hotel	244 W 56th St	212-489-4100	105-125	★★★
Days Inn Hotel Manhattan Midtown	790 Eighth Ave	212-581-7000	129-149	★★1/2*
Doubletree Guest Suites	1568 Broadway	212-719-1600	240-270	★★★
Dream	210 W 55th St	212-247-2000	239	★★★★
Dylan Hotel	52 E 41st St	212-338-0500	269	★★★
Flatotel International	135 W 52nd St	212-887-9400	270	★★★★
Four Seasons Hotel	57 E 57th St	212-758-5700	525-945	★★★★★
Helmsley Park Lane Hotel	36 Central Park S	212-371-4000	219-379	★★★★
Hilton New York	1335 Sixth Ave	212-586-7000	275-300	★★★★
Hilton Times Square	234 W 42nd St	212-840-8222	309	★★★
Hotel 41	206 W 41st St	212 703-8600	149	
Hotel Edison	228 W 47th St	212-840-5000	150	★★★
Hotel Shoreham	33 W 55th St	212-247-6700	180-210	★★★
Hotel St James	109 W 45th St	212-221-3600	100	
Howard Johnson	851 Eighth Ave	212-581-4100	160-180	★★★
Iroquois Hotel	49 W 44th St	212-840-3080	239-269	★★★★
Le Parker Meridien	119 W 56th St	212-245-5000	325	★★★★
Library Hotel	299 Madison Ave	212-983-4500	279	★★★
Mansfield Hotel	12 W 44th St	212-944-6050	159-189	★★★
Mayfair Hotel	242 W 49th St	212-586-0300	120	
Michelangelo	152 W 51st St	212-765-1900	195-245	★★★★
Milford Plaza	700 Eighth Ave	212-536-2200	119	★★★1/2*
Milford Plaza Hotel	270 W 45th St	212-869-3600	155	★★★
Millennium Broadway	145 W 44th St	212-768-4400	209	★★★★
Moderne Hotel	243 W 55th St	212-397-6767	175-185	★★★
The Muse	130 W 46th St	877-692-6873	229-259	★★★★
New York Inn	765 Eighth Ave	212-247-5400	85	
New York Marriott Marquis	1535 Broadway	212-398-1900	200	★★★
New York Palace Hotel	455 Madison Ave	212-888-7000	275-325	★★★★
Novotel New York	226 W 52nd St	212-315-0100	219	★★★1/2*
Omni Berkshire Place	21 E 52nd St	212-753-5800	179-289	★★★★
Paramount Hotel	235 W 46th St	212-764-5500	120-180	★★★★
Park Central Hotel	870 Seventh Ave	212-247-8000	129-239	★★★1/2*
Park Savoy Hotel	158 W 58th St	212-245-5755	95-105	

(309)

Map 12 · Midtown—continued

	Address	Phone	Rate $	Rating
Peninsula New York	700 Fifth Ave	212-956-2888	325	★★★★
Portland Square Hotel	132 W 47th St	212-382-0600	85-110	
The Premier	133 W 44th St	212-789-7670	179-295	★★★★
Quality Hotel Times Square	157 W 47th St	212-768-3700	197	★★1/2
Renaissance New York Times Square	714 Seventh Ave	212-765-7676	219-249	★★★★
Rihga Royal New York	151 W 54th St	212-468-8888	275-300	★★★★
Royalton Hotel	44 W 44th St	212-869-4400	205-260	★★★★
Salisbury Hotel	123 W 57th St	212-246-1300	90-139	★★★
Sheraton Manhattan	790 Seventh Ave	212-621-8500	179-379	★★★
Sheraton New York Hotel and Towers	811 Seventh Ave	212-581-1000	179-379	★★★
Sherry Netherland Hotel	781 Fifth Ave	212-355-2800	350-450	★★★★★
Sofitel	45 W 44th St	212-354-8844	209-229	★★★★1/2*
St Moritz Hotel/Ritz Carlton Central Park	50 Central Park S	212-308-9100	415-465	
St Regis	2 E 55th St	212-753-4500	550-610	★★★★★
Super 8 Times Square	59 W 46th St	212-719-2300	119	★★★
The Time	224 W 49th St	212-246-5252	179-199	★★★★
W New York Times Square	1567 Broadway	212-930-7400	279-299	★★★★
Wellington Hotel	871 Seventh Ave	212-247-3900	110-190	★★★
West Park Hotel	6 Columbus Cir	212-445-0200	149	★★★
Westin Essex House	160 Central Park S	212-247-0300	289-339	★★★★
Westin New York at Times Square	270 W 43rd St	212-201-2700	329	★★★★
Wyndham Hotels & Resorts	42 W 58th St	212-753-3500	140-155	

Map 13 · East Midtown

	Address	Phone	Rate $	Rating
Affinia 50	155 E 50th St	212-751-5710	239	★★★
Alex Hotel	205 E 45th St	212-867-5100	239	
Bedford Hotel	118 E 40th St	212-697-4800	125	★★★1/2*
Beekman Tower Suite Hotel	3 Mitchell Pl	212-355-7300	209	★★★
The Benjamin	125 E 50th St	212-715-2500	269	
Best Western	145 E 49th St	212-753-8781	249	★★1/2
Courtyard by Marriott Midtown East	866 Third Ave	212-644-1300	249	★★★
Crowne Plaza at the United Nations	304 E 42nd St	212-986-8800	239-269	★★★★
Doubletree Metropolitan Hotel	569 Lexington Ave	212-752-7000	299	★★★
Fitzpatrick Grand Central Hotel	141 E 44th St	212-351-6800	229-325	★★★★1/2*
Fitzpatrick Manhattan Hotel	687 Lexington Ave	212-355-0100	199-239	★★★★
Grand Hyatt Hotel	109 E 42nd St	212-883-1234	310-355	★★★★
Habitat Hotel	130 E 57th St	212-753-8841	75-125	★
Helmsley Middletowne Hotel	148 E 48th St	212-755-3000	159-289	★★★
Hotel Elysee	60 E 54th St	212-753-1066	275	★★★
Hotel Inter-Continental - The Barclay	111 E 48th St	212-755-5900	239-259	★★★★★
Hotel Lombary	111 E 56th St	212-753-8600	225	★★★
Kimberly Hotel	145 E 50th St	212-755-0400	189-209	★★★★
Marriott New York City East Side	525 Lexington Ave	212-755-4000	149-219	★★★★
Millenium UN Plaza	1 United Nations Plz	212-758-1234	269	
New York Helmsley Park	212 E 42nd St	212-490-8900	179-189	★★★
Pickwick Arms Hotel	230 E 51st St	212-355-0300	109-129	
Radisson Hotel East Side	511 Lexington Ave	212-755-4400	159-189	★★★
Roger Smith Hotel	501 Lexington Ave	212-755-1400	215-235	★★★
Roosevelt Hotel	45 E 45th St	212-661-9600	149-199	★★★★
San Carlos Hotel	150 E 50th St	212-755-1800	179	
Seton Hotel	144 E 40th St	212-889-5301	95 (60*)	
Swissotel New York	440 Park Ave	212-421-0900	249-299	★★★
W New York	541 Lexington Ave	212-755-1200	239-289	★★★★
Waldorf Astoria	301 Park Ave	212-872-4534	199-249	★★★★★
Waldorf Towers	100 E 50th St	212-355-3100	199	★★★★
YMCA Vanderbilt Hotel	224 E 47th St	212-756-9600	115 (67*)	

Map 14 · Upper West Side (Lower)

	Address	Phone	Rate $	Rating
Amsterdam Inn	340 Amsterdam Ave	212-579-7500	110 (80*)	
Amsterdam Residence	207 W 85th St	212-873-9402	110	
Comfort Inn Central Park West	31 W 71st St	212-721-4770	100-130	★★★
Country in the City	270 W 77th St	212-580-4183	150-230	
Excelsior Hotel	45 W 81st St	212-362-9200	129-169	★★★1/2*

Map 14 · Upper West Side (Lower)	Address	Phone	Rate $	Rating
Hayden Hall Hotel	117 W 79th St	212-787-4900	69-149	
Hotel Beacon	2130 Broadway	212-787-1100	145-175	★★★
Hotel Lucerne	201 W 79th St	212-875-1000	150-180	★★★★
Hotel Riverside Studios	342 W 71st St	212-873-5999	60	x
Inn New York City	266 W 71st St	212-580-1900	295-375	x
Mandarin Oriental New York	80 W 60th St	212-805-8800	429-615	★★★★★
Milburn Hotel	242 W 76th St	212-362-1006	149-159	x
On the Ave Hotel	2178 Broadway	212-362-1100	139-159	★★★1/2*
Phillips Club	155 W 66th St	212-835-8800	310	x
Riverside Tower Hotel	80 Riverside Dr	212-877-5200	84	★★
Trump International	1 Central Park W	212-299-1000	395-595	★★★★★
YMCA West Side Branch	5 W 63rd St	212-875-4100	100 (67*)	x

Map 15 · Upper East Side (Lower)				
1871 House	130 E 62nd St	212-756-8823	195-325	
Anco Studios	1202 Lexington Ave	212-717-7500	135	
Barbizon Melrose Hotel	140 E 63rd St	212-838-5700	229	★★★★
Bentley Hotel	500 E 62nd St	888-66-HOTEL	157	★★★
Carlyle Hotel	35 E 76th St	212-744-1600	360-420	★★★★
Gracie Inn	502 E 81st St	212-628-1700	129	
Helmsley Carlton	680 Madison Ave	212-838-3000	255	★★★★
Hotel Plaza Athenee	37 E 64th St	212-734-9100	329-5	★★★★
Lowell Hotel	28 E 63rd St	212-838-1400	415-445	★★★★
Lyden Gardens Suite Hotel	215 E 64th St	212-355-1230	199-209	★★★
The Mark New York	25 E 77th St	212-744-4300	299-400	★★★★
The Pierre Four Seasons	2 E 61st St	212-838-8000	380-495	★★★★
Regency Hotel	540 Park Ave	212-759-4100	269-319	★★★★
Surrey Suite Hotel	20 E 76th St	212-288-3700	259-289	★★★

Map 16 · Upper West Side (Upper)				
Belnord Residence Hotel	209 W 87th St	212-873-5222	175	★★
Central Park Hostel	19 W 103rd St	212-678-0491	75	
Hostelling International New York	891 Amsterdam Ave	212-932-2300	35 dorm, 135 private	
Hotel Belleclaire	250 W 77th St	212-362-7700	99-149	★★
Hotel Dexter House	345 W 86th St	212-873-9600	60	
Hotel Newton	2528 Broadway	212-678-6500	95	★★
Jazz on the Park	36 W 106th St	212-932-1600	86	
Malibu Hotel	2688 Broadway	212-222-2954	89	
Morningside Inn	235 W 107th St	212-316-0055	95 (80*)	
Quality Hotel on Broadway	215 W 94th St	212-866-6400	149-159	★★★
Riverside Inn	319 W 94th St	212-316-0656	80-90	
West End Studios	850 West End Ave	212-749-7104	69*	
West Side Inn	237 W 107th St	212-866-0061	60-70	★1/2*

Map 17 · Upper East Side / East Harlem				
92nd Steeet Y de Hirch Residence	1395 Lexington Ave	212-415-5650	30	
Franklin Hotel	164 E 87th St	212-369-1000	290	
Wales Hotel	1295 Madison Ave	212-876-6000	189-219	★★★

Map 19 · Harlem (Lower)				
102 Brownstone	102 W 118th St	212-662-4223	160-190	
Efuru Bed & Breakfast	106 W 120th St	212-961-9855	95-125 (79*)	

Map 21 · Manhattanville / Hamilton Heights				
Blue Rabbit International House	730 St Nicholas Ave	212-491-3892	25*	

Battery Park City				
Embassy Suites New York City	102 North End Ave	212-945-0100	280, 200	★★★★
Ritz-Carlton New York Battery Park	2 West St	212-344-0800	289-395	★★★★

Internet

A number of establishments around the city offer pay-as-you-go Internet access. In the list below you'll find everything from hotels to milkshake stores, as well as traditional "cyber-cafés" where you can check your email or the weather or whatever it is that can't wait until you get home. There are probably countless other hidden places to access the Internet in New York that are not listed here; many laundromats have installed machines to entertain idle washers. All Kinko's locations offer Internet access for 30-45 cents per minute, depending on which Kinko's you visit and which machine you use (it works out to $18-$27 per hour). Impeccably clean and open 24 hours a day, Kinko's is a good (but not cheap) Internet option.

Internet Café	Address	Phone	Website	Map
Internet Café NYC	17 John St	212-217-6043	www.internetcafenyc.com	1
Kinko's	110 William St	212-766-4646	www.fedexkinkos.com	1
Kinko's	100 Wall St	212-269-0024	www.fedexkinkos.com	1
Cyber Café	273A Lafayette St	212-334-5140	www.cyber-cafe.com	3
Kinko's	105 Duane St	212-406-1220	www.fedexkinkos.com:	3
Universal News	484 Broadway	212-965-0730		3
Six and Twelve	469 Sixth Ave	212-242-0580		5
Cyberfelds	20 E 13th St	212-647-8830		6
Dats Amore Pizza	347 E 14th St	212-529-3067		6
Gametime Nation	111 E 12th St	212-228-4260	www.gametimenation.com	6
Kinko's	21 Astor Pl	212-228-9511	www.fedexkinkos.com	6
Little Caesars	40 W 14th St	212-741-7499		6
Mr Fresh Bread, Inc	116 Second Ave	212-253-1046		6
Original New York Milkshake Co	1037 St Marks Pl	212-505-5200	www.nymilkshake.com	6
Rocket Wrapps	81 Third Ave	212-777-8000		6
Tasti D-Lite	137 Fourth Ave	212-228-5619	www.tastidlite.com	6
Village Juice Bar	200 E 14th St	212-673-0005		6
web2zone	54 Cooper Sq	212-614-7300	www.web2zone.com	6
alt.Coffee	139 Avenue A	212-529-2233	www.altdotcoffee.com	7
Café Pick Me Up	145 Avenue A	212-673-7231		7
Coffee Pot	41 Avenue A	212-614-0815		7
Kinko's	250 E Houston St	212-253-9020	www.fedexkinkos.com	7
Kudo Beans	49 1/2 First Ave	212-353-1477		7
William Christy Internet Cafe	392 E 10th St	212-477-6000		7
Brooklyn Bagel Café	319 Fifth Ave	212-532-0007		9
Ditto Internet Café	48 W 20th St	212-242-0841		9
ECT	417 Fifth Ave	212-684-8088		9
Hotel Grand Union	34 E 32nd St	212-683-5890	www.hotelgrandunion.com	9
Kinko's	350 Fifth Ave	212-279-3556	www.fedexkinkos.com	9
Kinko's	191 Madison Ave	212-685-3449	www.fedexkinkos.com	9
Kinko's	500 Seventh Ave	646-366-9166	www.fedexkinkos.com	9
Kinko's	650 Sixth Ave	646-638-9238	www.fedexkinkos.com	9
Kinko's	245 Seventh Ave	212-929-0623	www.fedexkinkos.com	9
News Bar	2 W 19th St	212-255-3996		9
Tasti D-Lite	236 Seventh Ave	212-414-4076	www.tastidlite.com	9
Universal News	50 W 23rd St	212-647-1761		9
Universal News	29 W 35th St	212-594-3113		9
Bistro 2 Go	316 Lexington Ave	212-685-2282		10
Kinko's	257 Park Ave S	646-602-0074	www.fedexkinkos.com	10
Kinko's	600 Third Ave	212-599-2679	www.fedexkinkos.com	10
Oxford Catering Café	399 Third Ave	212-252-1818		10
Coffee Pot	350 W 49th St	212-265-3566		11
Rocket Wrapps	609 Ninth Ave	212-333-2600		11
Tasti D-Lite	630 Ninth Ave	212-265-4977	www.tastidlite.com	11

Internet Café	Address	Phone	Website	Map
Cyber Café	705 Eighth Ave	212-245-3907	www.cyber-cafe.com	12
Cyber Café	250 W 49th St	212-333-4109	www.cyber-cafe.com	12
easyInternetcafé	16 W 48th St		www.easyinternetcafe.com	12
easyInternetcafé	234 W 42nd St	212-398-0775	www.easyinternetcafe.com	12
Kinko's	60 W 40th St	212-921-1060	www.fedexkinkos.com	12
Kinko's	1211 Sixth Ave	212-391-2679	www.fedexkinkos.com	12
Kinko's	16 E 52nd St	212-308-2679	www.fedexkinkos.com	12
Kinko's	233 W 54th St	212-977-2679	www.fedexkinkos.com	12
Kinko's	240 Central Park S	212-258-3750	www.fedexkinkos.com	12
Rick's Cyber Café at the Casablanca Hotel	147 W 43rd St	212-869-1212	www.casablancahotel.com	12
Universal News	977 Eighth Ave	212-459-0932		12
Bistro New York International	100 Park Ave, Ste 650	212-370-3911		13
easyInternetcafé	101 Park Ave		www.easyinternetcafe.com	13
Kinko's	230 Park Ave	212-949-2534	www.fedexkinkos.com	13
Kinko's	305 E 46th St	212-319-6600	www.fedexkinkos.com	13
Kinko's	747 Third Ave	212-753-7778	www.fedexkinkos.com	13
Kinko's	153 E 53rd St	212-753-7580	www.fedexkinkos.com	13
Kinko's	641 Lexington Ave	212-572-9995	www.fedexkinkos.com	13
NY Computer Place & Cafe	247 E 57th St	212-872-1704		13
Kinko's	221 W 72nd St	212-362-5288	www.fedexkinkos.com	14
Kinko's	1122 Lexington Ave	212-628-5500	www.fedexkinkos.com	15
Mr Rohrs Coffee	303 E 85th St	212-396-4456	www.rohrs.com	15
Mr Fresh Bread	336 E 86th St	212-717-2817		15
Broadway Bagel	2658 Broadway	212-662-0231		16
Delizia Pizzeria	1762 Second Ave	212-996-3720	www.delizia-ny.com	17

Wi-Fi

For those with a laptop or PDA that has wireless access, there are a ton of free public "Wi-Fi" connections available throughout the city. The NYC Wireless' website, www.nycwireless.net, provides a list and map of these locations. The majority of the listed hotspots are maintained by private citizens, though a few are run by the Downtown Alliance, including great spots at Bowling Green, City Hall, South Street Seaport, and the Winter Garden. Specific information about Downtown Alliance hotspot locations and how to sign on can be found at www.downtowny.com/wireless.asp. 58 branches of the NY Public Library in Manhattan and the Bronx (and one on Staten Island) offer Wi-Fi access, and the rest are sure to jump on the Wi-Fi bandwagon soon. Info about the libraries can be found at www.nypl.org/branch/services/wifi.html. Of course, it's always an option to simply plug in or turn on your wireless card and see what networks are available. If it doesn't offend your sense of ethics, you can often tap into other people's Wi-Fi networks for free.

There are plenty of fee-based services out there too. T-Mobile Hotspot subscribers ($6 per hour, $10 a day or $40 per month/$30 per month paid annually gives you unlimited access) can find access at most Kinko's, Borders, Starbucks, and T-Mobile retail locations. McDonald's offers Wi-Fi access at more than 50 locations in Manhattan: check out www.mcdwireless.com. Free Wi-Fi is offered at Penn Station for AT&T Wireless customers. Everyone else can get it for $9.99 per 24 hours. If you're the kind of person who likes to talk on your cell phone at restaurants, then you'll probably be partial to doing some emailing or Web browsing there too. A number of New York restaurants and hotels offer Wi-Fi: check out your options at www.subscriberdirect.com/the_new_yorker/zagat/ny.cfm. Intel's website (http://intel.jiwire.com) has a Hotspot Search function, where you can search for locations throughout the city.

There's recently been talk of a citywide Wi-Fi network in New York, similar to the one currently being implemented in Philadelphia and other major cities. Experts predict that it will take nine years to install, but, considering New York's track record for public projects, it will likely be a good time longer before a city-wide Wi-Fi system becomes reality.

Overview

We haven't checked (why should we?), but we're willing to bet that the highest concentration of art galleries in the world is contained in a rough box you can draw around Chelsea, Williamsburg, Dumbo, and SoHo. At any given time, more than 500 galleries are showing artwork created in every conceivable medium with, of course, varying levels of quality. But most galleries, especially in Chelsea and Williamsburg, are almost always showing something that's at least *provocative*, if not actually *good*. And since you can always hike up to the Met or the MoMA if you want to get comfortable, familiar masterworks, we're more than happy for the gallery scene to continue to provoke us.

SoHo Area

Five years ago, there were still hundreds of art galleries in SoHo. Now, it's swiftly becoming an outdoor mall. However, there are still some permanent artworks in gallery spaces, such as Walter DeMaria's excellent "The Broken Kilometer" (a Dia-sponsored space at 393 West Broadway), and his sublime New York Earth Room at 141 Wooster Street. And a short jaunt down to TriBeCa will land you in LaMonte Young's awesome aural experience "Dream House" at the **MELA Foundation.**

For rotating shows, **HEREArt** usually has some interesting things going on.

Chelsea

In case you weren't sure where all the galleries went after SoHo prices exploded, this is it. Over 200 galleries now reside in Chelsea, and there is always something new to see. Our recommendation is to hit at least two streets—W 24th Street between Tenth and Eleventh Avenues, and W 22nd Street between Tenth and Eleventh Avenues. W 24th Street is anchored by the almost-always-brilliant **Gagosian Gallery** and also includes the **Luhring Augustine, Charles Cowles, Mary Boone,** and **Matthew Marks** galleries. W 22nd has the brilliant **Dia: Chelsea** (temporarily closed for renovations), as well as the architecture-friendly **Max Protech** gallery and the **Julie Saul, Leslie Tonkonow, Marianne Boesky,** and **Yancey Richardson** galleries. Also check out the famous "artists" bookstore **Printed Matter** (535 W 22nd St).

If you're not tired from all that, there are tons more galleries to try on W 20th Street and W 26th Street. Take a cruise through the massive and cool Starrett-Lehigh Building (601 W 26th St) not only for the art but also for the great pillars, windows, and converted freight elevators (some big enough to fit trucks!).

Perhaps the final lid in the coffin for SoHo's art scene was **Exit Art's** move to 475 Tenth Avenue a couple years back. It's a truly original gallery that does everything from album covers to multimedia installations, and it's highly recommended.

Map 1 · Financial District

Water Street Gallery	241 Water St	212-349-9090

Map 2 · TriBeCa

A Taste of Art	147 Duane St	212-964-5493
Adelphi University	75 Varick St, 2nd Fl	212-965-8340
Anthem Gallery	41 Wooster St	212-334-9364
Apex Art	291 Church St	212-431-5270
Arcadia Gallery	51 Greene St	212-965-1387
Art at Format	50 Wooster St	212-941-7995
Artists Space	38 Greene St, 3rd Fl	212-226-3970
The Atlantic Gallery	40 Wooster St, 4th Fl	212-219-3183
Brooke Alexander Gallery	59 Wooster St	212-925-4338
Cheryl Hazan Gallery	35 N Moore St	212-343-8964
Cheryl Pelavin Fine Art	13 Jay St	212-925-9424
Coda Gallery	472 Broome St	212-334-0407
Dactyl Foundation for the Arts & Humanities	64 Grand St	212-219-2344
Deitch Projects	76 Grand St	212-343-7300
Desbrosses Gallery	9 Desbrosses St	212-343-3022
DFN Gallery	176 Franklin St	212-334-3400
The Drawing Center	35 Wooster St	212-219-2166
Ethan Cohen Fine Arts	37 Walker St	212-625-1250
Gallery Gen	158 Franklin St	212-226-7717
Latincollector	153 Hudson St	212-334-7813
Location One	26 Greene St	212-334-3347
Mela Foundation	275 Church St, 3rd Fl	212-925-8270
Organization of Independent Artists	19 Hudson St	212-219-9213
The Painting Center	52 Greene St	212-343-1060
PPOW	476 Broome St, 3rd Fl	212-941-8642
Spencer Brownstone Gallery	39 Wooster St	212-334-3455
Woodward Gallery	476 Broome St, 5th Fl	212-966-3411

Map 3 · City Hall / Chinatown

55 Mercer Gallery	55 Mercer St	212-226-8513
Agora Gallery	415 Varick St	212-226-4151
Animazing Art	461 Broome St	212-226-7374
Art in General	79 Walker St	212-219-0473
Bronwyn Keenan Gallery	3 Crosby St	212-431-5083
Broome Street Gallery	498 Broome St	212-226-6085
Canada	55 Chrystie St	212-925-4631
Franklin 54 Gallery	54 Franklin St	212-732-0009
Gallery 456	456 Broadway, 3rd Fl	212-431-9740
The Gallery at Dieu Donne Papermill	433 Broome St	212-226-0573
Gigantic Art Space	59 Franklin St	212-226-6762
Globe Institute Gallery	291 Broadway	212-349-4330
Grant Gallery	7 Mercer St	212-343-2919
K S Art	73 Leonard St	212-219-9918
Leo Koenig	249 Centre St	212-334-9255
Museum Salvador Rosillo	78 Reade St	212-349-7068
Paul Sharpe Contemporary Art	86 Walker St, 6th Fl	646-613-1252
Rhonda Schaller Studio	59 Franklin St	212-226-0166
Ronald Feldman Fine Arts	31 Mercer St	212-226-3232
S E Feinman Fine Arts	401 Broadway	212-431-6820
Studio 18 Gallery	18 Warren St	212-385-6734
Swiss Institute Contemporary Art	495 Broadway, 3rd Fl	212-925-2035
Synagogue for the Arts	49 White St	212-966-7141

Map 4 · Lower East Side

Abrons Art Center	466 Grand St	212-498-0400
maccarone	45 Canal St	212-431-4977
Michelle Birnbaum Fine Art	220 South St	212-427-8250

Map 5 · West Village

Akira Ikeda	17 Cornelia St, #1C	212-366-5449
Baron/Boisante	421 Hudson St	212-924-9940
Casey Kaplan	416 W 14th St	212-645-7335
Charles Street Gallery	160 Charles St	212-645-9700
Clockwork Gallery	32B Gansevoort St	212-229-1187
Cooper Classics Collection	137 Perry St	212-929-3909
DOMA	17 Perry St	212-929-4339
Gavin Brown's Enterprise	620 Greenwich St	212-627-5258

Hal Katzen Gallery	459 Washington St	212-925-9777
Heller Gallery	420 W 14th St	212-414-4014
HEREArt	145 Sixth Ave	212-647-0202
Jane Hartsook Gallery	16 Jones St	212-242-4106
at Greenwich House Pottery		
Parkett Editions	155 Sixth Ave, 2nd Fl	212-673-2660
Plane Space	102 Charles St	917-606-1268
Pratt Manhattan Gallery	144 W 14th St, 2nd Fl	212-647-7778
Sperone Westwater	415 W 13th St	212-999-7337
Synchronicity Fine Arts	106 W 13th St	646-230-8199
Tracy Williams Ltd	313 W 4th St	212-229-2757
Westbeth Gallery	57 Bethune St	212-989-4650
White Columns	320 W 13th St	212-924-4212
Wooster Projects	418 W 16th St	646-336-1999

Map 6 · Washington Sq / NYU / NoHo / SoHo

80 Washington Square East Galleries	80 Washington Sq E	212-592-5747
A/D	560 Broadway	212-966-5154
Agora	415 West Broadway, 5th Fl	212-226-4151
American Indian Community House Gallery	708 Broadway	212-598-0100
American Primitive	594 Broadway #205	212-966-1530
Andrei Kushnir/ Michele Taylor	208 E 6th St	212-254-2628
Axelle Fine Arts Ltd	148 Spring St	212-226-2262
Bottom Feeders Studio Gallery	195 Chrystie St, 2nd Fl	917-974-9664
Broadway Windows	Broadway & E 10th St	212-998-5751
The Broken Kilometer	393 West Broadway	212-925-9397
Bronfman Center Gallery at NYU	7 E 10th St	212-998-4114
Caldwell Snyder Gallery	451 West Broadway	212-387-0208
Cavin-Morris	560 Broadway, Ste 405B	212-226-3768
CFM	112 Greene St	212-966-3864
Chaim Gross Studio	526 LaGuardia Pl	212-529-4906
Deitch Projects	18 Wooster St	212-343-7300
Dia Center for the Arts - New York Earth Room	141 Wooster St	212-473-8072
Dia Center for the Arts - The Broken Kilometer	393 West Broadway	212-989-5566
Eleanor Ettinger	119 Spring St	212-925-7474
Entree Libree	66 Crosby St	212-431-5279
Exhibit A	160 Mercer St	212-343-0230
Flusso Gallery	568 Broadway	212-431-6925
Franklin Bowles Galleries	431 West Broadway	212-226-1616
Gallery Juno	568 Broadway #604B	212-431-1515
Gallery Revel	96 Spring St	212-925-0600
Gracie Mansion Gallery	407 E 6th St #2	212-925-9577
Grey Art Gallery	100 Washington Sq E	212-998-6780
Hebrew Union College - Jewish Institute of Religion	1 W 4th St	212-824-2205
ISE Foundation	555 Broadway	212-925-1649
Jacques Carcanagues	21 Greene St	212-925-8110
Janet Borden	560 Broadway	212-431-0166
John Szoke Editions	591 Broadway, 3rd Fl	212-219-8300
June Kelly	591 Broadway	212-226-1660
Kerrigan Campell Art + Projects	317 E 9th St	212-505-7196
Leslie-Lohman Gay Art Foundation	127B Prince St	212-673-7007
Louis K Meisel	141 Prince St	212-677-1340
Luise Ross	568 Broadway Ste 402	212-343-2161
Margarete Roeder Gallery	545 Broadway, 4th Fl	212-925-6098
Martin Lawrence	457 West Broadway	212-995-8865
Michael Ingbar Gallery of Architectural Art	568 Broadway	212-334-1100
Mimi Ferzt	114 Prince St	212-343-9377
Montserrat	584 Broadway	212-941-8899
Multiple Impressions	128 Spring St	212-925-1313
Nancy Hoffman	429 West Broadway	212-966-6676
National Association of Women Artists Fifth Avenue Gallery	80 Fifth Ave #1405	212-675-1616
New York Studio School	8 W 8th St	212-673-6466
Nolan/Eckman	560 Broadway Ste 604	212-925-6190

OK Harris Works of Art	383 West Broadway	212-431-3600
Opera Gallery	115 Spring St	212-966-6675
Parsons School of Design Exhibitions	2 W 13th St	212-229-8987
The Pen & Brush	16 E 10th St	212-475-3669
Peter Blum Gallery	99 Wooster St	212-343-0441
Peter Freeman	560 Broadway Ste 602	212-966-5154
Phyllis Kind Gallery	136 Greene St	212-925-1200
pop international galleries	473 West Broadway	212-533-4262
Rosenberg Gallery	34 Stuyvesant St	212-998-5702
Rosenberg + Kaufman Fine Art	115 Wooster St	212-431-4838
Salmagundi Club	47 Fifth Ave	212-255-7740
Sculptors Guild	110 Greene St Ste 603	212-431-5669
Silo	1 Freeman Aly	212-505-9156
Sragow	73 Spring St	212-219-1793
Staley-Wise Gallery	560 Broadway Ste 305	212-966-6223
Storefront for Art and Architecture	97 Kenmare St	212-431-5795
Suite 106/Popiashvili Newman Gallery	112 Mercer St	212-274-9166
Sundaram Tagore Gallery	137 Greene St	212-677-4520
Susan Teller Gallery	568 Broadway, Ste 103A	212-941-7335
Tenri Cultural Institute	43A W 13th St	212-645-2800
Terrain Gallery	141 Greene St	212-777-4490
Tobey Fine Arts	580 Broadway, Ste 902	212-431-7878
Walter Wickiser Gallery	568 Broadway, Ste 104B	212-941-1817
Ward-Nasse Gallery	178 Prince St	212-925-6951
Washington Sq Windows	80 Washington Sq E	212-998-5748
Weatherspoon Gallery	578 Broadway	212-925-5700
Wooster Arts Space	147 Wooster St	212-777-6338
Xanadu*	217 Thompson St	646-319-8597

Map 7 · East Village/Lower East Side

ATM Gallery	170 Ave B	212-375-0349
Gallery Onetwentyeight	128 Rivington St	212-674-0244
MF Gallery	157 Rivington St	917-446-8681
Rivington Arms	102 Rivington St	646-654-3213
The Phatory	618 E 9th St	212-777-7922

Map 8 · Chelsea

303 Gallery	525 W 22nd St	212-255-1121
511 Gallery	511 W 25th St, 3rd Fl	212-255-2885
ACA Galleries	529 W 20th St, 5th Fl	212-206-8080
AIR Gallery	511 W 25th St	212-255-6651
Alexander and Bonin	132 Tenth Ave	212-367-7474
Allen Sheppard Gallery	530 W 25th St	212-989-9919
Alona Kagan Gallery	540 W 29th St	212-560-0670
Amos Eno Gallery	530 W 25th St, 4th Fl	212-226-5342
Amsterdam Whitney	511 W 25th St	212-255-9050
Andrea Meislin Gallery	526 W 16th St	212-627-2552
Andrea Rosen Gallery	525 W 24th St	212-627-6000
Andrew Edlin Gallery	529 W 20th St, 6th Fl	212-206-9723
Andrew Kreps	516 W 20th St	212-741-8849
Annina Nosei	530 W 22nd St, 2nd Fl	212-741-8695
Anton Kern	532 W 20th St	212-367-9663
Ariel Meyerowitz Gallery	120 Eleventh Ave, 2nd Fl	212-414-2770
Art of this Century	530 W 25th St, 6th Fl	212-352-8131
Atelier A/E	323 W 22nd St	212-620-8106
Aurora Gallery	515 W 29th St, 2nd Fl	212-643-1700
Axel Raben Gallery	526 W 26th St #304	212-647-9064
Axis Gallery	453 W 17th St, 4th Fl	212-741-2582
Barbara Gladstone Gallery	515 W 24th St	212-206-9300
Baumgartner Gallery	522 W 24th St	212-243-6688
Bellwether	134 Tenth Ave	212-929-5959
Betty Cuningham Gallery	541 W 25th St	212-242-2772
Bill Maynes	529 W 20th St, 8th Fl	212-741-3318
Bitforms	529 W 20th St, 2nd Fl	212-366-6939
Blue Mountain Gallery	530 W 25th St, 4th Fl	646-486-4730
Bose Pacia Modern	508 W 26th St, 11th Fl	212-989-7074
Bound & Unbound	601 W 26th St #1201	212-463-7348
Bowery Gallery	530 W 25th St, 4th Fl	646-230-0655

Arts & Entertainment • **Art Galleries**

Map 8 • Chelsea—*continued*

Brent Sikkema	530 W 22nd St	212-929-2262
Briggs Robinson Gallery	527 W 29th St	212-560-9075
Bruce Silverstein Gallery	525 W 24th St	212-627-3930
Bryce Wolkowitz Gallery	601 W 26th St #1240	212-243-8830
Caelum Gallery	526 W 26th St, Ste 315	212-924-4161
Camhy Studio Gallery	526 W 26th St	212-741-9183
Caren Golden Fine Art	539 W 23rd St	212-727-8304
Ceres	547 W 27th St, 2nd Fl	212-947-6100
Chambers Fine Art	210 Eleventh Ave, 2nd Fl	212-414-1169
Chapel of Sacred Mirrors/ COSM NYC	540 W 27th St	212-564-4253
Chappell Gallery	526 W 26th St #317	212-414-2673
Charles Cowles Gallery	537 W 24th St	212-925-3500
Cheim & Read	547 W 25th St	212-242-7727
Chelsea Art Museum	556 W 22nd St	212-255-0719
Clementine Gallery	526 W 26th St, 2nd Fl	212-243-5937
COFA/Claire Oliver Fine Art	529 W 20th St #2W	212-929-5949
Cohan and Leslie	138 Tenth Ave	212-206-8710
CRG Gallery	535 W 22nd St, 3rd Fl	212-229-2766
Cristinerose/ Josee Bienvenu Gallery	529 W 20th St, 2nd Fl	212-206-0297
Cue Art Foundation	511 W 25th St	212-206-3583
D'Amelio Terras	525 W 22nd St	212-352-9460
Daniel Cooney Fine Art	511 W 25th St	212-255-8158
David Krut Fine Art	526 W 26th St #816	212-255-0394
David Zwirner	525 W 19th St	212-727-2070
DCA Gallery	525 W 22nd St	212-255-5511
Denise Bibro Fine Art	529 W 20th St, 4th Fl	212-647-7030
Derek Eller Gallery	526 W 25th St, 2nd Fl	212-206-6411
Dia	548 W 22nd St	212-989-5566
Dinter Fine Art	547 W 27th St	212-947-2818
DJT Fine Art/ Dom Taglialatella	511 W 25th St, 2nd Fl	212-367-0881
Dorfman Projects	529 W 20th St, 7th Fl	212-352-2272
Edition Schellmann	210 Eleventh Ave, 8th Fl	212-219-1821
Edward Thorp	210 Eleventh Ave, 6th Fl	212-691-6565
Elizabeth Dee Gallery	545 W 20th St	212-924-7545
Elizabeth Harris	529 W 20th St	212-463-9666
Esso Gallery	531 W 26th St	212-560-9728
Exit Art	475 Tenth Ave	212-966-7745
Eyebeam	540 W 21st St	718-222-3982
Feature	530 W 25th St	212-675-7772
Feigen Contemporary	535 W 20th St	212-929-0500
First Street Gallery	526 W 26th St #915	646-336-8053
Fischbach Gallery	210 Eleventh Ave #801	212-759-2345
Flomenhaft Gallery	547 W 27th St	212-268-4952
Florence Lynch Gallery	539 W 25th St	212-924-3290
Fredericks Freiser Gallery	504 W 22nd St	212-633-6555
Frederieke Taylor Gallery	535 W 22nd St, 6th Fl	646-230-0992
Friedrich Petzel	535 W 22nd St	212-680-9467
Gagosian Gallery	555 W 24th St	212-741-1111
Galeria Ramis Barquet	532 W 24th St	212-675-3421
Galerie Lelong	528 W 26th St	212-315-0470
Gallery Henoch	555 W 25th St	917-305-0003
Gary Tatintsian Gallery	525 W 25th St	212-633-0110
George Billis Gallery	511 W 25th St	212-645-2621
Gorney Bravin & Lee	534 W 26th St	212-352-8372
GR N'Namdi Gallery	526 W 26th St	212-929-6645
Greene Naftali	526 W 26th St, 8th Fl	212-463-7770
Haim Chanin Fine Arts	210 Eleventh Ave, Ste 201	646-230-7200
Heidi Cho Gallery	522 W 23rd St	212-255-6783
Henry Urbach Architecture	526 W 26th St	212-627-0974
Howard Scott	529 W 20th St, 7th Fl	646-486-7004
I-20 Gallery	529 W 20th St	212-645-1100
In Camera	511 W 25th St #401	212-647-7667
InterArt Gallery	225 Tenth Ave	212-647-1811
International Poster Center	601 W 26th St	212-787-4000
International Print Center New York	526 W 26th St, Rm 824	212-989-5090
J Cacciola Galleries	531 W 25th St	212-462-4646
Jack Shainman Gallery	513 W 20th St	212-645-1701
James Cohan	533 W 26th St	212-714-9500
Jeff Bailey Gallery	511 W 25th St #80	212-989-0156
JG Contemporary/ James Graham & Sons	505 W 28th St	212-564-7662

Jim Kempner Fine Art	501 W 23rd St	212-206-6872
John Connelly Presents	526 W 26th St,10th Fl	212-337-9563
John Davis Gallery	330 W 38th St	212-244-3797
John Elder Gallery	529 W 20th St #7W	212-462-2600
John Stevenson Gallery	338 W 23rd St	212-352-0070
Jonathan LeVine Gallery	529 W 20th St	212-243-3822
Josee Bienvenu Gallery	529 W 20th St	212-206-0297
Joseph Helman	601 W 26th St	212-929-1545
Julie Saul Gallery	535 W 22nd St, 6th Fl	212-627-2410
Kashya Hildebrand Gallery	531 W 25th St	212-366-5757
Katherine Markel Fine Arts	529 W 20th St	212-366-5368
Kent Gallery	541 W 25th St	212-627-3680
Kim Foster	529 W 20th St	212-229-0044
Kimcherova	532 W 25th St	212-929-9720
The Kitchen Gallery	512 W 19th St	212-255-5793
Klemens Gasser & Tanja Grunert	524 W 19th St, 2nd Fl	212-807-9494
Klotz Sirmon Gallery	511 W 25th St	212-741-4764
Kravets/Wehby Gallery	521 W 21st St	212-352-2238
Kustera Tilton Gallery	520 W 21st St	212-989-0082
Lehmann Maupin	540 W 26th St	212-255-2923
Lemmons Contemporary	210 Eleventh Ave	212-337-0025
Lennon, Weinberg	514 W 25th St	212-941-0012
Leslie Tonkonow Artworks and Projects	535 W 22nd St, 6th Fl	212-255-8450
LFL Gallery	530 W 24th St	212-989-7700
Linda Durham Contemporary Art	210 Eleventh Ave, 8th Fl	212-337-0025
Lohin Geduld Gallery	531 W 25th St	212-675-2656
Lombard-Freid Fine Arts	531 W 26th St	212-967-8040
Lost Art	515 W 29th St PH	212-594-5450
Lucas Schoormans	508 W 26th St #11B	212-243-3159
Luhring Augustine	531 W 24th St	212-206-9100
Lyons Wier Gallery	511 W 25th St #205	212-242-6220
Margaret Thatcher Projects	511 W 25th St #404	212-675-0222
Marianne Boesky Gallery	535 W 22nd St	212-680-9889
Marvelli Gallery	526 W 26th St	212-627-3363
Mary Boone Gallery	541 W 24th St	212-752-2929
Massimo Audiello	526 W 26th St #519	212-675-9082
Matthew Marks Gallery	523 W 24th St	212-243-0200
Max Protech	511 W 22nd St	212-633-6999
Maya Stendhal Gallery	545 W 20th St	212-366-1549
McKenzie Fine Art	511 W 25th St, 2nd Fl	212-989-5467
Medialia: Rack & Hamper Gallery	335 W 38th St, 4th Fl	212-971-0953
Messineo Wyman Projects	525 W 22nd St	212-414-0827
Metro Pictures	519 W 24th St	212-206-7100
Michael Perez Gallery	520 W 23rd St	212-366-6600
Mike Weiss Gallery	520 W 24th St	212-691-6899
Mixed Greens	601 W 26th St, 11th Fl	212-331-8888
Murray Guy	453 W 17th St	212-463-7372
MY Art Prospects	547 W 27th St 2nd Fl	212-268-7132
Nancy Margolis Gallery	523 W 25th St	212-242-3013
New Art Center	580 Eighth Ave	212-354-2999
New Century Artists	530 W 25th St Ste 406	212-367-7072
New Museum of Contemporary Art	556 W 22nd St	212-219-1222
Nicole Klagsbrun Gallery	526 W 26th St #213	212-243-3335
NoHo Gallery in SoHo	530 W 25th St, 4th Fl	212-367-7063
PaceWildenstein	534 W 25th St	212-929-7000
Paint Box Gallery	170 Ninth Ave	212-675-1680
Paul Kasmin Gallery	293 Tenth Ave	212-563-4474
Paul Morris Gallery	530 W 25th St	212-727-2752
Paul Rodgers/9W	529 W 20th St, 9th Fl	212-414-9810
Paula Cooper Gallery	534 W 21st St	212-255-1105
Pavel Zoubok Gallery	533 W 23rd St	212-675-7490
Perry Rubenstein Gallery	527 W 23rd St	212-627-8000
Phoenix	210 Eleventh Ave, 9th Fl	212-226-8711
Pleiades Gallery	530 W 25th St	646-230-0056
Plum Blossoms Gallery	555 W 25th St	212-719-7008
Postmasters Gallery	459 W 19th St	212-727-3323
PPOW	555 W 25th St, 2nd Fl	212-647-1044
Prince Street Gallery	530 W 25th St, 4th Fl	646-230-0246
Printed Matter	535 W 22nd St	212-925-0325
The Proposition: Ellen Donahue & Ronald Sosinski Art	559 W 22nd St	212-242-0035

Qui New York/ Zwicker Collective USA	601 W 26th St	212-691-2240
Randel Gallery	287 Tenth Ave, 2nd Fl	212-239-3330
Rare	521 W 26th St	212-268-1520
Reeves Contemporary	535 W 24th St, 2nd Fl	212-714-0044
Remy Toledo Gallery	529 W 20th St	212-242-7552
Ricco/Maresca Gallery	529 W 20th St, 3rd Fl	212-627-4819
Robert Mann Gallery	210 Eleventh Ave	212-989-7600
Robert Miller	524 W 26th St	212-366-4774
Robert Steele Gallery	511 W 25th St	212-243-0165
Rush Arts Gallery & Resource Center	526 W 26th St #311	212-691-9552
Sandra Gering Gallery	534 W 22nd St	646-336-7183
Sara Meltzer Gallery	516 W 20th St	212-727-9330
Sean Kelly Gallery	528 W 29th St	212-239-1181
Sears-Peyton Gallery	210 Eleventh Ave #802	212-966-7469
Sherry French	601 W 26th St	212-647-8867
Silas Seandel Studio	551 W 22nd St	212-645-5286
Skoto Gallery	529 W 20th St	212-352-8058
SoHo 20 Chelsea	511 W 25th St Ste 605	212-367-8994
Sonnabend	536 W 22nd St	212-627-1018
Spike Gallery	547 W 20th St	212-627-4100
Stefan Stux Gallery	530 W 25th St	212-352-1600
Stephen Haller	542 W 26th St	212-741-7777
Stricoff Fine Art	564 W 25th St	212-219-3977
Studio 601	511 W 25th St	212-367-7300
Susan Conde Gallery	521 W 23rd St	212-367-9799
Susan Inglett Gallery	535 W 22nd St, 6th Fl	212-647-9111
SVA Main Gallery	601 26th St	212-592-2145
Tanya Bonakdar Gallery	521 W 21st St	212-414-4144
Team	527 W 26th St	212-279-9219
Thomas Erben Gallery	516 W 20th St	212-645-8701
Thomas Werner Gallery	526 W 26th St #712	646-638-2883
Tony Shafrazi Gallery	544 W 16th St	212-274-9300
TRANS>area	511 W 25th St	646-486-0252
Transplant	525 W 29th St, 2nd Fl	212-505-0994
Van De Weghe Fine Art	521 W 23rd St	212-929-6633
Viridian Artists	530 W 25th St, #407	212-414-4040
Visual Arts Gallery	601 W 26th St	212-592-2145
Von Lintel Gallery	555 W 25th St, 2nd Fl	212-242-0599
WEISSPOLLACK Galleries	521 W 25th St	212-989-3708
WhiteBox	525 W 26th St	212-714-2347
Yancey Richardson Gallery	535 W 22nd St	646-230-9610
Yossi Milo Gallery	552 W 24th St	212-414-0370
Yvon Lambert	564 W 25th St	212-242-3611
Ziehersmith	531 W 25th St	212-229-1088
ZONEchelsea, Center for the Arts	601 W 26th St	212-205-2177

Map 9 • Flatiron / Lower Midtown

A Ramona Studio	65 W 37th St	212-398-1904
A-forest Gallery	134 W 29th St	212-673-1168
Alp Galleries	291 Seventh Ave, 5th Fl	212-206-9108
Art Center of the Graduate Center CUNY	365 Fifth Ave	212-817-7386
Avalanche	39 E 31st St, 3rd Fl	212-447-9485
Christine Burgin Gallery	243 W 18th St	212-462-2668
Gallery ArtsIndia	206 Fifth Ave	212-725-6092
H Heather Edelman Gallery	141 W 20th St	646-230-1104
Illustration House	110 W 25th St	212-966-9444
Jack Tilton	520 W 21st St	212-989-0082
Kavehaz	37 W 26th St	212-343-0612
Marlborough Chelsea	211 W 19th St	212-463-8634
Merton D Simpson Gallery	38 W 28th St, 5th Fl	212-686-6735
The Museum at the Fashion Institute of Technology	227 W 27th St	212-217-5800
Nabi Gallery	137 W 25th St	212-929-6063
Peter Hay Halpert Fine Art	223 W 21st St	646-220-8657
Peter Spinelli	29 W 26th St	917-468-2667
Senior & Shopmaker	21 E 26th St	212-213-6767
Sepia International	148 W 24th St	212-645-9444
Studio Annex at Madison Industries	279 Fifth Ave	212-652-0629
Tibet House Museum	22 W 15th St	212-807-0563
Yeshiva University Museum	15 W 16th St	212-294-8330

Map 10 • Murray Hill / Gramercy

Baruch College/ Sidney Mishkin Gallery	135 E 22nd St	212-802-2690
Blue Heron Arts Center	123 E 24th St	212-979-5000
East-West Gallery	573 Third Ave	212-687-0181
The National Arts Club	15 Gramercy Park S	212-475-3424
School of Visual Arts	209 E 23rd St	212-592-2144
Swann Galleries	104 E 25th St	212-254-4710
Talwar Gallery	108 E 16th St	212-673-3096
Tepper Galleries	110 E 25th St	212-677-5300

Map 11 • Hell's Kitchen

Archibald Arts	602 Tenth Ave	212-541-6366
Art for Healing NYC/ Art for Healing Gallery	405 W 50th St	212-977-1165
Fountain Gallery	702 Ninth Ave	212-262-2756
Gallery @49	322 W 49th St	212-767-0855
Hunter College/ Times Square Gallery	450 W 41st St	212-772-4991
Jadite	413 W 50th St	212-315-2740
NYCoo Gallery	408 W 46th St	212-489-0461

Map 12 • Midtown

Alexandre Gallery	41 E 57th St, 13th Fl	212-755-2828
American Folk Art Museum	45 W 53rd St	212-265-2350
Ameringer & Yohe Fine Art	20 W 57th St, 2nd Fl	212-445-0051
Anthony Grant	37 W 57th St, 2nd Fl	212-755-0434
Art Students League of NY	215 W 57th St, 2nd Fl	212-247-4510
Artemis Greenberg Van Doren Gallery	730 Fifth Ave, 7th Fl	212-445-0444
Asian Cultural Center	15 E 40th St	212-541-6366
Austrian Cultural Forum	11 E 52nd St	212-319-5300
AXA Gallery	787 Seventh Ave	212-554-4818
Babcock	724 Fifth Ave, 11th Fl	212-767-1852
Barbara Mathes	41 E 57th St, 3rd Fl	212-752-5135
Bernarducci - Meisel	37 W 57th St, 6th Fl	212-593-3757
Bill Hodges Gallery	24 W 57th St	212-333-2640
Bonni Benrubi	41 E 57th St, 13th Fl	212-517-3766
China 2000 Fine Art	5 E 57th St	212-588-1198
Dahesh Museum of Art	580 Madison Ave	212-759-0606
Danese	41 E 57th St, 6th Fl	212-223-2227
David Findlay Jr Fine Art	41 E 57th St Ste 1120	212-486-7660
DC Moore	724 Fifth Ave, 8th Fl	212-247-2111
Edwynn Houk	745 Fifth Ave, 4th Fl	212-750-7070
Fitch-Febvrel	5 E 57th St, 12th Fl	212-688-8522
Forum	745 Fifth Ave, 5th Fl	212-355-4545
Franklin Parrasch	20 W 57th St	212-246-5360
Frederick Schultz Ancient Art	41 E 57th St, 11th Fl	212-758-6007
Galeria Ramis Barquet	41 E 57th St, 5th Fl	212-644-9090
Galerie St Etienne	24 W 57th St Ste 802	212-245-6734
Gallery: Gertrude Stein	56 W 57th St, 3rd Fl	212-535-0600
Garth Clark	24 W 57th St #305	212-246-2205
Gemini GEL at Joni Moisant Weyl	58 W 58th St #21-B	212-308-0924
George Adams	41 E 57th St, 7th Fl	212-644-5665
Grant Selwyn Fine Art	37 W 57th St, 2nd Fl	212-755-0434
Hammer Galleries	33 W 57th St	212-644-4400
Herbert Arnot	250 W 57th St	212-245-8287
Howard Greenberg	41 E 57th St, 14th Fl	212-334-0010
International Center of Photography	1133 Sixth Ave	212-857-0000
Jain Marunouchi	24 W 57th St, 6th Fl	212-969-9660
James Goodman	41 E 57th St, 8th Fl	212-593-3737
Jason McCoy Inc	41 E 57th St	212-319-1996
Joan T Washburn	20 W 57th St, 8th Fl	212-397-6780
Joan Whalen Fine Art	24 W 57th St Ste 507	212-397-9700
Julian Jadow Ceramics	37 W 57th St #601	212-757-6660
Katharina Rich Perlow	41 E 57th St, 13th Fl	212-644-7171
Kennedy Galleries	730 Fifth Ave	212-541-9600

Arts & Entertainment • **Art Galleries**

Map 12 • Midtown—*continued*

Kraushaar	724 Fifth Ave	212-307-5730
Lang Fine Art	41 E 57th St	212-980-2640
Laurence Miller	20 W 57th St	212-397-3930
Leo Kaplan Modern	41 E 57th St, 7th Fl	212-872-1616
Leonard Hutton	41 E 57th St, 3rd Fl	212-751-7373
Littlejohn Contemporary	41 E 57th St, 7th Fl	212-980-2323
Littleton & Hennessey Asian Art	724 Fifth Ave	212-586-4075
Lori Bookstein Fine Art	37 W 57th St	212-750-0949
Marian Goodman	24 W 57th St, 4th Fl	212-977-7160
Marlborough	40 W 57th St, 2nd Fl	212-541-4900
Mary Boone	745 Fifth Ave, 4th Fl	212-752-2929
Mary Ryan	24 W 57th St, 2nd Fl	212-397-0669
Maxwell Davidson	724 Fifth Ave	212-759-7555
McKee	745 Fifth Ave, 4th Fl	212-688-5951
Meridian Gallery - Rita Krauss	41 E 57th St, 8th Fl	212-980-2400
Michael Rosenfeld	24 W 57th St, 7th Fl	212-247-0082
Museum of Arts & Design	40 W 53rd St	212-956-3535
Neuhoff	41 E 57th St, 4th Fl	212-838-1122
Nohra Haime	41 E 57th St, 6th Fl	212-888-3550
O'Hara	41 E 57th St, 13th Fl	212-355-3330
Pace MacGill	32 E 57th St, 9th Fl	212-759-7999
Pace Primitive	32 E 57th St, 7th Fl	212-421-3688
Pace Prints	32 E 57th St, 3rd Fl	212-421-3237
PaceWildenstein	32 E 57th St	212-421-3292
Patricia Laligant Gallery	24 W 57th St	212-252-9922
Peter Findlay	41 E 57th St, 3rd Fl	212-644-4433
The Project	37 W 57th St, 3rd Fl	212-688-4673
Reece	24 W 57th St Ste 304	212-333-5830
Rehs Galleries	5 E 57th St	212-355-5710
Rita Krauss/ Meridian Gallery	41 E 57th St	212-980-2400
Scholten Japanese Art	145 W 58th St #2H	212-585-0474
So Hyun Gallery	41 W 57th St	212-355-6669
Susan Sheehan	20 W 57th St, 7th Fl	212-489-3331
Tibor de Nagy	724 Fifth Ave, 12th Fl	212-262-5050
Tina Kim Fine Art	41 W 57th St, 2nd Fl	212-716-1100
UBS Art Gallery	1285 Sixth Ave	212-713-2885
UMA Gallery	30 W 57th St, 6th Fl	212-757-7240
Zabriskie	41 E 57th St, 4th Fl	212-752-1223

Map 13 • East Midtown

Dai Ichi Arts	249 E 48th St	212-230-1680
Gallery Korea	460 Park Ave, 6th Fl	212-759-9550
Japan Society	333 E 47th St	212-832-1155
National Sculpture Society	Park Ave Atrium, 237 Park Ave	212-764-5645
Spanierman Gallery	45 E 58th St	212-832-0208
St Peter's Lutheran Church	619 Lexington Ave	212-935-2200
Throckmorton Fine Art	145 E 57th St, 3rd Fl	212-223-1059
Trygve Lie Gallery	317 E 52nd St	212-319-0370
Ubu Gallery	416 E 59th St	212-753-4444
Wally Findlay Galleries	124 E 57th St	212-421-5390
Whitney Museum of American Art at Altria	120 Park Ave	917-663-2453

Map 14 • Upper West Side (Lower)

Linda Hyman Fine Arts	25 Central Park W	212-399-0112

Map 15 • Upper East Side (Lower)

Achim Moeller Fine Art	167 E 73rd St	212-988-4500
Acquavella	18 E 79th St	212-734-6300
Adam Baumgold	74 E 79th St	212-861-7338
Adelson Galleries	25 E 77th St, 3rd Fl	212-439-6800
American Illustrators Gallery	18 E 77th St Ste 1A	212-744-5190
Anita Friedman Fine Arts	980 Madison Ave	212-472-1527
Anita Shapolsky	152 E 65th St	212-452-1094
Barry Friedman	32 E 67th St	212-794-8950
Berry-Hill	11 E 70th St	212-744-2300
Bruton	40 E 61st St	212-980-1640
C&M Arts	45 E 78th St	212-861-0020

Cavalier Gallery	1100 Madison Ave	212-570-4696
CDS	76 E 79th St	212-772-9555
China Institute Gallery	125 E 65th St	212-744-8181
Conner & Rosenkranz	19 E 74rd St	212-517-3710
Cook Fine Art	1063 Madison Ave	212-737-3550
Craig F Starr Associates	5 E 73rd St	212-570-1739
D Wigmore Fine Art	22 E 76th St	212-794-2128
David Finlay	984 Madison Ave	212-249-2909
Davis & Langdale	231 E 60th St	212-838-0333
Debra Force Fine Art	14 E 73rd St Ste 4B	212-734-3636
Dickinson Roundell	19 E 66th St	212-772-8083
Ekstrom & Ekstrom	417 E 75th St	212-988-8857
Elkon Gallery	18 E 81st St	212-535-3940
Evan Janis Fine Art	70 E 79th St	212-639-1501
Ezair	905 Madison Ave	212-628-2224
Flowers	1000 Madison Ave, 2nd Fl	212-439-1700
Francis M Naumann Fine Art	22 E 80th St	212-472-6800
The Frick Collection	1 E 70th St	212-288-0700
Friedman & Vallois	27 E 67th St	212-517-3820
Frost & Reed	21 E 67th St	212-717-2201
Gagosian	980 Madison Ave	212-744-2313
Galerie Rienzo	20 E 69th St #4C	212-288-2226
Gallery 71	974 Lexington Ave	212-744-7779
Gallery Pahk	16 E 79th St	212-861-3303
Gallery Schlesinger	24 E 73rd St, 2nd Fl	212-734-3600
Gerald Peters	24 E 78th St	212-628-9760
Gitterman Gallery	170 E 75th St	212-734-0868
Godel & Co	39A E 72nd St	212-288-7272
Goedhuis Contemporary	42 E 76th St	212-535-6954
Hall & Knight	21 E 67th St	212-772-2266
Hilde Gerst	987 Madison Ave	212-288-3400
Hirschl & Adler Galleries	21 E 70th St	212-535-8810
Hollis Taggart Galleries	48 E 73rd St	212-628-4000
Hoorn-Ashby	766 Madison Ave, 2nd Fl	212-628-3199
Hubert Gallery	1046 Madison Ave	212-628-2922
Hunter College/Bertha & Karl Leubsdorf Gallery	E 68th St & Lexington	212-772-4991
Irena Hochman Fine Art	1100 Madison Ave	212-772-2227
Jacobson Howard	19 E 76th St	212-570-2362
James Francis Trezza	39 E 78th St Ste 603	212-327-2218
James Graham & Sons	1014 Madison Ave	212-535-5767
Jan Krugier	958 Madison Ave	212-755-7288
Jane Kahan	922 Madison Ave, 2nd Fl	212-744-1490
Janos Gat Gallery	1100 Madison Ave	212-327-0441
Kate Ganz USA	25 E 73rd St	212-535-1977
Keith De Lellis	47 E 68th St	212-327-1482
Knoedler & Co	19 E 70th St	212-794-0550
Kouros	23 E 73rd St	212-288-5888
L'Arc En Seine	15 E 82nd St	212-585-2587
Leila Taghinia-Milani Heller Gallery	22 E 72nd St	212-249-7695
Leo Castelli	18 E 77th St	212-249-4470
Leon Tovar Gallery	16 E 71st St	212-585-2460
M&R Sayer Fine Arts	129 E 71st St	212-517-8829
M Sutherland Fine Arts	55 E 80th St, 2nd Fl	212-249-0428
Marc Jancou Fine Art	801 Madison Ave	212-717-1700
Mark Murray Fine Paintings	39 E 72nd St	212-585-2380
Martha Parrish & James Reinish	25 E 73rd St, 2nd Fl	212-734-7332
Mary-Anne Martin Fine Art	23 E 73rd St	212-288-2213
McGrath Galleries	9 E 73rd St	212-737-7396
Megan Moynihan & Franklin Rielman	24 E 73rd St	212-879-2545
Menconi & Schoelkopt Fine Art	13 E 69th St	212-879-8815
Meredith Ward Fine Art	60 E 66th St	212-744-7306
Michael Werner	4 E 77th St	212-988-1623
Michail-Lombardo Gallery	19 E 69th St Ste 302	212-472-2400
Michelle Rosenfeld	16 E 79th St	212-734-0900
Mitchell-Innes & Nash	1018 Madison Ave, 5th Fl	212-744-7400
MMC Gallery	221 E 71st St	212-517-0692
MME Fine Art	74 E 79th St	212-439-6600
Nancy Schwartz Fine Art	710 Park Ave	212-988-6709
Neptune Fine Art & Brand X Projects	50 E 72nd St	212-628-0501
Praxis International Art	25 E 73rd St, 4th Fl	212-772-9478
Questroyal Fine Art	903 Park Ave, Ste 3A & B	212-744-3586
Rachel Adler Fine Art	24 E 71st St	212-308-0511

Richard Gray	1018 Madison Ave, 4th Fl	212-472-8787
Richard L Feigen & Co	34 E 69th St	212-628-0700
Roth Horowitz	160A E 70th St	212-717-9067
Salander-O'Reilly	20 E 79th St	212-879-6606
Sayer Fine Arts Gallery	129 E 71st St	212-517-8811
Schiller & Bodo	19 E 74th St	212-772-8627
Shepherd & Derom Galleries	58 E 79th St	212-861-4050
Skarstedt Fine Art	1018 Madison Ave, 3rd Fl	212-737-2060
Solomon & Co Fine Art	959 Madison Ave	212-737-8200
Soufer	1015 Madison Ave	212-628-3225
Ukrainian Institute of America	2 E 79th St	212-288-8660
Ursus Prints	981 Madison Ave	212-772-8787
Uta Scharf	42 E 76th St	212-744-3840
Vivian Horan Fine Art	35 E 65th St, 2nd Fl	212-517-9410
Wildenstein	19 E 64th St	212-879-0500
William Secord	52 E 76th St	212-249-0075
Winston Wachter Mayer Fine Art	39 E 78th St, Ste 301	212-327-2526
Yoshii	17 E 76th St, Ste 1R	212-744-5550
Zwirner & Wirth	32 E 69th St	212-517-8677

Map 16 · Upper W Side (Upper)

| Catherine Dail Fine Art | 40 W 86th St | 212-595-3550 |

Map 17 · Upper E Side / E Harlem

Allan Stone Gallery	113 E 90th St	212-987-4997
Casa Linda Galleries	300 E 95th St	212-860-8016
Doyle New York	175 E 87th St	212-427-2730
El Museo del Barrio	1230 Fifth Ave	212-831-7272
Gallery at the Marmara -Manhattan	301 E 94th St	212-427-3100
Jeffrey Myers Primitive & Fine Art	12 E 86th St	212-472-0115
The Jewish Museum	1109 Fifth Ave	212-423-3200
National Academy Museum	1083 Fifth Ave	212-369-4880
Neue Galerie New York	1048 Fifth Ave	212-628-6200
Samson Fine Arts	1150 Fifth Ave	212-369-6677
Taller Boricua Galleries	1680 Lexington Ave	212-831-4333
Uptown Gallery	1194 Madison Ave	212-722-3677

Map 18 · Columbia/Morningside Hts

| Galleries at the Interchurch Center | 475 Riverside Dr | 212-870-2200 |
| Miriam & Ira D Wallach Art Gallery | 116th & Broadway, Schermerhorn Hall, 8th Fl | 212-854-7288 |

Map 19 · Harlem (Lower)

| PCOG Gallery | 1902 Adam Clayton Powell Jr Blvd | 212-932-9669 |
| Studio Museum in Harlem | 144 W 125th St | 212-864-4500 |

Map 25 · Inwood

| 207 Art | 634 W 207th St | 212-304-0621 |

Map 27 · Long Island City

Dorsky Gallery	11-03 45th Ave	718-937-6317
Fisher Landau Center for Art	38-27 30th St	718-937-0727
Garth Clark Gallery's Project Space	45-46 21st St	718-706-2491
La Guardia Community College, CUNY	31-10 Thomson Ave	718-482-5696
Ro Gallery	47-15 36th St	800-888-1063
Sculpture Center	44-19 Purves St	718-361-1750
Socrates Sculpture Park	Broadway & Vernon Blvd	718-956-1819

Map 28 · Greenpoint

| Galeria Janet | 205 Norman St | 718-383-9380 |
| GV/AS | 140 Franklin St | 718-389-6847 |

Map 29 · Williamsburg

31 Grand	31 Grand St	718-388-2858
Artpage	781 N 7th St	718-302-1534
Barthelemy	329 Grand St	718-599-9772
Bench Dogs	60 Broadway	718-486-7338
Bicycle Paintings	35 Broadway	718-486-5490
Bingo Hall	212 Berry St	718-599-0844
Black & White	483 Driggs Ave	917-667-2332
Dollhaus	37 Broadway	718-387-4123
Elaint Kayne	475 Kapp St	718-783-0060
EX	872 Kent Ave	718-387-4320
Fishtank	93 N 6th St	718-599-8640
Fluxcore	340 Grand St	718-599-4962
Good/Bad	383 S 1st St	718-388-5022
Hogar	111 Grand St	718-782-0183
Jack the Pelican	487 Driggs Ave	718-384-9606
Jessica Murray Projects	210 N 6th St	718-218-6743
Landing	242 Wythe Ave	718-599-9205
Lunarbase	197 Grand St	718-302-9507
Modern Mediums	150 Kent Ave	718-609-4096
Naked Duck	66 Jackson St	718-384-3913
National Gallery of Brooklyn	90 Berry St	718-387-8226
Open Ground Photo Gallery of Williamsburg	252 Grand St	718-782-3433
Priska C Jushka	425 Keap St	718-782-4100
Roebling Hall	97 N 9th St	718-599-5352
S1	390 Wythe Ave	718-302-1521
Studio	242 S 1st St	718-302-4863
	84 S 1st St	

Map 30 · Brooklyn Heights / DUMBO/ Downtown

Antiquarius	183 Concord St	718-222-2434
Artisan's Gallery	221 Court St	718-330-3432
DUMBO Arts Center	30 Washington St	718-694-0831
Engels Galerie	45 State St	718-596-0850
Faith Art	393 Bridge St	718-852-1558
Howard Schickler	100 Water St	718-431-6363
Jubilee	117 Henry St	718-596-1499
Momose Art Studio	68 Jay St	718-403-9007
SouthFirst	60 N 6th St	718-599-2500
Spring	126 Front St	718-222-1054

Map 31· Fort Greene / Clinton Hill

| DEMU | 761 Fulton St | 718-596-8484 |
| Sarafina | 411 Myrtle Ave | 718-522-1083 |

Map 32 · BoCoCa / Red Hook

Artez'N	444 Atlantic Ave	718-596-2649
Axelle	312 Atlantic Ave	718-246-1800
David Allen	331 Smith St	718-488-5568
East End Ensemble	273 Smith St	718-624-8878
Felice Amara	121 3rd St	718-797-4414

Map 33 · Park Slope / Prospect Heights / Windsor Ter

| JK Flynn | 471 Sixth Ave | 718-369-8934 |
| Praxis | 610 Dean St | 718-398-0894 |

Map 35 · Jersey City

| Kearon-Hempenstall Gallery | 536 Bergen Ave | 201-333-8855 |
| New Jersey City University | 2039 Kennedy Blvd | 201-200-3246 |

Battery Park City

| World Financial Center Courtyard Gallery | 220 Vesey St | 212-945-2600 |

They don't call New York "the city that never sleeps" for nothing. There are a million reasons to stay out late in this town, and when most spots stay open until 4 in the am, you best take advantage. New York City boasts the best and largest assortment of bars per square foot on the planet. How many, you ask? A lot—a whole lot. While more and more places are opening up throughout the isle of Manhattan and its outer boroughs, the majority of these watering holes are still parked between 14th and Canal Streets, with new bars sprouting like weeds east of Avenue A and south of Houston in the East Village/Lower East Side. On any given night, you can also choose from over a hundred musical acts ranging from jazz to punk or practice your moves on some of the finest dance floors in the country. Faced with so many options, how do you decide where to go? Well, we've taken the liberty of selecting a few choice destinations for your basic nightlife variables: the dive, best beer selection, outdoor space, jukebox, smoker-friendly, music venue, and dance club. So put down that remote and go explore the best of what NYC has to offer.

Dive Bars

There are A LOT of dumps in this city, so we've done our best to single out the darkest and the dirtiest. A popular choice among our staff is the oh-so derelict **Mars Bar**—clean-freaks beware of the bathroom! Other favorites include **Milano's**, **The Subway Inn**, **International Bar**, **Cherry Tavern**, and **The Hole**. If you need to get down and dirty in Brooklyn, check out the **Turkey's Nest** in Williamsburg.

Best Beer Selection

When it comes to sheer beer selection, there are a number of worthy contenders. The heavily-trodden **Peculiar Pub** offers an expensive, yet extensive beer list. Visit this one on a weekday if you want some genuine one-on-one time with the bartender. The **Ginger Man** in lower Midtown stocks over 100 kinds of bottled brew, and has over 60 options on tap. **Vol de Nuit** has a large number of Belgian beers and a warm but reclusive atmosphere. Other places to try are **d.b.a.**, **Blind Tiger Ale House**, and **The Waterfront Ale House** (located in both Manhattan and Brooklyn).

Outdoor Spaces

What could be better than sipping a cocktail under the stars? How about sipping a cocktail *with a smoke* under the stars? That's right—bars with outdoor patios have circumvented the no-smoking legislation. Not only does these outdoor spaces offer solace to those cranky puffing pari-ahs, they provide us all with a short intermission from the commotion and clamor of city life…that is until the next fire truck screams by. We love the aptly named **Gowanus Yacht Club** in Carroll Gardens. This intimate beer garden serves up cold ones with dogs and burgers in a cook-out setting. Other patios to check out are **Barramundi**, **B Bar**, **Sweet & Vicious**, **The Porch**, **The Park**, and the **Heights**

Bar & Grill. Some other goodies in Brooklyn are **The Gate** in Park Slope and **Pete's Candy Store** in Williamsburg.

Best Jukebox

Again, this is truly a matter of personal taste, but here is a condensed list of NFT picks. For Manhattan: **Ace Bar** (indie rock/punk), **Cherry Tavern** (punk/rock), **HiFi** (a huge and diverse selection), **7B** (rock all the way), **Rudy's Bar & Grill** (blues). For Brooklyn: **The Charleston** (Williamsburg—old school), **Sweetwater Tavern** (Williamsburg—punk), **Great Lakes** (Park Slope—indie rock), **The Boat** (Carroll Gardens—indie rock), and the **Brooklyn Social Club** (Carroll Gardens—country/soul goodness).

Smoker-Friendly

Despite Bloomberg's efforts to create a smoke-free New York, there are a few loopholes in the current legislation. You can still light up in cigar bars and hookah bars, bars with outdoor spaces, and privately-owned establishments. Another exception is the separate smoking room, tightly sealed off from the rest of the bar and specially ventilated. Unless you bring a bottle of Febreze with you, we don't recommend trying this last option. Good places to puff are **Circa Tabac** (cigar bar) and **Swan's Bar & Grill**.

Music Venues

For smaller venues we love **Arlene's Grocery**, **CB's**, **Tonic**, the **Mercury Lounge**, **Sin-é**, **Magnetic Field** (Brooklyn) and **Trash** (Brooklyn). We also like the larger spaces at **Bowery Ballroom**, **Hammerstein Ballroom**, **Northsix** (Brooklyn), and **Warsaw** (Brooklyn). The best jazz can still be found at the **Village Vanguard**, **Birdland**, and **Iridium**. Terra Blues is a good small club for blues. **The Knitting Factory**, on many occasions, serves up the best of all of the above.

Dance Clubs

For those of you who don't believe in paying to dance, there are a number of great places to boogie for free. We like **Lit**, **Good World**, **Rififi** (free-$5), the **APT** (sometimes free, sometimes $5-10), and **Cielo**. If you're feeling adventurous, check out the panty party on Saturday nights at **Opaline**—that's right, no pants allowed!

If you don't mind shelling out the dough, definitely look into the cozy dance space at **Sapphire Lounge** ($5 after 10: 30 pm) and the new gargantuan-sized **Crobar** ($30-40). Some other new-ish clubs worth mentioning are **Avalon** (formerly Limelight) and **Capitale** (located in the old Bowery Savings Bank). On the weekends, entry into these clubs doesn't come without paying your dues in long lines and pricey cover charges ($20-$30), but many of them have reduced rates on weeknights. If you need to shake your tail feather in Brooklyn, we suggest checking out the lively dance scene at **Boogaloo** ($5).

Arts & Entertainment · **Nightlife**

Map 1 · Financial District

John Street Bar & Grill	17 John St	212-349-3278	Nightmarish underground nonsense.
Liquid Assets @ Millennium Hilton Hotel	55 Church St	212-693-2001	Plush seating and soft lighting.
Papoos	55 Broadway	212-809-3150	Popular Wall Street bar.
Ryan Maguire's Ale House	28 Cliff St	212-566-6906	Decent Irish pub.
Ryan's Sports Bar & Restaurant	46 Gold St	212-385-6044	Downtown sports bar.
Ulysses	95 Pearl St	212-482-0400	Slightly hipper downtown bar.
White Horse Tavern	25 Bridge St	212-668-9046	Downtown dive.

Map 2 · TriBeCa

46 Grand	46 Grand St	212-219-9311	Cramped and lacking in libations.
Brandy Library	25 North Moore St	212-226-5545	Refined but cozy.
Bubble Lounge	228 West Broadway	212-431-3433	Champagne bar.
Buster's Garage	180 West Broadway	212-226-6811	Sports bar for shitheads.
Church Lounge at the Tribeca Grand Hotel	25 Walker St	212-519-6600	Luxurious space with pricey drinks and occasional live music.
Circa Tabac	32 Watts St	212-941-1781	Smoker-friendly lounge.
Lucky Strike	59 Grand St	212-941-0772	Hipsters, locals, ex-smoky.
Naked Lunch	17 Thompson St	212-343-0828	Average lounge.
Nancy Whisky Pub	1 Lispenard St	212-226-9943	Good dive.
Puffy's Tavern	81 Hudson St	212-766-9159	Locals, hipsters.
Soho Grand Hotel	310 West Broadway	212-965-3000	Swank sophistication.
Tribeca Tavern	247 West Broadway	212-941-7671	Good enough for us.
Walker's	16 N Moore St	212-941-0142	Where old and new TriBeCa neighbors mix.

Map 3 · City Hall / Chinatown

The Beekman	15 Beekman St	212-732-7333	Guinness on tap and karaoke nights.
Capitale	130 Bowery	212-334-5500	Formerly the Bowery Savings Bank. Cool space.
Double Happiness	173 Mott St	212-941-1282	Downstairs hipster bar.
Happy Ending	302 Broome St	212-334-9676	Still taking the edge off.
Knitting Factory	74 Leonard St	212-219-3006	Great downstairs bar.
Metropolitan Improvement Company	3 Madison St	212-962-8219	Where the cops drink.
Milk & Honey	134 Eldridge St		Good luck finding the phone number.
Tribeca Blues	16 Warren St	212-766-1070	New space for live music.
Winnie's	104 Bayard St	212-732-2384	Chinese gangster karaoke!

Map 4 · Lower East Side

Bar 169	169 East Broadway	212-473-8866	Sometimes good, sometimes not.
Good World	3 Orchard St	212-925-9975	Great dance parties on the weekends.
Lolita	266 Broome St	212-966-7223	Hipster-haven.

Map 5 · West Village

2i's	248 W 14th St	212-807-1775	Hip-hop dance club.
APT	419 W 13th St	212-414-4245	If it makes you feel cool.
Art Bar	52 Eighth Ave	212-727-0244	Great spaces, cool crowd.
Automatic Slims	733 Washington St	212-645-8660	LOUD. Yes, that loud.
Blind Tiger Ale House	518 Hudson St	212-675-3848	Excellent beer selection.
Chumley's	86 Bedford St	212-675-4449	Former speakeasy. Top 10 bar.
Cielo	18 Little W 12th St	212-645-5700	Too much 'tude.
Cornelia Street Café	29 Cornelia St	212-989-9319	Cozy live music.
Culture Club	179 Varick St	212-243-1999	Bachelorette party heaven.
Don Hill's	511 Greenwich St	212-334-1390	Live rock music and dancing.
Duplex	61 Christopher St	212-255-5438	Everything's still fun.
Ear Inn	326 Spring St	212-226-9060	2nd oldest bar. A great place.
Henrietta Hudson	438 Hudson St	212-924-3347	Good lesbian vibe.
Jazz Gallery	290 Hudson St	212-242-1063	Jazz venue.
Lotus	409 W 14th St	212-243-4420	Don't forget your Seven jeans.
SOB'S	200 Varick St	212-243-4940	World music venue; salsa lessons on Mondays.
The Otherroom	143 Perry St	212-645-9758	Surprisingly decent beer selection.
Trust	421 W 13th St	212-645-7775	Large, laid-back lounge.

Arts & Entertainment · **Nightlife**

Map 5 · West Village—*continued*

Village Vanguard	178 Seventh Ave S	212-255-4037	Another classic for jazz.
Vol de Nuit	148 W 4th St	212-982-3388	Belgian beers, cool vibe.
West	425 West St	212-242-4375	Lounge with a view.
White Horse Tavern	567 Hudson St	212-243-9360	Another NYC classic.

Map 6 · Washington Sq / NYU / NoHo / SoHo

13	35 E 13th St	212-979-6677	Slam poetry on Monday nights.
Ace of Clubs	9 Great Jones St	212-420-1934	Cheap live music.
B Bar	40 E 4th St	212-475-2220	Great patio space. Crowded.
Baggot Inn	82 W 3rd St	212-477-0622	Live Bluegrass on Wednesdays.
Beauty Bar	231 E 14th St	212-539-1389	Just a little off the top, dahling?
The Bitter End	147 Bleecker St	212-673-7030	Live music with 2 drink minimum.
Blue & Gold	74 E 7th St	212-473-8918	Another fine East Village establishment.
Blue Note	131 W 3rd St	212-475-2462	Classic jazz venue. Pricey.
Bowery Ballroom	6 Delancey St	212-533-2111	Great space that attracts great bands.
Bowery Poetry Club	308 Bowery	212-614-0505	Slam poetry.
Burp Castle	41 E 7th St	212-982-4576	One of a kind. Faux monks.
CBGB & OMFUG	315 Bowery	212-982-4052	Punk classic.
Cedar Tavern	82 University Pl	212-741-9754	Classic NYU/actor hangout.
Continental	25 Third Ave	212-529-6924	Good for up-and-comers. Sometimes.
Crash Mansion	199 Bowery		Good live music in posh basement.
Decibel	240 E 9th St	212-979-2733	Go for the sake and the space.
Detour	349 E 13th St	212-533-6212	No cover jazz.
Eight Mile Creek	240 Mulberry St	212-431-4635	Relaxed downstairs bar.
Fanelli's	94 Prince St	212-226-9412	Old-time SoHo haunt. Nice tiles.
Fez	380 Lafayette St	212-533-7000	Great hangout space, gets crowded.
The Hole	29 Second Ave	212-473-9406	Dark and smoky.
Holiday Lounge	75 St Mark's Pl	212-777-9637	Where to go to lose your soul.
Joe's Pub	425 Lafayette St	212-539-8776	Good acts in problematic space.
KGB	85 E 4th St	212-505-3360	Former CP HQ. Meet your comrades.
Lion's Den	214 Sullivan St	212-477-2782	NYU rock venue. Bleh.
Lit	93 Second Ave	212-777-7987	Live rock and cavernous dancing.
Mannahatta	316 Bowery	212-253-8644	Newish lounge with huggable poles for dancing.
Marion's Continental	354 Bowery	212-475-7621	Classic cocktails with occasional live tunes.
Mars Bar	25 E 1st St	212-473-9842	The king of grungy bars. Recommended.
McSorley's Old Ale House	15 E 7th St	212-473-9148	Lights or darks?
Milady's	160 Prince St	212-226-9340	The only bar of its kind in this 'hood.
Milano's	51 E Houston St	212-226-8844	Grungy, narrow, awesome.
Nevada Smith's	74 Third Ave	212-982-2591	Gooooaaaaaallllllll!
Peculiar Pub	145 Bleecker St	212-353-1327	Large beer selection. NYU.
Pravda	281 Lafayette St	212-226-4696	Sophisticated lounge serving up inventive martinis.
Red Bench	107 Sullivan St	212-274-9120	Tiny, classy, quiet (sometimes).
Rififi	332 E 11th St	212-677-1027	Decent dancing.
Sapphire Lounge	249 Eldridge St	212-777-5153	Intimate dance floor.
Sin Sin/Leopard Lounge	248 E 5th St	212-253-2222	Sometimes good; sometimes not.
Sweet & Vicious	5 Spring St	212-334-7915	Great outdoor space.
Terra Blues	149 Bleecker St	212-777-7776	Live blues.
Village Underground	130 W 3rd St	212-777-7745	Average rock venue.
Webster Hall	125 E 11th St	212-353-1600	Dance club/ music venue. Amateur strip night.

Map 7 · East Village / Lower East Side

11th Street Bar	510 E 11th St	212-982-3929	Darts, Irish, excellent.
151	151 Rivington	212-228-4139	2 for 1 until 10pm.
2A	25 Ave A	212-505-2466	Great upstairs space.
7B	108 Ave B	212-473-8840	*Godfather II* shot here. What can be bad?
Ace Bar	531 E 5th St	212-979-8476	Loud, headbanger-y, good.
Arlene Grocery	95 Stanton St	212-995-1652	Cheap live tunes.
Bar 181	81 E 7th St	212-598-4394	It just feels good.
Barramundi	67 Clinton St	212-529-6900	Great garden in summer.
Bouche Bar	540 E 5th St	212-475-1673	Small, intimate.
Bua	124 St Marks Pl	212-979-6276	Friendly, great front deck.
C-Note	157 Ave C	212-677-8142	Cheap live music.
Cherry Tavern	441 E 6th St	212-777-1448	Get the Tijuana Special.
The Delancey	168 Delancey St	212-254-9920	Overrated, but the roof is cool if you can get up there.

d.b.a.	41 First Ave	212-475-5097	Lots of beers and hipsters.
The Edge	95 E 3rd St	212-477-2940	Biker hangout. Don't bring your camera.
Guernica	25 Ave B	212-674-0984	Dancing default. $5 cover after midnight.
The Hanger	217 E 3rd St	212-228-1030	Cute DJ on Monday nights.
International Bar	120 1/2 First Ave	212-777-9244	Small and unique.
Joe's Bar	520 E 6th St	212-473-9093	Classic neighborhood hangout. A favorite.
Korova Milk Bar	200 Ave A	212-254-8838	Everyone goes here.
Lakeside Lounge	162 Ave B	212-529-8463	Great jukebox, live music, décor, everything.
Lansky Lounge	104 Norfolk St	212-677-9489	Great space, packed with hyenas.
Living Room	154 Ludlow St	212-533-7235	Live music in your living room.
Manitoba's	99 Ave B	212-982-2511	Punk scene.
Max Fish	178 Ludlow St	212-529-3959	Where the musicians go.
Mercury Lounge	217 E Houston St	212-260-4700	Rock venue with occasional top-notch acts.
Mona's	224 Ave B	212-353-3780	Depressing. Recommended.
Motor City	127 Ludlow St	212-358-1595	Faux biker bar. Still good, though.
Nuyorican Poet's Café	236 E 3rd St	212-505-8183	Slam poetry.
Opaline	85 Ave A	212-995-8684	Panty parties on Saturday nights. Not as cool as it used to be.
Parkside Lounge	317 E Houston St	212-673-6270	Good basic bar.
The Phoenix	447 E 13th St	212-477-9979	$1 Wednesdays!
Pianos	158 Ludlow St	212-505-3733	Painful scene with decent live tunes.
The Porch	115 Ave C	212-982-4034	Just like back at home.
Rothko	116 Suffolk St	no phone	bleh.
Sidewalk	94 Ave A	212-473-7373	Classic open mic.
Sin-é	150 Attorney St	212-388-0077	Cozy live music.
Sophie's	507 E 5th St	212-228-5680	More crowded counterpart to Joe's.
Three of Cups Lounge	83 First Ave	212-388-0059	Live music and tasty pizza.
Tonic	107 Norfolk St	212-358-7501	Great avant-garde space. We hope it's still there!
WCOU Radio Bar	115 First Ave	212-254-4317	Great small neighborhood bar.
Welcome to the Johnsons	123 Rivington St	212-420-4317	Great décor, but too crowded mostly.
Zum Schneider	107 Ave C	212-598-1098	Get weisse, man.

Map 8 · Chelsea

Billymark's West	332 Ninth Ave	212-629-0118	Down and dirty dive.
Blarney Stone	340 Ninth Ave	212-502-4656	The only bar in purgatory.
Cajun	129 Eighth Ave	212-691-6174	A little taste of the French Quarter.
Chelsea Brewing Company	Pier 59	212-336-6440	When you're done playing basketball.
Copacabana	560 W 34th St	212-239-2672	Salsa Tuesdays with free buffet.
Coral Room	512 W 29th St	212-244-1965	Live mermaids and live music.
Crobar	530 W 28th St	212-629-9000	Hangar-like space for dancing.
Freight	410 W 16th St	212-242-6555	Huge lounge. Small crowds.
Hammerstein Ballroom	311 W 34th St	212-279-7740	Lofty rock venue.
The Park	118 Tenth Ave	212-352-3313	Good patio.
Red Rock West	457 W 17th St	212-366-5359	F--king loud!
Roxy	515 W 18th St	212-645-5156	Roller disco Wednesdays.
West Side Tavern	360 W 23rd St	212-366-3738	Local mixture.

Map 9 · Flatiron / Lower Midtown

Avalon	660 Sixth Ave	212-807-7780	You gotta go at least once.
Blarney Stone	106 W 32nd St	212-502-5139	The only bar in purgatory.
Club Shelter	20 W 39th St	212-719-4479	Dance until dawn.
Cutting Room	19 W 24th St	212-691-4065	Large, usually mellow vibe.
Discotheque	17 W 19th St	212-352-9999	Up close and personal dancefloor.
Dusk of Miami	147 W 24th St	212-924-4490	Raw, post-hip, good.
Ginger Man	11 E 36th St	212-532-3740	Excellent beer selection.
Kavehaz	37 W 26th St	212-343-0612	Jazz venue.
Live Bait	14 E 23rd St	212-353-2400	Still a great feel. A mainstay.
Merchants	112 Seventh Ave	212-366-7267	Good mixed space.
Old Town Bar & Restaurant	45 E 18th St	212-529-6732	Excellent old-NY pub. Skip the food.
Peter McManus	152 Seventh Ave	212-929-9691	Refreshingly basic.
Satalla	37 W 26th St	212-576-1155	World music venue.
Splash Bar	50 W 17th St	212-691-0073	Men dancing in waterfalls.
Suede	161 W 23rd St	212-633-2113	Be seen.
Tir Na Nog	5 Penn Plz	212-630-0249	Penn Station hangout.
Under The Volcano	12 E 36th St	212-213-0093	Relaxed, subdued; large selection of tequilas.

(**323**)

Arts & Entertainment · **Nightlife**

Map 10 · Murray Hill / Gramercy

Bar 515	515 Third Ave	212-532-3300	Local pseudo-frat hangout.
Belmont Lounge	117 E 15th St	212-533-0009	Be seen.
Irving Plaza	17 Irving Pl	212-777-6800	Staple rock venue.
The Jazz Standard	116 E 27th St	212-576-2232	Jazz venue.
Joshua Tree	513 Third Ave	212-689-0058	Murray Hill meat market.
Mercury Bar	493 Third Ave	212-683-2645	Lots of TVs for sports. You make the call.
Molly's	287 Third Ave	212-889-3361	Great Irish pub with a fireplace.
Revival	129 E 15th St	212-253-8061	Low maintenance beer drinking.
Rocky Sullivan's	129 Lexington Ave	212-725-3871	Lackadaisical trivia on Thursday nights. Free.
Rodeo Bar & Grill	375 Third Ave	212-683-6500	As close to a honky-tonk as you'll get, partner.
Waterfront Ale House	540 Second Ave	212-696-4104	Decent local vibe.

Map 11 · Hell's Kitchen

Bellevue Bar	538 Ninth Ave	212-760-0660	How low can you go?
Birdland	315 W 44th St	212-581-3080	Top-notch jazz.
Bull Moose Saloon	354 W 44th St	212-956-5625	Good local hangout.
Don't Tell Mama	343 W 46th St	212-757-0788	Good cabaret space.
Hudson Hotel Library	356 W 58th St	212-554-6000	Super-super-super pretentious.
Rudy's Bar & Grill	627 Ninth Ave	212-974-9169	Classic Hell's Kitchen. Recommended.
Siberia Bar	356 W 40th St	212-333-4141	Brrr…it's cold out there.
Xth	642 Tenth Ave	212-245-9088	Good local vibe.

Map 12 · Midtown

BB King Blues Club	237 W 42nd St	212-997-4144	Check out the live gospel brunch on Sundays.
China Club	268 W 47th St	212-398-3800	Think night at the Roxbury.
Heartland Brewery	127 W 43rd St	646-366-0235	Heartland HeartLAND HEARTLAND!
Heartland Brewery	1285 Sixth Ave	212-582-8244	Heartland HeartLAND HEARTLAND!
Howard Johnson's	1551 Broadway	212-354-1445	A Times Square haven in a sea of madness.
Iridium	1650 Broadway	212-582-2121	Good mainstream jazz venue. Pricey.
Paramount Bar	235 W 46th St	212-764-5500	Tiny, pretentious, unavoidable.
Roseland	239 W 52nd St	212-247-0200	Big-time rock venue.
The Royalton	44 W 44th St	212-768-5000	Phillipe Starcke is the SH--!
Russian Vodka Room	265 W 52nd St	212-307-5835	Russian molls and cranberry vodka. Awesome.
Show	135 W 41st St	212-278-0988	Show off your goods.
Town Hall	123 W 43rd St	212-840-2824	Attracts great musical acts.

Map 13 · East Midtown

Blarney Stone	710 Third Ave	212-490-0457	The only bar in purgatory.
The Campbell Apartment	Grand Central Terminal	212-953-0409	Awesome space, awesomely snooty!
Fubar	305 E 50th St	212-872-1325	The best option in the area by far.
Kate Kearney's	251 E 50th St	212-935-2045	Irish shenanigans.
Metro 53	307 E 53rd St	212-838-0007	Celebrities and suits.
PJ Clarke's	915 Third Ave	212-759-1650	An old-timer, resuscitated.

Map 14 · Upper West Side (Lower)

All-State Café	250 W 72nd St	212-874-1883	Great underground space.
Beacon Theater	2124 Broadway	212-496-7070	Official venue of the Allman Bros.
Café Des Artistes	1 W 67th St	212-877-3500	Endless wine menu. Snack on hard-boiled eggs at the bar.
Dead Poet	450 Amsterdam Ave	212-595-5670	Good Irish feel.
Dublin House	225 W 79th St	212-874-9528	Great dingy Irish pub. Recommended.
Emerald Inn	220 Columbus Ave	212-874-8840	Another good Irish pub!
Jake's Dilemma	430 Amsterdam Ave	212-580-0556	Sort of okay sometimes.
Makor	35 W 67th St	212-601-1000	Lots of different stuff.
P&G	279 Amsterdam Ave	212-874-8568	Depressing dive. Recommended.
Prohibition	503 Columbus Ave	212-579-3100	Cool space, music, people, etc.
Raccoon Lodge	480 Amsterdam Ave	212-874-9984	Everyone knows what these are like.
Shalel Lounge	65 W 70th St	212-799-9030	Very cool, semi-hidden lounge.

Map 15 · Upper East Side (Lower)

Banshee Pub	1373 First Ave	212-717-8177	Good, fun Upper East Sider.
Brandy's Piano Bar	235 E 84th St	212-650-1944	Good ol' New York vibe.

Brother Jimmy's	1485 Second Ave	212-288-0999	Crowded meat market.
Café Carlyle and Bemelmans Bar	35 E 76th St	212-744-1600	Classic cabaret venue. Hellishly expensive.
David Copperfield's	1394 York Ave	212-734-6152	Go for the beer.
Feinstein's at the Regency	540 Park Ave	212-339-4095	Cabaret.
Finnegan's Wake	1361 First Ave	212-737-3664	Standard Irish pub. Therefore, good.
Hi-Life	1340 First Ave	212-249-3600	Pseudo-retro, okay.
Session 73	1359 First Ave	212-517-4445	Live music and yuppies.
Ship of Fools	1590 Second Ave	212-570-2651	Loud sports with greasy vittles.
Subway Inn	143 E 60th St	212-223-8929	Sad, bad, glare, worn-out, ugh. Totally great.
Vudu	1487 First Ave	212-249-9540	They dance on the Upper East Side?

Map 16 · Upper West Side (Upper)

Abbey Pub	237 W 105th St	212-222-8713	Cozy Columbia hangout.
Broadway Dive	2662 Broadway	212-865-2662	Where everyone who reads this book goes.
Dive Bar	732 Amsterdam Ave	212-749-4358	Columbia hangout.
The Parlour	250 W 86th St	212-580-8923	Irish pub, two spaces, good hangout.
Smoke	2751 Broadway	212-864-6662	Local jazz hangout.

Map 17 · Upper East Side / East Harlem

Auction House	300 E 89th St	212-427-4458	Stylin' uptown lounge.
Big Easy	1768 Second Ave	212-348-0879	Cheap college dive. Beer Pong anyone?
Kinsale Tavern	1672 Third Ave	212-348-4370	Right-off-the-boat Irish staff. Good beers.
Rathbones Pub	1702 Second Ave	212-369-7361	Basic pub.
Ruby's Tap House	1754 Second Ave	212-987-8179	Lots of beer, lots of meat.

Map 18 · Columbia / Morningside Heights

1020 Bar	1020 Amsterdam Ave	212-961-9224	A nice break from the frat bars around Columbia.
Cotton Club	666 W 125th St	212-663-7980	Good, fun swingin' uptown joint.
Heights Bar & Grill	2867 Broadway	212-866-7035	Fun rooftop bar in summer.
Nacho Mama's Kitchen Bar	2893 Broadway	212-665-2800	Get your nacho on.
West End	2911 Broadway	212-662-8830	Long-time Columbia hangout.

Map 19 · Harlem (Lower)

Apollo Theatre	253 W 125th St	212-531-5300	The one and the only.
Lenox Lounge	288 Lenox Ave	212-427-0253	Old-time Harlem hangout, recently redone.

Map 21 · Manhattanville / Hamilton Heights

St Nick's Pub	773 St Nicholas Ave	212-283-9728	Great vibe, cool jazz.

Map 24 · Fort George / Fort Tryon

The Monkey Room	589 Ft Washington Ave	212-543-9888	Quirky, doubles as a coffee shop by day.

Map 25 · Inwood

Piper's Kilt	4944 Broadway	212-569-7071	Irish pub and sports bar.

Map 26 · Astoria

Bohemian Hall	29-19 24th Ave	718-274-4925	More than 90 years old, this bar is run by the Bohemia Citizens' Benevolent Society. Check out the Czech beers. Beer garden seats more than 500!
Brick Café	30-95 33rd St	718-267-2735	Great atmosphere with European lounge music piping through the speakers quiet enough so you can still chat.
Byzantio	28-31 31st St	718-956-5600	Greek-style café and bar.
Café Athens	32-07 30th St	718-626-2164	Greek café.
Crescent Lounge	32-05 Crescent St	718-728-9600	Great singles scene.
Gibney's	32-01 Broadway	718-545-8567	Authentic Irish pub.
McCann's Pub & Grill	3615 Ditmars Blvd	718-278-2621	Where the young and the Greek hang out.
McLoughlin's Bar	31-06 Broadway	718-278-9714	Another Irish local bar.

Map 27 · Long Island City

Café Bar	32-90 36th Ave	718-204-5273	Serves Cypriot cuisine and often features live jazz performances.

Map 28 · Greenpoint

Enid's	560 Manhattan Ave	718-349-3859	Trendy drinking space.
Europa	765 Manhattan Ave	718-383-5723	Strobe light extravaganza.
Lyric Lounge	278 Nassau Ave	718-349-7017	Neighborhood bar with a patio; hosts occasional live music.
The Mark Bar	1025 Manhattan Ave	718-349-2340	Wide selection of beer.
Matchless	557 Manhattan Ave	718-383-5333	Dark hipster bar with pool and foosball.
Pencil Factory	142 Franklin St	718-609-5858	Promising newcomer.
Tommy's Tavern	1041 Manhattan Ave		Dive with a pool table and often live music in the back room.
Warsaw	261 Driggs Ave	718-387-0505	Big space with live music.

Map 29 · Williamsburg

The Abbey	536 Driggs Ave	718-599-4400	Great jukebox and staff.
Black Betty	366 Metropolitan Ave	718-599-0243	Get the Black Betty Margarita…yum!
Boogaloo	168 Marcy Ave	718-599-8900	Intimate dancing to live music and DJs.
BQE	300 N 6th St	718-388-2211	Live music and great views of the BQE.
Brooklyn Ale House	103 Berry St	718-302-9811	When you just want to drink some beer.
Brooklyn Brewery	79 N 11th St	718-486-7422	Open Friday nights only. Tours on Saturdays.
Charleston	174 Bedford Ave	718-782-8717	Old school bar with pizza.
Galapagos	70 N 6th St	718-782-5188	Reflecting pools, candles, and attractive people.
Greenpoint Tavern	188 Bedford Ave	718-384-9539	Cheap beer in Styrofoam cups.
Iona	180 Grand St	718-384-5008	Plenty of choices on tap.
Laila Lounge	113 N 7th St	718-486-6791	Roomy space with pool and live music.
Pete's Candy Store	709 Lorimer St	718-302-3770	Cozy space—Scrabble on Saturdays!
Stinger Club	241 Grand St	718-218-6662	Good bands from time to time.
Sweetwater Tavern	105 N 6th St	718-963-0608	Punk dive.
Trash	256 Grand St	718-599-1000	Formerly Luxx.
Turkey's Nest	94 Bedford Ave	718-384-9774	Best dive in Williamsburg.
Union Pool	484 Union Ave	718-609-0484	Good starting point or finishing point.

Map 30 · Brooklyn Heights / DUMBO / Downtown

Eamonn Doran	174 Montague St	718-596-4969	Bland Irish bar.
Henry St Ale House	62 Henry St	718-522-4801	Cozy, dark space with good selections on tap.
Lunatarium	10 Jay St	718-813-8404	DJ playground.
Water Street Bar	66 Water St	718-625-9352	Roomy Irish pub.

Map 31 · Fort Greene / Clinton Hill

BAM Café	30 Lafayette Ave	718-636-4100	Highly recommended.
Frank's Lounge	660 Fulton St	718-625-9339	When you need to get funky.
Moe's	80 Lafayette Ave	718-797-9536	Fort Greene default.

Map 32 · BoCoCa / Red Hook

The Boat	175 Smith St	718-254-0607	Nice and dark with great tunes.
Brazen Head	228 Atlantic Ave	718-488-0430	Decent beer—mixed crowd.
Brooklyn Inn	148 Hoyt St	718-625-9741	When you're feeling nostalgic.
Brooklyn Social Club	335 Smith St	718-858-7758	Great addition to the Smith Street scene.
Gowanus Yacht Club	323 Smith St	718-246-1321	Dogs, burgers, and beer. Love it.
The Hook	18 Commerce St	718-797-3007	You can buy 40s at the bar!!! Live music.
Kili	81 Hoyt St	718-855-5574	Nice space & cool vibe.
Last Exit	136 Atlantic Ave	718-222-9198	Still trying to win trivia night—pails of PBR for $10.
Liberty Heights Tap Room	34 Van Dyke St	718-246-1793	A Red Hook must.
Lillie's	46 Beard St	718-858-9822	Retro Hideaway.
Magnetic Field	97 Atlantic Ave	718-834-0069	Great decor—even better beer specials. Live music on the weekends.
Moonshine	317 Columbia St		Great atmosphere and garden.
Quench	282 Smith St	718-875-1500	Mod space with fun drink specials.
Sunny's	253 Conover St	718-625-8211	No longer pay what you wish, but still cheap & good.
Waterfront Ale House	155 Atlantic Ave	718-522-3794	Great beer, food and service. This place has it all!
Zombie Hut	263 Smith St	718-875-3433	Drinks with bamboo umbrellas.

Arts & Entertainment · **Nightlife**

Map 33 · Park Slope / Prospect Heights / Windsor Ter

Babinga	78 St Marks Ave	718-857-8600	Yummy tropical drinks with a sweet happy hour.
Bar 4	444 Seventh Ave	718-832-9800	Replaced its previous glitz with stoop-sale furniture and (gulp) video poker.
Bar Reis	375 Fifth Ave	718-832-5716	Stylish lounge with a diverse crowd.
Bar Toto	411 11th St	718-768-4698	Great bar food.
Barbès	376 Ninth Ave	718-965-9177	Best entertainment in the Slope, from accordian trios to Delta Blues to McSweeney's sponsored readings.
Excelsior	390 Fifth Ave	718-832-1599	Decent bar with mixed gay crowd.
Freddy's	485 Dean St	718-622-7035	Music and readings and way-coolness.
The Gate	321 Fifth Ave	718-768-4329	THE best place to drink outdoors in the Slope, plus 20 great beers on tap.
Ginger's	363 Fifth Ave	718-788-0924	Nice and casual for center Slope.
Great Lakes	284 Fifth Ave	718-499-3710	Great, great bar.
Loki Lounge	304 Fifth Ave	718-965-9600	Darts and billiards tone down the classic wood bar. Good music.
Mooney's Pub	353 Flatbush Ave	718-783-6406	The real old Brooklyn deal—smells of many spilt beers.
O'Connor's	39 Fifth Ave	718-783-9721	The brick face and tiny windows say, "Run away!" but the friendly locals say, "Pull up a stool."
Park Slope Ale House	356 Sixth Ave	718-788-1756	The brewpub is gone, replaced with non-micro beers, but the bar food remains excellent.
Patio Lounge	179 Fifth Ave	718-857-3477	Verdant boozing.
Southpaw	125 Fifth Ave	718-no phone	Cozy music venue.
Up Over Jazz Café	351 Flatbush Ave	718-398-5413	Serious jazz at late hours.

Map 34 · Hoboken

Black Bear	205 Washington St	201-656-5511	Ordinary food but the bands and atmosphere compensate.
City Bistro	56 14th St	201-963-8200	Great summer scene, rooftop views to the city.
Leo's Grandezvous	200 Grand St	201-659-9467	Hoboken's Rat Pack bar. Bring a dame and have some booze.
Louise & Jerry's	329 Washington St	201-656-9698	Old style Hoboken saloon. A real throwback.
Maxwells	1039 Washington St	201-653-1703	Interesting bands, relax in the lounge with friends or grab a bite to eat.
Mile Square	221 Washington St	201-420-0222	Preppy bar where the food is good and the scene is lively.
Morans	501 Garden St	201-795-2025	Classic Irish tavern; darts, pool and a garrulous bartender.
Oddfellows	80 River St	201-656-9009	Happening happy hour. Close to the PATH so it catches the commuter crowd.
Texas Arizona	76 River St	201-420-0304	You can eat, you can drink, you can catch a band.

Map 35 · Jersey City

Dennis and Maria's Bar	322 1/2 7th St	201-217-6607	Popular with the locals.
Hamilton Park Ale House	708 Jersey Ave	201-659-9111	Relaxed *Cheers*-esque atmosphere with yummy food.
LITM	140 Newark Ave	201-536-5557	Artsy, laid-back lounge.
Lamp Post Bar and Grille	382 2nd St	201-222-1331	Look for the lamp post on the street to find this friendly neighborhood bar. If you're going to order food, do it from the front bar.
Markers	Harborside Financial Ctr, Plz II	201-433-6275	Happy hour heaven. The upscale after-work crowd selects from excellent beers on tap.
The Merchant	279 Grove St	201-200-0202	Classy bar where businessmen go to cut loose.
PJ Ryan's	172 First St	201-239-7373	A real Irish pub. Guaranteed to see your favorite sporting event. Enjoy a pint and watch the live entertainment.
White Star	230 Brunswick St	201-653-9234	Great bar & good eats.

Battery Park City

Rise Bar @ the Ritz	2 West St	212-344-0800	Great harbor and park views.

The New York City book scene has taken a sharp decline in terms of diversity in recent years, with many excellent bookshops—including A Different Light, Academy, A Photographer's Place, Rizzoli SoHo, Tower Books, Brentano's, Pageant, Spring Street Books, and Shortwave—all going the way of the dodo. The remaining independent stores are now the last outposts before everything interesting or alternative disappears altogether. And some of NYC's richest cultural neighborhoods—such as the East Village and the Lower East Side—don't have enough bookstores to even come close to properly serving their populations of literate hipsters. So we thought we'd take this opportunity to list some of our favorite remaining shops…

General New/Used

Strand is still the mother of all general bookshops with three locations and an impressive selection in every genre. Finding specific titles, of course, always remains a challenge, but it can't be beat for browsing. **Gotham Book Mart** remains Midtown's major literary watering hole, and **St. Mark's Bookshop** anchors the border between the NYU crowd and the East Village hipster contingent. Both Gotham and St. Mark's have excellent literary journal selections. **Argosy Book Store** on 57th Street is still a top destination for books and prints. Uptown, **Morningside Bookshop** and **Labyrinth** serve the Columbia area well. With four locations around the city, the punchy **Shakespeare & Company** is a local chain that somehow manages to maintain an aura of independence. In the West Village, **Three Lives and Co.** should be your destination. The **Barnes & Noble** on Union Square is their signature store, and has a great feel. The **Housing Works Used Book Café** is one of our favorite bookstores—and when you support your cerebral habit, you're also helping out some people in need!

Small Used

Fortunately there are still a lot of used bookstores tucked away all over the city. **Mercer Street Books** serves NYU, **Last Word** covers Columbia, **East Village**

Books takes care of hipster heaven, and **Skyline** remains a good Chelsea destination.

Travel

The city's travel book selection is possibly its greatest strength—from the **Hagstrom Map & Travel** near Bryant Park to several independents, such as the elegant **Complete Traveller Bookstore** and SoHo's **Traveler's Choice Bookstore**.

Art

Printed Matter houses one of the best collections of artists' books in the world and is highly recommended. Across the street, the **DIA** bookstore has a fantastic selection of books about art, with a special case reserved for artists' books. It's worth visiting the store for the Jorge Pardo design alone! The **New Museum of Contemporary Art Bookstore** also offers a brilliant selection of both artists' and art books. If you aren't on a budget and have a new coffee table to fill, try **Ursus** in Chelsea.

NYC/Government

The City Store in the Municipal Building is small, but carries a solid selection (and is still the only store we've seen that sells old taxicab medallions). The **Civil Service Bookstore** on Chambers Street has all the study guides you'll need when you want to change careers and start driving a bus. The **United Nations Bookshop** has a great range of international and governmental titles. The **New York Transit Museum** shop at Grand Central also has an excellent range of books on NYC.

Specialty

Books of Wonder in Chelsea has long been a Downtown haven for children's books. Mystery shops **Murder Ink**, **The Mysterious Book Shop**, and **Partners & Crime** slake the need for whodunits. **Biography Book Shop** speaks for itself. **Urban Center Books** is well-known for its architecture collection.

Map 1 • Financial District

Borders Books, Music, & Café	100 Broadway	212-964-1988	Chain.
Hagstrom Map and Travel Center	125 Maiden Ln	212-785-5343	Specialty - Travel/Maps.
National Museum of the American Indian	1 Bowling Green	212-514-3767	
Shakespeare & Co	1 Whitehall St	212-742-7025	Chain.
Strand	95 Fulton St	212-732-6070	Used; Remainders.

Map 2 • TriBeCa

Manhattan Books	150 Chambers St	212-385-7395	New and used textbooks.
NY Law School Bookstore	47 Worth St	212-334-2412	Specialty - Law textbooks.
Ruby's Book Sale	119 Chambers St	212-732-8676	General Interest.
Sufi Books	227 West Broadway	212-334-5212	Specialty - Spiritual.
Traveler's Choice	2 Wooster St	212-941-1535	Specialty - Travel.

Map 3 · City Hall / Chinatown

The City Store	1 Centre St	212-669-8246	Specialty - NYC.
Civil Service Book Shop	89 Worth St	212-226-9506	Specialty - Civil Services.
Computer Book Works	78 Reade St	212-385-1616	Specialty - Computer.
K-Mei	81 Bayard St	212-693-1989	Specialty - Chinese.
Ming Fay Book Store	42 Mott St	212-406-1957	Specialty - Chinese.
New York City Store	1 Centre St	212-669-8246	Specialty - NYC books and municipal publications.
Oriental Books, Stationery & Arts Co	29 East Broadway	212-962-3634	Specialty - Chinese.
Oriental Culture Enterprises	13 Elizabeth St	212-226-8461	Specialty - Chinese.
Pace University Bookstore	41 Park Row	212-349-8580	Academic - General.
Zakka	147 Grand St	212-431-3961	Specialty - Graphic design books.

Map 4 · Lower East Side

Eastern Books	15 Pike St	212-964-6869	Specialty - Chinese.

Map 5 · West Village

Barnes & Noble	396 Sixth Ave	212-674-8780	Chain.
Biography Book Shop	400 Bleecker St	212-807-8655	Specialty - Biography.
Bookleaves	304 W 4th St	212-924-5638	Used; Antiquarian.
Drougas Books	34 Carmine St	212-229-0079	Used, political, Eastern religious, etc.
Joanne Hendricks Cookbooks	488 Greenwich St	212-226-5731	Specialty - Wine & Cooking.
Libreria Lectorum	137 W 14th St	212-741-0220	Specialty - Spanish.
Macondo Books	221 W 14th St	212-741-3108	Specialty - Spanish.
Oscar Wilde Memorial Bookshop	15 Christopher St	212-255-8097	Specialty - Gay/Lesbian.
Partners & Crime Mystery Booksellers	44 Greenwich Ave	212-243-0440	Specialty - Mystery.
Slotnick Bonnie Cookbooks	163 W 10th St	212-989-8962	Specialty - Out of print cookbooks.
Three Lives and Co	154 W 10th St	212-741-2069	General Interest.

Map 6 · Washington Square / NYU / NoHo / SoHo

12th Street Books & Records	11 E 12th St	212-645-4340	Used.
Alabaster Bookshop	122 Fourth Ave	212-982-3550	Used.
Barnes & Noble	4 Astor Pl	212-420-1322	Chain.
Benjamin Cardozo School of Law Bookstore	55 Fifth Ave	212-790-0339/0200	Academic - Law.
Bilingual Publications	270 Lafayette St	212-431-3500	Specialty - Spanish.
East West Books	78 Fifth Ave	212-243-5994	Specialty - Spirituality; Self-Help.
Fine Art In Print	159 Prince St	212-982-2088	Specialty - Fine Art.
Forbidden Planet	840 Broadway	212-473-1576 212-475-6161	Specialty - Fantasy/Sci-fi.
Housing Works Used Book Café	126 Crosby St	212-334-3324	Used.
McNally Robinson	50 Prince St	212-274-1160	General Interest.
Mercer Street Books and Records	206 Mercer St	212-505-8615	Used.
New York Open Center Bookstore	83 Spring St	212-219-2527x109	Specialty - New Age; Spiritual.
New York University Book Center-Main Branch	18 Washington Pl	212-998-4667	Academic - General.
New York University Book Center -Professional Bookstore	530 LaGuardia Pl	212-998-4680	Academic - Management.
Scholastic Store	557 Broadway	212-343-6166	Specialty - Educational.
Science Fiction Shop	214 Sullivan St	212-473-3010	Specialty - Sci-Fi.
SF Vanni	30 W 12th St	212-675-6336	Specialty - Italian.
Shakespeare & Co	716 Broadway	212-529-1330	Chain.
St Mark's Bookshop	31 Third Ave	212-260-7853 212-260-0443	General Interest.
Strand	828 Broadway	212-473-1452	Used; Remainders.
Surma Book & Music	11 E 7th St	212-477-0729	Specialty - Ukrainian.
Village Comics	214 Sullivan St	212-777-2770	Specialty - Comics.
Virgin Megastore	52 E 14th St	212-598-4666	Chain.

Map 7 · East Village / Lower East Side

Aurora	43 Clinton St	212-477-0101	Specialty - Metaphysical.
Bluestockings Bookstore Café and Activist Center	172 Allen St	212-777-6028	Specialty - Political.
East Village Books and Records	99 St Mark's Pl	212-477-8647	Messy pile of used stuff.
May Day Books	155 First Ave		Anarchist bookstore and collective.
St Mark's Comics	11 St Mark's Pl	212-598-9439	Specialty - Comics.

Map 8 · Chelsea

New Museum of Contemporary Art Bookshop (Temporary Location)	556 W 22nd St	212-343-0460	Specialty - Art/ Artists Books.
Polish American	333 W 38th St	212-594-2386	Specialty - Polish.
Printed Matter	535 W 22nd St	212-925-0325	Specialty - Artist Books.

Map 9 · Flatiron / Lower Midtown

Aperture Book Center	20 E 23rd St	212-505-5555	Specialty - Photography.
Barnes & Noble	33 E 17th St	212-253-0810	Chain.
Barnes & Noble	675 Sixth Ave	212-727-1227	Chain.
Barnes & Noble College Bookstore	6 E 18th St	212-675-5500	Textbook mayhem.
Books of Wonder	16 W 18th St	212-989-3270	Specialty - Children's.
Center for Book Arts	28 W 27th St, 3rd Fl	212-481-0295	Specialty - Artist/Handmade.
Compleat Strategist	11 E 33rd St	212-685-3880	Specialty - Fantasy/ SciFi.
Complete Traveller	199 Madison Ave	212-685-9007	Specialty - Travel.
Fashion Design Books	250 W 27th St	212-633-9646	Specialty - Fashion design.
Hudson News	Penn Station	212-971-6800	Chain.
Jim Hanley's Universe	4 W 33rd St	212-268-7088	Specialty - Comics; SciFi.
Koryo Books	35 W 32nd St	212-564-1844	Specialty - Korean.
Metropolis Comics and Collectibles	873 Broadway	212-260-4147	Specialty - Comics.
Penn Books	1 Penn Plz	212-239-0311	General interest.
Revolution Books	9 W 19th St	212-691-3345	Specialty - Political.
Rudolf Steiner Bookstore	138 W 15th St	212-242-8945	Specialty - Metaphysics.
Russian Bookstore 21	174 5th Ave	212-924-5477	Specialty - Russian/Russia.
Samuel French	45 W 25th St	212-206-8990	Specialty - Plays and theater books.
Skyline Books & Records	13 W 18th St	212-759-5463	Used.
Ursus Books	132 W 21st St	212-627-5370	Specialty - Art.

Map 10 · Murray Hill / Gramercy

Baruch College Bookstore	55 Lexington Ave	646-312-4850	Academic - General.
Borders Books, Music, & Café	550 Second Ave	212-685-3938	Chain.
New York University Book Store	333 E 29th St	212-998-9990	Academic - Health Sciences.
Shakespeare & Co	137 E 23rd St	212-505-2021	Chain.

Map 11 · Hell's Kitchen

Hudson News	Port Authority Building, North Wing	212-563-1030	Chain.

Map 12 · Midtown

AMA Management Bookstore	1601 Broadway	212-903-8286	Specialty - Management.
Barnes & Noble	600 Fifth Ave	212-765-0592	Chain.
Bauman Rare Books	301 Park Ave	212-759-8300	Antiquarian.
Bauman Rare Books	535 Madison Ave	212-751-0011	Antiquarian.
Bookoff	12 E 41st St	212-685-1410	Used Japanese and English.
Chartwell Booksellers	55 E 52nd St	212-308-0643	General Interest; Antiquarian.
Coliseum Books	11 W 42nd St	212-803-5890	
Collector's Universe	31 W 46th St	212-398-2100	Specialty - Comics.
Dahesh Heritage Fine Books	1775 Broadway, Suite 501	212-265-0600	General interest.
Drama Book Shop	250 W 40th St	212-944-0595	Specialty - Theater & Drama.
FAO Schwarz Book Department	767 Fifth Ave	212-644-9400	Specialty - Children's.
Gotham Bookmart and Gallery	16 E 46th St	212-719-4448	Used; New.
Hagstrom Map and Travel Center	51 W 43rd St	212-398-1222	Specialty - Travel/Maps.
J N Bartfield-Fine Books	30 W 57th St	212-245-8890	Rare and antiquarian.
Kinokuniya	10 W 49th St	212-765-7766	Specialty - Japanese.
Librarie De France	610 Fifth Ave	212-581-8810	French and Spanish books, maps, foreign language dictionaries.
Metropolitan Museum of Art Bookshop at Rockefeller Center	15 W 49th St	212-332-1360	Specialty - Art books.
Midtown Comics - Times Square	200 W 40th St	212-302-8192	Specialty - Comics.
The Mysterious Book Shop	129 W 56th St	212-765-0900	Specialty - Mystery.
New York City Store	810 Seventh Ave, Information Center	212-669-8246	Specialty - NYC books and municipal publications.
New York Transit Museum	Grand Central Station	212-878-0106	Specialty - NYC/Transit.
Rakuza	16 East 41st St	212-686-5560	Specialty - Japanese.
Rizzoli	31 W 57th St	212-759-2424/ 800-52-BOOKS	Specialty - Art/Design.
Urban Center Books	457 Madison Ave	212-935-3595	Specialty - Architecture; Urban Planning.
Virgin Megastore	1540 Broadway, Level B-2	212-921-1020	Chain.

Map 13 • East Midtown

Argosy Book Store	116 E 59th St	212-753-4455	Used.
Asahiya	E 45th b/w Fifth & Madison Aves	212-883-0011	Specialty - Japanese.
Barnes & Noble	160 E 54th St	212-750-8033	Chain.
Barnes & Noble	750 Third Ave	212-697-2251	Chain.
Borders Books, Music, & Café	461 Park Ave	212-980-6785	Chain.
Come Again	353 E 53rd St	212-308-9394	Specialty - Erotica; Gay/Lesbian.
Hudson News	89 E 42nd St, Grand Central Station	212-687-0833	Chain.
Midtown Comics - Grand Central	459 Lexington Ave	212-302-8192	Specialty - Comics.
Posman Books	9 Grand Central Terminal	212-983-1111	General Interest.
Potterton Books	979 Third Ave	212-644-2292	Specialty - Decorative Arts/ Architecture/Design.
Quest Book Shop	240 E 53rd St	212-758-5521	Specialty - New Age.
Richard B Arkway Books	59 E 54th St	212-751-8135	Specialty - Rare maps and books.
United Nations Bookshop	General Assembly Building, Rm 32	212-963-7680/ 800-553-3210	Good range of everything.

Map 14 • Upper West Side (Lower)

Applause Theater Books	211 W 71st St	212-496-7511	Specialty - Theater & Drama.
Barnes & Noble	1972 Broadway	212-595-6859	Chain.
Barnes & Noble	2289 Broadway	212-362-8835	Chain.
Fordham University Bookstore	113 W 60th St	212-636-6079	Academic - General.
Juillard School Bookstore	60 Lincoln Center Plz	212-799-5000	Academic - Music.
New York Institute of Technology	1855 Broadway	212-261-1551	Specialty - Technical.
Westsider	2246 Broadway	212-362-0706	Used; Antiquarian.

Map 15 • Upper East Side (Lower)

Asia Society Bookstore	725 Park Ave	212-288-6400	Specialty - Asian.
The Black Orchid Bookshop	303 E 81st St	212-734-5980	Specialty - Mystery/Crime.
Blue Danube	217 E 83rd St	212-794-7099	Specialty - Hungarian.
Bookberries	983 Lexington Ave	212-794-9400	General Interest.
Bookstore Of The NY Psychoanalytic Institution	247 E 82nd St	212-772-8282	Specialty - Psychoanalysis.
Choices Bookshop- Recovery	220 E 78th St	212-794-3858	Specialty - Self-help and recovery.
Cornell University Medical College Bookstore	424 E 70th St	212-988-0400	Academic - Medical.
Crawford Doyle Booksellers	1082 Madison Ave	212-288-6300	General Interest.
Hunter College Bookstore	695 Park Ave	212-650-3970	Academic - General.
Imperial Fine Books	790 Madison Ave	212-861-6620	Antiquarian.
James Cummins Book Seller	699 Madison Ave, 7th Fl	212-688-6441	Antiquarian.
Lenox Hill	1018 Lexington Ave	212-472-7170	General Interest.
Metropolitan Museum of Art Bookshop	1000 Fifth Ave	212-650-2911	Specialty - Art books.
Shakespeare & Co	939 Lexington Ave	212-570-0201	Chain.
Ursus Books	981 Madison Ave	212-772-8787	Specialty - Art.
Whitney Museum of American Art Bookstore	945 Madison Ave	212-570-3614	Specialty - Art/ Artists Books.

Map 16 • Upper West Side (Upper)

Funny Business Comics	660B Amsterdam Ave	212-799-9477	Specialty - Comics.
Murder Ink	2486 Broadway	212-362-8905/ 800-488-8123	Specialty - Mystery.

Map 17 • Upper East Side / East Harlem

Barnes & Noble	1280 Lexington Ave	212-423-9900	Chain.
Barnes & Noble	240 E 86th St	212-794-1962	Chain.
Corner Bookstore	1313 Madison Ave	212-831-3554	General Interest.
Kitchen Arts & Letters	1435 Lexington Ave	212-876-5550	Specialty - Books on food and wine.
Mount Sinai Medical Bookstore	1425 Madison Ave	212-241-2665	Specialty - Medical.

Map 18 • Columbia / Morningside Heights

Augsburg Fortress	3041 Broadway	212-280-1554	Specialty - Spiritual and theological.
Bank Street College Bookstore	610 W 112th St	212-678-1654	Academic - Education/Children.
Columbia University Bookstore	2922 Broadway	212-854-4131	Academic - General.
Labyrinth Books	536 W 112th St	212-865-1588	General Interest.
Last Word Used Books	1181 Amsterdam Ave	212-864-0013	Used.
Morningside Bookshop	2915 Broadway	212-222-3350	General Interest; New and used.

Arts & Entertainment • **Bookstores**

Map 18 • Columbia / Morningside Heights—*continued*

Teachers College Bookstore (Columbia University Graduate School of Education)	1224 Amsterdam Ave	212-678-3920	Academic - Education

Map 19 • Harlem (Lower)

Hue-Man	2319 Frederick Douglass Blvd	212-665-7400	African American.

Map 20 • El Barrio

J P Medical Books	53 E 124th St	212-410-0593	Academic - Medical.

Map 21 • Manhattanville / Hamilton Heights

La Boheme	3441 Broadway	862-5500	Specialty - Spanish.
Sisters Uptown	1942 Amsterdam Ave	212-862-3680	African American books.

Map 23 • Washington Heights

Columbia Medical Books	3954 Broadway	212-923-2149	Academic - Medical.

Map 24 • Fort George / Fort Tryon

Libreria Caliope	170 Dyckman St	212-567-3511	Spanish and English.
Metropolitan Museum of Art Bookshop-Cloisters Branch	Ft Tryon Park	212-923-3700	Specialty - Art books.

Map 25 • Inwood

Libreria Continental	628 W 207th St	212-544-9004	Specialty - Spanish.

Map 28 • Greenpoint

Ex libris Polish Book Gallery	140 Nassau Ave	718-349-0468	Polish.
Polish American Bookstore	648 Manhattan Ave	718-349-3756	Polish.
Polish American Bookstore	946 Manhattan Ave	718-389-7790	Polish.
Polish Bookstore	739 Manhattan Ave	718-383-0739	Polish.
Polish Bookstore & Publishing	161 Java St	718-349-2738	Polish.
Polonia Book Store	882 Manhattan Ave	718-389-1684	Polish.

Map 29 • Williamsburg

Clovis Press	229 Bedford Ave	718-302-3751	General.
Spoonbill & Sugartown	218 Bedford Ave	718-387-7322	Art, architecture, design, philosophy, and literature. New and used.

Map 30 • Brooklyn Heights / DUMBO / Downtown

A&B Books	146 Lawrence St	718-596-0872	African American books.
Barnes & Noble	106 Court St	718-246-4996	Chain.
Heights Books	109 Montague St	718-624-4876	Rare, out of print, used.
Horizon Books	289 Livingston St	718-855-0053	African American books.
St Mark's Comics	148 Montague St	718-935-0911	Comics.
Trazar's Variety Book Store	40 Hoyt St	718-797-2478	African American books.
Waldenbooks	129 Montague St	718-858-2958	Chain.

Map 31 • Fort Greene / Clinton Hill

Big Deal Books	973 Fulton St	718-622-4420	General.
Dare Books	33 Lafayette Ave	718-625-4651	General.

Map 32 • BoCoCa / Red Hook

Anwaar Bookstore	428 Atlantic Ave	718-875-3791	Arabic books.
Bookcourt	163 Court St	718-875-3677	General.
Community Book Store	212 Court St	718-834-9494	Used.
Freebird Books	123 Columbia St	718-643-8484	Used.

Map 33 • Park Slope / Prospect Heights / Windsor Ter

Barnes & Noble	267 Seventh Ave	718-832-9066	Chain.
Comics Plus	302 Seventh Ave	718-768-5681	Comics.
Community Book Store	143 Seventh Ave	718-783-3075	General.
Nkiru International Bookstore	732 Washington Ave	718-783-6306	Excellent poetry and cultural books.
Park Slope Books	200 Seventh Ave	718-499-3064	General.
Seventh Avenue Kid's Books	202 Seventh Ave	718-840-0020	Children's.

Multiplexes abound in NYC, but unlike everywhere else, you'll need to cash in a savings bond to cover the steep $10.75 ticket price, the ridiculously expensive popcorn drenched in artificial grease, and costly carbonated syrup water. Needless to say, a trip to the movies here is a rather exorbitant affair, but hey, we don't live in the Big Apple 'cause it's cheap! No matter what kind of flick you're in the mood for, the city's bound to have a theater that'll suit your needs.

If you're after a first-run Hollywood blockbuster, we highly recommend the **Regal 16** in Battery Park City. It has spacious theaters with large screens, big sound, comfortable seats, plenty of aisle room, and most importantly, fewer people! The **Regal Union Square 14** is gargantuan too, but frequently so packed that the lines spill out onto the sidewalk. Stadium seating and an IMAX theater make **Loews Lincoln Square** a great place to catch a huge film, and its ideal location offers loads of after-movie options—we recommend grabbing a bite at the Whole Foods Market in the fancy new Time-Warner Center. If you'd like to save a little money and don't mind seeing a movie a few months after it's released, check out what's playing at the **Loews State** in the basement of the Times Square Virgin Megastore. The theater is a little threadbare, but they have popcorn and you can see a movie for half the regular price.

For the independent or foreign film, the **Landmark Sunshine** on Houston and Forsyth has surpassed the **Angelika** as the superior downtown movie house. Don't

get us wrong—the Angelika still presents some great movies, but the theater itself is a far cry from the Sunshine. Any list of hip venues wouldn't be complete without mentioning the **Two Boots Pioneer**, operated by the folks at Two Boots. The Pioneer specializes in the independent scene, featuring documentaries, short films, cool film series, and festivals (www.twoboots.com/pioneer). The best revival houses are **Cinema Classics** and the **Film Forum**—especially now that the Screening Room (now **Tribeca Cinemas**) is gone.

The most decadent and enjoyable movie experiences can be had at the theaters that feel the most "New York." The Upper East Side's **Cineplex Odeon Beekman**, while small, is featured in some of the best scenes in *Annie Hall*, so put on a big tie and vest to impress that date of yours. **Clearview's Ziegfeld** on 54th Street is a vestige from a time long past when movie theaters were real works of art. This space is so posh with its gilding and red velvet, you'll feel you're crossing the Atlantic on an expensive ocean liner. The **Paris Theatre** on 58th Street is one of our favorite theaters in the city—it has the best balcony, hands down!

Oh, and don't forget to use Moviefone (777-FILM; www.moviefone.com) or Fandango (www.fandango.com) to reserve your tickets ahead of time on an opening weekend!

Manhattan

	Address	Phone	Map	
92nd Street Y	Lexington Ave & 92nd St	212-415-5500	17	Upper East Side / East Harlem
AMC Empire 25	234 W 42nd St	212-398-3939	12	Midtown
American Museum of Natural History IMAX	Central Park W & 79th St	212-769-5100	14	Upper West Side (Lower)
Angelika Film Center	18 W Houston St	777-FILM #531	6	Washington Square / NYU / SoHo
Anthology Film Archives	32 Second Ave	212-505-5181	6	Washington Square / NYU / SoHo
Asia Society	725 Park Ave	212-327-9276	15	Upper East Side (Lower)
Bryant Park Summer Film Festival (outdoors)	Bryant Park, b/w 40th & 42nd Sts	212-512-5700	12	Midtown
Cinema Classics	332 E 11th St	212-677-5368	6	Washington Square / NYU / SoHo
Cinema Village	22 E 12th St	212-924-3363	6	Washington Square / NYU / SoHo
Cineplex Odeon: Beekman Theater	1254 Second Ave	212-737-2622	15	Upper East Side (Lower)
City Cinemas 1, 2, 3	1001 Third Ave	777-FILM #635	13	East Midtown
City Cinemas: East 86th Street	210 E 86th St	212-744-1999	17	Upper East Side / East Harlem
City Cinemas: Village East Cinemas	189 Second Ave	777-FILM #922	6	Washington Square / NYU / SoHo
Clearview's 62nd & Broadway	1871 Broadway	777-FILM #864	14	Upper West Side (Lower)
Clearview's Chelsea	260 W 23rd St	777-FILM #597	9	Flatiron / Lower Midtown
Clearview's Chelsea West	333 W 23rd St	777-FILM #614	8	Chelsea
Clearview's First & 62nd Street	400 E 62nd St	777-FILM #957	15	Upper East Side (Lower)
Clearview's Ziegfeld	141 W 54th St	777-FILM #602	12	Midtown
Czech Center	1109 Madison Ave	212-288-0830	15	Upper East Side (Lower)
Film Forum	209 W Houston St	212-727-8110	5	West Village
French Institute	55 E 59th St	212-355-6160	13	East Midtown
Goethe Institute	1014 Fifth Ave	212-439-8700	17	Upper East Side / East Harlem
Hudson Street Cinemas	5 Marineview Plz		34	Hoboken
The ImaginAsian	239 E 59th St	777-FILM #615	13	East Midtown
Instituto Cervantes	122 E 42nd St	212-661-6011	13	East Midtown
Italian Academy	1161 Amsterdam Ave	212-854-3570	18	Columbia / Morningside Heights
Japan Society	333 E 47th St	212-752-3015	13	East Midtown

Manhattan—*continued*

	Address	Phone	Map	
Landmark Sunshine Cinema	141 E Houston St	777-FILM #687	6	Washington Sq / NYU / SoHo
Leonard Nimoy Thalia	2537 Broadway	212-864-5400	16	Upper West Side (Upper)
Lincoln Plaza Cinemas	30 Lincoln Plz	212-757-2280	14	Upper West Side (Lower)
Loews 19th Street East	890 Broadway	50-LOEWS #858	9	Flatiron / Lower Midtown
Loews 34th Street	312 W 34th St	212-244-8686	8	Chelsea
Loews 42nd Street E Walk	247 W 42nd St	50-LOEWS #572	12	Midtown
Loews 72nd Street East	1230 Third Ave	50-LOEWS #704	15	Upper East Side (Lower)
Loews 84th St	2310 Broadway	50-LOEWS #701	14	Upper West Side (Lower)
Loews Astor Plaza	1515 Broadway	50-LOEWS #699	12	Midtown
Loews Cineplex Newport Center 11	30 Mall Dr W		35	Jersey City
Loews Cineplex Orpheum	1538 Third Ave	50-LOEWS #964	17	Upper East Side / East Harlem
Loews Cineplex Village VII	66 Third Ave	50-LOEWS #952	6	Washington Square / NYU / SoHo
Loews Kips Bay	550 Second Ave	50-LOEWS #558	10	Murray Hill / Gramercy
Loews Lincoln Square & IMAX Theatre	1992 Broadway	50-LOEWS #638	14	Upper West Side (Lower)
Loews State	1540 Broadway	50-LOEWS	12	Midtown
Magic Johnson Harlem USA	124th St & Frederick Douglass Blvd	212-665-8742	19	Harlem (Lower)
Makor	35 W 67th St	212-601-1000	14	Upper West Side (Lower)
Metropolitan Museum of Art	1000 Fifth Ave	212-535-7710	15	Upper East Side (Lower)
MOMA	11 W 53rd St	212-708-9480	12	Midtown
Museum of TV and Radio	25 W 52nd St	212-621-6800	12	Midtown
New Coliseum Theatre	703 W 181st St	212-740-1545	23	Washington Heights
New York Public Library Jefferson Market Branch	425 Sixth Ave	212-243-4334	5	West Village
New York Public Library -Donnell Library Center	20 W 53rd St	212-621-0618	12	Midtown
New York Twin	1271 Second Ave	212-249-4200	15	Upper East Side (Lower)
New York Youth Theater	593 Park Ave	212-888-0696	15	Upper East Side (Lower)
NYU Cantor Film Center	36 E 8th St	212-998-4100	6	Washington Square / NYU / SoHo
Paris Theatre	4 W 58th St	212-688-3800	12	Midtown
Quad Cinema	34 W 13th St	212-255-8800	6	Washington Square / NYU / SoHo
Regal Battery Park City 16	102 North End Ave (Embassy Suites)	800-326-3264 #629	p192	Battery Park City
Regal Union Square 14	850 Broadway	800-326-3264 #628	6	Washington Square / NYU / SoHo
Regal/UA	35-30 38th St		27	Long Island City
Scandinavia House	58 Park Ave	212-779-3587	10	Murray Hill / Gramercy
Solomon R Guggenheim Museum	1071 Fifth Ave	212-423-3500	17	Upper East Side (Upper)
Tribeca Cinemas	54 Varick St	212-334-2100	2	TriBeCa
Two Boots Pioneer Theater	155 E 3rd St	212-254-3300	7	East Village/Lower East Side
UA 64th & Second	1210 Second Ave	800-326-3264 #62615		Upper East Side (Lower)
UA East 85th Street	1629 First Ave	800-326-3264 #62715		Upper East Side (Lower)
Walter Reade Theater	70 Lincoln Plz	212-875-5600	14	Upper West Side (Lower)
Whitney Museum	945 Madison Ave	212-570-3600	15	Upper East Side (Lower)
YWCA	610 Lexington Ave	212-735-9717	13	East Midtown

Brooklyn

	Address	Phone	Map	
BAM Rose Cinemas	30 Lafayette Ave	718-777-3456	31	Fort Greene / Clinton Hill
Cinema Warsaw	261 Driggs Ave	718-383-5352	28	Greenpoint
Cobble Hill Cinemas	265 Court St	718-596-9113	32	BoCoCa / Red Hook
Pavilion Brooklyn Heights	70 Henry St	718-596-7070	30	Brooklyn Heights / DUMBO / Downtown
Pavilion Flatbush	314 Flatbush Ave	718-636-0170	33	Park Slope / Prospect Heights / Windsor Terrace
Pavilion Movie Theatres	188 Prospect Park W	718-369-0838	33	Park Slope / Prospect Heights Windsor Terrace
Regal/UA Court Street	108 Court St	718-246-7995	30	Brooklyn Heights / DUMBO / Downtown

General Information

NFT Map:	12
Address:	11 W 53rd St
Phone:	212-708-9400
Website:	www.moma.org
Hours:	Sun, Mon, Wed, Thurs, Sat: 10:30 am-5:30 pm; Fri 10:30 am-8 pm; closed Tues, Thanksgiving and Christmas
Admission:	$20 for adults, $16 for seniors, $12 for students; free to members and children under 16 accompanied by an adult

Overview

The Museum of Modern Art opened in 1929, back when impressionism and surrealism were truly modern art. Starting out in the Heckscher Building at 730 Fifth Avenue, MoMA moved to its current address on W 53rd Street in 1932. What started out as a townhouse eventually expanded into an enormous space, with new buildings and additions in 1939 (by Phillip L. Goodwin and Edward Durell Stone), 1953 (including a sculpture garden by Phillip Johnson), 1964 (another Johnson garden), and 1984 (by Cesar Pelli). During the summer of 2002, the museum closed its Manhattan location and moved temporarily to Long Island City. After a major expansion and renovation by Yoshio Taniguchi, MoMA reopened in September 2004.

The re-Manhattanized museum charges $20. If crowds on a typical Saturday afternoon are any indication, the hefty entry fee is not keeping patrons away. Taniguchi's new design is understated to the degree of actual boredom, but the art is the point, right?

Wrong. Museums are one of the last great bastions of inventive, exciting, and not-necessarily-practical architecture. Taniguchi's design uses all available space, which, considering the price of midtown real estate, must have been a selling point for his design. Other than that, you'll have to trek up to the Guggenheim, fly off to Bilbao, and/or wait for the New Museum of Contemporary Art to move in to its new Bowery digs to see better marriages of art and design.

What to See

The fourth and fifth floors are where the big names reside—Johns, Pollack, Warhol (fourth floor), Braque, Cezanne, Dali, Duchamp, Ernst, Hopper, Kandinsky, Klee, Matisse, Miro, Monet, Picasso, Rosseau, Seurat, Van Gogh, and Wyeth (fifth floor). More recent works can be found in the contemporary gallery on the second floor. Special exhibitions are featured on the third and sixth floors. The surrealism collection is definitely the bomb; however, we suspect that MoMA is only showing about 5% of its pop art collection. Well, you can't have everything...

Moving downstairs to the third floor, it's clear that the photography collection is, as always, one of the centerpieces of the museum, and is highly recommended (although the Gursky pieces are actually dotted throughout the building). The architecture and design gallery has all kinds of cool consumer product designs, from chairs to cars to airport arrival boards—there is a LOT more to see here than at the old museum, and it's by far the most fun thing to see at the new MoMA.

Breakdown of the Space

Floor One: Lobby, Sculpture Garden, Museum Store, Restaurant
Floor Two: Contemporary Galleries, Media Gallery, Prints and Illustrated Books, Café
Floor Three: Architecture and Design, Drawing, Photography, Special Exhibitions
Floor Four: Painting and Sculpture II
Floor Five: Painting and Sculpture I, Café
Floor Six: Special Exhibitions
There are two theater levels below the first floor.

Amenities

Bags are not allowed in gallery spaces, and the free coat check can become messy when the check-in and check-out lines become intertwined. Leave large items at home.

Bathrooms and water fountains are on floors one through five, and on the lower theater level. We don't think that there are enough of them, and the bathrooms themselves are way too small to handle the crowds.

There are three places to get food in the museum—you'll pay heavily for the convenience and Danny Meyer experience. Café 2, located on the second floor, offers "seasonal Roman fare," also known as "snooty Italian." They also have an espresso bar. Terrace 5, which overlooks the beautiful sculpture garden, has desserts, chocolates, and sandwiches, along with wine, cocktails, coffee, and tea. Both cafes open half an hour after the museum opens its doors and close half an hour before the museum closes.

For the ultimate museum dining experience, The Modern features the cuisine of Gabriel Kreuther. It has two main rooms—the Dining Room overlooks the sculpture garden and the Bar Room is more casual and overlooks the bar. An outdoor terrace is also made available when the weather permits. The Modern serves French and New American food and features wild game menu items—sounds great if you've got a platinum card.

The Modern is open beyond museum hours, with the Dining Room closing at 11 pm Monday-Thursday, and 11:30 pm on Friday and Saturday. The Bar Room closes at 11:30 pm Monday-Saturday and 10:30 on Sunday. There's a separate street entrance to allow diners access to The Modern after the museum closes.

Metropolitan Museum of Art

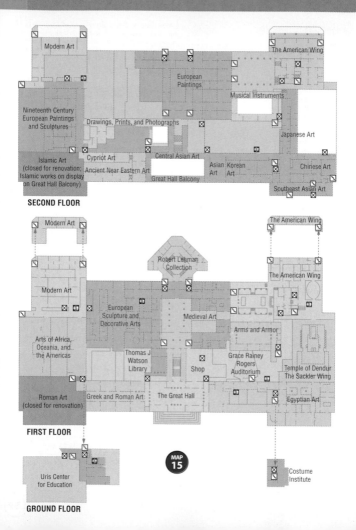

Modern Art

The American Wing

European Paintings

Musical Instruments

Nineteenth Century European Paintings and Sculptures

Drawings, Prints, and Photographs

Japanese Art

Islamic Art (closed for renovation; Islamic works on display on Great Hall Balcony)

Cypriot Art

Central Asian Art

Ancient Near Eastern Art

Great Hall Balcony

Asian Art

Korean Art

Chinese Art

Southeast Asian Art

SECOND FLOOR

Modern Art

The American Wing

Robert Lehman Collection

The American Wing

Modern Art

European Sculpture and Decorative Arts

Medieval Art

Arms and Armor

Arts of Africa, Oceania, and the Americas

Thomas J Watson Library

Shop

Grace Rainey Rogers Auditorium

Temple of Dendur The Sackler Wing

Roman Art (closed for renovation)

Greek and Roman Art

The Great Hall

Egyptian Art

FIRST FLOOR

Uris Center for Education

MAP 15

Costume Institute

GROUND FLOOR

General Information

NFT Map:	15
Address:	1000 Fifth Ave at 82nd St
Phone:	212-535-7710
Website:	www.metmuseum.org
Hours:	Sun, Tues-Thurs: 9:30 am-5:30 pm; Fri & Sat: 9:30 am-9 pm; Mon, New Year's Day, Christmas & Thanksgiving: closed
Admission:	A suggested $15 donation for adults, $7 for students, and $10 for senior citizens. Admission includes the Main Building and The Cloisters on the same day. Free to members and children under twelve with an adult.

Overview

The Metropolitan Museum of Art is touted as the largest and most comprehensive museum in the Western hemisphere. Established by a group of American businessmen, artists, and thinkers back in 1870, the museum was created to preserve and stimulate appreciation for some of the greatest works of art in history.

In the first few years of its inception, the museum moved from its original location at 681 Fifth Avenue to the Douglas Mansion at 128 W 14th Street, and then finally to its current Central Park location in 1880.

Calvert Vaux and Jacob Wrey Mold designed the museum's Gothic Revival red-brick facade, which was later remodeled in 1926 into the grand, white-columned front entrance that you see today. Part of the original facade was left intact and can still be seen from the Robert Lehman Wing looking toward the European Sculpture and Decorative Arts galleries.

The Met's annual attendance reaches over 5 million visitors who flock to see the more than 2 million works of art housed in the museum's permanent collection. The vast paintings anthology had a modest beginning in 1870 with a small donation of 174 European paintings and has now swelled to include works spanning 5,000 years of world culture, from the prehistoric to the present and from every corner of the globe.

The Met is broken down into a series of smaller museums within each building. For instance, the American Wing contains the most complete accumulation of American paintings, sculpture, and decorative arts, including period rooms offering a look at domestic life throughout the nation's history. The Egyptian collection is the finest in the world outside of Cairo, and the Islamic art exhibition remains unparalleled, as does the mass of 2,500 European paintings and Impressionist and Post-Impressionist works.

Other major collections include the arms and armor, Asian art, costumes, European sculpture and decorative arts, medieval and Renaissance art, musical instruments, drawings, prints, ancient antiquities from around the world, photography, and modern art.

The Greatest Hits

You can, of course, spend countless hours at the Met. But if you're rushed for time, check out the sublime space that houses the **Temple of Dendur** in the Sackler Wing, the elegant **Frank Lloyd Wright Room** in the American Wing, the fabulous **Tiffany Glass** and **Tiffany Mosaics**, also in the American Wing, the **Arms and Armor** exhibit, the **Caravaggios** and **Goyas** in the Renaissance Rooms, the wonderful **Clyfford Still** room in Modern Art, and that huge **canoe** in Arts of Africa and Oceania. When it's open, we highly recommend the **Roof Garden**, which has killer views of Central Park.

How to Get There—Mass Transit

Subway
Take the ❹ ❺ ❻ to the 86th Street stop and walk three blocks west to Fifth Avenue.

Bus
Take the ❹ bus along Fifth Avenue (from uptown locations) to 82nd Street or along Madison Avenue (from downtown locations) to 83rd Street.

Arts & Entertainment • **Museums**

Together, New York City's five boroughs have over a hundred different museums of varying reputation, from world famous institutions like the **Metropolitan Museum of Art** to lesser-known historical houses and buildings. However, this hasn't always been the case. In the 18th and 19th centuries, Manhattan quickly grew to become the capital of commerce, while culture was sorely neglected. Until the mid-1800's, most museums in the city were either small collections run by academic societies or individuals, or entertainment-focused, profit-making ventures, such as P.T. Barnum's American Museum.

The second half of the 19th-century saw the founding of the **American Museum of Natural History** and the **Met** with money donated by wealthy industrialists. This trend continued into the 20th century, with large donations of paintings to the Met by J.P. Morgan and B. Altman, the opening of **The Cloisters** with funding from John D. Rockefeller, and the creation of galleries based on the collections of Morgan and Henry Clay Frick. Other notable openings of this time include the **Brooklyn Children's Museum**, the **Museum of the City of New York**, and **Hayden Planetarium**.

Museums devoted to modern art, such as the **Whitney Museum of American Art**, the **Museum of Modern Art**, and the **Guggenheim**, were founded in the 1920's and '30s. Museum openings continued into the middle of the century with the **International Center of Photography**, the **American Folk Art Museum**, and the **Museum of Television and Radio**. This was also a period that

saw a growing awareness of cross-cultural art with the establishment of the **Asia Society** and **El Museo Del Bario**. Alternative spaces, such as **P.S.1**, also began to have a greater presence. In the last half of the 20th century, an increased interest in the city's historical structures after the destruction of Penn Station led to the installation of many small museums in historic houses across all five boroughs. The conversion of obsolete buildings into museums, such as the transformation of the Custom House into the **National Museum of the American Indian,** also occurred during this period. Quite a few large museums have been recently renovated, including the **Museum of Natural History** (which now has a planetarium), **MoMA** (now back in Manhattan and looking more modern than ever), and the Met.

Just about every museum in the city is worth a visit, and the major ones have so many exhibits and special collections that making the trek to them a few times a year isn't unreasonable. A few favorites include the **Transit Museum** (Brooklyn), the Museum of Television and Radio, the **Morgan Library** (closed until early 2006—has copies of Guttenberg's Bible on display), the **American Museum of the Moving Image** (Queens), the **Frick Collection**, the Cloisters, and the **Queens Museum of Art** (specifically the panorama of New York City), as well as the usual suspects—the Met, MoMA, Natural History, and the Whitney.

Our favorites for contemporary art are **Dia:Chelsea** on 22nd, the **New Museum of Contemporary Art** on Bowery, and **P.S.1** in Queens. Go crazy.

Manhattan

	Address	Phone	Map	
African American Institute	833 United Nations Plz	212-949-5666	13	East Midtown
African American Institute	40 Lexington Ave	212-949-5666	10	Murray Hill / Gramercy
America's Society	680 Park Ave	212-628-3200	15	Upper East Side (Lower)
American Academy of Arts & Letters	633 W 155th St	212-368-5900	21	Manhattanville / Hamilton Heights
American Folk Art Museum	45 W 53rd St	212-265-1040	12	Midtown
American Friends of Tel Aviv	545 Madison Ave	212-319-0555	12	Midtown
American Geographical Society	120 Wall St	212-422-5456	1	Financial District
American Institute of Graphic Arts	164 Fifth Ave	212-807-1990	9	Flatiron / Lower Midtown
American Museum of Natural History	Central Park W at 79th St	212-769-5400	15	Upper East Side (Lower)
American Numismatic Society	96 Fulton St	212-571-4470	1	Financial District
Anthology Film Archives	32 Second Ave	212-505-5181	6	Washington Square / NYU / SoHo
Arsenal Gallery	830 Fifth Ave	212-360-8163	15	Upper East Side (Lower)
Art in General	79 Walker St	212-219-0473	3	City Hall / Chinatown
Asia Society & Museum	725 Park Ave	212-288-6400	15	Upper East Side (Lower)
Asian American Art Centre	26 Bowery	212-233-2154	3	City Hall / Chinatown
Bard Graduate Center for Studies in the Decorative Arts	18 W 86th St	212-501-3000	16	Upper West Side (Upper)
Chaim Gross Studio Museum	526 LaGuardia Pl	212-529-4906	6	Washington Square / NYU / SoHo
Chelsea Art Museum	556 W 22nd St	212-255-0719	8	Chelsea
Children's Galleries for Jewish Culture	515 W 20th St	212-924-4500	8	Chelsea
Children's Museum of Manhattan	212 W 83rd St	212-721-1224	14	Upper West Side (Lower)
Children's Museum of the Arts	182 Lafayette St	212-941-9198	3	City Hall / Chinatown
Children's Museum of the Native Americans	550 W 155th St	212-283-1122	21	Manhattanville / Hamilton Heights
China Institute	125 E 65th St	212-744-8181	15	Upper East Side (Lower)
The Cloisters	Ft Tryon Park	212-923-3700	24	Fort George / Fort Tryon
Constitution Works	26 Wall St	212-785-1989	1	Financial District
Cooper Union for Foundation Building, the Advancement of Science and Art	E 7th & Third Ave	212-353-4200	6	Washington Square / NYU / SoHo
Cooper-Hewitt National Design Museum	2 E 91st St	212-849-8400	17	Upper East Side / East Harlem
Czech Center	1109 Madison Ave	212-288-0830	15	Upper East Side (Lower)
Dahesh Museum	580 Madison Ave	212-759-0606	12	Midtown
Dia:Chelsea	548 W 22nd St	212-989-5566	8	Chelsea
Drawing Center	35 Wooster St	212-219-2166	2	TriBeCa
Dyckman Farmhouse Museum	4881 Broadway	212-304-9422	25	Inwood
El Museo del Barrio	1230 Fifth Ave	212-831-7272	17	Upper East Side / East Harlem
Ellis Island Immigration Museum	Ellis Island, via ferry at Battery Park	212-269-5755	1	Financial District
Exit Art / The First World	475 Tenth Ave	212-966-7745	8	Chelsea
Fraunces Tavern Museum	54 Pearl St	212-425-1778	1	Financial District
Frick Collection	1 E 70th St	212-288-0700	15	Upper East Side (Lower)
Goethe-Institut	1014 Fifth Ave	212-439-8700	15	Upper East Side (Lower)
Gracie Mansion	East End Ave at 88th St	212-570-4751	17	Upper East Side / East Harlem
Grant's Tomb	W 122nd St & Riverside Dr		18	Columbia / Morningside Heights
Guggenheim Museum Soho	575 Broadway	212-423-3500	6	Washington Square / NYU / SoHo

Hayden Planetarium	175 Central Park W	212-769-5920	14	Upper West Side (Lower)
Hispanic Society of America	Broadway & 155th St	212-926-2234	21	Manhattanville / Hamilton Heights
International Center of Photography (ICP)	1133 Sixth Ave	212-857-0000	12	Midtown
Intrepid Sea-Air-Space Museum	Pier 86, W 46th St at the Hudson River	212-245-0072	12	Midtown
Japan Society	333 E 47th St	212-832-1155	13	East Midtown
Jersey City Museum	350 Montgomery St	201-413-0303	33	Jersey City
Jewish Museum	1109 Fifth Ave	212-423-3200	17	Upper East Side / East Harlem
Lower East Side Tenement Museum	90 Orchard St	212-431-0233	4	Lower East Side
Madame Tussauds NY	234 W 42nd St	800-246-8872	12	Midtown
Merchant's House Museum	29 E 4th St	212-777-1089	6	Washington Square / NYU / SoHo
Metropolitan Museum of Art	Fifth Ave & 82nd St	212-535-7710	15	Upper East Side (Lower)
Morgan Library	29 E 36th St	212-685-0610	9	Flatiron / Lower Midtown
Morris-Jumel Mansion	65 Jumel Ter	212-923-8008	23	Washington Heights
Mount Vernon Hotel Museum	421 E 61st St	212-838-6878	15	Upper East Side (Lower)
Municipal Art Society	457 Madison Ave	212-935-3960	12	Midtown
Museum at the Fashion Institute of Technology	Seventh Ave & 27th St	212-217-5800	9	Flatiron / Lower Midtown
Museum for African Art	593 Broadway	212-966-1313	6	Washington Square / NYU / SoHo
Museum of African American History and Arts	352 W 71st St	212-873-5040	14	Upper West Side (Lower)
Museum of American Financial History	28 Broadway	212-908-4110	1	Financial District
Museum of American Illustration	128 E 63rd St	212-838-2560	15	Upper East Side (Lower)
Museum of Arts & Design	40 W 53rd St	212-956-3535	12	Midtown
The Museum of Biblical Art	1865 Broadway	212-408-1500	14	Upper West Side (Lower)
Museum of Chinese in the Americas	70 Mulberry St	212-619-4785	3	City Hall / Chinatown
Museum of Jewish Heritage	36 Battery Pl	646-437-4200	p192	Battery Park City
Museum of Modern Art (MOMA)	11 W 53rd St	212-708-9400	12	Midtown
Museum of Sex	233 Fifth Ave	212-689-6337	9	Flatiron / Lower Midtown
Museum of Television & Radio	25 W 52nd St	212-621-6800	12	Midtown
Museum of the City of New York	1220 Fifth Ave	212-534-1672	17	Upper East Side / East Harlem
National Academy of Design	1083 Fifth Ave	212-369-4880	17	Upper East Side / East Harlem
National Museum of Catholic Art & History	443 E 115th St	212-828-5209	20	El Barrio
National Museum of the American Indian	1 Bowling Green	212-514-3700	1	Financial District
Neue Galerie: Museum for German & Austrian Art	1048 Fifth Ave	212-628-6200	17	Upper East Side / East Harlem
New Museum of Contemporary Art (Temporary Location)	556 W 22nd St	212-219-1222	8	Chelsea
New York City Fire Museum	278 Spring St	212-691-1303	5	West Village
New - York Historical Society	170 Central Park W	212-873-3400	14	Upper West Side (Lower)
New York Police Museum	100 Old Slip	212-480-3100	1	Financial District
New York Public Library for the Performing Arts	40 Lincoln Center Plz	212-870-1630	14	Upper West Side (Lower)
The New York Public Library Humanities & Social Sciences Library	Fifth Ave & 42nd St	212-869-8089	12	Midtown
New York Unearthed	17 State St	212-748-8628	1	Financial District
Nicholas Roerich Museum	319 W 107th St	212-864-7752	16	Upper West Side (Upper)
Rose Museum	154 W 57th St	212-247-7800	12	Midtown
Rubin Museum of Art	150 W 17th St	212-620-5000	9	Flatiron / Lower Midtown
Scandinavia House	58 Park Ave	212-879-9779	10	Murray Hill / Gramercy
School of Visual Arts Museum	209 E 23rd St	212-592-2144	10	Murray Hill / Gramercy
Skyscraper Museum	39 Battery Pl	212-968-1961	1	Financial District
Solomon R Guggenheim Museum	1071 Fifth Ave	212-423-3500	17	Upper East Side / East Harlem
Sony Wonder Technology Lab	550 Madison Ave	212-833-8100	12	Midtown
South Street Seaport Museum	12 Fulton St	212-748-8600	1	Financial District
Statue of Liberty Museum	Liberty Island, via ferry at Battery Park	212-363-3200	1	Financial District
Studio Museum in Harlem	144 W 125th St	212-864-4500	19	Harlem (Lower)
Tibet House	22 W 15th St	212-807-0563	9	Flatiron / Lower Midtown
Ukrainian Museum	222 E 6th St	212-228-0110	6	Washington Square / NYU / SoHo
US Archives of American Art	1285 Sixth Ave	212-399-5030	12	Midtown
Whitney Museum of American Art	945 Madison Ave	212-570-3676	15	Upper East Side (Lower)
Whitney Museum of American Art at Philip Morris	120 Park Ave	917-663-2453	13	East Midtown
Yeshiva University Museum	2520 Amsterdam Ave	212-960-5390	24	Fort George / Fort Tryon

Brooklyn

	Address	Phone	Map	
Brooklyn Historical Society	128 Pierrepont St	718-222-4111	30	Brooklyn Heights / DUMBO / Downtown
City Reliquary	Grand & Havemeyer Sts		29	Williamsburg
Kurdish Library and Museum	144 Underhill Ave	718-783-7930	33	Park Slope/Prospect Heights
Micro Museum	123 Smith St	718-797-3116	32	BoCoCa / Red Hook
New York Transit Museum	Boerum Pl & Schermerhorn St	718-243-8601	30	Brooklyn Heights / DUMBO / Downtown
The Old Stone House	336 Third St (b/w 4th and Fifth Ave)	718-768-3195	33	Park Slope / Prospect Heights
Simmons Collection African Arts Museum	1063 Fulton St	718-230-0933	31	Fort Greene / Clinton Hill

Queens

	Address	Phone	Map	
P.S.1	4601 21st St	718-784-2084	27	Long Island City
American Museum of the Moving Image	35th Avenue at 36th St	718-784-4520	27	Long Island City
Queens Museum of Art	New York City Building Corona Park, Flushing Meadows	718-592-9700	p189	

Eating out in New York. Why do we do it? Because cooking is probably only 15% cheaper. Or at least that's what we tell ourselves when we're spending $20 on a hamburger (**Union Square Café**), or $45 on pizza (**Otto**), or god knows what else. But hey—if you're into cooking, that's great. Just move where groceries are cheaper—say, Kansas.

As for the rest of us, eating out is a way of life, an art form, a topic of endless discussion. *Zagat Survey* restaurant ratings, started on a photocopied sheet handed out to friends in the 1970's, is now an institution in NYC. Half the time we think it's cool to actually even *find* a restaurant that's not "Zagat Rated." The other half of the time, it makes us very, very nervous.

But we *like* that nervous feeling; we can't wait to try a new cuisine; we don't mind eating in places that would clearly fail a Board of Health test—it's all part of eating out in New York. It never gets old….

Eating Old

Even though restaurant turnover continues at an astonishing rate, there are some old New York eateries worth checking out, for instance, the posh **'21' Club**, the former speakeasy **Chumley's**, the midtown watering hole **P.J. Clarke's**, the near-ancient **Bridge Café**, the classic Grand Central **Oyster Bar**, the Brooklyn staple **Ferdinando's Focacceria**, and the always-homey TriBeCa landmark **Walker's**.

Eating Cheap

Two words: go ethnic. Pizza, falafel, dumplings, burritos, bagels—this is what we eat to sustain ourselves on a daily basis for little $$$. For pizza, check out **Two Boots**, **Joe's**, **Ben's**, **Arturo's**, **John's**, and **Patsy's**. For cheap Chinese, you can go to any place on any corner, but two cheap Dim Sum meccas in Chinatown are **Mandarin Court** and **Triple Eight Palace**. Sharing at places like **Joe's Shanghai** and **Grand Sichuan International** will also not bleed your wallet. Middle Eastern and burrito places are also a dime a dozen—for these, we simply say: choose your poison. As for bagels, go with perennial winners **Ess-a-Bagel** and **H&H Bagels**, or take our two favorites: **David's Bagels** and **Kossar's Bialys**. If you're in an insane hurry, the New York street vendor hot dog is always an option…if you dare.

Eating Hip

You mostly can't eat cool, but sometimes you can come close, especially with favorites like **Florent** (great diner with décor by Tibor Kalman), **Pearl Oyster Bar** (mostly bar seating and the best lobster roll south of Portland), **Norma's** (a cool room and hands-down the best brunch in town), and the relatively pretentious **Tasting Room**.

Eating Late

Kang Suh's Korean barbeque runs all night, as well as **Bereket**, **Odessa**, **Florent** (weekends only), **7A**, **Yaffa Café**, and a host of generic diners. **Blue Ribbon** is still one of the best places to eat after midnight.

Eating Ethnic

New York has not only an example of every type of cuisine on the planet, but also a *good* version of every type of cuisine on the planet. To wit: **Sammy's Roumanian**, **Katz's Delicatessen**, and **Carnegie Deli** (Jewish); **Shun Lee**, **Grand Sichuan International**, and **Joe's Shanghai** (Chinese); **Banjara**, **Tabla**, and **Pongal** (Indian); **Alma**, **Maya**, and **Rosa Mexicano** (Mexican); **Kang Suh** and **Dok Suni's** (Korean); **Holy Basil** (Thai); **Nobu**, **Blue Ribbon Sushi**, and about 40 others (Japanese); **Il Giglio**, **Il Palazzo**, **Babbo**, **John's of 12th Street**, **Il Bagatto**, and about 20 others (Italian); **Ghenet** (Ethiopian); **Eight Mile Creek** (Australian); **Balthazar**, **Chanterelle**, **La Luncheonette**, **Le Gamin**, **Jules**, **French Roast**, and 50 others (French); **Good World** and **Aquavit** (Scandinavian); **Hallo Berlin** (German); **Charles' Southern Style**, **Sylvia's**, and **Old Devil Moon** (Southern); **Stamatis** (Greek); **Mingala Burmese** (Burmese); etc. etc. etc.

Eating Meat

New York is, of course, home to perhaps the world's best steakhouse, **Peter Luger's**. But getting closer to that quality every day is the new **Mark Joseph Steakhouse**, as well as such favorites like **Frank's Restaurant**, **Sparks**, **Palm**, **Smith & Wollensky**, **Angelo & Maxie's**, and, a top NFT pick, the **Strip House**. For the "all you can eat meatfest," **Churrascaria Plataforma** is the place. For poor man's steak (read: hamburger), nothing really comes close to **Corner Bistro**, although **Island Burgers 'N Shakes**, **7A**, **Cozy Soup & Burger**, **Big Nick's**, and even **Jackson Hole** have many admirers.

Eating Meatless

We're not sure, but we think the first McDonald's "veggie burger" ever sold was in the one on St. Mark's Place and Third Avenue. However, for less disgusting fare, try the veggie burgers at **Dojo East** and **West**, respectively, the great faux-sausages at **Kate's Joint**, a whole range of vegan/macrobiotic at **Angelica Kitchen**, the quality Indian fare at **Pongal**, and, for high-end eats, **Hangawi**.

Eating Your Wallet

Here's the rant: you can easily spend over $100 (per person) at any one of these places without even blinking an eye. Is it worth it? Sometimes, little grasshopper, sometimes. But it's almost always at least close at: **Craft**, **Gotham**, **Gramercy Tavern**, **Chanterelle**, **Le Bernardin**, **Oceana**, **Union Square Café**, **March**, **Jean-Georges**, **Babbo**, **Danube**, and a handful of other places. But you can eat at Joe's Shanghai for a full week for the same amount of money. So here we say: choose wisely.

Our Favorite Restaurant

It's **Blue Ribbon** on Sullivan Street. Why? A million reasons: it's open 'till 4 am, it's where the chefs of other restaurants go, it's got fondue, it's got beef marrow, it's got fried chicken, it's got pigeon, it's got a great vibe, great liquor, great service, and not-so-hellish prices. It's everything that's good and it's why we're in New York. Period.

Key: $: Under $10 / $$: $10–$20 / $$$: $20–$30 / $$$$: $30+; * : Does not accept credit cards / † : Accepts only American Express.

Map 1 · Financial District

The 14 Wall Street Restaurant	14 Wall St	212-233-2780	$$$$$	Top-end French from high-up.
American Café & Health Bar	160 Broadway	212-732-1426	$$	Kosher vegetarian.
Battery Gardens	Battery Park, across from 17 State St	212-809-5508	$$$	Panoramic views of NY harbor with a woodburning fireplace.
Burritoville	36 Water St	212-747-1100	$	Takeout Mexican.
Cafe Exchange	49 Broadway	212-425-5000	$*	Better than average cafeteria-style lunch, gets busy.
Carmela's	30 Water St	212-809-0999	$	Superior quick slices.
Cassis on Stone	52 Stone St	212-425-3663	$$	A mini European vacation.
Cosi Sandwich Bar	54 Pine St	212-809-2674	$	Sandwiches for the masses.
Cosi Sandwich Bar	55 Broad St	212-344-5000	$	Sandwiches for the masses.
Daily Soup	41 John St	212-791-7687	$*	Soup!
Financier Patisserie	62 Stone St	212-344-5600	$$	Have your cake and a light meal too.
Giovanni's Atrium	100 Washington St	212-513-4133	$$	Owner grows fresh herbs for meals!
The Grotto	69 New St	212-809-6990	$$	More quick, tasty Italian. Less nudity than that other grotto.
Heartland Brewery	93 South St	646-572-2337	$$	Decent pub grub.
Lemongrass Grill	84 William St	212-809-8038	$$	Serviceable Thai.
Les Halles	15 John St	212-285-8585	$$$	Excellent French steakhouse.
MJ Grill	110 John St	212-346-9848	$$$	Steaks, burgers, loud.
Papoos	55 Broadway	212-809-3150	$$$	Good, if pricey, Italian cuisine.
Red	19 Fulton St	212-571-5900	$$	Acceptable Mexican.
Romi	19 Rector St	212-809-1500	$$$	Tapas and sandwiches.
Rosario's	38 Pearl St	212-514-5763	$$*	Italian. Go for the small portions.
Roy's New York	130 Washington St	212-266-6262	$$$$	Hawaiian fusion seafood.
Sophie's	205 Pearl St	212-269-0909	$*	Great cheap Cuban/Carribean.
Sophie's	73 New St	212-809-7755	$*	Great cheap Cuban/Carribean.
St Maggie's Café	120 Wall St	212-943-9050	$$	Downtown lunch option.
Zeytuna	59 Maiden Ln	212-514-5858	$$	Gourmet take-out. NFT fave.

Map 2 · TriBeCa

66	241 Church St	212-925-0202	$$$$$	Trendy Asian fusion: beware the scene.
A&M Roadhouse	57 Murray St	212-385-9005	$$$	Down-south barbeque ribs meet Maine lobsters.
Azafran	77 Warren St	212-284-0578	$$$	Upscale tapas and Spanish dishes.
Bread Tribeca	301 Church St	212-334-8282	$$$	Country-style Italian.
Bubby's	120 Hudson St	212-219-0666	$$	Great atmosphere—good homestyle and homemade pies.
Burritoville	144 Chambers St	212-571-1144	$	Mexcellent.
Café Noir	32 Grand St	212-431-7910	$$$	Tapas. Open 'til 4am.
Capsouto Frères	451 Washington St	212-966-4900	$$$	Excellent brunch, great space.
Chanterelle	2 Harrison St	212-966-6960	$$$$$	Sublime French with prices to match.
City Hall	131 Duane St	212-227-7777	$$$$	Bright, expensive, lots of suits, but still cool.
Columbine	229 West Broadway	212-965-0909	$	Sandwiches made fresh to order; worth the wait.
Danube	30 Hudson St	212-791-3771	$$$$	Excellent food with an Austrian twist. Go for the tasting menu.
Della Rovere	250 West Broadway	212-334-3470	$$$	Booked until hell freezes over, apparently.
Duane Park Café	157 Duane St	212-732-5555	$$$$	Underrated New American.
Dylan Prime	62 Laight St	212-334-4783	$$$$	Cool looking steakhouse; prime rib is a special.
Edward's	136 West Broadway	212-233-6436	$$	Middle-of-the-road, NYC menu, mostly locals, sometimes great.
Elixir Juice Bar	95 West Broadway	212-233-6171	$	Fresh squeezed juices!
Félix	340 West Broadway	212-431-0021	$$$	Buzzing Brazilian with French overtones, and be seen.
Flor de Sol	361 Greenwich St	212-366-1640	$$$	Tapas with—of course—a scene.
fresh	105 Reade St	212-406-1900	$$$	Excellent seafood.
Ginger Ty	363 Greenwich St	212-925-7440	$$$	Reliable Thai.
The Harrison	355 Greenwich St	212-274-9310	$$$	Great New American—understandably popular.
Il Giglio	81 Warren St	212-571-5555	$$$$	Stellar Italian.
Ivy's Bistro	385 Greenwich St	212-343-1139	$$	Down-to-earth neighborhood Italian.
Karahi	508 Broome St	212-965-1515	$$	Authentic, delicious Indian.
Kitchenette	80 West Broadway	212-267-6740	$$	Great breakfast. Try the bacon.
Kori	253 Church St	212-334-4598	$$$	Korean.
Landmarc	179 West Broadway	212-343-3883	$$$	Modern American with extensive wine list.
Layla	211 West Broadway	212-431-0700	$$$	Belly dancer after nine!
Le Zinc	139 Duane St	212-513-0001	$$$$	French-influenced brasserie style.
Lucky Strike	59 Grand St	212-941-0772	$$	Good bar in front, reliable food in back.
Lupe's East LA Kitchen	110 Sixth Ave	212-966-1326	$$*	Tex-Mex. Quaint.
Montrachet	239 West Broadway	212-219-2777	$$$$	Wonderful French.
Nobu	105 Hudson St	212-219-0500	$$$$	Designer Japanese.
Nobu, Next Door	105 Hudson St	212-334-4445	$$$	Nobu's cheaper neighbor.
Odeon	145 West Broadway	212-233-0507	$$$	We can't agree about this one, so go and make your own decision.
Pace	121 Hudson St	212-965-9500	$$$	Newish upscale Italian with good cocktail bar.
Palacinka	28 Grand St	212-625-0362	$*	A tasty load of crepe.
Petite Abeille	134 West Broadway	212-791-1360	$*	Belgian waffle chain, great beer selection. Try the stoemp.
Roc	190 Duane St	212-625-3333	$$$	Lovely Italian, good for weekend brunch.
Salaam Bombay	317 Greenwich St	212-226-9400	$$	Indian; excellent lunch buffet.

Arts & Entertainment • **Restaurants**

Key: $: Under $10 / $$: $10–$20 / $$$: $20–$30 / $$$$: $30+; * : Does not accept credit cards / † : Accepts only American Express.

Map 2 • TriBeCa—continued

TShore	41 Murray St	212-962-3750	$$	Casual seafood.
Sosa Borella	460 Greenwich St	212-431-5093	$$	Louche Argentines and brilliant french toast.
Square Diner	33 Leonard St	212-925-7188	$*	Classic neighborhood diner.
Thalassa	179 Franklin St	212-941-7661	$$$	Greek. But it's cheaper and better in Astoria.
Tribeca Grill	375 Greenwich St	212-941-3900	$$$$	Are you looking at me?
Walker's	16 N Moore St	212-941-0143	$$	Surprisingly good food for a pub!
Yaffa's	353 Greenwich St	212-274-9403	$$	Cooly eclectic. Food 'til 1am.
Zutto	77 Hudson St	212-233-3287	$$$	Neighborhood Japanese.

Map 3 • City Hall / Chinatown

Bridge Café	279 Water St	212-227-3344	$$$$	Now extremely expensive.
Canton	45 Division St	212-226-4441	$$$*	Top-shelf Chinese.
Cup & Saucer	89 Canal St	212-925-3298	$*	Good greasy burgers.
Dim Sum Go Go	5 East Broadway	212-732-0797	$$	New, hip, inventive dim sum.
Excellent Dumpling House	111 Lafayette St	212-219-0212	$*	Excellent dumplings, really.
Ferrara	195 Grand St	212-226-6150	$	Classic Little Italy patisserie.
Fuleen's	11 Division St	212-941-6888	$$†	Chinese seafood shack.
Goody's	1 East Broadway	212-577-2922	$$	Almost as good as Joe's and one-eighth as crowded. 18 different soup varieties.
Il Palazzo	151 Mulberry St	212-343-7000	$$$	Excellent mid-range Italian.
Joe's Shanghai	9 Pell St	212-233-8888	$$*	Great crab soup dumplings, crowded.
L'Ecole	462 Broadway	212-219-3300	$$$	The restaurant of the French Culinary Institute; new student menu every 6 weeks.
Le Pain Quotidien	100 Grand St	212-625-9009	$$*	Excellent breads.
Lily's	31 Oliver St	212-766-3336	$$*	Official Japanese/Chinese takeout of NFT management.
Mandarin Court	61 Mott St	212-608-3838	$$	Consistently good dim sum.
Mark Joseph Steakhouse	261 Water St	212-277-0020	$$$$	Luger's wannabe: very good, and they take plastic.
New York Noodle Town	28 Bowery	212-349-0923	$*	Cheap Chinese.
Nha Trang	87 Baxter St	212-233-5948	$$	The best cheap Vietnamese.
Pho Viet Huong	73 Mulberry St	212-233-8988	$$	Very good Vietnamese.
Ping's	22 Mott St	212-602-9988	$$	Eclectic Asian seafood.
Pongsri Thai	106 Bayard St	212-349-3132	$$	Great, spicy Thai. Go for the jungle curry.
Positano Ristorante	122 Mulberry St	212-334-9808	$$	Good northern Italian fare.
Quartino	21 Peck Slip	212-349-4433	$$†	Good, clean pizza & pasta.
Triple Eight Palace	88 East Broadway	212-941-8886	$$	Dim sum madness under the Manhattan Bridge.
Umberto's Clam House	178 Mulberry St	212-431-7545	$$	Another (overpriced) Little Italy institution.
Wo Hop	17 Mott St	212-267-2536	$*	Chinatown mainstay.

Map 4 • Lower East Side

88 Orchard	88 Orchard St	212-228-8880	$$	Bridges the gap so you don't have to walk to the east village.
Congee Village	100 Allen St	212-941-1818	$$	Good neighborhood Asian.
Good World Bar & Grill	3 Orchard St	212-925-9975	$$	Excellent Scandinavian finger food.
Les Enfants Terribles	37 Canal St	212-777-7518	$$$	New French-African.
Pho Bang	3 Pike St	212-233-3947	$*	Vietnamese.

Map 5 • West Village

A Salt & Battery	112 Greenwich Ave	212-691-2713	$*	Great take-out fish 'n chips.
AOC	314 Bleecker St	212-675-9463	$$$	A fine French replacement for Grove.
Aquagrill	210 Spring St	212-274-0505	$$$$	Excellent seafood.
Benny's Burritos	113 Greenwich Ave	212-727-3560	$$	A NYC Mexican institution.
Blue Ribbon Bakery	33 Downing St	212-337-0404	$$$	Another Blue Ribbon success.
Café Asean	117 W 10th St	212-633-0348	$$*	Pan-Asian, via Mr. Wong.
Caffe Torino	139 W 10th St	212-675-5554	$$	Comfy, relaxed Italian.
Chez Brigitte	77 Greenwich Ave	212-929-6736	$*	You never thought a chicken sandwich could be this good.
Chumley's	86 Bedford St	212-675-4449	$$	Former speakeasy, great atmosphere & food.
Corner Bistro	331 W 4th St	212-242-9502	$*	Top NYC burgers. Open 'til 4am.
Cowgirl Hall of Fame	519 Hudson St	212-633-1133	$$	Good chicken fried steak.
Day-O	103 Greenwich Ave	212-924-3160	$$	Island fave, great cocktails.
Dragonfly	47 Seventh Ave	212-255-2848	$$	Try the Filipino specialties.
Florent	69 Gansevoort St	212-989-5779	$$*	One of the best places on the planet.
French Roast	458 Sixth Ave	212-533-2233	$$	Open 24 hours. French comfort food.
French Roast	78 W 11th St	212-533-2233	$$	Open 24 hours. French comfort food.
Gonzo Restaurant	140 W 13th St	212-645-4606	$$$	Cool Italian bistro with hearty food.
Grey Dog's Coffee	33 Carmine St	212-462-0041	$$*	Happy coffee, huge sandwiches.
Home	20 Cornelia St	212-243-9579	$$$	There's no place like it.
Ivo & Lulu	558 Broome St	212-226-4399	$$	Tiny inventive French-Caribbean (BYOB).
Jefferson	121 W 10th St	212-255-3333	$$$	Wong's American take.
Joe's Pizza	233 Bleecker St	212-366-1182	$*	Excellent slices.

John's Pizzeria	278 Bleecker St	212-243-1680	$$*	Quintessential NY pizza.
Le Gamin	27 Bedford St	212-243-2846	$$	New digs, same great food.
Lunchbox Food Company	357 West St	646-230-9466	$$*	Homemade doughnuts and ginger-sake lemonade.
Mary's Fish Camp	246 W 4th St	646-486-2185	$$$	Inventive but inconsistent seafood.
Mirchi	29 Seventh Ave S	212-414-0931	$$	Spicy Indian.
Moustache	90 Bedford St	212-229-2220	$$	Excellent sit-down falafel.
One If By Land, TIBS	17 Barrow St	212-228-0822	$$$	Exudes romance.
Ony	357 Sixth Ave	212-414-8429	$$	Noodles, sushi, NYU hangout.
Pastis	9 Ninth Ave	212-929-4844	$$$$	Great French vibe; LOUD.
Pearl Oyster Bar	18 Cornelia St	212-691-8211	$$$	For all your lobster roll cravings. NFT fave.
Petite Abeille	466 Hudson St	212-741-6479	$$	Tintin-infused waffle chain. Try the stoemp.
Pó	31 Cornelia St	212-645-2189	$$$$	Creative Italian.
Sapore	55 Greenwich Ave	212-229-0551	$$	Decent Italian, good lunch deal.
Souen	210 Sixth Ave	212-807-7421	$$$	High-end vegetarian.
Spotted Pig	314 W 11th St	212-620-0393	$$$	We're still waiting on line.
Tea & Sympathy	108 Greenwich Ave	212-989-9735	$$*	Eccentric English. Cult favorite.
Two Boots	201 W 11th St	212-633-9096	$	Cajun pizza.
Yama	38 Carmine St	212-989-9330	$$$	Sushi deluxe.

Map 6 • Washington Square / NYU / NoHo / SoHo

A Salt & Battery	80 Second Ave	212-254-6610	$	Fish. Chips. More chips.
Abbondazza's	193 Bleecker St	212-254-2542	$	Deli-style Italian.
Acme Bar & Grill	9 Great Jones St	212-420-1934	$$	Workmanlike Southern.
Angelica Kitchen	300 E 12th St	212-228-2909	$$$	Vegan/macrobiotic heaven.
Ápizz	217 Eldridge St	212-253-9199	$$$	Baseball-sized meatballs, and pizza of course.
Around the Clock	8 Stuyvesant St	212-598-0402	$$	Open 24 hours. NYU hangout.
Arturo's Pizzeria	106 W Houston St	212-677-3820	$$	Classic NYC pizza joint.
Babbo	110 Waverly St	212-777-0303	$$$$	Super Mario—eclectic Italian, fabulous wine list.
Balthazar	80 Spring St	212-965-1414	$$$	Simultaneously pretentious and amazing.
Baluchi's	104 Second Ave	212-780-6000	$$	Servicable Italian.
Ben's Pizza	177 Spring St	212-966-4494	$*	Decent pizza.
Blue Hill	75 Washington Pl	212-539-1776	$$$	Wonderful food in an unexpected location.
Blue Ribbon	97 Sullivan St	212-274-0404	$$$	Open 'til 4 am. Everything's great.
Blue Ribbon Sushi	119 Sullivan St	212-343-0404	$$$	Great sushi.
Bond Street	6 Bond St	212-777-2500	$$$	Japanese does not get trendier or better than this...
Borgo Antico	22 E 13th St	212-807-1313	$$$	Underrated Tuscan. Usually deserted.
Café Colonial	73 E Houston St	212-274-0044	$$†	Excellent American/Brazilian.
Café Habana	17 Prince St	212-625-2001	$$	Excellent Cuban takeout joint.
Café Spice	72 University St	212-253-6999	$$$	Designer Indian.
Chez Es Saada	42 E 1st St	212-777-5617	$$$	Dark and mysterious Moroccan.
Cozy Soup & Burger	739 Broadway	212-477-5566	$	Great burgers!
Cuba	224 Thompson St	212-420-7878	$$$	Authentic Cuban, bar, live music, etc.
DeMarco's	146 W Houston St	212-253-2290	$$$	Top Brooklyn pizza successfully transplanted—recommended.
Dojo East	24 St Mark's Pl	212-674-9821	$*	Cheap and cheerful in Studentville.
Dojo West	14 W 4th St	212-505-8934	$	Cheap and cheerful in Studentville.
Eight Mile Creek	240 Mulberry St	212-431-4635	$$$$	Awesome Australian.
Five Points	31 Great Jones St	212-253-5700	$$$	Excellent Noho destination.
Frank	88 Second Ave	212-420-0202	$$*	Good food, great breakfast.
Ghenet	284 Mulberry St	212-343-1888	$$$	Excellent, unpretentious Ethiopian.
Gotham Bar & Grill	12 E 12th St	212-620-4020	$$$$	Excellent New American—one of the best.
Great Jones Café	54 Great Jones St	212-674-9304	$$	Classic soul food. Sort of.
Hampton Chutney Co	68 Prince St	212-226-9996	$*	Good take-out dosas.
Haveli	100 Second Ave	212-982-0533	$$$	Most expensive of the 6th St. Indians. Good dosas.
Holy Basil	149 Second Ave	212-460-5557	$$$	Holy sh*t this is good Thai!
Il Buco	47 Bond St	212-533-1932	$$$	Lovely Italian food. Great wines by the glass.
Jane	100 W Houston St	212-254-7000	$$$	Good all-around!
John's of 12th Street	302 E 12th St	212-475-9531	$$	Classic Italian. Get the rollatini.
Jules	65 St Mark's Pl	212-477-5560	$$$	Small French bistro with live unimposing Jazz.
Kelley & Ping	127 Greene St	212-228-1212	$$$	Noodles and killer tea selection.
Khyber Pass	34 St Mark's Pl	212-473-0989	$$	Good Afghani.
L'Ulivo Focacceria	184 Spring St	212-343-1445	$$$	Good personal pizzas, quaint.
La Palapa Cocina Mexicana	77 St Mark's St	212-777-2537	$$	Loud, quality mexican.
Lupa	170 Thompson St	212-982-5089	$$$$	Italian, get reservations.
Mara's Homemade	342 E 6th St	212-598-1110	$$	Ragin' Cajun. Recommended.
Melampo Imported Foods	105 Sullivan St	212-334-5179	$*	Excellent sandwiches.
Mingala Burmese	21 E 7th St	212-529-3656	$$	Burmese.
Otto	1 Fifth Ave	212-995-9559	$$$	$45 pizza? Absolutely!
Paul's	131 Second Ave	212-529-3097	$*	Burger heaven.
Peep	177 Prince St	212-254-7337	$$$	Stylin' Thai. See-through bathroom mirrors.
Penang	109 Spring St	212-274-8883	$$$	Snooty but good Malaysian.
Pravda	281 Lafayette St	212-226-4944	$$$	Scene at the bar, tiny food.
Sala	344 Bowery	212-979-6606	$$	Wonderful décor, good tapas.

Key: $: Under $10 / $$: $10–$20 / $$$: $20–$30 / $$$$: $30+; * : Does not accept credit cards / † : Accepts only American Express.

Map 6 · Washington Square / NYU / SoHo—*continued*

Sammy's Roumanian	157 Chrystie St	212-673-0330	$	An experience not to be missed.
Snack	105 Thompson St	212-925-1040	$$*	Great Greek salads & spinach pie.
Soho Steak	90 Thompson St	212-226-0602	$$$	French. Not all that much steak.
Spice	60 University Pl	212-982-3758	$$	Trendy Thai.
Strip House	13 E 12th St	212-328-0000	$$$$	Super downtown steakhouse. NFT favorite.
Time Café	380 Lafayette St	212-533-7000	$$	Consistently good, great indoor & outdoor spaces.
Tomoe Sushi	172 Thompson St	212-777-9346	$$	Good sushi, long line.
Zoë	90 Prince St	212-966-6722	$$$$	Excellent New American, great desserts, a scene of course.

Map 7 · East Village / Lower East Side

1492 Food	60 Clinton St	646-654-1114	$$$	Tapas. It's cool.
71 Clinton Fresh Food	71 Clinton St	212-614-6960	$$$$	We still can't get in.
7A	109 Ave A	212-673-6583	$$	Open 24 hours. Great burgers.
AKA Café	49 Clinton St	212-979-6096	$$	Our favorite on Clinton.
Azul Bistro	152 Stanton St	646-602-2004	$$	Argentinean fare.
B3	33 Ave B	212-614-9755	$$$	Great default date restaurant.
Banjara	97 First Ave	212-477-5956	$$$	Best Indian on 6th Street, hands-down.
Benny's Burritos	93 Ave A	212-254-2054	$	A NYC Mexican institution.
Bereket Turkish Kebab House	187 E Houston St	212-475-7700	$*	Middle Eastern delights. Open late.
Boca Chica	13 First Ave	212-473-0108	$$	Excellent, fun South American.
Café Mogador	101 St Mark's Pl	212-677-2226	$$*	Perfect place for hummus and a latte.
Caracas Arepa Bar	91 E 7th St	212-228-5062	$$*	Authentic Venezuelan.
Crooked Tree Creperie	110 St Mark's Pl	212-533-3299	$*	Casual restaurant crepes.
The Delancey	168 Delancey St	212-254-9920	$$	Rooftop garden. Need we say more?
Dish	165 Allen St	212-253-8840	$$	Home cooking in a hip locale. Recommended.
Dok Suni's	119 First Ave	212-477-9506	$$$*	Excellent Korean fusion.
El Castillo de Jaqua	113 Rivington St	212-982-6412	$*	Great cheap Dominican.
Essex Restaurant	120 Essex St	212-533-9616	$$$	Great space, OK food.
Flea Market Café	131 Ave A	212-358-9280	$$†	French, good brunch.
Flor's Kitchen	149 First Ave	212-387-8949	$$	Authentic South American.
Grilled Cheese NYC	168 Ludlow St	212-982-6600	$*	Official selection of NFT interns.
The Hat (Sombrero)	108 Stanton St	212-254-4188	$$*	Cheap margaritas. Dates from an earlier LES.
Il Bagatto	192 E 2nd St	212-228-0977	$$$	Packed Italian.
Kate's Joint	58 Ave B	212-777-7059	$$	Inventive vegetarian and vegan.
Katz's Delicatessen	205 E Houston St	212-254-2246	$$	Great corned beef and fries.
Kuma Inn	113 Ludlow St	212-353-8866	$$*	Spicy southeast Asian tapas.
Kura Sushi	67 First Ave	212-979-6646	$$	Good sushi, good atmosphere, good music.
La Caverna	122 Rivington St	212-475-2126	$$$	It's got stalactites & stalagmites!
La Focaccia	128 First Ave	212-254-4946	$$	Simple Italian neighborhood joint.
Lavagna	545 E 5th St	212-979-1005	$$$	We hear it's great!
Le Gamin	536 E 5th St	212-254-8409	$$†	Great French Toast, overall brunch, etc.
Lil' Frankie's Pizza	19 First Ave	212-420-4900	$$*	Cheap, good pizzas and Italian.
The Lite Touch Restaurant	151 Ave A	212-420-8574	$	Authentic Moroccan and Middle Eastern.
Mama's Food Shop	200 E 3rd St	212-777-4425	$*	Great home-cooking and take-out.
Momofuku	163 First Ave	212-475-7899	$$*	Fresh noodles!
Moustache	265 E 10th St	212-228-2022	$*	Excellent Middle Eastern.
Odessa	117 Ave A	212-253-1470	$	Open 24 hours. Diner.
Old Devil Moon	511 E 12th St	212-475-4357	$$	Good southern food. Great biscuits.
Pylos	128 E 7th St	212-473-0220	$$	Delicious Greek, cool hanging-pot ceiling.
Raga	433 E 6th St	212-388-0957	$$$	Good Indian fusion.
Sapporo East	245 E 10th St	212-260-1330	$$	Cheap and cheerful sushi.
Schiller's	131 Rivington St	212-260-4555	$$$$	Loud, good, loud, good.
Share	406 E 9th St	212-777-2425	$$	Seasonal American.
The Sunburnt Cow	137 Ave C	212-529-0005	$	Aussie cooking featuring backyard garden.
Takahachi	85 Ave A	212-505-6524	$$$	Super-good Japanese and sushi.
Tasting Room	72 E 1st St	212-358-7831	$$$	Relatively pretentious.
Teany	90 Rivington St	212-475-9190	$	Cute café-vegan-drinks-whatever.
Two Boots	37 Ave A	212-505-2276	$	Cajun pizza.
Yaffa Café	97 St Mark's Pl	212-674-9302	$$	Eclectic food/decor. Open 24 hours.
Zum Schneider	107 Ave C	212-598-1098	$$*	Finally some downtown wurst.

Map 8 · Chelsea

Blue Moon Mexican Café	150 Eighth Ave	212-463-0560	$$	Great Mexican.
Bottino	246 Tenth Ave	212-206-6766	$$$	Good, clean Italian.
Bright Food Shop	216 Eighth Ave	212-243-4433	$$	Small, Asian-Mexican experience.
Burritoville	352 W 39th St	212-563-9088	$	Takeout Mexican.
Chelsea Bistro & Bar	358 W 23rd St	212-727-2026	$$$$	Charming French.
Cheyenne Diner	411 Ninth Ave	212-465-8750	$	NYC diner. You know the score.

Cupcake Café	522 Ninth Ave	212-465-1530	$*	Three words: sweet potato doughnuts.
El Cid	322 W 15th St	212-929-9332	$$$	Spanish/tapas.
Empire Diner	210 Tenth Ave	212-243-2736	$$	A Chelsea institution. 24 hours.
Frank's Restaurant	85 Tenth Ave	212-243-1349	$$$$	Noisy beef-fest.
Grand Sichuan Int'l	229 Ninth Ave	212-620-5200	$$	Some of the best Chinese in NYC.
Havana Chelsea	190 Eighth Ave	212-243-9421	$$*	Great Cuban sandwiches.
La Luncheonette	130 Tenth Ave	212-675-0342	$$$	A truly great French restaurant. Recommended.
La Taza de Oro	96 Eighth Ave	212-243-9946	$$*	Great local Puerto Rican.
Le Gamin	183 Ninth Ave	212-243-8864	$$	Great French toast.
Manganaro Foods	488 Ninth Ave	212-563-5331	$$*	Locals-only Italian sandwich joint. Recommended.
Moonstruck Diner	400 W 23rd St	212-924-3709	$$	24-hours on weekends only.
Pepe Giallo	253 Tenth Ave	212-242-6055	$$	Takeout Italian.
The Red Cat	227 Tenth Ave	212-242-1122	$$$$	Hip and expensive.
Sandwich Planet	534 Ninth Ave	212-273-9768	$*	Unlimited sandwich selection.
Skylight Diner	402 W 34th St	212-244-0395	$	24-hour diner.
Spice	199 Eighth Ave	212-989-1116	$$	Good, straightforward Thai.
Soul Fixins'	371 W 34th St	212-736-1345	$$	It would be an injustice not to include this soul food eatery.
Tazza	196 Eighth Ave		$$	Nice space.
Tick Tock Diner	481 Eighth Ave	212-268-8444	$	24-hour diner.
Viceroy	160 Eighth Ave	212-633-8484	$$$	Stargazin' American.

Map 9 • Flatiron / Lower Midtown

Basta Pasta	37 W 17th St	212-366-0888	$$$	Pac-rim Italian.
Blue Water Grill	31 Union Sq W	212-675-9500	$$$	Seafood. Overrated.
Burritoville	264 W 23rd St	212-367-9844	$	Mexcellent and cheap.
Cafeteria	119 Seventh Ave	212-414-1717	$$$	Comfort food, open all night.
Chat 'n Chew	10 E 16th St	212-243-1616	$$	Home cookin'.
City Bakery	3 W 18th St	212-366-1414	$$	Stellar baked goods.
Coffee Shop	29 Union Sq W	212-243-7969	$$	Open 24 hours. Diner.
Craft	43 E 19th St	212-780-0880	$$$$	Outstanding. A top-end place worth the $.
Eisenberg's Sandwich Shop	174 Fifth Ave	212-675-5096	$$	Old-school corned beef and pastrami.
Eleven Madison Park	11 Madison Ave	212-889-0905	$$$$	Where the elite meet to greet.
Elmo	156 Seventh Ave	212-337-8000	$$	Good for cocktails and oysters, in whatever order.
Francisco's Centro Vasco	159 W 23rd St	212-645-6224	$$$	Fun Spanish.
Giorgio's of Gramercy	27 E 21st St	212-477-0007	$$$	Cozy Italian.
Gramercy Tavern	42 E 20th St	212-477-0777	$$$$	Expensive, but good, New American.
Hangawi	12 E 32nd St	212-213-0077	$$$	Serene Korean.
Kang Suh	1250 Broadway	212-564-6845	$$$	Late-night Korean.
Kum Gang San	49 W 32nd St	212-967-0909	$$$	Another late-night Korean paradise.
Le Madri	168 W 18th St	212-727-8022	$$$	Chelsea Tuscan class.
Le Pain Quotidien	38 E 19th St	212-673-7900	$*	Excellent breads & such.
Le Zie 2000	172 Seventh Ave	212-206-8686	$$$	Venetian. That means it's Italian.
Luna Park	50 E 17th St	212-475-8464	$$$	Have meals May-October in Union Square Park.
Mandler's,	26 E 17th St	212-255-8999	$$	Sausage emporium.
The Original Sausage Co				
Mayrose	920 Broadway	212-533-3663	$$	Upscale diner.
Mesa Grill	102 Fifth Ave	212-807-7400	$$$	Southwestern heaven.
Periyali	35 W 20th St	212-463-7890	$$$$	Upscale Greek.
Petite Abeille	107 W 18th St	212-604-9350	$$*	Tintin-infused waffle chain. Try the stoemp.
Republic	37 Union Sq W	212-627-7172	$$	Noisy noodles.
Shake Shack	Madison Square Park	212-889-6600	$*	Shakes 'n burgers July-October.
Silver Swan	41 E 20th St	212-254-3611	$$	Beer, brats, 'n schnitzel.
Tabla	11 Madison Ave	212-889-0667	$$$	Inventive Indian-inspired American.
Tamarind	41 E 22nd St	212-674-7400	$$$	Lovely, intimate upscale Indian.
Toledo	6 E 36th St	212-696-5036	$$$	Classy Spanish.
Uncle Moe's	14 W 19th St	212-727-9400	$	Solid lunchtime burrito joint.
Union Square Café	21 E 16th St	212-243-4020	$$$	Someday we'll get in and like it.
Woo Chon	10 W 36th St	212-695-0676	$$$	All-night Korean.

Map 10 • Murray Hill / Gramercy

Angelo & Maxie's	233 Park Ave S	212-220-9200	$$$	Excellent steaks, burgers, etc.
Artisanal	2 Park Ave	212-725-8585	$$$	Eat the fondue and leave.
Blockheads Burritos	499 Third Ave	212-213-3332	$$*	Damn good burritos, a little pricey.
Coppola's	378 Third Ave	212-679-0070	$$	Neighborhood Italian.
El Parador Café	325 E 34th St	212-679-6812	$$$	NY's oldest and friendliest Mexican.
Gemini Restaurant	641 Second Ave	212-532-2143	$$	Open 24 hours. Diner.
Gramercy Restaurant	184 Third Ave	212-982-2121	$$	Open 24 hours. Diner.
Haandi	113 Lexington Ave	212-685-5200	$$*	Stellar Pakistani grilled meats.
I Trulli	122 E 27th St	212-481-7372	$$$$	Italian. Great garden.
Jackson Hole	521 Third Ave	212-679-3264	$$	Extremely large burgers.
Jaiya Thai	396 Third Ave	212-889-1330	$$$	Inventive, spicy Thai.
L'Express	249 Park Ave S	212-254-5858	$$	Always open French bistro.
Park Avenue Country Club	381 Park Ave S	212-685-3636	$$	Somewhat bearable sports bar.
Patsy's Pizza	509 Third Ave	212-689-7500	$$*	Classic NY pizza.

Arts & Entertainment · **Restaurants**

Key: $: Under $10 / $$: $10–$20 / $$$: $20–$30 / $$$$: $30+; *: Does not accept credit cards / †: Accepts only American Express.

Map 10 · Murray Hill / Gramercy—continued

Pete's Tavern	129 E 18th St	212-473-7676	$$$	Good pub food, especially after drinking!
Pongal	110 Lexington Ave	212-696-9458	$$	Possibly NY's best Indian. Vegetarian.
Pongsri Thai	311 Second Ave	212-477-4100	$$	Great, spicy Thai.
Rare Bar & Grill	303 Lexington Ave, Shelbourne Murray Hill Hotel	212-481-1999	$$$	Top-rated NYC burger.
Sarge's Deli	548 Third Ave	212-679-0442	$$	Open 24 hours. Jewish deli.
Shaheen's Sweets	130 E 29th St	212-251-0202	$*	Indian and Pakistani café and dessert shop.
Tatany	380 Third Ave	212-686-1871	$$$	Japanese.
Totonno Pizzeria Napolitan	462 Second Ave	212-213-8800	$$*	Manhattan wing of classic Coney Island Pizza.
Turkish Kitchen	386 Third Ave	212-679-6633	$$$	Excellent Turkish, great décor. NFT pick!
Union Pacific	111 E 22nd St	212-995-8500	$$$$	Top-end American.
Via Emilia	240 Park Ave S	212-505-3072	$$$	Emilia-Romagnan specialties.
Water Club	500 E 30th St	212-683-3333	$$$$	Romantic, good brunch.
Yama	122 E 17th St	212-475-0969	$$$	Sushi deluxe.
Zen Palate	34 Union Sq E	212-614-9291	$$$	Dependable vegetarian.

Map 11 · Hell's Kitchen

Afghan Kebab House	764 Ninth Ave	212-307-1612	$$	Great kebabs.
Ariana Afghan Kebab	787 Ninth Ave	212-262-2323	$	Afghan.
Burritoville	625 Ninth Ave	212-333-5352	$	Takeout Mexican.
Churruscaria Plataforma	316 W 49th St	212-245-0505	$$$	Popular but uneven Brazilian.
Daisy May's BBQ USA	623 Eleventh Ave	212-977-1500	$$	Takeout BBQ & sides Mon-Fri.
Grand Sichuan Int'l	745 Ninth Ave	212-582-2288	$$	Excellent weird Szechuan.
Hallo Berlin	402 W 51st St	212-541-6248	$$	Indeed the best wurst.
Hallo Berlin	626 Tenth Ave	212-977-1944	$$*	The best wurst in the city!
Hudson Cafeteria	356 W 58th St	212-554-6000	$$$$	Lovely and pricey and goody.
Island Burgers 'N Shakes	766 Ninth Ave	212-307-7934	$$	Aptly named.
Jezebel	630 Ninth Ave	212-582-1045	$$$	Southern charm.
Joe Allen	326 W 46th St	212-581-6464	$$$	De riguer stargazing, open late.
Les Sans Culottes	347 W 46th St	212-247-4284	$$$	Friendly French.
Meskerem	468 W 47th St	212-664-0520	$$	Standard Ethiopian.
Munson Diner	600 W 48th St	212-246-0964	$$	The diner of diners.
Old San Juan	765 Ninth Ave	212-262-6761	$$	Good, Puerto Rican-Argentinian fare.
Orso	322 W 46th St	212-489-7212	$$$$	Popular busy Italian.
Ralph's	862 Ninth Ave	212-581-2283	$$	Classic Italian cuisine.
Tout Va Bien	311 W 51st St	212-265-0190	$$$$	Warm, homey, pre-theater, French. NFT Pick.
Uncle Nick's	747 Ninth Ave	212-245-7992	$$$	Greek, noisy.
Zen Palate	663 Ninth Ave	212-582-1669	$$$	Dependable vegetarian.

Map 12 · Midtown

'21' Club	21 W 52nd St	212-582-7200	$$$$	Old, clubby New York.
Alain Ducasse	155 W 58th St	212-265-7300	$$$$$	Crème de la crème, dude.
Aquavit	13 W 54th St	212-307-7311	$$$	Top-drawer Scandinavian.
Baluchi's	240 W 56th St	212-397-0707	$$	Slightly above-average Indian.
Carnegie Deli	854 Seventh Ave	212-757-2245	$$$*	Still good.
Cosi Sandwich Bar	11 W 42nd St	212-398-6660	$*	Sandwiches for the masses.
Cosi Sandwich Bar	1633 Broadway	212-397-2674	$*	Sandwiches for the masses.
Cosi Sandwich Bar	61 W 48th St	212-265-2674	$*	Sandwiches for the masses.
Haru	205 W 43rd St	212-398-9810	$$	Excellent mid-range Japanese. Loud, good.
Joe's Shanghai	24 W 56th St	212-333-3868	$$*	Uptown version of killer dumpling factory.
Le Bernardin	155 W 51st St	212-554-1515	$$$$$	Top NYC seafood.
Molyvos	871 Seventh Ave	212-582-7500	$$$	Top Greek.
Nation Restaurant & Bar	12 W 45th St	212-391-8053	$$$$	Loud, pretentious, good.
Norma's	118 W 57th St	212-708-7460	$$$	Inventive and upscale brunch.
Pongsri Thai	244 W 48th St	212-582-3392	$$	Great, spicy Thai.
Pret a Manger	135 W 50th St		$	English sandwich chain.
Pret a Manger	1350 Sixth Ave	212-307-6100	$	British sandwich chain.
The Pump Energy Food	40 W 55th St	212-246-6844	$*	Just what you think it is.
Redeye Grill	890 Seventh Ave	212-541-9000	$$$	Sprawling and diverse.
Virgil's Real BBQ	152 W 44th St	212-921-9494	$$$	It's real.

Map 13 · East Midtown

BLT Steak	106 E 57th St	212-752-7470	$$$$	Pricey and good, not great.
Cosi Sandwich Bar	60 E 56th St	212-588-0888	$*	Sandwiches for the masses.
Dawat	210 E 58th St	212-355-7555	$$$$	Top-end Indian.
Docks Oyster Bar	633 Third Ave	212-986-8080	$$$	Great seafood, good atmosphere.
Felidia	243 E 58th St	212-758-1479	$$$$	Top Northern Italian.
Four Seasons	99 E 52nd St	212-754-9494	$$$$	Designer everything.

Les Halles	411 Park Ave	212-679-4111	$$$	Steak frites and French vibe.
March	405 E 58th St	212-754-6272	$$$$	Lovely. It's actually 8 dollar signs.
Menchanko-tei	131 E 45th St	212-986-6805	$	Japanese noodle shop.
Oceana	55 E 54th St	212-759-5941	$$$$$	Le Bernadin Jr.
Organic Harvest Café	235 E 53rd St	212-421-6444	$$	Vegetarian.
Oyster Bar	Grand Central, Lower Level	212-490-6650	$$$	Classic New York seafood joint.
Palm	837 Second Ave	212-687-2953	$$$$	Steak.
Pershing Square	90 E 42nd St	212-286-9600	$$$	Excellent food and awesome space.
PJ Clarke's	915 Third Ave	212-317-1616	$$$	Pub grub.
Rosa Mexicano	1063 First Ave	212-753-7407	$$$	Inventive Mexican. Great guac.
Shun Lee Palace	155 E 55th St	212-371-8844	$$$$	Top-end Chinese.
Smith & Wollensky	797 Third Ave	212-753-1530	$$$$	Don't order the fish.
Sparks Steak House	210 E 46th St	212-687-4855	$$$$	If you can't go to Luger's.
Vong	200 E 54th St	212-486-9592	$$$$	$38 pre-theater menu. Top Pan-Asian.

Map 14 · Upper West Side (Lower)

All-State Café	250 W 72nd St	212-874-1883	$$	Very comfy and friendly joint.
Asiate	80 Columbus Cir, 35th fl	212-805-8881	$$$$	Highest-end Japanese/French.
Baluchi's	283 Columbus Ave	212-579-3900	$$	Slightly above-average Indian.
Big Nick's	2175 Broadway	212-362-9238	$$	Death by burger.
Café Des Artistes	1 W 67th St	212-877-3500	$$$$	A fine romance.
Café Lalo	201 W 83rd St	212-496-6031	$$	Packed dessert & coffee destination.
Café Luxembourg	200 W 70th St	212 873 7411	$$$	Top-end bistro.
Caprice	199 Columbus Ave	212-580-6948	$$$	Spanish, Italian, African, whatever.
China Fun	246 Columbus Ave	212-580-1516	$$	Uptown dim sum option.
Edgar's Café	255 W 84th St	212-496-6126	$$*	24-hour desserts and atmosphere.
EJ's Luncheonette	447 Amsterdam Ave	212-873-3444	$$*	Homey diner.
Fairway Café	2127 Broadway	212-595-1888	$$	When it's all too much.
The Firehouse	522 Columbus Ave	212-595-3139	$$	Where to go for after-softball wings.
French Roast	2340 Broadway	212-799-1533	$$	Open 24 hours. Good croque monsieur.
Gabriel's	11 W 60th St	212-956-4600	$$$	Local-draw; good all-around.
Gray's Papaya	2090 Broadway	212-799-0243	$*	Open 24 hours. An institution.
Harry's Burrito Junction	241 Columbus Ave	212-580-9494	$$	What could they possibly serve here?
Hunan Park	235 Columbus Ave	212-724-4411	$$	Dependable Chinese.
Jackson Hole	517 Columbus Ave	212-362-5177	$$	Extremely large burgers.
Jean Georges	1 Central Park W	212-299-3900	$$$$	$20 prix fixe summer lunch!
Jean-Luc	507 Columbus Ave	212-712-1700	$$$$	Classy, expensive bistro.
Josie's	300 Amsterdam Ave	212-769-1212	$$	Good vegetarian option.
Krispy Kreme	141 W 72nd St	212-724-1100	$*	Health-food mecca.
La Caridad 78	2197 Broadway	212-874-2780	$$*	Cheap Cuban paradise.
La Fenice	2014 Broadway	212-989-3071	$$$	Good Italian.
Land Thai Kitchen	450 Amsterdam Ave	212-501-8121	$$	Standard Thai.
Le Pain Quotidien	50 W 72nd St	212-712-9700	$*	Good breads & such.
Lenge	200 Columbus Ave	212-799-9188	$$	Serviceable Japanese.
Manhattan Diner	2180 Broadway	212-877-7252	$	Diner.
Penang	240 Columbus Ave	212-769-3988	$$$	Snooty but good Malaysian.
Picholine	35 W 64th St	212-724-8585	$$$	Go for the cheese.
Planet Sushi	380 Amsterdam Ave	212-712-2162	$$	Decent sushi in a cheap raw fish no-man's land.
Rain West	100 W 82nd St	212-501-0776	$$	Asian fusion with a magnificent bar.
Rosa Mexicano	61 Columbus Ave	212-977-7700	$$$$	Inventive Mexican. Great guac.
Ruby Foo's Dim Sum & Sushi Palace	2182 Broadway	212-724-6700	$$$	Your parents will love it.
Santa Fe	73 W 71st St	212-724-0822	$$$	Calm Southwest.
Sarabeth's	423 Amsterdam Ave	212-496-6280	$$$	Go for brunch.
Taco Grill	146 W 72nd St	212-501-8888	$*	Mexican.
Vince and Eddie's	70 W 68th St	212-721-0068	$$$	Cosy comfort food.
Vinnie's Pizza	285 Amsterdam Ave	212-874-4382	$*	Good slice of pizza.
Whole Foods Café	10 Columbus Cir, downstairs	212-823-9600	$	Very good and by far the cheapest eats in Time Warner Center.

Map 15 · Upper East Side (Lower)

Afghan Kebab House	1345 Second Ave	212-517-2776	$$	Great kebabs.
Atlantic Grill	1341 Third Ave	212-988-9200	$$$$	Seafood galore.
Aureole	34 E 61st St	212-319-1660	$$$$	Well-done but unimaginative.
Baluchi's	1149 First Ave	212-371-3535	$$	Slightly above-average Indian.
Baluchi's	1565 Second Ave	212-288-4810	$$	Slightly above-average Indian.
Barking Dog Luncheonette	1453 York Ave	212-861-3600	$$*	Good diner/café food.
Brunelli	1409 York Ave	212-744-8899	$$$	Old-world Italian.
Canyon Road	1470 First Ave	212-734-1600	$$$	Southwest haven.
Daniel	60 E 65th St	212-288-0033	$$$$	Overated $150+ meal.
EJ's Luncheonette	1271 Third Ave	212-472-0600	$$*	Homey diner.
Ethiopian Restaurant	1582 York Ave	212-717-7311	$$$	Ethiopian in a sea of mediocre Italian.

(347)

Key: $: Under $10 / $$: $10–$20 / $$$: $20–$30 / $$$$: $30+; * : Does not accept credit cards / † : Accepts only American Express.

Map 15 • Upper East Side (Lower)—continued

Haru	1329 Third Ave	212-452-2230	$$	Sushi. Takeout recommended.
Heidelberg	1648 Second Ave	212-628-2332	$$$$	Olde German vibe.
Jackson Hole	1611 Second Ave	212-737-8788	$$	Extremely large burgers.
Jackson Hole	232 E 64th St	212-371-7187	$$	Extremely large burgers. Cozy.
JG Melon	1291 Third Ave	212-744-0585	$$*	Burgers. Open 'till 2:30 am.
John's Pizzeria	408 E 64th St	212-935-2895	$$	Quintessential NY pizza.
JoJo	160 E 64th St	212-223-5656	$$$$	Charming.
Le Pain Quotidien	1131 Madison Ave	212-327-4900	$*	Great breads & such.
Le Pain Quotidien	1336 First Ave	212-717-4800	$*	Great breads & such.
Le Pain Quotidien	833 Lexington Ave	212-755-5810	$*	Great breads & such.
Mary Ann's	1503 Second Ave	212-249-6165	$$	Good Mex, order margaritas.
Maya	1191 First Ave	212-585-1818	$$$$	Top-drawer Mexican.
Our Place	1444 Third Ave	212-288-4888	$$$	Next level Chinese.
Park Avenue Café	100 E 63rd St	212-644-1900	$$$$	Wonderful expensive American.
Pearson's Texas Barbecue	170 E 81st St	212-288-2700	$$$*	Stick with the brisket. For ribs you have to go to Memphis.
Penang	1596 Second Ave	212-585-3838	$$$	Snooty but good Malaysian.
Pintaile's Pizza	1237 Second Ave	212-752-6222	$	Tasty thin-crust stuff.
Pintaile's Pizza	1443 York Ave	212-717-4990	$	Tasty thin-crust stuff.
Pintaile's Pizza	1577 York Ave	212-396-3479	$	Tasty thin-crust stuff.
Post House	28 E 63rd St	212-935-2888	$$$$	Good bet: steak.
Rain East	1059 Third Ave	212-223-3669	$$	Pan-Asian.
rm	33 E 60th St	212-319-3800	$$$$	Simply excellent.
Serafina Fabulous Grill	29 E 61st St	212-702-9898	$$	Good pizza and pasta.
Totonno Pizzeria Napolitano	1544 Second Ave	212-327-2800	$$	Quality pizza.
Viand	1011 Madison Ave	212-249-8250	$$	Basic diner.
Viand	673 Madison Ave	212-751-6622	$$*	Basic diner.

Map 16 • Upper West Side (Upper)

A	947 Columbus Ave	212-531-1643	$$*	French-Caribbean café.
Afghan Kebab House	2680 Broadway	212-280-3500	$$	Kebabs for you!
AIX	2398 Broadway	212-874-7400	$$$$$	Upscale uptown French.
Barney Greengrass	541 Amsterdam Ave	212-724-4707	$$$*	Classic deli.
Bella Luna	584 Columbus Ave	212-877-2267	$$$	Italian.
Café Con Leche	726 Amsterdam Ave	212-678-7000	$$	Cuban-Dominican haven.
Carmine's	2450 Broadway	212-362-2200	$$$	Large-portion Italian.
City Diner	2441 Broadway	212-877-2720	$$	Neighborhood joint.
Docks Oyster Bar	2427 Broadway	212-724-5588	$$$	Consistently good seafood.
Flor de Mayo	2651 Broadway	212-595-2525	$$	Cuban-Chinese-Chicken-Chow.
Gabriela's	685 Amsterdam Ave	212-961-0574	$$	Cheery Mexican.
Gennaro	665 Amsterdam Ave	212-665-5348	$$$	Crowded Italian.
Henry's	2745 Broadway	212-866-0600	$$	Friendly uptown joint.
Lemongrass Grill	2534 Broadway	212-666-0888	$$	Serviceable Thai.
Mary Ann's	2452 Broadway	212-877-0132	$$	Good Mex, order margaritas.
Pampa	768 Amsterdam Ave	212-865-2929	$$*	Good Argentinian.
Popover Café	551 Amsterdam Ave	212-595-8555	$$	Kind of fun. Whatever.
Saigon Grill	620 Amsterdam Ave	212-875-9072	$$	Busy vietnamese/sushi.
Talia's Steakhouse	668 Amsterdam Ave	212-580-3770	$$$$	Your basic kosher steakhouse.
Trattoria Pesce Pasta	625 Columbus Ave	212-579-7970	$$	Italian.

Map 17 • Upper East Side / East Harlem

Barking Dog Luncheonette	1678 Third Ave	212-831-1800	$$*	Good diner/café food.
El Paso Taqueria	1642 Lexington Ave	212-831-9831	$$	Mexican
Elaine's	1703 Second Ave	212-534-8103	$$$$	It's still there.
Jackson Hole	1270 Madison Ave	212-427-2820	$$	Extremely large burgers.
La Fonda Boricua	169 E 106th St	212-410-7292	$$	Puerto Rican home-cookin'.
Pintaile's Pizza	26 E 91st St	212-722-1967	$	Tasty thin-crust stuff.
Saigon Grill	1700 Second Ave	212-996-4600	$$	Vietnamese.
Sarabeth's	1295 Madison Ave	212-410-7335	$$$	Good breakfast, if you can get in.
Viand	300 E 86th St	212-879-9425	$$	Open all night.

Map 18 • Columbia / Morningside Heights

Bistro Ten 18	1018 Amsterdam Ave	212-662-7600	$$$	Excellent uptown American bistro.
Hungarian Pastry Shop	1030 Amsterdam Ave	212-866-4230	$*	Exactly what it is—and excellent.
Kitchenette Uptown	1272 Amsterdam Ave	212 531 7600	$$	Good for everything.
Le Monde	2885 Broadway	212-531-3939	$$	Student brasserie.
M&G Soul Food Diner	383 W 125th St	212-864-7326	$$*	A soulful diner.
Massawa	1239 Amsterdam Ave	212-663-0505	$$	Neighborhood joint.

Max SoHa	1274 Amsterdam Ave	212-531-2221	$$	The Italian genius of Max, uptown.
The Mill Korean Restaurant	2895 Broadway	212-666-7653	$$	Great neighborhood Korean.
Ollie's	2957 Broadway	212-932-3300	$$	Only if you must.
Pisticci	125 La Salle St	212-932-3500	$$	Wonderful cozy Italian.
Sezz Medi	1260 Amsterdam Ave	212-932-2901	$$	Popular pizza/pasta place.
Symposium	544 W 113th St	212-865-1011	$$*	Good traditional Greek.
Terrace in the Sky	400 W 119th St	212-666-9490	$$$$	Rooftop French.
Toast	3157 Broadway	212-662-1144	$$*	Great diverse café menu. Recommended.
V&T Pizzeria	1024 Amsterdam Ave	212-666-8051	$*	Columbia pizza heaven.

Map 19 • Harlem (Lower)

Amy Ruth's	113 W 116th St	212-280-8779	$$	Soul food, incredible fried chicken.
Bayou	308 Lenox Ave	212-426-3800	$$$	Cajun, with a good bar, too.
Home Sweet Harlem Café	270 W 135th St	212-926-9616	$	Breakfast/lunch spot.
Keur Sokhna	225 W 116th St	212-864-0081	$*	Good cheap Senegalese.
Manna's Too	486 Lenox Ave	212-234-4488	$*	Soul food buffet!
Native	161 Lenox Ave	212-665-2525	$	Excellent soul food.
Papaya King	121 W 125th St	212-665-5732	$	Dawgs for all you dawgs.
Slice of Harlem	308 Lenox Ave	212-426-7400	$*	Harlem brick-oven pizza. Cool.
Sylvia's	328 Lenox Ave	212-996-0660	$$	An institution. Not overrated.
Yvonne Yvonne	301 W 135th St	212-862-1223	$*	Excellent Jamaican chicken, ribs, etc.

Map 20 • El Barrio

Camaradas	2241 First Ave	212-348-2703	$$*	Spanish/Puero Rican/tapas/music.
Creole Restaurant	2167 Third Ave	212-876-8838	$$	Local Creole.
La Hacienda	219 E 116th St	212-987-1617	$	Mexican.
Orbit East Harlem	2257 First Ave	212-348-7818	$$	We like it—dinner, brunch, music, etc.
Patsy's Pizza	2287 First Ave	212-534-9783	$$*	The original thin-crust pizza.
Rao's	455 E 114th St	212-722-6709	$$$$	We've heard it's an institution.
Sandy's Restaurant	2261 Second Ave	212-348-8654	$*	Neighborhood joint.

Map 21 • Manhattanville / Hamilton Heights

Copeland's	547 W 145th St	212-234-2357	$$$	Fine southern cooking.
Devin's Fish and Chips	747 St Nicholas Ave	212-491-5518	$*	Good take-out/counter sit-down.

Map 22 • Harlem (Upper)

Charles' Southern-Style Chicken	2841 Eighth Ave	212-926-4313	$*	The fried chicken they serve in heaven.
Flash Inn	107 Macombs Pl	212-283-8605	$$$	Old-timey New York Italian.
Londel's Supper Club	2620 Frederick Douglass Blvd	212-234-6114	$$$	Good Southern.
Margie's Red Rose	267 W 144th St	212-491-3665	$*	Fried chicken heaven.
Miss Maude's	547 Lenox Ave	212-690-3100	$	Harlem soul food.
Sugar Shack	2611 Frederick Douglass Blvd	212-491-4422	$$	Fried chicken, shrimp, catfish.

Map 23 • Washington Heights

Aqua Marina	4060 Broadway	212-928-0070	$	Uptown Italian.
Bohio	4055 Broadway	212-568-5029	$$$	Dominican destination.
Carrot Top Pastries	3931 Broadway	212-927-4800	$	Baked goods and coffee too!
Coogan's	4015 Broadway	212-928-1234	$$	Where med students and cops go.
Dallas BBQ	3956 Broadway	212-568-3700	$$	When you can't get to Virgil's.
El Conde Steak House	4139 Broadway	212-781-1235	$$$	Big slabs of MEAT.
El Malecon	4141 Broadway	212-927-3812	$	Mexican—fabulous roast chicken.
El Ranchito	4129 Broadway	212-928-0866	$$*	Central America in New York!
Empire Szechuan	4041 Broadway	212-568-1600	$$	Chinese.
Hispaniola	839 W 181st St	212-740-5222	$$	Tapas, bridge views—everything you need.
International Food House	4073 Broadway	212-740-1616	$*	Buffet-style. Open 24 hours.
Jessie's Place	812 W 181st St	212-795-4168	$$	Neighborhood joint.
Jimmy Oro Restaurant	711 W 181st St	212-795-1414	$	Chinese/Spanish. Huge variety.
Malibu Restaurant	1091 St Nicholas Ave	212-781-3150	$$*	Elegant with beautiful lighting.
Parrilla	3920 Broadway	212-543-9500	$$	Argentinean with cool-ass grill.
Reme Restaurant	4021 Broadway	212-923-5452	$	Comfort food.
Restaurant Tenares	2306 Amsterdam Ave	212-927-4190	$$*	Jukebox. Brush up your Spanish standards.
Taino Restaurant	2228 Amsterdam Ave	212-923-9035	$$	Neighborhood Latino w/ men constantly arguing outside.
Tipico Dominicano	4172 Broadway	212-781-3900	$	Family place to watch the game. Goooooal!
Tu Sonrisa	132 Audubon Ave	212-543-0218	$$*	Small sweet place. Stuffed bears in window.

Key: $: Under $10 / $$: $10–$20 / $$$: $20–$30 / $$$$: $30+; * : Does not accept credit cards / † : Accepts only American Express.

Map 24 · Fort George / Fort Tryon

107 West	811 W 187th St	212-923-3311	$$	Salads, burgers, etc.
Bleu Evolution	808 W 187th St	212-928-6006	$$	Uptown bohemian. Calm.
Caridad Restaurant	4311 Broadway	212-781-0431	$	Caribbean.
Frank's Pizzeria	94 Nagle Ave	212-567-3122	$$	Pizza.
New Leaf Café	1 Margaret Corbin Dr	212-568-5323	$$	Uptown haven.
Rancho Jubilee	1 Nagle Ave	212-304-0100	$$	Great Dominican destination.

Map 25 · Inwood

Bobby's Fish and Seafood Market and Restaurant	3842 Ninth Ave	212-304-9440	$$†	Fish! Fresh! Open late!
Capitol Restaurant	4933 Broadway	212-942-5090	$$*	Nice neighborhood diner.
Cloisters Restaurant Pizza	4754 Broadway	212-569-5035	$*	Guess what they have?
DR-K	114 Dyckman St	212-304-1717	$$$$	Nuevo Latino, uptown-style.
Hoppin' Jalapenos Bar & Grill	597 W 207th St	212-569-6059	$$*	Mexican bar and restaurant, good burrrrritos!
Mirage Restaurant	185 Dyckman St	212-567-9000	$$$	Piano bar. Sports bar. Restaurant.

Map 26 · Astoria

31 Pasta Pizza & Panni	2248 31st St	718-728-8288	$*	Our favorite polenta.
Amici Amore I	29-35 Newtown Ave	718-267-2771	$$*	Northern Italian.
Christos Hasapo-Taverna	41-08 23rd Ave	718-726-5195	$$	Get your red meat here!
Eastern Nights	25-35 Steinway St	718-204-7608	$$*	Egyptian cuisine.
Elias Corner	24-02 31st St	718-932-1510	$$*	Greek fish tavern.
Esperides	37-01 30th Ave	718-545-1494	$$$	Traditional Greek food, excellent place for large groups.
Fatty's Café	2501 Ditmars Blvd	718-267-7071	$$*	Great bunches. Even better bloody marys.
Kabab Café	25-12 Steinway St	718-728-9858	$$*	Cheap, casual kababs.
Lorusso Foods	18-01 26th Rd	718-777-3628	$	Pizzeria. Delicious focaccia.
Piccola Venezia	42-01 28th Ave	718-721-8470	$$$	Old-style traditional Italian fare.
Rizzo's Pizza	30-13 Steinway St	718-721-9862	$*	Arguably the best pizza in Astoria for over 70 years.
Stamatis	29-12 23rd Ave	718-278-9795	$$*	Classic Greek dishes. Our favorite.
Taverna Kyclades	33-07 Ditmars Blvd	718-545-8666	$$*	Greek seafood. Great swordfish kababs.
Tierras Colombianas	33-01 Broadway	718-956-3012	$$*	Huge platefuls of Colombian grill—not one for the veggies.
Tierras Colombianas	82-18 Roosevelt Ave	718-426-8868	$$*	Huge platefuls of Colombian grill—not one for the veggies.
Trattoria L'Incontro	21-76 31st St	718-721-3532	$$$	Amazing Italian. One of our all-time favorites.
Ubol's Kitchen	24-42 Steinway St	718-545-2874	$$*	Hyped-up Thai.
Uncle George's	33-19 Broadway	718-626-0593	$*	24-hour Greek.

Map 27 · Long Island City

Brooks 1890 Restaurant	24-28 Jackson Ave	718-937-1890	$$	10% off when you show your juror's card.
Court Square Diner	45-30 23rd St	718-392-1222	$*	Serves continental and Greek dishes.
Jackson Ave Steakhouse	12-23 Jackson Ave	718-784-1412	$$$$	Steakhouse.
La Vuelta	10-43 44th Dr	718-361-1858	$$*	Latino Bistro.
Manducatis	13-27 Jackson Ave	718-729-4602	$$$	Southern Italian.
Manetta's	10-76 Jackson Ave	718-786-6171	$$$	Brick-oven pizzas.
S'Agapo	34-21 34th St	718-626-0303	$$$	Greek restaurant with suberb outdoor dining for the warmer months.
Sage American Kitchen	26-21 Jackson Ave	718-361-0707	$$	Vegetarian-friendly American food.
Tournesol	50-12 Vernon Blvd	718-472-4355	$$$	French Bistro.
Water's Edge	44th Dr & East River	718-482-0033	$$$$	American fare with views of the skyline.

Map 28 · Greenpoint

Acapulco Deli & Restaurant	1116 Manhattan Ave	718-349-8429	$	Authentic Mexican food with some American standards.
Amarin Cafe	617 Manhattan Ave	718-349-2788	$	Good, cheap Thai food.
Bleu Drawes Café	97 Commericial St	718-349-8501	$$*	Jamaican home cookin'.
Casanova	338 McGuinness Blvd	718-389-0990	$$	Italian fare.
Christina's	853 Manhattan Ave	718-383-4382	$	Traditional Polish food, cheap breakfasts!
Divine Follie Café	929 Manhattan Ave	718-389-6770	$$	Large selection of meats, pastas and pizza. Small selection of sandwiches.
Enid's	560 Manhattan Ave	718-349-3859	$$	Popular brunch on weekends; just started serving dinners on weeknights.
God Bless Deli	818 Manhattan Ave	718-349-0605	$*	The only 24-hour joint in the 'hood. Sandwiches and burgers.
Kam Loon	975 Manhattan Ave	718-383-6008	$*	Chinese takeout and buffet.
Manhattan 3 Decker Restaurant	695 Manhattan Ave	718-389-6664	$$	Greek and American fare.
Old Poland Restaurant	181 Nassau Ave	718-389-9211	$*	Polish/American.
OTT	970 Manhattan Ave	718-609-2416	$$*	Thai.
Relax	68 Newell St	718-389-1665	$*	Polish diner with good prices and excellent soups—a neighborhood favorite.

SunView Luncheonette	221 Nassau Ave	718-383-8121	$*	Supercheap lunches.
Thai Café	925 Manhattan Ave	718-383-3562	$	Vast menu, veg options, eat in or take out.
Wasabi	638 Manhattan Ave	718-609-9368	$$	Japanese fare.
Valdiano	659 Manhattan Ave	718-383-1707	$$	Southern Italian.

Map 29 · Williamsburg

Acqua Santa	556 Driggs Ave	718-384-9695	$$*	Bistro Italian—amazing patio.
Allioli	291 Grand St	718-218-7338	$$*	Tapas heavy on the seafood, live mariachi.
Anna Maria Pizza	179 Bedford Ave	718-599-4550	$	A must after the late-night drinking.
Anytime	93 N 6th St	718-218-7272	$*	Greasy but good anytime, really.
Bliss	191 Bedford Ave	718-599-2547	$$*	Bland vegetarian with all vegan options.
Bonita	338 Bedford Ave	718-384-9500	$*	Inexpensive Americanized Mexican in a nice atmosphere. Bring your hot sauce.
Buffalo Cantina	149 Havemeyer St	718-218-7788	$$	Ameri-mexican. Anything with carne asada tastes good here.
Diner	85 Broadway	718-486-3077	$$	Amazing simple food like you've never tasted—never disappoints.
Du Mont	432 Union Ave	718-486-7717	$$	Continually changing market-fresh menu and yummy deserts.
Foodswings	295 Grand St	718-388-1919	$	Vegan fast-food joint. For those who like their tofu to taste like meat.
Kellogg's Diner	518 Metropolitan Ave	718-782-4502	$*	The ultimate diner/deli.
Miss Williamsburg Diner	206 Kent Ave	718-963-0802	$$	Creative Italian with pannacotta "to die for"!
M Shanghai Bistro & Den	129 Havemeyer St	718-384-9300	$$	Decent Chinese in a dark, ambient den.
Oznot's Dish	79 Berry St	718-599-6596	$$*	Lots of lentils and beans, Mediterranean. Good décor.
Peter Luger Steak House	178 Broadway	718-387-7400	$$$$*	The best steak on the planet.
Planet Thailand	133 N 7th St	718-599-5758	$$*	Hyped-up Thai/Japanese in a trendy locale.
Relish	225 Wythe St	718-963-4546	$$*	Comfort food gone eclectic with a touch of class.
Teddy's Bar and Grill	96 Berry St	718-384-9787	$$*	Best bar food ever, great beers on tap, hipster and Polish locals unite.
Vera Cruz	195 Bedford Ave	718-599-7914	$$*	Authentic Mexican. Great outdoor garden, fabulous frozen margaritas.

Map 30 · Brooklyn Heights / DUMBO / Downtown

Bubby's	1 Main St	718-222-0666	$$	It's all about the pie.
Fascati Pizzeria	80 Henry St	718-237-1278	$	Inexpensive pizza.
Five Front	5 Front St	718-625-5559	$$	Tasty newcomer with a beautiful garden.
Grimaldi's	19 Old Fulton St	718-858-4300	$	Excellent, though not the best, NY pizza.
Henry's End	44 Henry St	718-834-1776	$$$*	Inventive, game-oriented menu.
Noodle Pudding	38 Henry St	718-625-3737	$$	Excellent Northern Italian fare.
River Café	1 Water St	718-522-5200	$$$$*	Great view, but overrated.
Superfine	126 Front St	718-243-9005	$$*	Mediterranean-inspired menu, bi-level bar, local art and music.
Sushi California	71 Clark St	718-222-0308	$$*	Sushi Express, reasonable prices.

Map 31 · Fort Greene / Clinton Hill

1 Greene Sushi and Sashimi	1 Greene Ave	718-422-1000	$$*	The only place to get sushi in the 'hood.
À Table	171 Lafayette Ave	718-935-9121	$$*	French country. Small portions.
Academy Restaurant	69 Lafayette Ave	718-237-9326	$	Neighborhood joint.
BAM Café	30 Lafayette Ave	718-636-4100	$$	Café with live music weekend evenings.
Black Iris	228 DeKalb Ave	718-852-9800	$$	Middle Eastern.
Brooklyn Moon Cafe	747 Fulton St	718-855-7149		Food and performance space.
Café Fusion	99 S Portland Ave	718-624-1605	$$*	French/Asian Fusion—order the chocolate volcano!
Cambodian Cuisine	87 S Elliot Pl	718-858-3262	$$*	Cambodian/SE Asian—cheap and good!
Chez Oskar	211 DeKalb Ave	718-852-6250	$$$*	French cuisine in a good neighborhood bistro.
Good Joy Chinese Takeout	216 DeKalb Ave	718-858-8899	$	Best Chinese takeout.
Ici	246 DeKalb Ave	718-789-2778	$$$*	Beautiful new addition to FG restaurant scene, and worth the splurge.
Liquors	219 DeKalb Ave	718-488-7700	$$*	A great eclectic menu.
Locanda Vini & Olii	129 Gates Ave	718-622-9202	$$*	Rustic Italian, a neighborhood favorite.
Madiba	195 DeKalb Ave	718-855-9190	$$$*	South African—Bunny Chow, need we say more?
Mario's Pizzeria	224 DeKalb Ave	718-260-9520	$	The place to go for a slice.
Mo-Bay	112 DeKalb Ave	718-246-2800	$*	Caribbean/soul/bakery.
Pequena	86 S Portland Ave	718-643-0000	$$	Killer quesadillas.
Scopello	63 Lafayette Ave	718-852-1100	$$$	Decent Italian near BAM.
Thomas Beisl	25 Lafayette Ave	718-222-5800	$$$	Excellent pre-BAM complement.
Veliis	773 Fulton St	718-596-9070	$$*	New American/ European fusion

Map 32 · BoCoCa / Red Hook

360	360 Van Brunt St	718-246-0360	$$$*	Nouveaux French; excellent and pricey
Alma	187 Columbia St	718-643-5400	$$$	Top NYC Mexican with great views of lower Manhattan.
Bar Tabac	128 Smith St	718-923-0918	$$$	Open late; fabulous frites.
Buddy's Burrito & Taco Bar	260 Court St	718-488-8695	$*	Buddy always gets the job done.
Café Luluc	214 Smith St	718-625-3815	$$$	Friendly French bistro.
Chance	223 Smith St	718-242-1515	$$$$	Upscale Asian fusion—recommended.

Key: $: Under $10 / $$: $10–$20 / $$$: $20–$30 / $$$$: $30+; * : Does not accept credit cards / † : Accepts only American Express.

Map 32 • BoCoCa / Red Hook—continued

Cobble Hill Grill	212 DeGraw St	718-422-0099	$*	Tasty sandwiches and salads for takeout.
Delicatessen	264 Clinton St	718-852-1991	$$	Ready to go dinners @ 3pm, Euro deli.
Donut House	314 Court St	718-852-1162	$*	A classic greasy spoon. Don't get the donuts.
El Chulo	272 Smith St		$$*	Excellent Cuban sandwiches.
El Portal	217 Smith St	718-246-1416	$	Killer breaded steak.
Faan	209 Smith St	718-694-2277	$†	Pan-Asian in a chic setting.
Fatoosh	330 Hicks St	718-243-0500	$	Nicely priced Middle Eastern Food.
Ferdinando's	151 Union St	718-855-1545	$	Sicilian specialties you won't find anywhere else!
Hill Diner	231 Court St	718-522-2220	$$*	We liked it better before the renovations, but the breakfast still rocks.
Hope & Anchor	347 Van Brunt St	718-237-0276	$$	Great upscale diner.
The Grocery	288 Smith St	718-596-3335	$$$$	Magnificent. Reservations recommended.
Joya	215 Court St	718-222-3484	$$*	Excellent, inexpensive, but super-noisy Thai.
Le Petite Café	502 Court St	718-596-7060	*	Great bistro food—check out the garden.
Leonardo's Brick Oven Pizza	383 Court St	718-624-9620	$$	Excellent pizza and terrible hours.
Liberty Heights Tap Room	34 Van Dyke St	718-246-8050	$$*	Brick oven restaurant and bar.
Margaret Palca Bakes	191 Columbia St	718-802-9771	$	Tasty sandwiches and baked goods.
Osaka	272 Court St	718-643-0044	$$	Best sushi in BoCoCa.
Panino'teca	275 Smith St	718-237-2728	$$	Great paninis & fab cheese lasagna.
Patois	255 Smith St	718-855-1535	$$$$*	French bistro. Killer brunch.
Sal's Pizzeria	305 Court St	718-852-6890	$	The neighborhood staple.
Savoia	277 Smith St	718-797-2727	$$	Cozy Italian. Great individual pizzas.
Schnack	122 Union St	718-855-2879	$	Greasy goodness.
Sherwood Café/ Robin des Bois	195 Smith St	718-596-1609	$$	Mellow French vibe—best croque monsieur in town.
Siam Garden	172 Court St	718-596-3300	$$*	Good Brooklyn Thai.
Sonny's Bar & Grill	305 Smith St	718-643-3293	$$	Three kinds of french fries.
Soul Spot	302 Atlantic Ave	718-596-9933		American and Afro-Caribbean soul food.
Tuk Tuk	204 Smith St	718-222-5268	$$*	Authentic Thai—excellent curries.
Zaytoons	283 Smith St	718-875-1880	$$*	Excellent Middle Eastern pizzas and kebabs. Terrific falafel.

Map 33 • Park Slope / Prospect Heights / Windsor Ter

2nd Street Café	189 Seventh Ave	718-369-6928	$$*	Clamoring brunch crowd.
12th Street Bar and Grill	1123 Eighth Ave	718-965-9526	$$$*	Outstanding gourmet comfort fare.
Al Di La Trattoria	248 Fifth Ave	718-783-4565	$$$*	Chandelier, brick-walled Italian.
Beso	210 Fifth Ave	718-783-4902	$*	Great South American, good breakfast too.
Bistro St Mark's	76 St Mark's Ave	718-857-8600	$$$$	Expensive tastiness.
Blue Ribbon Brooklyn	280 Fifth Ave	718-840-0404	$$$$*	The one and only!
Café Steinhof	422 Seventh Ave	718-369-7776	$$*	Goulash Mondays: $5! German beers.
ChipShop	383 Fifth Ave	718-832-7701	$*	Brit boys dish fish, chips, and The Beatles.
Christie's Jamaican Patties	334 Flatbush Ave	718-636-9746	$*	Jamaican destination.
Convivium Osteria	68 Fifth Ave	718-857-1833	$$$†	Pretentious Portugese, rustic setting.
Cousin John's Café and Bakery	70 Seventh Ave	718-622-7333	$	Casual breakfast and lunch.
Dizzy's	511 Ninth Ave	718-499-1966	$$	Excellent brunch.
Franny's	295 Flatbush Ave	718-230-0221	$$*	Pizza with top-notch ingredients.
Garden Café	620 Vanderbilt Ave	718-857-8863	$$$*	Small, semi-formal intimate setting with delicious food.
Junior's	386 Flatbush Ave	718-852-5257	$*	American with huge portions.
La Taqueria	72 Seventh Ave	718-398-4300	$	Popular, pennywise burritos.
Long Tan	196 Fifth Ave	718-622-8444	$$*	Spartan Vietnamese goes mod.
Los Pollitos II	148 Fifth Ave	718-623-9152	$*	Chicken that dreams are made of.
Mamma Duke	243 Flatbush Ave	718-857-8700	$$	Southern take-out, tasty sides.
Maria's Mexican Bistro	669 Union St	718-638-2344	$$	Well worth the trek down to Fouth Ave.
The Minnow	442 9th St	718-832-5500	$$$	Excellent surf, not so good on the turf.
Mitchell's Soul Food	617 Vanderbilt Ave	718-789-3212	$	Seedy, cheap soul food.
Nana	155 Fifth Ave	718-230-3749	$$*	Absolutely delicious Pan-Asian.
New Prospect Café	393 Flatbush Ave	718-638-2148	$$*	Try the corn and shrimp chowder.
Olive Vine Café	441 Seventh Ave	718-499-0555	$	Tasty Middle Eastern fare.
Olive Vine Pizza	81 Seventh Ave	718-636-4333; 718-622-2626	$	Crispy Mediterranean pizzas.
Parkside Restaurant	355 Flatbush Ave	718-636-1190	$$	Standard diner fare.
Rose Water	787 Union St	718-783-3800	$$$*	Intimate, airy Mediterranean.
Santa Fe Grill	62 Seventh Ave	718-636-0279	$$*	Dinner? Chips, salsa, and icy piñas!
Tom's	782 Washington Ave	718-636-9738	$$	Old-school mom-and-pop diner since 1936. A cholesterol love affair.
Tutta Pasta	160 Seventh Ave	718-788-9500	$$*	Sidewalk seating, dependable penne.
Two Boots	514 2nd St	718-499-3253	$$*	Kid-friendly pizza and Cajun. Live music.

Arts & Entertainment · **Restaurants**

Map 34 · Hoboken

Amanda's	908 Washington St	201-798-0101	$$$	A touch of class in Hoboken, romantic and elegant. Catch the value-for-money really special.
Arthur's Tavern	237 Washington St	201-656-5009	$$*	The best steak for the price.
Baja	104 14th St	201-653-0610	$$*	Good Mexican food, good sangria.
Bangkok City	335 Washington St	201-792-6613	$$*	A taste of Thai.
Biggies Clam Bar	318 Madison St	201-656-2161	$*	Boardwalk fare and perfect raw clams. Order by the dozen.
Brass Rail	135 Washington St	201-659-7074	$$$	You can't beat the brunch deal.
Cucharamama	233 Clinton St	201-420-1700	$$$	Great Cuban and South American.
Delfino's	500 Jefferson St	201-792-7457	$$*	Pizza joint…Plus red checkered table cloths. BYO Chianti. The real thing.
East LA	508 Washington St	201-798-0052	$$*	Knock-your-socks-off margaritas and the food's not bad.
Far Side Bar & Grill	531 Washington St	201-963-7677	$$*	Hoboken's best pub food. Try the steak salad.
Frankie & Johnnie's	14th & Garden St	201-659-6202	$$$$	Power steakhouse. Keep an eye out for Tony Soprano.
Gas Light	400 Adams St	201-217-1400	$$*	Off the main drag, neighbourhood Italian, cozy and cute. Quiz nights and comedy.
Hoboken Gourmet Company	423 Washington St	201-795-0110	$$*	Hoboken's one true café. Rustic, yummy, quirky.
Karma Kafe	505 Washington St	201-610-0900	$$*	Ultra-friendly Tibetan staff, hip Indian food with a wild mix of flavors.
La Isla	104 Washington St	201-659-8197	$$*	A genuine taste of Havana.
La Tartufería	1405 Grand St	201-792-2300	$$*	Modern, imaginative, Northern Italian fare, specializing in truffle dishes.
Robongi	520 Washington St	201-222-8388	$$*	Consistently good sushi, friendly chefs, fun specials.
Trattoria Saporito	328 Washington St	201-533-1801	$$$	Lacks the old world Italian charm but has the old world taste and service. BYOB.
Zafra	301 Willow Ave	201-610-9801	$$*	Cozy with authentic Latino flavors. BYO wine—they'll magically turn it into sangria.

Map 35 · Jersey City

Amelia's Bistro	187 Warren St	201-332-2200	$$*	Try the crab cakes.
Casablanca Grill	354 Grove St	201-420-4072	$$*	Moroccan.
Ibby's Falafel	303 Grove St	201-432-2400	$*	One of the few JC restaurants open after 11pm, Ibby's is owned and operated by the nephew of the owner of the great Mamoun's.
Iron Monkey	97 Greene St	201-435-5756	$$*	Quiet, romantic atmosphere. From risotto to seafood it is all savory. Enjoy the beautiful summer evenings on the rooftop terrace which is equipped with a full bar.
Kitchen Café	60 Sussex St	201-332-1010	$$*	The Great American breakfast.
Komegashi	103 Montgomery St	201-433-4567	$$$*	Authentic Japanese restaurant. Watch the chefs create a master-piece at the open sushi bar.
Komegashi Too	99 Pavonia Ave	201-533-8888	$$$	The other Komegashi.
Light Horse Tavern	199 Washington St	201-946-2028	$$*	New American Cuisine
Madame Claude Café	364 4th St	201-876-8800	$$*	French café.
Marco and Pepe	289 Grove St	201-860-9688	$$$	Small, painfully hip French restaurant.
Miss Saigon	249 Newark Ave	201-239-1988	$*	Authentic and cheap Vietnamese fare.
Nicco's Restaurant	247 Washington St	201-332-8433	$$$	Romantic and fun.
Oddfellows Restaurant	111 Montgomery St	201-433-6999	$$*	It is always Mardi Gras with their happy hour specials. Enjoy authentic Cajun food served in a casual setting.
Presto's Restaurant	199 Warren St	201-433-6639	$$*	Italian BYOB.
Pronto Cena	87 Sussex St	201-435-0004	$$$*	Italian.
Rosie Radigans	10 Exchange Pl (Lobby)	201-451-5566	$*	Excellent after work venue—the food is terrific and the bar draws a friendly crowd.
Saigon Café	188 Newark Ave	201-332-8711	$$*	Compared to its neighbor (see above) the Saigon Café serves Southeast Asian cuisine of a quality that reflects its slightly higher prices.
Tania's	348 Grove St	201-451-6189	$$*	Homecooked Eastern European food. Beware: the cold borscht is addictive.
Unlimited Pizza Café & Diner	116 Newark Ave	201-333-0053	$$*	Best slice of pizza after St Marks.
Uno Chicago Bar & Grill	286 Washington St	201-395-9500	$$	Casual, family atmosphere. All-American eatery serving nachos, hamburgers and pizza. Go on an empty stomach because the sizes are large.
ZZ's Brick Oven Pizza	118 Pavonia Ave	201-626-8877	$$*	They deliver!!!

Battery Park City

Cove Restaurant	2 South End Ave	212-964-1500	$$$	New American cuisine.
Foxhounds	320 South End Ave	212-385-6190	$$	"English" pub; food, "American."
Gigino at Wagner Park	20 Battery Pl	212-528-2228	$$$	Lady Liberty is your companion as you dine Italian.
Grill Room	Winter Garden, World Financial Ctr	212-945-9400	$$$	Enter viewing palm trees; dine viewing the Hudson.
Picasso Pizza	303 South End Ave	212-321-2616	$$	Good thin crust pizza.
Samantha's Fine Foods	235 South End Ave	212-945-5555	$$	Italian take-out and catering.
Steamer's Landing	375 South End Ave	212-432-1451	$$$	Food from Italy, from the sea, and from the farms.
Wave Japanese Restaurant	21 South End Ave	212-240-9101	$$	Good Japanese.
Zen	311 South End Ave	212-432-3634	$$	Chinese and Thai.

353

New York's longstanding reputation as a fabulous place to shop is well deserved. From haute couture to vintage clothing, from house and garden to cars and sporting goods, you would be hard pressed to find something you couldn't purchase in this town. But unlike going to some ginormous, "convenient" boring mall, you'll probably end up spending most of your time schlepping between shopping destinations. Sigh. Such is the life of a savvy New Yorker. Here we've taken the liberty of listing a few key themes and some of the best places to give your credit card a workout.

Clothing

For the best of the haute couture labels, head for the area around Madison Avenue and Fifth Avenue in the 50s, 60s, and 70s. There you will find the likes of **Chanel**, **Donna Karan**, **Armani**, and **Gucci**. For department store shopping at its finest, try **Bloomingdale's**, **Macy's**, **Lord & Taylor**, and (for those with a little extra cash) **Saks Fifth Avenue**, **Bergdorf Goodman**, and **Barneys**. If you have the patience to deal with the crowds and to sift through the merchandise to find the real bargains, **Century 21** can yield great rewards of name brand clothing, shoes, make-up, accessories, and home wares at significantly discounted prices.

The past few years have seen the traditionally boutique-style SoHo welcome larger designers such as **Prada**, **DKNY**, **Tommy Hilfiger**, **BCBG**, and **Ralph Lauren**, as well as specialists like **Coach**. If your wallet is a little lighter, you'll also find a good cross-section of "middle of the road" stores such as **Banana Republic**, **Benetton**, and **French Connection**. SoHo is a great area for browsing and strolling, with Sullivan and Thompson Streets offering a glimpse of the smaller boutiques that once occupied the area.

For vintage clothing and fashions from up-and-coming designers, head to the area east of Broadway to Bowery, mainly below Houston, as well as to the East Village (just don't expect any cheap finds—their prices compare with those of the fancier label stores).

Sports

Paragon Sporting Goods in Union Square is hard to beat as a one-stop shop for everything sporting. The challenge is to find a recreation *not* listed on the store directory! For outdoor gear, try **Eastern Mountain Sports**. **Sports Authority**, **Foot Locker**, and **Modell's** provide a broad range of affordable sports clothing, shoes, and goods. **Blades Board & Skate** features groovy gear for boarding (both the wheeled and snow varieties) as well as a good selection of the latest equipment for these activities.

Housewares

You can lose hours in **ABC Carpet & Home** just off of Union Square. Its exotic array of furniture and other furnishings (much of it antique and imported from Asia and Europe) is fun to look at, even if you can't afford the steep prices. **Crate and Barrel**, **Fish's Eddy**, **Pottery Barn**, **Portico**, and **Bed Bath & Beyond** all are good houseware stores with a wide selection of styles and prices. For cheap kitchen outfitters, try some of the restaurant supply places on Bowery. For paint, window dressings, and other home decorating supplies, try **Janovic Plaza**.

Electronics

J&R provides most things electronic, including computers and accessories, games, cameras, music equipment, CDs, DVDs, and household appliances. **B&H** is another great place for photographic, audio, and video equipment. It's worth a visit just to witness the pure spectacle of this well-coordinated operation, as well as the outstanding selection of gear. Other places to shop for electronics include the SoHo **Apple** store, **DataVision**, and **Best Buy**.

Food

If the way to a person's heart is through their stomach, then no wonder we all love New York! Try the tasty delights of **Myers of Keswick** in the West Village, **East Village Cheese** in the East Village, **Sullivan Street Bakery** in SoHo, **Zabar's** gourmet foods on the Upper West Side, **Dylan's Candy Bar** on the Upper East Side, and **Settepani** for delicious baked goods in Harlem. The gigantic **Whole Foods** in the AOL/Time Warner Center would even please Martha Stewart. The introduction of online ordering and home delivery from Fresh Direct has brought New Yorker's a whole new level of convenience, with the highest quality fresh food delivered right to their doors. You can even specify a two-hour time frame for delivery. It doesn't get a great deal better than that!

Art Supplies

Running low on Cadmium Red? Use your last stick of charcoal drawing a nude? The best art stores in NYC are scattered loosely around the SoHo area, with **Pearl Paint** being the most well-known. Located where Mercer and Canal Streets meet, the store occupies a full 6-story building with every type of art supply you can imagine, including a great separate frame shop out back on Lispenard. Closer to NYU and Greenwich you can find the best selection of paper at **New York Central Art Supply** on Third Avenue. Further north on Fourth Ave is **Utrecht**, selling more than just the products with their name. **SoHo Art Materials** on Grand Street is a small, traditional shop that sells super premium paints and brushes for fine artists. Don't forget to check out both **Sam Flax** and **A.I. Friedman** in the Flatiron area—both great for graphic design supplies, portfolios, and gifts.

As the art scene has made its way to Williamsburg, having an art supply store close by is as important as a good supermarket (something folks in the 'burg are still waiting for). **Artist & Craftsman** on North 8th is a good bet for supplies.

*Remember to flash that student ID card if you've got it, as most art stores offer a decent discount!

Music Equipment & Instruments

There are as many starving musicians as there are artists in NYC, but that doesn't keep them from finding ways to fulfill their equipment needs. New York's large and vibrant music scene supports a thriving instrument trade. To buy a new tuba or get that banjo tuned, head over to 48th Street. You'll find the largest, most well-known stores, from generalist shops such as **Manny's** and **Sam Ash**, to more specialized shops like **Roberto's Woodwind Repair**. Just two blocks away, on 46th, you can delight in two shops dedicated solely to drummers—**Manhattan Drum Shop** and **Drummer's World**.

If you can't take the bustle of the Times Square area and are looking for used, vintage, or just plain cool, then you'll want to shop elsewhere. Some of our favorites include: **East Village Music, First Flight, 30th Street Guitars, Rogue Music**, and **Ludlow Guitars**. We're also surprisingly impressed with the nice salespeople at the **Guitar Center** on 14th Street.

For an exquisite purchase where money is no object, pick up a grand piano at **Klavierhaus** or a Strat at **Matt Umanov**.

The best remaining place for sheet music is still the **Joseph Patelson Music House**.

Music for Listening

NYC is a hotbed for music lovers, and its record stores house the best and the worst of what the world has to offer. Whether you're shopping for that Top Ten hit or a rare piece of '70s vinyl, your options for finding it are expansive. For those who like to dig, there's **Kim's Mediapolis**, where you're sure to find something to fill that void in your record collection. If you're not up for the smaller indie shops, head to **J&R Music World, Tower,**

or the **Virgin Megastore**, and be prepared to spend at least a good chunk of your paycheck.

The smaller stores carry more eclectic selections and, more often than not, the staff can help you out with musical queries. Head to **Footlight** in the East Village and you'll see what we're talking about. If you're not convinced, try **Other Music** and **Earwax** (Brooklyn)—two stores with unique vibes.

If all else fails, stroll down Bleecker Street to **Rebel Rebel, Kim's Underground**, and **Bleecker Street Records**.

Shopping "Districts"

Manhattan is famous for its shopping districts—a conglomeration of shops in one area where you go to find what you're looking for. Hit up the **Garment District** (25th to 40th Sts, Fifth to Ninth Aves) for buttons and zippers, rick-rack and ribbons; all the ingredients you'll need to fashion your own frocks. Attention men: The **Diamond and Jewelry District** (W 47th between Fifth and Sixth Aves), the world's largest market for diamonds, and the **Flower District** (26th to 29th Sts, along and off Sixth Ave) are where to go to make her swoon. **Music Row** (48th St between Sixth & Seventh Aves) is where to buy that accordion you've been meaning to try. The Bowery south of Houston is another well-known strip where you'll find the **Kitchenware District** for all your culinary endeavors, the **Lighting District** (past Delancey St) for all your illuminating needs, and the **Downtown Jewelry District** (turn the corner of Bowery to Canal St) for the more exotic baubles you can't get uptown. The **Flatiron District** (from 14th to 34th Sts, between Sixth & Park Aves) is a home furnishing mecca. Book Row (between 9th and 14th Sts) is sadly no more. What was once an assemblage of over 25 bookstores, now houses only the famous Strand Book Store and Alabaster Used Books, both tome troves unto themselves.

Map 1 · Financial District

Barclay Rex	75 Broad St	212-962-3355	For all your smoking needs.
Century 21	22 Cortlandt St	212-227-9092	Where most New Yorkers buy their underwear.
Christopher Norman Chocolates	60 New St	212-402-1243	Sweet chocolate shop.
Flowers of the World	80 Pine St	212-425-2234, 800-770-3125	Fulfill any feeling, mood, budget, or setting.
Godiva Chocolatier	33 Maiden Ln	212-809-8990	Everyone needs a fix now and then.
M Slavin & Sons	106 South St	212-233-4522	Fresh fish at the Seaport.
Modell's	200 Broadway	212-566-3711	Generic sporting goods.
Radio Shack	114 Fulton St	212-732-1904	Kenneth, what is the frequency?
Radio Shack	9 Broadway	212-482-8138	Kenneth, what is the frequency?
South Street Seaport	19 Fulton St		Mall with historic ships as backdrop.
The World of Golf	189 Broadway	212-385-1246	Stop here on your way to Briar Cliff Manor.
Yankees Clubhouse Shop	8 Fulton St	212-514-7182	25 and counting…

Map 2 · TriBeCa

Assets London	152 Franklin St	212-219-8777	Ultra-Mod British fashions for her.
Balloon Saloon	133 West Broadway	212-227-3838	We love the name.
Bazzini	339 Greenwich St	212-334-1280	Nuts to you!
Bell Bates Natural Food	97 Reade St	212-267-4300	No MSG?
Boffi SoHo	31 1/2 Greene St	212-431-8282	Hi-end kitchen and bath design.
Canal Street Bicycles	417 Canal St	212-334-8000	Bike messenger mecca.
Duane Park Patisserie	179 Duane St	212-274-8447	Yummy!

Arts & Entertainment • **Shopping**

Map 2 • TriBeCa—*continued*

Gotham Bikes	112 West Broadway	212-732-2453	Super helpful staff, good stuff.
Happy Baby Toys	51 Hudson St	212-406-7440	Children's store with clothing and educational toys.
Issey Miyake	119 Hudson St	212-226-0100	Flagship store of this designer.
Jack Spade	56 Greene St	212-625-1820	Barbie's got Ken, Kate's got Jack. Men's bags.
Janovic Plaza	136 Church St	212-349-0001	Top NYC paint store.
Kings Pharmacy	5 Hudson St	212-791-3100	Notary Public + discount days!
Korin Japanese Trading	57 Warren St	212-587-7021	Supplier to Japanese chefs and restaurants.
Let There Be Neon	38 White St	212-226-4883	Neon gallery and store.
Liberty Souveniers	275 Greenwich St	212-566-4604	Show your NY pride!
Lucky Brand Dungarees	38 Greene St	212-625-0707	Lucky you.
MarieBelle's Fine Treats & Chocolates	484 Broome St	212-925-6999	Top NYC chocolatier.
New York Nautical	158 Duane	212-962-4522	Armchair sailing.
Oliver Peoples	366 West Broadway	212-925-5400	Look as good as you see.
Shoofly	42 Hudson St	212-406-3270	Dressing your child for social success.
Stern's Music	71 Warren St	212-964-5455	World music.
Steven Alan	103 Franklin St	212-343-0352	Trendy designer clothing and accessories. One-of-a-kind stuff.
Urban Archaeology	143 Franklin St	212-431-4646	Retro fixtures.
We Are Nuts About Nuts	165 Church St	212-227-4695	They're nuts.
Willner Chemists	253 Broadway	212-791-0505	Free nutritional consultations for customers.

Map 3 • City Hall / Chinatown

Aji Ichiban	167 Hester St	212-925-1133	Japanese chain of Chinese candy.
Bangkok Center Grocery	104 Mosco St	212-349-1979	Curries, fish sauce, and other Thai products.
Bloomingdale's	504 Broadway	212-729-5900	Modern Bloomingdale's. Hottest young designers and exclusive collections.
Bowery Lighting	132 Bowery	212-941-8244	Got a match, anyone?
Catherine Street Meat Market	21 Catherine St	212-693-0494	Fresh pig deliveries every Tuesday.
Chinatown Ice Cream Factory	65 Bayard St	212-608-4170	Mango & redbean milkshakes.
Dipalo Dairy	200 Grand St	212-226-1033	Saying cheese since 1925.
Fountain Pen Hospital	10 Warren St	212-964-0580	They don't take Medicaid.
GS Food Market	250 Grand St	212-274-0990	Fresh veggies.
Hong Kong Seafood & Meat	75 Mulberry St	212-571-1445	Fresh seafood that you must eat today.
Industrial Plastic Supply	309 Canal St	212-226-2010	Plastic fantastic.
J&R Music & Computer World	33 Park Row	212-732-8600	Stereo, computer, and electronic equipment.
Kate Spade	454 Broome St	212-274-1991	Downtown design mecca.
Lung Moon Bakery	83 Mulberry St	212-349-4945	Chinese bakery.
Mitchell's Place	15 Park Pl	212-267-8156	Ca-ching for bling bling.
Modell's	55 Chambers St	212-732-8484	Generic sporting goods.
New Age Designer	38 Mott St	212-349-0818	Chinese emporium.
The New York City Store	1 Centre St	212-669-8246	Great NYC stuff—manhole cover pins, subway mugs, etc.
Pearl Paint	308 Canal St	212-431-7932	Mecca for artists, designers, and people who just like art supplies.
Pearl River Mart	477 Broadway	212-431-4770	Chinese housewares and more.
Radio Shack	280 Broadway	212-233-1080	Kenneth, what is the frequency?
SoHo Art Materials	127 Grand St	212-431-3938	A painter's candy store.
Tan My My Market	253 Grand St	212-966-7837	Fresh fish—some still moving!
Tent & Trails	21 Park Pl	212-227-1760	Top outfitter for gearheads.
Ting's Gift Shop	18 Doyers St	212-962-1081	Chinese emporium.
Two Lines Music	370 Broadway	212-227-9552	Music equipment.
Vespa	13 Crosby St	212-226-4410	Rosselini! Fellini! Spaghattini!
Yellow Rat Bastard	478 Broadway	877-YELL-RAT	Filled with young street clothes and skate gear.

Map 4 • Lower East Side

Doughnut Plant	379 Grand St	212-505-3700	Great, weird, recommended.
Gertel's Bake Shop	53 Hester St	212-982-3250	Great chocolate babka.
Hong Kong Supermarket	109 East Broadway	212-227-3388	A chance to see just how amazing food packaging can look.
Joe's Fabric Warehouse	102 Orchard St	212-674-7089	Designer fabrics and trimmings.
Kossar's Bialys	367 Grand St	212-473-4810	Oldest bialy bakery in the US.
Mendel Goldberg Fabrics	72 Hester St	212-925-9110	Small store and selection of great fabrics.
Moishe's Kosher Bake Shop	504 Grand St	212-673-5832	Best babka, challah, hamantaschen, and rualach.
Sweet Life	63 Hester St	212-598-0092	Gimme some CAN-DAY!

Map 5 • West Village

Alexander McQueen	417 W 14th St	212-645-1797	Brit bad boy designs.
Alphabets	47 Greenwich Ave	212-229-2966	Fun miscellany store.
American Apparel	373 Sixth Ave	646-336-6515	Sweatshop-free clothing for liberal New Yorkers.
Bleecker Street Records	239 Bleecker St	212-255-7899	Great selection.
CO Bigelow Chemists	414 Sixth Ave	212-533-2700	Classic village pharmacy.
Faicco's Pork Store	260 Bleecker St	212-243-1974	Pork! Just for you!
Flight 001	96 Greenwich Ave	212-691-1001	Cute hipster travel shop.
Geppetto's Toy Box	10 Christopher St	212-620-7511	Excellent toys and puppets.
Integral Yoga Natural Foods	229 W 13th St	212-243-2642	Shop in the lotus position.
Janovic Plaza	161 Sixth Ave	212-627-1100	Top NYC paint store.
The Leather Man	111 Christopher St	212-243-5339	No, you won't look like James Dean. But it'll help.
Little Pie Company	407 W 14th St	212-414-2324	A home-made dessert equals happiness.
Magnolia Bakery	401 Bleecker St	212-462-2572	Wait in a line for mediocre cupcakes.
Matt Umanov Guitars	273 Bleecker St	212-675-2157	Guitars. Guitars. Guitars.
Murray's Cheese Shop	254 Bleecker St	212-243-3289	We love cheese.
Mxyplyzyk	125 Greenwich Ave	212-989-4300	Great quirky mid-range tchochkes.
Myers of Keswick	634 Hudson St	212-691-4194	Killer English sausages, pasties, etc.
Porto Rico Importing Company	201 Bleecker St	212-477-5421	Sacks of coffee beans everywhere.
Radio Shack	360 Sixth Ave	212-473-2113	Kenneth, what is the frequency?
Radio Shack	49 Seventh Ave	212-727-7641	I need a multiplexer, Jim.
Rebel Rebel Records	319 Bleecker St	212-989-0770	Small CD & LP shop with knowledgeable staff.
Scott Jordan Furniture	137 Varick St	212-620-4682	Solid hardwood furniture.
Urban Outfitters	374 Sixth Ave	212-677-9350	College cool.
Vitra	29 Ninth Ave	212-929-3626	Modern stuff, just like we like it!

Map 6 • Washington Square / NYU / NoHo / SoHo

Academy Records & CDs	77 E 10th St	212-780-9166	Top Jazz/classical mecca.
American Apparel	121 Spring St	212-226-4880	Sweatshop-free clothing for liberal New Yorkers.
American Apparel	712 Broadway	646-336-3322	Sweatshop-free clothing for liberal New Yorkers.
Apple Store SoHo	103 Prince St	212-226-3126	Don't come looking for produce.
Aveda Environmental Lifestyle Store	456 West Broadway	212-473-0280	Expensive well-being.
Banana Republic	528 Broadway	212-334-3034	Destination for the modern, versatile, average wardrobe.
BCBG by Max Azria	120 Wooster St	212-625-2723	Tight clothes for loose women.
Benetton	749 Broadway	212-533-0230	Cheap(ly made) wardrobe basics.
Black Hound New York	170 Second Ave	212-979-9505	Killer desserts. NFT Favorite.
Blades Board & Skate	659 Broadway	212-477-7350	One-stop shop for skateboarding and inline skating gear.
Burberry	131 Spring St	212-925-9300	How to dress well without having to think about it.
Canal Jean	718 Broadway	212-353-2601	Where many New Yorkers buy their jeans.
CITE Design	120 Wooster St	212-431-7272	3 cool shops on Wooster.
Coach	143 Prince St	212-473-6925	Leather goods.
Daily 235	235 Elizabeth St	212-334-9728	A little tchotchke store; has great journals.
DKNY	420 West Broadway	646-613-1100	Sharp, wearable fashions by Donna.
East Village Cheese	40 Third Ave	212-477-2601	Great soy cheeses, laughably bad service.
East Village Music Store	85 E 4th St	212-979-8222	Excellent wares and repairs service. NFT top pick!
EMS	591 Broadway	212-966-8730	Excellent outdoor/hiking equipment and clothing.
Footlight Records	113 E 12th St	212-533-1572	Opera.
French Connection	700 Broadway	212-473-4486	Cool clothes for fashionable men and women. FCUK that.
Global Table	107 Sullivan St	212-431-5839	Quietly elegant tableware.
Guitar Center	25 W 14th St	212-463-7500	Guitar department store.
Jam Paper & Envelope	135 Third Ave	212-473-6666	And the envelope please…
Kar'ikter	19 Prince St	212-274-1966	Toys for kids and adults.
Kate's Paperie	561 Broadway	212-941-9816	Excellent stationery. NYC favorite.
Kiehl's	109 Third Ave	212-677-3171	Great creams, lotions, & unguents; laughably great service.
Kim's Underground	144 Bleecker St	212-260-1010	Where to blow $100 quickly.
Kim's Video	6 St Marks Pl	212-505-0311	Where to blow $100 quickly.
Knit New York	307 E 14th St	212-387-0707	Combo coffeehouse/knitting store w/ lessons.
Leekan Designs	93 Mercer St	212-226-7226	Bead shop for aspiring jewelry-makers.
Lighting by Gregory	158 Bowery	212-226-1276	Bowery lighting mecca. Good ceiling fans.
Meg	312 E 9th St	212-260-6329	Meg: unique designer…
Michael Anchin Glass	245 Elizabeth St	212-925-1470	The city's premier glassblower, still with good prices.
MOMA Design Store	81 Spring St	212-708-9669	Cutting-edge, minimalist, ergonomic, offbeat, and funky everything.
Moss	146 Greene St	212-204-7100	Awesome cool stuff you can't afford! Ever!
Nancy Koltes at Home	31 Spring St	212-219-2271	What's the thread-count?
National Wholesale Liquidators	632 Broadway	212-979-2400	They're not kidding.
New York Central Art Supply	62 Third Ave	212-473-7705	Great selection of art, papers, & supplies.

Arts & Entertainment • **Shopping**

Map 6 • Washington Square / NYU / NoHo / SoHo—continued

Other Music	15 E 4th St	212-477-8150	An excellent range of other music.
Paul Frank Store	195 Mulberry St	212-965-5079	Whimsical characters including that monkey on everything.
Porto Rico Importing Company	107 Thompson St	212-966-5758	Sacks of coffee beans everywhere.
Porto Rico Importing Company	40 St Marks Pl	212-533-1982	Sacks of coffee beans everywhere.
Prada	575 Broadway	212-334-8888	Big pretentious Rem Koolhaas-designed store!
Radio Shack	781 Broadway	212-228-6810	Kenneth, what is the frequency?
Ralph Lauren	381 West Broadway	212-625-1660	Love those little polo horses.
Saint Mark's Comics	11 St Mark's Pl	212-598-9439	Important comic book store.
Stereo Exchange	627 Broadway	212-505-1111	Just-under-obscenely-priced audiophile equipment.
Stuart Moore	128 Prince St	212-941-1023	Good for male depression.
Sullivan Street Bakery	73 Sullivan St	212-334-9435	Elegant, modern jewelry, $1000-$10,000 range.
Surprise, Surprise	91 Third Ave	212-777-0990	The best bakery, period.
Tommy Hilfiger	372 West Broadway	917-237-0983	Good just-moved-to-the-neighborhood store.
Tower Records	692 Broadway	212-505-1500	Soon it'll just be clothes made from the American flag.
Utrecht Art and Drafting Supplies	111 Fourth Ave	212-777-5353	For all your mainstream needs.
Veniero's	342 E 11th St	212-674-7070	Another fine downtown art store.
Virgin Megastore	52 E 14th St	212-598-4666	Another cookie, my dear?
White Trash	304 E 5th St	212-598-5956	Massive music store for the masses.
			Retro home furnishings.

Map 7 • East Village / Lower East Side

A Cheng	443 E 9th St	212-979-7324	Modern classic women's clothing.
Alphabets	115 Ave A	212-475-7250	Fun miscellany store.
Altman Luggage	135 Orchard St	212-254-7275	It's just you and that Samsonite gorilla, baby.
American Apparel	183 E Houston St	212-598-4600	Sweatshop-free clothing for liberal New Yorkers.
Dowel Quality Products	91 First Ave	212-979-6045	Super-cool Indian grocery. Great beer selection, too.
Earthmatters	177 Ludlow St	212-475-4180	Organic groceries with a garden out back.
Economy Candy	108 Rivington St	212-254-1531	Where Augustus Gloop can been seen hanging around late at night.
Etherea	66 Ave A	212-358-1126	Cool East Village record store.
Exit 9	64 Ave A	212-228-0145	Always fun and changeable hipster gift shop (The first place to sell NFT!)
First Flight Music	174 First Ave	212-539-1383	Good guitars and amps, spotty service.
Gringer & Sons	29 First Ave	212-475-0600	Kitchen appliances for every price range.
Lancelotti	66 Ave A	212-475-6851	Fun designer housewares, not too expensive.
Ludlow Guitars	164 Ludlow St	212-353-1775	New and used vintage guitars, accessories, and amps.
Masturbakers	511 E 12th St	212-475-0476	Erotic and custom cakes.
R&S Strauss Auto Store	644 E 14th St	212-995-8000	Sideview mirrors, tail lights, touch up paint—mecca for the urban car owner.
Russ & Daughters	179 E Houston St	212-475-4880	Get the nova, silly!
Schapiro Wine	126 Rivington St	212-674-4404	Kosher wine shop.
Spectra	293 E 10th St	212-529-3636	East Village photo print shop; great sepia processing.
TG170	170 Ludlow St	212-995-8660	Fun funky fresh women's clothing.
Toys in Babeland	94 Rivington St	212-375-1701	Sex toys and more.
Yonah Schimmel's Knishery	137 E Houston St	212-477-2858	Your run-of-the-mill knishery.

Map 8 • Chelsea

B&H Photo	420 Ninth Ave	212-444-5040	Where everyone in North America buys their cameras and film. Closed Saturdays.
Buon Italia	75 Ninth Ave	212-633-9090	Imported Italian food.
Chelsea Garden Center	455 W 16th St	212-929-2477	Urban gardener's delight.
Chelsea Market Baskets	75 Ninth Ave	212-727-1484	Gift baskets for all occasions.
Fat Witch Bakery	75 Ninth Ave	212-807-1335	Excellent chocolate brownies.
Kitchen Market	218 Eighth Ave	212-243-4433	Chiles, herbs, spices, hot sauces, salsas, and more.
New Museum Store	556 W 22nd	212-343-0460	One of our favorite stores on the planet Earth.
Portico	75 Ninth Ave	212-243-8515	Minimalist, urban sophistication.

Map 9 • Flatiron / Lower Midtown

17 at 17 Thrift Shop	17 W 17th St	212-727-7516	Proceeds go to Gilda's Club.
30th Street Guitars	236 W 30th St	212-868-2660	Ax heaven.
Al Friedman	44 W 18th St	212-243-9000	Art supplies, frames, office furniture, and more.
ABC Carpet & Home	888 Broadway	212-473-3000	Carpets, furniture, doodads—a NYC institution.
Abracadabra	19 W 21st St	212-627-5194	Magic, masks, costumes—presto!

Arts & Entertainment • **Shopping**

Academy Records & CDs	12 W 18th St	212-242-3000	Top jazz/classical mecca.
Adorama Camera	42 W 18th St	212-741-0052	Good camera alternative to B & H.
Ariston	69 Fifth Ave	212-929-4226, 800-422-2747	Excellent florist with orchids as well.
Aveda Environmental Lifestyle Store	140 Fifth Ave	212-645-4797	Great if you can afford it.
Bed Bath & Beyond	620 Sixth Ave	212-255-3550	De riguer destination when moving to a new apartment.
buybuy Baby	270 Seventh Ave	212-645-0187	Baby superstore.
Capitol Fishing Tackle	218 W 23rd St	212-929-6132	100+ year-old fishing institution.
The City Quilter	133 W 25th St	212-807-0390	Quilt for success!
CompUSA	420 Fifth Ave	212-764-6224	The Kmart of computer stores.
The Container Store	629 Sixth Ave	212-366-4200	For all your container needs.
Cupcake Café	18 W 18th St	646-307-5878	Pretty cupcakes.
DataVision	445 Fifth Ave	212-689-1111	Computers, printers, projectors
Fish's Eddy	889 Broadway	212-420-9020	The coolest used plates in the city.
Housing Works Thrift Shop	143 W 17th St	212-366-0820	Our favorite thrift store.
Jam Paper & Envelope	611 Sixth Ave	212-255-4593	And the envelope please…
Janovic Plaza	215 Seventh Ave	212-645-5454	Top NYC paint store.
Jazz Record Center	236 W 26th St	212-675-4480	All that jazz!
Jensen-Lewis	89 Seventh Ave	212-929-4880	Upgrade from Ikea!
Just Bulbs	5 E 16th St	212-228-7820	Do you have any lamps? How about shades?
Just Pickles	1 E 28th St	212-962-5733	Do you have any artichokes?
Just Pickles	168 Madison Ave	212-962-5734	Do you have any artichokes?
Krups Kitchen and Bath	11 W 18th St	212-243-5787	Good prices for top appliances.
Loehmann's	101 Seventh Ave	212-352-0856	Join the other thousands of bargain hunters sifting through clothing piles.
Lord & Taylor	424 Fifth Ave	212-391-3344	Classic NYC department store.
M&J Trimmings	1008 Sixth Ave	212-391-6200	For your DIY sewing projects.
Macy's	151 W 34th St	212-695-4400	Love the wooden escalators.
Manhattan Drum Shop & Music Studio	203 W 38th St	212-768-4892	Repairs and sells custom-made and vintage drums.
Paper Presentations	23 W 18th St	212-463-7035	Relatively cheap paper and such.
Paragon Sporting Goods	867 Broadway	212-255-8036	Good all-purpose sporting goods store.
Phoenix	64 W 37th St	212-564-5656	Bead shop for aspiring jewelry-makers.
Pleasure Chest	156 Seventh Ave	212-242-2158	Always a great window display.
Radio Shack	36 E 23rd St	212-673-3670	Kenneth, what is the frequency?
Rogue Music	251 W 30th St	212-629-5073	Used equipment you probably still can't afford.
Sam Flax	12 W 20th St	212-620-3038	Portfolios, frames, furniture, and designer gifts.
Sports Authority	636 Sixth Ave	212-929-8971	Sporting goods for the masses.
Tekserve	119 W 23rd St	212-929-3645	Apple computer sales and repairs.

Map 10 • Murray Hill / Gramercy

Alkit Pro Camera	222 Park Ave S	212-674-1515	Good camera shop; developing; rentals.
City Opera Thrift Shop	222 E 23rd St	212-684-5344	They always have something or other.
Foods of India	121 Lexington Ave	212-683-4419	Large selection of Indian ingredients including harder to find spices.
Housing Works Thrift Shop	157 E 23rd St	212-529-5955	Our favorite thrift store.
Ligne Roset	250 Park Ave S	212-375-1036	Modern, sleek furniture.
Nemo Tile Company	48 E 21st St	212-505-0009	Good tile shop for small projects.
Pastrami Factory	333 E 23rd St	212-689-8090	Pastrami, chopped liver, knishes, chicken soup and other kosher-style foods.
Pearl Paint	207 E 23rd St	212-592-2179	Not as big as the Canal St store, but still very useful.
Poggenpohl US	230 Park Ave	212-228-3334	By appointment only. $100,000 kitchens for all you grad students!
Quark Spy	240 E 29th St	212-889-1809	Spy shops are cool.
Urban Angler	206 Fifth Ave	212-689-6400, 800-255-5488	We think it's for fishermen.

Map 11 • Hell's Kitchen

Janovic Plaza	771 Ninth Ave	212-245-3241	Top NYC paint store.
Little Pie Company	424 W 43rd St	212-736-4780	A home-made dessert equals happiness.
Metro Bicycles	360 W 47th St	212-581-4500	New York's bicycle source.
Ninth Avenue Cheese Market	615 Ninth Ave	212-397-4700	Can I have some cheese, please?
Ninth Avenue International	543 Ninth Ave	212-279-1000	Mediterranean/Greek specialty store.
Pan Aqua Diving	460 W 43rd St	212-736-3483	SCUBA equipment and courses.
Poseidon Bakery	629 Ninth Ave	212-757-6173	Greek bakery.
Radio Shack	333 W 57th St	212-586-1909	Kenneth, what is the frequency?
Sea Breeze	541 Ninth Ave	212-563-7537	Bargains on fresh seafood.

Arts & Entertainment · **Shopping**

Map 12 · Midtown

Alkit Pro Camera	830 Seventh Ave	212-262-2424	Good camera shop; developing; rentals.
Baccarat	625 Madison Ave	212-826-4100	Top glass/crystal.
Bergdorf Goodman	754 Fifth Ave	212-753-7300	The widow dressed in Bergdorf-Goodman black…
Brooks Brothers	346 Madison Ave	212-682-8800	For hip, radical fashions from the Indian subcontinent.
Burberry	9 E 57th St	212-371-5010	How to dress well without having to think about it.
Carnegie Card & Gifts	56 W 57th St	212-977-2494	Great, diverse, always fresh.
Chanel	15 E 57th St	212-355-5050	Suits like grandma used to wear.
Colony Music	1619 Broadway	212-265-2050	Great sheet music store.
CompUSA	1775 Broadway	212-262-9711	The Kmart of computer stores.
Crate & Barrel	650 Madison Ave	212-308-0011	Housewares and furniture.
Drummer's World	151 W 46th St	212-840-3057	All-encompassing stop for professional to beginning drummers.
Ermenegildo Zegna	663 Fifth Ave	212-421-4488	A truly stylish and classic Italian designer.
ESPN Zone	1472 Broadway	212-921-3776	Brand experience for sports jocks
FAO Schwartz	767 Fifth Ave	212-644-9400	Noisy, crowded, overrated, awesome.
Felissimo	10 W 56th St	212-247-5656	Cool design store, great townhouse.
Gucci	685 Fifth Ave	212-826-2600	Largest Gucci store in the world.
Henri Bendel	712 Fifth Ave	212-247-1100	Expensive, classy, and expensive.
Joseph Patelson Music House	160 W 56th St	212-582-5840	Where Beethoven would shop, if he weren't dead.
Kate's Paperie	140 W 57th St	212-459-0700	Excellent stationery. NYC favorite.
Klavierhaus	211 W 58th St	212-245-4535	Unique pianos from the 19th, 20th, and 21st centuries.
Manny's Music	156 W 48th St	212-819-0576	Uptown musical instruments mecca.
Mets Clubhouse Shop	11 W 42nd St	212-768-9534	For Amazin' stuff!
Mikimoto	730 Fifth Ave	212-457-4600	Beautiful jewelry, mostly pearls.
MoMA Design Store	44 W 53rd St	212-767-1050	Cutting-edge, minimalist, ergonomic, offbeat, and funky everything.
Museum of Arts and Design Shop	40 W 53rd St	212-956-3535	Not your average museum store.
NBA Store	666 Fifth Ave	212-515-6221	Brand experience for basketball junkies
Niketown	6 E 57th St	212-891-6453	Just do it brand experience.
Orvis Company	522 Fifth Ave	212-827-0698	For the angler in all of us. Or, for Halloween.
Petrossian Boutique	911 Seventh Ave	212-245-2217	Caviar and other delectables.
Radio Shack	1134 Sixth Ave	212-575-2361	Kenneth, what is the frequency?
Roberto's Woodwind Repair Shop	146 W 46th St	212-391-1315	Saxophones, horns, clarinets, and flutes. If it blows, bring it here.
Saks Fifth Avenue	611 Fifth Ave	212-753-4000	When Bloomie's just gets to be too much…
Sam Ash	160 W 48th St	212-719-2299	The original, so not that bad.
Smythson of Bond Street	4 W 57th St	212-265-4573	High quality stationery.
Steinway and Sons	109 W 57th St	212-246-1100	Great store and free delivery!
Takashimaya	693 Fifth Ave	212-350-0100	Elegant tea, furniture, accessory store. Highly recommended.
Tiffany & Co	727 Fifth Ave	212-755-8000	Gaudy and overblown but still interesting.

Map 13 · East Midtown

Adriana's Caravan	Grand Central Station	212-972-8804	Number 1 rated herb and spice shop.
Bridge Kitchenware	214 E 52nd St	212-688-4220	A mecca.
Godiva Chocolatier	560 Lexington Ave	212-980-9810	Everyone needs a fix now and then.
Ideal Cheese	942 First Ave	212-688-7579	All cheese is ideal.
Innovative Audio	150 E 58th St	212-634-4444	Quality music systems and home theaters.
Mets Clubhouse Shop	143 E 54th St	212-888-7508	For Amazin' stuff!
Modell's	51 E 42nd St	212-661-4242	Generic sporting goods.
New York Transit Museum	Grand Central, Main Concourse	212-878-0106	Great subway fun.
Pottery Barn	117 E 59th St	917-369-0050	Mainstream, quality home goods.
Radio Shack	940 Third Ave	212-750-8409	Kenneth, what's the frequency?
Sam Flax	900 Third Ave	212-935-5353	Portfolios, frames, furniture, and designer gifts.
Sports Authority	845 Third Ave	212-355-9725	Sporting goods for the masses.
Terence Conran Shop	407 E 59th St	212-755-9079	Wonderful design store—furniture, accessories, tableware, and more.
The World of Golf	147 E 47th St	212-775-9398	Stop here on your way to Briar Cliff Manor.
Yankee Clubhouse Shop	110 E 59th St	212-758-7844	26 and counting…
Zaro's Bread Basket	89 E 42nd St	212-292-0160	They've got bread. In baskets.

Map 14 · Upper West Side (Lower)

Alphabets	2284 Broadway	212-579-5702	Fun miscellany store.
Assets London	464 Columbus Ave	212-874-8253	Ultramodern British fashions for her.
Balducci's	155 W 66th St	212-653-8320	One third of the gourmet "holy trinity."
Bed Bath & Beyond	1932 Broadway	917-441-9391	De rigueur destination when moving to a new apartment.
Bonne Nuit	30 Lincoln Plz	212-677-8487	Pretty, feminine underthings and sleepwear.
Bruce Frank	215 W 83rd St	212-595-3746	Great bead shop.

Bruno the King of Ravioli	2204 Broadway	212-580-8150	Gourmet market with a shocking specialty.
Claire's Accessories	2267 Broadway	212-877-2655	Fun for the young.
Eastern Mountain Sports (EMS)	20 W 61st St	212-397-4860	For all of your outdoor sporting needs.
Ethan Allen	103 West End Ave	212-201-9840	Furniture for the mature set.
Fish's Eddy	2176 Broadway	212-873-8819	Great used plates.
Godiva Chocolatier	245 Columbus Ave	212-787-5804	Everyone needs a fix now and then.
Gracious Home	1992 Broadway	212-231-7800	The definition of the word "emporium."
Harry's Shoes	2299 Broadway	212-874-2035	Mecca for reasonably priced footwear.
Housing Works Thrift Shop	306 Columbus Ave	212-579-7566	Our favorite thrift shop.
Janovic Plaza	159 W 72nd St	212-595-2500	Top NYC paint store.
Lincoln Stationers	1889 Broadway	212-459-3500	Classic stationery store.
NYCD	173 W 81st St	212-724-4466	Excellent CD shop.
Patagonia	426 Columbus Ave	917-441-0011	Environmentally conscious store selling outstanding outdoor clothing.
Tower Records/Video	1961 Broadway	212-799-2500	Lincoln Center location with emphasis on classical, show tunes (ugh), and jazz.
Tumi	10 Columbus Cir	212-823-9390	When your luggage gets lost and insurance is paying.
West Side Records	233 W 72nd St	212-874-1588	Cool record store.
Whole Foods Market	10 Columbus Cir	212-823-9600	Organic & pricey.
Yarn Co	2274 Broadway	212-787-7878	The stories we could tell…
Zabar's	2245 Broadway	212-787-2000	The third gourmet shop in the "holy trinity."

Map 15 · Upper East Side (Lower)

A Bear's Place	789 Lexington Ave	212-826-6465	Excellent toys and children's furniture.
American Apparel	1090 3rd Ave	212-772-7462	Sweatshop-free clothing for liberal New Yorkers.
Aveda Environmental Lifestyle Store	1122 Third Ave	212-744-3113	Pamper yourself.
Bang & Olufsen	952 Madison Ave	212-879-6161	Sleek, expensive home entertainment products.
Barneys New York	660 Madison Ave	212-826-8900	Wonderful(ly) expensive clothing.
Bed Bath & Beyond	410 E 61st St	646-215-4702	De riguer destination when moving to a new apartment.
Bloomingdale's	1000 Third Ave	212-705-2000	An upscale version of Macy's.
Bra Smyth	905 Madison Ave	212-772-9400	Need a new bra?
Diesel	770 Lexington Ave	212-308-0055	Why spend $60 on a pair of jeans when you can spend $150?
DKNY	655 Madison Ave	212-223-3569	Sharp, wearable fashions by Donna.
Dolce & Gabbana	825 Madison Ave	212-249-4100	Jeans, sunglasses, suits, and known for their animal prints.
Donna Karan	819 Madison Ave	212-861-1001	Sophisticated clothing for sophisticated people.
Dylan's Candy Bar	1011 Third Ave	646-735-0078	Keeping NYC dentists in business since 2001.
Elk Candy	1628 Second Ave	212-650-1177	Store-made marzipan and chocolates.
Garnet Wines & Liquors	929 Lexington Ave	212-772-3211	Top NYC wine store.
Giorgio Armani	760 Madison Ave	212-988-9191	Fantastic store, fantastic clothes, fantastic(ally high) prices.
Gracious Home	1217 Third Ave	212-517-6300	The definition of the word "emporium."
Hermes	691 Madison Ave	212-751-3181	Is that an Hermes tie?
Housing Works Thrift Shop	202 E 77th St	212-772-8461	Our favorite thrift store.
Janovic Plaza	1150 Third Ave	212-772-1400	Top NYC paint store.
Kate's Paperie	1282 Third Ave	212-396-3670	Excellent stationery. NYC favorite.
Lyric Hi-Fi	1221 Lexington Ave	212-439-1900	Friendly top-end stereo shop.
Morgane Le Fay	746 Madison Ave	212-879-9700	Where Jodie got her wedding dress.
Neuhaus Chocolate Boutique	922 Madison Ave	212-861-2800	Belgian chocolatier.
Ottomanelli Brothers	1549 York Ave	212-772-7900	Meat chain.
Radio Shack	1267 Lexington Ave	212-831-2765	Kenneth, what is the frequency?
Radio Shack	1477 Third Ave	212-327-0979	Kenneth, what is the frequency?
Radio Shack	782 Lexington Ave	212-421-0543	Kenneth, what is the frequency?
Radio Shack	925 Lexington Ave	212-249-3028	Kenneth, what is the frequency?
Steuben	667 Madison Ave	212-752-1441	Glass you can't afford.
Venture Stationers	1156 Madison Ave	212-288-7235	Great neighborhood stationers.
Yorkville Meat Emporium	1560 Second Ave	212-628-5147	Hungarian specialties, fresh meat, cured pork, etc.

Map 16 · Upper West Side (Upper)

Ann Taylor	2380 Broadway	212-721-3130	For the businesswoman. Conservative, classic and clean.
Banana Republic	2360 Broadway	212-787-2064	Destination for the modern, versatile, average wardrobe.
Ben & Jerry's	2722 Broadway	212-866-6237	Cherry Garcia, Phish Food, and Half Baked.
Gothic Cabinet Craft	2652 Broadway	212-678-4368	Real wood furniture.
Gourmet Garage	2567 Broadway	212-663-0656	Less greasy food than most garages.
Health Nuts	2611 Broadway	212-678-0054	Standard health food store.
Janovic Plaza	2680 Broadway	212-769-1440	Top NYC paint store.
Metro Bicycles	231 W 96th St	212-663-7531	New York's bicycle source.
Mommy Chic	2449 Broadway	212-769-9099	Because being pregnant is chic.
Planet Kids	2688 Broadway	212-864-8705	Outfitter of newborns to teens.

361

Arts & Entertainment • **Shopping**

Map 17 • Upper East Side / East Harlem

Best Buy	1280 Lexington Ave	917-492-8870	Test the electronics before you buy.
Blacker & Kooby	1204 Madison Ave	212-369-8308	Good selection of pens, stationery, and novelty items.
Blades Board & Skate	120 W 72nd St	212-996-1644	One-stop shop for skateboarding and inline skating gear.
Capezio	1651 Third Ave	212-348-7210	Dance apparel & shoes.
Cooper-Hewitt National Design Museum Shop	2 E 91st St	212-849-8355	Cool design stuff.
Eli's Vinegar Factory	431 E 91st St	212-987-0885	Gourmet market with prepared foods, cheeses, meats, seafood, and produce.
FACE Stockholm	1263 Madison Ave	212-987-1411	Skincare and makeup.
La Tropezienne	2131 First Ave	212-860-5324	Bakery.
Martha Frances Mississippi Cheesecake	1707 Second Ave	212-360-0900	Southern-style bakery with big selection of cheesecakes.
New York Replacement Parts Corp	1456 Lexington Ave	212-534-0818	Plumbing supplies and bath fixtures.
Piece of Cake Bakery	1370 Lexington Ave	212-987-1700	Bakery.
Schatzie's Prime Meats	1200 Madison Ave	212-410-1555	Butcher with good prime meat and poultry.
Soccer Sport Supply	1745 First Ave	212-427-6050	Omni soccer.
Steve Madden	150 E 86th St	212-426-0538	Trendy and modern, though not the highest quality.
Super Runners Shop	1337 Lexington Ave	212-369-6010	Brand name sneakers, apparel, and gadgets.
Williams-Sonoma	1175 Madison Ave	212-289-6832	Fine cookware.

Map 18 • Columbia / Morningside Heights

JAS Mart	2847 Broadway	212-866-4780	Japanese Asian Specialty. Japanese imports.
Kim's Mediapolis	2906 Broadway	212-864-5321	Audiovisual heaven.
Labyrinth Books	536 W 112th St	212-865-1588	NFT favorite.
Mondel Chocolates	2913 Broadway	212-864-2111	Mom-and-pop candy shop with great chocolates.

Map 19 • Harlem (Lower)

The Body Shop	1 E 125th St	212-348-4900	Naturally inspired skin and hair care products.
Champs	208 W 125th St	212-280-0296	Sports and street shoes and wear.
Dr Jays Harlem NYC	256 125th St	212-665-7795	Inner-city urban fashions.
H&M	125 W 125th St	212-665-8300	Disposable fashion.
Harlem Underground Clothing Co	2027 Fifth Ave	212-987-9385	Embroidered Harlem t-shirts.
Harlemade	174 Lenox Ave	212-987-2500	Clothes/gifts/art.
Jimmy Jazz	132 W 125th St	212-665-4198	Urban designers with a range of sizes
MAC Cosmetics	202 W 125th St	212-665-0676	Beauty products in many colors and shades.
Malcolm Shabazz Harlem Market	58 W 116th St	n/a	An open-air market for all your daishiki needs.
Settepani	196 Lenox Ave	917-492-4806	Lovely baked goods.
Studio Museum of Harlem Gift Shop	144 W 125th St	212-864-0014	Art produced by African Americans.
Wimp's Southern Style Bakery	29 W 125th St	212-410-2296	What it says.
Xukuma	183 Lenox Ave	212-222-0490	Capitalize Harlem.

Map 20 • El Barrio

Capri Bakery	186 E 116th St	212-410-1876	Italian El Barrio bakery.
Casa Latina	151 E 116th St	212-427-6062	El Barrio's oldest record store.
The Children's Place	163 E 125th St	212-348-3607	Cute clothes for little ones.
Don Paco Lopez Panaderia	2129 Third Ave	212-876-0700	Spanish El Barrio bakery.
Gothic Cabinet Craft	2268 Third Ave	212-410-3508	Real wood furniture.
La Marqueta	Park Ave & 114th St	212-534-4900	Mainly Puerto Rican foodstuffs.
Mexico Lindo Bakery	2267 Second Ave	212-410-4728	Mexican El Barrio bakery.
Morrone Bakery	324 E 116th St	212-722-2972	Italian bakery with prosciutto break, whole wheat loaves, and baguettes.
Motherhood Maternity	163 E 125th St	212-987-8808	Casual maternity wear.
Payless Shoe Source	2143 Third Ave	212-289-2251	Inexpensive shoes.
R&S Strauss Auto	2005 Third Ave	212-410-6688	Power steering fluid and windshield wipers 'till 9pm!
VIM	2239 Third Ave	212-369-5055	Streetwear—jeans, sneakers, tops—for all.

Map 21 • Manhattanville / Hamilton Heights

Foot Locker	3549 Broadway	212-491-0927	Get your sneakers here.
VIM	508 W 145th St	212-491-1143	Streetwear—jeans, sneakers, tops—for all.

Arts & Entertainment • **Shopping**

Map 22 • Harlem (Upper)

Baskin-Robbins	2730 Frederick Douglass Blvd	212-862-0635	31 flavors and other frozen treats.
New York Public Library Shop	515 Malcolm X Blvd, Schomburg Ctr	212-491-2206	Shop specializing in Black history and culture.

Map 23 • Washington Heights

Baskin-Robbins	728 W 181st St	212-923-9239	31 flavors and other frozen treats.
Carrot Top Pastries	3931 Broadway	212-927-4800	Top carrot cake, muffins, chocolate cake, rugalach, and more.
The Children's Place	600 W 181st St	212-923-7244	Cute clothes for little ones.
Fever	1387 St Nicholas Ave	212-781-6232	For ladies, at night.
FootCo	599 W 181st St	212-928-3330	Sneakers galore.
Footlocker	621 W 181st St	212-568-6091	New in area.
Goodwill Industries	512 W 181st St	212-923-7910	Jeans, business attire, baby and children's clothing, housewares and appliances, furniture, and more.
Modell's	606 W 181st St	212-568-3000	Generic sporting goods.
Payless Shoe Source	617 W 181st St	212-795-9183	Inexpensive shoes.
Planet Girls	3923 Broadway	212-927-0542	Cute clothes. Plants all over the store.
Range	659 W 181st St	212-740-3499	Hot alternative clothing.
Santana Banana	661 W 181st St	212-568-4096	Leather shoes for men and women who are in to leather.
Tribeca	655 W 181st St	212-543-3600	Trendy store for women. Good soundtrack.
VIM	561 W 181st St	212-781-8801	Streetwear—jeans, sneakers, tops—for all.

Map 25 • Inwood

Carrot Top Pastries	5025 Broadway	212-569-1532	Top carrot cake, muffins, chocolate cake, rugalach, and more.
The Cloisters	Ft Tryon Park	212-650-2277	Dark Age trinkets.
Foot Locker	146 Dyckman St	212-544-8613	There's a lot of shoe stores around here.
K&R Florist	4955 Broadway	212-942-2222	The best flower shop in the area.
Payless Shoe Source	560 W 207th St	212-544-9328	Inexpensive shoes.
Radio Shack	180 Dyckman St	212-304-0364	Electronics. What else?
Radio Shack	576 W 207th St	212-544-2180	Electronics. What else?
Tread Bicycles	225 Dyckman St	212-544-7055	Where to fix your bike after riding through Inwood Hill Park.
VIM	565 W 207th St	212-942-7478	Streetwear—jeans, sneakers, tops—for all.

Map 26 • Astoria

Bagel House	3811 Ditmars Blvd	718-726-1869	Hand-rolled bagels baked on the spot.
Book Value	3318 Broadway	718-267-7929	Bookstore.
Top Tomato	33-15 Ditmars Blvd	718-721-1400	24-hour produce stand—you never know when you'll need fresh herbs in the wee hours.

Map 28 • Greenpoint

The City Mouse	1015 Manhattan Ave	718-361-5832	Toy shop.
Dee & Dee	777 Manhattan Ave	718-389-0181	Mega-dollar store, cheap stuff.
Mini Me	123 Nassau Ave	718-349-0333	Baby and kid's clothing.
Polam	952 Manhattan Ave	718-383-2763	Quality Polish meat market with cheap bulk pickles.
Pop's Popular Clothing	7 Franklin St	718-349-7677	Great second-hand clothing, especially jeans.
Syrena Bakery	207 Norman Ave	718-349-0560	Very nice Polish bakery with an espresso bar and bagels.
The Thing	1001 Manhattan Ave	718-349-8234	This unusual second-hand store's basement contains thousands of old LPs.
Uncle Louie G's	172 Greenpoint Ave	718-349-5955	So many flavors, so little time.
The Vortex	1084 Manhattan Ave	718-609-6066	Interesting junk shop full of collectable and vintage items.
Wizard Electroland	863 Manhattan Ave	718-349-6889	Electronics store.
Z&J Liquor	761 Manhattan Ave	718-383-6818	Discounts when you buy a lot!

Map 29 • Williamsburg

American Apparel	104 N 6th St	718-218-0002	Sweatshop-free clothing for liberal New Yorkers.
Artist & Craftsman	221 N 8th St	718-782-7765	Art supplies.
Beacon's Closet	88 N 11th St	718-486-0816	Rad resale with lots of gems.
Bedford Cheese Shop	218 Bedford Ave	718-599-7588	Best cheese selection in the borough.
Brooklyn Industries	154 Bedford Ave	718-486-6464	Bags and tops—think St Marks-esque t-shirt shop.

Arts & Entertainment • **Shopping**

Map 29 • Williamsburg—*continued*

Domsey's Warehouse	431 Broadway	718-384-6000	Ready to dig? Picked over by hipsters, but bargains still abound.
Earwax Records	218 Bedford Ave	718-486-3771	Record store with all the indie classics.
Isa	88 N 6th St	718-387-3363	Fashion-forward boutique, doubles as performance/art/party space.
The Mini-Market	218 Bedford Ave	718-302-8030	Hodge-podge of tchotchkes and fun clothes.
MTC Drum Shop	536 Metropolitan Ave	718-963-2777	Friendly, knowledgeable staff.
Spacial Etc	199 Bedford Ave	718-599-7962	Overpriced housewares, baby clothes, and knitted goods.
Spoonbill & Sugartown	218 Bedford Ave	718-387-7322	Excellent indie bookstore.
Yarn Tree	347 Bedford Ave	718-384-8030	Knitting trend hit you yet? Visit and it will!

Map 30 • Brooklyn Heights / DUMBO / Downtown

ABC Carpet & Home	20 Jay St	718-643-7400	Carpets, furniture, doodads—a NYC institution.
Heights Prime Meats	59 Clark St	718-237-0133	Butcher.
Lassen & Hennigs	114 Montague St	718-875-6272	Specialty foods and deli.
Soho Art Materials	111 Front St	718-855-2929	Art supplies.
Tapestry the Salon	107 Montague St	718-522-1202	Spa.
West Elm	75 Front St	718-875-7757	Cool home decor at reasonable prices.

Map 31 • Fort Greene / Clinton Hill

Cake Man Raven Confectionary	708 Fulton St	718-694-2253	Get the red velvet cake!
Carol's Daughter	1 S Elliot Pl	718-596-1862	Skincare.
The Greene Grape	756 Fulton St	718-797-WINE	Nice new wine shop.
Indigo Café and Books	672 Fulton St	718-488-5934	Caffeine and literature.
Jacob Eyes	114 DeKalb Ave	718-625-7534	A little bit of everything: candles, bags, shoes?
L'Epicerie	270 Vanderbilt Ave	718-636-0360	French gourmet.
Malchijah Hats	225 DeKalb Ave	718-643-3269	Beautiful and unique hats.
The Midtown Greenhouse Garden Center	115 Flatbush Ave	718-636-0020	Fully stocked with plants and gardening supplies.
My Little India	96 S Elliot Pl	718-855-5220	Furniture, candles, textiles.
Target	139 Flatbush Ave	718-290-1109	Bulls eye!
Yu Interiors	15 Greene Ave	718-237-5878	Modern furniture, bags, and candles.

Map 32 • BoCoCa / Red Hook

American Apparel	112 Court St	718-855-4627	Sweatshop-free clothing for liberal New Yorkers.
American Beer Distributors	256 Court St	718-875-0226	International beer merchant.
Astro Turf	290 Smith St	718-522-6182	Kitschy retro furniture that you'll pay top dollar for.
Bopkat	113 Union St	718-222-1820	Funky vintage.
Breukelen	369 Atlantic Ave	718-246-0024	Gorgeous and expensive home furnishings.
Caputo's Fine Foods	460 Court St	718-855-8852	Italian gourmet specialties.
D'Amico Foods	309 Court St	718-875-5403	The best coffee in the 'hood, if not the city.
Frida's Closet	296 Smith St	718-855-0031	Women's skirts, shirts, and sweaters with a Frida Kahlo feel.
Granny's Attic	305 Smith St	718-624-0175	Find unique collectibles amongst the junk.
The Green Onion	274 Smith St	718-246-2804	Fine children's clothing, but service with an attitude.
Kimera	366 Atlantic Ave	718-422-1147	Great pillows.
Knitting Hands	398 Atlantic Ave	718-858-6548	Great stock of interesting yarns.
Lowes	118 Second Ave	718-249-1154	For all your home improvement needs.
Marquet	221 Court St	718-855-1289	Top NYC croissants and quiches.
Mazzola Bakery	192 Union St	718-643-1719	Top bakery in CG.
Monte Leone's Pasticceria	355 Court St	718-624-9253	Bakery with great bread!
Refinery	254 Smith St	718-643-7861	Great bags and accessories.
Sahadi Importing Company	187 Atlantic Ave	718-624-4550	Specialty goods at bargain prices.
Stacia	267 Smith St	718-237-0078	Designer women's clothes by Stacy Johnson.
Staubitz Meat Market	222 Court St	718-624-0014	Top NYC butcher.
Swallow	361 Smith St	718-222-8201	Excellent glass, excellent jewelry, fun books.
Sweet Melissa	276 Court St	718-855-3410	Good deserts, tea, and coffee.
Tuller	199 Court St	718-222-9933	Delectable and expensive gourmet shop. Great cheese.
Uncle Louie G's	517 Henry St	718-246-5300	So many flavors, so little time.
Urban Monster	396 Atlantic Ave	718-855-6400	Fantastic, friendly baby store.
Zipper	333 Smith St	718-596-0333	Excellent home accessories and great books.

Map 33 · Park Slope / Prospect Heights / Windsor Ter

Barnes & Noble	267 Seventh Ave	718-832-9066	Books and such.
Beacon's Closet	220 Fifth Ave	718-230-1630	Rad resale with lots of gems.
The Bicycle Station	560 Vanderbilt Ave	718-638-0300	New, used, vintage, sales, repairs.
Bird	430 Seventh Ave	718-768-4940	Unique women's clothes and accessories.
Bob and Judi's Collectibles	217 Fifth Ave	718-638-5770	Antiques, vintage novelties.
Boing Boing	204 Sixth Ave	718-398-0251	Boutique for mother and child.
Brooklyn Industries	152 Fifth Ave	718-789-3447	Bags and tops—think St Marks-esque T-shirt shop.
Brooklyn Superhero Supply	372 Fifth Ave	718-499-9884	Egger's latest brainchild.
Castor & Pollux	76 Sixth Ave	718-398-4141	Slightly overpriced boutique store selling mainly fashion items and accessories
Clay Pot	162 Seventh Ave	718-788-6564	Hand-crafted gifts, jewelry.
Community Book Store	143 Seventh Ave	718-783-3075	Books, coffee, garden.
Eidolon	233 Fifth Ave	718-638-8194	Local designer labels.
Heidi Story	453 Seventh Ave	718-965-1119	Susana Monaco, A Cheng, and a host of other designers.
Hibiscus	564A Vandebilt Ave	718-638-6850	Flowers, plants, and arrangements for all occasions.
Hooti Couture	321 Flatbush Ave	718-857-1977	Girlie Vintage.
Jack Rabbit Sports	151 Seventh Ave	718-636-9000	Mecca for runners, swimmers, and cyclists.
Kimera	274 Fifth Ave	718-965-1313	Great pillows.
Leaf and Bean	83 Seventh Ave	718-638-5791	Coffees and teas.
Nancy Nancy	244 Fifth Ave	718-789-5262	Cards, gifts, novelties.
Nkiru International Bookstore	732 Washington Ave	718-783-6306	Excellent selection of poetry and cultural books.
Pieces	671 Vanderbilt Ave	718-857-7211	Urban clothes for sleek hip-hop crowd.
RedLipstick	64 Sixth Ave	718-857-9534	Luxurious hand-knitted originals. Sign up for a class.
Sound Track	119 Seventh Ave	718-622-1888	CDs & LPs.
Uncle Louie G's	741 Union St	718-623-6668	So many flavors, so little time.
Uprising Bread Bakery	328 Seventh Ave	718-499-8665	Artisanal breads, goodies.
Uprising Bread Bakery	138 Seventh Ave	718-499-5242	Artisanal breads, goodies.

Map 34 · Hoboken

Air Studio	55 First St	201-239-1511	Cutting edge women's clothing boutique, featuring the hot designers of tomorrow.
Arts on Sixth	155 Sixth St	201-217-4311	Hand-blown glass; hand-wrought iron. Furniture and art. Screw the registry!
Basic Foods	204 Washington St	201-610-1100	Not so personal, but a good selection.
Battaglia's	319 Washington St	201-798-1122	Interesting gifts and homewares.
Big Fun Toys	602 Washington St	201-714-9575	Go for the gift wrap…the toys aren't bad.
City Paint & Hardware	130 Washington St	201-659-0061	Everything, including kitchen sinks.
Gallatea	1224 Washington St	201-963-1522	Elegantly lusciuos lingerie, chosen with an expert eye.
Hand Mad	86 Park Ave	201-653-7276	Folk, Funk, Fine Art. Plus groovy gift-wrapping.
Hoboken Farmboy	127 Washington St	201-656-0581	It doesn't come much healthier. Good advice for your health needs.
Makeovers	302 Washington St	201-420-1444	Every hair care product known to womankind. A fantasy for your follicles.
Peper	1030 Washington St	201-217-1911	Hoboken's sexiest clothing. A must for your next high school reunion.
Sobsey's Produce	92 Bloomfield St	201-795-9398	Expert greengrocer. Exotic produce and gourmet foods.
Sparrow Wine and Liquor	1224 Shipyard Ln	201-659-1501	Good selection of local and imported products. Staff are helpful with selections.
Sparrow Wine and Liquor	126 Washington St	201-659-1500	Good selection of local and imported products. Staff are helpful with selections.
Tunes New & Used CDs	225 Washington St	201-653-3355	Support your local indie music store. They'll order stuff for you.
Yes I Do	312 Washington St	201-659-3300	Elegant cards, stationary, invitatons, printing, and gifts.

Map 35 · Jersey City

Harborside Shopping Complex			Mall.
Newport Center Mall	30 Mall Dr W	201-626-2025	Mall.

Battery Park City

DSW Shoe Warehouse	102 North End Ave	212-945-7419	Fabulous choices for men's and women's shoes.

Here is, as best as we can figure out, a list of all the theaters in Manhattan. The difference between "Off" and "Off-Off," you ask? Size, of course. "Off-Off" refers to a theater with less than 100 seats, while "Off" means the theater holds 100-500 seats.

If it's a Broadway show you're after, check out www.broadway.com for a comprehensive list of what's playing and when. You can buy tickets from their website or you can go through the usual Ticketmaster or Telecharge routes, or just call the theaters directly.

If you're short on cash and long on time and patience, you might try standing in line at the tkts booths in Times Square or South Street Seaport for discounted (by 25-50%) tickets (cash only). Tickets for shows such as *Avenue Q* (**John Golden Theatre**), *The Lion King* (**New Amsterdam Theatre**), *Aida* (**Palace Theatre**), *Beauty and the Beast* (**Lunt-Fontanne Theatre**), *Chicago* (**Ambassador Theatre**), *Little Shop of Horrors* (**Virginia Theatre**), *Movin' Out* (**Richard Rodgers Theatre**), *Rent* (**Nederlander Theatre**), and *Thoroughly Modern Millie* (**Marquis Theatre**) are featured often at the tkts booths.

Off-Broadway shows tend to not sell out too often, so tkts offers plenty of discounted tickets to Off-Broadway shows as well. You can usually score discounted tickets to such long-running acts as *Forbidden Broadway* (**Douglas Fairbanks Theatre**), *I Love You, You're Perfect, Now Change* (**Westside Theatre**), *Naked Boys Singing* (**47th Street Theatre**), and *Stomp* (**Orpheum Theatre**).

There are two tkts booths—one in Times Square at 47th and Broadway and one at the South Street Seaport on the corner of Front and John Streets. The one at the Seaport is by far the less busy of the two, with a wait time that doesn't usually last more than half an hour compared to a couple of hours in Times Square. The Seaport location opens at 11 am from Monday to Saturday and only sells tickets to evening performances. The Times Square booth starts selling tickets at 3 pm daily for evening performances, 10 am for Wednesday and Saturday matinees, and 11 am for Sunday matinees.

If you're after something further off Broadway, check out the fare at some of our favorite theaters:

Pearl Theatre Company, presently located at 80 St. Mark's Place, is one of the 15 or so largest institutional theaters in New York City. 2004 marked their 20th anniversary, and they continue to grow as a resident company and a classical repertory, offering delights from Sheridan, Shakespeare, Aeschylus, Marivaux, and Ibsen. www.pearltheatre.org

Now in its seventh season, Horse Trade continues its commitment to producing a varied program of performance series, readings, workshops, and fully-realized productions. Most events are performed at **The Kraine Theater**, which also houses the **Red Room** on its third floor. The theaters are also available to rent for rehearsals and performances. www.httheater.org

HERE not only houses two small theaters, but it also has an amazing gallery space and a cozy café/bar—perfect for pre- or post-show drinks. www.here.org

In Chelsea, **The Kitchen** literally began in the unused kitchen of the Mercer Arts Center, housed in the Broadway Central Hotel in Greenwich Village. In 1985, The Kitchen moved into its new and permanent home at 512 W 19th Street. The venue plays host to new performance artists blending music, dance, video, art, and spoken word. www.thekitchen.org

Located in a former public school on First Avenue and 9th Street in the East Village, **P.S. 122** is a not-for-profit arts center serving New York City's dance and performance community. Shows rotate through on a regular basis, so check the website for the latest schedule. www.ps122.org

The outdoor **Delacorte Theater** in Central Park hosts performances only during the summer months. Tickets to the ridiculously popular and free Shakespeare in the Park performances are given away at 1 pm at the Delacorte and also at the **Public Theate**r (425 Lafayette St) on the day of each performance. Hopefully you enjoy camping, because people line up for days in their tents and sleeping bags just to secure a ticket!

Just on the other side of the Manhattan Bridge in Brooklyn is the world famous **Brooklyn Academy of Music**. A thriving urban arts center, BAM brings domestic and international performing arts and film to Brooklyn. The center includes two theaters (Harvey Lichtenstein Theater and Howard Gilman Opera House), the Bam Rose Cinemas, and the BAMcafé, a restaurant and live music venue. Our favorite season is the *Next Wave*, an annual three-month celebration of cutting-edge dance, theater, music, and opera. www.bam.org

Broadway

			Map
Ambassador Theatre	219 W 49th St	212-239-6200	12
American Airlines Theatre	227 W 42nd St	212-719-1300	12
Apollo Theater	253 W 125th St	212-531-5300	18
Belasco Theatre	111 W 44th St	212-239-6200	12
Biltmore Theatre	261 W 47th St	212-245-2266 212-245-2288	12
Booth Theatre	222 W 45th St	212-239-6200	12
Broadhurst Theatre	235 W 44th St	212-239-6200	12
Brooks Atkinson Theatre	256 W 47th St	212-307-4100	12
Cadillac Winter Garden Theatre	1634 Broadway	212-239-6200	12
Carnegie Hall	154 W 57th St	212-247-7800	12
Circle in the Square Theatre	1633 Broadway	212-307-0388	12
Cort Theatre	138 W 48th St	212-239-6200	12
Ethel Barrymore Theatre+C71	243 W 47th St	608-241-2345	12
Eugene O'Neill Theatre	230 W 49th St	212-239-6200	12
Gershwin Theatre	222 W 51st St	212-307-4100	12
Golden Theatre	252 W 45th St	212-239-6200	12
Helen Hayes Theatre	240 W 44th St	212-239-6200	12
Henry Miller Theatre	124 W 43rd St	212-239-6200	12
Imperial Theater	249 W 45th St	212-239-6200	12
Longacre Theatre	220 W 48th St	212-239-6200	12
Lunt-Fontanne Theatre	205 W 46th St	212-307-4747	12
Lyceum Theatre	149 W 45th St	212-239-6200	12
Majestic Theater	245 W 44th St	212-239-6200	12
Marquis Theatre	1535 Broadway	212-307-4100	12
Minskoff Theatre	200 W 45th St	212-869-0550	12
Music Box Theatre	239 W 45th St	212-239-6200	12
Nederlander Theatre	208 W 41st St	212-307-4100	12
Neil Simon Theatre	250 W 52nd St	212-307-4100	12
New Amsterdam Theatre	214 W 42nd St	212-307-4100	12
New Victory Theatre	209 W 42nd St	212-239-6200	12
Palace Theatre	1564 Broadway	212-307-4747	12
Plymouth Theatre	236 W 45th St	212-239-6200	12
Radio City Music Hall	1260 Sixth Ave	212-247-4777	12
Richard Rodgers Theatre	226 W 46th St	212-221-1211	12
Roundabout/ Laura Pels Theatre	111 W 46th St	212-719-9300	12
Royale Theatre	242 W 45th St	212-239-6200	12
Shubert Theatre	225 W 44th St	212-239-6200	12
St James Theatre	246 W 44th St	212-239-6200	12
The Theater at Madison Square Garden	2 Penn Plz	212-307-4111	9
Virginia Theatre	245 W 52nd St	212-239-6200	12
Vivian Beaumont Theatre	Lincoln Ctr, 150 W 65th St	212-362-7600	14
Walter Kerr Theatre	219 W 48th St	212-239-6200	12

Off- and Off-Off Broadway

			Map
13th Street Theatre	50 W 13th St	212-675-6677	6
29th Street Repertory Theatre	212 W 29th St	212-465-0575	9
45 Bleecker Theater	45 Bleecker St	212-253-7017	6
45th St Theater	354 W 45th St	212-279-4200	11
47th Street Theatre	304 W 47th St	212-239-6200	12
47th Street Theatre	304 W 47th St	212-265-1086	12
59E59 Theaters	59 E 59th St	212-279-4200	13
74A	E 4th St b/w Bowery & Second Ave	212-475-7710	6
78th Street Theatre Lab	236 W 78th St	212 873-9050	14
92nd Street Y Theatre	1395 Lexington Ave	212-996-1100	17
Abingdon Mainstage Theatre	312 W 36th St	212-206-1515	8
Access Theatre	380 Broadway, 4th Fl	212-966-1047	3
Acorn Theatre	410 W 42nd St	212-239-6200	11
Actor's Playhouse	100 Seventh Ave S	212-239-6200	9
Actor's Theater Workshop	145 W 28th St	212-947-1386	8
Al Hirschfeld Theatre	302 W 45th St	212-239-6200	12

			Map
Alice Tully Hall at Lincoln Center	150 W 65th St	212-721-6500	14
Amato Opera	319 Bowery	212-228-8200	6
American Globe Theater	145 W 46th St	212-869-9809	12
American Place Theatre	520 Eighth Ave	212-239-6200	8
American Theatre of Actors	314 W 54th St	212-239-6200	11
Apocalypse Lounge	189 E 3rd St	212-228-4811	7
ArcLight Theatre	152 W 71st St	212-595-0355	14
Arno Ristorante	141 W 38th St	800-687-3374	9
Astor Place Theatre	434 Lafayette St	212-254-4370	6
Atlantic Theater Company	336 W 20th St	212-239-6200	8
Axis Theater	1 Sheridan Sq	212-807-9300	5
Barrow Group Arts Center	312 W 36th St		8
Barrow Street Theater	27 Barrow St	212-239-6200	5
Baruch Performing Arts Center	55 Lexington Ave	212-239-6200	10
Beacon Theater	2124 Broadway	212-496-7070	14
Belt Theater	336 W 37th St	718-670-7234	8
Bernie West Theatre at Baruch College	17 Lexington Ave	646-623-3488	10
Blue Heron Arts Center	123 E 24th St	212-868-4444	10
Bouwerie Lane Theatre	330 Bowery	212-279-4200	6
CAMI Hall	165 W 57th St	212-841-9650	12
Castillo Theater	543 W 42nd St	212-941-1234	11
CBGB's 313 Gallery	313 Bowery	212-677-0455	6
Cedar Lake	547 W 26th St	212-868-4444	8
Century Center for the Performing Arts	111 E 15th St	212 239-6200	10
Chashama	217 W 42nd St	212-391-8151	12
Chelsea Playhouse	125 W 22nd St	212-366-9176	9
Cherry Lane Theater	38 Commerce St	212-239-6200	5
Chicago City Limits Theatre	318 W 53rd St	212-888-5233	12
City Center Main Stage	131 W 55th St	212-581-7907	12
Classic Stage Co	136 E 13th St	212-279-4200	6
Clemente Soto Velez Cultural Center	107 Suffolk St	212-260-4080	7
Club El Flamingo	547 W 21st St	212-307-4100	8
Collective: Unconscious	279 Church St	212-352-3101	1
Community Service Council of Greater Harlem	207 W 133rd St	212-368-9314	19
Creative Artists Laboratory	303 W 42nd St, 3rd Fl	212-316-0400	12
Culture Club	179 Varick St	212-352-3101	5
The Culture Project	45 Bleecker St	212-307-4100	6
Dance Theatre Workshop	219 W 19th St	212-924-0077	9
Daryl Roth Theatre	20 Union Sq E	212-239-6200	10
Delacorte Theater	Central Park, W 81st St	212-539-8750	15
Dicapo Opera Theatre	184 E 76th St	212-288-9438	15
Dodger Stages	340 W 50th St	212-239-6200	11
Dominion Theatre	428 Lafayette St	212-868-4444	6
Douglas Fairbanks Theatre	432 W 42nd St	212-239-6200	11
DR2 Theatre	103 E 15th St	212-239-6200	10
Duffy Theater	1553 Broadway	212-695-3401	12
Duo Theatre	62 E 4th St	212-598-4320	6
Duplex Cabaret Theatre	61 Christopher St	212-255-5438	5
East 13th Street Theatre	136 E 13th St	212-206-1515	6
Fez Under Time Café	380 Lafayette St	212-533-2680	6
Flea Theatre	41 White St	212-226-0051	3
French Institute– Florence Gould Hall	55 E 59th St	212-355-6160	13
Gene Frankel Theatre	24 Bond St	212-777-1767	6
The Gerald W Lynch Theater at John Jay College	899 Tenth Ave	212-279-4200	11
Gertrude Stein Repertory Theater	15 W 26th St	212-725-7254	9
Gloria Maddox Theater	151 W 26th St		9
Grace Rainey Rogers Auditorium	Metropolitan, Museum 1000 Fifth Ave	212-570-3949	15

367

Off- and Off-Off Broadway—*continued*

Greenwich Street Theatre	547 Greenwich St	212-206-1515	5
Grammery Arts Theatre	138 E 27th St	212-889-2850	10
Harold Clurman Theatre	412 W 42nd St	212-279-4200	11
Harry DeJur Playhouse	466 Grand St	212-598-0400	4
Hartley House Theater	413 W 46th St	212-246-9885	11
HERE	145 Sixth Ave	212-868-4444	5
Hilton Theater	213 W 42nd St	212-556-4750	12
HSA Theater	645 St Nicholas Ave	212-868-4444	21
Hudson Guild	119 Ninth Ave	212-760-9800	8
Hudson Theater	145 W 44th St	212-307-7171	12
Intar Theatre	508 W 53rd St	212-279-4200	11
Irish Arts Center	553 N 51st St	212-581-4125	11
Irish Repertory Theatre	133 W 22nd St	212-727-2737	9
Jean Cocteau Repertory	330 Bowery	212-677-0060	6
Jewish Community Center	334 Amsterdam Ave	800-994-3347	14
Joe's Pub at the Public Theater	425 Lafayette St	212-239-6200	6
John Houseman Theater	450 W 42nd St	212-239-6200	11
Joseph Papp Public Theater	425 Lafayette St	212-260-2400	6
Joyce Theater	175 Eighth Ave	212-242-0800	8
June Havoc Theater	312 W 36th St	212-868-4444	8
Kirk Theatre	410 W 42nd St	212-279-4200	11
The Kitchen	512 W 19th St	212-255-5793	8
Knitting Factory– Alterknit Theater	74 Leonard St	212-219-3006	3
The Kraine Theater	85 E 4th St	212-868-4444	6
Lambs Theater	130 W 44th St	212-239-6200	12
Lillie Blake Auditorium at PS 6	45 E 81st St	212-737-9774	15
Lincoln Center for the Performing Arts	Broadway & 64th St	212-875-5456	14
Lions Theatre	410 W 42nd St	212-279-4200	11
Little Shubert Theatre	422 W 42nd St	212-239-6200	11
The Looking Glass Theatre	422 W 57th St	212-307-9467	11
Lucille Lortel Theatre	121 Christopher St	212-279-4200	5
Manhattan Ensemble Theatre	549 W 52nd St	212-247-3405	11
Manhattan School of Music	120 Claremont Ave	212-749-2802	18
Manhattan Theatre Source	177 MacDougal St	212-868-4444	6
Mazer Theater	197 East Broadway	212-239-6200	4
McGinn/Cazale Theatre	2162 Broadway	212-352-3101	14
Medicine Show Theatre	549 W 52nd St	212-352-3101	11
Merkin Concert Hall	129 W 67th St	212-501-3330	14
Metropolitan Playhouse	220a E 4th St, 2nd Fl	212-995-5302	7
The Milagro Theatre at the CSV Cultural Center	107 Suffolk St	212 279-4200	7
Miller Theater– Columbia University	200 Dodge Hall, Broadway & 116th St	212-854-7799	18
Minetta Lane Theatre	18 Minetta Ln	212-307-4100	6
Mint Theatre	311 W 43rd St 5th Fl	212-315-0231	11
Mitzi E Newhouse Theater	150 W 65th St	212-239-6200	14
Music Room	Frick Museum, 1 E 70th St	212-288-0700	15
National Arts Club	15 Gramercy Park	212-362-2560	10
National Black Theatre	2031 Fifth Ave	212-722-3800	19
New Perspectives	750 Eighth Ave, 6th Fl	212-719-0500	12

New York State Theatre	Lincoln Ctr, Columbus Ave at 63rd St	212-870-5570	14
New York Theatre Workshop	79 E 4th St	212-239-6200	6
Nuyorican Poets Café	236 E 3rd St	212-505-8183	7
Ohio Theatre	66 Wooster St	800-965-4827	6
Ontological– Hysteric Theatre	131 E 10th St	212-533-4650	6
The Ontological Theater at St Mark's Church-in-the-Bowery	131 E 10th St	212-533-4650	6
Orpheum Theatre	126 Second Ave	212-477-2477	6
Ottendorfor Public Library	135 Second Ave	212-674-0947	6
Pan Asian Repertory Theatre	520 Eighth Ave	212-868-4030	8
Partners & Crime	44 Greenwich Ave	212-462-3027	5
Pearl Theatre Co	80 St Mark's Pl	212-598-9802	6
Pelican Studio Theatre	750 Eighth Ave	212-730-2030	12
People's Improvisation Theatre	154 W 29th St, 2nd Fl	212 563-7488	9
Perfoming Garage	38 Water St	212-966-3651	0
Perry St Theatre	31 Perry St	212-868-4444	5
Phil Bosakowski Theatre	354 W 45th St	212-352-3101	11
Players Theatre	115 MacDougal St	212-254-8138	6
Playhouse 91	316 E 91st St	212-307-4100	17
Playwrights Horizons Theater	416 W 42nd St	212-279-4200	11
Primary Stages	59 E 59th St	212-333-4052	13
The Producers Club	358 W 44th St	212-315-4743	11
Producers Club II	616 Ninth Ave	212-496-4571	11
Promenade Theatre	2162 Broadway	212-239-6200	14
PS 122	150 First Ave	212-477-5288	7
Public Theater	425 Lafayette St	212-539-8500	6
Rattlestick Theatre	224 Waverly Pl	212-206-1515	5
The Red Room	85 E 4th St	212-539-7686	6
Repertorio Español	138 E 27th St	212-889-2850	10
Reprise Room at Dillon's	245 W 54th St	212-239-6200	12
Riant Theatre	161 Hudson St	212-623-3488	2
Riverside Church	490 Riverside Dr	212-870-6700	18
Samuel Beckett Theatre	412 W 42nd St	212-307-4100	11
Sanford Meisner Theatre	164 Eleventh Ave	917-334-1780	8
Second Stage Theatre	307 W 43rd St	212-246-4422	12
Signature Theatre	555 W 42nd St	212-244-7529	11
Soho Playhouse	15 Vandam St	212-691-1555	5
Soho Repertory Theatre/ Walker Street Theater	46 Walker St	212-941-8632	3
Sol Goldman Y of the Educational Alliance	344 E 14th St	212-868-4444	6
St Bart's Playhouse	Park Ave & E 50th St	212-378-0248	13
St Lukes Church	308 W 46th St	212-352-3101	12
Stage 36 @ TBG	312 W 36th St	212-352-3101	8
Stella Adler Theatre	31 W 27th St	212-260-0525	9
Storm Theatre	145 W 46th St	212-868-4444	12
Studio 54	254 W 54th St	212-239-6200	12
Studio at Cherry Lane Theatre	38 Commerce St	212-727-3673	5
Surf Reality	172 Allen St, 2nd Fl	212-673-4182	7
Sylvia and Danny Kaye Playhouse	695 Park Ave	212-772-5207	15
Symphony Space	2537 Broadway	212-864-5400	16
T Schreiber Studio	151 W 26th St	212-352-3101	9
Tenement Theater	97 Orchard St	212-431-0233	4

Arts & Entertainment • Theaters

			Map
Theater at St Clement's	423 W 46th St	212-868-4444	11
Theater for the New City	155 First Ave	212-352-3101	7
Theater Ten Ten	1010 Park Ave	212-288-3246	15
Theatre Studio	750 Eighth Ave	212-719-0500	12
Times Square Theater and Entertainment Center at Show World	42nd St & 8th Ave	212-586-7829	12
Town Hall	123 W 43rd St	212-840-2824	12
Triad Stage	158 W 72nd St	212-239-6200	14
TriBeCa Performing Arts Center	199 Chambers St	212-220-1460	2
Union Square Theater	100 E 17th St	212-307-4100	10
Urban Stages	259 W 30th St	212-868-4444	9
Village Theater	158 Bleecker St	212-307-4100	6
Vineyard Theatre	108 E 15th St	212-352-3101	10
Vinnie Black's Coliseum at the Edison Hotel	221 W 46th St	212-352-3101	12
West End Theatre	263 W 86th St	212-352-3101	16
West Park Presbyterian Church	165 W 86th St	212-868-4444	16
Westside Theatre	407 W 43rd St	212-239-6200	11
Wings Theater	154 Christopher St	212-627-2961	5
Women's Project Theatre	424 W 55th St	212-765-1706	11
WOW Café	59 E 4th St	212-777-4280	6
York Theatre at St Peter's Church	619 Lexington Ave	212-868-4444	13
The Zipper Theatre	336 W 37th St	212-239-6200	8

Performing Arts

			Map
Amato Opera	319 Bowery	212-228-8200	6
Beacon Theater	2124 Broadway	212-496-7070	14
CAMI Hall	165 W 57th St	212-841-9650	12
Century Center for the Performing Arts	111 E 15th St	212 239-6200	10
City Center Main Stage	131 W 55th St	212-581-7907	12
Dance Theatre Workshop	219 W 19th St	212-924-0077	9
Ford Center for the Performing Arts	214 W 43rd St	212-307-4100	12
Grace Rainey Rogers Auditorium	Metropolitan Museum, 1000 Fifth Ave	212-570-3949	15
Joyce Theater	175 Eighth Ave	212-242-0800	8
Manhattan School of Music	120 Claremont Ave	212-749-2802	18
Manhattan Theatre Club	131 W 55th St	212-581-1212	12
Merkin Concert Hall	129 W 67th St	212-501-3330	14
Music Room	Frick Museum, 1 E 70th St	212-288-0700	15
Riverside Church	490 Riverside Dr	212-870-6700	18
Town Hall	123 W 43rd St	212-840-2824	12
Warren St Performance Loft	46 Warren St	212-732-3149	2

Brooklyn

			Map
651 Arts	651 Fulton St	718-636-4181	31 Fort Greene / Clinton Hill
BAX	421 Fifth Ave	718-832-9189	33 Park Slope / Prospect Heights
BRIC Studio	57 Rockwell Pl	718-855-7882	30 Brooklyn Heights / DUMBO / Downtown
Brick Theatre	575 Metropolitan Ave	718-907-6189	29 Williamsburg
Brooklyn Arts Council	195 Cadman Plz W	718-625-0080	30 Brooklyn Heights / DUMBO / Downtown
Brooklyn Arts Exchange	421 Fifth Ave	718-832-0018	33 Park Slope / Prospect Heights
Brooklyn Family Theatre	1012 Eighth Ave	718-670-7205	33 Park Slope / Prospect Heights
Brooklyn Lyceum	227 Fourth Ave	718-857-4816	33 Park Slope / Prospect Heights
Charlie's Pineapple Theater Company	208 N 8th St	718-907-0577	29 Williamsburg
Gallery Players Theater	199 14th St	718-595-0547	33 Park Slope / Prospect Heights
Harvey Theater (Brooklyn Academy of Music)	651 Fulton St	718-636-4100	31 Fort Greene / Clinton Hill
The Heights Players	26 Willow Pl	718-237-2752	30 Brooklyn Heights / DUMBO / Downtown
National Asian American Theater	674 President St	718-623-1672	33 Park Slope / Prospect Heights
One Arm Red	100 Water St	718-797-0046	30 Brooklyn Heights / DUMBO / Downtown
Paul Robeson Theatre	54 Greene Ave	718-783-9794	31 Fort Greene / Clinton Hill
Puppetworks	338 Sixth Ave	718-965-3391	33 Park Slope / Prospect Heights
St Ann's Warehouse	38 Water St	718-858-2424	30 Brooklyn Heights / DUMBO / Downtown
The Waterloo Bridge Playhouse	475 Third Ave	212-502-0796	33 Park Slope / Prospect Heights

News.

Culture.

Life.

Visit any one of our **18 offices** citywide.

Upper West Side
465 Columbus Ave.

Upper West Side
222 West 72nd St.

Upper East Side
400 East 84th St.

Upper East Side
400 East 76th St.

Midtown West
346 West 57th St.

Midtown East
937 Second Ave.

Murray Hill
30 East 33rd St.

Murray Hill
206 East 38th St.

Chelsea
155 Seventh Ave.

Gramercy/Flatiron
32 East 22nd St.

Gramercy/Flatiron
27 East 22nd St.

West Village
114 Perry St.

Corp. Headquarters
Sales Headquarters
250 Park Ave So.

East Village
37 Third Ave.

SoHo
62 Greene St.

Greenwich Village
1 Great Jones St.

Financial District
100 John St.

Luxurious lofts to first studios, Citi Habitats has Manhattan covered.

Manhattan's Real Estate Leader
www.citihabitats.com
Owned and operated by NRT, Incorporated.

CITI HABITATS
NEW YORK

THE BIG APPLE
(worms and all)

Saving is Always in Style!

Century 21

Legendary for Values
Top Fashion Brands

DISCOUNT PRICES ON
Mens, Ladies & Childrens Designer Apparel
Footwear for the Entire Family ∎ Handbags ∎ Luggage ∎ Linens
Housewares ∎ Lingerie ∎ Gifts ∎ Cosmetics ∎ Fragrances

40–70% OFF RETAIL

Free Gift*
With this ad and any purchase
*Valid only in Manhattan Store

CENTURY 21 DEPARTMENT STORES
22 Cortlandt Street, NYC   212/227-9092
Mon – Wed & Fri.: 7:45 am – 8 pm ∎ Thurs.: 7:45 am – 8:30 pm ∎ Sat.: 10 am – 8 pm ∎ Sun.: 11 am – 7 pm

VISIT OUR OTHER LOCATIONS
Long Island: 516/333.5200   Brooklyn: 718/748.3266   Morristown, NJ: 973/401.9500

WWW.C21STORES.COM

Think with your deck.

"The coolest thing ever!" - *CBS Morning News & DailyCandy.com*

"These restaraunts are first rate spots." - *Sky Magazine*

"A blessing for our palates and pocketbooks." - *Gothamist*

"I wish I had one for every city I visit." - *Rachael Ray, The Food Network*

Introducing **The Diner's Decks**. Pick a card. Discover a Restaurant. Save Money. Every card is a **$10 Gift Certificate** at the restaurant it describes. 52 restaurants in a deck. Now picking a place is as easy as picking a card.

www.dinersdeck.com

find Subway Directions *Online*

① enter **Start address** »

ADDRESS
Penn Station

② enter **Destination address** »

ADDRESS
60 Wall Street

A Penn Station, Manhattan
B 60 Wall Street, Manhattan

 Take the Number 2 train from 34 Street - Penn Station
Pass 14 Street, Pass Chambers Street, Pass Park Place, Pass Fulton Street
Exit Wall Street station, Start out going on Wall St towards Hanover St
Total travel time: 20mins

www.hopstop.com

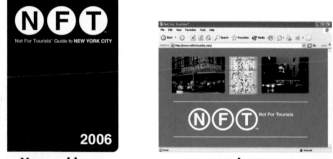

NOT FOR TOURISTS™ Custom Mapping

We'll map your world.

Have us make you an **NFT™** map! **Not For Tourists™** can bring its award-winning graphic functionality to helping put your organization or event and put you on the map.

The same trademark design that makes our Guidebooks stunning and unique can put your information into a clear and beautiful map package.

NFT™'s team will come up with something new or put a fresh face on something you already have.

We provide custom map-making and information design services to fit your needs—whether simply showing where your organization is located on one of our existing maps, or creating a completely new visual context for the information you wish to convey. **NFT™** will help you—and your audience—make the most of the place you're in, while you're in it.

For more information, call us at 212-965-8650 or visit www.notfortourists.com.

 Not For Tourists™   www.notfortourists.com
New York City · Brooklyn · Los Angeles · Chicago · San Francisco · Boston · Washington DC · Atlanta · Philadelphia

THE MANHATTAN SKYLINE

Two detailed panoramas portraying the city prior to September 11, 2001. Drawn by John Wagner

One of the world's most breathtaking sights is the New York City skyline, now captured as never before in two new panoramas called **The Manhattan Skyline Portraits**. Although photographic in appearance, these images are actually illustrations drawn by artist John Wagner. Using a computer as a pen and paintbrush, he carefully crafted a faithful likeness of each building based largely on thousands of photographs he took from the air as well as at ground level.

40 Months from Start to Finish

Drawing the 6.5 miles of Manhattan pictured in both portraits took Wagner more than three years to complete. He began in May 1998 and finished two weeks after the World Trade Center towers were destroyed in September 2001. More than 1,000 buildings take center stage in each drawing. Another 2,500 less-visible structures serve as the skyline's supporting cast, conveying the density of construction so characteristic of Manhattan.

The East River Portrait faithfully records the eastern side of the skyline as seen from Brooklyn and Queens across the East River. **The Hudson River Portrait** shows the west side of the city, looking across the Hudson River from the New Jersey shoreline. Each portrait is sold separately.

Drawn One Building at a Time

World Trade Center
Tower No. 2
1972-2001
110-1362'/415m
Minoru Yamasaki & Assocs.,
Emery Roth & Sons

In order to fit the entire 12 feet of city depicted in each portrait on a single sheet of poster paper, the image is presented in two decks with a pause at 29th Street. Each panorama reads like a two-line sentence, left to right and top to bottom. The size of each print is 18.5 x 75 inches (47 x 190.5 cm). All buildings in the panoramas are drawn using the same scale, which means no structure is diminished in size because of its distance from you, the viewer. All skyscrapers stand tall in these group portraits, even those in the back row. How tall? The Empire State Building measures 5.75 inches tall (15 cm). More than 500 buildings in each Manhattan Skyline portrait are identified. The stories of these buildings are told in these labels, such as the date completed, the street address and the architect. Labels for skyscrapers taller than 700 feet (213 m) also list the height in stories, feet and meters. In addition, many labels include further information of historic interest.

Available at www.notfortourists.com

Street Index

Street Index

Street Index

NOT FOR TOURISTS™ Wallmaps

Map 6 · Washington Sq./NYU/SoHo

Blown up and hung.

Your favorite **NFT** map as a poster. Any **Not For Tourists** map can be made into a 24"x 36" poster. These large wall maps are taken directly from the pages of the **Not For Tourists** Guidebooks.

Order at www.notfortourists.com